Wissenschaftliche Untersuchungen
zum Neuen Testament

Herausgegeben von
Martin Hengel und Otfried Hofius

84

World map (10 × 15 cm) with orientation on the East and Jerusalem
in the center accompanying a thirteenth-century manuscript
of the Psalms

British Library Add MS 28681 f9

Paul and the Nations

The Old Testament
and Jewish Background of Paul's Mission
to the Nations with Special Reference
to the Destination of Galatians

by

James M. Scott

J. C. B. Mohr (Paul Siebeck) Tübingen

Die Deutsche Bibliothek – CIP-Einheitsaufnahme

Scott, James M.:
Paul and the nations: the Old Testament and Jewish background of Paul's mission
to the nations with special reference to the destination of Galatians /
by James M. Scott. – Tübingen: Mohr, 1995
   (Wissenschaftliche Untersuchungen zum Neuen Testament; 84)
   ISBN 3-16-146377-3
NE: GT

This book was typeset and printed by Gulde-Druck in Tübingen on acid-free paper from
Papierfabrik Weissenstein in Pforzheim and bound by Heinrich Koch in Tübingen.

ISSN 0512-1604

Meinem Lehrer
Professor Dr. Dr. Peter Stuhlmacher
in aufrichtiger Dankbarkeit

Preface

The present study is the result of research and writing that I carried out as a Humboldt fellow at the University of Tübingen during the 1992−93 academic year. My original research proposal was to concentrate solely on the problem of the Galatian addressees from the perspective of Greco-Roman historical geography, hoping that, with the aid of new resources, I would be able to break the deadlock into which the worn-out discussion of the problem had slipped. Soon, however, I found it necessary to modify my approach by entertaining the possibility of a uniquely Jewish conception of geography and by extending the scope of my study to Paul's missionary strategy as a whole, thus setting the problem of the destination of Galatians within a new and broader context.

I would like to express my profound thanks to Professors Otto Betz, Martin Hengel, and Peter Stuhlmacher, to Privatdozent Rainer Riesner, and to Frau Anna Maria Schwemer of the Evangelisch-theologische Fakultät for their friendly encouragement and critical interaction during my research stay in Tübingen. I am especially grateful to my host, Professor Stuhlmacher, to whom this volume is dedicated, for assisting my family and me in many practical ways. We shall not forget his and his wife's kind hospitality. The incomparable resources of the Theologisches Seminar greatly facilitated my work from start to finish. The Seminar staff is to be thanked for all their helpfulness.

I would also like to express my gratitude to the Alexander von Humboldt Foundation for providing the fellowship that made this year of research and writing financially possible. I owe many thanks to Professors Hengel and Otfried Hofius for their willingness to include the present study in WUNT 1. For her painstaking work in compiling the indices I am much obliged to Catherine Porter. Finally, I would like to express my love and appreciation for my wife Gail, who, despite her own busy schedule, labored with me at every stage in the production of this volume.

November, 1993   James M. Scott

Contents

Chapter 1
The Table of Nations in Old Testament and Jewish Tradition

Chapter 2
Paul's Use of ΕΘΝΟΣ

Chapter 3
The Table of Nations in Paul

Chapter 4
The Table of Nations and the Destination of Galatians

Abbreviations

AB	Anchor Bible
ABD	D. N. Freedman (ed.), *Anchor Bible Dictionary*
AGJU	Arbeiten zur Geschichte des antiken Judentums und des Urchristentums
AJP	*American Journal of Philology*
AJT	*American Journal of Theology*
ALGHJ	Arbeiten zur Literatur und Geschichte des hellenistischen Judentums
AnBib	Analecta Biblica
AnOr	Analecta Orientalia
ANRW	*Aufstieg und Niedergang der römischen Welt*
ANTJ	Arbeiten zum Neuen Testament und Judentum
AOAT	Alter Orient und Altes Testament
ASNU	Acta seminarii neotestamentici upsaliensis
ATANT	Abhandlungen zur Theologie des Alten und Neuen Testaments
ATD	Das Alte Testament Deutsch
AusBR	*Australian Biblical Review*
BBET	Beiträge zur biblischen Exegese und Theologie
BDR	F. Blass, A. Debrunner, and F. Rehkopf, *Grammatik des neutestamentlichen Griechisch*
BETL	Bibliotheca ephemeridum theologicarum lovaniensium
BEvT	Beiträge zur evangelischen Theologie
BHH	B. Reicke and L. Rost (eds.), *Biblisch-historisches Handwörterbuch*
BHT	Beiträge zur historischen Theologie
Bib	*Biblica*
Bib. Ant.	Ps.-Philo, *Biblical Antiquities*
BibOr	Biblica et Orientalia
BJRL	*Bulletin of the John Rylands University Library of Manchester*
BJS	Brown Judaic Studies
BKAT	Biblischer Kommentar: Altes Testament
BSac	*Bibliotheca Sacra*
BZ	*Biblische Zeitschrift*
BWANT	Beiträge zur Wissenschaft vom Alten und Neuen Testament
CBQ	*Catholic Biblical Quarterly*
CIG	*Corpus Inscriptionum Graecarum*
CIJ	*Corpus Inscriptionum Iudaicarum*
CIL	*Corpus Inscriptionum Latinarum*
ConBOT	Coniectanea Biblica, Old Testament
CP	*Classical Philology*
CPSSup	Cambridge Philological Society Supplements
CRINT	Compendia Rerum Iudaicarum ad Novum Testamentum

DJD	Discoveries in the Judaean Desert
EKKNT	Evangelisch-katholischer Kommentar zum Neuen Testament
EncJud	*Encyclopaedia Judaica*
EPRO	Etudes préliminaires aux religions orientales dans l'empire Romain
EvQ	*Evangelical Quarterly*
EvT	*Evangelische Theologie*
EWNT	H. Balz and G. Schneider (eds.), *Exegetisches Wörterbuch zum Neuen Testament*
FRLANT	Forschungen zur Religion und Literatur des Alten und Neuen Testaments
GCS	Griechischen christlichen Schriftsteller
GTA	Göttinger theologische Arbeiten
HeyJ	*Heythrop Journal*
HNT	Handbuch zum Neuen Testament
HNTC	Harper's NT Commentaries
HSM	Harvard Semitic Monographs
HSS	Harvard Semitic Studies
HTKNT	Herders theologischer Kommentar zum Neuen Testament
HUCA	*Hebrew Union College Annual*
HUT	Hermeneutische Untersuchungen zur Theologie
ICC	International Critical Commentary
IDB	G. A. Buttrick (ed.), *Interpreter's Dictionary of the Bible*
IDBSup	Supplementary volume to *IDB*
IEJ	*Israel Exploration Journal*
IG	*Inscriptiones Graecae*
IGRR	*Inscriptiones Graecae ad Res Romanas pertinentes*
ILS	H. Dessau (ed.), *Inscriptiones Latinae Selectae*
ISBE	G. W. Bromiley (ed.), *International Standard Bible Encyclopedia*
JAOS	*Journal of the American Oriental Society*
JBL	*Journal of Biblical Literature*
JJS	*Journal of Jewish Studies*
Jos. As.	*Joseph and Aseneth*
JQR	*Jewish Quarterly Review*
JRS	*Journal of Roman Studies*
JSHRZ	Jüdische Schriften aus hellenistisch-römischer Zeit
JSJ	*Journal for the Study of Judaism in the Persian, Hellenistic and Roman Period*
JSNT	*Journal for the Study of the New Testament*
JSNTSup	Journal for the Study of the New Testament – Supplement Series
JSOT	*Journal for the Study of the Old Testament*
JSOTSup	Journal for the Study of the Old Testament – Supplement Series
JSP	*Journal for the Study of the Pseudepigrapha*
JSS	*Journal of Semitic Studies*
JTS	*Journal of Theological Studies*
Jub.	*Jubilees*
LSJ	Liddell-Scott-Jones, *Greek-English Lexicon*
MAMA	*Monumenta Asiae Minoris Antiqua*
MGWJ	*Monatsschrift für Geschichte und Wissenschaft des Judentums*
NICNT	New International Commentary on the New Testament

NIDNTT	Colin Brown (ed.), *The New International Dictionary of New Testament Theology*
NIGTC	The New International Greek Testament Commentary
NovT	*Novum Testamentum*
NovTSup	Novum Testamentum, Supplements
NTD	Das Neue Testament Deutsch
NTOA	Novum Testamentum et Orbis Antiquus
NTS	*New Testament Studies*
NTTS	New Testament Tools and Studies
OBO	Orbis Biblicus et Orientalis
OCD	*Oxford Classical Dictionary*
OGIS	W. Dittenberger (ed.), *Orientis Graeci Inscriptiones Selectae*
OTP	J. H. Charlesworth (ed.), *The Old Testament Pseudepigrapha*
OTS	*Oudtestamentische Studiën*
Pss. Sol.	*Psalms of Solomon*
PTMS	Pittsburgh (Princeton) Theological Monograph Series
PVTG	Pseudepigrapha Veteris Testamenti graece
PW	Pauly-Wissowa, *Realencyclopädie der classischen Altertumswissenschaft*
QD	Quaestiones disputatae
RAC	*Reallexikon für Antike und Christentum*
RB	*Revue biblique*
RevQ	*Revue de Qumran*
RNT	Regensburger Neues Testament
RSR	*Recherches de science religieuse*
SANT	Studien zum Alten und Neuen Testament
SBLDS	Society of Biblical Literature Dissertation Series
SBLRBS	SBL Resources for Biblical Study
SBLTT	SBL Texts and Translations
SC	Sources chrétiennes
Sib. Or.	*Sibyline Oracles*
SNTSMS	Society for New Testament Studies Monograph Series
SO	Symbolae osloenses
SPB	Studia Postbiblica
STDJ	Studies on Texts of the Desert of Judah
Str-B	[H. Strack and] P. Billerbeck, *Kommentar zum Neuen Testament*
SUNT	Studien zur Umwelt des Neuen Testaments
SVTP	Studia in Veteris Testamenti Pseudepigrapha
TBei	*Theologische Beiträge*
T. Ben.	*Testament of Benjamin*
THKNT	Theologischer Handkommentar zum Neuen Testament
T. Jud.	*Testament of Judah*
T. Lev.	*Testament of Levi*
Tg. Neof.	*Targum Neofiti I*
Tg. Onq.	*Targum Onqelos*
Tg. Ps.-J.	*Targum Pseudo-Jonathan*
Tg. Yer.	*Targum Yerushalmi*
TQ	*Theologische Quartalschrift*
TRE	*Theologische Realenzyklopädie*

TU	Texte und Untersuchungen
TWAT	G.J. Botterweck and H. Ringgren (eds.), *Theologisches Wörterbuch zum Alten Testament*
TWNT	G. Kittel and G. Friedrich (eds.), *Theologisches Wörterbuch zum Neuen Testament*
TynBul	*Tyndale Bulletin*
USQR	*Union Seminary Quarterly Review*
VP	*Vitae Prophetarum*
VT	*Vetus Testamentum*
VTSup	Vetus Testamentum, Supplements
WBC	Word Biblical Commentary
WMANT	Wissenschaftliche Monographien zum Alten und Neuen Testament
WO	*Die Welt des Orients*
WUNT	Wissenschaftliche Untersuchungen zum Neuen Testament
ZAH	*Zeitschrift für Althebraistik*
ZAW	*Zeitschrift für alttestamentliche Wissenschaft*
ZDPV	*Zeitschrift des deutschen Palästina-Vereins*
ZNW	*Zeitschrift für neutestamentliche Wissenschaft*
ZTK	*Zeitschrift für Theologie und Kirche*

Introduction

> ... geographical knowledge is an essential element in any view of the world in a more immediate and direct way than is historical knowledge, and full understanding of the outlook of any individual in antiquity – or indeed at any period before the modern era – depends to a considerable extent on our ability to assess his geographical horizon.[1]

The Destination of Galatians

Who are the addressees in Paul's letter "to the churches of Galatia" (Gal 1:2)? Who are the ones apostrophized as "O foolish Galatians!" (3:1)? As is well known, the discussion on this question has centered for the last century on two basic answers:

(1) the *North Galatian Hypothesis*, the traditional and still most widely accepted view, which holds that Paul wrote his letter to churches presumably founded on his so-called Second Missionary Journey in Galatia proper (cf. Acts 16:6), the original territory of the three Gaulic tribes who settled in central Anatolia;

(2) the *South Galatian Hypothesis*, a more recent view articulated in its classic form by W. M. RAMSAY in 1899, which holds that Paul wrote his letter to churches founded on his so-called First Missionary Journey at Antioch, Iconium, and Lystra (and Derbe), located in the southern part of the more extensive Roman province of Galatia.

According to the North Galatian position, "Galatians" is an ethnic term and would not have been used by Paul to address the inhabitants of South Galatia.[2] According to the South Galatian position, on the other hand, there is no evidence from Acts that Paul ever established churches in North Galatia, and, departing from Antioch, he would have never deviated from his course toward the northwest by travelling over the Sultan Dagh into the land of North Galatia.[3] The debate has been kept alive over the years mostly by proponents of the South Galatian Hypothesis, who, mostly by reiterating the classic argu-

---

[1] P. M. FRASER, *Ptolemaic Alexandria* (3 vols.; Oxford: Clarendon Press, 1972), 1:520.

[2] Cf. Hans HÜBNER, "Galaterbrief," *TRE*, 12 (1984) 6; Jürgen BECKER, *Paulus. Apostel der Völker* (Tübingen: Mohr-Siebeck, 1989), p. 287; Werner Georg KÜMMEL, *Einleitung in das Neue Testament* (21st ed.; Heidelberg: Quelle & Meyer, 1983), p. 259.

[3] Cf., most recently, Rainer RIESNER, *Die Frühzeit des Apostels Paulus. Studien zur*

ments of RAMSAY, have sought to effect a paradigm shift in the scholarly community. However, cumbersome arguments from Greco-Roman historical geography, based on sometimes obscure epigraphic evidence about a remote and recondite part of Asia Minor,[4] coupled with an interpretation of Paul's missionary strategy as one of concentration on the main roads and centers of communication in the Roman provinces, have failed as yet to tip the scales. In fact, nowadays, the sentiment seems to be growing that the debate is either inconsequential and/or undecidable.[5]

A Jewish Perspective on the Problem

The curious thing about this whole debate is that it has proceeded almost exclusively on the basis of considerations from Greco-Roman historical geography without considering the possibility of a Jewish perspective on the matter. Paul may have been born in Tarsus, but he was raised and educated in Jerusalem.[6] Therefore, the possibility of a Jewish background must always be considered when discussing Paul. In his important but unfortunately unpublished and little known Cambridge dissertation on "The Toponymy of the Targumim,"[7] Philip S. ALEXANDER argues that Jews learned geography in conjunction with their study of the Bible, just as Greeks learned geography from their study of Homer.[8] "Thus the Bible," writes ALEXANDER, "functioned

---

Chronologie, Missionsstrategie und Theologie (WUNT 71; Tübingen: Mohr-Siebeck, 1994), pp. 250–254.

[4] Not even historians and archaeologists in the field of Anatolian studies, let alone NT scholars, find it easy to discuss this area. For example, David FRENCH, after many years of collecting and interpreting evidence of Roman roads in Asia Minor (including Galatia), must admit: "My knowledge is uneven. Much is still *terra incognita* to me" (*Roman Roads and Milestones of Asia Minor, Fasc. 2.1* [British Institute of Archaeology at Ankara Monograph 9; BAR International Series 391(i); Oxford: BAR, 1988], p. i).

[5] Cf. Hans Dieter BETZ, *Galatians: A Commentary on Paul's Letter to the Galatians* (Hermeneia; Philadelphia: Fortress, 1979), p. 5: "It is not necessary at this point to discuss fully the pros and cons of the two theories. The arguments used on both sides are mostly speculative. [...] ... we are not in the position to say with certainty on which of his journeys Paul founded the churches." Also Heinrich SCHLIER, *Der Brief an die Galater* (12th ed.; Kritisch-exegetischer Kommentar über das Neue Testament 7; Göttingen: Vandenhoeck & Ruprecht, 1962), p. 17 n. 1, who describes the two theories as a question, "die exegetisch längst nicht die Bedeutung hat, die ihr oft zugeschrieben wird ..." Even F. F. BRUCE, who clearly favors the South Galatian view, concludes his survey of the topic with this sobering statement: "The fact that so many competent scholars can be cited in support of either position suggests that the evidence for neither is absolutely conclusive" ("Galatian Problems 2. North or South Galatians?" *BJRL* 52 [1969–70] 243–266 [here p. 266]).

[6] Cf. Martin HENGEL, *The Pre-Christian Paul* (London: SCM Press; Philadelphia: Trinity Press International, 1991), pp. 1–62.

[7] P. S. ALEXANDER reports that he is preparing a monograph on *Early Jewish Geographical Lore* (cf. idem, "Notes on the 'Imago Mundi' of the Book of Jubilees," *JJS* 33 (1982) 197–213 [here p. 203 n. 11]).

[8] P. S. ALEXANDER, "The Toponymy of the Targumim, with Special Reference to the Table

for the Rabbis in geography as a co-ordinating frame of reference and an information storage system. A new geographical fact was not assimilated until it was put on the 'Biblical map',"[9] for, as he goes on to explain, the Bible has an excellent range of texts that could be (and were) used as the basis of a comprehensive program of geographical study: (1) The Creation story in Genesis 1−3 provided the framework for a general and theoretical geography; (2) the Table of Nations in Genesis 10 provided a basic regional geography and ethnography; and (3) the Boundaries of the Land in Numbers 34 provided an outline geography of the Land of Israel.[10]

If the Bible was thus so fundamental to the Rabbinic understanding of geography, what place might it have had in the thinking of Paul about his mission in general and about the Galatians in particular? We know that Paul is otherwise deeply indebted to OT and Jewish traditions for his perspectives. Why not also for his geography? Of course, we are not interested here so much in a possible theoretical geography based on Genesis 1−3 or in the geography of the Land of Israel from Numbers 34 but rather in the Table of Nations of Genesis 10, for the Table of Nations provides the regional geography and ethnography that formed the basis not just of Rabbinic tradition but, as we shall see, of pre-Rabbinic tradition as well.[11] Is it possible that the Apostle to the ἔθνη derived his fundamental orientation to the nations from the Table of Nations? Here is a question that, oddly enough, has not even been considered. Yet, this is also a question that can contribute to our understanding of the identity of the Galatian addressees from Paul's perspective.

Method

In order to consider the possible influence of the Table of Nations on Paul's understanding of the Galatians, the following discussion is divided into three parts. First of all, we shall examine the Table of Nations itself along with the OT and Jewish tradition that develops from it (Chap. 1). Second, we shall consider whether there is evidence that Paul appropriates the Table-of-Nations tradition. This will necessitate not only an extensive study of Paul's use of ἔθνος against its OT and Jewish background (Chap. 2) but also an investigation into

---

of Nations and the Boundaries of the Land of Israel" (D. Phil. thesis, Oxford University, 1974), pp. 11−17. In ALEXANDER's view, the geographic material of the Targumim has as its *Sitz im Leben* the instruction of children in the *Bet Sepher* (ibid., pp. 13−14).

[9] Ibid., p. 13.

[10] Ibid., pp. 16−17. See now, for example, Nadav NA'AMAN, *Borders and Districts in Biblical Historiography: Seven Studies in Biblical Geographical Lists* (Jerusalem Biblical Studies 4; Jerusalem: Simor, 1986).

[11] As ALEXANDER points out, the Table of Nations provided a basic regional geography and ethnography for Judaism and Christianity all the way up to the late Middle Ages ("Toponomy," p. 16; cf. idem, "Imago Mundi," pp. 212−213). We are dealing here with a very fundamental and pervasive tradition.

geographical aspects of Paul's missionary strategy (Chap. 3). Third, in light of these considerations, we shall turn to the question of the Galatian addressees itself (Chap. 4).

Chapter 1

The Table of Nations in Old Testament
and Jewish Tradition

Introduction

The genealogy in Genesis 10, commonly known as the "Table of Nations," represents an ethnographic and geographic tradition that is quite pervasive in the OT and in Jewish literature. Not only does the Chronicler appropriate this so-called "table" at the very beginning of his two-volume work (1 Chr 1:1–2:2), but other OT writers also make extensive use of the tradition (e. g., Ezekiel 27, 38–39; Daniel 11; Isa 66:18–20). Jewish literature of the Second Temple period continues and modifies this tradition, often combining it with prevalent Hellenistic conceptions of ethnography and geography.

The Table of Nations in the Old Testament

The Table of Nations in Genesis 10

The Table of Nations in Genesis 10 concludes with a summary, in which the plural term "nations" occurs for the first time in the Hebrew Bible in reference to all "the nations" of the world: "These are the families of Noah's sons, according to their genealogies, in their nations (גוים, ἔθνη); and from these the nations (הגוים, τὰ ἔθνη) spread abroad after the flood" (v. 32).[1] Thus after the Deluge, in which "all flesh died that moved on the earth" (Gen 7:21; cf. vv. 22–23), Noah became, in essence, the father of all postdiluvian nations on earth. Noah, his three sons – Shem, Ham, and Japheth – and their wives emerged from the ark, receiving a mandate to be fruitful and multiply and to fill the earth (Gen 9:1), which is an exact reiteration of the mandate to Adam (Gen 1:28). Hence, from these sons the whole earth was repopulated (Gen 9:19). Genesis 10 gives a list of the (traditionally 70 or 72[2]) nations that descended

---

[1] Here, we are concerned with the final form of the text and its reception in later Jewish tradition. The text of Genesis 10 is usually understood as combining material from both P (vv. 1a, 2–7, 20, 22–23, 31–32) and J (1b, 8–19, 21, 24–30). See Table 1 for an overview. For a cartographic reconstruction of the territories covered by P and J, see H. Graf REVENTLOW, "Völkertafel," in *BHH*, 3 (1966) 2112–2115 (here cols. 2113–2114).

[2] The Jewish tradition that humanity is made up of 70 nations is based on the count in the

from Noah's sons (see Table 1). Although several of the identifications in the list remain uncertain,[3] and the criteria by which the nations were distinguished are disputed,[4] nevertheless, the main contours of the earth's division among the three sons are relatively clear: the nations of *Japheth* in the northern and western lands, including Asia Minor[5] and Europe (Gen 10:2−5);[6] the nations

Table of Nations (see Table 1) although the sum itself is not stated in the text. The same number of Nations seems to underlie Deut 32:8 MT, which speaks of God's dividing mankind "in accordance with the number of the sons of Israel." According to Gen 46:27; Ex 1:5; Deut 10:22, this number was 70 (cf. *Num. Rab.* 9:14). On the other hand, the Septuagint and the 4Q Deuteronomy fragment, which read "the sons of God" (i.e. angels) instead of "the sons of Israel" reflect the notion, dated as early as the Persian period (Dan 10:20) and possibly earlier (Ps 82:7), that every nation has a divine patron. Note that *Tg. Yer.* to Gen 46:27 combines both of these interpretations. In some Jewish and Christian sources, the number of nations is assumed to be 72, following the Septuagintal version of Genesis 10. See further Samuel KRAUSS, "Die Zahl der biblischen Völkerschaften," *ZAW* 19 (1899) 1−14; idem, "Zur Zahl der biblischen Völkerschaften," *ZAW* 20 (1900) 38−43; Samuel POZNANSKI, "Zur Zahl der biblischen Völker," *ZAW* 24 (1904) 301−308; R. MEYER, "Die Bedeutung des Deuteronomium 32, 8f.43 (4Q) für die Auslegung des Moseliedes," in *Verbannung und Heimkehr. Beiträge zur Geschichte und Theologie Israels im 6. und 5. Jahrhundert v. Chr. Wilhelm Rudolf zum 70. Geburtstag* (ed. Arnulf Kuschke; Tübingen: Mohr-Siebeck, 1961), pp. 197−210; Daniel SPERBER, "Nations, the Seventy," *EncJud*, 12 (1971) 882−886; Isaiah GAFNI, "Seventy Shepherds, Vision of," *EncJud*, 14 (1971) 1198−1199; Christoph UEHLING-ER, *Weltreich und "eine Rede". Eine neue Deutung der sogenannten Turmbauerzählung (Gen 11,1−9)* (OBO 101; Freiburg: Universitätsverlag Freiburg; Göttingen: Vandenhoeck & Rup-recht, 1990), pp. 51−55; Martin HENGEL, *Judentum und Hellenismus. Studien zu ihrer Begeg-nung unter besonderer Berücksichtigung Palästinas bis zur Mitte des 2. Jh.s v. Chr.* (3rd ed.; WUNT 10; Tübingen: Mohr-Siebeck, 1988), pp. 342−343 (on *1 Enoch* 85−90); Brendon BYRNE, *'Sons of God' - 'Seed of Abraham': A Study of the Idea of the Sonship of God of all Christians against the Jewish Background* (AnBib 83; Rome: Biblical Institute Press, 1979), pp. 10 n. 3, 12, 22; Harry M. ORLINSKY, "The Septuagint and its Hebrew Text," in *The Cambridge History of Judaism, Vol. 2: The Hellenistic Age* (ed. W. D. Davies, et al.; Cam-bridge: Cambridge University Press, 1989), pp. 537−540.

[3] Cf., e. g., Claus WESTERMANN, *Genesis* (3 vols.; 3rd ed.; BKAT 1; Neukirchen-Vluyn: Neukirchener Verlag, 1983), 1:673ff.; J. SIMONS, "The 'Table of Nations' (Gen. X): Its General Structure and Meaning," *OTS* 10 (1954) 155−184; Alan P. Ross, "The Table of Nations in Genesis 10 – Its Structure," *BSac* 137 (1980) 340−353; idem, "The Table of Nations in Genesis 10 – Its Content," *BSac* 138 (1981) 22−34. See further John Van SETERS, *Prologue to History: The Yahwist as Historian in Genesis* (Zürich: Theologischer Verlag, 1992), pp. 174−187; John HAMLIN, "Three Metaphors for the Inhabited World [Genesis 10; Jer 25:15−29; Ezekiel 27]," *Proceedings of the Eastern Great Lakes and Midwest Bible Societies* 9 (1989) 49−58.

[4] Cf. B. ODED, "The Table of Nations (Genesis 10) – A Socio-cultural Approach," *ZAW* 98 (1986) 14−31; Philip S. ALEXANDER, "Geography and the Bible (Early Jewish)," *ABD*, 2 (1992) 977−988 (here p. 980).

[5] Although Lud in western Asia Minor (Lydia) is grouped with Shem (Gen 10:22) and not, as might be expected, with Japheth.

[6] For the modern, often uncertain, identifications of the sons and grandsons of Japheth, of which only a representative sample is given here, see Édouard LIPIŃSKI, "Les Japhétites selon Gen 10,2−4 et 1 Chr 1,5−7," *ZAH* 3 (1990) 40−52; P.-R. BERGER, "Ellasar, Tarschisch und Jawan, Gn 14 und 10," *Die Welt des Orients* 13 (1982) 50−78; Édouard DHORME, "Les peuples issus de Japhet," in *Études bibliques et orientales* (Paris: Imprimerie Nationale, 1951),

Table 1
The Table of Nations According to the Sequence of Genesis 10.
P-source in roman type; J-source in italic.

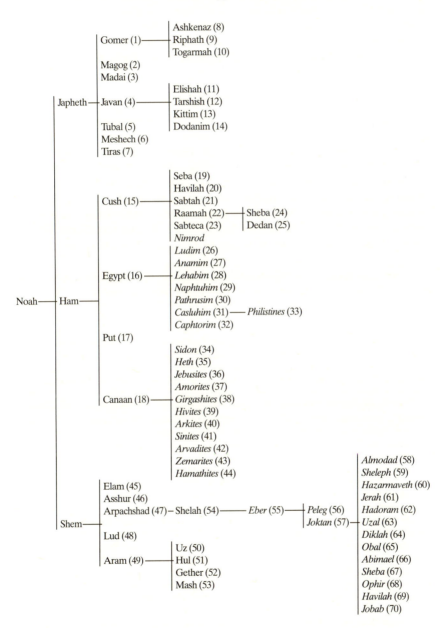

of *Ham* in Egypt and North Africa (vv. 6–20); and the nations of *Shem* in Mesopotamia and Arabia (vv. 21–31). As Yohanan AHARONI observes, "All of the human family is divided into three main groups which *surrounded Palestine*: the sons of Shem to the east, the sons of Ham to the south and the sons of Japheth to the north and west. [...] The Table of Nations ... gives a faithful sketch of Palestine's position among the peoples and kingdoms of the ancient Near East, where the three spheres of Shem, Ham and Japheth intersected."[7]

The Table of Nations in 1 Chronicles 1:1–2:2

The centrality of Israel among the nations is brought out more clearly in 1 Chr 1:1–2:2. Whereas Genesis recounts a development that led to Israel, 1 Chronicles describes the world and the relationship of nations to Israel as they were at the time of writing in the postexilic period.[8] According to Magnar KARTVEIT,[9] the Chronicler weaves the Genesis Table of Nations into a genealogical context that extends from Adam to Israel (1 Chr 1:1–2:2), thereby putting special emphasis on Israel. After briefly listing the sons of Japheth (vv. 5–7) and the sons of Ham (vv. 8–16), the text delves into an extensive listing of the sons of Shem (1:17–2:2), particularly the sons of

---

167–189; David NEIMAN, "The Two Genealogies of Japhet," in *Orient and Occident: Essays Presented to Cyrus H. Gordon on the Occasion of his Sixty-fifth Birthday* (ed. Harry A. Hoffner, Jr.; AOAT 22; Kevelaer: Verlag Butzon & Becker; Neukirchen-Vluyn: Neukirchener Verlag, 1973), 119–126; Friedrich SCHMIDTKE, *Die Japhetiten der biblischen Völkertafel* (Breslauer Studien zur historischen Theologie 7; Breslau: Verlag Müller & Seiffert, 1926); WESTERMANN, *Genesis*, 1:673–681; John SKINNER, *A Critical and Exegetical Commentary on Genesis* (2nd ed.; ICC; Edinburgh: T. & T. Clark, 1930), pp. 196–200; E. A. SPEISER, *Genesis* (AB 1; Garden City, NY: Doubleday, 1964), pp. 65–66. On the idea of the "islands of the nations" in Gen 10:5, see Wayne HOROWITZ, "The Isles of the Nations: Genesis X and Babylonian Geography," in *Studies in the Pentateuch* (ed. J. A. Emerton; VTSup 41; Leiden: Brill, 1990), pp. 35–43. Arguing that some OT toponyms can be explained in terms of "symbolic-metaphorical or even theological geography," Manfred GÖRG speculates, for example, that Tarshish is to be understood not as a concrete place but as a "distant land full of valuable things" ("Ophir, Tarschisch und Atlantis. Einige Gedanken zur symbolischen Topographie," *Biblische Notizen* 15 [1981] 76–86).

[7] Yohanan AHARONI, *The Land of the Bible: A Historical Geography* (London: Burns & Oates, 1979), pp. 6, 8. See also Yohanan AHARONI and Michael AVI-YONAH, *The Macmillan Bible Atlas* (2nd ed.; trans. A. F. Rainey; New York: Macmillan; London: Collier, 1968), p. 21 (with a map showing the intersection of the three spheres); REVENTLOW, "Völkertafel," 3:2115: "um Israel als Mittelpunkt (Nabel) gruppiert, das jedoch selbst nicht genannt ist." But see D. J. WISEMAN, ed., *Peoples of Old Testament Times* (Oxford: Clarendon Press, 1973), p. xviii; Jamie SCOTT and Paul SIMPSON-HOUSLEY, eds., *Sacred Places and Profane Spaces: Essays in the Geographics of Judaism, Christianity, and Islam* (New York: Greenwood, 1991).

[8] Cf. Thomas WILLI, *Chronik* (BKAT 24.1; Neukirchen-Vluyn: Neukirchener Verlag, 1991), p. 23. For a convenient comparison between Genesis 10 and 1 Chr 1:5–23, see Jürgen KEGLER, *Synopse zum Chronistischen Geschichtswerk* (Beiträge zur Erforschung des Alten Testaments und des antiken Judentums 1; Frankfurt a. M.: Lang, 1984), pp. 74–75.

[9] Magnar KARTVEIT, *Motive und Schichten der Landtheologie in I Chronik 1–9* (ConBOT 28; Stockholm: Almquist & Wiksell, 1989), pp. 110–117.

Abraham (vv. 28ff.). In v. 34, the text lists Esau and *Israel*, instead of Esau and Jacob. In 2:1−2, the "sons of Israel" are enumerated. The text wants to show that in the middle of the nations of the world, there is Israel.[10] In fact, KARTVEIT argues that 1 Chronicles lists the nations of the world "in a circle" that moves counterclockwise – from the North, to the West, to the South, and to the East – with Israel in the center.[11] Thus, according to KARTVEIT,

I [Chronik] 1 ist nicht nur eine Genealogie, sondern auch eine *mappa mundi*, vielleicht sogar ein Ausdruck einer *imago mundi*, wo Israel in der Mitte liegt. Es ist die einzige Stelle des ATs, wo die Genealogien der Urgeschichte mit der Völkertafel und den Angaben zu den südlichen Nachbarvölkern verbunden werden, und dadurch eine einzigartige Konzeption. Hier ist zwar kein *Wort* von einer *tabbur ha'araes* ["navel of the earth"]. Ist aber das Kapitel nicht von der Vorstellung beherrscht, dass Israel das Volk inmitten der Völker ist und in einem Land inmitten der Länder wohnt? Aus einer späteren Zeit ist eine solche "Weltkarte" bekannt, die deutlich die Vorstellung ausspricht, dass Sem das Los der Mitte der Welt zufiel, Jub 8,12−9,15, vgl. besonders 8,12.[12]

Manfred OEMING agrees with KARTVEIT's interpretation of 1 Chronicles 1 as "Israel-centric,"[13] adducing an astrological inscription from the synagogue of En-Gedi (5th-6th cent. A.D.) as an example that the passage was indeed interpreted this way in early Judaism.[14] Already in the OT, however, there is the concept that Yahweh set Jerusalem "in the middle of the nations" (Ezek 5:5) and that Jerusalem is the "navel of the earth" (Ezek 38:12).[15] We may

---

[10] Ibid., p. 112.

[11] Ibid., p. 114.

[12] Ibid., pp. 116−117. On the exposition of the Table of Nations in *Jubilees 8−9*, see further below.

[13] Cf. Manfred OEMING, *Das wahre Israel. Die "genealogische Vorhalle" 1 Chronik 1−9* (BWANT 7.8; Stuttgart: Kohlhammer, 1990), pp. 90−91.

[14] Ibid., pp. 90−95. In the inscription, the first thirteen names of 1 Chronicles 1 are directly connected with the Twelve Signs of the Zodiac; these are, in turn, connected with the names of the twelve months of the year. The series is completed with the three Patriarchs (Abraham, Isaac, and Jacob) and the three friends of Daniel. Thus, the beginning and the end of Israel's salvation history in the canonical OT are coupled with the order of the cosmos. On the En-Gedi inscription, see further WILLI, *Chronik*, pp. 49−51. On the Zodaic in Judaism (incl. early Palestinian synagogues), see James H. CHARLESWORTH, "Jewish Interest in Astrology during the Hellenistic and Roman Period," in *ANRW* II.20.2 (ed. Wolfgang Haase; Berlin/New York: de Gruyter, 1987), pp. 926−952; also idem, "Die 'Schrift des Sem': Einführung, Text und Übersetzung," in ibid., pp. 953−987; Pierre PRIGENT, *Le Judaïsme et l'image* (Texte und Studien zum Antiken Judentum 24; Tübingen: Mohr-Siebeck, 1990), pp. 159−173 (on En Gedi, pp. 164−165). See further Hans Georg GUNDEL, *Zodiakos. Tierkreisbilder im Altertum: Kosmische Bezüge und Jenseitsvorstellungen im antiken Alltagsleben* (Kulturgeschichte der antiken Welt 54; Mainz am Rhein: Philipp von Zabern, 1992). On the connection between the Zodiac and the twelve tribes of Israel, see Philo *Fug.* 185; *Praem.* 65.

[15] Cf. Walther ZIMMERLI, *Ezechiel* (2 vols.; 2nd ed.; BKAT 13.1; Neukirchen-Vluyn: Neukirchener Verlag, 1979), 1:132−133; 2:955−957. On the other hand, S. TALMON denies that Ezek 5:5 and 38:12 can be interpreted in terms of the center of the world, charging that this amounts to foisting later Greek and Jewish ideas onto the text ("הר," *TWAT*, 2:459−483 [here

compare the funerary inscription of Darius I (522–486 B.C.) from Naqsh-i-
Rustam, which contains a map of Darius' empire consisting of three concentric
circles, with lists of the thirty nations in the empire arrayed about "Parsa
(Persepolis)," the capital, in the center (i.e., the center of the earth!).[16] In the
second circle, nations are listed in four columns radiating out perpendicularly
from the center according to the cardinal points of the compass, beginning with
the North and proceeding clockwise to the West. In the outermost circle,
nations are listed counterclockwise along the inside perimeter. We are dealing
here with a common geographical conception of ancient Near-Eastern empires.[17]

The Table of Nations in OT Eschatology

In the OT, the Table of Nations is valid not only as a description of the past
(Genesis 10) and of the present (1 Chr 1:1–2:2) but also of the eschatological
future. The Table of Nations is seen as timeless in its applicability. Examples
from Ezekiel, Daniel, and Isaiah will suffice for the moment to establish this
point.

Ezekiel 38–39. The concept of Jerusalem as the navel of the earth as found in
Ezek 38:12 reveals contact with the Table of Nations since it comes within the
eschatological context of the Gog and Magog oracles (Ezekiel 38–39). After
Israel and Judah are reunited and restored to the Land in safety (Ezekiel
36–37; 38:8, 11–12, 14), they can expect an invasion by hostile nations that will
culminate in a final, decisive battle between God and the nations. These nations
are called by names familiar from the Table of Nations: Magog (Ezek 38:2;
39:6; cf. Gen 10:2), Meshech (38:2, 3; 39:1; cf. Gen 10:2), Tubal (38:2, 3; 39:1;
cf. Gen 10:2), Cush (38:5; cf. Gen 10:6, 7, 8), Put (38:5; cf. Gen 10:6), Gomer
(38:6; cf. Gen 10:2, 3), Togarmah (38:6; cf. Gen 10:3), and Tarshish (38:13; cf.
Gen 10:4).[18] Most of these nations are listed as sons of Japheth in Genesis 10

---

cols. 471–473]; cf. also idem, "*Tabûr ha'arez* and the Comparative Method," *Tarbiz* 45
[1975–76] 163–177 [English summary, p. XI]).

[16] For a drawing of the map and commentary, see Paul GOUKOWSKY, "L'espace impérial de
Darios Ier," in *Essai sur les origines du mythe d'Alexandre (336–270 av. J.-C.), Vol. 1: Les
origines politiques* (Nancy: Bialec, 1978), pp. 222–224.

[17] See the Babylonian world map, containing two concentric circles with Babylon in the
center. Cf. Wayne HOROWITZ, "The Babylonian Map of the World," *Iraq* 50 (1988) 147–163,
which includes drawings of the map, together with transcriptions of the accompanying inscriptions, translations, and commentary.

[18] Cf. Walther ZIMMERLI, *Ezechiel*, 2:941: "Gn 10 (P) steht traditionsgeschichtlich in der
Nähe von Ez 38f." The influence of the Table-of-Nations tradition is also apparent in the
extensive list of Tyre's international trading partners in Ezekiel 27:

Ezekiel 27	Nation	Genesis 10	Noah's Son
v. 6	Kittim	v. 4	Japheth
v. 7	Mizraim	v. 6	Ham
v. 7	Elishah	v. 4	Japheth

(Magog, Meshech, Tubal, Gomer, Togarmah, Tarshish); the other two are listed as sons of Ham (Cush, Put). Hence, according to Ezekiel's oracle, nations from both the north and the south will converge on the center of the earth to destroy and plunder Israel of the Restoration.

Daniel 11. We find a similar eschatological expectation in the Book of Daniel. After "the kingdom of Javan" is divided among the successors (Dan 11:2—4), "the king of the south" (Egypt) will engage in battle with "the king of the north" (vv. 7ff.). After being thwarted by the Kittim (v. 30) and setting up the abomination of desolations in the Jerusalem Temple (v. 31), the king of the north will eventually defeat the king of the south, as well as the Libyans and the Cushites (vv. 42—43), thereby becoming the new world empire. Finally, he will enter a battle in order to completely destroy all peoples (v. 44).[19] The text states that he will pitch his tents "between the sea and the beautiful Holy Mountain" (v. 45a). Yet he shall meet his end, with no one to help him (v. 45b). According to Hartmut GESE, this conception is based on the tradition, found in Ezekiel 38—39 and elsewhere, of the final battle for Mount Zion, the cosmic center,[20] when the world power assembled against God is defeated.[21] Like Ezekiel 38—39, furthermore, Daniel 11, with its mention of several nations (Javan,[22]

Ezekiel 27	Nation	Genesis 10	Noah's Son
v. 8	Sidon	v. 15	Ham
v. 8	Zemer	v. 18	Ham
v. 10	Lud	v. 22	Shem
v. 10	Put	v. 6	Ham
vv. 12, 25	Tarshish	v. 4	Japheth
vv. 13, 19	Javan	vv. 2, 4	Japheth
v. 13	Tubal	v. 2	Japheth
v. 13	Meshech	v. 2	Japheth
v. 14	Togarmah	v. 3	Japheth
vv. 15, 20	Dedan	v. 7	Ham
vv. 22, 23	Sheba	v. 7	Ham
v. 22	Raamah	v. 7	Ham
v. 23	Asshur	vv. 11, 22	Shem

As this table shows, descendants of all three sons of Noah are represented in the list: Japhethites and Hamites seven times each and Shemites twice.

[19] As Hartmut GESE points out, the Hebrew word רבים ("many") means "all" here ("Das Geschichtsbild des Danielbuches und Ägypten," in *Alttestamentliche Studien* [Tübingen: Mohr-Siebeck, 1991] p. 198 n. 36).

[20] Once there is an explicit reference to "the middle of the earth" (Dan 4:7), although it is not Jerusalem. The tree at the center of the earth that was visible to the ends of the whole earth (4:7—8) is interpreted as referring to Nebuchadnezzar (cf. v. 19). Cf. Ezekiel 31, where Assyria is called a tree (v. 3), under whose shadow "the whole multitude of nations" dwelled (v. 6). Nevertheless, Daniel strongly implies that Jerusalem is the center of the earth by referring to it as "the Holy Mountain" (cf. Dan 9:20; 11:45).

[21] GESE, "Das Geschichtsbild des Danielbuches und Ägypten," p. 198.

[22] יון/ Ἕλληνες (8:21; 10:20; 11:2; cf. Gen 10:2, 4).

Kittim,[23] Mizraim,[24] Cushites,[25] Lubim[26]) and its implication of Jerusalem as the center of a tripartite world (north, south, and center), seems to be influenced by the Table-of-Nations tradition.[27] This is substantiated not only by Daniel's recurrent emphasis on "all peoples, nations, and tongues" (cf. Dan 3:4, 7, 29, 31; 6:26; 7:14), which reflects the scope of the Table of Nations (cf. Gen 10:5, 20, 31) but also by Daniel's explicit reference to the origin of the nations (cf. Dan 12:1)[28] and to the angelic princes who were set over them.[29]

Isaiah 66:18–20. Despite the impression that Ezekiel 38–39 and Daniel 11 may leave, eschatological texts of the OT do not always portray the relationship of the nations to Israel as hostile, especially when Zion is seen as the goal of the pilgrimage of the nations at the time of the Restoration of Israel.[30] In that day, the nations will come to Zion in order to bring tribute (Isaiah 60) and to be taught (Isa 2:2–5 = Mic 4:1–5). The post-exilic prophets expect that in Jerusalem, the nations will acknowledge the one true God of all people (Zech 8:22–23; cf. Isa 45:14–15; 56:3–8). Zion will become the Mother of all peoples (Psalm 87). The Isaiah Apocalypse (Isaiah 24–27) foresees a feast for all peoples, to be provided "on this mountain" by the Lord of Hosts (25:6–7). According to Isa 19:23–24, "On that day there will be a highway from Egypt to

---

23 כתים/Κίτιοι (11:30; cf. Gen 10:4).

24 מצרים/Αἴγυπτος (9:15; 11:8, 24, 42, 43; cf. Gen 10:6, 13).

25 כשים/Αἰθίοπες (11:43; cf. Gen 10:6, 7).

26 The relationship of the Lubim (Libyans) to Lehabim, the third son of Mizraim in the Table of Nations (cf. Gen 10:13), is obscure, although by their location in North Africa, they would clearly belong to the descendants of Ham. Josephus states both that Put, the third son of Ham (cf. Gen 10:6), colonized Libya (*Ant.* 1.132) and that Labimus (biblical Lehabim) settled in Libya (§ 137).

27 Daniel also includes other names from the Table of Nations: Babylon (1:1; 2:12, 14, 18, 24, 48, 49; 3:1, 12, 97; 4:3, 26, 27; cf. Gen 10:10), Shinar (1:2; cf. Gen 10:10), Medes (5:28, 31; 6:8, 12, 15; 8:20; cf. Gen 10:2), Elam (8:2; cf. Gen 10:22). Many other nations are mentioned in Daniel: Judah (1:1, 2; 5:13; 6:13; 9:7; cf. 11:16, 41), Chaldeans (1:4; 2:2, 4, 5, 10; 4:4; 5:11, 30; 7:1; 9:1), Persians (5:28; 6:8, 12, 15, 28; 8:20; 10:1, 13, 20; 11:2), Edom, Moab, and Ammon (11:41). Cf. J. SIMONS, *The Geographical and Topographical Texts of the Old Testament* (Leiden: Brill, 1959), pp. 460–461. Furthermore, Dan 11:18 refers to "the coastlands/islands" (איים, νῆσοι), which recalls Gen 10:5.

28 Actually, the singular is used in the MT (גוי) and in the LXX (ἔθνος), but the plural rendering seems to convey the meaning better here.

29 Michael, the ruler of the Jews (Dan 10:13, 21; 12:1); "the ruler of the kingdom of the Persians" (10:13); "the ruler of Javan" (10:20). The idea goes back to Deut 32:8. Cf. Michael MACH, *Entwicklungsstadien des jüdischen Engelglaubens in vorrabbinischer Zeit* (Texte und Studien zum Antiken Judentum 34; Tübingen: Mohr-Siebeck, 1992), pp. 257–262.

30 On the centrality of Zion in OT eschatology, cf. Donald E. GOWAN, *Eschatology in the Old Testament* (Philadelphia: Fortress Press, 1986), pp. 9–16. On the nations in OT eschatology, see ibid., pp. 48–57; Andrew WILSON, *The Nations in Deutero-Isaiah: A Study on Composition and Structure* (Ancient Near Eastern Texts and Studies 1; Lewiston, NY: Edwin Mellen Press, 1986), pp. 232–244; D. W. van WINKLE, "The Relationship of the Nations to Yahweh and to Israel in Isaiah xl–lv," *VT* 35 (1985) 446–458; Graham DAVIES, "The Destiny of the Nations in the Book of Isaiah," in *The Book of Isaiah/Le Livre d'Isaïe. Les oracles et leurs reflectures unité complexité de l'ouvrage* (ed. Jacques Vermeylen; BETL 81; Leuven: University Press, 1989), pp. 93–120.

Assyria, and the Assyrian will come to Egypt, and the Egyptian to Assyria, and the Egyptians will worship with the Assyrians. On that day Israel will be the third with Egypt and Assyria, a blessing in the midst of the earth . . ." Here the motive of Israel and Jerusalem "in the midst of the nations" (cf. Ezek 5:5) is evidently combined with the promise that in Abraham, all the nations of the earth shall be blessed (Gen 12:3). As the nations carried Israel into exile, so they will carry them back to their homeland (Isa 49:22; cf. 60:4−9). As the nations removed the wealth of Israel, including the temple treasures, so the day will come when the world's treasures will be lavished on Jerusalem (Isa 45:14; cf. 60:6−7, 13; 61:6). As Israelites served the nations, so one day the nations will serve Israel (Isa 49:23; cf. 60:10, 12, 14; 61:5).

Isa 66:18−20 stands among these OT texts containing a positive eschatological expectation for the nations. In the context of God's gathering the nations to Jerusalem, this passage clearly reflects the Table-of-Nations tradition:

. . . and I am coming to gather all nations and tongues (כל הגוים והלשנות/πάντα τὰ ἔθνη καὶ τὰς γλώσσας); and they will come and see my glory. And I will set a sign among them, and from them I will send survivors to the nations (הגוים/τὰ ἔθνη) – to Tarshish, Put,[31] and Lud, to Meshech,[32] Tubal, and Javan, and to the distant islands that have neither heard my fame nor seen my glory. And they shall declare my glory among the nations (בגוים/ἐν τοῖς ἔθνεσι). And they shall bring all your brothers from all the nations (מכל הגוים/ἐκ πάντων τῶν ἐθνῶν) as an offering to the Lord . . . to my Holy Mountain Jerusalem, says Yahweh.

First of all, the reference to "all nations and tongues" (v. 18) must be seen in the light of Genesis 10, the fundamental text that lists all the "nations" of the world according to their "tongues" (cf. vv. 5, 20, 31). Second, the list of the six "nations" in Isa 66:19 obviously stems from the list of the traditional seventy nations in the Table of Nations.[33] Particularly telling in this regard is the reference to the "coastlands/islands" (איים, νῆσοι) in connection with Javan/Greece (v. 19), for in Gen 10:5, the peoples of the "coastlands/islands" (איים, νῆσοι) are connected with the sons of Javan, who is elsewhere identified with "Ionia and all Greeks."[34] Regardless of the exact identification of the nations listed in Isa 66:19, it is clear that descendants of each of the three sons of Noah

---

[31] Reading Φούδ (Put) with the LXX instead of פול in the MT.

[32] Reading Μοσοχ (Meshech) with the LXX instead of משכי קשת ("those who draw the bow") in the MT.

[33] Tarshish (Gen 10:4), Put (v. 6), Lud (v. 22), Meshech (v. 2), Tubal (v. 2), Javan (vv. 2, 4).

[34] Cf. Josephus *Ant.* 1.124; Dan 8:21; 10:20; 11:2. The Hebrew "Javan" (יון) is the equivalent of the Greek "Ion" (Ἴων), the ancestor of the Ionians. By the Hellenistic period, Javan refers to all of Greece, but the precise identification of Javan in the biblical sources is uncertain. They mention Javanites, along with Tubal and Meshech, as merchants in trade with the Phoenicians of Tyre (Ezek 27:13; cf. v. 19) and as slave traders who bought Judean captives from Phoenicians and Philistines (Joel 4:6). According to Zech 9:13, Judah and Ephraim are to take revenge on the Javanites at the time of the ingathering of Israel.

are represented: *Shem* (Lud),[35] *Ham* (Put), and, most of all again,[36] *Japheth* (Tarshish, Tubal, Meshech, Javan).[37] In other words, by alluding to the Table of Nations, the partial list of nations in v. 19 explicates what is meant by "the nations," which, in turn, provides concrete examples of God's intention to gather "all nations" in v. 18.[38] Third, the focus on Jerusalem in this text (cf. v. 20) is characteristic of the OT and Jewish tradition based on the Table of Nations.

Conclusion

We have seen that the Table of Nations in Genesis 10 forms part of a tradition that pervades the OT. For example, 1 Chr 1:1–2:2 appropriates this tradition, presupposing that the readers are well acquainted with it.[39] A passage like Ezekiel 27 shows that the ethnography and geography of the Table-of-Nations tradition applies not just to the distant past but to the present as well. Furthermore, texts such as Ezekiel 38–39, Daniel 11, and Isa 66:18–20 demonstrate that the tradition even applies to the eschatological future.[40]

The Table of Nations in Early Judaism

The Table of Nations continued to exert a significant influence on Early Judaism. Far from being considered obsolete, the Table of Nations remained a fundamental point of orientation for thinking about world geography and ethnography, particularly about Israel and her place among the nations. "The assumption was that, being Scripture, the Table must be an accurate and comprehensive picture of the world."[41] In the following, we will trace the

---

[35] In the Table of Nations, Lud, the fifth son of Shem (Gen 10:22), is distinguished from Ludim, the first son of Mizraim (Gen 10:13; cf. Jer 46:9, where a reference to the Ludim occurs in a list with Cush and Put).

[36] See the discussion on Ezekiel 38–39 above, where the Japhethites also figure most prominently.

[37] This corresponds to the fact that the Japhethites are given pride of place in Genesis 10. Furthermore, the first three nations listed in Isa 66:19 (Tarshish, Put, and Lud) follow the general order of presentation in the Table of Nations of Genesis 10 (Japheth, Ham, and Shem).

[38] Cf. Jer 32:17–26, where "all the kingdoms which are on the face of the earth" (v. 26) are summarized in an extensive list of nations that will come under Yahweh's judgment.

[39] Cf. WILLI, *Chronik*, p. 23 (also p. 28): "Sowohl die beiden Stammreihen wie die Stammbäume setzen beim Hörer bzw. Leser Vertrautheit mit der dahinterliegenden Tradition voraus, und zwar nicht nur im allegemeinen. Ganz deutlich ist das bei Sem, Ham und Jafet V. 4. Wer die Chr[onik] zur Hand nimmt, muß einfach wissen, daß sie alle drei Söhne Noachs auf einer Ebene sind."

[40] As another example, Mic 5:6(5), in a passage on the future Restoration of Israel and the defeat of Israel's enemies, calls Assyria "the land of Nimrod" (cf. Gen 10:9–11).

[41] ALEXANDER, "Geography and the Bible (Early Judaism)," p. 980.

Table-of-Nations tradition through a number of Jewish texts of the Second Temple period and beyond. We begin with the *Book of Jubilees*.

The Table of Nations in Jubilees 8–9

Jubilees 8–9 as an Exposition of Genesis 10. In its exposition of the Table of Nations in Genesis 10, *Jubilees* 8–9 does not merely list the nations around Israel but actually describes the geography of the world – a world extending from the Garden of Eden in the east (*Jub.* 8:16) to Gadir (= Cádiz)[42] in Spain (8:23, 26; 9:12) – and Israel's central position in it.[43]

Jubilees 8–9 contains two accounts of the division of the earth.[44] In the first account (*Jub.* 8:10–30), Noah divides the earth by lot among his three sons: Shem receives the temperate "middle of the earth" (vv. 12–21 = Asia), with Mount Zion "in the midst of the navel of the earth" (v. 19); Ham, the hot southern portion (vv. 22–24 = Africa); and Japheth, the cold northern portion (vv. 25–30 = Europe). The geographical extent of these portions and the physical boundaries between them are described in great and explicit detail, following a circular path in each case.[45] Finally, each description ends with a formula indicating that the portion allotted to that son became a possession to him and his descendants "forever" (vv. 17, 24, 29). In the second account (*Jub.* 9:1–15), the sons of Noah, still in the presence of Noah (cf. v. 14), divide the portions given to them among their own sons: the sons of Ham (v. 1), the sons of Shem (vv. 2–6), and the sons of Japheth (vv. 7–13). Using a method inspired by Genesis 10 itself (see Table 1), this second account "blocks in" the portions of the first account with actual nations, often indicating the geographical extent of their territories. Thereupon, Noah compels his sons and grandsons to swear an oath to curse anyone who desires to seize a portion that does not belong to his lot (vv. 14–15). Thus, the Table of Nations – and Israel's central position in it – is seen to have timeless value and eternal validity, even for the second

---

[42] Cf. E. Hübner, "Gades," *PW* 13 (1910) 439–461; Johann Maier, "Zu ethnographisch-geographischen Überlieferungen über Japhetiten (Gen 10,2–4) im frühen Judentum," *Henoch* 13 (1991) 157–194 (here pp. 183–184).

[43] Add to the bibliography on Jubilee's geographical ideas given in P.S. Alexander, "Notes on the 'Imago Mundi' of the Book of Jubilees," *JJS* 33 (1982) 197–213 (here p. 210 n. 13): Paul Riessler, "Zur Geographie der Jubiläen und der Genesis," *TQ* 96 (1914) 341–367; Doron Mendels, *The Land of Israel as a Political Concept in Hasmonean Literature: Recourse to History in Second Century B. C. Claims to the Holy Land* (Texte und Studien zum Antiken Judentum 15; Tübingen: Mohr-Siebeck, 1987), pp. 57–88; Maier, "Japhetiten," pp. 179–184.

[44] Cf. O.S. Wintermute, "Jubilees," in *OTP*, 2:72–75.

[45] The descriptions of Shem and Japheth make a counterclockwise circuit beginning at the source of the Tina, while the description of Ham makes a clockwise circuit beginning at a place beyond the Gihon, to the right of the Garden of Eden. Cf. Francis Schmidt, "Jewish Representations of the Inhabited Earth during the Hellenistic and Roman Periods," in *Greece and Rome in Eretz Israel: Collected Essays* (ed. A. Kasher, et al.; Jerusalem: Yad Izhak Ben-Zvi/The Israel Exploration Society, 1990), pp. 119–134 (here p. 127).

century B.C., when *Jubilees* was written.[46] The original division of the earth among the sons and grandsons of Noah as given in Genesis 10 and 1 Chronicles 1 represents the God-ordained order of the world: it is static and inviolable.[47] According to Deut 32:8 MT, referring evidently to the same postdiluvian division of the earth and in the same "Israel-centric" way, "When the Most High apportioned the nations, when he divided mankind, he fixed the boundaries of the nations according to the number of the sons of Israel [= 70!]."[48] Thereafter, the situation is inalterable from a biblical point of view. As we have seen, OT prophecies about the eschatological future continue to presuppose the geography and ethnography based on the Table-of-Nations (cf., e.g., Ezekiel 38–39; Isa 66:18–20). This helps to explain the abiding influence that the Table of Nations has had on both Jewish and Christian thinking.[49]

Jubilees 8–9 and the Ionian World Map. Given that *Jubilees* 8–9 is an exposition of Genesis 10 with a fundamentally OT and Jewish perspective, it seems surprising that, according to P.S. ALEXANDER, "The Jubilees world map is one of the clearest examples we possess of the impact of Hellenistic thought on the Palestinian Jewish cultural milieu at this period [i.e., the mid-second century B.C.]."[50] He suggests that the "Jubilees world map" (see Map

---

[46] On the dating of *Jubilees*, see J.C. VANDERKAM, *Textual and Historical Studies in the Book of Jubilees* (HSM 14; Missoula, MT: Scholars Press, 1977), pp. 207–288. The attempt of Albert HERRMANN (*Die Erdkarte der Urbibel* [Braunschweig: Westermann, 1931]) to show by geographical means that the core of the Book of *Jubilees* dates to a time before the sources of Genesis (i.e., to the time of King Solomon) need not be considered in this study.

[47] So also Klaus E. MÜLLER, *Geschichte der antiken Ethnographie und ethnologischen Theoriebildung von den Anfängen bis auf die byzantinischen Historiographen* (2 vols.; Studien zur Kulturkunde 29 and 52; Wiesbaden: Franz Steiner Verlag, 1972–80), 2:270–274 (esp. pp. 272, 274). *Jubilees* does, however, mention two exceptions in which descendants of Noah (i.e., Canaan and Madai) violated the original division of the world by occupying territories in the land of Shem, which were not allotted to them, and thus incurred the aforementioned curse (cf. *Jub.* 9:1, 9; 10:29–33, 35–36).

[48] See further nn. 2 and 29 above.

[49] ALEXANDER, "Imago Mundi," pp. 201–203, 212–213; MÜLLER, *Geschichte der antiken Ethnographie*, 2:296–303. See further below on the influence of *Jubilees* 8–9 upon subsequent cartographic tradition.

[50] ALEXANDER, "Imago Mundi," p. 211; see further p. 212 (also idem, "Geography and the Bible [Early Judaism]," pp. 983–985): "We could see in Jubilees [8–9] and I Enoch [17–18, 24–36, 77] two distinct, and, perhaps, to some extent, opposed, 'schools' of early Jewish geography – one, the Hellenistic school, deriving its ideas from and invoking the authority of the Greek 'scientific' tradition; the other, the Oriental school, looking for its inspiration and doctrine to the ancient scholarly traditions of Babylonia. Further investigation might show that these two 'schools' simply reflect a conflict between Orientalism and Hellenism which ran across the whole field of early Jewish 'science' and culture, a conflict between educated Jews open specifically to Greek ideas, and those who set greater store by the traditions of the older civilizations of the Middle East." Cf. James C. VANDERKAM, "1 Enoch 77,3 and a Babylonian Map of the World," *RevQ* 11 (1983) 271–278; Wayne HOROWITZ, "Mesopotamian Cosmic Geography" (Ph.D. diss., University of Birmingham, 1986); idem, "The Babylonian Map of the World," 147–163; also A.R. MILLARD, "Cartography in the Ancient Near

Map 1
Jubilees 8−9, reconstructed by P. S. Alexander

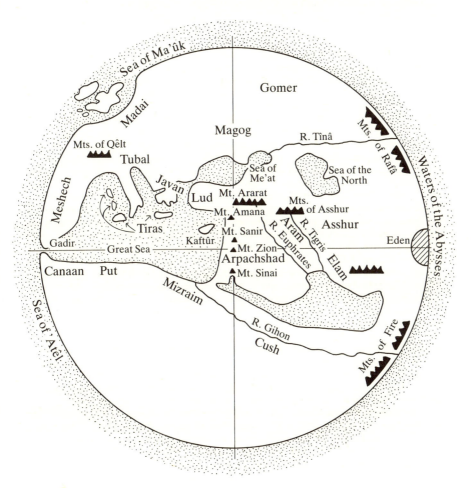

1) was framed by the Ionian world map, which was very popular and widespread in antiquity.[51] According to ALEXANDER, the main elements of the Ionian map can be reconstructed from various literary sources as follows:[52]

East," in *The History of Cartography, vol. 1: Cartography in Prehistoric, Ancient, and Medieval Europe and the Mediterranean* (ed. J.B. Harley and David Woodward; Chicago: University of Chicago Press, 1987), pp. 107–116 (here pp. 111–113). However, as Martin HENGEL has pointed out in his deliberations on the lack of a strict division between "Hellenistic" Diaspora and Palestinian Judaism (*The 'Hellenization' of Judaea in the First Century after Christ* [London: SCM Press; Philadelphia: Trinity Press International, 1989], pp. 46–47), "The 'mythological geography' of Ethiopian Enoch similarly has numerous points of contact with Greek ideas. This is true first of the kingdom of the dead in the distant West, with a realm of light and a refreshing spring for the righteous. Here one thinks of the Elysian fields and the spring of Mnemosyne; the stream of fire recalls the Pyriphlegeton and the dark places of punishment recall Tartarus. Possibly these conceptions go back to common myths shared by the Greeks and the Near East which now circulated more widely during the Hellenistic period in changed circumstances. The utopian journey of Enoch into the fabulous lands beyond the Erythraean Sea, i.e. the Indian Ocean, which is said to be the location of paradise with its miraculous herbs (Ethiopian Enoch 30–32), recalls motives of the utopian travel romance." Francis SCHMIDT ("Géographie politique et espaces imaginaires dans le Judaïsme à l'époque hellénistique et romaine," *Annuaire de l'École pratique des Hautes Études, Vᵉ Section (Sciences Religieuses)* 89 [1980–81] 443–449 [here pp. 446–447]; idem, "Naissance d'une géographie juive," in *Moïse géographie. Recherches sur les représentations juives et chrétiennes de l'espace* [ed. Alain Desreumaux and Francis Schmidt; Études de Psychologie et de Philosophie 24; Paris: Librairie philosophique J. Vrin, 1988], pp. 13–30; reproduced substantially in idem, "Jewish Representations," pp. 132–134) argues that the point of *Jubilees* 8–9 is precisely a reaction of conservative Jews against the Hellenistic reformers of the second century B.C., warning the latter, on the threat of a curse, both to acknowledge the preeminence of Shem over the nations and to preserve the distinction between Judaism and Hellenism. When *Jubilees* paradoxically uses a Greek representation of the world (i.e., the Ionian map) to fight Hellenism, SCHMIDT explains this as an example of the "counter-acculturation" that is so characteristic of apocalyptic Judaism.

[51] ALEXANDER, "Imago Mundi," pp. 198–199, 211; idem, "Geography and the Bible (Early Jewish)," pp. 980–982; cf. Gustav HÖLSCHER, *Drei Erdkarten. Ein Beitrag zur Erdkenntnis des hebräischen Altertums* (Sitzungsberichte der Heidelberger Akademie der Wissenschaften, Philosophisch-historische Klasse, Jahrgang 1944/48, 3. Abhandlung; Heidelberg: Winter, 1948), p. 57; SCHMIDT, "Géographie," p. 445; idem, "Jewish Representations," pp. 126–127. See also MÜLLER, *Geschichte der antiken Ethnographie*, 2:270: "Mit dieser noch geradezu altionisch anmutenden Erdzonenlehre kombiniert der Verfasser im weiteren dann die eratosthenische Golfen-Theorie. ..." On the other hand, Forentino G. MARTINEZ attributes the account of the partition of the earth among Noah's sons in *Jubilees* 8–9 to the influence of the lost *Book of Noah*, whose contents he reconstructs from several sources ("4QMess AR and the Book of Noah," in *Qumran and Apocalyptic: Studies on the Aramaic Texts from Qumran* [STDJ 9; Leiden: Brill, 1992], pp. 1–44 [here p. 39]; see further Emil SCHÜRER, *The History of the Jewish People in the Age of Jesus Christ [175 B.C. – A.D. 135]* [3 vols. in 4; rev. ed.; ed. Geza Vermes, et al.; Edinburgh: T. & T. Clark, 1973–1987], 3.1:332–333).

[52] Cf. ALEXANDER, "Imago Mundi," pp. 198–199. For a brief survey of Greco-Roman conceptions of world geography, see my article, "Luke's Geographical Horizon," in *The Book of Acts in Its First Century Setting, Vol. 2: The Book of Acts in Its Graeco-Roman Setting* (ed. David W.J. Gill and Conrad Gempf; Grand Rapids: Eerdmans; Carlisle: Paternoster, 1994), pp. 483–544 (here pp. 484–492).

Map 2
Jubilees 8–9, reconstructed by F. Schmidt

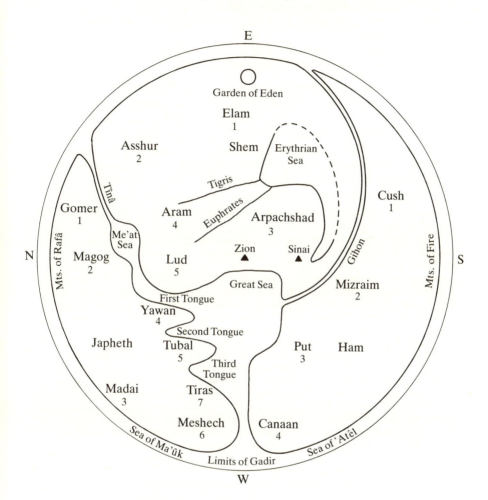

(1) the earth is represented as a disk surrounded by Ocean, which penetrates into the land-mass through three inlets (e.g., the Pillars of Hercules) to form three seas (the Caspian, the Erythrean, and the Mediterranean);

(2) the earth-disk is described as having a center (Delphi), which is called the navel (ὀμφαλός) of the world;[53]

(3) the earth is divided into three continents (Europe, Asia, and Libya [= Africa]) by means of two rivers (the Tanais [= the Don] and the Nile).

As to (1), ALEXANDER admits that *Jubilees* mentions neither the general shape of earth nor the surrounding Ocean; he merely assumes that the *Jubilees* earth was disk-shaped on the basis of Ionian and early Christian maps.[54] This is not a bad assumption in itself (despite the circular reasoning); however, in view of the overwhelming dependence of *Jubilees* 8–9 on the OT, the assumption might also be drawn from the OT.[55] As to (2), *Jubilees* does indeed portray Mt. Zion as being "in the midst of the navel of the earth" (*Jub.* 8:19b), but, as ALEXANDER himself rightly points out, that conception "may be based on Ezek 5:5; 38:12."[56] Indeed, that possibility is very probable, especially if the Table of

---

[53] On the Delphic omphalos in literary sources, see, for example, Strabo *Geogr.* 9.3.6; Plutarch *Mor.* 409E; Pausanius 10.6.3. For numismatic evidence, see Barclay V. HEAD, *Catalogue of Greek Coins: Central Greece (Locris, Phocis, Boeotia and Euboea)* (Bologna: Arnaldo Forni, 1963), p. 24, with Plate IV. 4 (obverse: tripod; reverse: a point in the center of a circle inscribed by a square); Charles SELTMAN, *Greek Coins: A History of Metallic Currency and Coinage down to the Fall of the Hellenistic Kingdoms* (2nd ed.; Methuen's Handbook of Archaeology; London: Methuen, 1955), p. 113, with Plate XVII.14 (a mound flanked by two eagles). See further Leon LACROIX, "L'omphalos, attribut d'Asclépios, selon le témoinage des monnaies," *Revue belge de Numismatique* 97 (1951) 6–18.

[54] ALEXANDER, "Imago Mundi," p. 203. Actually, little is known about these so-called "Ionian" maps. According to J. B. HARLEY and David WOODWARD, "We have almost no details of Anaximander's map, but is is traditionally accepted that 'ancient maps' (which are probably those from Ionia), were circular, with Greece in the middle and Delphi at the center" ("The Foundations of Theoretical Cartography in Archaic and Classical Greece," in *The History of Cartography*, pp. 130–147 [here p. 135]). Nevertheless, HARLEY and WOODWARD go on to adduce evidence that circular maps were common among the Greeks and that they were repeatedly subjected to critique even down to the first century B.C. (ibid., p. 135). Neverthe-less, by the first century B.C., the educated class largely seems to have preferred to ignore new scientific discoveries in cartography in favor of earlier Hellenistic concepts like the circular, flat earth (cf. HARLEY and WOODWARD, "Greek Cartography in the Early Roman World," in *The History of Cartography*, pp. 161–176 [here p. 171]). On Ionian conceptions of world geography, see further Wanda WOLSKA-CONUS, "Geographie," *RAC* 10 (1978) 155–222 (here cols. 156–159).

[55] Cf. Isa 40:22; Job 26:10; Ps 24:2; 136:6; Prov 8:27; also Josephus *Ant.* 1.38 (on Gen 2:10ff.).

[56] ALEXANDER, "Imago Mundi," p. 204. Cf. *1 Enoch* 26:1, which describes Jerusalem as "the center of the earth." From this center, Enoch makes a journey to the four corners of the earth – East (*1 Enoch* 28–33), North (34), West (35), and South (36) – in a counterclockwise direction that corresponds approximately to the orientation and movement of the Table of Nations in 1 Chronicles 1. On the geography of *1 Enoch*, see further n. 48 above. See also *Tanchuma B*, Lev. 78: "As the navel is set in the middle of a person, so is Eretz Israel the navel of the world, as it is said: 'They who dwell in the navel of the earth' [Ezek 38:12]. Eretz Israel is located in the center of the world; Jerusalem is the center of Eretz Israel; the Temple, in the

Nations in Genesis 10 and 1 Chronicles 1 is already "Israel-centric." *Jubilees* further emphasizes the position of Zion as the God-ordained center of the world by stating that the Garden of Eden, Mount Sinai, and Mount Zion "were created as holy places, one facing the other" (*Jub.* 8:19c). As ALEXANDER plausibly suggests, "This probably means that they are at right-angles to each other, i.e., a median runs east-west though the centre of Paradise and Zion, and another north-south through Zion and Sinai." [57] In addition, *Jubilees* has the standard OT and Jewish orientation on the East. [58] How, then, can we speak of exclusively Ionian influence at this point? [59] Finally, as to (3), *Jubilees* does

---

center of Jerusalem; the היכל, in the center of the Temple; the ark, in the center of the היכל; and in front of the היכל is the even foundation stone from which the world was started." The antiquity of this concept is attested by a parallel in *2 Enoch* 23:45, in which the metaphor of "the navel of the earth" is connected with the site of Adam's creation. Furthermore, *m. Kelim* 1:6−9 has a similar concept of the centrality of Jerusalem when, beginning with the nations and focussing stepwise in concentric circles on Jerusalem according to degrees of holiness, the Holy of Holies is seen as the holiest place on earth. See further Hermann LICHTENBERGER, "'Im Lande Israel zu wohnen, wiegt alle Gebote der Tora auf'. Die Heiligkeit des Landes und die Heiligung des Lebens," in *Die Heiden. Juden, Christen und das Problem des Fremden* (ed. Reinhard Feldmeier and Ulrich Heckel; WUNT 70; Tübingen: Mohr-Siebeck, 1994), pp. 92−107 (esp. pp. 94−96); Beate EGO, *Im Himmel wie auf Erden. Studien zum Verhältnis von himmlischer und irdischer Welt im rabbinischen Judentum* (WUNT 2.34; Tübingen: Mohr-Siebeck, 1989), pp. 86ff., 89 n. 58, et passim; Luis I. J. STADELMANN, *The Hebrew Conception of the World: A Philological and Literary Study* (AnBib 39; Rome: Pontifical Biblical Institute, 1970), pp. 147−154; Samuel TERRIEN, "The Omphalos Myth and Hebrew Religion," *VT* 20 (1970) 315−338.

[57] ALEXANDER, "Imago Mundi," p. 204. According to Agathemerus (*Geographiae informatio* 1.5; cf. also Strabo *Geogr.* 2.10.1−2), Dicaearchus (fl. ca. 326−296 B.C.) included a map in his *Circuit of the Earth* (Περίοδος γῆς) in which he drew a parallel called the *diaphragma* extending eastward from the Straits of Gibraltar, passing through Sardinia, Sicily, Caria, Lycia, Pamphylia, Cilicia, and along the Taurus range as far as Mount Himaeus (the Himalayas). The main difference is that Dicaearchus drew the perpendicular meridian to pass approximately through Rhodes, rather than through Zion as in *Jub.* 8:19.

[58] Cf. *Jub.* 8:22−23: "And to Ham was assigned the second portion toward the other side of Gihon, toward the *south* on the *right* of the Garden [of Eden]. [. . .] And it goes along the Gihon River until it approaches the *right* side of the Garden of Eden." This suggests that south was on the right side of the map (cf. ALEXANDER, "Imago Mundi," p. 204; SCHMIDT, "Géographie," p. 445; idem, "Jewish Representations," pp. 128−129). Thus ALEXANDER's reconstruction of the *Jubilees* world map, with its apparent northward orientation, requires modification (cf. ibid., p. 213; see now his corrected map in "Geography and the Bible [Early Jewish]," p. 982). On the eastward orientation of the OT, see AHARONI and AVI-YONAH, *Atlas*, p. 2; T. KRONHOLM, "קדם," *TWAT*, 6 (1989) 1165; Robert NORTH, *A History of Biblical Map Making* (Beihefte zum Tübinger Atlas des vorderen Orients B32; Wiesbaden: Ludwig Reichert Verlag, 1979), pp. 142−143.

[59] Even if the background for the "navel of the earth" in *Jub.* 8:19b should be sought outside OT/Jewish tradition, which is improbable, why would it necessarily be Ionian? The concept is found widely in antiquity, including the Ancient Near East. See the bibliography in TERRIEN, "The Omphalos Myth and Hebrew Religion," pp. 315ff. In the second century A.D., Claudius Ptolemaeus (*Apotelesmatica* 2.3.29; cf. 2.40.1−2) lists Judea among the nations, including Idumea, Coele-Syria, Phoenicia, Chaldea, Orchinia, and Arabia Felix, that are situated "around the center of the whole inhabited world" (περὶ τὸ μέσον τῆς ὅλης οἰκουμένης).

conceive of a tripartite division of the world corresponding to the three continents. Yet that division of the world corresponds *approximately* to that which is
found already in the Table of Nations itself.[60] To that degree, the tripartite
division of the world in *Jubilees* is not a specifically Ionian conception. However, insofar as the river Tina (= Tanais) and the river Gihon (= the Nile)[61]
form boundaries between the three divisions (i.e., between Japheth and Shem
[*Jub.* 8:12], on the one hand, and between Shem and Ham [8:22−23], on the
other),[62] Greek influence may be suspected.[63] Nevertheless, it may be asked
whether *Jubilees* introduces biblical elements into a basically Ionian framework
or rather Greek elements into a fundamentally biblical structure.[64]

ALEXANDER tries to clinch his interpretation that *Jubilees* is "adapting and
forcing a pre-existing [Ionian] scheme" by showing that the presumed correla-
tion of the three sons of Noah with the Ionian continents necessitated several
awkward assignments that are in no way implicit in the biblical text. Thus
Madai, as a son of Japheth, had to be assigned a portion in Europe (*Jub.* 9:9),
and Canaan, as a son of Ham, had to be assigned a portion in Africa (*Jub.*
9:1).[65] According to ALEXANDER, these assignments then required *Jubilees* to
fabricate legends in order to account for the intrusion of Madai and Canaan into
the portion of Shem, where they actually ended up (cf. *Jub.* 10:29−33, 35−36).

---

[60] Cf. Othmar KEEL, et al., *Orte und Landschaften der Bibel* (2 vols.; Zürich: Benziger
Verlag; Göttingen: Vandenhoeck & Ruprecht, 1982−84), 1:191: "Diese Völkerfamilie wird
in Gen 10 aufgrund ihrer Abstammung von den drei Noachsöhnen Sem, Ham und Jafet in drei
Gruppen geteilt, die ungefähr den drei Kontinenten entsprechen, in deren Schnittpunkt
Palästina liegt." Note, however, that MAIER denies that *Jubilees* divides the world according to
the three continents ("Japhetiten," p. 180).

[61] On the identification of the Gihon with the Nile, see Joseph A. FITZMYER, *The Genesis
Apocryphon of Qumran Cave 1: A Commentary* (2nd ed.; BibOr 18A; Rome: Biblical
Institute Press, 1971), pp. 152−153.

[62] 1QapGen 16.16 and 17.16 also use the river Tina as a boundary.

[63] Cf., e.g., Strabo *Geogr.* 2.5.26: "Now as you sail into the strait at the Pillars, Libya lies on
your right hand as far as the stream of the Nile, and on your left hand across the strait lies
Europe as far as the Tanais. And both Europe and Libya end at Asia." On the three
continents, see further below on Philo *Legat.* 283.

[64] ALEXANDER does not consider the question of the origin of *Jubilees'* concept of a table of
nations. For a Hellenistic parallel we may point, for example, to the *Geography* of Claudius
Ptolemaeus (ca. A.D. 90−168), which often includes a list of ἔθνη for the lands covered in his
survey of the world (cf., e.g., Georg HOLZ, *Über die germanische Völkertafel des Ptolemaeus*
[Beiträge zur deutschen Altertumskunde; Halle: Niemeyer, 1894]). We could also mention
the list of nations in the *Res Gestae* of Augustus (see Chap. 2 below) or in Pliny *Nat. Hist.*
6.211−220 (see further in Chap. 2). As an exposition of Genesis 10, however, *Jubilees* 8−9 is
obviously most directly influenced by the biblical Table of Nations. See now MAIER, "Japhetiten," p. 179: "Im Grundschema entspricht manches dem alten ionischen Weltbild und dem,
was von Hekataios bekannt ist. Aber sowohl im Ganzen wie in den Details sind Beson-
derheiten festzustellen, die auf andere Traditionen weisen." MAIER considers HÖLSCHER'S
(and ALEXANDER'S) reconstruction of the world map in *Jubilees* 8−9 in need of revision,
especially in regard to "die zu starke Einbindung in den hellenistischen Kontext" (ibid.,
p. 180).

[65] ALEXANDER, "Imago Mundi," p. 200.

These considerations notwithstanding, however, the assignments can be shown to stem from inferences drawn from Genesis itself rather than from the imposition of an Ionian model, for on the basis of the biblical Table of Nations, Madai would logically be expected in the northern and western lands with the rest of the sons of Japheth, and Canaan would be expected in Egypt or North Africa with the rest of the sons of Ham. Thus, *Jubilees* simply puts these two nations where they would be expected on the basis of the biblical record and then later accounts for their intrusion into the territory of Shem as a violation of the world order that God had originally ordained.[66]

By the same token, the fact that *Jubilees* sees the territory of Shem as including Anatolia and thus all of Asia is due not to the influence of an Ionian world map but more probably to the inclusion of Lud (= Lydia in western Asia Minor[67]) among the sons of Shem in the original Table of Nations (cf. Gen 10:22). In order to occupy a continuous territory between Palestine and western Asia Minor, which *Jubilees'* principle of "blocking-in" would require,[68] the sons of Shem had to displace some of the sons of Japheth on the world map, forcing them to occupy places in Europe. Hence, when *Jubilees* views the sons of Shem as occupying practically all of Asia Minor (9:6, 10), this is evidence of a harmonizing tendency in Jewish exegesis of the biblical text.

Jubilees 8−9 and Ancient Cartography. Whether *Jubilees* presupposes an actual map or merely a mental construct remains uncertain since there is no direct evidence and analogies from antiquity are few.[69] Nevertheless, there are

---

[66] See now ALEXANDER, "Geography and the Bible (Early Jewish)," p. 982: "*Jubilees'* aim in all this is, presumably, to prove that the Jews have an ancient right to settle in the 'land of Canaan' (it was Canaanites, not themselves, who were usurpers), and to justify the territorial expansion of the Hasmonaean state." See further MENDELS, *The Land of Israel as a Political Concept in Hasmonean Literature*, pp. 57−88. Note that in his *Chronicon*, a biblical chronology based on the distribution of the earth among Shem, Ham, and Japheth (Genesis 10), Hippolytus lists the Medes at first under the Japhethites (cf. *Chron.* 59; 80[1]; 82[5]) and then later under the Shemites (§§ 190[3]; 192[3]). Cf. Adolf BAUER and Rudolf HELM, eds., *Hippolytus Werke, Bd. 4: Die Chronik* (2nd ed.; GCS 46; Berlin: Akademie-Verlag, 1955). The purpose of the *Chronicon* is to show how the development of the seed of Israel came to its fulfillment in Christ (*Chron.* 20).

[67] Cf., e.g., WESTERMANN, *Genesis*, 1:684−685.

[68] *Jubilees* strives to make the individual portions assigned to the sons of Noah as continuous and as mutually exclusive as possible, demarcated from one another by clear, natural boundaries. In the case of Shem's portion, where generosity was obviously shown, the furthest, westerly extent of the territory was determined by Lud, whose boundary was the Mediterranean on the west (*Jub.* 9:6) and – by "blocking-in" the territory to the next closest son in the east (i.e., Asshur) and assigning it to Lud – Mount Asshur on the east (*Jub.* 9:5, 6). In this way, the whole, uninterrupted land mass between the western shore of Asia Minor and the Gihon River on the border to Ham could be assigned to Shem.

[69] In classical Greek cartography, for example, there are relatively few surviving artifacts in the form of graphic representations that may be considered maps even though world maps are known as early as the sixth century B.C. in Ionia (cf. Strabo *Geogr.* 1.1.11; Agathemerus, *Geographiae informatio* 1.1). Our cartographic knowledge must therefore be gleaned largely from literary descriptions, often expressed in poetic language and difficult to interpret. Cf. J.B. HARLEY and D. WOODWARD, "The Foundations of Theoretical Cartography in Archaic

at least two reasons to suspect that such a map existed in antiquity. First, Palestinian Jews would have been well acquainted with world geography because of the reciprocal contact between Palestine and the worldwide Diaspora.[70] In particular, the collection of the Temple tax from the Diaspora[71] very likely presupposes that priestly circles in Jerusalem possessed an actual map of the world based, probably, on the Table of Nations.[72] Second, the account in *Jubilees* 8—9 is "so full of precise, visual detail that it is hard to avoid the suspicion that the author was describing not merely an image which he saw with the mind's eye, but one which lay physically before him in the shape of a world map."[73] ALEXANDER attempts to reconstruct the presumed *Jubilees* world map[74] by comparing various patristic and medieval maps with the description in *Jubilees* 8—9.[75] The following survey builds on his seminal observations.

---

and Classical Greece," p. 130; M. HENGEL, "Luke the Historian and Geographer in the Acts of the Apostles," in *Between Jesus and Paul: Studies in the Earliest History of Christianity* (London: SCM Press, 1983), pp. 97—128 (here pp. 98—99).

[70] Cf. P. S. ALEXANDER, "The Toponymy of the Targumim, with Special Reference to the Table of Nations and the Boundaries of the Land of Israel" (D. Phil. thesis, Oxford University, 1974), pp. 18—27. See further the geographical survey of the Jewish Diaspora in SCHÜRER, *Hist.*, 3.1:3—86.

[71] Cf. Shmuel SAFRAI, *Die Wallfahrt im Zeitalter des Zweiten Tempels* (Forschungen zum jüdisch-christlichen Dialog 3; Neukirchen-Vluyn: Neukirchener Verlag, 1981), pp. 65—93.

[72] For a cartographic reconstruction of the Table of Nations according to P, see REVENTLOW, "Völkertafel," 3:2113—2114. According to Wisd 18:24 (based on Ex 28:15—21), Aaron's high-priestly vesture was endowed with symbolic and cosmic significance: "For on his long robe the whole world was depicted ..." (ἐπὶ γὰρ ποδήρους ἐνδύματος ἦν ὅλος ὁ κόσμος). The earliest reference to an actual physical "map" of the world from the Land of Israel seems to be the first-century epigram of Philip of Thessalonica, which describes a tapestry given as a gift by a queen to the reigning Roman Emperor, containing "a perfect copy of the harvest-bearing earth, all that the land-encircling ocean girdles, obedient to great Caesar, and the gray sea too" (*Anth. Gr.* 9.778). If, as commonly assumed, the word καρπός in the manuscript should be emended to Κύπρος, then the queen who gave the tapestry could be Cyprus, a granddaughter of Herod and the wife of Agrippa I (see Menachem STERN, *Greek and Latin Authors on Jews and Judaism* [3 vols.; Jerusalem: The Israel Academy of Sciences and Humanities, 1976—84], 1:375—376).

[73] ALEXANDER, "Imago Mundi," p. 197.

[74] Ibid., p. 213; followed by KEEL, et al., *Orte und Landschaften*, 1:403. Cf. HÖLSCHER's very similar attempt at the reconstruction (*Drei Erdkarten*, p. 58) and Francis SCHMIDT's critique of it for including too many geographic details that are not explicitly mentioned in the text ("Géographie," p. 445; idem, "Jewish Representations," pp. 128, 133). Nevertheless, SCHMIDT does postulate that *Jubilees* 8—9 presupposes a diagram or map of the world ("Jewish Representations of the Inhabited Earth," pp. 127—128), and he attempts to represent this by means of a "schematic diagram" (ibid., p. 122; see Map 2).

[75] ALEXANDER, "Imago Mundi," pp. 201—203: the World Map of Cosmas Indicopleustes, the T-O maps, and the Macrobius maps.

I. The World Map of Cosmas Indicopleustes.

First of all, *Jubilees* 8—9 can be compared to the world map of Cosmas Indicopleustes (fl. A.D. 540), which accompanies his twelve-volume *Christian Topography*.[76] The manuscripts that have come down to us are thought to be fairly faithful to the original, so we can take their illustrations as similar to the ones actually drawn by Cosmas himself. On this map, the inhabited world is drawn as a rectangle surrounded by an Ocean with a rectangular frame.[77] Four gulfs of the Ocean break the regular outline of the inhabited world: the Caspian on the north; the Arabian (Red Sea) and Persian Gulfs on the south; and the Romaic Gulf (the Mediterranean) on the west. Whether or not *Jubilees* 8—9 presupposes the encircling Ocean (see above),[78] it does refer to Caspian Sea (*Jub.* 8:21), the Red Sea (*Jub.* 8:14; 9:4; 10:2), and the "Great Sea" or the Mediterranean (*Jub.* 8:15; 9:6).

Cosmas' world map also contains several biblical elements, including the Garden of Eden in the east and the four rivers of Gen 2:10—14 flowing out of it into the inhabited world, passing under the Ocean: The Gihon (Nile) flows into the Romaic Gulf, while the Tigris, the Euphrates, and the Pishon flow into the Persian Gulf. Likewise in the *Jubilees* conception, the Gihon flows from the Garden of Eden (or near it) in the east and into the Great Sea (cf. *Jub.* 8:15, 22—23). Surrounding the rectangular Ocean in Cosmas' world map is "the earth beyond the Ocean, where men used to live before the Flood" (γῆ πέραν τοῦ Ὠκεανοῦ ἔνθα πρὸ τοῦ κατακλυσμοῦ κατῴκουν οἱ ἄνθρωποι). Like *Jubilees* 8—9, therefore, Cosmas' map is oriented on the Deluge. The overall impression of the Cosmas' map is somewhat similar to that of *Jubilees* 8—9: "Taken as a whole, this particular map of Cosmas's is a strange mixture of classical and Hellenistic knowledge . . . and of biblical teaching. . . ."[79]

II. The Madaba Mosaic Map.

Another map that might also be compared to *Jubilees* 8—9 is the Madaba Mosaic Map, a Christian work dating from the sixth century and situated in a church of Madaba in modern Jordan.[80] In its present state of preservation, the

---

[76] Cf. Wanda WOLSKA-CONUS, *Cosmas Indicopleustès, Topographie chrétienne* (3 vols.; SC 141, 159, 197; Paris: Cerf, 1968—1973). See further WOODWARD, "Cartography in the Byzantine Empire," in *The History of Cartography*, pp. 261—263.

[77] See the reproductions in HARLEY and WOODWARD, *The History of Cartography*, pp. 263, 351, and the line drawing in WOLSKA-CONUS, *Cosmas Indicopleustès*, 1:545.

[78] Cf. ALEXANDER, "Imago Mundi," p. 205.

[79] DILKE, "Cartography in the Byzantine Empire," p. 262. Nevertheless, it appears that Cosmas' world map may have even more affinities with both Josephus' exposition of the Table of Nations (*Ant.* 1.122—147) and his description of the Garden of Eden and the rivers of Paradise (*Ant.* 1.37—39). See, for example, Cosmas' description of the distribution of the earth among the sons of Noah in *Christian Topography* 2.26.

[80] Photographs of the map are published in Herbert DONNER and Heinz CÜPPERS, *Die Mosaikkarte von Madeba, Teil 1: Tafelband* (Abhandlungen des deutschen Palästinavereins;

map is highly fragmentary and includes only biblical Palestine and parts of the adjacent lands, especially Lower Egypt.[81] However, according to the local villagers who were consulted immediately after its discovery in the 1880's, the names Ephesus, Smyrna and even Constantinople could be seen on the map.[82] If this is correct, the map would have originally included all of Syria and Asia Minor and would start to take on worldwide proportions. Although this eyewitness testimony has been all but dismissed in the modern research on the map,[83] it remains interesting for comparison with the world map presupposed by *Jubilees* 8–9.

The text of *Jubilees* in its Greek and Latin versions was certainly known to the church fathers,[84] and some patristic accounts of the Table of Nations, such as the *Chronicon* of Hippolytus, may have drawn upon it.[85] Furthermore, the

---

Wiesbaden: Otto Harrassowitz, 1977), which, unfortunately, does not provide an adequate overview of the map as a whole (cf. ibid., p. VIII). For text and commentary, see H. DONNER, *The Mosaic Map of Madaba: An Introductory Guide* (Palaestina Antiqua 7; Kampen: Kok Pharos, 1992); Michael AVI-YONAH, *The Madaba Mosaic Map with Introduction and Commentary* (Jerusalem: Israel Exploration Society, 1954). See further NORTH, *A History of Biblical Map Making*, pp. 85–88.

[81] Cf. AVI-YONAH, *The Madaba Mosaic Map*, pp. 15–16.

[82] Cf. ibid., *The Madaba Mosaic Map*, p. 15.

[83] Cf. Adolf JACOBY, *Das geographische Mosaik von Madaba. Die älteste Karte des heiligen Landes* (Studien über christliche Denkmäler 3; Leipzig: Dieterisch'sche Verlagsbuchhandlung, 1905), p. 35. AVI-YONAH (*The Madaba Mosaic Map*, p. 15 [emphasis mine]) argues rather circularly: "A wide extension to include Asia Minor must be rejected if we consider the purpose of the map. It was obviously intended to show Bible lands, and an extension beyond Syria could have only two meanings in this context: either the author intended to illustrate *the tenth chapter of Genesis* [the Table of Nations!], or he meant to show *the voyages of St. Paul*. In either case we should expect the map to show much more than Asia Minor. Genesis X includes at least part of Europe and Africa; whereas St. Paul visited Macedonia, Greece and finally Italy. We may therefore safely refuse to believe that the map extended beyond southern Syria."

[84] As J.C. VANDERKAM explains, *Jubilees* was translated from Hebrew, its original language, into Greek and Syriac; from Greek, it was translated into Latin and Ethiopic (*Textual and Historical Studies in the Book of Jubilees*, pp. 1–18).

[85] On the question of whether Hippolytus used *Jubilees* as the source of his ethnography and geography, see Alfred von GUTSCHMID (*Kleine Schriften, Vol. 5: Schriften zur römischen und mittelalterlichen Geschichte und Literatur* [ed. Franz Rühl; Leipzig: Teubner, 1894], p. 239), who speaks in favor of a connection, and Adolf BAUER (*Hippolytus Werke, Bd. 4: Die Chronik*, p. XI; idem, *Die Chronik des Hippolytus in Matritensis Graecus 121* [TU 19.1; Leipzig: Hinrichs, 1905], p. 151 n. 2), who speaks against it. Others reckon with a less direct appropriation of the *Jubilees* tradition by Hippolytus: cf. Wanda WOLSKA-CONUS ("Geographie," in *RAC* 10 [1978] 155–222 [here col. 214]); MÜLLER (*Geschichte der antiken Ethnographie*, 2:297–299); F. SCHMIDT, "Jewish Representations," p. 129, with n. 45. The Ps.-Clementine *Recognitiones* (1.30) contain the lots of the three sons of Noah: the oldest brother received the middle of the earth, including Judea; the youngest received the East; and the other received the West (ed. Bernard REHM, *Die Pseudoklementinen II. Rekognitionen in Rufins Übersetzung* [GCS 51; Berlin: Akademie-Verlag, 1965], p. 25; cf. Wilhelm FRANKENBERG, *Die syrischen Clementinen mit griechischen Paralleltext. Eine Vorarbeit zu dem literargeschichtlichen Problem der Sammlung* [TU 48.3; Leipzig: Heinrichs, 1937], p. 37). For an example from seventh-century Armenian tradition, see Michael E. STONE, *Signs of the*

imago mundi represented in *Jubilees* 8–9 "predominated in Christian circles right through the patristic and mediaeval periods down almost to the time of Christopher Columbus."[86] Is it, therefore, a coincidence that, like *Jubilees* 8–9, the Madaba Map has an orientation on the East,[87] that it is deeply influenced by biblical toponymy,[88] and that it makes Jerusalem central (on a scale ten times larger than the rest)?[89] Furthermore, it is striking that the Madaba Map portrays the Nile as if its source were in the East instead of the South. As H. DONNER points out, the explanation for this is twofold: (1) the space available on a church floor, and (2) the traditional conception of the Nile as one of the four rivers in Gen 2:10–14 that had their source in the Garden of Eden, in the East (cf. v. 8), and thus flowed from east to west.[90] Indeed, according to *Jub.* 8:15, 22–23, the source of the Gihon (Nile) is said to be to the

---

Judgment, Onomastica Sacra, and the Generations from Adam (University of Pennsylvania Armenian Texts and Studies 3; Chico, CA: Scholars Press, 1981), pp. 221–227. For an example from Sethian Gnostic tradition, see the *Apocalypse of Adam* 71.1–4; 72.15–23; 73.13–29; 74:11; 76:13–14 (George W. MacRae, in *Nag Hammadi Codices V, 2–5 and VI* [ed. Douglas M. Parrott; NHS 11; Leiden: Brill, 1979], pp. 165–173). For an example from Samaritan tradition, see *Asatir* 4.27–32 (ed. Moses Gaster, *The Asatir: The Book of the 'Secrets of Moses' together with the Pitron or Samaritan Commentary and the Samaritan Story of the Death of Moses* [London: Royal Asiatic Society, 1927]; cf. Alan D. Crown, ed., *The Samaritans* [Tübingen: Mohr-Siebeck, 1989], pp. 223–224, 465–467). See also Tryggve Kronholm, *Motifs from Genesis 1–11 in the Genuine Hymns of Ephrem the Syrian with Particular Reference to the Influence of Jewish Exegetical Tradition* (ConBOT 11; Lund: Gleerup, 1978), pp. 210–211; F. Nau, "Méthodius – Clément – Andronicus. Textes édités, traduits et annotés," *Journal asiatique* 9 (1917) 415–471 (here pp. 462–471, on Andronicus Philosophicus, a Greek chronographer contemporary with Emperor Justinian).

[86] Alexander, "The Imago Mundi," pp. 212–213; Schmidt, "Jewish Representations," pp. 129–130. Genesis 10 had a powerful influence on Christian cartography (cf., e.g., Jörg-Geerd Arentzen, *Imago Mundi Cartographica. Studien zur Bildlichkeit mittelalterlicher Welt- und Ökumenenkarten unter besonderer Berücksichtigung des Zusammenwirkens von Text und Bild* [Münstersche Mittelalter-Schriften 53; Munich: Wilhelm Fink, 1984], pp. 112–123). Nevertheless, in discussing the possible sources of the Madaba map, Donner discounts the influence that Genesis 10 (particularly Hippolytus' *Diamerismos*) may have had on the map (*The Mosaic Map of Madaba: An Introductory Guide*, pp. 21–27 [here p. 25]).

[87] Cf. Avi-Yonah, *The Madaba Mosaic Map*, p. 9.

[88] Cf. ibid., *The Madaba Mosaic Map*, pp. 27–28. This toponymy is not dependent solely on Eusebius' *Onomasticon* (cf. Donner, "Transjordan and Egypt on the Mosaic Map of Madaba," *Annual of the Department of Antiquities, Jordan* 18 [1984] 249–257 [here p. 255]; Avi-Yonah, *The Madaba Mosaic Map*, pp. 11, 30–31). Yet, Eusebius' *Onomasticon* shows influence from Josephus' exposition of the Table of Nations in *Ant.* 1.122–147 (cf. Michael E. Hardwick, *Josephus as an Historical Source in Patristic Literature through Eusebius* [BJS 128; Atlanta, GA: Scholars Press, 1989], pp. 96–97).

[89] Cf. Avi-Yonah, *The Madaba Mosaic Map*, pp. 10, 11, 16, 21, 30. On the medieval-Christian view of Jerusalem as the middle of the earth, see Woodward, "Medieval *Mappaemundi*," in *The History of Cartography*, pp. 307, 312, 317, 340–342, 348; Müller, *Geschichte der antiken Ethnographie*, pp. 283–284.

[90] Cf. Donner, "Transjordan and Egypt on the Mosaic Map of Madaba," pp. 255–256. See also Avi-Yonah, *The Madaba Mosaic Map*, p. 11.

south of the Garden of Eden in the East.[91] Is it possible, therefore, that, as W. KUBITSCHEK suggested, the Madaba Map originally portrayed the Garden of Eden in the East?[92] We know that ancient Christian scholars were vexed by question of the concrete, geographical location of Paradise and that they appropriated Jewish tradition in this regard.[93] May we assume therefore that, to preserve symmetry,[94] the western portion of the map was at least as extensive as the eyewitnesses claimed? The preliminary archaeological report indicates that the original map was limited to Syria-Palestine, Transjordan, and Lower Egypt.[95]

III. Medieval T-O Maps.

In the medieval T-O maps, the inhabited world is schematically divided into three parts by a "T" that is circumscribed by an "O," representing the encircling Ocean.[96] The top crossbar of the "T" represents the Tanais and Nile rivers, while the vertical leg stands for the Mediterranean. The world is thus divided into three continents: Asia in the top semicircle, Europe in the lower left-hand quarter, and Africa in the lower right-hand quarter. It is debated whether Jerusalem is normally conceived of as situated at the intersection of the "T."[97] Some T-O maps include the names of Shem, Ham, and Japheth on the continents which they settled.[98] The comparison to *Jubilees* 8–9 is obvious.[99]

---

[91] Cf. ALEXANDER, "Imago Mundi," p. 207. On the equation of the Gihon with the Nile in Jewish tradition, see HÖLSCHER, *Drei Erdkarten*, p. 44.

[92] AVI-YONAH dismisses this suggestion as unfounded (*The Madaba Mosaic Map*, p. 11).

[93] Cf. MÜLLER, *Geschichte der antiken Ethnographie*, 2:284–286.

[94] Ancient cartography strove for symmetry (cf. ALEXANDER, "Toponymy," p. 47).

[95] Cf. H. DONNER and H. CÜPPERS, "Die Restauration and Konservierung der Mosaikkarte von Madeba," *ZDPV* 83 (1967) 1–33 (esp. pp. 11–14); AVI-YONAH, *The Madaba Mosaic Map*, p. 15.

[96] For an illustrated survey of the many kinds of medieval T-O maps, see WOODWARD, "Medieval *Mappaemundi*," pp. 343–347. Of particular interest is the *mappa mundi* that accompanies a thirteenth-century Psalms manuscript, for it depicts the cosmic Christ holding a miniature T-O globe in his hand and looming above the disk-shaped earth, which is oriented on the East with Jerusalem in the center (see the Frontispiece; also Peter WHITFIELD, *The Image of the World: 20 Centuries of World Maps* [London: The British Library, 1994], pp. 18–19). The map explicity mentions "Noah" and portrays the four rivers of Paradise.

[97] Cf. SCHMIDT, "Jewish Representations," p. 130; WOODWARD, "Medieval *Mappaemundi*," pp. 340–342.

[98] For example, the various Isidorian T-O maps dating from the seventh century (cf., e. g., ibid., p. 302) or the eleventh-century manuscript of the *Commentary on the Apocalypse of Saint John* by Beatus of Liebana (see the reproduction in HARLEY and WOODWARD, eds., *The History of Cartography*, p. 346). When Shem receives the largest portion, the semi-circle at the top of the T-O map (i. e., Asia), this may reflect his primogeniture (cf. Gen 10:21) or his relative importance.

[99] Cf. ALEXANDER, "Geography and the Bible (Early Judaism)," p. 982: "It is unclear whether the Christian T-O maps go back to the lost drawings of the *Jubilees* map, or whether they are derived from the written text of *Jubilees* alone." Curiously, WOODWARD ("Medieval *Mappaemundi*," p. 328) regards the tripartite division of the earth among the sons of Noah in

Conclusion. The exposition of the Table of Nations in the *Book of Jubilees* has had a powerful *Wirkungsgeschichte*. We can trace its influence even into medieval Christian maps. We now turn our attention to the influence of *Jubilees* 8–9 on texts from the Second Temple period.

The Table of Nations in the Qumran Genesis Apocryphon

The Dependence of 1QapGenesis on Jubilees. Dating probably from the first century B.C. or A.D.,[100] the *Genesis Apocryphon* can be compared to many other Jewish writings that are part of what is sometimes called the "rewritten Bible," a broad category that includes targum, midrash, and rewritten biblical narratives like *Jubilees*.[101] In fact, passage for passage, *Jubilees* parallels the contents of 1QapGenesis so closely that dependence one way or the other is usually assumed. Whereas the original editors consider the scroll a source for *Jubilees*,[102] FITZMYER argues rather that the *Genesis Apocryphon* is dependent on *Jubilees*.[103] In support of this position, FITZMYER points out, first, that the dependency of 1QapGenesis on *Jubilees* is "more in accord with the general tendency of the scroll to fill out and embellish the Genesis narrative."[104] He argues, second, that the *Genesis Apocryphon* includes a chronological detail about Abraham's life that is also found in *Jubilees* but that has a special function only in the latter; therefore, the Qumran scroll is most likely dependent on *Jubilees*.[105] Although neither of these arguments seems compelling in itself, the priority of *Jubilees* is assumed for purposes of the present study. The fragments

---

medieval *mappaemundi* to be a late development: "As the influence of the classical tradition declined, biblical sources became more prominent. Although originally Roman, the basic structure of the tripartite diagrams *now* owed their form to the tradition of the peopling of the earth by the descendants of Noah" (emphasis mine). Even the predominantly eastern orientation of these T-O maps is said to "follow the late Roman Sallustian tradition adopted by the Christian world" (ibid., p. 337). Likewise, the concept of placing Jerusalem at the center of the world is considered an idea that was "introduced in the seventh century but was not generally established until the twelfth or even the thirteenth" (ibid., p. 342).

[100] Cf. FITZMYER, *The Genesis Apocryphon*, pp. 14–19.

[101] Cf. P.S. ALEXANDER, "Retelling the Old Testament," in *It is Written: Scripture Citing Scripture. Essays in Honour of Barnabas Lindars* (ed. D.A. Carson and H.G.M. Williamson; Cambridge: Cambridge University Press, 1988), pp. 99–121 (here pp. 104–107); Craig A. EVANS, "The Genesis Apocryphon and the Rewritten Bible," *RevQ* 49–52 (1988) 153–165.

[102] Nahman AVIGAD and Yigael YADIN, *A Genesis Apocryphon: A Scroll from the Wilderness of Judaea* (Jerusalem: The Magnes Press of the Hebrew University and Heikhal Ha-Sefer, 1956), p. 38. Geza VERMES considers it possible that "Jubilees may be no more than an abridgment of Genesis Apocryphon" (*Scripture and Tradition in Judaism: Haggadic Studies* [SPB 4; Leiden: Brill, 1961], p. 124).

[103] FITZMYER, *Genesis Apocryphon*, pp. 16–17 (cf. p. 6).

[104] Ibid., p. 16. On the other hand, embellishment of the biblical narrative would seem to be precisely what the *Genesis Apocryphon* has in common with *Jubilees* and other rewritten biblical narratives (cf. ibid., pp. 10–11).

[105] Ibid., pp. 16–17.

of *Jubilees* found in Qumran[106] establish conclusively that the desert community used the text.

The Comparison of 1QapGenesis 16–17 and Jubilees 8–9. The extant portions of the *Genesis Apocryphon* can be divided into two main sections: (1) a poorly preserved section that embellishes Gen 6:8–9; 9:2–3, 4, 20; 10, that is, the life of Noah, the Flood, and the subsequent division of the earth among the sons of Noah (cols. 2–17);[107] and (2) a section that elaborates on Gen 12:8–15:4, that is, Abram's sojourns in Canaan, Egypt, and the Promised Land, his defeat of the four invading kings, and his vision concerning his future heir (cols. 18–22).[108] We are interested here particularly in the division of the earth among the sons of Noah after the Flood in columns 16–17 and its connection with the Table-of-Nations tradition.[109]

Although these two columns are poorly preserved, their contents can be deduced to a certain degree by comparing them to the very similar account in *Jubilees* 8–9 (see Table 2).[110] Like *Jubilees* 8, 1QapGenesis 16 must have originally contained a description of the division of the world among the three sons of Noah, giving the geographical boundaries of each portion. By the same token, column 17 must have given a description of the division of the portions of Shem, Ham, and Japheth among their sons much like that in *Jubilees* 9. Within the extant text, we find many of the same physical features as in *Jubilees*: the Great Sea,[111] the rivers Tina[112] and Tigris,[113] and probably also the Mount of the Ox.[114] We also find the same ethnography based on the Table of Nations:

---

[106] Cf. J. A. FITZMYER, *The Dead Sea Scrolls: Major Publications and Tools for Study* (rev. ed.; SBLRBS 20; Atlanta, GA: Scholars Press, 1990), pp. 17, 21, 23, 53, 64, 65, 72; James C. VANDERKAM, "The Jubilees Fragments from Qumran Cave 4," in *The Madrid Qumran Congress: Proceedings of the International Congress on the Dead Sea Scrolls* (2 vols.; STDJ 11; Leiden: Brill, 1992), 2:635–648. Nevertheless, MAIER expresses caution about the Ethiopic version, arguing that since the Qumran fragments of *Jubilees* do not contain chapters 8–9, we cannot be certain whether some of the toponymns may not go back to a later redactor or translator ("Japhetiten," p. 183).

[107] Noah figures prominently in the Dead Sea Scrolls. Cf., e.g., 1QNoah; CD 3.1–2; 1QapGen 6.6; 4Q534–536 (ed. Robert EISENMAN and Michael WISE, *The Dead Sea Scrolls Uncovered: The First Complete Translation and Interpretation of 50 Key Documents Withheld for over 35 Years* [Rockport, MA: Element, 1992], pp. 35–37); 4Q243–245.5 (ibid., pp. 66–67); 4Q252 1.1–2.7 (ibid., pp. 86–88); 4Q213–214 A 5.3 (ibid., pp. 139–141).

[108] See the more detailed outline of 1QapGenesis in FITZMYER, *The Dead Sea Scrolls*, pp. 137–138.

[109] Cf. also 1QapGen 12.10–11 ("[and became the father of] Arpachshad two years after the Flood, . . . all the sons of Shem . . . Put and Canaan . . ."); 19.13 ("Now we crossed [the border of] our land and entered the land of the sons of Ham, the land of Egypt").

[110] Cf. AVIGAD and YADIN, *A Genesis Apocryphon*, pp. 21–22; FITZMYER, *Genesis Apocryphon*, pp. 102–105.

[111] 1QapGen 16.12; cf. *Jub.* 8:15; 9:6.

[112] 1QapGen 16.16; 17.16; cf. *Jub.* 8:12, 16, 28; 9:2, 8.

[113] 1QapGen 17.8; cf. *Jub.* 9:5.

[114] On the equation of the Mount of the Ox with Mount Asshur in *Jub.* 8:21; 9:5, 6, see FITZMYER, *Genesis Apocryphon*, p. 104; AVIGAD and YADIN, *A Genesis Apocryphon*, pp. 29–30.

Table 2

A Comparison of Jubilees 8−9 with 1QapGen 16−17

		Jubilees 8−9		1QapGen 16−17
I. The Division of the World among the Sons of Noah (*Jubilees* 8)	Shem's Portion (vv. 12−21)			
	Ham's Portion (vv. 22−24)	(23) And it goes forth in the north to the east of Gadir. And it goes forth along the edge of the water of the sea into the waters of the Great Sea until it approaches the river Gihon.		(16.11) all the land north until it reached (16.12) [as far as] this boundary, the waters of the Great Sea
	Japheth's Portion (vv. 25−30)	(25) And for Japheth, the third portion was assigned, beyond the Tina River toward the north of the mouth of its waters.		(16.16) the Tina River
II. The Division of the Portions of Shem, Ham, and Japheth among their Sons (*Jubilees* 9)	Ham's Portion (v. 1)			
	Shem's Portion (vv. 2−6)	(2) And the first portion was assigned to Elam and his sons, toward the east of the Tigris River . . . (3) And also Asshur was assigned the second portion . . .		(17.8) to the west, to Asshur, until it reached the Tigris
		(4) And to Arpachshad was assigned the third portion, all of the land of the region of Chaldea toward the east of the Euphrates, which is near the Red Sea, and all of the waters of the desert as far as the vicinity of the tongue of the sea that faces toward Egypt, all of the land of Lebanon and Senir and Amana as far as the vicinity of the Euphrates.		(17.11) and upon the head of the three portions . . . for Arpachshad
		(5) And to Aram, the fourth portion was assigned, all of the land of Mesopotamia, between the Tigris and the Euphrates, toward the north of the Chaldeans up to the vicinity of Mount Asshur and the land of Arara.		(17.9) To Aram, the land that . . . until it reached the head of (17.10) this Mount of the Ox and he crossed this portion toward the west, until it reached
	Japheth's Portion (vv. 7−13)	(8) And the first portion was assigned to Gomer, toward the east from the north side up to the river Tina. And in the north, to Magog was assigned all of the inner parts of the north until it approaches toward the Sea of Me'at.		(17.16) to Gomer, he gave the east in the north, until it reached the Tina River and its circuit; to [Mag]og

Asshur, Arpachshad, Aram, Gomer, and Magog. Finally, we find the same basic order of presentation as in *Jubilees*,[115] replete with similar directional indications ("until it reached," "to the west," etc.).

Other Comparisons between Jubilees 8–9 and 1QapGenesis. As we have seen above, *Jubilees* 8 describes the boundaries of the territories of the three sons of Noah by following a circular path in each case. The descriptions of Shem and Japheth make a counterclockwise circuit beginning at the source of the Tina (cf. *Jub.* 8:12–21, 25–30), while the description of Ham makes a clockwise circuit beginning at a place beyond the Gihon, to the right of the Garden of Eden (vv. 22–24). The *Genesis Apocryphon* also describes territory in terms of circuits. In 1QapGen 17.16, for example, Gomer is said to have been given "the east in the north, until it reached the Tina River and its circuit (וכתרה)." This "circuit," if that is the correct translation,[116] refers to the territory bounded by the river Tina. The text 1QapGen 21.15–19 provides a very clear example of a territorial description in a clockwise circuit, beginning and ending with the river Gihon (Nile), much like the description of the territory of Ham in *Jub.* 8:22–24. In an attempt to correct the embarrassing fact that, in Genesis, Abraham never explicitly obeys the divine command to "Rise up, walk though the land in the length and breadth of it ..." (Gen 13:17), the *Genesis Apocryphon* includes a unique description of Abraham's journey:

> So I, Abram, set out to go around and look at the land. I started going about from the Gihon River, moving along the Sea [= the Mediterranean], until I reached the Mount of the Ox [= the Taurus range]. I journeyed from [the coast] of this Great Salt Sea and moved along the Mount of the Ox toward the east through the breadth of the land, until I reached the Euphrates River. I travelled along the Euphrates, until I came to the Red Sea in the east. (Then) I moved along the Red Sea, until I reached the tongue of the Red Sea, which goes forth from the Red Sea. (From there) I journeyed to the south, until I reached the Gihon River.[117]

In other words, Abraham made a complete, clockwise circuit around the Promised Land, which, in this case, seems to correspond to the portion of Arpachshad according to *Jub.* 9:4.[118] Several of the physical features from 1QapGen 16–17 also reappear in 21.15–19: the Gihon River, the Great Sea, and the Mount of the Ox.[119] Since columns 16–17 are evidently based

---

[115] In 1QapGen 17, however, Aram (*l.* 9) comes before Arpachshad (*l.* 11), instead of after him as in *Jub.* 9:4–5 and Gen 10:22.

[116] On the conjectured meaning of כתר here, see FITZMYER, *Genesis Apocryphon*, p. 104. However, Klaus BEYER reads instead בתר, a shortened form of באתר ("nach, hinter") and construes it with the succeeding clause: "und nach ihm dem Magog" (*Die aramäischen Texte vom Toten Meer* [Göttingen: Vandenhoeck & Ruprecht, 1984], p. 171; cf. p. 526, s.v. אתר).

[117] FITZMYER, *Genesis Apocryphon*, p. 69.

[118] Cf. ALEXANDER, "Imago Mundi," p. 206 n. 12.

[119] The fact that Abraham journeyed east along the Mount of the Ox (1QapGen

on *Jubilees* 8−9, ALEXANDER appears correct in suggesting that 21.15−19 "may be based on the Jubilees map."[120]

The Table of Nations in the War Scroll (1QM 2.10−14)

The *War Scroll*[121] is another Qumran text that contains the Table-of-Nations tradition.[122] According to column 1, after the Sons of Light return to Jerusalem "from the wilderness of the peoples" (ממדבר העמים),[123] they will engage in a series of campaigns against the Sons of Darkness led by the Japhethite nation of Kittim[124] together with, apparently, "the kings of the north" (1QM 1.1−15). The influence of Daniel 11 and Ezekiel 38−39 is readily apparent here.[125] The Kittim in the Qumran scrolls are generally understood as the Romans.[126] So,

---

21.16−17) may presuppose the notion of the *diaphragma* found already, possibly, in *Jub.* 8:19 (see above).

[120] Cf. ALEXANDER, "Imago Mundi," p. 206 n. 12.

[121] Cf. Yigael YADIN, *The Scroll of the War of the Sons of Light against the Sons of Darkness* (trans. Batya and Chaim Rabin; Oxford: Oxford University Press, 1962). On the dating of the War Scroll, see SCHÜRER, *Hist.*, 3.1:402−404 ("the final decades of the first century B.C.; or, if the paleographic data may be stretched a little, to the early decades of the first century A.D"); Devorah DIMANT, "Qumran Sectarian Literature," in *Jewish Writings of the Second Temple Period: Apocrypha, Pseudepigrapha, Qumran Sectarian Writings, Philo, Josephus* (CRINT 2.2; Assen: Van Gorcum; Philadelphia: Fortress, 1984), pp. 483−550 (here p. 517: "the early phase of the sect's life, namely the second half of the second century B.C.E"); Hermann LICHTENBERGER, *Studien zum Menschenbild in Texten der Qumrangemeinde* (SUNT 15; Göttingen: Vandenhoeck & Ruprecht, 1980), p. 27 ("von ca. 170 v.Chr. bis zur Zeitenwende").

[122] Philip R. DAVIES considers whether the roots of 1QM 2−9 might be the Deuteronomic dichotomy between "Israel" and "the nations" found in 1 Maccabees (*1QM, the War Scroll from Qumran: Its Structure and History* [BibOr 32; Rome: Biblical Institute Press, 1977], pp. 64−65).

[123] 1QM 1.3; cf. Ezek 20:35 ("the wilderness of the peoples"); 4Q266.8−12: "He [sc. the priest] is to stand and say, 'Blessed are you; you are all; everything is in your hand and (you are) the maker of everything, who established [the peo]ples according to their families and their national languages. You 'made them to wander astray in a wilderness without a way,' but you chose our fathers, and to their seed you gave the laws of your truth and the judgments of your holiness, 'which man shall do and thereby live'" (EISENMAN and WISE, *The Dead Sea Scrolls Uncovered*, pp. 218−219).

[124] On the Kittim as sons of Japheth, see Gen 10:4 and the parallelism between the "sons of Japheth" and the "Kittim" in 1QM 1.5−6; 18.2−3.

[125] On "the king (sg.) of the north," see Dan 11:40−45. On the Kittim, see Dan 11:30. Note that Ezek 38:5−6 expects Gog, together with other nations in the north (cf. Ezek 38:5−6, 15; 39:1−2), to join in with the attack on Jerusalem.

[126] Cf. George J. BROOKE, "The Kittim in the Qumran Pesharim," in *Images of Empire* (ed. Loveday Alexander; JSOTSSup 122; Sheffield: JSOT Press, 1991), pp. 135−159; Mireille HADAS-LEBEL, "L'évolution de l'image de Rome auprès des Juifs en deux siècles de relations judéo-romaines – 164 à +70," in *ANRW* II.20.2 (ed. Wolfgang Haase; Berlin/New York: de Gruyter, 1987), pp. 715−856 (here pp. 747−755); SCHÜRER, *Hist.*, 1:241 n. 30; 3.1:402−404, 434−435; YADIN, *The Scroll of the War of the Sons of Light against the Sons of Darkness*, pp. 6, 22−26; Henry A. REDPATH, "The Geography of the Septuagint," *AJT* 7 (1903) 289−307 (here p. 300); Rita EGGER, *Josephus Flavius und die Samaritaner. Eine terminologische Unter-*

when the *War Scroll* refers to "the Kittim of Asshur" (1QM 1.2) and "the Kittim in Egypt" (*l.* 4), this evidently shows that the Japhethite nation of the Kittim had encroached on and stationed legions in the territories of Shem[127] and Ham,[128] respectively. This would be another indication of the universal sovereignty of the Kittim.

Column 2 goes on to describe how the community will conduct a forty-year war against all its enemies on earth, including 29 years against all the nations of the world listed in Genesis 10 (1QM 2.10–14).[129] Thus, following the order of both the seniority of the sons of Noah and their proximity to Israel,[130] the first nine years of this final period are devoted to the war against the sons of Shem, who are listed individually along with the number of years needed to fight each one (2.10–13).[131] The next ten years are concentrated on the war with "all the sons of Ham according to their families (למשפחותם)[132] in their dwelling places (במושבותם)[133]" (2.13–14). And the last ten years are dedicated to the war with "all the sons of Japheth in their dwelling places (במושבותיהם)" (2.14).[134] Here, we see that the final battle in Ezekiel 38–39 has been expanded to include not just the nations of Japheth and Ham but those of Shem as well.[135] Again, we are struck by the fact that the Table of Nations has continuing relevance, even for

---

suchung zur Identitätsklärung der Samaritaner (NTOA 4; Freiburg: Universitätsverlag; Göttingen: Vandenhoeck & Ruprecht, 1986), pp. 179–183; Louis H. FELDMAN, *Josephus and Modern Scholarship (1937–1980)* (New York/Berlin: de Gruyter, 1984), pp. 245–247. Additional Qumran texts on the Kittim are now available in EISENMAN and WISE, *The Dead Sea Scrolls Uncovered*, pp. 27–29 (4Q285 1.2; 6.5; 7.6), 41–46 (4Q554 11.16), 167 (4Q424 1.13). On the identification of the Kittim with the Romans, see further Louis H. FELDMAN, *Jew and Gentile in the Ancient World: Attitudes and Interactions from Alexander to Justinian* (Princeton, NJ: Princeton University Press, 1993), p. 494 n. 59.

[127] For Asshur as a son of Shem, see Gen 10:22; 1QM 2.12.

[128] For Egypt (מצרים) as a son of Ham, see Gen 10:6.

[129] The connection between 1QM 1 and 2 is uncertain. Most scholars who are convinced of the composite nature of the *War Scroll* agree that these columns belong to different layers of redaction (cf. LICHTENBERGER, *Menschenbild*, pp. 20–26; SCHÜRER, *Hist.*, 3.1: 401–402; DIMANT, "Qumran Sectarian Literature," pp. 516–517). In their present form, the first two columns of the *War Scroll* seem to indicate that the war against the Kittim (Rome) in 1QM 1 precedes the campaigns of 2.10–14, in which the whole world is gradually conquered (cf. DAVIES, *1QM, the War Scroll from Qumran*, p. 119).

[130] For the order, cf. Gen 9:18; 10:1. The Table of Nations itself lists the descendants of each son in the reverse order – Japheth, Ham, Shem.

[131] See the table in YADIN, *The Scroll of the War of the Sons of Light against the Sons of Darkness*, p. 27.

[132] Restored after Gen 10:20.

[133] Restored after Num 31:10.

[134] The "sons of Ham" and the "sons of Shem" are also mentioned in 4Q529.7 (EISENMAN and WISE, *The Dead Sea Scrolls Uncovered*, pp. 38–39). Cf. "Ham and Japheth" in 4Q462 1.1 (ibid., pp. 268–269). On the fate of the "sons of Japheth," see also 1QM 1.6; 18.2; 4QM6 13, 3.4. Gog does not figure prominently in the *War Scroll* (cf. merely 1QM 11.16) and Magog not at all. The latter, however, is mentioned in 4QpIsa[a] 7–10 iii 25.

[135] Cf. 1QM 1.1–2, where the war against the Sons of Darkness includes the troop of Edom and Moab, the sons of Ammon, and the offenders against the covenant.

the future conquest of the world by the twelve tribes of Israel.[136] Taken together in its present form, therefore, 1QM 1–2 suggests that the nations will fall under divine judgment,[137] and the universal sovereignty of the Kittim will pass to Israel.

The Table of Nations in the Sibylline Oracles, Book 3

Noachic Traditions in The Sibylline Oracles. Although they stem from different times and places, several of the Jewish *Sibylline Oracles* contain references to Noah and his family.[138] In fact, the Sibyl herself is said to be a daughter (or daughter-in-law) of Noah.[139] Books 1 and 2, which deal extensively with the Flood story, provide a convenient point of departure for our discussion. Structured on the familiar Sibylline division of the world into ten generations,[140] the *Grundschrift* of these books, without the Christian passage on the incarnation and career of Christ (1.324–400), stems from between 30 B. C. and A. D. 70 in Phrygia.[141] This provenance is derived from the reference to Phrygia as the first land to emerge after the Flood (1.196–198) and as the location of Mt. Ararat and the springs of the river Marsyos, where the Ark landed (1.261–267).[142] Since the springs of the Marsyos are situated just behind Apamea, P. R. TREBILCO suggests that Books 1 and 2 stem specifically from the Jewish community in Apamea.[143] This would be significant for our study insofar as Apamea belongs to the part of the Phyrgian mainland bordering Galatia on the west.

---

[136] On the expected universal sovereignty of Israel, see, e.g., Jacob's vision at Bethel in *Jub.* 32:18–19, an interpretation of Gen 17:6 and 28:14 in light of Dan 7:9–28: "And there will be kings from you; they will rule everywhere that the tracks of mankind have been trod. And I shall give to your seed all the land under heaven and they will rule in all nations as they have desired. And after this all of the earth will be gathered together and they will inherit it forever." See further Chap. 2 on the OT promise of land for Abraham and his seed and on the interpretation of Gen 28:14 in Philo *Somn.* 1.175; also J. SCOTT, *Adoption as Sons of God: An Exegetical Investigation into the Background of* ΥΙΟΘΕΣΙΑ *in the Pauline Corpus* (WUNT 2.48; Tübingen: Mohr-Siebeck, 1992), pp. 134–135.

[137] The conclusion of the exposition of the Table of Nations in *Jubilees* 8–9 likewise expects "the day of judgment in which the Lord God will judge them [sc. the descendants of Noah] with a sword and with fire on account of all the evil of the pollution of their errors which have filled the earth with sin and pollution and fornication and transgression" (9:15).

[138] Cf. *Sib. Or.* 1.125–136, 147–306; 3.824–828; 7.8.

[139] Cf. *Sib. Or.*, Prologue 33; 1.288–290; 3.827.

[140] Cf. John J. COLLINS, *The Sibylline Oracles of Egyptian Judaism* (SBLDS 13; Missoula, MT: Scholars' Press, 1974), pp. 101–102.

[141] Cf. J. COLLINS, "Sibylline Oracles," in *OTP*, 1:331; idem, "The Development of the Sibylline Tradition," in *ANRW* II.20.1 (ed. Wolfgang Haase; Berlin: de Gruyter, 1987), pp. 421–459 (here p. 442).

[142] Ararat is generally identified as a mountain in Armenia (cf. Josephus *Ant.* 1.90). See further Jack P. LEWIS, *A Study of the Interpretation of Noah and the Flood in Jewish and Christian Literature* (Leiden: Brill, 1968), pp. 33, 94, et passim.

[143] Cf. Paul R. TREBILCO, *Jewish Communities in Asia Minor* (SNTSMS 69; Cambridge: Cambridge University Press, 1991), p. 95.

A rich Noachic tradition is associated with the Apamea area.[144] The city itself was "nicknamed" Κιβωτός ("box, chest, ark"),[145] the usual term for Noah's Ark in the Septuagint.[146] This nickname may have given the impetus for identifying the four local (Phrygian) flood traditions with the biblical Flood story.[147] Coins minted in Apamea from the end of the second century A.D. picture Noah and his wife[148] with the Ark, a rectangular box that bears the name ΝΩΕ.[149]

Similarities between Sibylline Oracles 3 and Jubilees 8−9. Although Book 3 of the *Sibylline Oracles* is not intended to be an exposition of the Table of Nations,[150] it nevertheless contains many striking similarities to *Jubilees* 8−9.[151] First, the *Third Sibyl* stems from the same period of time as *Jubilees*, i.e., the second century B.C.[152] Second, the *Third Sibyl* recounts the biblical story of Noah and his three sons in much the same way as *Jubilees* does, albeit with a thick overlay of Greek mythology. The Sibyl, herself a daughter (or daughter-in-law) of Noah,[153] explains that after the Flood,[154] the earth was divided by lot (κατὰ κλῆρον) into three territories according to the three sons of Gaia and Ouranos: Kronos, Titan, and Iapetos (*Sib. Or.* 3.110−114). The Iapetos of Hesiod,[155] who is equivalent to the biblical Japheth,[156] facilitates the

---

[144] Cf. Schürer, *Hist.*, 3.1:28−30. See further G.A. Caduff, *Antike Sintflutsagen* (Hypomnemata 82; Göttingen: Vandenhoeck & Ruprecht, 1986).

[145] Cf. Strabo *Geogr.* 12.8.13. See further Trebilco, *Jewish Communities in Asia Minor*, pp. 90−91.

[146] Cf. Gen 6:15, 16, 17, 19, etc.

[147] So Trebilco, *Jewish Communities in Asia Minor*, pp. 91, 96−97. On the various local flood legends, see ibid., pp. 88−90.

[148] Note, however, that J. Geffcken thought the coins depicted Noah and the Sibyl (*Komposition und Entstehung der Oracula Sibyllina* [TU 23.1; Leipzig: Hinrichs, 1902], p. 49; followed by J.J. Collins, "Sibylline Oracles," *OTP*, 1:331). On the tradition of Noah and his wife, see further Rainer Stichel, *Die Namen Noes, seines Bruders und seiner Frau. Ein Beitrag zum Nachleben jüdischer Überlieferungen in der außerkanonischen und gnostischen Literatur und in den Denkmälern der Kunst* (Abhandlungen der Akademie der Wissenschaften, Philologisch-historische Klasse 3.112; Göttingen: Vandenhoeck & Ruprecht, 1979).

[149] Cf. Trebilco, *Jewish Communities in Asia Minor*, pp. 86−88. The coins bear the image and inscriptions of five emperors: Septimius Severus (A.D. 193−211), Macrinus (A.D. 217−218), Severus Alexander (A.D. 222−235), Philippus Arabs (A.D. 244−249), and Trebonianus Gallus (A.D. 251−253).

[150] On the nature and purpose of the *Third Sibyl*, see Collins, *The Sibylline Oracles of Egyptian Judaism*; Valentin Nikiprowetsky, *La troisième Sibylle* (Études Juives 9; Paris: Mouton, 1970). See further H.W. Parke, *Sibyls and Sibylline Prophecy in Classical Antiquity* (London/New York: Routledge, 1988).

[151] So also Schmidt, "Jewish Representations," p. 129.

[152] Cf. Collins, *OTP*, "Sibylline Oracles," 1.354−355; idem, *The Sibylline Oracles of Egyptian Judaism*, pp. 21−22.

[153] See nn. 137 and 146 above.

[154] Cf. *Sib. Or.* 3.108−109.

[155] Cf. Hesiod *Theog.* 18, 134, 507, 746 (ed. M.L. West, *Hesiod: Theogony, Edited with Prolegomena and Commentary* [Oxford: Clarendon Press, 1966]). Iapetos is mentioned, along with Kronos, also in Homer *Il.* 8.479.

[156] On the identification of Iapetos and Japheth, cf. Westermann, *Gen.*, 1:674; Neiman,

connection between the Greek myth and the Table-of-Nations tradition.[157]
Each son reigned over his own territory and was bound by oath not to violate
the others' portions (vv. 115—116). The parallel to *Jubilees* 8—9 is obvious, for
there too, the three sons are assigned portions by lot (cf. *Jub.* 8:11), and the
territories are held inviolable by an oath imposed by their father, which, if
broken, would bring a curse upon the offender and ultimately divine judgment
by sword and fire (cf. *Jub.* 9:14—15). The point of the *Third Sibyl* is that the
oath imposed by their father was broken, that a struggle for world domination
began among the three sons, and that, before setting up his own kingdom, God
would judge all nations by sword and fire. Third, Book 3 contains a number of
the same formal geographic features as in *Jubilees* 8—9: the three continents,[158]
the eastward orientation,[159] several seas (Oceanus,[160] Lake Maeotis,[161] the
Western Sea[162]), the Tanais River,[163] and Mt. Sinai.[164]

   The Ethnography of the Third Sibyl. The *Third Sibyl* goes far beyond *Jubilees*
in listing the nations of world. After the distribution of the earth among
Kronos, Titan, and Iapetos, Ouranos died, and the sons began to transgress the
aforementioned oaths by stirring up strife against each other "as to who should
have royal honor and reign over all men" (*Sib. Or.* 3.110—120). At first,
diplomacy was able to bring about an uneasy truce that allowed the eldest son,
Kronos, to rule over all on a provisional and temporary basis (vv. 121—131).
However, when Titan discovered that Kronos had deceived him, a war broke

---

"The Two Genealogies of Japhet," pp. 123ff.; M. C. ASTOUR, "Japheth," in *IDBSup*, p. 470;
WEST, *Hesiod: Theogony*, pp. 202—203. See also Erika SIMON, "Iapetos," in *Lexicon Iconographicum Mythologiae Classicae*, 5.1 (1990) 523—524.

   [157] According to [Pseudo-]Eupolemus (in Eusebius *Pr. Ev.* 9.17.9), the Babylonians hold
that Kronos was the father of Canaan, the father of Phoenicians, who was the father of Chus
(= Ethiopia) and Mitzraim (= Egypt). Thus, Kronos occupies a genealogical position analogous to that of Ham, who was the father of Cush, Mitzraim, Put, and Canaan (cf. Gen 10:6).
On J. FREUDENTHAL's widely-followed emendation of Χαναav to Χαμ, see R. DORAN,
"Pseudo-Eupolemus," *OTP*, 2:881 n. *u*. On the similarity of this text to the *Third Sibyl*, see
further HENGEL, *Judentum und Hellenismus*, pp. 163—164.

   [158] Cf. *Sib. Or.* 3.295—380: Libya (v. 323), Asia (v. 342), and Europe (v. 346). In other
words, this passage pronounces woes against all the nations of the world (cf., similarly, *Sib.
Or.* 3.489—544, esp. vv. 517—519).

   [159] *Sib. Or.* 3.26; cf. *Jub.* 8:22—23.

   [160] *Sib. Or.* 3.223. Several bodies of water probably constitute Oceanus in *Jubilees* 8 (cf.
ALEXANDER, "Imago Mundi," p. 205).

   [161] *Sib. Or.* 3.338; equivalent to the Sea of Me'at in *Jub.* 8:27; 9:8.

   [162] *Sib. Or.* 3.176; equivalent to the Great Sea in *Jub.* 8:15; 9:6. In the Hebrew Bible, the
Mediterranean is called both the Great Sea (cf. Josh 1:4) and the Western Sea (cf. Deut 11:24).
The word ים itself denotes "west" or "western."

   [163] *Sib. Or.* 3.338; equivalent to the Tina river in *Jub.* 8:12, 16; 9:8. The one account states
that the Tanais leaves Lake Maeotis (*Sib. Or.* 3.338—340), the other that the Tina runs into
Sea of Me'at (*Jub.* 8:12). The same geography is obviously presupposed in both cases.

   [164] *Sib. Or.* 3.256; cf. *Jub.* 8:19. On the other hand, the *Third Sibyl* frequently mentions
Jerusalem and the Temple (cf. *Sib. Or.* 3.213, 274, 281, 290, 294, 302, 565, 575, 657, 702, 718)
but not as the center of the earth. Cf. *Sib. Or.* 5.250, which describes Jerusalem as πόλις ἐν
μεσογαίοις.

out between the families (vv. 147–153), which is described as "the first beginning of war for mortals" (vv. 154–155). The subsequent list of nations shows
that the struggle for world empire continued even after all the descendants of
Titans and of Kronos had died (vv. 156–158): "But then as time pursued its
cyclic course, the kingdom of Egypt arose, then that of the Persians, Medes,
and Ethiopians, and Assyrian Babylon, then that of the Macedonians, of Egypt
again, then of Rome" (vv. 158–161).[165] The cyclical nature of this succession of
nations derives evidently from the fact that, as the following diagram shows,
descendants of each of the three sons of Noah reign according to the sequence:
Ham, Shem, and Japheth.

Cycle	Nation	Noah's Sons
I	Egypt	Ham
	Persians	Shem
	Medes	Japheth
II	Ethiopians	Ham
	Assyrian Babylon	Shem
	Macedonia	Japheth
III	Egypt	Ham
	Rome	Japheth
	[Jews]	[Shem]

This shows that, despite the Greek mythology with which the Table-of-
Nations tradition has been overlaid here, the three sons of Noah have not been
forgotten.[166] That a descendant of Ham begins each of the three cycles of
nations (Egypt-Ethiopia-Egypt) may be attributed to the Egyptian provenance
of the *Third Sibyl*.[167] A subtle reversal takes place at the end of the list, where
Rome, a Japhethite nation, appears second instead of third in the final cycle,

---

[165] On the origin of the kingdoms in the aftermath of the Tower of Babel, cf. *Sib. Or.*
3.105–107: "But when the Tower fell, and the tongues of men were diversified by various
sounds, the whole earth of humans was filled with fragmenting kingdoms."

[166] Cf. *Sib. Or.* 3.293, which refers to "three great-spirited kings" who come at the time of
the Flood, that is, the three sons of Noah.

[167] Cf. COLLINS, *The Sibylline Oracles*, p. 26.

thus allowing the descendants of Shem (the Jews!) to be the implied final kingdom.[168] This illustrates the political nature of the Sibyllines.[169]

The influence of the Table-of-Nations tradition can be seen very clearly in the prophecy of universal disasters in *Sib. Or.* 3.489−544.[170] The oracle is billed as a prophecy "concerning the earth" (κατὰ γαῖαν).[171] Thereupon, the oracle proceeds to list woes against various nations,[172] including Magog,[173] one of the seven sons of Japheth in Genesis 10 (v. 2). Yet the Sibyl stops short of completing the list, exclaiming: "Why should I proclaim each one according to its fate? For on all nations, as many as inhabit the earth, will the Most High send terrible affliction."[174] Here, again, is evidence that the *Third Sibyl* is oriented on the Table-of-Nations tradition.[175] In that case, the nations in this oracle, even those with Greek names, may have been assumed to have biblical equivalents in Genesis 10. For example, the Αἰθίοπες mentioned in *Sib. Or.* 3.516[176] could be the Greek equivalent of כוש, just as it usually is in the Septuagint.[177] Likewise, the Ἕλληνες mentioned in 3.520[178] could be the Greek equivalent of

---

[168] Cf. *Sib. Or.* 3.701−761, 767−795. That the final empire is strongly implied in the list can also be shown by the fact that in the *Sibylline Oracles*, the usual number of world kingdoms is ten (cf. COLLINS, *The Sibylline Oracles*, pp. 26, 101−102; idem, "Sibylline Oracles," *OTP*, 1.365 note). For example, the immediately following list of nations in *Sib. Or.* 3.161−195 contains the full complement of ten kingdoms. If we include the kingdom of Kronos as the first kingdom and assume an expected eschatological kingdom as the tenth, then the list in *Sib. Or.* 3.158−161 gives the usual number (ibid., p. 26 n. 27). Note, however, that the Fourth Sibyl reckons with four kingdoms (cf. David FLUSSER, "The Four Empires in the Fourth Sibyl and in the Book of Daniel," *IOS* 2 [1972] 148−175).

[169] Cf. COLLINS, "Sibylline Oracles," *OTP*, 1.322: "The main historical value of the books lies in their representation of popular attitudes in the realm of politics, the legend-laden view of kings and empires, and the hopes and fears of Eastern peoples under first Greek and then, for most of the books, Roman rule. In particular they are a major source for ideology of resistance to Rome throughout the Near East."

[170] Yehoshua AMIR argues that *Sib. Or.* 3.520−572 applies the curses of Deuteronomy 28 against the foreign nations instead of against Israel ("Homer und Bibel als Ausdrucksmittel im 3.Sibyllenbuch," in *Studien zum antiken Judentum* [Beiträge zur Erforschung des Alten Testaments und des antiken Judentums 2; Frankfurt a. M.: Peter Lang, 1985], pp. 83−100).

[171] *Sib. Or.* 3.491.

[172] I. e., the nation of Phoenicians and all maritime cities (*Sib. Or.* 3.492−503), Crete (3.504−506), Thrace (3.508−511), the sons of the Lycians and Mysians and Phrygians (3.514), many nations of Pamphylians and Lydians (3.515), Maurians and Ethiopians and barbaric-speaking nations, Cappadocians, and Arabs (3.516−517). Note that the Cappadocians are listed among the sons of Egypt in *Bib. Ant.* 4:7.

[173] *Sib. Or.* 3.512−513; cf. also 3.319, both with Gog (Ezek 38:1). The *Third Sibyl* contains other terms from the Table-of-Nations tradition (cf., e.g., Babylon [3.104, 160, 301, 303, 307, 384], Gaza [3.345], Medes [3.160], Lydians [3.515], and Assyrians [3.207, 268, 303]).

[174] *Sib. Or.* 3.517−519: τί δὴ κατὰ μοῖραν ἕκαστον ἐξαυδῶ; πᾶσιν γάϱ, ὅσοι χθόνα ναιετάουσιν, Ὕψιστος δεινὴν ἐπιπέμψει ἔθνεσι πληγήν.

[175] Other books of the *Sibylline Oracles* are also interested in "all nations" or "every nation" (cf. *Sib. Or.* 11.76; 12.106).

[176] Cf. also *Sib. Or.* 3.160, 208, 320.

[177] Cf. REDPATH, "The Geography of the Septuagint," pp. 292−293.

[178] Cf. also *Sib. Or.* 3.171, 193, 202, 536, 553, 609.

יון, just as constantly not only in the Septuagint but also in the other versions of Daniel.[179] What might this imply about the other nations, such as the Galatians, listed in the *Third Sibyl*?[180] As we shall see below, Josephus "updates" the toponymy in the Table of Nations, providing the contemporary Greek name for the nations alongside the original.

The Table of Nations in Josephus Ant. 1.120–147

Josephus' exposition of the Table of Nations interacts with the *Jubilees* tradition in a highly complex way, for Josephus not only appropriates the tradition directly and possibly indirectly, he also corrects it at important points.[181]

Sibylline Tradition in Josephus' Exposition of the Table of Nations. L. H. FELDMAN argues that throughout the part of the *Antiquities* that parallels the Bible, Josephus Hellenizes the account in order to make it intelligible to his Greek readers.[182] These Hellenizations include geographic and ethnographic details, such as the notion of a stream (Oceanus) surrounding the earth, the equation of the Gihon with the Nile, and the identification of lands settled by Japheth's sons with various Greek countries.[183] In particular, FELDMAN argues that Book 1 of the *Antiquities* interprets the prehistory of Genesis 1–8 in light of the Hesiodic tradition of the Golden Age and humanity's decline there-from.[184] If this is correct, we may ask whether Josephus understands the division of the earth among the three sons of Noah in terms of the Hesiodic tradition of Iapetos and the other sons of Ouranos which we have seen in *Sib. Or.* 3.110–120. Josephus may have been acquainted with this section of the *Third Sibyl*, for in *Ant.* 1.118 he cites *Sib. Or.* 3.99–106 to adduce pagan evidence for the biblical account of the confusion of tongues at the Tower of Babel.[185] This would, in general, fit in with Josephus' polemic in the context of

---

[179] Cf. REDPATH, "The Geography of the Septuagint," p. 300.

[180] The Galatians are mentioned three times: *Sib. Or.* 3.485, 509, 599; cf. also 5.340.

[181] If, as Tessa RAJAK argues ("Josephus and the 'Archaeology' of the Jews," *JJS* 33 [1982] 465–477), Josephus' aim in writing the *Antiquities* was to convince Greek readers of the antiquity of the Jewish people (cf. *Ap.* 1.2), then his exposition of the Table of Nations is crucial for his endeavor.

[182] Louis H. FELDMAN, "Hellenizations in Josephus' Portrayal of Man's Decline," in *Religions in Antiquity: Essays in Memory of Erwin Ramsdell Goodenough* (ed. Jacob Neusner; Studies in the History of Religions 14; Leiden: Brill, 1968), pp. 336–353; also idem, "Josephus' Commentary on Genesis," *JQR* 72 (1981/82) 121–131; idem, "Josephus' Portrait of Noah and its Parallels in Philo, Pseudo-Philo's *Biblical Antiquities*, and Rabbinic Midrashim," *PAAJR* 55 (1988) 31–57. FELDMAN's thesis is taken up and developed by Arthur J. DROGE, *Homer or Moses? Early Christian Interpretation of the History of Culture* (HUT 26; Tübingen: Mohr-Siebeck, 1989), pp. 35–47.

[183] Cf. FELDMAN, "Hellenizations," pp. 339–340.

[184] Cf. ibid., pp. 341–352.

[185] However, Josephus' citation is often considered to be based on Alexander Polyhistor

his complaint against the Greeks' tampering with ancient nomenclature (see further below). In the absence of positive evidence, the possibility of an indirect appropriation of the *Jubilees* Table-of-Nations tradition through the *Third Sibyl* must remain open.

Differences between Josephus and Jubilees on the Table of Nations. Josephus' exposition of the Table of Nations in *Ant.* 120–147 differs sharply from that in *Jubilees* 8–9.[186] Josephus' perspective may be, broadly speaking, "Israel-centric" since it comes within the work entitled *Jewish Antiquities*; however, his perspective is not at all "Israel-centric" in a geographic sense, for according to Josephus, Canaan, far from being an intruder from western North Africa into Shem's territory (so *Jubilees*), was actually the original, divinely-ordained settler of Judea (*Ant.* 1.133; cf. § 120). Indeed, for Josephus, the western boundary of Shem begins at the Euphrates (§ 143), rather than at the Nile (so *Jubilees*); thus, Judea is excluded from the territory of Shem altogether and included rather as part of the territory of Ham.[187] Furthermore, when Josephus does refer to Jerusalem as the ὀμφαλός (*BJ* 3.52), he restricts the concept to mean to the "navel of the country [sc. Judaea]," rather than the middle of the earth (so *Jubilees*).[188]

Many other differences could be mentioned between the two accounts. For example, whereas *Jubilees* follows the order of Gen 10:1 in discussing the sons of Noah (Shem, Ham, Japheth), Josephus follows the order of Gen 10:2–31: Japheth (*Ant.* 1.122–129), Ham (§§ 130–142), and Shem (§§ 143–147).

(cf. STERN, *Greek and Latin Authors on Jews and Judaism*, 3:17–19; SCHÜRER, *Hist.*, 3.1:646; C. UEHLINGER, *Weltreich und "eine Rede"*, pp. 133–137).

[186] Note that in his speech to dissuade the Jews from war with Rome (*BJ* 2.345–401), Agrippa lists and briefly describes the many nations that are subject to the rule of Rome (§ 358–387). Although Agrippa asserts that "the universe" (τὰ πάντα) is subject to Rome (§ 361; also 5.366) and that therefore "all who are in the inhabited world are Romans" (§ 388), the somewhat more limited boundaries of the Roman Empire that he subsequently gives according to the four points of the compass reveal this as an exaggeration: the Euphrates in the east, the Ister (= the Danube) in the north, Libya in the south, and Gades in the west (§ 363; cf. 375, 382). The division of the earth into the three continents is presupposed throughout: Asia (§§ 358, 359, 366), Libya (§§ 363, 382), and Europe (§ 358). In a similar vein, Josephus himself urges the Jews besieged in Jerusalem to surrender to the Romans, who had God on their side (*BJ* 5.362–419). Evidently, Josephus believes that Rome is the fourth kingdom of Daniel, for he uses as part of his argument the fact that "God who went the round of the nations, bringing to each in turn the rod of empire, now rested over Italy" (§ 367). See further in Chap. 2.

[187] Whereas *Jubilees* assumes that Palestine was originally allotted to Shem, Josephus assumes that it was allotted to Ham (*Ant.* 1.136). Thus, Josephus is more realistic, reflecting the historical geopolitical situation in the OT before the Conquest, whereas *Jubilees* is more idealistic, attempting to harmonize the Biblical with the preconceived idea, based on the principle of inviolability of the God-ordained world order, that the Promised Land was originally assigned to Shem.

[188] In this way, Josephus may be following the use of ὀμφαλός τῆς γῆς in Judg 9:37, understood in the sense of the "middle of the land" of Shechem. On the other hand, Judg 9:37 may represent a competing tradition of Gerizim as the center of the world (cf. Jn 4:20–21; EGO, *Im Himmel wie auf Erden*, pp. 105–107; STADELMANN, *The Hebrew Conception of the World*, pp. 147–148).

Whereas *Jubilees* has the descendants of Noah assigned their portions by lot in the presence of Noah *before* the discussion of the confusion of languages, Josephus' exposition of the Table of Nations comes *after* his discussion of the confusion of languages at the Tower of Babel (§§ 113—119); for up to that point, the sons of Noah refused to obey the divine command to colonize the earth, opting instead to settle on the Plain of Shinar (§§ 109—112). It was at Babel, therefore, that the sons of Noah "were dispersed through their diversity of languages and founded colonies everywhere, each group occupying the country that they lit upon and to which God led them, so that every continent was peopled by them ..." (§ 120). Moreover, Josephus' use of the Table of Nations differs from that of *Jubilees*, for whereas (in the face of a Hellenistic threat in Palestine?[189]) *Jubilees* uses the Table of Nations to affirm the inviolable nature of the portions assigned by God to the descendants of Noah, Josephus uses it to critique the way that "the Greeks" changed the names of the nations that were originally given to them by their founders, i.e, the grandsons of Noah (§§ 121—122a).[190] Thereupon follows the list of the descendants of Noah, which in each case supplies the original name of the nation and then the Greek alteration or substitution. Although the list of differences between Josephus and *Jubilees* could go on,[191] it will suffice to mention a final one that is important for our considerations here: Whereas *Jubilees* assigns Asia Minor to Shem, Josephus assigns it to Japheth (§§ 122ff.), thus allowing Lud (= the Lydians [§ 144]) to occupy a territory that is well outside the portion of Shem. Unlike *Jubilees*, therefore, Josephus evidently resists the urge to harmonize at this point.

Jubilees as a Source for Josephus' Exposition of the Table of Nations? Despite the serious differences between the two texts, T. W. FRANXMAN suggests that, "for a while at least," Josephus uses *Jubilees* 8—9 as a source.[192] If that is correct, then Josephus is quite free with his source and obviously very critical of

---

[189] Cf. SCHMIDT, "Jewish Representations," pp. 133—134; ALEXANDER, "Imago Mundi," p. 212. See n. 50 above.

[190] In *contra Apionem*, Josephus gives more scope to his polemical attitude toward the Greeks. Cf. DROGE, *Homer or Moses?* pp. 41ff.; ALEXANDER, "Toponymy," pp. 54—55; Thomas W. FRANXMAN, *Genesis and the "Jewish Antiquities" of Flavius Josephus* (BibOr 35; Rome: Biblical Institute Press, 1979), pp. 100—101. Josephus claims that the Grecized form of the nations' names is "not that used in our country, where their structure and termination always remain the same" (*Ant.* 1.129). This refers to the Hebrew form of the names.

[191] For example, the sons of Ham are given much more scope in Josephus' exposition than in *Jubilees*, more in fact than the other two sons of Noah; Josephus assigns the Arameans to Syria (*Ant.* 1.144) rather than to Mesopotamia (*Jub.* 9:5).

[192] FRANXMAN, *Genesis and the "Jewish Antiquities" of Flavius Josephus*, pp. 100—116 (here p. 101). This point is contested by MAIER, "Japhetiten," pp. 170, 187n. 120, 188. Note also that Josephus is aware of a Babylonian record that enumerates Noah's descendants (*Ap.* 1.130—131).

it at many points.[193] What is the main evidence for literary dependence?[194] First of all, the *Antiquities* of Josephus does show familiarity either with the *Book of Jubilees* or at least with the traditions found there. This applies even to Book 1 of the *Antiquities*, which we are currently considering.[195] Second, there are a number of minor agreements between Josephus and *Jubilees*. For example, the western extent of the world is the same in both: Gadeira (*Ant.* 1.122) or Gadir (*Jub.* 8:23, 26; 9:12), which is Gades (Cádiz), on the Spanish coast northwest of Gibraltar.[196] Furthermore, the Tanais River (= Tina) is used in Josephus as a boundary between Asia and Europe just as it is in *Jubilees* (cf. *Ant.* 1.122; *Jub.* 8:12, 16, 25, 28; 9:8).[197] The difference, of course, is that *Jubilees* also sees the Tina as a boundary between Shem and Japheth, whereas in Josephus, the sons of Japheth occupy territory on both sides of the Tanais. Third, the technique of "blocking-in" is used in both Josephus and *Jubilees*: Just as *Jubilees* first describes the portion allotted to each son of Noah and then "blocks-in" the descendants of the sons within that general territory, so also Josephus first describes the general extent of the territory assigned to the sons of Noah and then the specific area granted to their descendants.[198] The difference is that

---

[193] Here, it is interesting to note that the *Chronicles of Jerahmeel* (31.1), a 13th-14th century collection of Jewish sources (cf. H. SCHWARZBAUM, "Prolegomenon," in *The Chronicles of Jerahmeel* [ed. M. Gaster; London: Oriental Translation Fund, 1899; reprint ed., New York: Ktav, 1971], pp. 1–2), juxtaposes both the *Jubilees* and the Josephus traditions without noting any contradiction (cf. ibid., p. 43). On the one hand, the world is divided, as in *Jubilees* 8–9, among the sons of Noah according to the three continents (Shem in Asia, Ham in Africa, and Japheth in Europe) with even the same boundaries between them (the Tanais River and Gadeira). On the other hand, the *Chronicles of Jerahmeel* go on, as in the *Antiquities*, to identify Gomer with the Galatians. This fusion of traditions is made possible by the *Chronicles'* inclusion of Asia Minor as part of "Europe," which thus embraces the whole territory from "Syria and Cilicia" to "Gadeira."

[194] The following considerations are adapted in part, with modifications, from FRANXMAN, *Genesis and the "Jewish Antiquities" of Flavius Josephus*, pp. 100–116.

[195] E.g., *Ant.* 1.41 (cf. *Jub.* 3:28), 52 (cf. *Jub.* 4:1, 8), 70–71 (cf. *Jub.* 8:3); 2.224 (cf. *Jub.* 47:5).

[196] On the other hand, however, the eastern extent of the world is different in each case: the Indian Ocean (*Ant.* 1.143) or Seria (= a country adjacent to India, probably China; cf. G.J. REININK, "Das Land 'Seiris' [Shir] und das Volk der Serer in jüdischen und christlichen Traditionen," *JSJ* 6 [1975] 72–85) in Josephus (*Ant.* 1.147) and the Garden of Eden in *Jubilees* (8:16). Two 10th-century writers suggest that descendants of Amur (Gomer?), a son of Japheth, reached China (cf. Leslie D. DONALD, "Japhet in China," *JAOS* 104 [1984] 403–409).

[197] Cf. FRANXMAN, *Genesis and the "Jewish Antiquities" of Flavius Josephus*, p. 102.

[198] For example, after describing the general extent of the territory held by the Hamites (*Ant.* 1.130: "The children of Ham held the countries branching from Syria and the mountain-ranges of Amanus and Libanus, occupying all the district in the direction of the sea and appropriating the regions reaching to the ocean"), Josephus lists the four sons of Ham and their contemporary equivalents (§§ 131–134) before blocking in this general territory with the particular portion held by each son of Ham and his descendants (§§ 134ff.). Thus, Mersaios, the second son of Ham, who is identified with Egypt and the Egyptians (§ 132), is said to have had "eight sons, all of whom occupied the territory extending from Gaza to Egypt..." (*Ant.* 1.136). On Josephus' general method here and its similarity to that in *Jubilees*, see further

Josephus is not as rigorous in his use of "blocking-in." As we have seen above, for example, Lud (a Shemite) is allowed to stand isolated among the sons of Japheth in Asia Minor. Finally, in both Josephus and *Jubilees*, the Table of Nations has abiding validity as a geographical guide to the world order. In no way is the Table of Nations considered archaic, a relic of the distant past.[199] In their own way, both texts try to reaffirm the relevance of the Table of Nations as a description of the world, the one by asserting its eternal inviolability, the other by updating the names of the nations.[200] The difference is that Josephus does not use Genesis 10 to argue the eternal centrality and inviolability of Israel among the nations of the world, for, on the one hand, Josephus recognizes that Israel did not always possess the land but, rather, took it by force from its original occupants at the time of the Conquest (cf. *Ant.* 1.139). On the other hand, Josephus probably considered it impossible to argue for the eternal inviolability and centrality of Israel in view of both A. D. 70 and the oppressive reign of Domitian, when the *Antiquities* was being compiled (cf. *Ant.* 20.267).

In light of these similarities and differences, it seems possible that Josephus' exposition of the Table of Nations represents an exegetical and ideological confrontation with that in *Jubilees*. Josephus and *Jubilees* may even represent rival schools of interpretation within Judaism – schools that disputed, for example, both the distribution of Asia Minor among the sons of Noah and the geographical centrality of Jerusalem in the world.

Josephus and the OT/Jewish Tradition on the Sons of Japheth. Josephus begins his exposition of the Table of Nations by considering the sons of Japheth in *Ant.* 1.122–129. This section, the most carefully developed part of Josephus' exposition of the Table of Nations,[201] commences with a description of the migration and geographical distribution of the Japhethites:

Japheth, son of Noah, had seven sons. These, beginning by inhabiting the mountains of Taurus and Amanus, advanced in Asia up to the river Tanais and in Europe as far as Gadeira, occupying the territory (γῆν) upon which they lit, and, as no inhabitant had preceded them, giving their own names to the nations (τὰ ἔθνη). (§ 122)

FRANXMAN, *Genesis and the "Jewish Antiquities" of Flavius Josephus*, pp. 101–102, 107–108, 113.

[199] Cf. ALEXANDER, "Toponymy," p. 53: "Fundamental to Josephus' toponymy is the belief that the Biblical account of the origin of the nations is primary; it is not only historically true and ancient, but preserves above all others the original names and places of settlement of the peoples of the world." Contra Arno BORST, *Der Turmbau von Babel. Geschichte der Meinungen über Ursprung und Vielfalt der Sprachen und Völker* (4 vols. in 6; Stuttgart: Hiersemann, 1957–1963), 1:173.

[200] As a realist, however, Josephus allows for the destruction of several of the original nations of Ham, including those that Israel destroyed at the time of the Conquest because of the sin of Canaan (cf. *Ant.* 1.137, 139).

[201] Cf. FRANXMAN, *Genesis and the "Jewish Antiquities" of Flavius Josephus*, pp. 103–104. As we noted above, however, Josephus places the Tower of Babel (*Ant.* 113–119) *before* his exposition of the Table of Nations.

If, according to Josephus, Noah's ark landed on a peak in Armenia (*Ant.* 1.90),[202] then the sons of Japheth began settling at a point not far from there in southwest Asia Minor, for the Taurus and Amanus mountains bound the region that, in Josephus' day, was the Roman province of Cilicia.[203] According to Jewish tradition, including 1QapGen 21:16−17 (see above), the "Taurus Amanus" mountain range forms the northern border of Israel.[204] This is the region that was settled by Tarshish, son of Javan, son of Japheth; for, as Josephus goes on to explain, "[Tharsia?] was the ancient name of Cilicia, as is proved by the fact that its principal and capital city is called Tarsus, the theta having been converted into a tau" (*Ant.* 1.127). From there, the sons of Japheth spread out over the rest of Asia Minor and throughout Europe as far as Gadeira in Spain.[205] This migration of the Japhethites from the Taurus Mountains to Gadeira can be compared to the map of Dicaearchus of Messana (fl. ca. 326−296), which bisects the world by a central east-west parallel called a *diaphragma*, drawn from the Pillars of Hercules, through Sardinia, Sicily, Caria, Lycia, Pamphylia, Cilicia, and along the Taurus range as far as Mount Himaeus (the Himalayas).[206] Eratosthenes, working about a century later (ca. 275−194), took up the idea and developed it further.[207] As we will discuss

---

[202] This agrees with the Septuagint, Aquila, Symmachus, and Theodotion (cf. REDPATH, "The Geography of the Septuagint," pp. 296−297). This tradition was familiar to Apollonius Molon, a renowned Carian rhetor of the first century B.C.: "Molon, who composed the invective against the Jews, relates that the man who survived the flood left Armenia with his sons, having been expelled from his native place by the inhabitants of the land. Having traversed the immediate country, he came to the mountainous part of Syria, which was desolate. After three generations Abraam was born..." (quoted in Eusebius, *Pr. Ev.* 9.190.1−3). The Table-of-Nations tradition was also known very early in the non-Jewish literature of the Near East (cf. Josephus, *Ap.* 1.130−131).

[203] Vespasian made Cilicia a separate province from Syria in A.D. 72 (cf. Terence Bruce MITFORD, "Roman Rough Cilicia," in *ANRW* II.7.2 [ed. Hildegard Temporini; Berlin: de Gruyter, 1980] pp. 1230−1261 [here pp. 1239, 1241, 1246−1248]).

[204] Cf. *m. Sheb.* 6:1; *y. Hal.* 4.4; *Ex. Rab.* 23:5; *b. Git.* 8a. See further AVIGAD and YADIN, *A Genesis Apocryphon*, p. 30; FITZMYER, *The Genesis Apocryphon*, pp. 136, 153; ALEXANDER, "Geography and the Bible (Early Jewish)," p. 986: "This [sc. the 'Taurus Amanus' Formula], the earliest border definition, states that 'all that runs from Taurus Amanus and inwards is the Land of Israel; from Taurus Amanus and outwards is outside the Land' (*t. Ter.* 2:12; *t. Hall.* 2:11; *y. Hall.* 60a; *y. Sheb.* 32d). 'Taurus Amanus' (with which the P[alestinian] T[argum] identifies 'Mt. Hor' in Num 34:7) refers to the range of mountains just N of Antioch on the Orontes. ..." According to Jdt 2:25, occuring within a geographically problematic passage (Judith 1−2) that is influenced throughout by the Table-of-Nations tradition (cf. MAIER, "Japhetiten," pp. 185−186), Holofernes, a general of Nebuchadnezzar, seized the territory of Cilicia and then came "to the borders of Japheth which are to the south facing Arabia" (ἕως ὁρίων Ιαφεθ τὰ πρὸς νότον κατὰ πρόσωπον τῆς Ἀραβίας).

[205] Compare the counterclockwise listing of nations in 1 Chronicles 1. Note that, according to Josephus (*BJ* 2.363), Gadeira is also the western boundary of the Roman Empire. Note that, according to Herodotus, the famous Royal Road of the Persians made its way through the Cilician Gates, over the Halys River, past Ankara, to Sardis.

[206] Agathemerus *Geographiae informatio* 1.5 (ed. Karl Müller, *Geographi Graeci minores* [2 vols.; Paris: Didot, 1861], 2:471−487). See also on *Jub.* 8:19 above.

[207] Cf. Strabo *Geogr.* 2.1.1: "Eratosthenes, in establishing the map of the inhabited world,

further in Chap. 3, *this migration of the sons of Japheth corresponds almost exactly to the projected scope and actual direction of Paul's mission to the* ἔθνη. Could it be that Paul was purposely retracing the steps of the Japhethites?

Who are the Japhethites from a Jewish point of view? In this regard, Noah's blessing of Japheth in Gen 9:27 is of signal importance: "May God make space[208] for Japheth, and let him dwell in the tents of Shem; and let Canaan be his slave." Of the Jewish texts that construe the subject of the second verb (ישכן) as Japheth rather than God,[209] the idea of dwelling in the tents of Shem is interpreted either literally or metaphorically. First, some Jewish texts interpret Gen 9:27 quite *literally* of the Japhethites' physically dwelling in the land of Shem and particularly in the Land of Israel. For example, *Gen. Rab.* 36:6 reads: "The Holy One, blessed be he, said to Japheth: 'You covered your father's nakedness: By my life, I will reward you, for it shall come to pass in that day, that I will give unto Gog a place fit for burial in Israel.'"[210] This alludes to Ezekiel 38–39, which predicts that Gog and his hoards will attack Jerusalem, "the navel of the earth" (Ezek 38:12), but that God will marshal all the forces of nature against Gog and defeat him in a decisive, eschatological battle. Thus, assuming that Gog – the king of Magog (Ezek 38:2), the chief prince of Meshech and Tubal (v. 3), and the leader of other Japhethite troops (v. 6) – is himself a Japhethite, *Gen. Rab.* 36:6 sees Ezek 39:11, where God promises to "give Gog a place for burial in Israel, the Valley of the Travelers east of the sea . . .," as the ironic fulfillment of the promise that Japheth will dwell in the land of Shem. The *Tg. Ps.-J.* to Gen 9:27 may also be cited as a possible example of the literal interpretation: "May the Lord beautify the borders of Japheth and may his sons be proselytes and dwell in the school of Shem." Although this text could be taken figuratively of successful proselytism among the Japhethites, more probably, it recalls Isa 66:18–21, the clearest missionary text in the OT,[211] in which, as we have seen above, God promises to

---

divides it into two parts by a line drawn from west to east, parallel to the equatorial line. . . . He draws the line from the Pillars [of Heracles] through the Strait of Sicily and also through the southern capes both of the Peloponnesus and of Attica, and as far as Rhodes and the Gulf of Issus; . . . then the line is produced in an approximately straight course along the whole Taurus Range as far as India, for the Taurus stretches in a straight course with the sea that begins at the Pillars, and divides all Asia lengthwise into two parts, thus making one part of it northern, the other southern; so that in like manner both the Taurus and the Sea from the Pillars up to the Taurus lie on the parallel of Athens." On the possible relation of Josephus' conception of a *diaphragma* to that of the Agrippa World Map, see Chap. 2.

[208] The verb יפת is the Hiph. juss. of פתה ("enlarge"), which is supported by πλατύναι in the Septuagint. The Rabbis, however, sometimes construe the verb as coming from יפה ("beautify" [cf. *y. Meg.* 71b; *Pes. R.* 35, §1.3; *Tg. Ps.-J.* to Gen 9:27]).

[209] For texts that take the subject as God, see *Jub.* 7:12; *Gen. R.* 36.8; *Pesiq. R.* 35, §1.3; Philo *Sobr.* 65; *Tg. Onq.* to Gen 9:27; *b. Yoma* 10a. See further Louis GINZBERG, *The Legends of the Jews* (5 vols.; trans. Henrietta Szold; Philadelphia: Jewish Publication Society of America, 1937–1968), 1:170; 5:192–193.

[210] Cf. *b. Meg.* 9b.

[211] According to Claus WESTERMANN, Isa 66:19 is the only text in the OT (excluding the Servant passages in Isaiah) that speaks of preaching to the Gentiles by human messengers (*Das*

send to the nations survivors of the Exile[212] in order to gather all nations and tongues to participate in the Temple cult in Jerusalem (cf. also v. 23).[213] Interestingly enough, the nations that are singled out in Isaiah 66 for special mention as the object of this eschatological mission are mostly sons of Japheth (v. 19). Therefore, when *Targum Ps.-Jonathan* interprets Gen 9:27 as referring to proselytes dwelling in the school of Shem, this could be seen against the background of the eschatological pilgrimage of the nations to Jerusalem. This could also explain the central design in the mosaic floor of the fifth-century synagogue of Jerash (Gerasa) in Transjordan, the left corner of which features the heads of two people, labeled ΣΗΜ and ΙΑΦΕΘ, while a dove with a twig in its beak sits on a branch above them.[214]

Of the literal interpretations of Gen 9:27, a fragment from the fourth cave of Qumran (4Q252 2.6−7) provides the most innovative, for it assumes that the blessing of Gen 9:26−27 applies not just to Japheth but to all three sons of Noah: "He [sc. God] did not curse Ham, but rather his son, for God had already blessed the sons of Noah [cf. Gen 9:1]: 'And in the tents of Shem he will dwell.'"[215] What it means concretely for God to dwell in the tents of Shem becomes apparent from the next line, which alludes to the promise of Gen 12:1: "The Land he gave to Abraham, his friend" (*l.* 8). In other words, the "tents of Shem" in Gen 9:27 is interpreted here in terms of the Abrahamic Promise of Land (Gen 12:1). In that case, the idea all three sons of Noah are blessed is apparently equated with the promise that, in Abraham, all the families/nations of the earth will be blessed (Gen 12:3; cf. 18:18; 22:18; 26:4; 28:14), for in context, Gen 12:3 refers back to the Table of Nations of Genesis 10 (i.e., the nations that descended from Shem, Ham, and Japheth).[216] On the other hand,

---

Buch Jesaja, Kapitel 40−66 [5th ed.; ATD 19; Göttingen: Vandenhoeck & Ruprecht, 1986], p. 337).

[212] Whereas WESTERMANN interprets the פליטים in terms of Isa 45:20−25, as referring to the nations that escape the judgment (*Jesaja, Kapitel 40−66*, p. 337), more likely, the "survivors" are to be understood in light of the idea of the remnant, with which the derivatives of פלט are often associated in Isaiah (cf. Gerhard F. HASEL, "פלט," *TWAT* 6 [1989] 589−606 [here cols. 602−603], which represents a change from an earlier opinion [cf. idem, "Remnant," in *IBDSup*, p. 735]).

[213] Cf. *Ex. Rab.* 23:10: "R. Johanan said, 'Jerusalem will one day become the Metropolis of the whole world, for its says: Ashdod, its daughters (Josh 15:47).'"

[214] Cf. A. BARROIS, "Chronique," *RB* 39 (1930) 257−265 (here p. 259 and Plate IXb); Prigent, *Le Judaïsme et l'image*, pp. 85−96 (esp. 85−88); Erwin R. GOODENOUGH, *Jewish Symbols in the Greco-Roman Period, Vol. 1: The Archeological Evidence from Palestine* (Bollinger Series 37; New York: Pantheon Books, 1953), pp. 259−260. Note also that Gen 10:21 emphasizes that Shem was the brother of Japheth.

[215] Timothy H. LIM, "Notes on *4Q252* fr.1, cols. i-ii," *JJS* 44 (1993) 121−126 (esp. p. 123); EISENMAN and WISE, *The Dead Sea Scrolls Uncovered*, pp. 86, 88. I am grateful to Professor Otto Betz for indicating this reference to me.

[216] Cf. CD 3.1−2: the "sons of Noah and their families" who went astray are contrasted to Noah, who was recorded as a "friend" of God through his keeping of the commandments of God.

4Q462 1.1–3 seems to interpret Gen 9:27 as a promise that God will enslave the sons of Canaan to Jacob.[217]

Second, other Jewish texts interpret Gen 9:27 *figuratively* of the language of Japheth (i.e., Greek) dwelling in the tents of Shem in the form of the Septuagint.[218] For example, b. Meg. 9b reads:

R. Simeon b. Gamaliel says that books [of the scripture] also are permitted to be written only in Greek. R. Abbahu said in the name of R. Johanan: the halachah follows R. Simeon b. Gamaliel. R. Johanan further said: What is the reason of R. Simeon b. Gamaliel? Scripture says, God enlarge Japheth, and he shall dwell in the tents of Shem; [this means] that the words of Japheth shall be in the tents of Shem. But why not say Gomer and Magog? – R. Chiyya b. Abba replied: The real reason is because it is written, Let God enlarge (יפת) Japheth: implying, let the chief beauty (יפיות) of Japheth [i.e., the Greek language] be in the tent of Shem.

Evidently, texts like this[219] associate the Greek language particularly with Japheth because Javan, whom Josephus identifies with "Ionia and all Greeks" (*Ant.* 1.124), is reckoned among the sons of Japheth in Gen 10:2.[220] Indeed, Ἑλλάς or Ἕλλην is a constant rendering of Javan both in the Septuagint and in the other versions of Daniel. The descendants of Japheth can be associated with Greek and the Greeks since much of the territory of the Japhethites (Asia Minor and Europe) was Greek-speaking in the Hellenistic period.[221] *There-*

---

[217] Cf. EISENMAN and WISE, *The Dead Sea Scrolls Uncovered*, pp. 268–269.

[218] Cf. Marguerite HARL, *La Langue de Japhet. Quinze études sur la Septante et le grec des chrétiens* (Centre Lenain de Tillemont; Paris: Cerf, 1992), pp. 11–15; P.S. ALEXANDER, "Jewish Aramaic Translations of Hebrew Scriptures," in *Mikra: Text, Translation, Reading and Interpretation of the Hebrew Bible in Ancient Judaism and Early Christianity* (CRINT 2.1; Assen: Van Gorcum; Philadelphia: Fortress, 1988), pp. 217–254 (here pp. 217–218). For an allegorical interpretation of Gen 9:27, see Philo *Quaest. Gen.* 2.76, which seeks to answer the question, "Why in praying for Japheth, does (Noah) say, 'God shall enlarge Japheth, and he shall dwell in the house of Shem, and Canaan shall be their servant' (Gen 9:27)?" Philo sets aside the literal meaning of the prayer as clear (cf. *Sobr.* 65, which interprets the prayer literally as applying to God's dwelling in the tents of Shem) and tries instead to examine its deeper meaning: If the one who is morally indifferent (neither bad nor good) receives an enlargement of such bodily and external things as health, perceptiveness, beauty, power, wealth, glory, nobility, friends, and offices, his possession are liable to bring him harm unless, as Noah prays, he dwells in the house of the wise man in order that he may set straight his own way by the example of all good.

[219] This tradition is very widely represented in Rabbinic literature: cf. *Gen. Rab.* 36.8; *y. Meg.* 1:9 (71b); *Deut. Rab.* 1:1. Cf. ALEXANDER, "Jewish Aramaic Translations of Hebrew Scriptures," pp. 217–218.

[220] As S.J. BASTOMSKY points out, Japheth can be regarded as the ancestor of the Greeks from both the Hebrew and the Greek point of view, for not only is Japheth, according to Gen 10:2, the father of Javan (= the Hebrew word for Greece), Iapetos (a phonetically identical name to Japheth) is, according to Greek mythology, the great-grandfather of Hellen, who named the Greeks after himself ("Noah, Italy, and the Sea-Peoples," *JQR* 67 [1977] 146–153 [here p. 148 n. 7]). As we observed above, *Sib. Or.* 3.110–116, a Jewish collection from the second century B.C., appropriates this Greek myth in recounting the story of the Flood and explicitly mentions Iapetos.

[221] On the distribution of the Greek language in the Roman Empire, see Edgar C. POLOMÉ,

fore, if Paul is retracing the steps of the Japhethites, it may be significant that his gospel is "to the Jew first and also to the Greek" (Rom 1:16).[222]

The Nature of Josephus' Update of the Table of Nations. As already common in the ancient Near East, the Greeks and the Romans consider the population of the whole world and each of its parts as completely divided into "nations."[223] Therefore, Josephus' task is merely to establish the proper correspondences.[224] The tendency to "update" the original Table of Nations by identifying the original names with peoples and places in his own day (νῦν) is something that Josephus has in common with much Jewish exegesis (see Table 3).[225] For Josephus, the Roman Empire was the ruling world power, and his patrons were Romans. Therefore, he naturally identifies the biblical Table of Nations in terms of Roman nomenclature that are familiar to him even though he claims that the "Greeks" were responsible for the name changes.[226] Josephus' method is similar to that in the Targumim, where the loanword איפרכייה (= ἐπαρχεία, "province") is often used to introduce the contemporary identifications of the sons of Noah.[227] As we shall see in Chap. 4, Josephus' identification of Gomer with the contemporary Galatians provides a classic example of updating the Table of Nations in terms of official Roman nomenclature.[228]

"The Linguistic Situation in the Western Provinces of the Roman Empire," in *ANRW* II.29.2 (ed. Wolfgang Haase; Berlin: de Gruyter, 1983), pp. 509−553 (here pp. 511−513); Rüdiger SCHMITT, "Die Sprachverhältnisse in den östlichen Provinzen des Römischen Reiches," in ibid., pp. 554−586 (here pp. 556−561).

[222] See further Chap. 2 below.

[223] Cf. Fritz GSCHNITZER, "Volk, Nation, Nationalismus, Masse (II. Altertum)," in *Geschichtliche Grundbegriffe. Historisches Lexikon zur politisch-sozialen Sprache in Deutschland*, 7 (1992) 151−171 (here p. 165); A. N. SHERWIN-WHITE, "The Roman World as *Omnes Gentes* or Τὰ Ἔθνη," in *The Roman Citizenship* (2nd ed.; Oxford: Clarendon Press, 1973), pp. 437−444.

[224] It is interesting to note that the name of the ancient Tabalians (biblical Tubal) survived into the time of Roman Republic as the *Tibarani* (cf. Cicero *Fam.* 15.4). Thus, some of the biblical names did not need to be "updated" since they were still in use (see also on the name Cush below).

[225] Cf. Samuel KRAUSS, "Die biblische Völkertafel im Talmud, Midrasch und Targum," *MGWJ* N. F. 3 (1895) 1−11, 49−63, who argues that in later Jewish tradition, this updating of the nations in Genesis 10 is always based on official nomenclature in the Greco-Roman world (p. 50). Cf. also ALEXANDER, "Jewish Aramaic Translations of Hebrew Scriptures," pp. 226−227, 246. On the tendencies of the Septuagint, see REDPATH, "The Geography of the Septuagint," pp. 289−307. Note that Herodotus commonly gives the Greek name for ancient peoples (cf., e.g., Herodotus 4.6: Σκύθας δὲ Ἕλληνες ὠνόμασαν).

[226] See further in Chap. 2 on Josephus' use of ἔθνος.

[227] On the Targumim, see further below.

[228] On Josephus' method in identifying biblical nations with contemporary ones, see further Fergus MILLAR, "Hagar, Ishmael, Josephus and the Origins of Islam," *JJS* 44 (1993) 23−45, who argues that Josephus was influenced by the Greek ethnographic tradition of identifying contemporary "peoples" in terms of their descent from mythical "founders" or "forefathers."

The Table of Nations in Ps.-Philo Bib. Ant. 4—5

Dating probably from the first century A. D., Ps.-Philo's *Biblical Anti-quities*[229] recounts the history of Israel from Adam to David by an imaginative retelling of the narrative from Genesis to 2 Samuel by the means of joining the OT text with other traditional material. Thus, *Biblical Antiquities* stands closest in form to the *Book of Jubilees*, the Qumran *Genesis Apocryphon*, and Josephus' *Antiquities*. However, Ps.-Philo's exposition of the Table of Nations differs significantly from any of these, for whereas *Jubilees* gives full geographi-cal details of the territories allotted to the three sons of Noah, *Biblical Anti-quities* provides only the bare names of places, most of which are now hope-lessly corrupt.[230] Furthermore, whereas Josephus seeks to update the Table of Nations, Ps.-Philo's *Biblical Antiquities* seeks to expand and reshape it to a certain extent.

Based on Genesis 5, *Biblical Antiquities* commences with a genealogy of Adam (1:1) that ends with Noah and his three sons: Shem, Ham, and Japheth (v. 22). After recounting the story of the Flood (*Bib. Ant.* 3), Ps.-Philo proceeds to devote a major section to the genealogy of Noah's sons (chap. 4) and their census (chap. 5).[231] The genealogy, with which we are chiefly con-cerned here, follows the general order of the Table of Nations in Genesis 10 – Japheth (*Bib. Ant.* 4:2—5), Ham (vv. 6—8), and Shem (vv. 9—15) – and even concludes with a summary statement similar to that in Gen 10:32. Within three parts, however, *Biblical Antiquities* evidences significant additions and modifi-cations to the biblical text as to ethnography and geography.

Ethnography. The list of the sons of Japheth in *Biblical Antiquities* 4 provides a good example of how the text deviates from Genesis 10 in terms of ethnogra-phy. First, the two sons of Japheth, Meshech and Tiras, who are combined at first in "Mocteras," are later listed separately as "Tiras" and "Mellech" (*Bib. Ant.* 4:2). Second, Japheth's grandsons in Gen 10:2—4 (i.e., the seven sons of Gomer and Javan) are enumerated in *Biblical Antiquities* as his own sons (4:2). As a result, both Gomer, who is omitted from the initial list of Japheth's sons, and Javan are given a different set of sons than those in the biblical Table of Nations (see Table 1). Third, the list of Japheth's descendants in Genesis 10 is greatly expanded by including not only the grandsons in each case (except for Madai) but the great-grandsons as well. Fourth, the list of Japheth's descen-dants in Genesis 10 often undergoes inversions of order in *Biblical Antiquities*

---

[229] Cf. Daniel J. HARRINGTON and Jacques CAZEAUX, *Pseudo-Philon, Les Antiquités Bibli-ques* (2 vols.; SC 229—230; Paris: Cerf, 1976).

[230] Cf. M. R. JAMES, *The Biblical Antiquities of Philo* (London: The Society for Promoting Christian Knowledge; New York: Macmillan, 1917), p. 45.

[231] The abiding influence of *Biblical Antiquities* 4—5 is documented by the *Chronicles of Jerahmeel*, which date to the 13th to 14th century (see n. 193 above). Cf. Daniel J. HARRING-TON, *The Hebrew Fragments of Pseudo-Philo's Liber Antiquitatum Biblicarum Preserved in the Chronicles of Jerahmeel* (SBLTT 3; SBLPS 3; Missoula, MT: Society of Biblical Literature, 1974), pp. 16—25.

(e.g., the sons of Tiras come before the sons of Meshech and the sons of Kittim before the sons of Tarshish). Similar deviations from the biblical Table of Nations could be documented in the rest of *Biblical Antiquities* 4.

Geography. *Biblical Antiquities* is more explicit than Genesis 10 in providing geographical details, especially for the sons of Japheth. According to *Bib. Ant.* 4:3, the sons of Japheth "were scattered abroad and dwelt on the earth among the Persians and the Medes, in the islands that are in the sea" (cf. Gen 10:5). "And then," the text goes on to state, "a third part of the earth was divided up" (et tunc divisa est pars tercia terre). This seems to refer to the tripartite division of the world among the three sons of Noah, perhaps according to the three continents.[232] Thereupon, the text lists the names of the countries received by each of the sons of Japheth and their sons (v. 4). Unfortunately, however, these names are for the most part unintelligible.[233] Gomer (Domereth) and his sons, for example, are said to have received "Ladech."

The Table of Nations in Rabbinic Judaism

Rabbinic literature deals with the Table of Nations in a number of passages.[234] While Table 3 summarizes the contemporary equivalents that some of these passages give for the Japhethite nations in Genesis 10, B. GROSSFELD supplies full rabbinic parallels.[235] The following overview cites a few of these texts.

y. Megilla 71b. Redacted in the first half of the fifth century A.D., the Jerusalem Talmud is the commentary of the Palestinian Amoraim on the Mishnah.[236] For example, commenting on *m. Meg.* 1:8 ("Scripture may be written in any language"), the Jerusalem Talmud discusses the languages of the world in terms of a commentary on the Table of Nations, in which Greek is seen as "the language of Japheth":

> Rabban Simeon b. Gamaliel says, "Even sacred scrolls, they have permitted only that they be written in Greek." It is written, "Now the whole earth had one language and a few words" (Gen 11:1). R. Eleazar and R. Yohanan: One of them said, "For they were

---

[232] HARRINGTON suggests that this refers to a third part of the earth destroyed by the Flood but now being resettled, citing in support Rev 8:7–12; 9:15, 18 ("Pseudo-Philo," *OTP*, 2:308 n. *q*).

[233] Cf. ALEXANDER, "Geography and the Bible (Early Jewish)," p. 983: "If they [sc. the names] had any real geographical reference, it must be assumed that they have become hopelessly garbled in the transmission of the text from Hebrew, through Greek, into its present Latin form."

[234] Cf. ibid., p. 983; Samuel KRAUSS, ed., *Monumenta Talmudica, Bd. 5.1: Geschichte – Griechen und Römer* (Monumenta Hebraica 1; Wien/Leipzig: Orion-Verlag, 1914), pp. 1–8.

[235] Cf. Bernard GROSSFELD, *An Analytical Commentary of the Targum Neofiti to Genesis, Including Full Rabbinic Parallels* (New York: Ktav, forthcoming). See also Adolphe NEUBAUER, *La géographie du Talmud* (Amsterdam: Meridian, 1965), pp. 420–429.

[236] Cf. Hermann L. STRACK and Günter STEMBERGER, *Einleitung in Talmud und Midrasch* (7th ed.; Beck'sche Elementarbücher; Munich: Beck, 1982), pp. 163ff.

speaking seventy languages." The other said, "For they were speaking the language of the Unique One of the World, the language of God." Bar Qappara taught, "'God enlarge Japheth, and let him dwell in the tents of Shem; [and let Canaan be his slave'] (Gen 9:27) means that they will speak the language of Japheth in the tents of Shem." "The sons of Japheth: Gomer, Magog, Madai, Javan, Tubal, Meshech, and Tiras" (Gen 10:2). Gomer is Garmamia; Magog is Gitayya; Madai is as he stated here [Midia]; Javan is Issus; Tubal is Vitanayya; Meshech is Misiyya. As to Tiras: R. Simon said, "It is Persia." And the rabbis say, "It is Tarqa." "'The Sons of Gomer: Ashkenaz, Riphath, and Togarmah' (Gen 10:3). These are Asia, Adiabene, and Germanica." "And the sons of Javan: Elishah, Tarshish, Kittim, and Dodanim" (Gen 10:4). These are Hellas and Taras, Abiah and Dardanayyah.[237]

b. Yoma 10a. More comprehensive than the Jerusalem Talmud, the Babylonian Talmud was redacted about A.D. 500. It presents an exposition of the Table of Nations in order to answer the question, "Whence do we know that the Persians are derived from Japheth?" The rabbinic debate recounted here focuses particularly on whether or not Tiras (Gen 10:2) is to be identified with Persia. In the process, the other sons of Japheth are identified:

The sons of Japheth: Gomer, and Magog, and Madai and Javan, and Tubal, and Meshech, and Tiras. Gomer, i.e., Germania; *Magog,* i.e., Kandia; *Madai,* i.e., Macedonia; *Javan,* in its literal sense; *Tubal,* i.e., Beth-Unyaki; *Meshech,* i.e., Mysia; *Tiras* – its identification is a matter of dispute between R. Simai and the Rabbis, one holding that it is to be identified with Beth Tiryaka, and the other [authorities] declaring it is Persia.

Genesis Rabbah 37:1−8. Dating from approximately the fifth century A.D., *Genesis Rabbah* is a midrash on Genesis whose provenance is probably Palestine.[238] Although the commentary on the Japhethites is much shorter (37:1) than that on either the Hamites (37:2−6) or the Shemites (37:7−8), it is actually more complete and geographical:

The sons of Japheth: Gomer, and Magog, etc. (Gen 10:2). R. Samuel b. Ammi said: These are Africa, Germania, Media, Macedonia and Mysia. *And Tiras:* R. Simon said: That is the Euphrates region; the Rabbis said: It is Trace.
And the sons of Gomer: Ashkenaz, and Riphath and Togarmah (10:3): i.e., Asia, Adiabene, and Germania. R. Berekiah said: Germanicia.
And the sons of Javan: Elishah, and Tarshish, Kittim, and Dodanim (10:4): i.e., Hellas and Taras [Tarantum], Italia, and Dardania. One verse calls them Dodanim, while another verse calls them *Rodanim* (1 Chr 1:7)? R. Simon said: They are called *Dodanim* because they are the descendants of Israel's kinsmen (*dodim*); *Rodanim*, because they come and oppress (*rodim*) them. R. Hanan said: When Israel are elevated, they say to

---

[237] Cf. Jacob NEUSNER, *The Talmud of the Land of Israel, Vol. 19: Megillah* (Chicago Studies in the History of Judaism; Chicago: University of Chicago Press, 1987), p. 49. See further above on Jewish interpretations of Gen 9:27.
[238] Cf. STRACK and STEMBERGER, *Einleitung in Talmud und Midrasch*, pp. 258−260.

them, "We are the descendants of your kinsmen," but when they are low, they come and oppress them.[239]

Targumim. Redacted between the fourth and the eighth centuries A. D., the three recensions of the Palestinian Targum to the Pentateuch – *Neofiti I, Fragmentary Targum*, and *Ps.-Jonathan* – systematically interpret the names on the Table of Nations.[240] In doing so, the Targumim employ two different methods to introduce identifications of the sons of Noah.[241] In the first method, the biblical names are transliterated, and then, their contemporary identifications are introduced by the formula, "And the names of their provinces. ..." Thus, *Targum Ps.-Jonathan* explains Gen 10:2 as follows: "*The sons of Japheth: Gomer, Magog, Madai, Javan, Tubal, Meshech, and Tiras.* And the names of their provinces: Phrygia, Germania, Media, Macedonia, Bithynia, Asia, and Thrace."[242] The Aramaic word for "province" (איפרכייה) here is the Greek loan word ἐπαρχεία.[243] In the second method of updating, the biblical names are not transliterated; rather, the identification is introduced directly in the form of a gentilic plural. For example, the *Fragmentary Targum* renders Gen 10:15−18 ("And Canaan begot ... the Zemarite") as: "And Canaan begot the inhabitants of Emesa."

This tendency of the Targumim to "update" the Table of Nations by identifying biblical peoples and places with peoples and places from their own times provides us with a virtual map of the world as known to the meturgemanim. According to ALEXANDER, few geographical terms in the Targumim of the Pentateuch relate exclusively to the Byzantine or Arabic geographical onomastica; the vast majority belong to an earlier period. For example, the equivalents that *Targum Neofiti* gives for Genesis 10 fit best with the world of the third to fourth centuries A. D.[244]

---

[239] Cf. H. FREEDMAN and Maurice SIMON, *Midrash Rabbah* (10 vols.; 2nd ed.; London: Soncino, 1951), 1:295.

[240] The Targum to 1 Chronicles 1 also contains many equivalents, drawn mainly from the Palestinian Targum to the Pentateuch. Cf. ALEXANDER, "Toponymy," pp. 72 ff.

[241] ALEXANDER, "Toponymy," pp. 77−78.

[242] Cf. Michael MAHER, *Targum Pseudo-Jonathan: Genesis* (The Aramaic Bible 1B; Edinburgh: Clark, 1992), pp. 46−47.

[243] Cf. Michael SOKOLOFF, *A Dictionary of Jewish Palestinian Aramaic of the Byzantine Period* (Dictionaries of Talmud, Midrash and Targum 2; Ramat-Gan, Israel: Bar Ilan University Press, 1990), s.v., p. 53; Hugh J. MASON, *Greek Terms for Roman Institutions: A Lexicon and Analysis* (American Studies in Papyrology 13; Toronto: Hakkert, 1974), pp. 135−136 (ἐπαρχεία = *provincia*).

[244] Cf. ALEXANDER, "Jewish Aramaic Translations of Hebrew Scriptures," pp. 226−227. But see also ALEXANDER's earlier judgment on the date of the Targumic tradition. The identifications of the sons of Japheth belong to the primary strata ("Toponymy," pp. 79, 106). Concretely, according to ALEXANDER ("Toponymy," p. 168) that means the following: "The world as depicted by the Palestinian Targum is, in fact, very little removed from that of Josephus' Table of the Nations. Though the equivalents of the sons of Japhet are in many cases not the same, they belong to the same Greek onomasticon, and paint a similar picture of the northern peoples of the inhabited world. All the indications appear to point in the same

Pirqe Rabbi Eliezer 23. Dating from the eighth or ninth century A. D., *Pirqe Rabbi Eliezer* represents an example of the "rewritten Bible" that begins with the Creation and ends abruptly with the judgment of Miriam in Numbers 12.[245] The section on Noah includes the following exposition of the Table of Nations:

Noah brought his sons and his grandsons, and he blessed them with their (several) settlements, and he gave them as an inheritance all the earth. He especially blessed Shem and his sons, (making them) dark but comely, and he gave them the habitable earth. He blessed Ham and his sons, (making them) dark like the raven, and he gave them as an inheritance the coast of the sea. He blessed Japheth and his sons, (making) them entirely white, and he gave them for an inheritance the desert and its fields. . . .[246]

We may note several parallels between this passage and *Jubilees* 8 even though the latter mentions nothing about skin color. First of all, Noah is the one who assigns portions of the earth to his sons (cf. *Jub.* 8:11). Second, the territorial allotment to the sons is called an "inheritance" (cf. *Jub.* 8:10). Third, Shem receives the choicest portion of land because of Noah's special blessing on him (cf. *Jub.* 8:18—21, 30). Fourth, Ham's territory lies along the coast of the Sea (cf. *Jub.* 8:23). It appears, therefore, that the *Jubilees* tradition of the Table of Nations continues into medieval Judaism.[247]

Conclusion

We have seen that the Table of Nations exerted a significant influence on the OT and Jewish literature. Genesis 10 provided the fundamental point of orientation for describing Israel's place among the nations of the world and the basis for envisioning world geography and ethnography both in the present and for the eschatological future.

For example, the Japhethite nation of the Kittim (Gen 10:4), originally designating the inhabitants of Kition (a Phoenician colony on Cyprus),[248] continues to be used in Jewish writings of the Greco-Roman period to describe

---

direction, and suggest that the Targumic equivalents of the sons of Japhet originated before AD 100. The stratum of material, consequently, in which they are found must date from the same period." See further B. Barry Levy, *Targum Neophyti 1: A Textual Study, Vol. 1: Introduction, Genesis, Exodus* (Studies in Judaism; Lanham, NY/London: University Press of America, 1986), pp. 121, 122 (on *Tg. Neof.* to Genesis 10): "Japhet's genealogy (vv. 2—5) is supplemented by correlations with contemporary places. [. . .] That these glosses are added only for the descendents of Japhet may imply a political perspective that limited Greek control to those areas, but the presence of similar glosses in other targumim argues against any such conclusion."

[245] Cf. Strack and Stemberger, *Einleitung in Talmud und Midrasch*, pp. 298—299.

[246] Cf. Gerald Friedlander, *Pirkê de Rabbi Eliezer* (London: Kegan Paul; New York: Block, 1916), pp. 172—173.

[247] But see Alexander, "Imago Mundi," p. 213: ". . . for a thousand years after it was written Jubilees VIII—IX remained virtually unparalleled within Jewish tradition."

[248] Cf. Josephus *Ant.* 1.128.

various nations of the past, the present, and the future. In Dan 11:30, the Kittim refers to the Greeks. In 1 Macc 1:1, Alexander the Great, the "king of Greece" (cf. Dan 8:21), is portrayed as proceeding "from the land of the Kittim" (ἐκ γῆς Χεττιιμ) to defeat Darius, the king of the Medes and the Persians, and to succeed him as king of that empire, advancing even "to the ends of the earth" (ἕως ἄκρων τῆς γῆς) and plundering "many nations" (v. 3). 1 Macc 8:1−13 lists the nations conquered by the Romans, including the Kittim (v. 5), which in this case refers to the Macedonian kingdom of Perseus defeated in 168 B. C. Since the Romans replace the Greeks as a world empire, the name "Kittim" can also be applied to them[249] based on Num 24:24 (Κιτιαῖοι) and Dan 11:30 (LXX: Ῥωμαῖοι; Theodotion: Κίτιοι).[250] There is a broad consensus that the victorious Kittim in Qumran literature stand for the Romans.[251]

On this point, Elias BICKERMANN argues that the main difference between Hebrew and Greek ethnography consists in the difference between a *static* world view and a *dynamic* one: "the Jews could mechanically transfer an old name to some new people," whereas the Greeks, truer to actual historical development, thought that "nations continued to be formed through expansion and division."[252] There is evidence, however, for the development of at least two different schools of interpretation on the Table of Nations in this period, both of which were vying to affirm the abiding significance of Genesis 10 as a description of the world. On the one hand, the conservative school as represented by *Jubilees* 8−9, perhaps in the face of Hellenistic reform, tried to make the world fit into the Table of Nations, often radically harmonizing individual aspects of the text to conform with the fundamental tenet of territorial inviolability. For *Jubilees*,

---

[249] We may compare this terminological usage to that of the Byzantines, who called themselves not Byzantines but Romans and liked to see themselves as heirs of the Roman Empire (cf. Robert BROWNING, *The Byzantine Empire* [New York: Charles Scribner's Sons, 1980], p. 8).

[250] Another biblical name applied to the Roman Empire is Esau/Edom, the brother of Israel. Cf. Clemens THOMA, "Die Weltvölker im Urteil rabbinischer Gleichniserzähler," in *Judentum − Ausblicke und Einsichten. Festgabe für Kurt Schubert zum siebzigsten Geburtstag* (ed. Clemens Thoma, et al.; Judentum und Umwelt 43; Frankfurt a.M.: Lang, 1993), pp. 115−133 (here pp. 120−128); FELDMAN, *Jew and Gentile*, pp. 102−103; Friedrich AVEMARIE, "Esaus Hände, Jakobs Stimme. Edom als Sinnbild Roms in der frühen rabbinischen Literatur," in *Die Heiden. Juden, Christen und das Problem des Fremden*, pp. 177−208. On the prophets' use of Esau as a symbol of the nations, see Gary V. SMITH, "Alienation and Restoration: A Jacob-Esau Typology," in *Israel's Apostasy and Restoration: Essays in Honor of Roland K. Harrison* (ed. Avraham Gileadi; Grand Rapids, MI: Baker, 1988), pp. 165−174 (here esp. pp. 169−170).

[251] See the literature in n. 126 above.

[252] Elias J. BICKERMAN, "Origines Gentium," *CP* 47 (1952) 65−81 (here pp. 77−78). Contrast Thorlief BOMAN, *Das hebräische Denken im Vergleich mit dem griechischen* (7th ed.; Göttingen: Vandenhoeck & Ruprecht, 1983), which portrays Greek thinking up to the time of Aristotle as "static" and Hebrew thinking in the same period as "dynamic"; after Alexander the Great, however, there was only a mixture of both types of thinking.

Jerusalem is the indisputable geographical center of the world, which God apportioned to Israel forever. On the other hand, the Hellenistic school as represented by Josephus (*Ant.* 1.120−147), while openly repudiating the change of nomenclature perpetrated by the Greeks, abandons the OT and Jewish tradition both of Jerusalem as the geographical center of the world and of Palestine as the God-given land of Israel. In other respects, however, Josephus is more faithful to OT and Jewish tradition than *Jubilees* is (e. g., in the assignment of Asia Minor to Japheth rather than to Shem), for he resists the urge to harmonize the text. Josephus also illustrates that official nomenclature was often used in updating the list of nations in Genesis 10. Despite the major differences in these two texts, however, both in their own way represent attempts to "update" the Table of Nations, for *Jubilees* does in fact appropriate aspects of Hellenistic geography, while Josephus explains the Greek equivalents for the biblical names.

Chapter 2
Paul's Use of ΕΘΝΟΣ

Introduction

Having examined the Table-of-Nations tradition in Chap. 1, we procede now to widen our scope by investigating the use of "nation" (גוי, ἔθνος) in the OT and Jewish tradition. As we shall see, Paul's use of ἔθνος clearly rests on the usage prevalent in the Second Temple period, as documented by the Greek OT and the so-called "Hellenistic-Jewish" writings.

A glance at the secondary literature reveals why this rather extensive survey is indispensable to the present study, for neither the relatively few monographs on the subject[1] nor the standard reference works[2] suffice to provide the necessary background of Paul's concept of ἔθνος. Furthermore, there is still much confusion about the translation of the term.[3] While the following survey does not claim to be exhaustive, it does strive to be comprehensive, giving a representative sample of the usage in its various contexts.

---

[1] Cf., e.g., Charles H. H. SCOBIE, "Israel and the Nations: An Essay in Biblical Theology," *TynBul* 43/2 (1992) 283–305, and the literature cited there. Clemens THOMA observes that at present only a few monographs are available on the "Mega-Thema" of "Judentum und Weltvölker" ("Die Weltvölker im Urteil rabbinischer Gleichniserzähler," in *Judentum – Ausblicke und Einsichten. Festgabe für Kurt Schubert zum siebzigsten Geburtstag* [Judentum und Umwelt 43; Frankfurt a.M.: Lang, 1993], pp. 115–133 [here p. 116]). After writing this chapter, I was given a pre-publication copy of Reinhard FELDMEIER and Ulrich HECKEL, eds., *Die Heiden. Juden, Christen und das Problem des Fremden* (WUNT 70; Tübingen: Mohr-Siebeck, 1994), which does much to fill the void. The following discussion now takes account of this rich resource.

[2] Cf., e.g., N. WALTER, "ἔθνος," *EWNT*, 1 (1980) 924–929; Georg BERTRAM and Karl Ludwig SCHMIDT, "ἔθνος," *TWNT*, 2 (1935) 362–369.

[3] Cf. Rolf DABELSTEIN, *Die Beurteilung der 'Heiden' bei Paulus* (BBET 14; Frankfurt a.M.: Peter Lang, 1981), p. 11, who speaks of a "Sprachverwirrung." See further Douglas R. A. HARE and Daniel J. HARRINGTON, "'Make Disciples of all Gentiles' (Mt 28:19)," *CBQ* 37 (1975) 359–369, and the response by I. P. MEIER, "Nations or Gentiles in Matthew 28:19?" *CBQ* 39 (1977) 94–102.

Old Testament and Jewish Background

ΕΘΝΟΣ *in the Septuagint*

Introduction. Tracing the use of the word ἔθνος reveals one of the most fundamental aspects of the OT: the interplay between Israel as a nation and the other nations of the world. That Israel herself is an ἔθνος precludes that the term is wholly pejorative in its OT usage.[4] Already in the postdiluvian world, the Table of Nations shows the common origin of all humanity from the three sons of Noah and, implicitly, the central position of Israel among the nations. Furthermore, the seed of Abraham is specially selected to be a great nation within the world of nations and, at the same time, the hope of blessing for all nations. Hence, from its foundation at the Exodus to its Restoration at the Second Exodus, the nation Israel is constantly involved with the other nations of the world.

The Septuagint uses the plural ἔθνη in three interrelated senses. First of all, ἔθνη is used in the sense of the "nations" of the world, including Israel. We find this usage already in the Table of Nations, which traces the origin of all nations back to Noah and his sons (cf. Gen 10:32). Israel may occupy a central position among the nations, but it is still one nation among others (cf. Deut 32:8−9; Jer 38:7). The Abrahamic Promise expects that Abraham will become a "great nation," and that in him (or his seed) "all the tribes/nations of the earth" will be blessed (Gen 12:3; 18:18; 22:18; 26:4; 28:14). In context, "all the tribes/nations of the earth" obviously refers back to the Table of Nations in Genesis 10.[5] According to Jer 1:5, Jeremiah is appointed "a prophet to the nations" (προφήτης εἰς ἔθνη), which obviously includes not just the foreign nations but Israel as well.[6]

The first usage leads to the second, which further distinguishes Israel from the other nations: (πάντα) τὰ ἔθνη is used in the sense of "(all) the nations" of the world apart from the nation Israel.[7] There are many texts that juxtapose the "nation" Israel to other "nations," and even to "all the (non-Israelite) nations"

---

[4] Cf., similarly, R. E. CLEMENTS, "גוי," *TWAT*, 1 (1973) 965−973 (here col. 972).

[5] This is especially clear in a text like 4Q252 2.6−7, which interprets Gen 9:26−27 as an expectation for all three sons of Noah (including Ham) and links it, by means of the Table of Nations, with the Abrahamic Promise of blessing for all nations (Gen 12:3). See Chap. 1 above.

[6] The scope of the prophet's mission to the nations is given in Jeremiah 32: not only the extensive list of nations in vv. 18−26a but "all the kingdoms which are on the face of the earth" (v. 26b).

[7] Since about the time of Aristotle, there was a propensity to use ἔθνη for the "nations" other than the Greeks (cf. LSJ, s.v., p. 480). There is a parallel development in the Latin *gens* ("race, nation, people"), which in the plural can be used not only in the sense of all the "nations" of the world, but also of all the "nations" of the world apart from the Romans or Italians (cf. *Oxford Latin Dictionary*, s.v., 1 [1968] 759; Fritz GSCHNITZER, "Volk, Nation, Nationalismus, Masse [II. Altertum]," in *Geschichtliche Grundbegriffe. Historisches Lexikon zur politisch-sozialen Sprache in Deutschland*, 7 [1992] 151−171 [here pp. 166−168]).

of the earth. For example, Ex 19:5–6 (cf. 23:22) reads: ". . . you shall be to me a peculiar people above all [other!] nations (λαὸς περιούσιος ἀπὸ πάντων τῶν ἐθνῶν); for the whole earth is mine. And you shall be to me a royal priesthood and a holy nation (ἔθνος ἅγιον)." According to Deut 4:6–8, the Law is Israel's wisdom "before all nations" (ἐναντίον πάντων τῶν ἐθνῶν), which causes the nations to exclaim in admiration: "Behold, this great nation is a wise and understanding people (ἰδοὺ λαὸς σοφὸς καὶ ἐπιστήμων τὸ ἔθνος τὸ μέγα τοῦτο)."[8]

This second use of ἔθνη in the sense of "(foreign) nations" develops naturally into the third: "foreign nationals," i.e., individuals of any nation other than the nation of the Jews. This third use of the term is found only in the plural; there is no corresponding usage in the singular for an individual "foreign national" or "foreigner." Furthermore, it must be stressed that this third use of ἔθνη retains the idea of "nation" and does not denote "pagan" per se although it may have that connotation at times. We may translate ἔθνη in this sense by "Gentiles" if we keep in mind the historical roots of the latter, for "Gentiles" comes from the Latin *gens* ("nation")[9] and, as a substantive, has much the same denotation as

---

[8] For further examples, see Deut 28:64 ("And the Lord your God will scatter you to all nations [εἰς πάντα τὰ ἔθνη]"); Josh 4:24 (God led the Israelites out of Egypt and through the Red Sea "that all the nations of the earth [πάντα τὰ ἔθνη τῆς γῆς] might know that the power of the Lord is mighty"); Ezek 37:21–23 ("Behold, I will take the whole house of Israel from the midst of the nations [ἐκ μέσου τῶν ἐθνῶν], among whom they have gone, and I will gather them from all that are round them, and I will bring them into the land of Israel. And I will make them one nation [ἔθνος ἕν] in my land, even on the mountains of Israel; and they shall have one ruler; and they shall be no more two nations [δύο ἔθνη], neither shall they be divided any more at all into two kingdoms; that they may no more defile themselves with their idols, and I will deliver them from all their transgressions whereby they have sinned, and will cleanse them; and they shall be to me a people [λαός] and I the Lord will be to them God"); Mal 3:12 ("And all nations [πάντα τὰ ἔθνη] shall call you blessed"); Esth 3:8 ("And he [sc. Haman] spoke to king Artaxerxes, saying, There is a nation [ἔθνος] scattered among the nations [ἐν τοῖς ἔθνεσιν] in all your kingdom, and their laws differ from all the nations [πάντα τὰ ἔθνη] . . ."); 1 Macc 13:6 ("But I [sc. Simon] will avenge my nation [ἔθνος μου] . . ., for all nations [πάντα τὰ ἔθνη] have gathered together out of hatred to destroy us"); also 2 Kgdms 7:23 ("And what other nation on earth [ἔθνος ἄλλο ἐν τῇ γῇ] is as your people [λαός] Israel?"). In Am 9:12, the parallelism between "the rest of men" (οἱ κατάλοιποι τῶν ἀνθρώπων) and πάντα τὰ ἔθνη shows that the latter denotes "all the nations" of the world apart from Israel. Even in 1 Maccabees, where (τὰ) ἔθνη could be thought to be used throughout in the sense of "(the) Gentiles" (cf., e.g., 1 Macc 1:13–14, 42; 2:12, 18, 19, 40, 44; 14:36), the term clearly retains the meaning "nations" at points. In 1 Macc 3:58, for example, τὰ ἔθνη ταῦτα must mean "these nations" by contrast with the "nation" of the Jews (τὸ ἔθνος ἡμῶν) in v. 59. The use of the term is also clear in 1 Macc 1:3–4, where Alexander is said to have slain "kings of the earth, " to have taken spoils "of many nations," and to have ruled "over countries of nations." Moreover, ἔθνος ἁμαρτωλόν in 1 Macc 1:34 could not mean that a "sinful Gentile" was put in the City of David. See further 1 Macc 2:10 ("What nation has not inherited a kingdom and and taken of her spoils?"), 48 ("So they recovered the law out of the hand of the nations and of kings . . ."); etc. On ἔθνη in the sense of the non-Jewish "nations" of the world, see further 2 Chr 32:17; Ps 2:1; 46:3; 56:10; 66:3–5; 95:3; 107:4; Ezek 25:7.

[9] Cf. J. A. Simpson and E. S. C. Weiner, eds., *The Oxford English Dictionary* (20 vols.; 2nd ed.; Oxford: Clarendon, 1989), s. v., 6:448. Similarly, the German *Heiden* etymologically

ἔθνη.[10] It is often difficult to distinguish between the second and third uses of ἔθνη, that is, whether the foreign nations themselves are being emphasized or, rather, the individuals who compose them. Context must decide in each case. It is helpful to note, however, that when ἔθνη stands in parallel with terms such as λαοί[11] or χῶραι,[12] the meaning "nations" is beyond doubt.

The following survey of ἔθνος in the OT is framed by the basic salvation-historical scheme of the texts in which the term occurs.[13] Hence, beginning with the Table of Nations, the survey proceeds to trace the complex interaction between Israel and the other nations from initial plight to ultimate solution and from the Abrahamic Promise to the fulfillment of that Promise in the Restoration of Israel and the eschatological Pilgrimage of the Nations to Zion.

The Table of Nations. In a description of the origin of the nations from the descendants of Noah, Genesis 10 divides the descendants of the three sons of Noah "according to their tongues in their countries and in their nations" (Gen 10:5, 20, 31; cf. v. 32).[14] Elsewhere, this origin of the nations is merely presupposed without much elaboration. For example, Ex 9:24 states: "And the hail was very great, such as was not in Egypt, from the time there was a nation (ἔθνος) upon it." Other passages assume that God made and established the nations.[15] Thus Deut 32:8 states: "When the Most High divided the nations

---

stems from τὰ ἔθνη (cf. Elmar SEEBOLD, "Das germanische Wort für den Heiden," *Beiträge zur Geschichte der deutschen Sprache und Literatur*, Tübingen 93 [1971] 29–45; Friedrich KLUGE, *Etymologisches Wörterbuch der deutschen Sprache* [22nd ed.; ed. Elmar Seebold; Berlin/New York: de Gruyter, 1989], p. 300). Thus, DABELSTEIN's criterion for translating ἔθνη with "Heiden" seems overly influenced by a secondary meaning of the term (*Beurteilung der 'Heiden' bei Paulus*, pp. 27–28, 37).

[10] According to *The Oxford English Dictionary* (s. v., 6:448), the first definition of the substantive "Gentile" is "one of any nation other than the Jewish."

[11] Cf. Gen 25:23; 2 Chr 32:17; Ps 2:1; 43:15; 46:3; 56:10; 66:3–5; 95:3; 107:4; Isa 60:5; Mic 4:3; 5:6–7; Ezek 25:7; 28:25; Wisd 3:8. On the synonymy of the underlying Hebrew in some of these cases, see CLEMENTS, "גוי," 1:967: "In einigen Belegen, wo עם and גוי zusammen vorkommen (z.B. Ez 33, 13; Deut 4, 6), ist keine grundsätzliche Unterscheidung zwischen den beiden beabsichtigt, beide Wörter werden synonym gebraucht." See further A. R. HULST, "עם/גוי," *THAT*, 2 (1979) 290–325. According to HARE and HARRINGTON ("'Make Disciples of All the Gentiles' (Mt 28:19)," pp. 360–361; also BERTRAM, "ἔθνος," 2:363), however, λαοὶ τῶν ἐθνῶν (עמי הארצות) in 2 Esdr 9:11 (Ezra 9:11) refers to all the peoples of "non-Jewish mankind"; otherwise, ἔθνη would be redundant. We might add that similar expressions occur in Ezek 31:12 (πάντες οἱ λαοὶ τῶν ἐθνῶν; MT: . . . כל עמי הארץ) and *Pss. Sol.* 17:30 (λαοὶ ἐθνῶν).

[12] Cf. Gen 10:20, 31; 36:40; 4 Kgdms 18:33; Esth 3:12, 14; Ezek 5:5; 6:8; 11:16–17; 12:15; 20:23; 22:4, 15; 29:12; 30:23, 26; 35:10; 36:19; Ps 104:44; 105:27; Lam 1:1.

[13] Text: A. RAHLFS, *Septuaginta* (2 vols.; 9th ed.; Stuttgart: Würtembergische Bibelanstalt, 1935).

[14] The expression "islands of the nations" within the territory of Japheth (Gen 10:5) is applied to the other sons of Noah in v. 32. For the expression, see also Zeph 2:11; 1 Macc 11:38.

[15] Cf. Ps 21:28–29 ("All the ends of the earth will remember and turn to the Lord; and all the families of the nations [πᾶσαι αἱ πατριαὶ τῶν ἐθνῶν] will worship before you. For the kingdom is the Lord's, and he rules over the nations [τὰ ἔθνη]"); 85:9 ("All nations [πάντα τὰ

(ἔθνη), when he scattered the sons of Adam, he set the boundaries of the nations (ὅρια ἐθνῶν) according to the number of the angels of God [MT: sons of Israel]."[16] This is a fundamental text on the relation of Israel and "the nations," for as the passage goes on the explain, "And his people (λαός) Jacob became the portion of the Lord" (v. 9).[17]

The Abrahamic Promise. Gen 12:1−3 contains a threefold promise for Abraham and his seed: the promise of nationhood, of land, and of blessing for all nations. In the following, we shall discuss each of these aspects in sequence.

I. The Promise of Nationhood for Abraham and his Seed. The promise in Gen 12:2 that God would make Abraham "a great nation" (ἔθνος μέγα) runs like a thread throughout Genesis, where it is reiterated not only to Abraham himself on several occasions[18] but also to others who stand in the line of promise: Rebecca,[19] Jacob,[20] and Joseph.[21]

II. The Promise of Land for Abraham and his Seed. In the OT, a גוי/ἔθνος signifies the whole population of a particular land.[22] Hence, the Abrahamic

---

ἔθνη], as many has you have made, will come and worship before you, O Lord, and they will glorify your name").

[16] Cf. Sir 17:17: "For each nation he set a ruler, and Israel is the portion of the Lord." On "the boundaries of the nations," see Isa 10:13, with concrete examples of the nations given in vv. 9−12.

[17] According to *3 Enoch* 2:3, the Holy One chose Israel from the seventy nations to be his people.

[18] Cf. Gen 17:4, 16; 18:18; also Sir 44:19.

[19] Cf. Gen 25:23.

[20] Cf. Gen 28:3 ("And may my God bless you and increase you and multiply you, and you will become assemblies of nations"); 35:11 ("nations and assemblies of nations shall come from you, and kings shall come from your loins"); 46:3 ("Do not be afraid to go down to Egypt, for I will make you there a great nation").

[21] Cf. Gen 48:4.

[22] Cf. Leonhard ROST, "Die Bezeichnungen für Land und Volk im Alten Testament," in *Das kleine Credo und andere Studien zum Alten Testament* (Heidelberg: Quelle & Meyer, 1965), pp. 76−101 (here pp. 86−89). Although CLEMENTS critiques ROST at this point for putting too much emphasis on the possession of a territory ("גוי," 1:968), nevertheless, he himself recognizes that this aspect is "eminently important for a גוי" (ibid., cols. 968−969), particularly in regard to the promise to Abraham and his seed (ibid., col. 970): "Abraham erhält die Zusage, daß seine Nachkommen ein גוי werden sollen (Gen 12, 2; vgl. 17, 5; 18, 18), und ihre Existenz als Nation ist eng an die gleichzeitig ergangene Verheißung des Landesbesitzes geknüpft (Gen 12, 7, vgl. 17, 8; 18, 18). Obwohl die erweiterte Familie der Nachkommen Abrahams natürlich ein עם bilden, sind der Erwerb eines Gebietes und eine politische Struktur nötig, um wirklich ein גוי unter den übrigen גוים der Welt zu werden." See further Steven CROSBY, "Kinship, Territory, and the Nation in the Historiography of Ancient Israel," *ZAW* 105 (1993) 3−18. Very frequently in the Septuagint, the terms ἔθνος and χώρα ("land, territory") stand in parallel to one another (see n. 11 above). For instance, 2 Macc 5:19−20 refers directly to the close relationship between ἔθνος and land in regard to Israel: "But the Lord did not choose the nation for the sake of the place, but the place for the sake of the nation. Therefore the place itself shared in the misfortunes that befell the nation and afterward participated in its benefits." Nevertheless, it should be noted that in some cases, a nation that has been deprived of its land in the course of deportation and resettle-

promise of nationhood includes a promise of land: "And the Lord said to Abram, 'Go forth out of your land and out from your kindred, and out of the house of your father to the land which I shall show you'" (Gen 12:1). Like the promise of nationhood, the promise of land is frequently reiterated in Genesis not only to Abraham himself[23] but also to those who stand in the line of promise (i.e., Isaac[24] and Jacob[25]). Of course, until this promise was fulfilled, the Patriarchs were forced to live as nomads, travelling "from nation to nation (ἐξ ἔθνους εἰς ἔθνος), and from kingdom to another people" (Ps 104:13; cf. 1 Chr 16:20).

In certain OT texts, especially those associated with the messianic expectation, the land promised as an inheritance to Abraham and his seed extends beyond the borders of Canaan to include *the whole world*. In OT tradition, the king was an integral aspect of the concept of a גוי/ἔθνος.[26] Since the messianic King, the seed of Abraham in the strict sense,[27] was expected to rule the world,[28] the Abrahamic Promise of land was expanded to include the whole world. The classic example is Sir 44:21, where the Abrahamic Promise is expressed in terms of the promise of universal sovereignty for the King in Ps 71:8 (= Zech 9:10):

Therefore, he [sc. God] assured him [sc. Abraham] by an oath that he would bless the nations (ἔθνη) in his seed, and that he would multiply him as the dust of the earth and would exalt his seed as the stars, and cause them to inherit from sea to sea, and from the River unto the end of the earth.

To illustrate the universal sovereignty of the King, Psalm 71 provides a list of nations, drawn from the Table-of-Nations tradition,[29] that will be subjugated to him, including perhaps a reference to the centrality of Jerusalem:

The Ethiopians shall fall down before him, and his enemies shall lick the dust. The kings of Tharsis (Tarshish) and the islands will bring gifts; the kings of the Arabs and Saba will bring gifts. And all kings will worship him; all the nations (πάντα τὰ ἔθνη) will serve him. [...] There shall be an establishment[30] on the earth on the tops of the

---

ment is still called a "nation" (cf. 4 Kgdms 17:26, 29, 32, 33, 41; Esth 3:8). This usage persists throughout the Second Temple period and beyond (see further below).

[23] Cf. Gen 15:18−21, where the Abrahamic Promise of land is set out very geographically, with western and eastern boundaries and a list of ten nations that would be dispossessed of their land.

[24] Cf. Gen 26:3−4.

[25] Cf. Gen 28:4: "And may he give you the blessing of my father Abraham, even to you and to your seed after you, to inherit the land of your sojourning, which God gave to Abraham."

[26] Cf. CLEMENTS, "גוי," 1:968.

[27] Cf. J. SCOTT, *Adoption as Sons of God: An Exegetical Investigation into the Background of ΥΙΟΘΕΣΙΑ in the Pauline Corpus* (WUNT 2.48; Tübingen: Mohr-Siebeck, 1992), pp. 180−182, on Gal 3:16.

[28] Cf. Ps 2:8; 109:5−6; Isa 55:4.

[29] In the Septuagint, "Ethiopians" is the standard Greek translation for Cush (Gen 10:6, 7, 8; see further below on *VP* 1:8). For "Tharsis and the islands," see Gen 10:4−5.

[30] For στήριγμα in the sense of an "establishment" on Zion, see 2 Esdr 9:8.

mountains; its fruit shall be exalted above Lebanon, and they shall shall burst forth from the city like grass of the land.[31]

This expectation also has links to Isaac's blessing on Jacob: "And let the nations serve you, and may rulers bow down to you. . ." (Gen 27:29).[32] Furthermore, the reiteration of the Abrahamic Promise to Jacob at Bethel in Gen 28:13−14 (cf. 13:14) takes on global dimensions: "The earth (γῆ) on which you lie, I will give it to you and to your seed. And your seed shall be as the sand of the earth (γῆ); and it shall spread abroad to the sea, and to the south, and to the north, and to the east. And in you and in your seed shall all the tribes of the earth (γῆ) be blessed."[33] By the end of Genesis, Jacob's blessing of his twelve sons starts to narrow the focus of this aspect of the Abrahamic Promise to Judah: "A ruler shall not fail from Judah, nor a prince from his loins, until there come the things stored up for him; and he is the expectation of the nations (προσδοκία ἐθνῶν)" (Gen 49:10). Similarly, in Num 24:7: "A man will come from his [sc. Jacob's] seed, and he shall rule many nations (ἐθνῶν πολλῶν). . . ."[34] In this way, the Abrahamic Land Promise becomes identified with the expectation of universal sovereignty for the King.[35]

Even in passages that do not mention the King, the universalization of the Abrahamic Land Promise can be seen. The address to exilic Zion as a barren mother in Isa 54:1−3 is a case in point: "Rejoice, you barren one who does not bear, break forth and cry out, you who does not suffer birth-pangs; for more are the children of the desolate one than of her that has a husband. For the Lord has said, 'Enlarge the place of your tent and of your curtains. . . . Spread forth to the right and the left; and your seed shall inherit the nations (καὶ τὸ σπέρμα σου ἔθνη κληρονομήσει) . . .'" Clearly, the language of the passage points to the Abrahamic Promise, for to call exilic Zion a "barren" woman recalls Sarah from the previous context (cf. Isa 51:2), the superabundance of progeny recalls the expectation of a great nation, and the vocabulary of inheritance recalls the land promise. In other words, this passage expects that the Abrahamic Promise of seed and of becoming a great nation is the means by which, spreading out

---

[31] Ps 71:9−11, 16. Note that v. 17 applies the Abrahamic blessing (Gen 12:3; 28:14) to the King: "and all the tribes of the earth shall be blessed in him . . . ."

[32] The expectation of Israel's univeral sovereignty over the nations is a recurrent theme in the OT. Cf. Deut 15:6; Ps 46:2−3, 9−10; Isa 54:3; 60:11, 16; Jer 38:7.

[33] See esp. Philo *Somn.* 1.175, which takes Gen 28:14 as a promise rendering its possessor the "heir of the world" (τοῦ κόσμου κληρονόμος). Cf. Rom 4:13.

[34] Martin HENGEL stresses the importance of Num 24:7 for understanding Jewish nationalism and revolutionary thinking ("Messianische Hoffnung und politischer 'Radikalismus' in der 'jüdisch-hellenistischen Diaspora'. Zur Frage der Voraussetzungen des jüdischen Aufstandes unter Trajan 115−117 n. Chr.," in *Apocalypticism in the Mediterranean World and the Near East: Proceedings of the International Colloquium on Apocalypticism* [2nd ed.; ed. David Hellholm; Tübingen: Mohr-Siebeck, 1989], pp. 655−686 [here pp. 679−680]). On Jewish nationalism, see further Doron MENDELS, *The Rise and Fall of Jewish Nationalism* (Anchor Bible Reference Library; New York: Doubleday, 1992).

[35] Compare the passages on the Isaianic Servant: Isa 42:1, 4 (cf. 11:10); 49:1, 6.

from Zion, Israel will gradually take over possession ("inherit") all the nations of the world.[36]

III. The Promise of Blessing for all Nations in Abraham and his Seed. In Gen 12:3, God promises Abraham that "in you shall all the tribes of the earth be blessed." In the context of Genesis, πᾶσαι αἱ φυλαὶ τῆς γῆς obviously refers back to αἱ φυλαὶ υἱῶν Νῶε, which, according the the Table of Nations, "scattered over the earth after the flood" (Gen 10:32). Like the other two aspects of the Abrahamic Promise, this one is reiterated in the subsequent context of Genesis to Abraham and his seed. This time, however, πάντα τὰ ἔθνη τῆς γῆς is used instead of πᾶσαι αἱ φυλαὶ τῆς γῆς (cf. Gen 18:18; 22:18; 26:4; also Sir 44:21). Like Gen 28:14, which, as we saw above, contains the Abrahamic Promise of universal sovereignty for Jacob and universal blessing for the nations, Psalm 71 contains the Abrahamic promise of universal sovereignty (v. 8) and universal blessing (v. 17: ". . . all the tribes of the earth will be blessed in him [sc. the King]"). Moreover, Jer 4:2 applies the same promise to Israel of the Restoration: ". . . and the nations (ἔθνη) will bless in him [sc. Israel], and by him they shall praise God in Jerusalem."

The Covenant with Israel.

I. The Establishment of the Covenant with Israel as a Nation. When God led the Israelites out of Egypt, "that all the nations of the earth (πάντα τὰ ἔθνη τῆς γῆς) might know that the power of the Lord is mighty" (Josh 4:24),[37] he took Israel to himself as "a nation from the midst of a nation" (Deut 4:34: ἔθνος ἐκ μέσου ἔθνους).[38] With this, the promise that Abraham would be made "a great nation" (ἔθνος) was on its way toward fulfillment.[39]

Whereas Deut 26:5 (cf. Gen 46:3; Josh 24:4) dates the beginning of the "nation" very nebulously from the Sojourn in Egypt, where Jacob became "a great nation (ἔθνος μέγα) and a numerous and great multitude," Ex 19:5–6 dates it more specifically to the revelation at Sinai, where Israel enters into a special, covenantal relationship with God: "And now if you will indeed hear my voice, and keep my covenant, you will be to me a peculiar people above [lit. 'from'] all nations (λαὸς περιούσιος ἀπὸ πάντων τῶν ἐθνῶν); for the whole earth is mine. And you shall be to me a royal priesthood and a holy nation (ἔθνος ἅγιον)."[40] The idea that Israel is a peculiar people "above all nations" is often repeated in Deuteronomy,[41] and in Qumran, at least, this indicates

---

[36] As we shall see below, Philo develops this point in very great detail.

[37] Cf. Ezek 20:22, which states that Israel came out of Egypt in the sight of the nations.

[38] Cf. Esth 4:17m: the Lord "took Israel out of all the nations. . . ."

[39] Cf. Ex 33:13, where Moses refers to Israel as "this great nation" (τὸ ἔθνος τὸ μέγα τοῦτο).

[40] Cf. also Ex 23:22. Wisd 17:2 calls Israel the "holy nation."

[41] Cf. Deut 7:6–7; 10:14–15; 14:2; 26:19; 28:1.

universal sovereignty.[42] A similar concept is found in Leviticus: "And you shall be holy to me, for I the Lord your God am holy, who separated you from all the nations (ἀπὸ πάντων τῶν ἐθνῶν) to be mine" (Lev 20:26; cf. v. 24). Balaam's first oracle goes so far as to completely dissociate Israel from the nations: "Behold, a people will dwell alone, and they will not be reckoned among the nations" (Num 23:9).

Even the laws themselves distinguish Israel from all other nations. They are Israel's "wisdom and understanding before all nations (ἐναντίον πάντων τῶν ἐθνῶν)" (Deut 4:6a).[43] When it comes to the giving of the Law, God "has not done so with every nation (παντὶ ἔθνει), and his judgments he has not shown to them" (Ps 147:9).

II. The Settlement of Canaan. When God wanted to destroy Israel in the wilderness for her disobedience, Moses was able to appeal to the Abrahamic Promise, and thus to God's reputation before the nations, in order to dissuade him: "And if you destroy this people (λαός) as one man, then the nations (τὰ ἔθνη), as many as have heard your name, shall speak, saying, 'Because the Lord could not bring this people into the land which he swore to them, he has overthrown them in the wilderness'" (Num 14:15–16). Nevertheless, the conquest of Canaan was conditional on Israel's obedience to God if the Lord was to cast out before them "all these nations" (πάντα τὰ ἔθνη ταῦτα) and if they were to "inherit nations greater and stronger" (ἔθνη μεγάλα καὶ ἰσχυρότερα) than themselves (Deut 11:22–24).[44] Moreover, even after God "removes great nations from before you, the Hittite, and Gergesite, and Amorite, and Canaanite, and Perizzite, and Hivite, and Jebusite, seven nations (ἑπτὰ ἔθνη) more numerous and stronger than you . . ." (Deut 7:1; cf. 9:1), Israel was obligated to remain obedient in the land (cf. Ex 23:18). They were to have nothing to do with the nations they had conquered: "For if you turn aside and associate yourselves with these nations that are left with you, and you intermarry with them, and you are mingled with them and they with you, know that the Lord will surely not destroy these nations from before you; and they will be to you snares and stumbling-blocks, and nails in your heels, and arrows in your eyes. . . (Josh 23:12–13). According to the OT, this is precisely what happened. For despite the very great things that God had done in removing the nations for Israel,[45] certain "nations" were left to put Israel to the test (Judg 3:1, with the list of the nations given in v. 3).

As the people became established in the land and emerged from the dark period of the Judges, they demanded of Samuel that a king be appointed to

---

[42] Cf. 4Q381 76–77, 14–16 (cited below).

[43] See further on Deut 4:6b above.

[44] Note the boundaries of the Land that they would conquer: "from the wilderness and Antilebanon, and from the Great River, the River Euphrates, and even as far as the Western Sea" (v. 24).

[45] Cf. Josh 23:3.

judge them "as also the other nations have" (καθὰ καὶ τὰ λοιπὰ ἔθνη).[46] By popular acclamation, Saul became the first king of Israel, though it was David, the second king, whom God chose to found an eternal dynasty. In response to this and to the peace that God had given from all his enemies round about him, David exclaims before the Lord: "And what other nation (ἔθνος ἄλλο) on the earth is as your people (ὁ λαός σου) Israel? God led him, to redeem for himself a people (λαός), to make yourself a name, to make greatness and appearance, that you may cast out nations (ἔθνη) and (their) tents from before your people, whom you redeemed for yourself from Egypt. And you have prepared for yourself your people Israel to be a people forever, and you, Lord, have become their God" (2 Kgdms 7:23−24).

III. The Sin of Israel. Once the Israelites entered the land, they fell continually into two related forms of sin: "they did according to all the abominations of the nations (βδελύγματα τῶν ἐθνῶν) which the Lord cast out from the face of the sons of Israel,"[47] and "they worshipped the gods of the nations round about them (τοὺς θεοὺς τῶν ἐθνῶν τῶν κύκλῳ αὐτῶν)."[48] According to the Pentateuch, Moses had often warned the Israelites about the pitfalls that would be encountered in the new land,[49] but to no avail. For upon entering the land, "They did not destroy the nations (τὰ ἔθνη) which the Lord told them [to destroy], and they mingled with the nations (ἐν τοῖς ἔθνεσιν) and learned their works" (Ps 105:34−35). Thus already of the period of the Judges, it could be said: "Inasmuch as this nation (τὸ ἔθνος τοῦτο) has forsaken my covenant which I commanded their fathers, and they have not obeyed my voice, I will no longer cast out a man of the nations from before their face, which Joshua also left..." (Judg 2:20−21). In the course of Israel's subsequent history, the situation continued to deteriorate. During the United Monarchy, for example, Solomon took numerous foreign wives "from the nations concerning which the Lord forbade the sons of Israel: You shall not go in to them, and they shall not

---

[46] 1 Kgdms 8:5; cf. v. 20. According to Deuteronomy, however, this was a matter to be decided by God himself: "And when you shall enter into the land which the Lord your God will give you by lot, and you inherit it and dwell in it, and you say, I will set a ruler over me, as also the other nations around about me (καθὰ καὶ τὰ λοιπὰ ἔθνη τὰ κύκλῳ μου), you shall surely set over yourself the ruler whom the Lord your God shall choose" (Deut 17:14−15).

[47] Cf. 3 Kgdms 14:24; 4 Kgdms 16:3; 21:2; 2 Chr 28:3; 36:14. See further 4 Kgdms 17:8; 4 Kgdms 17:11, 15; 1 Esdr 1:47.

[48] Cf. Josh 24:33b. "The gods of the nations" is a major theme in the OT, which goes back to the idea that each nation has its national deity (cf. Deut 32:8; CLEMENTS, "גוי," 1:969). Although Judah is taunted with the question, "Have the gods of the nations at all delivered each their own land out of the hand of the king of the Assyrians?" (4 Kgdms 18:33; cf. 19:12), nevertheless, the Lord is to be feared above all gods; "for all the gods of the nations are idols, and our God made heaven" (1 Chr 16:26; cf. Ps 95:5; 113:12; 134:15; Jer 14:22; Wisd 15:15). According to Jdt 3:8, Holofernes had decreed to destroy all the gods of the earth, "that all nations should worship Nebuchadnezzar only, and that all tongues and tribes should call upon him as god." Eventually, however, God himself will destroy "all the gods of the nations of the earth" (Zeph 2:11; cf. Wisd 14:11).

[49] Cf. Lev 18:24−25; 20:23; Deut 6:14; 12:29; 13:8; 18:9; 32:21.

come in to you, lest they turn away your hearts after their idols. . . (3 Kgdms 11:2).[50] Yahweh addresses Judah and Jerusalem as "a sinful nation (ἔθνος ἁμαρτωλόν), a people full of sins, an evil seed, lawless sons" (Isa 1:4). After the demise of the northern kingdom as a result of sin, Manasseh brought Judah into its worst period of apostasy, leading the people astray to evil in the sight of the Lord "*beyond* the nations (ὑπὲρ τὰ ἔθνη) which the Lord destroyed from before the face of the sons of Israel" (4 Kgdms 21:9).[51] Jeremiah was instructed to say to Judah: "This is the nation (τὸ ἔθνος) which neither listened to the voice of the Lord nor received instruction" (Jer 7:27−28). Israel became "a nation that has lost counsel, neither is there understanding in them" (Deut 32:28). The Lord reveals the fundamental problem: "For all the nations (πάντα τὰ ἔθνη) are uncircumcised in the flesh, and the whole house of Israel are uncircumcised in their hearts" (Jer 9:25b).[52] Jerusalem, which had been given pride of place "in the midst of the nations" (Ezek 5:5), became "the lawless one of the nations" (ἡ ἄνομος ἐκ τῶν ἐθνῶν) (v. 6).[53] "Therefore, thus says the Lord, 'Because your pretext [for sin] is from the nations round about you (ἐκ τῶν ἐθνῶν τῶν κύκλῳ ὑμῶν),[54] and you have not walked in my statutes, nor done my ordinances, indeed you have not even done according to the ordinances of the nations round about you (κατὰ τὰ δικαιώματα τῶν ἐθνῶν τῶν κύκλῳ ὑμῶν); therefore, thus says the Lord: Behold, I am against you, and I will execute judgment in the midst of you in front of the nations (ἐνῶπιον τῶν ἐθνῶν). . .'" (Ezek 5:7−8).

IV. The Exile of Israel. In the Pentateuch, God repeatedly threatens that he will send Israel into exile by scattering them "to/among the nations." For example, Deut 28:64 warns: "And the Lord your God will scatter you to all nations (εἰς πάντα τὰ ἔθνη), from one end of the earth to the other. . . ."[55] Similarly, the prophets threaten Israel and Judah that God will disperse them "among the nations." In Jer 9:15, for instance, Yahweh inveighs against the people: "And I will scatter them among the nations (ἐν τοῖς ἔθνεσιν), unto those which neither they nor their fathers knew. . . ."[56]

---

[50] Cf. 2 Esdr 23:26: "Did not Solomon king of Israel sin thus? And among many nations there was not a king like him, and he was beloved of God, and God made him king over all Israel. And foreign women turned him aside."

[51] Cf. Jer 18:13 ("Enquire among the nations [ἐν ἔθνεσιν]: Who has heard such terrible things as the virgin Israel has done?"); 1 Macc 7:23.

[52] For this reason, the prophet Jeremiah predicts Yahweh's judgment on the "circumcised who are uncircumcised" and groups Judah with Egypt, Edom, Ammon, Moab, and those who live in the desert (Jer 9:24−25a). Elsewhere as well, Jeremiah's treats the apostate nation of Israel like one of the nations that are ripe for judgment. Cf. Gary V. Sмітн, "Alienation and Restoration: A Jacob-Esau Typology," in *Israel's Apostasy and Restoration: Essays in Honor of Roland K. Harrison* (ed. Avraham Gileadi; Grand Rapids, MI: Baker, 1988), pp. 165−174 (here p. 171).

[53] The ἐκ stands for a comparative מן in the MT: רשעה מן הגוים.

[54] Cf. Ezek 23:30: ". . . you went whoring after the nations and defiled yourself with their devices."

[55] Cf. Deut 4:27; Lev 26:33, 38. See further Deut 28:32, 36; Ezek 20:23.

[56] Cf. Ezek 12:15; Hos 8:10; 9:17; Zech 7:14.

Eventually, the sins of both the northern and the southern kingdoms caught up with them, and they were sent into their respective exiles. First, Israel was deported into Assyrian Captivity. In their place, other "nations" (τὰ ἔθνη) were transplanted from Mesopotamia into the cities of Samaria (4 Kgdms 17:26). Then, the Lord also became angry with "his nation" (τὸ ἔθνος αὐτοῦ) Judah because of her great ungodliness (1 Esdr 1:49), and so, Judah was deported into Babylonian Captivity, where she could be found "dwelling among the nations" (ἐκάθισεν ἐν ἔθνεσιν) (Lam 1:3). Thus, at a later time, Haman could say to king Artaxerxes, "There is a nation scattered among the nations (ἔθνος διεσπαρμέ-νον ἐν τοῖς ἔθνεσιν) in all your kingdom, and their laws differ from all the nations (πάντα τὰ ἔθνη); and they disobey the laws of the king. . ." (Esth 3:8; cf. v. 13d). Here, we begin to see that ἔθνος can be used of Israel even in Exile, a usage that will be encountered often in Jewish sources of the Second Temple period. This corresponds to the Greek usage of ἔθνος that allows the term to be applied to groups of people who are thought to belong together on some basis (e.g., common descent, language, customs, characteristics, or name) whether or not they are a politically unified entity.[57]

Originally, the length of the Exile was to be relatively short: ". . . they shall serve among the nations (ἐν τοῖς ἔθνεσιν) seventy years" (Jer 25:11). By the time of Daniel 9, however, the original figure had been multiplied sevenfold (cf. vv. 2, 24), signifying that the Exile would last much longer than at first expected.[58] Thus, even into the second century B.C., the appeal for an end to the protracted Exile can be heard: "Let your wrath turn from us, for we have been left few among the nations (ἐν τοῖς ἔθνεσιν) where you have scattered us" (Bar 2:13). This is in accordance with the word of the Lord given through Moses, "If you will not hear my voice, surely this very great bustling multitude will turn back into a small number among the nations (ἐν τοῖς ἔθνεσιν) where I will scatter them" (Bar 2:29, alluding to Deut 4:27).

During the Exile, the captives did not mend their ways and keep the Law. According to Tob 1:10, Israel failed to keep the dietary laws while in Exile: "And when we were taken captive to Nineveh, all my brethren and those who

---

[57] Cf. GSCHNITZER, "Volk, Nation, Nationalismus, Masse (II. Altertum)," pp. 164–165: "Ein ἔθνος in diesem [unpolitischen] Sinne bleibt auch, was seine politische Einheit längst verloren hat, etwa alle Arkader (vor der Wiedervereinigung ebenso wie nach dem Zerfall des Bundes), alle Dorier, alle Ioner (obwohl durch Wanderungen und Kolonisation weit zerstreut) . . .," See further Michael V. Fox, *Character and Ideology in the Book of Esther* (Studies in Personalities of the Old Testament; Columbia, SC: University of South Carolina, 1991), pp. 230–234.

[58] On the protracted Exile, see Odil Hannes STECK, "Das Problem theologischer Strömungen in nachexilischer Zeit," *EvT* 28 (1968) 445–458 (here p. 454); J. SCOTT, "'For as many as are of works of the Law are under a curse' (Galatians 3.10)," in *Paul and the Scriptures of Israel* (ed. James A. Sanders and C. A. Evans; JSNTSup 83; SSEJC 1; Sheffield: JSOT Press, 1993), pp. 187–220; Willem Cornelius VAN UNNIK, *Das Selbstverständnis der jüdischen Diaspora in der hellenistisch-römischen Zeit* (ed. Pieter Willem van der Horst; AGJU 17; Leiden: Brill, 1993).

were of my nation (οἱ ἐκ τοῦ γένους μου) ate of the food of the nations (ἐκ τῶν ἄρτων τῶν ἐθνῶν)." This is in accordance with the prophecy of Ezek 4:13: "Thus shall the sons of Israel eat unclean things among the nations (ἐν τοῖς ἔθνεσιν)." Even more grievous, however, God's name was blasphemed because of Israel's Exile. Hence Isa 52:5 makes the indictment, "On account of you [sc. Israel] my name is continually blasphemed among the nations (ἐν τοῖς ἔθνεσιν)." According to Ezek 36:19−22, God's name was profaned by Israel herself:

And I dispersed them to the nations (εἰς τὰ ἔθνη) and scattered them like chaff to the countries (εἰς τὰς χώρας). I judged them according to their way and according to their sin. And they went into the nations (εἰς τὰ ἔθνη), among which they have gone, and they profaned my holy name, while it was said of them, "These are the people of the Lord (λαὸς κυρίου), and they came forth out of his land." And I spared them for the sake of my holy name, which the house of Israel profaned among the nations (ἐν τοῖς ἔθνεσιν), among which they went. Therefore, say to the house of Israel, "Thus says the Lord: I do not do this, O house of Israel, for your sakes, but because of my holy name, which you have profaned among the nations (ἐν τοῖς ἔθνεσιν), among which you have gone."

In other words, Israel's Exile provides the nations an opportunity to ridicule the reputation of the God of Israel.[59] To prevent just such a thing from happening, Joel cries out before the Lord: "Spare your people, O Lord, and do not give your inheritance to disgrace, that the nations (ἔθνη) should rule over them, lest they should say among the nations (ἐν τοῖς ἔθνεσιν), 'Where is their God?'" (Joel 2:17; cf. v. 19).

Texts in which the word ἔθνος occurs reveal that the purpose of Exile was multifaceted: to humiliate Israel among the nations,[60] to winnow her among all the nations,[61] to give Israel an opportunity to declare all her iniquities among the nations,[62] to make her jealous by another nation,[63] and to remove her uncleanness.[64] In no case, however, is the purpose for which Israel was "sold to the nations" to destroy Israel (Bar 4:6: ἐπράθητε τοῖς ἔθνεσιν οὐκ εἰς ἀπώ-

---

[59] Compare the Assyrian taunt against Judah: "Have the gods of the nations at all delivered each his own land out the hand of the king of the Assyrians?" (4 Kgdms 18:33; cf. 19:12; 2 Chr 32:13−14).

[60] Cf. Tob 3:4: "You gave us as plunder and captivity and death and as a proverb of reproach to all the nations (πᾶσιν τοῖς ἔθνεσιν) among which we are dispersed."

[61] Cf. Amos 9:9.

[62] Cf. Ezek 12:16: "And I will leave of them a [few] men in number [spared] from the sword, from famine and from death, in order that they may declare all their iniquities among the nations (ἐν τοῖς ἔθνεσιν) whence they have gone."

[63] Cf. Deut 32:21: "They have provoked me to jealousy with that which is no god; they have made me angry with their idols. And I will provoke them to jealousy with that which is no nation (ἐπ' οὐκ ἔθνει); I will make them angry with a nation lacking understanding (ἐπ' ἔθνει ἀσυνέτῳ)."

[64] Cf. Ezek 22:15: "And I will scatter you among the nations (ἐν τοῖς ἔθνεσιν) and disperse you among the the countries (ἐν ταῖς χώραις), and your uncleanness will be removed from you."

λειαν).[65] Rather, the ultimate purpose of the Exile was that Israel might return to God: "When some of you are rescued from the sword among the nations (ἐν τοῖς ἔθνεσιν), and when you are scattered among the countries (ἐν ταῖς χώραις), then those of you who are rescued among the nations (ἐν τοῖς ἔθνεσιν), whence they were taken captive, will remember me" (Ezek 6:8−9).[66] Hence, Tobit exhorts, "Confess him [sc. God] before the nations (ἐνώπιον τῶν ἐθνῶν), you sons of Israel, for he has scattered us among them" (Tob 13:3).

V. The Restoration of Israel. The end of the Exile and the beginning of the Restoration is an issue that is viewed differently in various streams of tradition within the OT.[67] According to one perspective, which can be identified with theocratic circles associated with the Temple, the Restoration of Israel took place in the so-called "Post-Exilic Period." According to another major perspective, however, the Restoration of Israel was yet to take place in the eschatological future. These two perspectives must be distinguished when discussing the use of ἔθνος in reference to the Restoration of Israel.

From a *theocratic* perspective, the Restoration of Israel took place under Cyrus, when Israel was allowed to return to Jerusalem and rebuild the Temple. Thus, we read in 1 Esdr 2:3: "If any of you, therefore, are of his nation [i.e., the Lord's nation, Israel], let his Lord be with him; let him go up to Jerusalem, which is in Judea, and build the house of the Lord of Israel – he is the Lord who dwells in Jerusalem."[68] Despite some encouraging initial signs,[69] however, it gradually became clear that this "restoration" had some fundamental flaws, particularly in regard to "the nations of the land" and Israel's relationship to them. For, on the one hand, "the nations of the land" were persecuting the returning exiles,[70] and, on the other hand, they were causing Israel to fall back into old patterns of sin. According to 1 Esdr 8:66−67 (cf. also v. 89), for example, "The nation of Israel (τὸ ἔθνος τοῦ Ἰσραήλ) and the rulers and the

---

[65] But see Ps 43:12−13.

[66] Cf. Deut 30:1−2 ("And it will be when all these words have come upon you, the blessing and the curse, which I have set before your face, and you take them to heart among all the nations to which the Lord will have scattered you, and you return to the Lord your God..."); Tob 13:8 ("In the land of my captivity I will confess him and show his power and majesty to a nation of sinners [Israel? the host nation?]: Turn back, you sinners, and do righteousness before him. Who knows if he will take pleasure in you and have mercy on you?").

[67] Cf. STECK, "Das Problem theologischer Strömungen in nachexilischer Zeit," pp. 445−458. See also my article on "The Restoration of Israel," in *The Dictionary of Paul and his Letters* (ed. R. P. Martin, et al.; Downers Grove: InterVarsity Press, 1993), pp. 796−805.

[68] Cf. also 1 Esdr 8:10: "In accordance with my gracious decision, I have given orders that those of the nation of the Jews (ἐκ τοῦ ἔθνους τῶν Ἰουδαίων) and of the priests and Levites and others in our realm, those who freely choose to do so, may go with you to Jerusalem." In 1 Esdras, Israel is regularly referred to as a "nation" (cf. 8:64, 66−67).

[69] Cf. 1 Esdr 7:13 ("And the sons of Israel who came out of the captivity ate [the passover], all those that had separated themselves from the abominations of the nations of the land and sought the Lord"); 8:64 ("And they [sc. the governors of Coelesyria and Phoenicia] honored the nation [i.e., Israel] and the temple of the Lord").

[70] Cf. 1 Esdr 5:49, 69.

priests and the Levites have not separated themselves from the foreign nations of the land (τὰ ἀλλογενῆ ἔθνη τῆς γῆς) and their pollutions, from the Canaanites, the Hittites, Perizzites, the Jebusites, and the Moabites, the Egyptians, and the Edomites. For both they and their sons have married with their daughters, and the holy seed has been mixed with the foreign nations of the land (τὰ ἀλλογενῆ ἔθνη τῆς γῆς). . . .," Ezra's prayer in response to this admission characterizes the postexilic period as a period of renewed apostasy: ". . . we have turned back again to transgress your law in order to mingle ourselves with the uncleanness of the nations of the land (τῇ ἀκαθαρσίᾳ τῶν ἐθνῶν τῆς γῆς)" (1 Esdr 8:84). According to 2 Esdr 9:7, the situation of Israel's sin and therefore of her judgment has not really changed: "From the days of our fathers we have been in a great sin until this day. And because of our iniquities, we and our kings and our sons have been delivered into the hand of the kings of the nations (ἐν χειρὶ βασιλέων τῶν ἐθνῶν) by sword and by captivity and by plunder and by the shame of our face, as it is this day."[71] Obviously, therefore, this was not the glorious Restoration that the prophets envisioned. Furthermore, it was not until 141 B.C. that "the yoke of the nations (ὁ ζυγὸς τῶν ἐθνῶν) was taken away from Israel" (1 Macc 13:41), but even that was relatively short-lived.

From the *eschatological* perspective, the Restoration had not yet occurred fully and finally but was yet to come in the future. Jeremiah looks forward to a day when God will make a New Covenant with Israel (Jer 38:31−34), and the existence of Israel as a "nation" will be as certain as the natural order (vv. 35−36). Ezekiel presents the Restoration as a new Exodus,[72] when Israel will be reconstituted as an ἔθνος gathered from the nations and brought into a new covenantal relationship with God (note the Covenant Formula):

Behold, I will take the whole house of Israel from the midst of the nations (ἐκ μέσου τῶν ἐθνῶν), whence they have gone, and I will gather them from all that are around them, and I will bring them into the land of Israel. And I will make them one nation (ἔθνος ἕν) in my land, even on the mountains of Israel; and they shall have one ruler; and they will no longer be two nations (δύο ἔθνη),[73] nor will they be divided any longer into two kingdoms, that they may no longer defile themselves with their idols. And I will deliver them from all their transgressions whereby they have sinned, and will cleanse them; and they shall be my people (λαός), and I the Lord will be their God" (Ezek 37:21−23; cf. 38:12).[74]

Just as, at the first Exodus, God took Israel to himself out of Egypt as "a

---

[71] Reform was still necessary: "And now by confessing give glory to the Lord God of our fathers, and do his will, and separate yourselves from the nations of the land, and from the foreign women" (1 Esdr 9:8−9).

[72] Cf. Lev 26:45: "And I will remember their former covenant, when I brought them out of the land of Egypt, out of the house of bondage before the nations, to be their God."

[73] Cf. Ezek 35:10, where Israel and Judah are called "the two nations and the two countries" (τὰ δύο ἔθνη καὶ αἱ δύο χῶραι).

[74] This corresponds to the Exodus typology elsewhere in Ezekiel. Cf. Ezek 20:34−35, where bringing Israel into "the wilderness of the peoples" is directly analogous to bringing the people into the wilderness at the time of the Exodus (cf. vv. 10−24).

nation from the midst of a nation" (Deut 4:33), so also, in the future, God will gather Israel "from the midst of the nations" and will make them one, new "nation."[75] In that day, Israel will be "a nation gathered from many nations, that has acquired property, dwelling on the navel of the earth."[76]

Unlike the partial return from Exile and failed attempt at Restoration in the so-called "post-exilic period," the eschatological Restoration will be complete and comprehensive. According to Deut 30:3−4, the Lord "will again gather you out from *all* the nations (ἐκ πάντων τῶν ἐθνῶν) to which he has scattered you.[77] If your dispersion (ἡ διασπορά σου) is from one end of the heaven to the other, the Lord your God will gather you from there. . . .." A similar expectation is found about the remnant in Isa 11:11−12: God will raise "a sign for the nations" (σημεῖον εἰς τὰ ἔθνη) by which he will gather both the lost ones of Israel and the dispersed ones of Judah from the four corners of the earth.[78] According to Jer 38:8, the Lord will "bring them [sc. the remnant of Israel] from the north, and will gather them from the end of the earth. . . ." Or again, in Ezek 36:24: "And I will take you out from the nations (ἐκ τῶν ἐθνῶν) and will gather you from all the lands (ἐκ πασῶν τῶν γαιῶν) and will bring you into your land."

The Restoration will bring relief for the exiles and a new relationship with the nations of the world. According to Ezek 34:28−29, "And they shall no longer be plunder to the nations (ἐν προνομῇ τοῖς ἔθνεσιν), and the wild beasts of the land shall no longer devour them, and they shall dwell in peace, and there shall be none to make them afraid. And . . . they shall no longer bear the reproach of the nations (ὀνειδισμὸν ἐθνῶν)." In fact, according to Mal 3:12, "And all nations (πάντα τὰ ἔθνη) will call you blessed, because you will be a desirable land. . . ." Whereas they were once a "curse among the nations" (κατάρα ἐν τοῖς ἔθνεσιν), Judah and Israel will be a "blessing" (Zech 8:13). According to Jer 38:7, the regathered remnant of Israel is expected to become the "head of the nations" (κεφαλὴ ἐθνῶν).[79] We might say that, corresponding to its central position in the Table of Nations, Israel will return to a place of prominence among the nations in the middle of the world (Ezek 38:12).

Although the eschatological Restoration is first and foremost for Israel, it will also affect all other nations, whether positively or negatively. First, in a positive way, all nations of the world will participate in the eschatological pilgrimage to Zion. Israel will be a light to the nations (Isa 60:3; cf. 51:4).[80] Thus Isa 2:2−4 (= Mic 4:1−3) states:

---

[75] Cf. Mic 4:7: "And I will make the crushed one a remnant, and the rejected one a mighty nation; and the Lord will reign over them in Mount Zion from now and for ever."

[76] Ezek 38:12: ἔθνος συνηγμένον ἀπὸ ἐθνῶν πολλῶν πεποιηκότας κτήσεις κατοικοῦντας ἐπὶ τὸν ὀμφαλὸν τῆς γῆς.

[77] Cf. Tob 13:5: "And he will have mercy again and will gather us out of all nations (ἐκ πάντων τῶν ἐθνῶν), among which he has scattered us."

[78] Cf. Isa 52:10; 62:10−11.

[79] See further above on the Abrahamic Promise of Land interpreted as universal sovereignty.

[80] The expression is applied to the Servant of the Lord in Isa 42:6; 49:6.

For in the last days the mountain of the Lord will be visible, and the house of God on the tops of the mountains, and it will be exalted above the hills. And all nations (πάντα τὰ ἔθνη) will come to it. And many nations (ἔθνη πολλά) will go and say, 'Come and let us go up to the mountain of the Lord and to the house of the God of Jacob; and he will teach us his way, and we will walk in it.' For from Zion will go forth the Law, and the word of the Lord from Jerusalem. And he will judge in the midst of the nations (ἀνὰ μέσον τῶν ἐθνῶν) and will reprove many people (λαὸν πολύν); and they will beat their swords into plowshares, and their spears into sickles; and nation will not take up sword against nation (ἔθνος ἐπ᾽ ἔθνος), neither will they learn to make war any more.

Isaiah is full of this expectation. The nations will bring Israel back to their land (Isa 14:2) together with many riches (cf. 60:1–6).[81] On Zion "the Lord of Hosts will be for all nations (πᾶσι τοῖς ἔθνεσιν) on this Mount; they will drink gladness. . ." (Isa 25:6). The Lord who gathers the dispersed of Israel will say that "my house will be called a house of prayer for all nations (ὁ γὰρ οἶκός μου οἶκος προσευχῆς κληθήσεται πᾶσιν τοῖς ἔθνεσιν)."[82] In that day, according to Isa 11:10, the root of Jesse will arise "to rule over the nations" (ἄρχειν ἐθνῶν), and "the nations will trust in him" (ἐπ᾽ αὐτῷ ἔθνη ἐλπιοῦσιν). As we have seen, Isa 66:18–20 expects, under influence of the Table-of-Nations tradition, that God will gather "all nations and tongues" (πάντα τὰ ἔθνη καὶ τὰς γλώσσας) to Jerusalem. According to Jeremiah, "the prophet to the nations" (cf. Jer 1:5), "all nations" (πάντα τὰ ἔθνη) will be gathered to Jerusalem, "and they will not walk any longer after the imaginations of their evil heart" (Jer 3:17). The nations, which will come from "the end of the earth," will acknowledge that their idols are worthless (Jer 16:19).[83] "And many nations (ἔθνη πολλά) will flee to the Lord in that day, and they shall become his people (καὶ ἔσονται αὐτῷ εἰς λαόν), and they shall dwell in the midst of you [sc. the daughter of Zion]. . ." (Zech 2:15).[84]

The ultimate goal of the Restoration is that Israel and the nations might worship the Lord together in Zion. Israel's cry in Exile is that God might gather them together "from the nations (ἐκ τῶν ἐθνῶν), that we might confess your holy name and boast in your praise" (Ps 105:47 = 1 Chr 16:35). According to Jer 4:2, if Israel will return to the Lord, "the nations (ἔθνη) will bless in him (cf. Gen 12:3), and by him they shall praise God in Jerusalem." The nations (ἔθνη) are exhorted to rejoice with God's people Israel (μετὰ τοῦ λαοῦ αὐτοῦ) at the time of the Restoration (Deut 32:43). The Lord's holy name, which had formerly been profaned "among the nations" (ἐν τοῖς ἔθνεσιν), will be sanctified when "the nations" (τὰ ἔθνη) realize that he is the Lord (Ezek 36:22–24;

---

[81] Cf. Isa 49:22; 66:18–20; also Zech 8:22–23; Tob 13:13.

[82] Isa 56:7–8. On the question of whether the end-time pilgrims are expected to be full proselytes to Judaism or merely God-fearers, see Terence L. DONALDSON, "Proselytes or 'Righteous Gentiles'? The Status of Gentiles in Eschatological Pilgrimage Patterns of Thought," *JSP* 7 (1990) 3–27.

[83] Cf. Tob 14:6: "And all nations (πάντα τὰ ἔθνη) will turn and fear the Lord truly and bury their idols. And all nations (πάντα τὰ ἔθνη) will praise the Lord."

[84] Note that the Covenant Formula is applied to the nations here! Cf. 2 Cor 6:16.

cf. 39:7),[85] for then "all nations" (πάντα τὰ ἔθνη) will know that the Exile was not caused by the impotence of God but by the sin of Israel (Ezek 39:23). When the Lord has been manifested to them "among the nations," Israel will also know that he is the Lord (Ezek 39:28).

Second, in a negative way, the Restoration of Israel will result in the destruction of the nations of the world. As Ezekiel 38–39 describes in detail,[86] the nations will wage war against the returned exiles only to be defeated in a final, eschatological battle. According to Ezek 30:3, "the day of the Lord is near, a day [which] will be the end of the nations" (πέρας ἐθνῶν).[87] Thus, two traditions are allowed to coexist in the OT – one universalistic (salvation for Israel and all nations) and another particularistic (salvation for Israel alone). The same tension will be seen in many of the Jewish writings of the Greco-Roman period.

EΘNOΣ in Jewish Writings of the Greco-Roman Period

Introduction. We are interested here in the use of ἔθνος in the so-called "Hellenistic-Jewish" writings from approximately the third century B.C. to the third century A.D. regardless of their place of origin (whether Palestine or the Diaspora) and their original language (whether Semitic[88] or Greek).[89] As we shall see, there is not only a great deal of continuity between the OT and early Judaism on the subject of "nation(s)" but some interesting developments as well.

Demetrius the Chronographer. Eusebius' *Praeparatio Evangelica*[90] preserves six fragments of Demetrius, which probably stem originally from the third century B.C. in Egypt.[91] As such, these fragments represent the earliest datable writings of a Jewish author writing in Greek. The second fragment (*Pr. Ev.* 9.21.1–19) repeats twice that "Abraham was chosen from among the nations" (ἀφ' οὗ [δὲ] ἐκλεγῆναι Ἀβραὰμ ἐκ τῶν ἐθνῶν) and migrated into Canaan (vv. 16, 18). This alludes to the idea both that Abraham was chosen to be a great nation (Gen 12:2) and that Israel was elected "above all nations" (cf. Deut 7:6–7; 10:15; 14:2).

The Sibylline Oracles.[92] The documents that are collectively called the *Sibyl-*

---

[85] Cf. 2 Macc 1:27: "Gather together our dispersion, deliver those who serve among the nations (ἐν τοῖς ἔθνεσιν) . . ., and let the nations (τὰ ἔθνη) know that you are our God."

[86] Cf. also Joel 4:1–3, 11–12. See further in Chap. 1.

[87] Cf. Obad 15.

[88] Hebrew is considered a "Semitic" language even though in the Hebrew Bible, it is called "the language (שׂפה, 'lip') of Canaan" (Isa 19:18), one of the descendents of Ham (cf. Gen 10:6).

[89] For the use of ἔθνος by Greco-Roman writers in connection with the Jews and Judaism, see Menahem STERN, *Greek and Latin Authors on Jews and Judaism, edited with Introduction, Translations and Commentary* (3 vols.; Jerusalem: The Israel Academy of Sciences and the Humanities, 1974–84), 3:157, s.v. ἔθνος.

[90] Text: K. MRAS, *Eusebius Werke 8.1, Praeparatio Evangelica* (GCS 43.1; Berlin: Akademie-Verlag, 1954–56).

[91] Cf. J. HANSON, "Demetrius the Chronographer," *OTP*, 2:844.

[92] Text: J. GEFFCKEN, *Die Oracula Sibyllina* (GCS 8; Leipzig: Hinrichs, 1902).

line Oracles stem from various times and places.[93] Of the 26 occurrences of ἔθνος in this corpus, the Third Sibyl, which originates from the second century B.C. in Egypt, has by far the most occurrences, with 10.[94] That the term normally denotes "nation(s)," often in distinction to the Jews,[95] is beyond doubt, for as was shown in Chap. 1, the *Sibylline Oracles*, particularly Book 3, are deeply influenced by the Table-of-Nations tradition. The *Sibyllines* are concerned with "all nations, as many as inhabit the earth" (3.518–519).[96] In the end time, the "kings of the nations" (βασιλῆες ἐθνῶν) will launch an attack together against the Temple and the Land (3.663–666; cf. Ezekiel 38–39), but God will send judgment upon them (vv. 669–701). Then, the sons of the great God will dwell securely around his Temple, and the nations will come confessing their sins and acknowledging him as God (vv. 702–731). When God ushers in his everlasting kingdom, all the nations will bring him tribute (vv. 767–795). The oracles also refer to a large number of individual nations.[97]

Joseph and Aseneth.[98] Based on Gen 41:45, *Joseph and Aseneth* is the story of the daughter of an Egyptian priest who, as a prototypical proselyte from polytheism to the one true Creator-Father,[99] converts to Judaism and then marries Joseph. Although it is impossible to be certain about the date of the Jewish *Grundschrift*, which has obviously undergone Christian redaction, the Egyptian provenance of the document seems very likely.[100] The term ἔθνος occurs four times in *Joseph and Aseneth*. First, after Aseneth confesses her sin and takes refuge (κατέφυγον)[101] in the Lord (*Jos. As.* 12–13), an angel descends from heaven and announces to Aseneth her new status as prototypical proselyte: "And your name shall no longer be called Aseneth, but your name shall be City of Refuge (πόλις καταφυγῆς),[102] because in you many nations will take refuge with the Lord God, the Most High (διότι ἐν σοι καταφεύξονται ἔθνη πολλὰ ἐπὶ κύριον τὸν θεόν τὸν ὕψιστον), and under your wings many

---

[93] Cf. J.J. COLLINS, "Sibylline Oracles," *OTP*, 1:322 et passim.

[94] Followed by Book 8 (4 times); Book 11 (3 times); Books 1, 2, 5, and 14 (2 each); and Book 14 (1 time).

[95] Cf. *Sib. Or.* 1.345 (Christian!); 2.73; 3.663. Elsewhere, Israel is called "the nation of the great God" (*Sib. Or.* 3.194), "a true nation" (5.149), "the nation of the Hebrews" (8.141), and "the holy nation" (14.360).

[96] Cf. *Sib. Or.* 11.76 ("every nation of men"); 12.106 ("every nation").

[97] Cf. *Sib. Or.* 3.172 (Macedonia as "another great, diverse nation"), 515 ("many nations of Pamphylians and Lydians"), 516 (Cappadocians and Arabs as "barbaric-speaking nations"), 520 (Rome [or possibly the Gauls] as "a vast barbarian nation" that comes against the Greeks [cf. also 8.95; 14.313]), 598–599 ("and many other nations of others, Persians and Greeks and all Asia"); 5.132 ("the race and savage nation of the Tauri"); 8.12 ("nations to the west"), and 11.64 ("the Median nation").

[98] Text: Christoph BUCHARD, "Ein vorläufiger griechischer Text von Joseph und Aseneth," *Dielheimer Blätter zum Alten Testament* 14 (1979) 2–53.

[99] On Aseneth as a prototypical proselyte, see SCOTT, *Adoption*, pp. 95–96.

[100] Cf. C. BURCHARD, "Joseph and Aseneth," *OTP*, 2:187–188.

[101] *Jos. As.* 13:1.

[102] On this expression as applied to Aseneth, see further BURCHARD, *OTP*, 2:189–190.

peoples (λαοὶ πολλοί) trusting in the Lord will be sheltered, and behind your walls will be guarded those who attach themselves to the Most High God in the name of Repentance."[103] This alludes to the expectation in Zech 2:15[104] that, in the Restoration, many nations will take refuge in the Lord in Jerusalem, that they will become part of the people of God, and that God will dwell among them in Zion.

The second and third occurrences of the term come when Aseneth later repeats to Joseph what the angel said to her: "Your name will no longer be called Aseneth, but your name will be called City of Refuge, and the Lord God will reign as king over many nations for ever (καὶ κύριος ὁ θεὸς βασιλεύσει ἐθνῶν πολλῶν εἰς τοὺς αἰῶνας), because in you many nations will take refuge with the Lord, the Most High (διότι ἐν σοι καταφεύξονται ἔθνη πολλά ἐπὶ κύριον τὸν θεόν).[105] The idea that God reigns over the nations is, of course, widespread in the OT.[106]

The final occurrence of ἔθνος comes in the context of the wedding feast for Joseph and Aseneth: "And he [sc. Pharaoh] called together all the chiefs of the land of Egypt and all the kings of the nations (πάντας τοὺς βασιλεῖς τῶν ἐθνῶν) and proclaimed to the whole land of Egypt, saying, 'Every man who does work during the seven days of Joseph's and Aseneth's wedding shall surely die.'" We may compare the summons to the wedding feast for Esther and King Ahasuerus in Esth 2:17–19 and the tradition dependent on it.[107]

The Testaments of the Twelve Patriarchs.[108] Of the 40 occurrences of ἔθνος in the *Testament of the Twelve Patriarchs*, all are plural and refer to "the nations" (or perhaps in some cases to "the Gentiles") in distinction to Israel.[109] If the *Testaments* is a basically Jewish document of the second century B.C. that has undergone Christian redaction,[110] then we must reckon with the possibility of

---

[103] *Jos. As.* 15:7.

[104] καὶ καταφεύξονται ἔθνη πολλά ἐπὶ τὸν κύριον ἐν τῇ ἡμέρᾳ ἐκείνῃ καὶ ἔσονται αὐτῷ εἰς λαὸν καὶ κατασκηνώσουσιν ἐν μέσῳ σου. . . .

[105] *Jos. As.* 19:5.

[106] Cf., e. g., 1 Chr 16:31; Ps 46:2–3, 9; Mal 1:14.

[107] Cf., e. g., Josephus *Ant.* 11.203.

[108] Text: M. de JONGE, *The Testaments of the Twelve Patriarchs: A Critical Edition of the Greek Text* (PVTG 1.2; Leiden: Brill, 1978).

[109] Cf., e. g., *T. Sim.* 7:2 (πάντα τὰ ἔθνη καὶ τὸ γένος τοῦ Ἰσραήλ); *T. Ash.* 7:3 (τὸν Ἰσραὴλ καὶ πάντα τὰ ἔθνη); *T. Jos.* 19:6 (πάντα τὰ ἔθνη καὶ τὸν Ἰσραήλ).

[110] One of the central issues in research on the *Testaments* is whether it is basically a Jewish document of the second century B.C. (cf. Jürgen BECKER, *Untersuchungen zur Entstehungsgeschichte der Testamente der Zwölf Patriarchen* [AGJU 3; Leiden: Brill, 1970], p. 25; Howard Clark KEE, "Testaments of the Twelve Patriarchs," *OTP*, 1:777–778; James H. CHARLESWORTH, *The Old Testament Pseudepigrapha and the New Testament: Prolegomena for the Study of Christian Origins* [SNTSMS 54; Cambridge: Cambridge University Press, 1985], p. 40) or a Christian document of about A.D. 200 whose Jewish original, if any, is irrecoverable (cf. M. de JONGE, "The Testaments of the Twelve Patriarchs: Christian and Jewish. A Hundred Years after Friedrich Schnapp," *Nederlands Theologisch Tijdchrift* 39 [1985] 265–275; H.W. HOLLANDER and M. de JONGE, *The Testaments of the Twelve Patriarchs: A Commentary* [SVTP 8; Leiden: Brill, 1985], pp. 83–85).

various uses of the term from different periods. It seems likely, however, that, like the Septuagint, the *Grundschrift* uses ἔθνος in the sense of "nation." This can be seen, for example, from Isaac's instructions to Levi concerning the priesthood in *T. Levi* 9:6–14, which are clearly based on OT and Jewish tradition and are devoid of distinctively "Christian" influence. Included among these instructions is the command that Levi take a wife who is not "of a race of foreigners or of nations" (ἀπὸ γένους ἀλλοφύλων ἢ ἐθνῶν [v. 10]).[111] Although, at first glance, the parallelism between the words ἀλλόφυλος[112] and ἔθνος might seem to indicate that the terms are synonymous and that the latter therefore denotes "Gentiles,"[113] nevertheless, in other examples of this parallelism from Jewish writings of the period, ἔθνη obviously denotes "(foreign) nations."[114] In the following, we shall see that the term occurs in many of the same contexts that were observed in the Greek OT, with a similar interplay between Israel and the other nations.

I. The Table of Nations. In conformity with the general character of the *Testaments* as deathbed exhortations and predictions by the twelve patriarchs of Israel,[115] Benjamin exhorts his sons to keep the commandments of God "until the Lord reveals his salvation to all the nations" (ἕως ὅτε ὁ κύριος ἀποκαλύψῃ τὸ σωτήριον αὐτοῦ πᾶσι τοῖς ἔθνεσιν).[116] "Then," as he goes on to say, "you will see Enoch, Noah and Shem and Abraham and Isaac and Jacob rising on the right hand in gladness" (v. 6). This reference to "all the nations" in the context of the genealogical line leading from Noah[117] and Shem to Jacob reflects the Table-of-Nations tradition. In fact, the line itself seems to be a compression of 1 Chr 1:1–2:2,[118] for *T. Ben.* 10:7 goes on to mention the patriarchs over the twelve tribes of Israel, who conclude the Table of Nations in 1 Chronicles (cf. 1 Chr 2:1–2).

The influence of the Table-of-Nations tradition can also be seen in *T. Sim.* 5:4–7:3, which expects both the final destruction of Israel's enemies (6:3–4b) and the ultimate salvation of all nations and the tribe of Israel through the king who will arise from Judah (7:2). First, the enemies of Israel will be destroyed:

---

[111] Cf. Lev 21:14.

[112] Cf. also *T. Jud.* 22:2.

[113] Cf. HOLLANDER and de JONGE, *The Testaments of the Twelve Patriarchs: A Commentary*, p. 158.

[114] Cf. 1 Chr 18:11 ("And these things David consecrated to the Lord, with the silver and the gold which he took from all the nations [ἐκ πάντων τῶν ἐθνῶν], from Idumea, and Moab, and from the sons of Ammon, and from the foreigners [ἐκ τῶν ἀλλοφύλων], and from Amalek"); Josephus *BJ* 2.412 ("Their forefathers, they said, had adorned the sanctuary mainly at the expense of foreigners [ἐκ τῶν ἀλλοφύλων] and had always accepted the gifts of foreign nations [ἀπὸ τῶν ἔξωθεν ἐθνῶν]"); *Ant.* 8.39; Ep Jer 3–4; *T. Jud.* 22:2.

[115] Cf. HOLLANDER and de JONGE, *The Testaments of the Twelve Patriarchs: A Commentary*, pp. 29–41.

[116] *T. Ben.* 10:5.

[117] For further references to the Flood (ὁ κατακλυσμός), see *T. Rub.* 5:6; *T. Naph.* 3:5; *T. Ben.* 7:4.

[118] Cf. esp. 1 Chr 1:1–4, 17, 24–28, 34.

"Then the seed of Canaan (σπέρμα Χανάαν) will perish, and there will not be a remnant to Amalek, and all the Cappadocians (πάντες οἱ Καππάδοκες) will perish, and all the Hittites (πάντες οἱ Χετταῖοι) will be utterly destroyed. Then the land of Ham (ἡ γῆ Χάμ) will fail and the whole people (πᾶς ὁ λαός) will perish" (6:3—4b). It is interesting to note that all these enemies, except Amalek,[119] are Hamites. Canaan is the son of Ham who was cursed for his father's impropriety.[120] Even the Cappadocians, who have at times been identified as descendants of Japheth,[121] are now usually identified with the Hittites, the descendants of Heth, the son of Canaan (Gen 10:15).[122] This would make good sense in context since the Hittites are mentioned together with the Cappadocians and the seed of Canaan (*T. Sim.* 6:3). In the exposition of the Table of Nations in *Bib. Ant.* 4:7, furthermore, the Cappadocians are listed among the sons of Ham as descendants of Egypt. After the destruction of the Hamites follows a period of peace on earth and glory for Shem (6:4c-5a). With this reference to Shem, we have further evidence of the Table-of-Nations tradition.

II. The Abrahamic Promise. The *Testaments* frequently mention Abraham[123] but not the Abrahamic Promise itself.[124] Israel is not referred to as a "nation" in the *Testaments*.

III. The Covenant with Israel. This is the most developed aspect in the document, for the traditional Sin-Exile-Restoration schema provides the framework for most of the Testaments.[125]

A. The Sin and Exile of Israel. The blessings and the curses of Leviticus 26 and Deuteronomy 28—30 are well known to the *Testaments*. If Naphtali's children do the good, then they will be blessed, "and God will be gloried through you among the nations" (καὶ θεὸς δοξασθήσεται δι' ὑμῶν ἐν τοῖς ἔθνεσι).[126] If, on the other hand, they do evil, then they will be cursed, "and

---

[119] Amalek is considered the grandson of Esau (cf. Gen 36:12, 16) although the Amalekites are mentioned already in the time before Esau (cf. Gen 14:7). The Amalekites lived in the Negev (Num 13:29), bordering the land traditionally ascribed to Canaan (cf. Gen 10:19).

[120] Cf. Gen 9:22—27; 10:6, 15, 18—19.

[121] For example, Josephus identifies the Cappadocians with Meshech (*Ant.* 1.125; cf. Gen 10:2), whereas Hippolytus identifies them with Gomer (*Chron.* 57; cf. Gen 10:2, 3).

[122] Cf., e.g., Claus WESTERMANN, *Genesis* (3 vols.; 3rd ed.; BKAT 1; Neukirchen-Vluyn: Neukirchener Verlag, 1983), 1:696; E. A. SPEISER, *Genesis* (AB 1; Garden City, NY: Doubleday, 1964), p. 69.

[123] Cf. *T. Levi* 6:9; 8:15; 9:12; 15:4; 18:6, 14; 19:5; *T. Jud.* 17:5; 25:1; *T. Dan* 7:2; *T. Naph.* 1:10; *T. Ash.* 7:7; *T. Jos.* 6:7; *T. Ben.* 1:2; 10:4, 6.

[124] *T. Levi* 8:15 refers to the expectation of a "prophet from the seed of Abraham our father." In *T. Levi* 15:4, the patriarch expresses his outlook on the salvation of his descendants: "And if it were not for the sake of Abraham and Isaac and Jacob our fathers, not one of my seed would be left on earth" (cf. *T. Ash.* 7:7). The inheritance of Abraham is the law of the Lord and his commandments (*T. Ben.* 10:4).

[125] On the Sin-Exile-Return (better: Restoration) passages in the *Testaments*, see HOLLANDER and de JONGE, *The Testaments of the Twelve Patriarchs: A Commentary*, pp. 51—56.

[126] *T. Naph.* 8:4.

God will be dishonored among the nations through him" (καὶ ὁ θεὸς ἀδοξήσει ἐν τοῖς ἔθνεσι δι᾽ αὐτοῦ).[127] As Naphtali foretells, however, his sons will "walk according to all the wickedness of the nations" (πορευόμενοι κατὰ πᾶσαν πονηρίαν ἐθνῶν).[128] Many of the patriarchs predict that Israel will indeed sin so grievously that God will thrust them into Exile among the nations, where they will then become a laughingstock.[129] The Levites, for example, will take as wives "daughters of the nations" (θυγατέρες ἐθνῶν),[130] the union with whom will be like Sodom and Gomorrah.[131] For this and other violations, the Levites will be "darkened"[132] and "scattered as captives among the nations" (καὶ διασπαρήσεσθε αἰχμάλωτοι ἐν τοῖς ἔθνεσι), where they will be for a reproach and for a curse.[133] The *T. Levi* 15:1 predicts that they will be captives throughout "all the nations" (καὶ ὑμεῖς αἰχμάλωτοι ἔσεσθε εἰς πάντα τὰ ἔθνη).[134] The descendants of Judah will mingle "in the abominations of the nations" (ἐν βδελύγμασιν ἐθνῶν),[135] which will result both in "their enslavement among the nations" (αὐτῶν δουλείαν ἐν ἔθνεσιν)[136] and in the termination of Judah's kingship "among foreigners" (ἐν ἀλλοφύλοις).[137] For their wickedness, the children of Issachar "will be dispersed among the nations" (καὶ διασπαρήσονται ἐν τοῖς ἔθνεσι) and will serve their enemies.[138] The children of Zebulon will be led captive by their enemies, and they "will be afflicted among the nations with all infirmities and tribulations and anguish of soul" (καὶ κακωθήσεσθε ἐν τοῖς ἔθνεσιν ἐν πάσαις ἀσθενείαις καὶ θλίψεσι καὶ ὀδύναις ψυχῆς).[139] As a result of their sins, the descendants of Dan will be led away into captivity with the sons of Levi and Judah, and there, they will receive all the plagues of Egypt and "all the evils of the nations" (πᾶσα πονηρία τῶν ἐθνῶν).[140] During the time of Israel's lawlessness, the Lord will leave Israel "and pass to the nations who do his will" (καὶ μετελεύσεται ἐπὶ ἔθνη ποιοῦντα τὸ θέλημα αὐτοῦ).[141]

---

[127] *T. Naph.* 8:6.

[128] *T. Naph.* 4:1.

[129] Cf., e.g., *T. Levi* 14:1.

[130] For the expression, see Ezek 32:16; 3 Kgdms 3:11; 1 Esdr 8:66–67.

[131] *T. Levi* 14:6.

[132] Cf. *T. Levi* 14:4, which describes this darkening as bad for "all the nations" (πάντα τὰ ἔθνη) and a curse for Israel; 18:9.

[133] *T. Levi* 10:4; cf. 16:5. See, e.g., Tob 3:4.

[134] Cf. *T. Ash.* 7:3: ". . . and you will be scattered to the four corners of the earth (καὶ ὑμεῖς διασκορπισθήσεσθε εἰς τὰς τέσσαρας γωνίας τῆς γῆς), and you will be in dispersion (καὶ ἔσεσθε ἐν διασπορᾷ)."

[135] For the expression, see *T. Dan.* 5:5; Deut 18:9; 3 Kgdms 14:24; 4 Kgdms 16:3; 21:2; 2 Chr 28:3; 33:2; 36:14; 1 Esdr 7:13.

[136] *T. Jud.* 23:2–3. On Israel's enslavement among the nations, see *T. Iss.* 6:2; *T. Naph.* 4:2; Jer 25:11; 2 Macc 1:27; Josephus *Ap.* 2.125.

[137] *T. Jud.* 22:2.

[138] *T. Iss.* 6:2.

[139] *T. Zeb.* 9:6.

[140] *T. Dan* 5:8. For the expression, see Wisd 10:5.

[141] *T. Dan* 6:6–7; cf. *T. Ben* 9:4. As HOLLANDER and de JONGE (*The Testaments of the Twelve Patriarchs: A Commentary*, p. 292) point out, however, this passage may be the

C. The Restoration of Israel. The *Testaments* emphasize the eschatological Restoration of Israel, often with universalistic tones. In fact, when the *Testaments* use ἔθνος in the context of the Restoration, this universalistic aspect always stands out. Thus the tribe of Dan is exhorted to repent in order that it may be accepted by "the Savior of the nations" (ὁ σωτὴρ τῶν ἐθνῶν).[142] The tribe of Benjamin is exhorted to keep the commandments of God "until the Lord reveals his salvation to all the nations" (ἕως ὅτε ὁ κύριος ἀποκαλύψῃ τὸ σωτήριον αὐτοῦ πᾶσι τοῖς ἔθνεσιν).[143] This will be accomplished through a Benjamite called "a beloved of the Lord," who will enlighten all the nations with a new knowledge (γνῶσιν καινὴν φωτίζων πάντα τὰ ἔθνη).[144] The *T. Jud.* 24:5–6 expects that a stem will arise from the root of Judah, "and in it will arise a rod of righteousness to the nations" (καὶ ἐν αὐτῷ ἀναβήσεται ῥάβδος δικαιοσύνης τοῖς ἔθνεσι)[145] to judge and save all who call upon the Lord.[146] In this connection, the *Testament of Levi* expects that a king from Judah will establish a new priesthood "after the fashion of the nations for all the nations" (κατὰ τὸν τύπον τῶν ἐθνῶν, εἰς πάντα τὰ ἔθνη).[147] This evidently refers to the priesthood of Melchizedek over against that of Moses and Aaron.[148] In that day, the Lord "will turn all the nations to zeal for him" (καὶ ἐπιστρέψει πάντα τὰ ἔθνη εἰς παραζήλωσιν αὐτοῦ).[149] God will save "the nation of Israel" (τὸ γένος Ἰσραήλ) and gather the "righteous from among the nations" (δικαίους ἐκ τῶν ἐθνῶν).[150] That God "will save Israel and all the nations" echoes like a refrain throughout the *Testaments*.[151] According to *T. Ben.* 9:2, the twelve tribes and "all the nations" will be gathered at "the last [Temple],"[152] which will be more glorious than the first.

---

product of Christian influence. On this tradition in early Judaism, see Richard H. BELL, "The Origin and Purpose of the Jealousy Motif in Romans 9–11: A Case Study in the Theology and Technique of Paul" (Dr. theol. diss., University of Tübingen, 1990).

[142] *T. Dan* 6:9.

[143] *T. Ben.* 10:5. Cf. Ps 66:3–5; 97:2–3; Isa 49:6; 52:10.

[144] *T. Ben.* 11:2. HOLLANDER and de JONGE interpret this as a reference to the Apostle Paul, who, according to Phil 3:5, was a Benjamite (cf. *The Testament of the Twelve Patriarchs: A Commentary*, pp. 442–444). The *T. Ben.* 11:3 goes on to state that this beloved Benjamite will be "in the gatherings of the nations" (ἐν συναγωγαῖς ἐθνῶν) until the consummation. For the expression, see Gen 35:11; 48:4; Jer 27:9; Zeph 3:8.

[145] For the expression, see Prov 26:3: οὕτως ῥάβδος ἔθνει παρανόμῳ.

[146] Cf. also *T. Levi* 4:4 ("... the Lord will visit all nations [πάντα τὰ ἔθνη] in the tender mercies of his son forever"); *T. Ben.* 10:9–10.

[147] *T. Levi* 8:14.

[148] Cf. HOLLANDER and de JONGE, *The Testaments of the Twelve Patriarchs: A Commentary*, pp. 154.

[149] *T. Zeb.* 9:8. Cf. Tob 14:6: καὶ πάντα τὰ ἔθνη ἐπιστρέψουσιν ἀληθινῶς φοβεῖσθαι κύριον τὸν θεόν.

[150] *T. Naph.* 8:3. Cf. Tob 13:5 S.

[151] Cf. *T. Ash.* 7:3; *T. Sim.* 7:2; *T. Jos.* 19:6; *T. Ben.* 3:8.

[152] On the gathering of Israel and "all the nations" (πάντα τὰ ἔθνη) to the Temple, see esp. Isa 56:7–8; 66:18–20.

The Epistle of Aristeas.[153] In this document, which stems from Alexandria in Egypt in the second century B. C.,[154] ἔθνος occurs only twice. The first occurrence, in *Ep. Arist.* 36, refers to "the nation of the Egyptians" (τὸ τῶν Αἰγυπτίων ἔθνος). The second occurrence is more important, coming in the context of an explanation of the purpose of the Law: "In his wisdom the legislator [i.e., Moses], in a comprehensive survey of each particular part, and being endowed by God for the knowledge of universal truths, surrounded us with unbroken palisades and iron walls to prevent our mingling with any other nations in any manner (ὅπως μηθενὶ τῶν ἄλλων ἐθνῶν ἐπιμισγώμεθα κατὰ μηδέν),[155] being thus kept pure in body and soul, preserved from false beliefs, and worshipping the only God omnipotent over all creation" (*Ep. Arist.* 139). The subsequent context goes on to make clear that this separation from the nations extends to every area of life: "So, to prevent our being perverted by contact with others or by mixing with bad influences, he hedged us in on all sides with purifications connected with meat and drink and touch and hearing and sight, after the manner of the Law" (v. 142). We are reminded of the many passages in the OT that either admonish Israel not to mingle with the nations or acknowledge that it had already failed in this regard.[156]

Theodotus. Eusebius' *Praeparatio Evangelica* preserves fragments of Theodotus' epic poem, entitled "On the Jews," (9.22.1–11), which stems from the first to second century B. C.[157] Since the extant fragments all pertain to the story of the rape of Jacob's daughter Dinah at Shechem (Genesis 34), which is called a "holy city" (*Pr. Ev.* 9.22.1), this has led to the theory that Theodotus was a Samaritan.[158] Indeed, the only passage in which ἔθνος occurs could be read as betraying Samaritan sympathies, insofar as it refers to giving the ten lost tribes of Israel into the hands of Abraham's descendants:[159]

As Hamor went into the city and encouraged his subjects to be circumcised, one of the sons of Jacob – Simeon by name – decided to kill Hamor and Sychem, since he was unwilling to bear in a civil manner the violent attack upon his sister. When he had decided this, he shared it with his brother. Seizing him, he urged him to agree to the act by producing an oracle which said that God had determined to give ten nations (δέκα ἔθνη) to the descendants of Abraham. Simeon says the following to Levi: For I have indeed

---

153 Text: A. PELLETIER, *Lettre d'Aristée à Philocrate* (SC 89; Paris: Cerf, 1962).

154 Cf. R. J. H. SHUTT, "Letter of Aristeas," *OTP*, 2:8–9.

155 Contrast Eph 2:14–15.

156 Cf., e.g., Josh 23:12–13; 1 Esdr 8:84 ("We turned back again to transgress your Law by mixing with the uncleanness of the nations [ἐθνῶν] of the land"); Ps 105:34–35 ("They did not utterly destroy the nations [τὰ ἔθνη] which the Lord told them to, and they mingled with the nations [ἐν τοῖς ἔθνεσιν] and learned their deeds").

157 Cf. F. FALLON, "Theodotus," *OTP*, 2:785–788.

158 Cf. SCHÜRER, *Hist.*, 3.1:561–562.

159 So J. FREUDENTHAL, *Alexander Polyhistor* (Hellenistische Studien 1.2; Breslau: Skutsch, 1875), pp. 99–100.

learned the word from God, for of old he said that he would give ten nations (δέκ' ἔθνεα) to the children of Abraham.[160]

More likely, however, this is a reference not to the ten lost tribes of Israel but to the ten tribes listed in Gen 15:18–21, which God promised to give to Abraham and his seed.[161] By claiming this promise, Simeon and Levi could justify their slaying the Shechemites, for they would simply be giving the "Canaanites" and "Perizzites" into the hands of Abraham's descendants.

The Psalms of Solomon. This collection of psalms probably stems from the first century B. C. in Jerusalem.[162] Of the 22 occurrences of ἔθνος in the *Psalms of Solomon*, almost all are plural.[163] Very likely, all of the occurrences of the term are used in the sense of foreign "nation(s)", as distinguished from Israel. That the term is not used in the sense of "Gentile(s)" can be shown by several observations. First, as in the Greek OT, ἔθνος sometimes stands in parallel to λαός.[164] Second, ἔθνη ἀλλότρια in *Pss. Sol.* 2:2 must mean "foreign nations"[165] rather than "Gentile foreigners."[166] Third, the *Psalms of Solomon* use other terms for "foreigners."[167] Fourth, a number of passages either allude to OT texts in which ἔθνος denotes "nation" or else use biblical language.[168] Despite the relative infrequency of the term in the *Psalms of Solomon*, ἔθνος is used in all three contexts that we observed in the OT.

I. The Table of Nations. Although there is no direct reference to the Table of Nations in the *Psalms of Solomon*, the tradition seems to influence the text at several points. In *Pss. Sol.* 8:23, "the nations of the earth" (τὰ ἔθνη τῆς γῆς) gives the worldwide scope of the work.[169] Furthermore, the psalmist declares that "the Diaspora of Israel [is/was] among every nation (ἐν παντὶ ἔθνει), according to the saying of God" (*Pss. Sol.* 9:2; cf. Deut 30:3–4). Most significantly, *Pss. Sol.* 17:31 expects "nations (ἔθνη) to come from the ends of the earth to see his [sc. the Messiah's] glory, to bring as gifts (δῶρα) her [Jerusalem's] sons who had been driven out. . . ." This alludes to Isa 66:18–20,

---

[160] Eusebius *Pr. Ev.* 9.22.8–9, as translated by F. FALLON, "Theodotus," *OTP*, 2:792–793.

[161] Cf. Carl R. HOLLADAY, *Fragments from Hellenistic Jewish Authors, Vol. 2: Poets* (SBLTT 30; SBLPS 12; Atlanta, GA: Scholars Press, 1989), pp. 62–63, 187–188.

[162] Cf. R. B. WRIGHT, "Psalms of Solomon," *OTP*, 2:640–642.

[163] Cf., however, *Pss. Sol.* 7:6.

[164] Cf. *Pss. Sol.* 9:2; 17:29, 30.

[165] Cf. Ex 21:8; Sir 29:18; 36:1–2; 39:4; 49:5; Bar 4:3; Josephus *Ant.* 8.191; 9.16.

[166] Contra WRIGHT, "Psalms of Solomon," *OTP*, 2:652, ἔθνη is not used as an adjective.

[167] Cf. *Pss. Sol.* 17:28 (πάροικος καὶ ἀλλογενής).

[168] *Pss. Sol.* 1:8 (cf. 4 Kgdms 21:9); 2:19 (cf. Zech 12:3; 1 Macc 4:60), 22 (cf. Zech 12:9; 14:2, 16); 8:13 (cf. 4 Kgdms 21:9), 30 (cf. Isa 16:8); 9:2 (cf. Deut 30:3–4; 2 Macc 1:27), 9 (cf. Deut 7:6; 10:15); 17:3 (cf. Ps 46:9), 14 (cf. 4 Kgdms 17:29), 22 (cf. Zech 12:3), 24 (cf. Deut 4:38; 12:29; 31:3; 33:18), 25 (cf. Zech 2:15; 1 Macc 4:14), 29 (cf. Isa 2:4; Mic 4:3; Ps 66:5; 95:10; 105:6; Wisd 3:8), 30 (cf. 2 Esdr 9:11; Ezek 31:12; Ps 71:11; Gen 27:29), 31 (cf. Isa 2:2–3; Isa 49:22; 66:18).

[169] The parallel term πᾶσα ἡ γῆ in v. 24 militates against translating the expression "the nations of the land." See also *Pss. Sol.* 17:30.

which, as we have seen, supplies a *pars pro toto* list of "all nations and tongues" (πάντα τὰ ἔθνη καὶ τὰς γλώσσας), based on the Table-of-Nations tradition, that God will gather and to which God will send surviving exiles, so that " from all the nations" (ἐκ πάντων τῶν ἐθνῶν) their exiled "brethren" will be brought back to Jerusalem as a "gift" (δῶρον) to the Lord (v. 20).

II. The Abrahamic Promise. There is one direct reference to the Abrahamic Promise of nationhood. Alluding to Deut 10:15,[170] the psalmist declares: "For you chose the seed of Abraham above all the nations (παρὰ πάντα τὰ ἔθνη), and you put your name upon us, Lord, and it will not cease forever" (*Pss. Sol.* 9:9). As we shall see, this becomes the basis of the psalmist's petition for Restoration.

III. The Covenant with Israel.

A. The Sin and Exile of Israel. The establishment of the covenant with Israel – "the sons of the covenant"[171] – and the settlement of the Land are simply presupposed in the *Psalms of Solomon*. However, the text does emphasize the Exile, which resulted from the nation's sin. Thus *Pss. Sol.* 2:6–7 laments: "The sons and daughters [are/were] in harsh captivity, their neck in a seal, a spectacle among the nations (ἐν τοῖς ἔθνεσιν). He did this to them in accordance with their sins, so that he abandoned them to the hands of those who prevailed." For the psalmist, the situation of "Exile" still continues in the time after Pompey's capture of Jerusalem in 63 B.C.[172] Therefore, he expresses the situation in terms of the traditional "doxology of judgment,"[173] which acknowledges the righteousness of God for his continuing judgment on the nation: "The Diaspora of Israel is among every nation (ἐν παντὶ ἔθνει), according to the word of God, that in your righteousness you might be justified, O God, in our lawless deeds. For you are a righteous judge over all the peoples of the earth (ἐπὶ πάντας τοὺς λαοὺς τῆς γῆς)."[174] The only thing left for Israel to do in this situation is to pray

---

[170] πλὴν τοὺς πατέρας ὑμῶν προείλατο κύριος ἀγαπᾶν αὐτοὺς καὶ ἐχελέξατο τὸ σπέρμα αὐτῶν μετ' αὐτοὺς ὑμᾶς *παρὰ πάντα τὰ ἔθνη* κατὰ τὴν ἡμέραν ταύτην.

[171] Cf. *Pss. Sol.* 17:15.

[172] For references to this capture, see *Pss. Sol.* 1:8; 2:2 ("Foreign nations [ἔθνη ἀλλότρια] went up to your altar; they arrogantly trampled [it] with their sandals"), 19; 8:13; 17:14–15 ("So he [sc. the lawless one who invaded Judea (cf. v. 11)] did in Jerusalem all the things that the nations [τὰ ἔθνη] do for their gods in their cities. And the sons of the covenant [living] among the rabble of the nations [ἐθνῶν] adopted these [practices].").

[173] The term stems from Gerhard von RAD, "Gerichtsdoxologie," in *Gesammelte Studien zum Alten Testament* (2 vols.; ed. Rudolf Smend; München: Chr. Kaiser Verlag, 1973), 2:245–254. Von RAD argues that the "doxologies of judgment" in Daniel 9; Ezra 9; Nehemiah 9; and Bar 1:15–3:8, containing unmistakable Deuteronomistic language, reflect groups who felt the catastrophe of 587 B.C. as an undiminished reality, for, although 587 had long passed, they considered themselves still under the judgment of Yahweh. On the presence of this tradition in *Pss. Sol.* 9:2, see O.H. STECK, *Israel und das gewaltsame Geschick der Propheten. Untersuchungen zur Überlieferung des deuteronomistischen Geschichtsbildes im Alten Testament, Spätjudentum und Urchristentum* (WMANT 23; Neukirchen-Vluyn: Neukirchener Verlag, 1967), pp. 170–171.

[174] *Pss. Sol.* 9:2; cf. 17:3.

for the deliverance based on God's mercy and the eternal Abrahamic Promise.[175]

B. The Restoration of Israel. Since the *Psalms of Solomon* assume that the situation of Exile persists into the present, they refer only to the eschatological Restoration. In the future, the son of David will "cleanse Jerusalem from the nations (ἀπὸ ἐθνῶν) who trample her to destruction" and "drive out sinners from the inheritance" (*Pss. Sol.* 17:22−23; cf. v. 30). As in the OT, *Psalms of Solomon* 17 expresses both positive and negative attitudes toward the nations and their fate at the time of the Restoration. On the one hand, the nations are to be destroyed[176] and to have no place among the regathered people of Israel.[177] On the other hand, the nations are expected to make a pilgrimage to Jerusalem, bringing the exiles with them,[178] and to experience the mercy of the Davidic king.[179] He will judge "peoples and nations" (λαοὺς καὶ ἔθνη) in the wisdom of his righteousness, and he will have "peoples of nations" (λαοὺς ἐθνῶν)[180] serving under his yoke.[181]

Philo.[182] Of the 280 occurrences of ἔθνος in the works of Philo of Alexandria,[183] the majority are used of "the nation of the Jews" (τὸ Ἰουδαίων

---

[175] Cf. *Pss. Sol.* 8:30; 9:8−11; also 7:6.

[176] Cf. *Pss. Sol.* 17:24: Undergird the son of David "... to shatter all their substance with an iron rod; to destroy the unlawful nations [ἔθνη παράνομα] with the word of his mouth."

[177] Cf. *Pss. Sol.* 17:30: "He [sc. the Davidic king] will distribute them [the regathered people of Israel] upon the land according to their tribes; the alien and the foreigner will no longer live near them."

[178] Cf. *Pss. Sol.* 17:31 (cited above). According to one rabbinic perspective, "the nations have part in the world to come" (*t. Sanh.* 13:2, a statement by the Tannaite Rabbi Eliezer).

[179] Cf. *Pss. Sol.* 17:34: "He will be merciful to all the nations before him in fear."

[180] Whereas HARE and HARRINGTON argue that in such a construction ἐθνῶν would be redundant unless it means "non-Jewish mankind, i.e. Gentiles" ("'Make Disciples of All the Gentiles' [Mt 28:19]," pp. 360−361), λαοὺς καὶ ἔθνη in v. 29 shows that "nations" are in view.

[181] *Pss. Sol.* 17:29−30; cf. Ps. 71:8−11.

[182] Cf. Naoto UMEMOTO, "Juden, 'Heiden' und das Menschengeschlecht in der Sicht Philons von Alexandria," in *Die Heiden. Juden, Christen und das Problem des Fremden*, pp. 22−51, a shortened version of a more extensive study soon to be published; Francis SCHMIDT, "Idée de 'nation' et sentiment d'appartenance au peuple dans le Judaïsme de l'époque hellénistique et romaine," *Annuaire de l'École Pratique des Hautes Études, Vᵉ Section (Sciences religieuses)* 85 (1975−76) 323−329 (here pp. 323−326). On Philo's idea of Jewish nationalism in the sense of the movement for independence from foreign rule, see Ray BARRACLOUGH, "Philo's Politics. Roman Rule and Hellenistic Judaism," in *ANRW* II.21.1 (ed. Wolfgang Haase; Berlin/New York: de Gruyter, 1984), pp. 417−553 (here pp. 476−486).

[183] For the statistics, see UMEMOTO, "Juden, 'Heiden' und das Menschengeschlecht in der Sicht Philos," pp. 23−24.

ἔθνος), [184] or simply "the nation" (τὸ ἔθνος), [185] "our nation," [186] etc., whether it is located in Palestine or the Diaspora. [187] Although Philo never uses the term in the sense of "Gentile(s)," he does use it in reference to other nations [188] and sometimes even to all nations apart from Israel. [189] As we will see in the following survey, the interplay between Israel and the other nations of the world that was observed in the Septuagint also finds expression in Philo.

I. The Table of Nations. Philo has very few direct references to Genesis 10 [190]

---

[184] Cf., e.g., *Mos.* 1.7; *Decal.* 96; *Spec. Leg.* 2.166; 4.244; *Flacc.* 170. Philo's use of this name for the nation is sometimes quite anachronistic: "The most ancient member of the nation of the Jews was a Chaldean by birth" (*Virt.* 212; cf. also *Mos.* 1.7, despite Solomon ZEITLIN, "The Jews: Race, Nation or Religion – Which? A Study Based on the Literature of the Second Jewish Commonwealth," *JQR* N. S. 26 [1935–36] 313–347 [here pp. 335–336]). Only once is the "nation" called Israel: "Its high position is shown by the name; for the nation is called in the Hebrew tongue Israel, which, being translated, is 'He who sees God'" (*Abr.* 57). As Peder BORGEN points out, one of the basic questions in Philonic research is to determine the relationship in Philo's thinking between the concrete Jewish nation and his universal and abstract (mystical) notions about it ("Philo of Alexandria. A Critical and Synthetic Survey of Research since World War II," in *ANRW* II.21.1 [ed. Wolfgang Haase; Berlin/New York: de Gruyter, 1984], pp. 98–154 [here pp. 113–115]). BORGEN argues that "the Jewish nation was the life-setting for his philosophical and mystical ideas" (ibid., p. 115).

[185] Cf., e.g., *Quis Her.* 174; *Mut.* 191; *Mos.* 1.4 ("some of the elders of the nation"), 71; 2.250; *Virt.* 42 (Moses as "the leader of the nation"); *Legat.* 373.

[186] Cf., e.g., *Decal.* 1.

[187] See further below on the "populous nation" motif.

[188] Cf., e.g., *Leg. All.* 3.187 ("Amelek the first of the nations"); *Abr.* 188 ("the nation of the Chaldeans"); *Mos.* 1.263 ("all the Asian nations"); *Virt.* 34 (the Arabs as "a very populous nation").

[189] Cf., e.g., *Mos.* 1.278 ("But I [sc. Balaam] shall not be able to harm the people which shall dwell alone, not reckoned among other nations...");*Abr.* 98 (Israel as "the dearest of the nations to God"); *Mos.* 2.271 (before the Golden Calf incident, Israel "had excelled every nation in clearness of vision"); *Legat.* 116–117, 240 ("our right to be treated no worse than all the nations"); *Spec. Leg.* 4.179 ("... the whole nation of the Jews is in the position of an orphan compared with all the nations on every side"). UMEMOTO underplays the ethnic distinction between Israel and the other nations, emphasizing instead that Philo interprets "Israel" anthropologically as the "Verkörperung der Wesensbestimmung der Menschheit ..., die Gott für jedes Volk gelten läßt" ("Juden, 'Heiden' und das Menschengeschlecht in der Sicht Philos," p. 22).

[190] According to J. ALLENBACH, ed., et al., *Biblia Patristica: Index des citations et allusions bibliques dans la littérature patristique, Supplément: Philon d'Alexandrie* (Paris: Centre National de la Recherche Scientifique, 1982), p. 39, Philo refers to Genesis 10 in two passages: *Quaest. Gen.* 2.79, 80, 81, 82 (on Gen 10:1, 4–5, 6, 8–9, respectively) and *Gig.* 66–67 (on Gen 10:8, 10). In *Quaest. Gen.* 2.79, Philo answers the question, "Why, among the three sons of Noah, does Ham always appear in the middle, while the extremes vary? When they are born, Shem is mentioned first, as follows: 'Shem, Ham, and Japheth' [Gen 10:1; cf. also *Quaest. Gen.* 2.65 on Gen 9:18–19], but when they beget children, Japheth is put first in order, and the family begins to reckon from Japheth [Gen 10:2]?" In *Quaest. Gen.* 2.80, he answers the question, "Why do 'the Kittians and Rhodians and the islands of the Gentiles' (spring) from Japheth [Gen 10:4–5]?" In *Quaest. Gen.* 2.81, "Why is Ham's eldest son Cush [Gen 10:6]?" In *Quaest. Gen.* 2.82, "Why did Cush beget Nimrod, who began to be 'a giant hunter' before the Lord, wherefore they said, 'like Nimrod a giant hunter before God'' [Gen 10:8–9]?" The passage in *Gig.* 66–67 also concerns Nimrod and his kingdom Babylon (Gen

and nothing like the exposition of the Table of Nations in Josephus.[191] Nevertheless, the influence of the Table-of-Nations tradition can be demonstrated at several points. First, Philo develops the idea that God established the bounds of the nations (Deut 32:8)[192] and that people were separated into different nations,[193] which clearly presupposes the Table-of-Nations tradition. Although, unlike the OT itself, Philo assumes the existence of "nations" even before the Flood,[194] these nations were destroyed by the Deluge, making it necessary for Noah and his sons to establish new nations in their place.[195]

Second, Philo's cosmological frame of reference recalls the Table-of-Nations tradition. The universe is divided into four basic parts (τὰ μέρη τοῦ παντός): earth (γῆ), sea (θάλαττα), air (ἀήρ), and heaven (οὐρανός).[196] The earth, in turn, is divided into a hierarchy that Philo calls an "orderly series,"[197] proceeding from specific to general: individual men (ἄνδρες),[198] families/households (οἶκοι), cities (πόλεις), countries and nations (χῶραι καὶ ἔθνη),[199] and major

---

10:8, 10). On this, see further Pieter W. van der Horst, "Nimrod after the Bible," in *Essays on the Jewish World of Early Christianity* (NTOA 14; Freiburg: Universitätsverlag; Göttingen: Vandenhoeck & Ruprecht, 1990), pp. 220–232.

[191] Cf., however, *Virt.* 34, which shows Philo recognized that contemporary Gentilics had biblical counterparts: "The Arabians, whose name in the old times was Midianites...." According to Maier, "Philo von Alexandrien, der ansonsten die Anfangskapitel der Genesis nicht nur intensiv ausdeutet sondern überhaupt zur Darlegung seines Denkens benützt, hat Gen 10 mit seiner Thematik offenbar *bewußt ausgeklammert*" ("Japhetiten," p. 186 [emphasis mine]).

[192] Cf. *Post.* 89, 91; *Plant.* 59–60; *Congr.* 58.

[193] Cf. *Conf.* 10.

[194] Whereas Genesis does not refer to "nations" until after the Flood (chap. 10), Philo considers that the time of Noah before the Flood "bore its harvest of iniquities, and every country and nation (πᾶσα χώρα καὶ ἔθνος) and city and household and every private individual was filled with evil practices..." (*Abr.* 40). Similarly, 4 Ezra 3:7–10 presupposes the existence of antediluvian nations: "From him [sc. Adam] there sprang nations and tribes, peoples and clans, without number. And every nation walked after its own will and did ungodly things before you and scorned you, and you did not hinder them. But again, in its time you brought the Flood upon the inhabitants of the world and destroyed them. And the same fate befell them: As death came upon Adam, so the flood upon them."

[195] Cf. *Abr.* 56, where, in contrast to Adam, who is the first man and father of all that were born up to the Deluge, Noah is the father of the new race of men that would spring up afresh. Likewise, in 2 Enoch 70:10, God promises to make another world rise up from Noah's seed.

[196] Cf. *Flacc.* 123; *Abr.* 43; *Somn.* 1.135.

[197] Cf. *Praem.* 7. For this series, see also *Ebr.* 34; *Mig.* 120; *Gig.* 51; *Conf.* 46; *Somn.* 1.177; 2.287; *Plant.* 67–68; *Abr.* 40; *Jos.* 56, 134; *Mos.* 2.19–20; *Spec. Leg.* 2.82; *Virt.* 119; *Legat.* 48, 116.

[198] Individuals are divided into two classes: "fellow-countryman" and "alien" (cf. *Spec. Leg.* 2.123). The proselyte, however, was considered a full-fledged member of the nation of the Jews and was to be treated as such (cf. *Virt.* 103).

[199] Does this imply a distinction between χώρα and ἔθνος, as Zeitlin suggests ("The Jews," p. 336 n. 81), or are the terms basically synonymous, as often in the Septuagint? The nations are divided equally into two classes: "Greek" and "barbarian" (ἔθνη βαρβαρικά τε καὶ ἑλληνικά). Cf. *Cher.* 91; *Legat.* 8; *Jos.* 134; *Mos.* 2.20, 27; *Quod Omn. Prob.* 138; *Plant.* 67; *Legat.* 8. Philo seems to include the Jews among the "barbarians" (cf. *Mos.* 2.27).

regions/climates (κλίματα γῆς μεγάλα).[200] Clearly, this hierarchy reflects the general structure of the Table of Nations.[201]

Two concrete examples of this hierarchy can be adduced from *De Legatione ad Gaium* in order to show how Philo appropriates the Table-of-Nations tradition. In the first example, Philo remonstrates against Gaius' bid for universal sovereignty. For, already lawful ruler of the whole earth,[202] Gaius exceeded the bounds of human propriety by seeking to be worshipped as a god in the Jerusalem Temple and thereby to include the whole universe within his domain:

> Do you a mere man seek to annex also ether and heaven, not satisfied with the sum of so many mainlands, islands, nations (ἔθνη), regions, over which you assumed sovereignty, and do you deem God worthy of nothing in our world here below, no country (χώρα), no city, but even this tiny area hallowed for him and sanctified by oracles and divine messengers you propose to take away, so that in the circumference (περίβολος) of this great earth no trace or reminder should be left of the reverence and honor due to the truly existing veritable God?[203]

---

[200] This means the "continents" of Europe, Asia, and Libya (cf. *Legat.* 283; *Jos.* 134; *Legat.* 48, 144). Thus, Philo refers to "all the nations of Asia" (*Mos.* 1.263). The inhabited world is further divided into two types: "mainland" and "island" (cf. *Jos.* 134; *Mos.* 2.19–20; *Legat.* 283, 347).

[201] The Table of Nations begins with individual men (Shem, Ham, and Japheth) and their families, who, in turn, found cities (e.g., Nineveh, Rehoboth-ir, Calah, Resen, Sidon, Gerar, Gaza, Sodom, Gomorrah, Admah, and Zeboiim) and nations. The Table-of-Nations tradition in *Jubilees* 8–9 includes both the three continents and the three climatic zones (i.e., cold, hot, and temperate).

[202] Cf. *Legat.* 8, 10: "For who that saw Gaius when after the death of Tiberius he succeeded to the sovereignty of the whole earth and sea (τὴν ἡγεμονίαν πάσης γῆς καὶ θαλάσσης), gained not by faction but established by law, with all parts, east, west, south, north, harmoniously adjusted, the Greek in full agreement with the barbarian, the civil with the military, to enjoy and participate in peace – who I say was not filled with admiration and astonishment at his prodigious and indescribable prosperity? [. . .] (10) . . . a dominion not confined to the really vital parts which make up most of the inhabited world (οἰκουμένη), and indeed may properly bear that name, the world, that is, which is bounded by the two rivers, the Euphrates and the Rhine, the one dissevering us from the Germans and all the more brutish nations (θηριωδέστερα ἔθνη), the Euphrates from the Parthians and from the Sarmatians and Scythians, races which are no less savage than the Germans, but a dominion extending, as I said above, from the rising to the setting sun both within the ocean and beyond it. All these things were a joy to the Roman people and all Italy and the Asian and European nations ('Ασιανὰ καὶ Εὐρωπαῖα ἔθνη)." Contrast the situation before Augustus brought in law and order (*Legat.* 143–147). Compare P. R. Hardie's description of the Chigi relief, which depicts the figures of Europe and Asia on either side of, and supporting, a round shield upon which is shown the decisive victory of Alexander the Great over Darius at the battle of Arbela, by means of which Alexander realized his ambition of rule over both continents, i.e. the *oikoumene* ("Imago mundi: Cosmological and Ideological Aspects of the Shield of Achilles," *JHS* 105 [1985] 11–31 [here esp. pp. 29–30]).

[203] *Legat.* 347; cf. *Plant.* 67–68; Isa 14:13; *Pss. Sol.* 1:4–5. Philo accuses the Egyptians of doing much the same thing when they worship the earth (cf. *Mos.* 2.194). In contrast, the Jews were the only nation in the whole inhabited world that refused to worship Gaius: "For all others, men, women, cities, nations, countries, regions of the earth, I might almost say the whole inhabited world . . . magnified him out of all proportion and augmented his vanity. [. . .]

From this example we see that Philo not only appropriates the same hierarchy as that in the Table-of-Nations tradition, he also contains the same focus on Jerusalem as the center.

In the second example, again dealing with Gaius' proposed violation of the Jerusalem Temple, the centrality of Jerusalem in Philo's appropriation of the Table-of-Nations tradition comes out even more strongly. In his account of the events, Philo includes Agrippa I's initial, horrified reaction to the plan (*Legat.* 261–275) and his alleged letter to Gaius appealing for consideration of the Jewish nation, the city of Jerusalem, and the Temple (§§ 276–329).[204] Agrippa introduces himself in the letter as one who is personally affected by Gaius' plan to violate the Jerusalem Temple, for he was "born a Jew,"[205] his "native city" (πατρίς) is Jerusalem, and his ancestors were "kings, most of whom also held the office of high priest . . . ." (§§ 278–279). "As my lot is cast in such a nation (ἔθνος), city and Temple," writes Agrippa, "I beseech you for them all" (§ 279). Then, reiterating that Jerusalem is his πατρίς,[206] Agrippa goes on to state that Jerusalem is also the μητρόπολις of the Jewish Diaspora scattered throughout the world (§§ 281–283).

Agrippa asserts that Jerusalem is "the mother city not of one country Judea but also of most of the others in virtue of the colonies (ἀποικίαι) sent out at various times . . ." (*Legat.* 281). In describing the places to which these Jewish colonies had been sent, Agrippa proceeds systematically according to three categories, supplying in the process a *pars pro toto* table of nations:[207]

One nation only standing apart, the nation of the Jews, was suspected of intending opposition..." (cf. *Legat.* 116–117).

[204] On the Philonic authorship of Agrippa's letter to Gaius, see Daniel R. Schwartz, *Agrippa I: The Last King of Judaea* (Texte und Studien zum Antiken Judentum 23; Tübingen: Mohr-Siebeck, 1990), pp. 179, 200–202; Solomon Zeitlin, "Did Agrippa write a letter to Gaius Caligula?" *JQR* N.S. 56 (1965) 22–31. On Agrippa's intervention in the affair, see Schwartz, *Agrippa I*, pp. 77–89.

[205] Although Agrippa was in fact three quarters Idumaean and only one quarter Jewish by descent, Schwartz argues that Agrippa could legitimately claim to be Jewish, since his father, if not his grandfather, was probably born to parents who were Jews by conversion (*Agrippa I*, pp. 219–222).

[206] Both at the beginning and at the end of the section.

[207] In the following, the systematic progression between parts of the list is somewhat marred by the apparent lack of order within the individual parts, especially in the description of the distant lands. This hodgepodge is, however, paralleled in other lists. In 1 Macc 15:22–23, for example, the Hellenistic cities and states to which the Roman circular of 139 B.C. is addressed are listed in fairly random order: "He [sc. Lucius, consul of the Romans (cf. v. 16)] wrote the same thing [i.e., a letter prohibiting rulers from harming the Jewish people or from making war against them and their cities and their country or from making alliances with those who war against them; cf. v. 19] to King Demetrius and to Attalus and Ariarathes and Arsaces, and to all the countries, and to Sampsames, and to the Spartans, and to Delos, and to Myndos, and to Sicyon, and to Caria, and to Samos, and to Pamphylia, and to Lycia, and to Halicarnassus, and to Rhodes, and to Phaselis, and to Cos, and to Side, and to Aradus and Gortyna and Cnidus and Cyprus and Cyrene." On 1 Macc 15:22–23, see further Maier, "Japhetiten," pp. 164–167.

The Mainlands (αἱ ἤπειροι μεσταί) [in relative distance from both Jerusalem and the χώρα Ἰουδαία]:
Neighboring lands (αἱ ὅμοροι [χῶραι]): Egypt, Phoenicia, and Syria
Distant lands (αἱ πόρρω διῳκισμέναι [χῶραι]):
  • [Asia Minor:] Pamphylia, Cilicia, most of Asia up to Bithynia, and the
    corners of Pontus,
  • Europe: Thessaly, Boeotia, Macedonia, Aetolia, Attica, Argos, Corinth,
    and most of the best parts of Peloponnese
The most highly esteemed of the Islands (νῆσοι): Euboea, Cyprus, and Crete
The Countries beyond the Euphrates: all (Babylon is explicitly mentioned) except for a
  very few.

From this survey of the Diaspora, Agrippa concludes that if Gaius shows
goodwill to his πατρίς (i.e., Jerusalem), "the benefit extends not to one city but
to myriads of others situated *in every region of the inhabited world* (καθ᾽
ἕκαστον κλίμα τῆς οἰκουμένης) ..." (§ 283).[208] Agrippa explains what he
means by "every region of the inhabited world," again using three categories
(this time overlapping categories): (1) Europe, Asia, and Libya;[209] (2) the
mainlands and the islands; (3) the seaboard and the inland. With this pleonasm,
Agrippa obviously wants to stress that Jewish colonies sent out from Jerusalem
are found in the whole inhabited world.[210] A comparison of Agrippa's table of

---

[208] Cf. *Legat.* 284: "through every part of the inhabited world" (διὰ πάντων τῶν τῆς
οἰκουμένης μερῶν).

[209] Libya, the Greek word for Africa, is a geographical term for the continent when it occurs
in the context of the tripartite division of the inhabited world. Philo mentions this tripartite
division one other time in his writings, in a circumlocution for the whole world (cf. *Somn.*
2.54). Dio Chrysostomus reports that Alexander "did not care to live at all unless he might be
king of Europe, Asia, Libya, and any islands which might lie in the Ocean" (*Or.* 4.49); in other
words, king of the whole world. Erotian, a medical writer of the first century A.D., refers to
the three continents as τὰ τρία κλίματα τῆς οἰκουμένης (*Vocum Hippocraticarum* 91.11).
Strab. *Geogr.* 17.3.25 describes the organization of the Roman Empire as having two parts –
one for Caesar (imperial provinces) and another for the people (senatorial provinces), the
latter type of which is further subdivided into two varieties according to the three continents:
consular provinces in Libya and Asia and praetorial provinces in Europe. Plutarch relates that
Pompey celebrated his first triumph over Libya, his second over Europe, and his last over Asia
so that he seemed to have included "the whole world" in his three triumphs (*Pomp.* 45.5). We
may compare the world map of Marcus Vipsanius Agrippa, an official Roman map that was
executed in marble under Augustus and may have included a threefold division of the world
into Europe, Asia, and Africa (cf. O. A. W. DILKE, "Maps in the Service of the State: Roman
Cartography to the End of the Augustan Era," in *Cartography in Prehistoric, Ancient, and
Medieval Europe and the Mediterranean* [ed. J. B. Harley and David Woodward; The History
of Cartography 1; Chicago/London: University of Chicago Press, 1987], pp. 201–211 [here
pp. 207–209]; see further SCHÜRER, *Hist.*, 1:409–410).

[210] The concept of a worldwide Diaspora goes back to the OT (cf., e.g., Deut 28:64: καὶ
διασπερεῖ σε κύριος ὁ θεός σου εἰς πάντα τὰ ἔθνη ἀπ᾽ ἄκρου τῆς γῆς ἕως ἄκρου τῆς γῆς) and
continues into the Roman era. Cf. Harald HEGERMANN, "The Diaspora in the Hellenistic
Age," in *The Cambridge History of Judaism, Vol. 2: The Hellenistic Age*, pp. 115–166 (here
p. 149): "At the outset of the Roman era there is a prevailing impression that the Jews are to be
found all over the world. 'There is no part of the earth that has not admitted this people or been
possessed by them' (thus Strabo in Josephus, *Antiquitates Judaicae* xiv.7.2). 'Land and sea are

nations with Josephus' exposition of the biblical Table of Nations reveals a number of similarities. Besides the obvious overlap in the nations listed,[211] both texts divide the world into three continents (Europe, Asia, Libya), and both consider the Euphrates as the boundary of a territory lying to the east of it.[212]

In Agrippa's description of the Jewish Diaspora, Jerusalem is seen not only as the center of world Judaism but also as the center of the world itself.[213] The orientation of lands and peoples is relative to Jerusalem,[214] and the general movement of the list is counterclockwise around the eastern Mediterranean, with Jerusalem in the middle. Jerusalem is the μητρόπολις, which is used in the double sense of "mother city" (in contrast to πατρίς)[215] and, especially, of

full of them' (*the Sibylline Oracles* [3.271], circa 140 B.C.E.)." According to Josephus *BJ* 2.398, Agrippa II points out to his Jewish audience in Jerusalem that "there is not a people in the inhabited world which does not contain a portion of our people." To match this saturation of the earth with the Jewish nation is the worldwide respect for Jewish institutions: "They attract and win attention of all, of barbarians, of Greeks, of dwellers on the mainland and islands, of nations of the east and the west, of Europe and Asia, of the whole inhabited world from end to end" (Philo *Mos.* 2.19–20).

[211] E.g., Αἴγυπτος, Φοινίκη, Συρία, Κιλικία, Μακεδονία, Κύπρος, Βαβυλών.

[212] In Josephus *Ant.* 1.143, Shem's sons are said to have "inhabited Asia as far as the Indian Ocean, beginning at the Euphrates." In *Legat.* 282, Philo declares through the alleged letter of Agrippa that he says nothing of the countries "beyond the Euphrates." Of course, this could also be due to the fact that the Euphrates formed the eastern frontier of the Roman Empire (cf. Philo *Legat.* 10; Josephus *BJ* 2.363). Note also that both tables employ the wording τῆς 'Ασίας ἄρχι (cf. Philo *Legat.* 281; Josephus *Ant.* 1.122).

[213] Hence, Agrippa's description of the world from a Jewish perspective differs radically from his wife's depiction of the world on a tapestry presented to Gaius to celebrate the universal sovereignty of the Roman emperor (see my article, "Luke's Geographical Horizon," in *The Book of Acts in Its First Century Setting, Vol. 2: The Book of Acts in Its Graeco-Roman Setting* [ed. David W.J. Gill and Conrad Gempf; Grand Rapids: Eerdmans; Carlisle: Paternoster, 1994], pp. 483–544 [here p. 495]).

[214] Note that neither Rome nor Italy is mentioned here.

[215] On the relationship between πατρίς and μητρόπολις in Philo's political terminology, see Aryeh KASHER, *The Jews in Hellenistic and Roman Egypt: The Struggle for Equal Rights* (Texte und Studien zum Antiken Judentum 7; Tübingen: Mohr-Siebeck, 1985), pp. 232–261; idem, "Jerusalem as 'Metropolis' in Philo's National Consciousness," *Cathedra* 11 (1979) 5–56 (Hebrew; English summary), who discusses especially the parallel passages to *Legat.* 281–283 in *Flacc.* 46 and *Conf.* 77–78. Philo uses μητρόπολις in the sense of a πόλις that, because of overpopulation, has sent out a portion of its population to another region, where this group forms a colony, its new "fatherland" (πατρίς), which still maintains ties to the "mother city." Cf. also Berndt SCHALLER, "Philon von Alexandreia und das 'Heilige Land,'" in *Das Land Israel in biblischer Zeit. Jerusalem-Symposium 1981 der Hebräischen Universität und der Georg-August-Universität* (ed. Georg Strecker; GTA 25; Göttingen: Vandenhoeck & Ruprecht, 1983) pp. 172–187 (here pp. 174, 186 n. 51); Hermann LICHTENBERGER, "'Im Lande Israel zu wohnen, wiegt alle Gebote der Tora auf'. Die Heiligkeit des Landes und die Heiligung des Lebens," in *Die Heiden. Juden, Christen und das Problem des Fremden*, pp. 92–107 (here esp. pp. 92–93); Shalom ROSENBERG, "The Link to the Land of Israel in Jewish Thought: A Clash of Perspectives," in *The Land of Israel: Jewish Perspectives* (ed. Lawrence A. Hoffman; University of Notre Dame Center for the Study of Judaism and Christianity in Antiquity 6; Notre Dame: University of Notre Dame, 1986), pp. 139–169 (here pp. 141–146).

"capital city"[216] of the whole world,[217] for Isa 1:26 foresees that after the judgment of Exile, Jerusalem will be called "the faithful Metropolis Zion" (μητρόπολις πιστὴ Σιών), in a context that portrays Zion as "the highest of the mountains," to which "all nations" (πάντα τὰ ἔθνη) will come (Isa 2:2), and as "in the middle of the nations" (v. 4 LXX). Hence, although Agrippa's letter does not explicitly state that Jerusalem is the "navel of the earth," it nevertheless strongly implies just that. In this respect, Jerusalem is being compared perhaps to Delphi, for in establishing a Greek colony, a founder first sought sanction from the Delphic oracle, situated from the Greek perspective at the very omphalos of the earth.[218]

Philo's concept of Jerusalem as Mother also stems from Isa 54:1−3, which expects that, in the time of the Restoration, Zion, a barren woman up to that point, will have so many children that the place of her tent will need to be continually enlarged to the right and to the left until her seed inherits the nations.[219] For Philo, the reason that colonies had to be sent out from Jerusalem in the first place was because of overpopulation.[220] As the following excursus shows, the motif of the Jews as a populous nation – or rather the most populous nation – runs throughout the writings of Philo.

Excursus: The Jews as the Most Populous Nation

According to Philo, "the most populous of the nations" (τὸ πολυανθρωπότατον τῶν ἐθνῶν) sprang from Sarah.[221] The secret of Israel's tremendous fertility lies in the sign of the Abrahamic Covenant, circumcision (Gen 17:9−14), for circumcision "causes the semen to travel aright without being scattered or dropped into the folds of the foreskin, and therefore the circumcised nations appear to be the most prolific and populous."[222]

---

[216] In the Septuagint, there are a number of examples of this usage. In Josh 10:2, for example, Gibeon is described as "a great city . . ., as one of the mother-cities" (μεγάλη πόλις . . ., ὡσεὶ μία τῶν μητροπόλεων). In 2 Sam 20:19, Abel is considered a πόλις and a μητρόπολις. See further Josh 14:15; 15:13; 21:11; Neh 1:1 (S). Thus, the (fortified) daughter cities of a great city can be called "daughters" (cf. Num 21:25, 32; 32:42; Josh 15:45, 47; 17:16; Judg 1:27; 11:26; Neh 11:25−31; 1 Chr 2:23; 7:28−29; 8:12; 18:1; 2 Chr 13:19; 28:18).

[217] Cf. *Ex. Rab.* 23:10: "R. Johanan said, 'Jerusalem will one day become the Metropolis of the whole world. . . .'"

[218] Cf. Alexander J. GRAHAM, "Greek Colonization," *OCD*, pp. 264−265 (here p. 265). On Delphi as the omphalos, see Chap. 1.

[219] Cf. Isa 49:19−20.

[220] Cf. *Flacc.* 45−46: "For so populous are the Jews that no one country can hold them, and therefore they settle in Europe and Asia and in the islands and on the mainland, and while they hold the Holy City where stands the sacred Temple of the Most High God to be their mother city, yet those which are theirs by inheritance from their fathers, grandfathers, and ancestors even farther back, are in each case accounted by them to be their fatherland in which they were born and reared, while to some of them they have come at the time of their foundation as immigrants to the satisfaction of the founders." See further *Mos.* 2.232.

[221] *Congr.* 3.

[222] *Spec. Leg.* 1.7; cf. 1.2. Of course, more to the point is the promise that Abraham's seed

Hence, when Israel was in Egypt, "the nation" was constantly growing so numerous that the king of Egypt feared they would show their superiority by contesting the chief power with the Egyptians.[223] Thus, fundamental to Israel's liturgy is the creed to be repeated at the presentation of the basket of fruit (cf. Deut 26:1–11): "The founders of our race abandoned Syria and migrated to Egypt and, though few in number, increased to a populous nation."[224] As a reward for his renouncing the lordship of Egypt, which he held as the adopted son of the then-reigning king, Moses became the king of a nation more populous and mightier than Egypt.[225] The time of the Exodus was "the beginning of the prosperity of the nation, when its many myriads set out as colonists from Egypt to the cities of Syria."[226] Moses' successor would preside "not over some ordinary nation but over the most populous of all the nations on earth" (οὐκ ἐπί τῷ τυχόντι ἔθνει γενη-σομένης, ἀλλὰ πολυανθρωποτάτῳ μὲν τῶν ἀπανταχοῦ πάντων).[227] "All the nations of Asia" feared the advancing Israelites, and Balak, himself the ruler of "a great and populous portion of the East," lost heart.[228] After the Conquest, Israel settled in the land and remained most populous until the Exile.[229] As Philo ruefully comments, however, apparently in reference to the plight of his own people: "Even so the good fortune which has flooded a great and populous nation sometimes turns the stream of its current elsewhere and leaves not even a tiny trickle behind it, that no trace of the old richness may remain."[230]

During the Second Temple period, the description of "most populous nation" is still seen to apply to the Jews. A considerable part of "the very populous nation of the Jews" lives in Palestinian Syria, including the four-thousand-strong Essenes.[231] Furthermore, the nation is so numerous that "the offering of firstfruits are naturally exceedingly abundant. In fact, practically in every city there are banking places for the holy money where people regularly come and give their offerings."[232] "As the nation is very populous," says Philo, "the firstfruits are necessarily also on a lavish scale, so that even the poorest of the priests has so superabundant a maintenance that he seems exceedingly well-to-do."[233] Philo goes so far in carrying through this motif that he makes Petronius, the Roman governor of Syria who was charged with introducing Gaius' statue into the Temple, balk at the sheer size of the Jewish nation.[234] First, Petronius "considered the vast number of people comprised in the nation (ἔθνος), which needed to contain it not like every other the circumference of a single country (χώρα) allotted to itself alone, but,

---

would be made as many as the dust of the earth and the stars in the heaven (Gen 13:16; 15:5) and that "Abraham shall become a great and populous nation" (Gen 18:18).

[223] *Mos.* 1.8.

[224] *Spec. Leg.* 2.217; cf. *Mos.* 1.34.

[225] *Mos.* 1.149. On Moses as "god and king of the whole nation" (ὅλου τοῦ ἔθνους θεὸς καὶ βασιλεύς), see *Mos.* 1.158.

[226] *Mos.* 2.246. Cf. *Mos.* 1.222.

[227] *Virt.* 64. The Edomites are also described as a populous nation (*Mos.* 1.239–240).

[228] *Mos.* 1.263.

[229] Cf. *Spec. Leg.* 2.170.

[230] *Quod Deus* 178. Cf. *Spec. Leg.* 2.170.

[231] *Quod Omn. Prob.* 75.

[232] *Spec. Leg.* 1.78. Sacrificial animals are also available in great supply (*Spec. Leg.* 1.136).

[233] *Spec. Leg.* 1.133; cf. 1.141; *Mos.* 2.159.

[234] On the other hand, it was feared that "the overthrow of the Temple" would be accompanied by an order for the annihilation of the Jewish nation (*Legat.* 194).

one might almost say, the whole inhabited world (πᾶσα ἡ οἰκουμένη).[235] For it is spread abroad over all the continents and islands so that it seems to be not much less than the indigenous inhabitants. To draw all these myriads into war against him was surely very dangerous. Heaven forbid indeed that the Jews in every quarter should come by common agreement to the defence. The result would be something too stupendous to be combated."[236] Thus, like the king of Egypt, Petronius considers the Jewish nation as a force to be reckoned with. Later, a multitude of Jews came to Petronius and "suddenly descended like a cloud and occupied the whole of Phoenicia, to the profound astonishment of those who did not know how populous the nation was."[237] Gaius chides Petronius for attempting to have the order rescinded: "You concern yourself with the institutions of the Jews, the nation (ἔθνος) which is my worst enemy; you disregard the imperial commands of your sovereign. You feared the great numbers (τὸ πλῆθος). Then had you not with you the military forces which are feared by the nations of the east (ἔθνη τὰ ἑῷα) and their rulers the Parthians?"[238] One wonders whether Philo envisions a day when the nation will simply overwhelm the world with its numbers.[239] In any case, he does expect a final eschatological battle against the most populous nations of the world (cf. *Praem.* 95).

II. The Abrahamic Promise. Of the three aspects of the Abrahamic Promise that we observed in Gen 12:1–3,[240] Philo allegorizes the first and practically ignores the other two.[241] Thus, in Philo's allegorical scheme, the promise of seed focuses on the two nations in Rebecca's womb (Gen 25:23), which symbolize either rational and irrational,[242] virtue and vice,[243] or good and evil.[244] The promise that Abraham will become a "great nation" (Gen 12:2) is explained in terms of the individual's quantitative and qualitative progress in

---

[235] Cf. ZEITLIN, "The Jews," pp. 313–347, who tried to argue that during the Second Commonwealth, Jews did not regard themselves as constituting a "nation."

[236] *Legat.* 214–215.

[237] *Legat.* 226–227.

[238] *Legat.* 256.

[239] Josephus seems to have a similar, perhaps even dependent, eschatological expectation for his people Israel (cf. Betsy Halpern AMARU, "Land Theology in Josephus' *Jewish Antiquities*," *JQR* 71 [1980–81] 201–229 [here p. 228]). Compare also what Josephus has Agrippa say to the Jews who want to wage war on the Romans and defy the unconquered empire: "I ask you, then, are you ... more numerous than the peoples of the world?" (*BJ* 2.364). Interestingly enough, the tremendous population of the Jewish nation was a persistent cause of anti-Jewish bigotry in the ancient world (cf., e.g., Ex 1:8–9; Hecataeus of Abdera, preserved in Diodorus Siculus 40.3.8; Strabo, preserved in Josephus *Ant.* 14.115; Tacitus *Hist.* 5.5.3; see further Louis H. FELDMAN, *Jew and Gentile in the Ancient World: Attitudes and Interactions from Alexander to Justinian* [Princeton, NJ: Princeton University Press, 1993], pp. 84–102, 106).

[240] This passage is cited at the beginning of *De migratione Abrahami* (§ 1).

[241] Although Gen 26:4 ("and all the nations of the earth shall be blessed in your seed") is cited in *Quis Her.* 8, that is only to show that God praises the loyalty of Abraham's service. Philo does not develop the idea of all the nations being blessed in Abraham's seed (cf., however, the citation of Gen 28:14 in *Somn.* 1.176).

[242] *Leg. All.* 3.88.

[243] *Congr.* 129.

[244] *Sac.* 4.

the principles of virtue: The term "nation" implies the number and the term "great," their improvement in quality.[245] Thus, the person who is "law-abiding and obedient to God is equal in worth to a whole nation, even the most populous, or rather to all nations, and if we may go still farther, even to the whole world."[246] Nevertheless, Philo does not completely lose track of the idea that Abraham is "the founder of the nation" in the literal sense,[247] for Moses is regarded as "seventh in descent from Abraham, who became the founder of the whole nation of the Jews."[248] Because of the virtues of the founders, the nation of Israel was set apart from others.[249]

Although the Abrahamic Promise of Land does not receive much attention in contexts where the term ἔθνος occurs,[250] it must be suspected that the idea of "the most populous nation," with its connection with circumcision (the sign of the Abrahamic Covenant), has a relationship to the Land Promise.[251] We have seen that in early Judaism, this promise is frequently interpreted in terms of sovereignty over the whole world. Therefore, the most populous nation, which has spread out to the whole inhabited world, is in a position to inherit the nations, in accordance with the expectation of Isa 54:1−3,[252] which, as we have seen, alludes to Abraham and Sarah and the Abrahamic Promise. We may also compare here Philo's interpretation of the Abrahamic Promise reiterated to Jacob in Gen 28:14, which expects that Jacob's seed will be like the dust of the earth and will spread abroad throughout the world: "And this, in accordance with the Divine promises, is broadening out to the very bounds of the universe (τὸ πᾶν), and renders its possessor inheritor of the four quarters of the world, reaching to them all, to East, and West, and South and North; for it is said, 'It shall spread abroad to the West and to the South and to the North and to the East.'"[253] This expectation also converges with Philo's messianic hope: "There shall come forth from you one day a man and he shall rule over many nations, and his kingdom spreading every day shall be exalted on high."[254]

II. The Covenant with Israel.

---

[245] *Mig.* 53. Note, however, that in *Mig.* 54, Ex 1:9 is cited to show that the promise of a great nation was fulfilled.

[246] *Decal.* 37.

[247] *Abr.* 276; cf. *Praem.* 57−58. On Abraham as "the most ancient member of the nation of the Jews," see *Virt.* 212.

[248] *Mos.* 1.7. Cf. Ex 6:14−20, where Moses is listed as fifth from Jacob and therefore seventh from Abraham.

[249] *Spec. Leg.* 4.179−181.

[250] See merely *Sac.* 57 and *Congr.* 119.

[251] Cf. *Mig.* 53−54.

[252] Philo cites this passage in *Praem.* 158.

[253] *Somn.* 1.175. Cf. Scott, *Adoption*, pp. 134−135.

[254] *Mos.* 1.290. Cf. *Praem.* 95: " For 'there shall come forth a man,' says the oracle [Num 24:7, 17 LXX], and leading his host to war he will subdue great and populous nations, because God has sent to his aid the reinforcement which befits the godly, that is dauntless courage of soul and all-powerful strength of body, either of which strikes fear into enemy and the two if united are quite irresistible." See further below on the Restoration of Israel.

A. The Establishment of the Covenant with Israel as a Nation. We have seen that, in accordance with Deut 26:1−11, Philo reckons the establishment of the populous nation already in Egypt[255] rather than at Sinai. Whereas the Greeks and barbarians wrongly failed to acknowledge God as Creator, this was corrected by the nation of the Jews, which passed over all created objects and chose service to the Uncreated and Eternal God.[256] Although every other nation has laws diametrically opposite to those of the Jews,[257] the *halakoth* that Moses delivered to the Jewish nation are universally acknowledged as desirable and precious.[258] Philo stresses repeatedly that the institutions of Israel are, to a large extent, not just for the nation itself but indeed for the whole human race.[259] In fact, "the nation of the Jews is to the whole inhabited world what the priest is to the state."[260] Therefore, Philo cannot understand the charge of misanthropy that is often leveled against the nation,[261] for the nation of the Jews is ready for agreement and friendship with all like-minded nations.[262] This is precisely what Moses desires to create through his regulations: "unanimity, neighborliness, fellowship, reciprocity of feeling, whereby houses and cities and nations and countries and the whole human race may advance to supreme happiness."[263] Those who accuse the nation of misanthropy must reckon with the fact that even animals are protected by Mosaic legislation.[264]

If the goal of the Mosaic Law is fellowship among all human beings, then the nation must be willing to accept proselytes into their ranks, those who have abandoned "their kinfolk by blood, their country, their customs, and the temples and images of their gods."[265] Therefore, Moses expressly "commands

---

[255] See further *Mos.* 1.71, 73, 86, 88, 123; 2.250, 254; *Decal.* 15.

[256] *Spec. Leg.* 2.166. Cf. *Quod Deus* 148 ("But in the school of Moses it is not one man only who may boast that he has learned the first elements of wisdom, but a whole nation, a mighty people"); *Legat.* 210 (the nation of the Jews carries "the likeness of the commandments enshrined in their souls").

[257] *Ebr.* 193−194. For example, whereas many other nations complacently expose infants, to the Jews, this is a sacrilegious and inhumane practice that is punishable by law (*Spec. Leg.* 3.110).

[258] Cf. *Mos.* 2.20 ("They attract and win the attention of all, of barbarians, of Greeks, of dwellers on the mainland and islands, of nations of the east and the west, of Europe and Asia, of the whole inhabited world from end to end"), 43. See, however, *Spec. Leg.* 4.179, where Philo admits that the nation stands alone as an orphan among other nations because its severe laws are repulsive to the pleasure-seeking mass of humanity.

[259] Cf. *Spec. Leg.* 1.168−190 (lists a number of sacrifices offered on behalf of the human race); 2.150 (the Feast of Unleavened Bread), 162−163, 171 (Sheaves), 188 (Feast of Trumpets).

[260] *Spec. Leg.* 2.163.

[261] *Spec. Leg.* 2.167.

[262] *Spec. Leg.* 4.224.

[263] *Virt.* 119. According to *Legat.* 161, Tiberius charged his procurators in every place to deal gently with the Jewish nation, assuring them that the Jewish institutions promoted orderly conduct.

[264] *Virt.* 141.

[265] *Virt.* 102.

all members of the nation to love the incomers, not only as friends and kinfolk but as themselves both in body and soul. ..."[266]

B. The Settlement of Canaan. As Balaam predicted, the nation of the Jews had God as its guide and therefore would devour many nations of its enemies.[267] Israel "devoted" the first kingdom that they conquered, as Philo explains, "For, just as every pious person gives firstfruits of the year's produce, whatever he reaps from his own possessions, so too the whole nation set apart the kingdom which they took at the outset, and thus gave a great slice of the great country into which they were migrating as the firstfruits of their settlement."[268]

C. The Sin and Exile of Israel. Although Philo often emphasizes the nation's virtue,[269] he also recognizes that the whole nation can fall into sin and indeed did so from time to time.[270] Early on, the most serious offence was when the people worshipped the Golden Calf and thus turned their back on the one true God: "Moses was cut to the heart to think that ... the whole people had suddenly been blinded who a few hours ago had excelled every nation in clearness of vision. ..."[271] This blinding of Israel seems to mark the beginning of nation's downfall, for by Philo's day, the cities of the once populous Land of Israel "have been stripped of their inhabitants and the whole nation, except for a small fraction, has disappeared, partly through wars, partly through heaven-sent visitations, a consequence of their strange and monstrous practices of iniquity and all their heinous acts of impiety aimed at the subversion of the statutes of nature."[272] "Our nation has not prospered for many a year," Philo acknowledges.[273]

D. The Restoration of Israel. We have already suggested that Philo's concept of "the most populous nation" may be connected with his eschatological expectation for Israel.[274] Philo was convinced that God had not withdrawn from the nation of the Jews.[275] The hopeful words of comfort in the Song of Moses about Israel's Restoration, Philo reasons, "must be followed by their happy fulfillment."[276] Likewise, he notes, some of the blessings of Moses on the twelve

---

[266] *Virt.* 103.

[267] *Mos.* 1.291.

[268] *Mos.* 1.254.

[269] Cf., e.g., *Virt.* 79; *Mos.* 1.189; 2.15, 202; *Spec. Leg.* 2.166; *Quod Deus* 148; *Legat.* 210.

[270] Cf. *Spec. Leg.* 1.230, 233. For example, part of the nation began to have sexual relations with Moabite women (*Mos.* 1.300–304).

[271] *Mos.* 2.271; cf. *Spec. Leg.* 1.79. Moses made prayers and supplications for the nation, begging that their sins might be forgiven (*Mos.* 2.166).

[272] *Spec. Leg.* 2.170.

[273] *Mos.* 2.43.

[274] Philo does not use ἔθνος in reference to the events of the postexilic period.

[275] This is the message of *In Flaccum* (cf. § 191; also the confession of Flaccus in § 171).

[276] *Virt.* 75. Deuteronomy 32 contains the familiar Deuteronomic salvation-historical scheme: God's election and care for Israel (vv. 6–14), Israel's rebellion (vv. 15–18; cf. v. 5), God's judgment upon them (vv. 19–35), and, ultimately, God's final deliverance and vindication of his own people (vv. 36–43). On the Deuteronomic scheme, see further Scott,

tribes of the nation (Deut 33:1—29) have already taken place, which inspires confidence that the others will be fulfilled in the future.[277] Thus, in his treatment of Deut 30:1—10 and Lev 26:40—45, Philo expects that when it repents, the nation, which has come under the Deuteronomic curses and thus finds itself in Exile, will be delivered and restored to the Land: "When they have gained this unexpected liberty, those who but now were scattered in Greece and the outside world over islands and continents[278] will arise and post from every side with one impulse to the one appointed place, guided in their pilgrimage by a vision divine and superhuman unseen by others but manifest to them as they pass from Exile to their home."[279]

Philo's confidence about the future of his nation is based also on his view of the succession of world empires, which he evidently derives from Daniel:[280] "For circlewise moves the revolution of that divine plan which most call Fortune (τύχη). Presently in its ceaseless flux it makes distribution city by city, nation by nation, country by country (κατὰ πόλεις καὶ ἔθνη καὶ χώρας). What these had once, those have now. What all had, all have. Only from time to time is the ownership changed by its agency, to the end that the whole world (ἡ οἰκουμένη πᾶσα) should be as a single city-state (ὡς μία πόλις), enjoying that best of constitutions, democracy."[281] As examples of this flux of Fortune among the nations, Philo adduces, among others, the Persians and the

---

"Restoration of Israel." As H. W. BASSER points out, the traditional assumption has been that Deuteronomy 32 "is a summary of Israel's total history, from inception until the end of days" (*Midrashic Interpretations of the Song of Moses* [American University Studies 7/2; New York/ Frankfurt/Berne: Peter Lang, 1984], p. 4). Cf. Josephus *Ant.* 4.302—303.

[277] *Mos.* 2.288. In *Praem.* 107, Philo applies Deut 15:6 to the future ("in those days").

[278] On the worldwide extent of the Jewish Diaspora, see above on *Legat.* 281—283.

[279] *Praem.* 162—169 (here § 165). Cf. UMEMOTO, "Juden, 'Heiden' und das Menschengeschlecht in der Sicht Philons," pp. 47—48. According to SCHALLER ("Philon von Alexandreia und das 'Heilige Land,'" pp. 172—187), it was only towards the end of his life that Philo began to reconsider the eschatological significance of the Land of Israel. In fact, Philo is the only known witness in the Hellenistic-Jewish Diaspora literature of the Roman period who considered the Return of the Jews to the Land as an eschatological goal for the Jews scattered throughout the world (ibid., p. 182). On the other hand, Betsy Halpern AMARU argues that Philo uses the theme of the "ingathering of the exiles" as a metaphor for returning to wisdom and knowledge of God rather than as a literal recovery of real estate ("Land Theology in Philo and Josephus," in *The Land Of Israel: Jewish Perspectives*, pp. 65—93 [here p. 85]).

[280] According to the Scripture index in ALLENBACH, ed., et al., *Biblia Patristica: Index des citations et allusions bibliques dans la littérature patristique, Supplément: Philon d'Alexandrie*, there is no citation of or allusion to Daniel in the works of Philo.

[281] *Quod Deus* 176. Cf. BARRACLOUGH, "Philo's Politics," p. 521.

Greeks.[282] If Philo views Rome as the Fourth Empire of Daniel,[283] then the "city-state" to which he refers here might be Jerusalem, which meanwhile spreads its tent to encompass the whole earth.[284]

Philo believes that if his nation flourishes again, "each nation would abandon its peculiar ways, and, throwing overboard their ancestral customs, turn to honoring our laws alone. For when the brightness of their shining is accompanied by national prosperity, it will darken the light of the others as the risen sun darkens the stars."[285] Philo prays that, by adopting the Mosaic Law,

---

[282] Cf. *Quod Deus* 173–175 (also § 178): "If you do not care to test the fortunes of individual men, scan the vicissitudes, for better and worse, of whole countries and nations. Greece was once at its zenith, but the Macedonians took away its power. Macedonia flourished in its turn, but when it was divided into portions it weakened until it was utterly extinguished. Before the Macedonians fortune (εὐτυχία) smiled on the Persians, but a single day destroyed their vast and mighty empire, and now Parthians rule over Persians, the former subjects over their masters of yesterday. The breath that blew from Egypt of old was clear and strong for many a long year, yet like a cloud its great prosperity passed away. What of the Ethiopians, what of Carthage, and the parts towards Libya? What of the kings of Pontus? What of Europe and Asia, in a word of the whole civilized world? It is not tossed up and down and kept in turmoil like ships at sea, subject now to prosperous, now to abject winds?" Compare the list of kingdoms in *Sib. Or.* 3.156–161 (Egyptian provenance! cf. also 8.4–13): "Then God inflicted evil upon the Titans, and all the descendants of Titans and of Cronos died. But then as time pursued its cyclic course, the kingdom of Egypt arose, then that of the Persians, Medes, and Ethiopians, and Assyrian Babylon, then that of the Macedonians, of Egypt again, then of Rome." See further Philo *Jos.* 134–136: "That these [sc. external goods] are dreams is attested not only by single men, but by cities, nations, countries, by Greeks, by the world of the barbarians, by the dwellers on the mainland, by dwellers on islands, by Europe, by Asia, by West, by East. For nothing at all anywhere has remained in the same condition; everywhere all has been subject to changes and vicissitudes. Egypt once held the sovereignty over many nations, but now is in slavery. The Macedonians in their day of success flourished so greatly that they held dominion over all the habitable world, but now they pay to the tax-collectors the yearly tributes imposed by their masters. Where is the house of the Ptolemies, and the fame of the several Diodochoi whose light once shone to the utmost boundaries of land and sea? Where are the liberties of the independent nations and cities, where again the servitude of the vassals? Did not the Persians once rule the Parthians, and now the Parthians rule the Persians? So much do human affairs twist and change, go backward and forward as on the draught-board."

[283] This view is strengthened by the way that Josephus apparently appropriates Philo's concept of Fortune in *BJ* 5.367 (see below). Furthermore, in *Legat.* 346, Philo styles Gaius as a successor to the Kingdom of the Greeks (particularly Antiochus Epiphanes) when he reacts against making the Jerusalem Temple into a sanctuary bearing the name, "the new Zeus made manifest" (Διὸς Ἐπιφανοῦς Νέου).

[284] See the excursus above on "the most populous nation," where it is explained that because of overpopulation, Jerusalem has sent colonies out to every part of the world. This image is also generally compatible with that of the stone that destroyed the statue, became a great mountain, and filled the whole earth (Dan 2:35, 44–45). Philo expects that Israel will one day be the prominent nation among all peoples of the world (cf., e.g., *Mos.* 2.44; *Quaest. Ex.* 2.76).

[285] *Mos.* 2.43–44. Is this Philo's version of the eschatological pilgrimage of the nations? Israel of the Restoration will be a light to the nations (cf. Isa 51:4; 60:3).

houses, cities, nations, and indeed the whole human race might advance to supreme happiness, and he is firmly convinced that this will come about.[286]

Josephus.[287] Of the approximately 413 occurrences of ἔθνος in the works of Flavius Josephus, the overwhelming majority are used of "the nation of the Israelites" (τὸ τῶν Ἰσραηλιτῶν ἔθνος),[288] "the nation of the Hebrews" (τὸ Ἑβραίων ἔθνος),[289] "the nation of the Jews" (τὸ [τῶν] Ἰουδαίων ἔθνος),[290] "the nation" (τὸ ἔθνος),[291] "his [sc. God's] nation,"[292] "our nation,"[293] etc. whether it is located in Palestine or in the Diaspora.[294] The term is never used in the sense of "Gentile(s)," for which Josephus prefers ἀλλόφυλος[295]; however, ἔθνος is used in reference to other nations[296] and sometimes even as a collective

---

[286] *Virt.* 119–120.

[287] Cf. SCHMIDT, "Idée de 'nation'," pp. 326–328.

[288] Cf. *Ant.* 11.3.

[289] Cf. *Ant.* 4.308: "Moses therefore commanded these things, and the nation of the Hebrews, obeying these things, continues to do them." It would appear from this that this name still applies to the nation as of the time of Josephus. See further *Ant.* 7.356, which distinguishes between "the nation of the Hebrews" and "the tribe of Judah"; 7.391; 8.120.

[290] Cf. *BJ* 2.197; *Ant.* 11.123; 12.357.

[291] Cf. *Ant.* 6.32. Here, as often elsewhere in Josephus, "the nation" refers unequivocally to "the nation of the Jews" even when the full name of the nation has not been specified in the previous context.

[292] Cf. *Ant.* 11.229.

[293] In *Contra Apion* (1.5), Josephus is concerned to explain the reasons why "our nation" is mentioned by only a few of the Greek historians (cf. 1.68, 213).

[294] For the use of ἔθνος in reference to the Jewish nation in the Diaspora, see, e.g., *BJ* 6.442 (the Jews as "the nation spread over the whole inhabited world [τὸ διαπεφοιτηκὸς ὅλης τῆς οἰκουμένης ἔθνος]); *Ant.* 15.16 (Hyrcanus was honored by those in Babylon and "all the nation of the Jews occupying the region as far as the Euphrates"); 18.378; 19.278.

[295] Cf., e.g., *Ant.* 20.262: μήτε Ἰουδαῖος μήτε ἀλλόφυλος. The same term is used on the inscriptions in the Temple prohibiting the "foreigner," on penalty of death, from going beyond the parapet that separates the Court of the Gentiles from the steps leading to the Court of the Women (*BJ* 5.193–194; but cf. *Ant.* 15.417 [τὸν ἀλλοεθνῆ]). Two almost identical copies of one of these Greek inscriptions has been found, but they use the term ἀλλογενῆ, in accordance with the prohibition of the foreigner (ὁ ἀλλογενῆς) from touching the sanctuary in Num 1:51; 3:10, 38; 18:7 (cf. Peretz SEGAL, "The Penalty of the Warning Inscription from the Temple of Jerusalem," *IEJ* 39 [1989] 79–84; see further E. P. SANDERS, *Judaism: Practice and Belief 63 BCE – 66 CE* [London: SCM; Philadelphia: Trinity Press International, 1992] pp. 61, 69, 72–76). According to *BJ* 2.412–413 (cf. Eupolemus in Eusebius *Pr. Ev.* 9.34.2), the sanctuary had been adorned mainly at the expense of "foreigners" (ἀλλοφύλοι) and it had always accepted the gifts of "foreign nations" (τῶν ἔξωθεν ἐθνῶν). Cf. also *Ant.* 8.39: "The king [sc. Solomon] also had governors, who ruled the land of the Syrians and the foreigners (Σύρων γῆς καὶ τῶν ἀλλοφύλων), extending from the Euphrates river to Egypt, and collected tribute for him from the nations (τὰ ἔθνη)." On the Qumran position regarding foreigners in the Temple, see Roland DEINES, "Die Abwehr der Fremden in den Texten aus Qumran. Zum Verständnis der Fremdenfeindlichkeit in der Qumrangemeinde," in *Die Heiden. Juden, Christen und das Problem des Fremden*, pp. 59–91 (here pp. 74–82). In the Temple Scroll, the description of the Temple leaves no room for a "court of the Gentiles" (ibid., p. 81).

[296] For the expression "the other nations" (τὰ ἄλλα ἔθνη) with respect to the nation of the Jews, see *Ant.* 11.285, 329; also 12.241 (τὰ τῶν ἀλλοεθνῶν ἔργα). Of course, Josephus' exposition of the Table of Nation contains many references to other "nations" (cf. *Ant.* 1.124,

whole in opposition to Israel.[297] As we will see in the following survey, the interplay between Israel as an ἔθνος and the other nations of the world that was observed in the Greek OT also finds expression in Josephus.

I. The Table of Nations. In recounting the history of the nation of the Jews, Josephus begins where the OT itself begins, that is, with the Table of Nations (*Ant.* 1.120−147). After the confusion of tongues at the Tower of Babel,[298] the people dispersed throughout the world, claimed territory, and founded colonies so that every continent was filled with them (§ 120). Those who occupied a certain territory (γῆ) then conferred upon the nations (τὰ ἔθνη) that they had founded the names of Noah's grandsons (§ 122).

By the time of Josephus, however, some of "the nations" (τὰ ἔθνη) that were thus formed still preserved the names that they had originally been given by their founders, some had changed their names, and still others had modified their names in some way (§ 121). The Greeks, says Josephus, were responsible for the change of nomenclature: "for when in subsequent ages they rose to power, they appropriated even the glories of the past, embellishing the nations (τὰ ἔθνη) with names which they could understand and imposing on them forms of government, as though they were descended from themselves" (§ 121). Here, we begin to see that Josephus' concept of the nations is controlled by the idea of the succession of the four world empires in Daniel. For Josephus, "the Greeks," whom he identifies with Javan in the Table of Nations,[299] constitute the Third Kingdom[300]; the Romans, to whom his own nation was currently subjected, embody the Fourth Kingdom.[301] As Josephus himself expressed it to

---

125, 135). See further *Ant.* 4.300 ("the nation of the Canaanites"); 6.138 ("the nation of the Amelikites"); 6.140 ("the nation of the Sikimites"); 18.85 ("the nation of the Samaritans"); 18.106 ("the nation of the Bataneans"). Josephus wants to touch on a subject that is profitable "to cities, peoples and nations" and that should instill into the hearts of "kings of nations" a noble desire (*Ant.* 6.343).

[297] Cf., e.g., *Ant.* 9.16 (τὰ ἀλλόφυλα ἔθνη); *BJ* 2.412 (τὰ ἔξωθεν ἔθνη). According to *Ap.* 2.282 (cf. 1.166), "The masses have long since shown a keen desire to adopt our religious observances; and there is not one city, Greek or barbarian, nor a single nation (ἕν ἔθνος), to which our custom of abstaining from work on the seventh day has not spread, and where the fast and the lighting of lamps and many of our prohibitions in the matter of food are not observed."

[298] Josephus puts the Tower of Babel (Gen 11:1−9) before the Table of Nations (Genesis 10). It is interesting to note that Josephus claims the Jewish people do not put stock in learning foreign languages: "For our people do not favor those persons who have mastered the speech of many nations (πολλῶν ἐθνῶν διάλεκτον). . ." (*Ant.* 20.264).

[299] Cf. *Ant.* 1.124.

[300] Cf. *Ant.* 10.273, where Josephus recounts the interpretation of Daniel's vision in Dan 8:16: "The goat, he [sc. God] said, indicated that there would be a certain king of the Greeks (ἐκ τῶν Ἑλλήνων) who would encounter the Persian king twice in battle and defeat him and take over all his empire."

[301] Cf. *Ant.* 15.385−387, which contains the sequence: Babylonia, Persia, Macedonia, and Rome. According to *Ant.* 10.276, the rule of the Romans over the Jews was foretold by Daniel: "In the same manner [as the prophecy about Antiochus Ephiphanes], Daniel also wrote about the empire of the Romans and that Jerusalem would be taken by them and the Temple laid

the Jewish rebels in the beleaguered city of Jerusalem, "Fortune, indeed, had from all quarters passed over to them [sc. the Romans], and God who went the round of the nations, bringing to each in turn the rod of empire (καὶ κατὰ ἔθνος τὸν θεὸν ἐμπεριάγοντα τὴν ἀρχήν), now rested over Italy" (*BJ* 5.367).[302] Hence, the Table of Nations forms the basic presupposition for Josephus' understanding of the eschatological events in Daniel.[303]

The description of the universal sovereignty of the Roman Empire that Josephus puts in the mouth of King Agrippa II at the beginning of the war (*BJ* 2.345–401) is most instructive in this regard.[304] However, far from being brittle and crumbly like the Fourth Empire in Dan 2:41–43, the Roman Empire is portrayed by Josephus as the strongest and most extensive empire yet to emerge of the four.[305] Thus, whereas the Persian Empire extends "from India to Ethiopia"[306] and embraces "many nations" (*Ant.*

---

waste." On Rome as the Fourth Kingdom in Jewish tradition, see Philip R. DAVIES, "Daniel in the Lions' Den," in *Images of Empire* (ed. Loveday Alexander; JSOTSup 122; Sheffield: JSOT Press, 1991), pp. 160–178. The Palestinian Targumim and the midrashim (e.g., *Mek.* to Ex 20:18; *Gen. Rab.* 44:17; *Ex. Rab.* 51:7; *Lev. Rab.* 13:5) frequently find a reference to the four kingdoms of Daniel in Gen 15:12, a passage describing the covenant ceremony with Abraham.

[302] Philo has a similar concept of "Fortune" and the succession of world empires (see above on *Quod Deus* 173–176). In fact, we may wonder whether Philo has influenced Josephus at this point, since this is the case elsewhere in the writings of Josephus (cf. SCHÜRER, *Hist.*, 1:49; Louis H. FELDMAN, *Josephus and Modern Scholarship [1937–1980]* [New York/Berlin: de Gruyter, 1984], pp. 14, 410–418; see further below on the Restoration). On Josephus' concept of "Fortune" as a mixture of Jewish apocalyptic and Roman imperial ideology, see HENGEL, "Messianische Hoffnung," p. 671 n. 59; Helgo LINDNER, *Die Geschichtsauffassung des Flavius Josephus im Bellum Judaicum. Gleichzeitig ein Beitrag zur Quellenfrage* (AGJU 12; Leiden: Brill, 1972), pp. 42–48. See also Menaham STERN, "Josephus and the Roman Empire as Reflected in The Jewish War," in *Josephus, Judaism, and Christianity* (ed. Louis H. Feldman and Gehei Hata; Leiden: Brill, 1987), pp. 71–80. On Josephus' interpretation of Daniel, see further FELDMAN, *Josephus and Modern Scholarship*, pp. 178–181; idem, "Josephus' Portrait of Daniel," *Henoch* 14 (1992) 37–96 (here esp. pp. 66–71); Geza VERMES, "Josephus' Treatment of the Book of Daniel," *JJS* 42 (1991) 149–166. On Fortune and Roman imperial ideology, see further Iiro KAJANTO, "Fortuna," in *ANRW* II.17.1 (ed. Wolfgang Haase; Berlin/New York: Walter de Gruyter, 1981), pp. 502–558.

[303] See further below on the Restoration of Israel. See also MAIER's considerations on why Josephus' exposition of the Table of Nations does not explicitly mention either Rome or the real political situation in the Roman Empire ("Japhetiten," pp. 192–194).

[304] The similarities between this speech and Josephus' own speech in *BJ* 5.362–419 show that the latter is primarily responsible for this material. Cf. Tessa RAJAK, "Friends, Romans, Subjects: Agrippa II's Speech in Josephus's *Jewish War*," in *Images of Empire*, pp. 122–134 (here pp. 123–125).

[305] Cf. LINDNER, *Geschichtsauffassung*, p. 44. As VERMES points out, Josephus avoids formulating anything that his patrons might find objectionable, so the feet of statue are made purely of iron (*Ant.* 10.206) and not of a mixture of iron and clay as in Dan 2:41 ("Josephus' Treatment of the Book of Daniel," pp. 155, 165). Josephus also refuses to comment on the "stone," i.e., the new kingdom established by God, which is to shatter the "iron" empire (*Ant.* 10.210).

[306] Cf. Esth 1:1; 8:9.

11.216),[307] the Greek Empire is even greater, covering, at the death of Alexander, Asia, Babylon and the surrounding nations, the Hellespont, Macedonia, and Egypt (*Ant.* 12.2). Yet, as Agrippa sets out in great and explicit detail, the Romans rule "the universe" (τὰ πάντα),[308] and their imperialistic ambition compels them to the ends of the inhabited world.[309] To underscore this universal sovereignty[310] and to dissuade the excited crowd in Jerusalem from revolting against the invincible Romans,[311] Agrippa includes an impressive *table of nations* under Roman control: Greeks and the Macedonians, as well as "myriads of [other] nations,"[312] including the five hundred cities of the province of Asia and other nations of Asia Minor,[313] the Thracians, the Illyrians, the Dalmatians, the Gauls, the Iberians, the Germans, the Britons,[314] the Parthians, the Carthaginians, the Cyrenians, the numerous nations of the continent of Africa,[315] and Egypt (*BJ* 2.358–387).[316] There appears to be no particular order to this list, other than perhaps a generally counterclockwise movement beginning with the North, familiar from the Table-of-Nations tradition. Furthermore, it is interesting to note that many nations listed here have biblical correspondents in Josephus' exposition of the Table of

---

[307] According to *Ant.* 11.3, Cyrus was the divinely appointed "king of the inhabited world" (τῆς οἰκουμένης βασιλεύς).

[308] Cf. *BJ* 2.361. Compare also *BJ* 5.367: "To scorn meaner masters might, indeed, be legitimate, but not those to whom the universe was subject. For what was there that had escaped the Romans, save maybe some spot useless through heat or cold?" On the other hand, Samuel exhorts Saul that he should obey God, for, while Saul had dominion over the nations, God had dominion over him and over the universe (*Ant.* 6.131).

[309] Cf. *BJ* 2.363: "Not even that world [the inhabited world (ἡ οἰκουμένη)] has sufficed for their ambition. For, not content with having their frontiers on the east the Euphrates, on the north the Ister [the Danube], on the south Libya explored into desert regions, on the west Gadeira, they have sought a new world beyond the ocean and carried their arms as far as the Britons, previously unknown to history." Note that in Josephus' exposition of the Table of Nations, Gadeira forms the westernmost boundary of the territory of the Japhethites (*Ant.* 1.122). Diodorus Siculus (40.4) gives the contents of a tablet that Pompey had inscribed with his conquests over "all the nations that dwell between the Pontic and the Red Seas" whereby he extended the frontiers of the Empire "to the limits of the earth."

[310] Much to the consternation of the Jews, the theater that Herod built in Jerusalem was lined all around with gold and silver trophies of the nations (τρόπαια τῶν ἐθνῶν) that Caesar had won in war (*Ant.* 15.272, 276). Josephus points out that the Romans have imparted their name to almost all humanity, not only to individuals but to great nations as a whole, so that those who were once Iberians, Tyrrhenians, and Sabines were now called Romans (*Ap.* 2.40).

[311] As Agrippa points out, the Jewish forces have been constantly defeated even by the neighboring nations, whereas the Roman forces have never been defeated throughout the whole inhabited world (*BJ* 2.362).

[312] Thus, Josephus breaks with the Jewish tradition of 70 or 72 nations in the world.

[313] I.e., Bithynia, Cappadocia, the Pamphylian nation, Lycians, and Cilicians.

[314] Cf. *BJ* 2.378: ". . . they inhabit an island no less in extent than the part of the world in which we live. . . ."

[315] Cf. *BJ* 2.382, which gives a geographical description of Africa: "This third part of the inhabited world, the mere enumeration of whose nations is no easy task, bounded by the Atlantic Ocean and the Pillars of Hercules, and supporting right up to the Red Sea, Ethiopians innumerable, they [sc. the Romans] have subdued it all. . . ."

[316] See further A. N. SHERWIN-WHITE, "The Roman World as *Omnes Gentes* or Τὰ Ἔθνη," in *The Roman Citizenship* (2nd ed.; Oxford: Clarendon, 1973), pp. 437–444.

Nations.[317] Nevertheless, we may also consider whether or not or to what extent, this description of the Roman Empire also goes back to the world map of M. Vipsanius Agrippa, which was commissioned by emperor Augustus (27 B.C. – A.D. 14) and set up in the colonnade named after Agrippa, Porticus Vipsania, in what is now the Via del Corso area of Rome.[318] Josephus resided in Rome after the Jewish War (cf. *Vit.* 423; *Ap.* 1.50) and may have come into contact with the map there. The fact that Agrippa had shown himself to be a friend of the Jews could have added to the impression that the map made on Josephus.[319] Furthermore, we may consider whether Josephus' description goes back either to the *Breviarium totius imperii* of Augustus, which contains, among other things, a list of the kingdoms and provinces in the Roman Empire (cf. Tacitus *Ann.* 1.11.7),[320] or to the *Res Gestae*, which announces the completion of the conquest of the *orbis terrarum* (Preamble) and provides a geographical survey of the Empire (§§ 26–33).[321] The text of the latter appears almost as

---

[317] E.g., the Greeks (= Javan; cf. *Ant.* 1.124), the Thracians (= Tiras; cf. § 125), the Iberians (= Tubal; cf. § 124), and Egypt (= Mizraim; cf. § 132).

[318] Cf. Claude NICOLET, "Representation of Space: Agrippa's Geographical Work," in *Space, Geography, and Politics in the Early Roman Empire* (Jerome Lectures 19; Ann Arbor: University of Michigan Press, 1991), pp. 95–122; DILKE, "Maps in the Service of the State: Roman Cartography to the End of the Augustan Era," pp. 207–209; idem, *Greek and Roman Maps* (Aspects of Greek and Roman Life; London: Thames and Hudson, 1985), pp. 39–54. If, as NICOLET suggests (*Space, Geography, and Politics,* p. 105), Agrippa's map had a *diaphragma* (a central parallel that passed through the Pillars of Hercules, the southern part of Asia Minor, and along the Taurus range, etc.), then Josephus may indeed have been influenced by this map, for, as we have seen in Chap. 1, Josephus' exposition of the Table of Nations presupposes a *diaphragma.*

[319] Agrippa sacrificed at the Temple in Jerusalem and was enthusiastically received by the people (Josephus *Ant.* 16.14–15). A Jewish community in Rome was named after Agrippa (cf. *CIJ* I² nos. 365, 425, 503). Agrippa protected the rights of Jews in Asia Minor (Josephus *Ant.* 12.125–126; 16.27–65).

[320] Cf. NICOLET, "The 'Geographical' Work of Augustus," in *Space, Geography, and Politics in the Early Roman Empire,* pp. 171–187 (here esp. 178–183). NICOLET argues that Josephus' description recalls geopolitical data that are encountered not only in the *Breviarium* but also in the *Res Gestae* and geographical sources like the Agrippa World Map (ibid., pp. 181–182). Compare also the extensive table of nations in Pliny's list of the regions of the world (*Nat. Hist.* 6.211–220). See now MAIER, "Japhetiten," p. 169 n. 47: "Josephus schöpfte im Wesentlichen aus einer lateinischen Quelle, siehe schon: L. Friedländer, *De fonte quo Josephus B.J. II,16,4 usus sit,* Königsberg 1873 (zu Grunde liege ein Breviarium des Augustus)."

[321] Cf. P.A. BRUNT and J.M. MOORE, eds., *Res Gestae Divi Augusti: The Achievements of the Divine Augustus with An Introduction and Commentary* (Oxford: Oxford University Press, 1967), pp. 18–29, 31–35, 69–75; NICOLET, "The *Res Gestae* of Augustus: Announcing the Conquest of the World," pp. 15–27. As NICOLET points out (ibid, p. 20), the *Res Gestae* contains no less than 55 geographical names divided into four large categories: "First come Rome and Italy along with the names of fourteen provinces: Achaia, Aegyptus, Africa, Asia, Cyrenae, Galliae [sic], Germania, Hispaniae [sic], Illyricum, Macedonia, Narbonensis, Pisidia, Sicilia, and Syria. Secondly, there are the names of countries and peoples: peoples defeated and annexed, peoples subjected, countries to which expeditions or exploratory missions were sent, ancient enemies or peoples with whom Augustus was the first to have contact, distant peoples who sent deferential embassies, and finally peoples who requested or received kings from the Romans. There are twenty-four such peoples or countries: the Adiabeni, Aethiopia, the Albani, Arabia Eudaimon, Armenia, the Bas-

a commentary to a map and seems to require the guidance of a drawing. That drawing, Agrippa's map, was not far away: The portico where it was displayed was a few hundred meters from the Mausoleum where the *Res Gestae* was posted after Augustus' death.[322]

II. The Abrahamic Promise. Of the three aspects of the Abrahamic promise, Josephus uses the term ἔθνος in reference to the promise of nationhood and land but not in reference to the blessing for all nations. In *Ant.* 1.191, the promise of nationhood comes to expression: God announces to Abraham that Sarah would have a son named Isaac, from whom would spring "great nations" (ἔθνη μεγάλα) and kings. In *Ant.* 1.235, furthermore, God foretells that the descendants of Abraham and Isaac would swell into "a multitude of nations" (ἔθνη πολλά). Finally, the promise of nationhood is extended to the twin sons of Isaac (*Ant.* 1.257).

The promise of land can be seen in *Ant.* 1.191: The kings who would spring from Abraham would win possession of all of Canaan from Sidon to Egypt by means of war. Josephus does not bring in a concept of universal sovereignty at this point even though elsewhere he does mention the widespread expectation that someone from Judea would become ruler of the world.[323]

III. The Covenant with Israel.

A. The Establishment of the Covenant with Israel as a Nation. Josephus clearly assumes that already in Egypt, Israel was a nation, for Amaram, the father of Moses, was fearful there that "the whole nation would be extinguished through lack of the succeeding generation" (*Ant.* 2.210). Thus, Josephus partakes of the tradition in Deut 26:5 (cf. Gen 46:3; Josh 24:4), that Israel became a "great nation" in Egypt (cf., explicitly, *Ant.* 2.212, 214, 243). As a consequence, the term "nation" does not appear in connection with the covenant at Sinai, although it does occur at the conclusion of the giving of the Law at Abile

---

tarnae, the Britanni, the Charydes (or Herudes), the Cimbri, the Daci, the Dalmati, the Germani, the Hiberi, India, the Marcomani, the Medi, the Pannoni, the Parthi, the Sabaei, the Sarmatae, the Scythae, the Semnones, the Suevi, and the Sugambri." On the notion of Rome's universal sovereignty in the two centuries before the *Res Gestae*, see NICOLET, "Symbolism and Allegories of the Conquest of the World: Pompey, Caesar, Augustus," pp. 29–56.

[322] Cf. ibid., p. 9.

[323] Cf. *BJ* 6.312–313, which presumably refers to the prophecy of Dan 7:14 and/or Num 24:17 (cf. Martin HENGEL, *Die Zeloten. Untersuchungen zur jüdischen Freiheitsbewegung in der Zeit von Herodes I. bis 70 n. Chr.* [AGJU 1; Leiden: Brill, 1976], pp. 243–246): "But what more than all else incited them [sc. the Jews] to the war was an ambiguous oracle, likewise found in their sacred scriptures, to the effect that at that time one from their country would become ruler of the world. This they understood to mean someone of their own household, and many of their wise men went astray in their interpretation of it. The oracle, however, in reality signified the sovereignty of Vespasian, who was proclaimed Emperor on Jewish soil." Thus, even though he identifies the Roman Empire with the Fourth Kingdom of Daniel, which was destined to perish, Josephus appropriates the Jewish messianic expectation as evidence for the divine origin of Roman invincibility. As we have seen above on *BJ* 5.367, this goes along with the fact that, in contrast to Daniel, Josephus actually views the Fourth Kingdom as the strongest and most extensive of the four world empires.

near the Jordan: "Such were the ordinances of Moses, and the nation of the Hebrews continues to act in conformity with them" (*Ant.* 4.308).

B. The Settlement of Canaan. Josephus recounts the history of the conquest of "the nation(s) of the Canaanites"[324] and the subsequent interaction between Israel and the other nations that remained unconquered until the time of the Monarchy. We may skip over much of this very traditional and familiar material.

C. The Sin of Israel. Joshua's farewell address contains a warning about the dire consequences for turning aside "to imitate other nations" (*Ant.* 5.98). Nevertheless, Solomon, in clear violation of the laws of Moses, married many women from "foreign nations" and began to worship their gods (*Ant.* 8.191−192).

D. The Exile of Israel. According to Josephus, the warning that Israel would be exiled for disobedience had been issued by the prophet Azariah: "If, then, he said, they so continued, God would grant them always to overcome their foes and live happily, but, if they abandoned his worship, everything would turn out to the contrary and the would would come 'when no prophet will be found among your people nor any priest to give righteous judgment, but your cities shall be laid waste and the nation (τὸ ἔθνος) scattered over all the earth to lead the life of aliens and wanderers'" (*Ant.* 8.297). Accordingly, both the Northern and the Southern Kingdoms were deported into their respective countries of Exile. Josephus expresses it as follows in *Ant.* 10.184−185: "Now, when Salmanasses removed the Israelites, he settled in their place the nation of the Chuthaeans (τὸ τῶν Χουθαίων ἔθνος),[325] who had formerly lived in the interior of Persia and Media and who were then, moreover, called Samaritans because they assumed the name of the country in which they were settled. But the king of Babylonia, when he carried off the two tribes, did not settle any nation (ἔθνος) in their country, and for this reason all of Judea and Jerusalem and the Temple remained deserted for seventy years."

E. The Restoration of Israel.[326] The Jews were to survive this period of exile, which almost saw the extermination of the people as a nation.[327] Josephus

---

[324] Cf., e.g., *Ant.* 4.300; 5.49, 55, 88.

[325] Elsewhere Josephus refers to "nations (plural!) from a region called Chuthos" (*Ant.* 9.279), which accords with 2 Kgdms 17:24.

[326] Cf. Marianus de JONGE, "Josephus und die Zukunftserwartung seines Volkes," in *Josephus-Studien. Untersuchungen zu Josephus, dem antiken Judentum und dem Neuen Testament. Otto Michel zum 70.Geburtstag gewidmet* (ed. Otto Betz, et al.; Göttingen: Vandenhoeck & Ruprecht, 1974), pp. 205−219.

[327] Cf. *Ant.* 11.184 ("During the time when he [sc. Ahasuerus = Artaxerxes] ruled the Persian empire, the entire nation of the Jews, with their wives and children, was in danger of being destroyed"); 11.211 ("And although he [Haman] wished to be avenged on Mordecai, he considered it too little to ask that he alone be punished by the king, but decided to exterminate his whole nation, for he naturally hated the Jews because his own people, the Amelekites, had been destroyed by them"). Haman accuses the Jews of being "an unfriendly nation mingled with all mankind, which has a peculiar law, is insubordinate to kings, is different in its customs, hates monarchy, and is disloyal to our government" (*Ant.* 11.217). The way out of the crisis,

recounts that "the nation of the Israelites" returned under Cyrus, king of Persia, in accordance with the prophecy of Isa 44:28.[328] Nevertheless, work on the Temple and on the walls of Jerusalem was severely hampered by "the surrounding nations" (τὰ πέριξ ἔθνη),[329] especially by the Chuthaeans.[330] In the midst of this distressing situation, Nehemiah called out to heaven, "How long, O Lord, will you look away while our nation (τὸ ἔθνος ἡμῶν) suffers these things, having become the prey and spoil of all?" (*Ant.* 11.162). Clearly, the Persian empire did not usher in the expected Restoration of the nation, and neither did the two subsequent world empires.

Josephus goes on to describe the continuing struggles of his nation during the Greek and Roman empires. In fact, Josephus must defend his people against the charge that their laws can be shown to be unjust because the Jews are the slaves first of one nation then of another (*Ap.* 2.125) – a concept that fits very well with the aforementioned succession of world empires.

If the Greek Empire was basically a reign of terror for the nation of the Jews,[331] the Roman Empire was even worse, while the surrounding nations remained as hostile as ever to the nation.[332] In dealing with the Roman Empire, Josephus tries to show that, despite signs of goodwill to the nation from the Romans,[333] the recalcitrance of the Jews themselves – fueled by Roman out-

---

through the traditional national confession of sin and petition for divine intervention on behalf of the nation (*Ant.* 11.229), is paradigmatic in Josephus for subsequent crises that the Jews would face, as a substitute for armed resistance (cf., e.g., *Ant.* 11.326; *BJ* 5.375–419). In this case, the salvation of the Jews proved so dramatic that "from fear of the Jews many of the other nations also had themselves circumcised" (*Ant.* 11.285).

[328] Cf. *Ant.* 11.4–5. For the return under Xerxes, see *Ant.* 11.123. Josephus does not present a hope for the restoration to the Land (cf. AMARU, "Land Theology in Philo and Josephus," in *The Land Of Israel: Jewish Perspectives*, p. 80).

[329] Also called "the surrounding nations" (cf. *Ant.* 11.161).

[330] Cf. *Ant.* 11.19, 76, 88; see further 11.170, 175, 180.

[331] Already, the fear of Alexander's march on Jerusalem caused the nation both to petition God to deliver them from the impending dangers (*Ant.* 11.326) and to send out a reception committee that would be different from that of other nations (§ 329). The reign of Antiochus Ephiphanes proved particularly disastrous. For, on the one hand, many Jews, with the encouragement of Antiochus, gave up their "national customs," concealing their circumcision in order to be Greeks even when unclothed, and imitated "the works of the other nations" (τὰ τῶν ἄλλων ἐθνῶν ἔργα [*Ant.* 12.241; cf. 13.4]). On the other, Antiochus himself desecrated the sacred institutions of the nation, especially the Temple, and enforced the process of Hellenization (cf., e.g., *Ant.* 12.357). Furthermore, the oppression of the Jews under Bac-chides, an ally of Antiochus, is described as the worst the nation had experienced since their return from Babylon (*Ant.* 13.5). The resistance movement under Mattathias and his sons may have improved the situation of the nation and purged it of the offending Hellenistic Jews, some of whom escaped into the neighboring nations (*Ant.* 12.278); nevertheless, the surrounding nations, which resented the resurgence of the Jewish nation, banded together against them and destroyed many of freedom fighters (*Ant.* 12.327; cf. also § 330). Eventually, of course, the movement prevailed, hailing Judas Maccabaeus as the one who freed his nation and rescued them from slavery to the Macedonians (*Ant.* 12.434).

[332] Cf. *Ant.* 13.195–196.

[333] Josephus uses the Roman treaties and decrees in favor of the Jewish nation to show the

rages[334] – led to their own demise in the war against the Romans,[335] a war that was "the greatest not only of the wars of our own time, but, as far as accounts have reached us, well nigh of all that ever broke out between cities or nations" (*BJ* 1.1). According to Josephus, Agrippa II had warned the nation of what would happen if they went to war with Rome: The Romans would make them an example to the other nations, they would burn Jerusalem to the ground, and they would exterminate their people (*BJ* 2.397).[336] Josephus' perspective on the culpability of the Jews during this period becomes particularly clear in his own appeals to the intransigent Jews in Jerusalem during the siege (*BJ* 5.362–419; 6.96–110). Josephus exclaims: "But, pray, who enlisted the Romans against the nation (κατὰ τοῦ ἔθνους)? Was it not the impiety of its inhabitants? Whence did its servitude arise? Was it not from party strife among our forefathers, when the madness of Aristobulus and Hyrcanus and their mutual dissensions brought Pompey against the city, and God subjected to the Romans those who were unworthy of liberty?" (*BJ* 5.395–396).[337]

While emphasizing the Jewish responsibility for their situation under the Romans, Josephus also stresses divine sovereignty over the plight of the nation: ". . . God who went the round of the nations, bringing to each in turn the rod of

---

basic goodwill of Rome (cf. *Ant.* 12.417; 13.163; 14.186, 189, 196, 199, 265, 323; 16.162–163; 19.284–285, 290). As M. STERN points out, however, "There seems to be only a single allusion in *The Jewish War* [i.e., *BJ* 7.100–111] to the view that at least the Jews in the Diaspora benefited from Roman rule, and that within the Roman Empire the Jewish communities in the Hellenistic East were more secure than the Hellenistic cities without Roman control and supervision" ("Josephus and the Roman Empire," p. 77). By abstaining from all interference with the customs of the country, Tiberius Alexander kept the nation at peace (*BJ* 2.220). On the Roman hatred for the nation of the Jews, however, see *BJ* 3.133; 6.214.

[334] For example, Pompey's penetration into the Holy Place is said to have affected the nation more deeply than all the other calamities of that time (*BJ* 1.152). Much to the consternation of the nation, Herod's theater was lined with trophies of the nations that Caesar had won in war (*Ant.* 15.272, 276). Gaius ordered that his statue be erected in the Temple and, in case of resistance, that the whole nation be reduced to slavery (*BJ* 2.186). The overbearing and lawless actions of Gessius Florus provoked the nation foolishly to rebel against the Romans (*Ant.* 18.25). Albanus burdened the whole nation with extraordinary taxes (*BJ* 2.273). The Syrians in Caesarea obtained a rescript from Nero cancelling Jewish rights, which led to the misfortunes that befell the nation of the Jews (*Ant.* 20.184).

[335] Cf. *Ant.* 16.277 ("Such was the great madness that settled upon the nation because they had no king of their own to restrain the populace by his pre-eminence. . ." [cf. Judg 21:25]); 18.7 (". . . and so these men [sc. Judas the Gaulanite and Saddok the Pharisee] sowed the seed of every kind of misery, which so afflicted the nation that words are inadequate"), 25. The defeat of Cestius Gallus, the Roman governor of Syria, by Jewish revolutionaries in Palestine proved disastrous for the whole nation, for those who were bent on war with Rome hoped to continue victorious to the end (*Vit.* 24). Titus addresses the leaders of the besieged city of Jerusalem: "Thus, when the empire found refuge in us [i.e., the Romans], when throughout its length was universal tranquility, and foreign nations were sending embassies of congratulations, once again the Jews were in arms" (*BJ* 6.342).

[336] Cf. Jn 11:48: ". . . and the Romans will come and destroy both the place [i.e., the Temple] and the nation (τὸ ἔθνος)."

[337] Cf. *Ant.* 14.41.

empire, now rested over Italy" (§ 367). If God had wanted to free the Jews or to punish the Romans, he could have done so (§§ 408–409). But, God is now with the Romans (§ 368). The destruction of Jerusalem was already prophesied in Daniel and was, therefore, a foregone conclusion (cf. *Ant.* 10.276). Thus, Josephus concludes his account of the siege of Jerusalem with these words: "However, neither its [Jerusalem's] antiquity, nor its ample wealth, nor the nation spread over the whole inhabited world (οὔτε τὸ διαπεφοιτηκὸς ὅλης τῆς οἰκουμένης ἔθνος), nor yet the great glory of its religious rites, would aught avail to avert its ruin" (*BJ* 6.442).

Josephus does not use the term ἔθνος in reference to an expectation for the Jewish nation after the war.[338] Did he nevertheless tacitly maintain the hope of Dan 2:34, 44–45, that the stone of the Kingdom of God would finally smash the Fourth Kingdom?[339] All we can say with certainty is that Josephus encouraged his readers to read Daniel if they wanted to understand the meaning of the stone for the future (*Ant.* 10.210).[340]

For Josephus, the Temple and Jerusalem occupy a special position in relation to the nation and the nations. As the capital of the whole nation (*BJ* 4.89),[341] Jerusalem contained two fortified places, one guarding the city itself and the other the Temple; whoever controlled these places had the whole nation in his power (*Ant.* 15.248). The Temple had been adorned mainly at the expense of "foreigners" (ἀλλοφύλοι) and had always accepted gifts of "the foreign nations" (τῶν ἔξωθεν ἐθνῶν), which exposes the absurdity of the pretext for suspending the daily offerings on behalf of the emperor and the Roman nation (*BJ* 2.412–413). Josephus exhorts those trapped in Jerusalem: "Oh! iron-hearted men, fling away your weapons, take compassion on your country even now tottering to its fall, turn around and behold the beauty of what you are betraying: what a city! what a Temple! what countless nations' gifts!" (*BJ* 5.416–417).

---

[338] Nevertheless, we may note that Josephus' eschatology sounds strangely similar to Philo's at this point: "Josephus replaces the classical messianic eschatology with his own vision of future blessings: a glorious people whose eternal existence is assured by divine blessing and promise; a people who have a motherland, but whose population is so great that they overflow into every island and continent . . . – a motherland (as a point of reference) with an extensive eternal diaspora *which might even be seen as colonial in character*" (AMARU, "Land Theology in Josephus' *Jewish Antiquities*," p. 228 [emphasis mine]). Philo makes explicit reference to the Diaspora as colonies of Jerusalem (see above on *Legat.* 281).

[339] So SANDERS, *Judaism: Practice and Belief 63 BCE – 66 CE*, pp. 288–289; de JONGE, "Josephus und die Zukunftserwartungen seines Volkes," p. 212. Cf. RAJAK, "Agrippa II's Speech in Josephus's *Jewish War*," p. 132 (also p. 133): "The implication of the Josephan doctrine that God is siding with the Romans [*BJ* 5.367–368] must surely be that the day will come when the tables will be turned, when he will change sides once more."

[340] See further FELDMAN, "Josephus' Portrait of Daniel," pp. 66–71. Note that Josephus affirms the veracity of Daniel's prophecies by pointing to their fulfillment in Antiochus Ephiphanes and the recent conquest of Jerusalem by the Romans (*Ant.* 10.276).

[341] Cf. *BJ* 4.261, which refers to Jerusalem as "the front and head of the whole nation."

The Vitae Prophetarum (VP).[342] The sixth-century manuscript[343] in which this (possibly first-century) Palestinian pseudepigraphon is preserved summarizes its contents as follows: "The names of the prophets, and where they are from, and where they died, and how and where they lie."[344] From this description it is clear that the *Lives of the Prophets* has a fundamentally geographical structure.[345] What this summary fails to mention, however, is that the prophets, some of whom either began or ended their lives in foreign lands, were also otherwise active and/or resident in foreign countries.[346] Altogether, therefore, there are even more toponyms in this work than the summary would suggest.

I. The Table-of-Nations Tradition. The scope of eschatology in the *Lives* is universalistic, encompassing "all the earth" (πᾶσα ἡ γῆ)[347] and "all nations" (πάντα τὰ ἔθνη),[348] often in connection with Jerusalem.[349] To match this universal scope, the *Lives of the Prophets* presupposes a geographical horizon for the prophets that includes not only Palestine and adjoining regions but also representatives of all three continents of the world. Asia, of course, is the best represented, since all the prophets in the *Lives* have contact there, and Jerusalem receives particular emphasis.[350] Africa is represented chiefly by Jeremiah, who was very active in Egypt.[351] Europe is represented both by Jonah, who was from "the district of Kariathmos near Azotos, the city of the Greeks by the sea" (*VP* 10:1),[352] and by Habakkuk, who prophesied about a "western nation" (ἔθνος δυτικόν), that is, the Romans (12:11).[353]

---

[342] Text: T. SCHERMANN, *Prophetarum vitae fabulosae indices apostolorum discipulorumque Domini Dorotheo, Epiphanio, Hippolyto aliisque vindicate* (Leipzig: Teubner, 1907). In the following, I am indebted to Anna Maria SCHWEMER for kindly providing me with portions of her dissertation, Studien zu den frühjüdischen Prophetenlegenden. Vitae Prophetarum, Band 1: Die Viten der großen Propheten: Jesaja, Jeremia, Ezechiel und Daniel, eingeleitet, übersetzt und kommentiert (Tübingen, 1993).

[343] The oldest and most reliable Greek text is Codex Marchalianus (Vat. gr. 2125).

[344] ὀνόματα προφητῶν καὶ πόθεν εἰσὶ καὶ ποῦ ἀπέθανον καὶ πῶς καὶ ποῦ κεῖνται. SCHWEMER argues that the *Lives* is "eine lexikonartige, jüdische Sammlung von Kurzbiographien."

[345] The *Lives* have a northern orientation, for "the mountains which are above Babylon" lie to the "north" (*VP* 4:21).

[346] To this degree, the *Vitae Prophetarum* resemble ancient itineraries (on which, see O. A. W. DILKE, "Itineraries and Geographical Maps in the Early and Late Roman Empires," in *The History of Cartography*, pp. 234–257; Claus-Jürgen THORNTON, *Der Zeuge des Zeugen. Lukas als Historiker der Paulusreisen* [WUNT 56; Tübingen: Mohr-Siebeck, 1991], pp. 280–299).

[347] Cf. *VP* 4:21, 22; also 10:8 (ὅλην τὴν γῆν). See further *VP* 3:7: "to the end of the earth."

[348] Cf. *VP* 2:10; 4:21; 10:8. See further *VP* 13:2; 15:5.

[349] Cf. *VP* 3:7; 10:8; 13:2; 15:5.

[350] Cf. *VP* 1:1, 3, 4, 7; 3:7, 14, 15; 4:3; 10:8; 12:2, 3, 4; 13:2; 14:1; 15:2, 4, 5; [17:2]; 21:3; 22:2; 23:1; 24:1.

[351] Cf. *VP* 2:1–8. On the Egyptian Diaspora, see also 12:4. When Nebuchadnezzar entered Jerusalem, Habakkuk fled to Ostrakine in Egypt (12:3).

[352] For another reference to a Greek city, cf. *VP* 2:6: "Argos of the Peloponnesus."

[353] On the Romans as the nation of the west, cf. *Sib. Or.* 3.175–176; 8.9–12. Philo *Flacc.* 45 refers to "the western nations" (ἔθνη τὰ ἑσπέρια).

Given the universal scope of the *Lives* and its interest in "all nations,"[354] we
are struck by the fact that the toponomy of the *Vitae Prophetarum* appropriates
the Table-of-Nations tradition at several points. Ezekiel, for example, was
buried "in the field of Maour in the grave of Shem and Arpachshad, ancestors
of Abraham" (*VP* 3:3). According to Genesis 10, Shem is the father of all the
sons of Eber (v. 1) and thus the ancestor of Abraham and his descendants (cf.
Gen 11:10−26). Arpachshad was born to Shem two years after the Flood (Gen
10:22; 11:10). According to Jewish tradition, Arpachshad became the ruler of
the territory corresponding to the land of the Chaldeans,[355] that is, the very
place of the Babylonian Diaspora. As we have seen in 1QapGenesis 15−19, the
territory around which Abraham made a complete, clockwise circuit in
response to the promise of Gen 13:14 is equivalent to the portion allotted to
Arpachshad in the exposition of the Table of Nations in Jubilees (9:4).[356] Thus,
by resorting to the eternally valid Table-of-Nations tradition, the text is able to
claim that Ezekiel was buried not in foreign soil but in the land promised to
Abraham. If the field of "Maour" (Μαούρ) is to be identified with Mamre,[357]
the original place of Abraham's grave (Gen 23:17, 19), then this would underscore Abraham's claim to the Land.

Another example of the Table-of-Nations tradition is found in *VP* 1:8, which
refers to "the gold from Ethiopia (Αἰθιοπία) and the spices" kept in the tombs
Solomon made. According to 1 Kgs 10:10, gold and spices were among the gifts
given to Solomon by the Queen of Sheba. What, therefore, is the connection
between "Ethiopia" and the biblical Queen of "Sheba" (שבא/Σαβά)? In the
(updated) Table-of-Nations tradition, Ethiopia is the Greek name for the
territory of Cush, the first son of Ham (cf. Gen 10:6, 7). Thus, in his exposition
of the Table of Nations, Josephus explains that "of the four sons of Ham, the
name of one, Chusaeus [Cush], has escaped the ravages of time: the Ethiopians,
his subjects, are to this day called by themselves and by all in Asia Chusaeans
[Cushites]" (*Ant.* 1.131).[358] In the Septuagint, the inhabitants of Cush are

---

[354] Note also the implicit references to the four world empires: Babylon (*VP* 3:17; 4:21;
12:7, 8, 17; 14:1; 15:7); Media (3:19) and Persia (4:19); Alexander the Macedonian (2:5); and
Rome (12:11).

[355] Cf. *Jub.* 9:4. According to Josephus (*Ant.* 1.144), Arpachshad (ארפכשד) is the older
name for those who are now called Chaldeans (כשדים). The latter are frequently mentioned in
the *Lives of the Prophets* (cf. 3:1, 9; 4:1; 12:4; 15:1).

[356] Cf. Philip S. ALEXANDER, "Notes on the 'Imago Mundi' of the Book of Jubilees," *JJS* 33
(1982) 197−213 (here p. 206 n. 12). On the dependence of the *Genesis Apocryphon* on
Jubilees, see Chap. 1.

[357] So A. M. SCHWEMER, who suggests that this "Mamre" refers to a Babylonian "Ur-
mamre" after which the Palestinian "Mamre" was patterned.

[358] See further Torgny SÄVE-SÖDERBERGH, "Kusch," in *Lexikon der Ägyptologie*, 3 (1980)
888−893; Jean LECLANT, "Kuschitenherrschaft," in ibid., cols. 893−901. Inge HOFMANN
(*Studien zum meroitischen Königtum* [Monographies Reine Élisabeth 2; Brussels: Fondation
Égyptologique Reine Élisabeth, 1971], p. 10) notes, however, that the modern usage of
"Cush" is more limited than the ancient: "Seit dem Mittleren Reich bezeichneten die Ägypter
das Gebiet südlich des 2. Kataraktes als 'Kusch', welcher Name später für das gesamte, südlich

usually rendered by Αἰθίοπες, and Αἰθιοπία stands in general for the Hebrew כוש; only in the Table of Nations itself does the transliteration Χούς occur (Gen 10:6, 7, 8; 1 Chr 1:8, 9, 10).[359] According to Josephus, whom L. H. SILBERMAN considers idiosyncratic at this point,[360] the Queen of Sheba was the "queen of Egypt and Ethiopia" (*Ant.* 8.159, 165, 175), and Saba (Sheba) was the capital of the Ethiopian realm (*Ant.* 2.249).[361] Yet the *Lives* seems to appropriate the same tradition when it refers to the "the gold from Ethiopia and the spices" (1:8).

II. The Use of ἔθνος. The word ἔθνος occurs seven times in the *Lives*, most often in the sense of "nation" but possibly once or twice in the sense of "Gentiles." Because Hezekiah showed τοῖς ἔθνεσι the aforementioned tombs made by Solomon, God swore that Hezekiah's seed would be enslaved to his enemies (*VP* 1:9). Since, according to 2 Kgs 20:12–18, Hezekiah showed his treasures only to an embassy from Merodach-baladan, king of Babylon, it is possible that ἔθνη refers here to a group of individual non-Jews or "Gentiles." On the other hand, however, since either translation – "the Gentiles" or "the nations" – represents a generalization of the account in 2 Kings, ἔθνη here may denote "nations," especially since, as we have just seen, the reference to "Ethiopia" in the immediately preceding verse presupposes the updated Table-of-Nations tradition. Furthermore, the *Lives* otherwise uses ἀλλόφυλοι to designate "foreigners" (cf. 1:3; also 10:2).

Another passage in which the meaning of ἔθνος is open to interpretation appears to be either a Christian interpolation or a Christian redaction. Just before the capture of the Temple, Jeremiah – "the prophet to the nations"[362] – explains why he has hidden the ark of the Law and its contents in a rock: "The Lord has gone away from Sinai (or Zion)[363] into heaven and will come again in power. And this will be a sign (σημεῖον) of his coming, when all the nations

---

an Ägypten grenzende Territorium verwendet wurde. Von einem 'kuschitischen' Königreich zu sprechen, führt aber unweigerlich zu Missverständnissen, da seit Lepsius der Begriff 'kuschitisch' für die hamito-semitischen Sprachen zwischen Nil und Rotem Meer reserviert ist und ethnologisch für die verhältnismässig einheitliche Kultur Abessiniens Anwendung findet."

[359] Cf. Henry A. REDPATH, "The Geography of the Septuagint," *AJT* 7 (1903) 289–307 (here pp. 292–293). Thus, the association of Gog and Magog with Ethiopia in *Sib. Or.* 3:319 is probably due to the mention of Cush (LXX: Αἰθίοπες) in Ezek 38:5, whose whole immediate context (Ezekiel 38–39) stands in the Table-of-Nations tradition (see Chap. 1). Whereas Num 12:1 refers to the "Cushite woman" whom Moses had married, Josephus speaks of Moses' having married "Tharbis, the daughter of the king of the Ethiopians" (*Ant.* 2.252–253; cf. Tessa RAJAK, "Moses in Ethiopia: Legend and Literature," *JJS* 29 [1978] 111–122).

[360] Cf. Lou H. SILBERMAN, "The Queen of Sheba in Judaic Tradition," in *Solomon & Sheba* (ed. James B. Pritchard; London: Phaidon Press, 1974), pp. 65–84.

[361] See further in Chap. 3 on the eunuch who was an official in the court of the queen of the Ethiopians (Acts 8:27; cf. Lk 11:31).

[362] Cf. Jer 1:5: προφήτην εἰς ἔθνη τέθεικά σε.

[363] In v. 10a, the mss. vacillate between "Zion" and "Sinai." SCHWEMER argues that the latter is the *lectio difficilior*.

(πάντα τὰ ἔθνη) worship a tree (ξύλον)."[364] If this text was shaped by Christian redaction, the original Jewish substratum may have had Jer 10:2 in mind, which refers to "the nations."[365] As it stands now, however, the sign of the coming of the Lord probably refers to the "sign" (σημεῖον) of the cross,[366] and thus the meaning of πάντα τὰ ἔθνη is less certain.

The other occurrences of ἔθνη more clearly refer to the "nations." First, Jonah is said to have "sojourned in Sour, a country of foreign nations" (παρῴκησε τὴν Σοὺρ χώραν ἀλλοφύλων ἐθνῶν).[367] The modifying adjective ἀλλόφυλος ("foreign") ensures that ἔθνη denotes "nations" here. If, as in Ezek 16:28 (A), Σούρ stands for אשור ("Assyria"),[368] the "foreign nations" might be a reference to "the nations" (τὰ ἔθνη) composing Assyria.[369] Second, Jonah "gave a portent concerning Jerusalem and the whole earth (ὅλην τὴν γῆν), that whenever they should see a stone crying out piteously the end was at hand. And whenever they should see all the nations (πάντα τὰ ἔθνη) in Jerusalem, the entire city would be razed to the ground."[370] This appropriates the widespread OT tradition of the attack on Jerusalem by the nations.[371] Third, Habakkuk predicted concerning the end of the Temple: "By a western nation it will happen" (ὑπὸ ἔθνους δυτικοῦ γενήσεται).[372] This evidently refers to the Romans,[373] whom the Jews feared would destroy the Temple in the turbulent years preceding A.D. 70.[374] Fourth, Zephaniah "prophesied concerning the city (περὶ τῆς πόλεως) and about the end of the nations (περὶ τέλους

---

[364] *VP* 2:10.

[365] In that case, "the signs of heaven" (τὰ σημεῖα τοῦ οὐρανοῦ) in Jer 10:2 have been interpreted as the futile customs of "the nations" (τὰ ἔθνη), which include "a tree" (ξύλον) cut out of the forest and a molten image (v. 3).

[366] Cf. D. R. A. Hare, "The Lives of the Prophets," *OTP*, 2:388 n. 2q. Schwemer appeals to G. Q. Reijners, *The Terminology of the Holy Cross in Early Christian Literature as Based on Old Testament Typology* (Graecitas Christianorum Primaeva 2; Nijmegen: Dekker & Vande Vegt, 1965), pp. 118–187, which discusses σημεῖον as a name for the cross possibly as early as Did. 16:6. On ξύλον as a term for the cross, see ibid., pp. 6ff.

[367] *VP* 10:2.

[368] This would make sense since in v. 3, Jonah's sojourn in "Sour" is connected with the prophet's desire to remove his reproach for falsely prophesying against Nineveh, the capital of the Assyrian empire. Charles Cutler Torrey understood it as a reference to Tyre (*Lives of the Prophets: Greek Text and Translation* [JBLMS 1; Philadelphia: Society of Biblical Literature and Exegesis, 1946], p. 41).

[369] Josephus refers to "the nations of the Assyrians" that Tiglath-Pileser, king of Assyria, resettled in Damascus (*Ant.* 9.253). See also 2 Kgs 17:26.

[370] *VP* 10:8.

[371] Cf. Zech 12:3 (καὶ ἐπισυναχθήσονται ἐπ' αὐτὴν [sc. Jerusalem] πάντα τὰ ἔθνη τῆς γῆς), 9; 14:2, 16.

[372] *VP* 12:11.

[373] See n. 353 above.

[374] See above on Josephus *BJ* 2.397; 5.416–417. This expectation is also found in Jesus' eschatological discourse in Mark 13, which is not to be explained wholly as a *vaticinium ex eventu* (cf. M. Hengel, "The Gospel of Mark: The Time and Origin of the Situation," in *Studies in the Gospel of Mark* [London: SCM, 1985], pp. 1–30). See also Jn 11:48.

ἐθνῶν)."[375] Likewise, Zechariah's "prophesying in Jerusalem was based on his visions about the end of the nations (περὶ τέλους ἐθνῶν), Israel, the Temple, the laziness of prophets and priests. . . ."[376]

Paraleipomena Jeremiou (4 Baruch).[377] This possibly first-century (Palestinian) pseudepigraphon deals with certain events between the destruction of Jerusalem by the Babylonians and the stoning of Jeremiah.[378] Our term occurs three times in this document: twice in the Jewish *Grundschrift* and once in the Christianized ending (i.e., 8:12−9:32).[379] In the first of these occurrences, Baruch sent "to the market place of the nations/Gentiles" (εἰς τὴν ἀγορὰν τῶν ἐθνῶν) for papyrus and ink, so that he could write a letter to Jeremiah in Babylon (*4 Bar.* 6:19). Whereas J. R. HARRIS interpreted this reference to a market as evidence of the provenance of the document, since the author thereby betrays a thorough familiarity with Jerusalem, S. E. ROBINSON suggests that this detail may have been added merely for verisimilitude.[380] It is beyond the scope of this survey to delve further into this question, which would require consideration not only of the role of foreign merchants in Jerusalem during the post-exilic situation[381] but also of the nature of the market place(s) in the city.[382]

The second occurrence of ἔθνος comes in *4 Bar.* 7:37, according to which Jeremiah took the figs which Baruch had sent with his letter to Babylon and distributed them to the sick among the people, admonishing them to abstain "from the pollutions of the nations/Gentiles of Babylon" (ἐκ τῶν ἀλισγημάτων τῶν ἐθνῶν τῆς Βαβυλῶνος). Although this may recall the more common expression, "abominations of the nations" (βδελύγματα τῶν ἐθνῶν),[383] the genitive τῆς Βαβυλῶνος seems to preclude the possibility that ἐθνῶν denotes "nations" in this case.

---

[375] *VP* 13:2. Cf. Zeph 2:11; 3:8.

[376] *VP* 15:5. Cf. Zech 1:15; 2:4, 12, 15; 8:22−23; 9:10; 12:3; 12:9; 14:2, 16, 18−19.

[377] Text: Robert A. KRAFT and Ann-Elizabeth PURINTUN, *Paraleipomena Jeremiou* (SBLTT 1; Pseudepigrapha Series 1; Missoula, MT: Society of Biblical Literature, 1972).

[378] On the date and provenance, see S. E. ROBINSON, "4 Baruch," *OTP*, 2:414−415.

[379] Cf. *4 Bar.* 9:20: "For he [sc. Jesus Christ] shall come, and he shall go out and choose for himself twelve apostles that they might preach the good news among the nations (ἵνα εὐαγγελίζωνται ἐν τοῖς ἔθνεσιν). . . ." See further Peter STUHLMACHER, *Das paulinische Evangelium, Teil 1: Vorgeschichte* (FRLANT 95; Göttingen: Vandenhoeck & Ruprecht, 1968), p. 177 n. 2.

[380] Cf. ROBINSON, "4 Baruch," 2:415.

[381] Cf., e.g., Zech 14:21; Neh 13:15−22. Was there a connection between this alleged "market of the nations/Gentiles" and the so-called Court of the Gentiles (on which, see further above under Josephus)? In this regard, the Gospel accounts of Jesus' Cleansing of the Temple should also be consulted (cf. Mk 11:15−17 par.; Jn 2:13−17).

[382] Josephus uses ἀγορά of a plurality of market places in Jerusalem (cf. *BJ* 5.513; *Ant.* 11.22), particularly "the upper agora" (cf. *BJ* 2.305, 315; 5.137), "the timber market" (*BJ* 2.530), and "the clothes-market" (*BJ* 5.331). Cf. Henry St. John THACKERAY, *A Lexicon to Josephus, Part 1* (Publications of the Alexander Kohut Memorial Foundation; Paris: Librairie orientaliste Paul Geuthner, 1930), s.v. ἀγορά, p. 5.

[383] Cf., e.g., Deut 18:9; 4 Kgdms 16:3; 21:2; 2 Chr 28:3.

The Greek Apocalypse of Baruch (3 Baruch).[384] In this probably first-to-second-century pseudepigraphon, Baruch, the friend and secretary of Jeremiah, weeps over the destruction of Jerusalem and its Temple and the mockery of its destroyers. The Lord sends an angel to comfort him and to guide him through the heavens, showing him their mysteries. The term ἔθνος occurs only three times in *3 Baruch*. In the first occurrence, Baruch laments the destruction of Jerusalem by asking God why he "handed us over to such nations so that they reproach us, saying, 'Where is their God?'" (ἀλλὰ παρέδωκας ἡμᾶς εἰς ἔθνη τοιαῦτα, ὅπως ὀνειδίζοντες λέγουσιν· ποῦ ἐστιν ὁ θεὸς αὐτῶν;).[385] Israel as a "reproach to the nations" is a common motif in the OT and Jewish literature.[386] Here, the text alludes particularly to Joel 2:17.

The next two occurrences of the term allude to Deut 32:21:[387] "But since they [sc. the sons of men] have provoked me to anger by their deeds, go and provoke them to jealousy, and provoke them to anger, and embitter them against those who are no nation, against a nation without understanding."[388] Originally, of course, Deut 32:21 applied to Israel in Exile, but here it receives a generalized application.

Greek Apocalypse of Ezra.[389] This obviously Christianized pseudepigraphon of uncertain date and provenance contains the visions of Ezra, who prays that the mysteries of God be revealed to him (1:1−5). In answer to his request, Ezra is shown, among other things, the signs of the end: "And God said, 'First, I shall cause by shaking the fall of four-footed beasts and men. And when you see that brother delivers brother over to death and children will rise up against parents and a wife abandons her own husband, and when nation will rise up against nation in war (καὶ ὅταν ἔθνος πρὸς ἔθνος ἐπαναστῇ ἐν πολέμῳ), then you will know that the end is near.'"[390] Although this probably alludes most directly to 2 Chr 15:6,[391] it may also be influenced by the signs of the end in the Olivet Discourse (Mk 13:3−8 par.).[392]

Qumran Texts.[393] For the sake of completeness, this survey of Second Temple literature closes with a brief overview of the Qumran texts containing

---

[384] Text: J. C. PICARD, *Apocalypsis Baruchi Graece* (PVTG 2; Leiden: Brill, 1967).

[385] *3 Bar.* 1:2.

[386] Cf. Tob 3:4; 2 Esdr 15:9; 1 Macc 4:58; Joel 2:19; Jer 51:8; Ezek 34:29; 36:6.

[387] αὐτοὶ παρεζήλωσάν με ἐπ' οὐ θεῷ, παρώργισάν με ἐν τοῖς εἰδώλοις αὐτῶν· κἀγὼ παραζηλώσω αὐτοὺς ἐπ' οὐκ ἔθνει, ἐπ' ἔθνει ἀσυνέτῳ παροργιῶ αὐτούς.

[388] *3 Bar.* 16:2: ἀλλ' ἐπειδὴ παρώργισάν με ἐν τοῖς ἔργοις αὐτῶν, πορευθέντες, παραζηλώσατε αὐτοὺς καὶ παροργίσατε, καὶ παραπικράνατε ἐπ' οὐκ ἔθνει, ἐπὶ ἔθνει ἀσυνέτῳ. Cf. Rom 10:19.

[389] Text: Konstantin von TISCHENDORF, *Apocalypses Apocryphae* (Leipzig, 1866; reprint ed., Hildesheim: Georg Olms, 1966).

[390] *Gk. Apoc. Ezra* 3:11−13.

[391] καὶ πολεμήσει ἔθνος πρὸς ἔθνος καὶ πόλις πρὸς πόλιν, ὅτι ὁ θεὸς ἐξέστησεν αὐτοὺς ἐν πάσῃ θλίψει. Cf. also 4 Ezra 13:31.

[392] Cf. Mk 13:8 (par.): ἐγερθήσεται γὰρ ἔθνος ἐπ' ἔθνος καὶ βασιλεία ἐπὶ βασιλείαν. . . .

[393] Cf. DEINES, "Die Abwehr der Fremden in den Texten aus Qumran," pp. 59−91.

גּוֹי, the Hebrew word that usually stands behind ἔθνος in the Septuagint.[394] The plural גוים (or an orthographic variation)[395] predominates in the Qumran texts, although the singular does occur sporadically. The term occurs very frequently in citations of or allusions to the OT.[396]

Like ἔθνη, גוים is used in three interrelated senses that are sometimes difficult to distinguish in any given context.[397] First of all, the term is used in the sense of the "nations"[398] of the world, including Israel. Israel may occupy a central position among the nations, but it is still one nation among others. According to 4Q381 76−77.14-16: "He [sc. God] chose y[ou from m]any [peoples] and from great nations (ומגויים גדולים) to be his people (עם), to rule ... as most high over every nation of the earth (על כל גוי הארץ)."[399] Based ostensibly on Deut 28:1 ("the Lord your God will set you high above all the nations of the earth"), this expectation of Israel's universal sovereignty clearly implies that Israel is itself one of the nations from which it was chosen.[400] Other Qumran texts also either express or imply that Israel is a גוי.[401] Furthermore, the term "foreign nation(s)" (גוי נכר)[402] makes sense only if Israel itself is a nation among other nations; otherwise, נכר would be superfluous.

---

[394] Cf. Edwin HATCH and Henry A. REDPATH, *A Concordance to the Septuagint and the Other Greek Versions of the Old Testament* (2 vols.; Oxford: Clarendon, 1897; reprint ed., Graz: Akademische Druck- u. Verlagsanstalt, 1975), 1:368−373.

[395] גואים (e.g., 1QpHab 3.5; 4QpIsaᵃ 7−10 iii 8; 4QpHosᵃ 2.13, 16; 11QTemple 64:10); גוויים (e.g, 1QM 14.5; 4QFlor 1.18).

[396] Cf. 1QpHab 2.11 (Hab 1:6a); 8.5 (Hab 2:5); 9.3 (Hab 2:8a); 4QpNah 3−4 ii 7 (Nah 3:4), 11 (Nah 3:5); 1QapGen 21.23 (Gen 14:1, 9); 4QFlor 1.18 (Ps 2:1); 11QTemple 60.16−17 (Deut 18:9); CD 5.17 (Deut 32:28a).

[397] Cf., e.g., the difficult and much discussed text of CD 9:1 ("As for every case of devoting, namely that a man be devoted so that he ceases to be a living man, he is to be put to death [Lev 27:29] by the ordinances of the nations/Gentiles"), on which see further DEINES, "Die Abwehr der Fremden in den Texten aus Qumran," p. 84 n. 71. See also 11QTemple 48.11 ("And you shall not do as the Gentiles/nations [הגויים] do: everywhere they bury their dead; even within their houses they bury"); 57.15−17 ("And he [sc. the king] shall not take a wife from all the daughters of the nations [בנות הגויים], but from his father's house he shall take unto himself a wife from the family of his father").

[398] In response to HARE and HARRINGTON, who argue that in Qumran, גוים "refers to the whole collection of non-Jews rather than to specific national groups" ("'Make Disciples of All the Gentiles' [Mt 28:19]," p. 360), it should be mentioned that גוים often stands in parallel with either עמים (1QpHab 3.5−6; 8.5; 4QpIsaᵃ 7−10 iii 25−26; 4QDibHam 4.5, 8; cf. 11QTemple 58.3; CD 5.16−17) or לאומים (4QFlor 1.18; 1QH 6.12; 4Q434,436 2.7−8; 3.2), demonstrating that גוים denotes "nations" in these cases.

[399] For the text and translation, see Eileen M. SCHULLER, *Non-Canonical Psalms from Qumran: A Pseudepigraphic Collection* (HSS 28; Atlanta: Scholars Press, 1986), pp. 215, 219. SCHULLER considers l. 16 to be based specifically on Deut 28:1 (cf. ibid., p. 225).

[400] 4QpPs37 1.3−4, 9−13 represents another Qumran text that expects universal sovereignty: The community of the poor will be the "heir of the whole world," whose middlepoint is Jerusalem and the Temple.

[401] Cf. 1QpZeph 1.2 (in a restored citation of Zeph 2:1); 4Q381 33.10; CD 5.17 (citation of Deut 32:28a).

[402] Cf. CD 14.15; 11QTemple 57.11; 64.7. This combination is not found in the Hebrew Bible (cf. τὰ ἔξωθεν ἔθνη [Josephus *BJ* 2.412; 6.342] or ἔθνη ἀλλότρια [*Pss. Sol.* 2:2]). The

The first usage prepares the way for the second, which further distinguishes Israel from the other nations: הגוים[403] or כול הגוים[404] is used in the sense of the "(all) the nations" of the world apart from Israel. The *War Scroll*, for example, refers several times to the wicked "nations of vanity" (גוי הבל) which will be destroyed in the end time.[405] When used in this sense, גוים often has a double connotation: religious (i.e., idolatrous nations) and national (i.e., enemy nations).[406]

This second use of גוים in the sense of "(foreign) nations" flows naturally into the third: "foreign nationals, Gentiles," i.e., individuals of any nation other than the nation of the Jews. This third use of the term is found only in the plural and primarily in halakic contexts; there is no corresponding usage of גוי in the singular for an individual "Gentile."[407] The passage CD 11.14−15 provides an example of this plural usage: "No man shall rest in a place near Gentiles (גוים) on the Sabbath." As HARE and HARRINGTON rightly point out, "This statement makes more sense if *gôyîm* refers to Gentile settlements in Palestine (or elsewhere) rather than to specific national groups such as the Egyptians or Greeks."[408] Similarly, CD 12.8−9 states: "No man shall sell an animal or bird that is clean to Gentiles (גוים), in order that they may not sacrifice them."

I. The Table of Nations. As we have noted above, the Qumran texts focus on "all nations." In particular, the *War Scroll*, which expects a final "battle with all the nations" and the "annihilation of all nations of wickedness" (1QM 15.1−2), plans a series of major offensives based on the geography and ethnography of the Table of Nations. With the goal of world domination, these campaigns proceed over a 29-year period: first against the Shemites, then against the

---

most famous of these texts is 11QTemple 64.6−8 because of its reference to crucifixion in conjunction with Deut 21:22: "And if a man informs against his people, and delivers his people up to a foreign nation (גוי נכר), and does harm to his people, you shall hang him on a tree, and he shall die." See further Johann MAIER, *The Temple Scroll: An Introduction, Translation and Commentary* (JSOTSup 34; Sheffield: JSOT Press, 1985), pp. 132−134.

[403] Cf., e.g., 1QpHab 5.3; 11QTemple 48.11.

[404] Cf., e.g., 1QpHab 3.4−5; 5.4; 8.5; 13.1; 4QpIsa^a 7−10 iii 8; 1QH 6.12; 1QM 15.1; 16.1; 4QDibHam 3.3, 5; 4.8.

[405] Cf. 1QM 4.12; 6.6; 9.9; 11.9. In these examples, גוי is evidently a defective spelling for the plural construct (cf., Jer 26:6; 44:8; 2 Chr 32:13; Ezra 6:21). The expression may be a rhetorical inversion of the wording in Jer 14:22 (הבלי הגוים), which refers to "the vanities (i.e., the idols) of the nations."

[406] Cf. Yigael YADIN, *The Temple Scroll* (3 vols.; Jerusalem: The Israel Exploration Society/The Institute of Archaeology of the Hebrew University of Jerusalem/The Shrine of the Book, 1983), 1:290.

[407] Despite the considerations of HARE and HARRINGTON, "'Make Disciples of all the Gentiles' (Mt 28:19)," p. 360. On the later rabbinic use of the term, see Gary G. PORTON, *Goyim: Gentiles and Israelites in Mishnah-Tosefta* (BJS 155; Atlanta, GA: Scholars Press, 1988).

[408] HARE and HARRINGTON, "'Make Disciples of All the Gentiles' (Mt 28:19)," p. 360.

Japhethites, and finally, against the Hamites (1QM 2.10−14).[409] Nevertheless, the Qumran perspective on the nations is not all negative. As we shall see below on 4QDibHam 4.4−12, the Qumran community maintains the hope of Isa 66:18−20 for "all nations," a hope that, in its original context, is based on the Table-of-Nations tradition (cf. v. 19).

II. The Abrahamic Promise.

A. The Promise of Land for Abraham and his Seed. Although this aspect of the Abrahamic Promise is not prominent in the Qumran texts containing the word גוים, it is implied in the citations of Deut 7:8 and 9:5 in CD 8.14−15 (cited below).

B. The Promise of Blessing for all Nations in Abraham and his Seed. As we discussed in Chap. 1, 4Q252 2.6−7 applies the blessing of Gen 9:26−27 not just to Japheth but to all three sons of Noah, apparently under the influence of the promise in Gen 12:3, that in Abraham all the families/nations of the earth will be blessed (cf. 18:18; 22:18; 26:4; 28:14).

III. The Covenant with Israel.

A. The Establishment of the Covenant with Israel as a Nation. As we have seen above, 4Q381 76−77.14-16 refers to the election of Israel as a nation from among other nations. The language of this passage is thoroughly Deuteronomic.[410] Similarly, 4QDibHam 3.3−5 states the following:

> Behold, all the nations (כול הגוים) are as nothing beside you; they are counted as void and nought before you. We have called on your name alone. You have created us for your glory and have made us your children in the sight of all the nations (כול הגוים). For you have called [I]srael 'my firstborn son' (Ex 4:22), and you have chastised us as one chastises his son.

These are expressions of the special covenantal relationship that God established with his people Israel.

B. The Settlement in Canaan. The passage CD 8.14−15 (cf. also 19.27) cites Deuteronomy in this regard: "And as for which Moses said to Israel: 'Not for your righteousness, or for the uprightness of your heart, are you going in to possess these nations' (Deut 9:5; 7:8), 'but because He loved your fathers and because he would keep the oath' (Deut 7:8a)." The *War Scroll* refers to the troops of Belial as "the seven nations of vanity" that will be destroyed in the end time (1QM 11.7−9),[411] alluding to the "seven nations" that Israel was to conquer upon entering Canaan (Deut 7:1).

---

[409] See further in Chap. 1, which also discusses the Japhethite nation of Kittim (1QM 1.2, 4, 6, 9, 12; 11.11; 15.2; 16.3, 6, 8, 9; 17.12, 14, 15; 18.2, 4; 19.10, 13; cf. Gen 10:4).

[410] Cf. SCHULLER, *Non-Canonical Psalms from Qumran*, pp. 223−224, 225.

[411] As YADIN suggests (*The Scroll of the War of the Sons of Light against the Sons of Darkness* [trans. Batya and Chaim Rabin; Oxford: Oxford University Press, 1962], p. 311 n.), here are meant the nations enumerated in 1QM 1.1−2, i.e., "the sons of darkness, the army of Belial, the troop of Edom and Moab, and the sons of Ammon and the army of the dwellers of Philistia and the troops of the Kittim of Asshur, and in league with them the offenders against the covenant."

C. The Sin of Israel. The Qumran texts are acutely aware of Israel's sin, and several passages cite the words of Moses in linking this sin to the influence of the nations. The passage 11QTemple 60.17 cites Deut 18:9, in which Moses exhorts Israel not to follow the "abominations of the nations" (תועבות הגויים).[412] In 1QDM 1.6–7, furthermore, Moses announces that Israel will one day prefer the "detestable things of the nations" (שקוצי הגוים).[413]

D. The Exile of Israel. The concept of protracted Exile is very well developed in the Qumran literature.[414] 4Q385–389 4–6.2-10 states:

... and sovereignty will devolve upon the nations (גוים) for [m]any [years], while the children of Israe[l...] a heavy yoke in the lands of their Exile (בארצות שבים),[415] and they will have no deliverer, because ... they have rejected my laws, and their soul has scorned my teaching. Therefore, I have hidden my face from [them, until] they fill up the measure of their sins. This will be the sign for them, when they fill up the measure of their sin ... I have abandoned the land because they have hardened their hearts against me, and they do not kno[w] tha[t ... they have] done evil again and again ... [and they broke my covenant that I had made] with Ab[raham, I]saac and [Jacob. [In] those [days] a blasphemous king will arise among the Gentiles/nations (גוים), and do evil things ... Israel from (being) a people (עם).[416]

Despite its fragmentary nature, the text apparently describes Israel's protracted Exile due to sin. During this time of judgment, the nations prevail over Israel.[417]

E. The Restoration of Israel. Although some of the Qumran texts containing גוי presuppose a flawed restoration in the Second Temple period,[418] the

---

[412] Cf. also 11QTemple 51.19–21: "You shall not behave in your land as the nations behave: in every place they are accustomed to sacrifice and plant for themselves *asherim* and set up for themselves *mazzeboth* and place for themselves stone images, to bow down before them and to build for themselves. ..."

[413] Cf. Deut 29:16: "You have seen their [sc. the nations'] detestable things."

[414] Cf. Michael A. KNIBB, "Exile in the Damascus Document," *JSOT* 25 (1983) 99–117; idem, "The Exile in the Literature of the Intertestamental Period," *HeyJ* 17 (1976) 253–272; Donald E. GOWAN, "The Exile in Jewish Apocalyptic," *Scripture in History and Theology: Essays in Honor of J. Coert Rylaarsdam* (ed. Arthur L. Merrill and Thomas W. Overholt; PTMS 17; Pittsburgh: Pickwick, 1977), pp. 205–223; Philip R. DAVIES, "Eschatology at Qumran," *JBL* 104/1 (1985) 39–55 (here pp. 49, 52–53); John J. COLLINS, "Was the Dead Sea Sect an Apocalyptic Movement?" in *Archaeology and History in the Dead Sea Scrolls: The New York University Conference in Memory of Yigael Yadin* (ed. Lawrence H. Schiffman; JSPSup 8; JSOT/ASOR Monographs 2; Sheffield: JSOT, 1990), pp. 25–51 (esp. pp. 28, 41, 43–44); Robert P. CARROLL, "Israel, History of (Post-Monarchic Period)," *ABD* 3 (1992) 567–576 (esp. p. 575).

[415] For the expression, see Jer 30:10; 46:27; 2 Chr 6:37, 38; Neh 3:36 *v.l.*

[416] Robert EISENMAN and Michael WISE, *The Dead Sea Scrolls Uncovered: The First Complete Translation and Interpretation of 50 Key Documents Withheld for over 35 Years* (Rockport, MA: Element, 1992), pp. 62–63.

[417] Cf. 4QpPs[a] 1–10 ii 20 (commenting on Ps 37:14–15): "and afterwards they [sc. the wicked ones of Ephraim and Manasseh] will be given into the hand of the ruthless ones of the nations for judgment."

[418] See, for example, the emphasis on the Wicked Priest who has plundered many nations

majority concentrate on the eschatological Restoration of Israel, when the nation is regathered from Exile.[419] As 4QDibHam 5.1—14 shows,[420] the Qumran community identifies itself as the remnant that returns from Exile:

> ... [they forsook] the fount of living waters ... and served a strange god in their land. Also, their land was ravaged by their enemies; for your fury and the heat of your wrath overflowed, in the fire of your jealousy, making it a desert where no man could go and return. Yet in spite of all this, you did not reject the seed of Jacob, nor did you cast away Israel to destruction, breaking your covenant with them. For you alone are a living God, and there is none beside you. You remembered your covenant; you who rescued us before the eyes of the nations (הגוים) and did not forsake us amidst the nations (בגוים). You were gracious toward your people Israel in all the lands to which you exiled them (הדחתם), that they might remember to return to you and to listen to your voice [according to] all you have commanded by the hand of Moses your servant.

While many Restoration texts expect the judgment and complete annihilation of the nations,[421] others anticipate merely the subjugation of the nations,[422] the eschatological reign of Israel or the Davidide over the nations,[423] and/or the eschatological pilgrimage of the nations to Jerusalem.[424] Thus Qumran appropriates both the universalistic and particularistic perspectives on the Restoration.[425]

---

and will eventually be given over to the nations (1QpHab 8.15—17; 9.3—7; 4QpPs[a] 1—10 iv 8—10).

[419] Cf. 1QM 19.5—6; 4Q*434,436* 2.7—8.

[420] See also CD 1.3—11a, where, in accordance with Ezek 4:4—8, the establishment of the remnant in the land occurs 390 years after the beginning of the Babylonian Exile under Nebuchchadnezzar.

[421] Cf. 1QpHab 5.4 ("but into the hand of his holy ones God will give the judgment of all the nations"); 12.13—14; 13.1—3 ("The interpretation of it [sc. Hab 2:20] concerns all the nations (כול הגוים) who have served stone and wood, but on the day of judgment God will wipe out completely all who serve idols. ..."); 1QM 4.12 ("When they close for battle, they shall write upon their banners ... 'Annihilation by God of all nations of vanity'"); 11.7—9; 12.10—11; 14.5, 7; 15.1—3; 16.1; 19.10.

[422] Cf. 1QSa 1.21 ("the war for the subjugation of the nations"); 1QM 11.15 (despite the destruction, there will be a "remnant of the nations").

[423] Cf. 4QpIsa[a] 7—10 iii 22—26 (interpreting Isa 11:1—5): "[And God will place a scepter] in his [sc. the scion of David's] hand, and over all the n[ation]s (כול הגואים) he will rule, and Magog ... [al]l the peoples (כול העמים) will his sword judge... " (cf. *3 Enoch* 45:5; Rev 20:8). The previous context interprets Isa 10:28ff. as a reference to the battle with the Kittim, in which Israel will prevail: "[They are the] Kittim, wh[o] will fa[ll] by the hand of Israel. And the poor ones of [Judah will judge] all nations (כול הגואים) ... " (*ll.* 7—8).

[424] Cf. 1QM 12:12—14 (cf. Isa 60:11, 14): "Zion, rejoice exceedingly, and shine forth in songs of joy, O Jerusalem, and be joyful, all you cities of Judah. Open [your] gates forever, to let enter into you the wealth of the nations, and their kings shall serve you. All they that afflicted you shall bow down to you, and the dust of your feet they shall lick." See further DEINES, "Die Abwehr der Fremden in den Texten aus Qumran," p. 66: "Mit der endgültigen Unterwerfung der Heidenwelt unter den König auf dem Zion beginnt die zweite Stufe des universalen Heils, die Zeit, in der die Völker der Erde zum Zion wallfahren, um dorthin ihre Schätze zu bringen und von dorther Belehrung und Erleuchtung zu erfahren."

[425] Cf. DEINES, "Die Abwehr der Fremden in den Texten aus Qumran," pp. 66, 69.

For our purposes, 4QDibHam 4.4—12 provides an important example of the positive expectation about the nations:

> For you have loved Israel above all the peoples (מכול העמים). You have chosen the tribe of Judah and have established your covenant with David, that he might be as a princely shepherd over your people and sit before you on the throne of Israel forever. And all the nations (כול הגוים) shall see your glory, (you) who has sanctified yourself in the bosom of your people Israel. And to your great name they [sc. the nations] will bring their offering (מנחתם): silver and gold and precious stones, together with all the treasures from their lands, to honor your people and Zion your holy city and the house of your majesty. From then on (there will be there) neither enemy nor misfortune, just peace and blessing. . . .

This alludes to Isa 66:18—20, which likewise expects that "all nations (כל הגוים) . . . shall see my [sc. Yahweh's] glory" and bring their "offering" (מנחה) to Yahweh in Zion. As we have seen in Chap. 1, "all nations" in Isa 66:18 is elaborated in v. 19 by a partial list of nations drawn from all three sons of Noah in the Table of Nations.

Conclusion. In our brief survey of "Hellenistic-Jewish" literature, we have found abundant evidence of all three uses of ἔθνη occurring in the Septuagint. First, ἔθνη is used in the sense of the "nations" of the world, including Israel.[426] As in the Septuagint, Israel is consistently viewed as a "nation" among other "nations," from initial Election to ultimate Restoration. The use of ἔθνος for "the nation of the Jews" continues at least until the third century A.D., as a Jewish inscription from Smyrna attests.[427] Therefore, Theodor MOMMSEN's argument – that the Jews existed as an ἔθνος (*gens Iudaeorum*) only until the destruction of Jerusalem, and after that "in the place of the privileged nation, the privileged confession, the *religio licita*," appeared – seems improbable.[428] Second, ἔθνη is used in the sense of "(all) the nations" in distinction to the nation Israel.[429] Finally, the term is used in the sense of the (individual) "Gentiles" in distinction to the Jews.[430]

Our survey of "Hellenistic-Jewish" literature also shows that, as in the OT, ἔθνος occurs within three basic contexts that provide a salvation-historical framework for understanding the concept: (1) the Table of Nations; (2) the Abrahamic Promise; and (3) the Covenant with Israel, from its inital establishment to its ultimate restoration. Within this framework, the nation Israel is

---

[426] Cf., e.g., Philo *Abr.* 98; *Congr.* 3; *T. Ben.* 10:5—6; Josephus *Ant.* 1.146.

[427] In *CIJ* II, no. 741, the unauthorized user of the grave must pay a fine τῷ ἔθνει τῶν Ἰουδαίων. Cf. Paul R. TREBILCO, *Jewish Communities in Asia Minor* (SNTSMS 69; Cambridge: Cambridge University Press, 1991), pp. 213, 228, 257; SCHÜRER, *Hist.*, 3.1:20, 90. For the expression τὸ τῶν Ἰουδαίων ἔθνος, see, e.g., 1 Esdr 8:10; 1 Macc 8:23, 25, 27; 10:25; 11:33; 12:3; 15:2; 2 Macc 10:8.

[428] Theodor MOMMSEN, "Der Religionsfrevel nach römischen Recht," *Historische Zeitschrift* 64 (1890) 389—429 (here pp. 421—426). Cf. SCHÜRER, *Hist.*, 3.1:114 n. 28. FELDMAN entertains a similar argument ("Josephus' Portrait of Daniel," p. 87 n. 116).

[429] Cf., e.g., *T. Sim.* 7:2; *T. Ash.* 7:3; *Pss. Sol.* 9:9; *Ep. Arist.* 139; Philo *Virt.* 64.

[430] Cf., e.g., *VP* 1:12; *4 Bar* 6:19; 7:37; *T. Levi* 9:10 (?).

involved in a constant interplay with the other nations of the world. First, the Table of Nations in Genesis 10 and especially in 1 Chr 1:1−2:2 provides the basis for understanding the central position of Israel among the other nations of the world. Second, the oft-reiterated Abrahamic Promise sets in motion a trajectory whose ultimate fulfillment takes place in the time of Israel's Restoration, when Israel will again become a great nation, and all nations (i.e., those listed in the Table of Nations) will be blessed in Abraham and his seed. Third, having consistently followed the ways of the nations and having forsaken her covenantal responsibility as a holy nation under God, Israel meanwhile languishes in protracted exile among the nations, anticipating that day when God will restore her fortunes and gather all nations to himself. As we shall see, this interplay between Israel and the other nations of the world forms the background of Paul's own understanding of ἔθνος.

Pauline Letters

Introduction

Usage.[431] Paul's use of ἔθνος follows that of the Septuagint and other "Hellenistic-Jewish" literature of the Greco-Roman period. This can be seen first and foremost by the many OT citations in which ἔθνος occurs. Of the 45 times that ἔθνος appears in Paul's letters,[432] approximately 30 percent occur in conjunction with OT citations.[433]

The singular ἔθνος occurs only in a citation of Deut 32:21 (Rom 10:19). Otherwise, Paul uses exclusively the plural. In accordance with OT and "Hellenistic-Jewish" usage, Paul uses the plural in three related senses.[434] First, ἔθνη is used in the sense of the "nations" of the world, including the nation

---

[431] Cf. Ulrich HECKEL, "Das Bild der Heiden und die Identität der Christen bei Paulus," in *Die Heiden. Juden, Christen und das Problem des Fremden*, pp. 269−296; DABELSTEIN, *Die Beurteilung der 'Heiden' bei Paulus*.

[432] The term occurs predominantly in the authentic Pauline letters (45 times): Romans (28); 1 Corinthians (3); 2 Corinthians (1); Galatians (10); Colossians (1); 1 Thessalonians (2). The term also occurs in Ephesians (5), 1 Timothy (2), and 2 Timothy (1).

[433] Cf. Rom 2:24 (Isa 52:5); 4:17 (Gen 17:5), 18 (Gen 15:5); 9:24−26 (Hos 2:25; 2:1); 10:19 (Deut 32:21); 15:9−12 (Ps 17:50; 2 Kgdms 22:50; Deut 32:43; Ps 116:1; Isa 11:10); Gal 3:8 (Gen 12:3; 18:18).

[434] Because of the negative connotations of the term *Heiden*, DABELSTEIN prefers to render ἔθνη with *Völker*, although he also acknowledges other uses of the term (*Die Beurteilung der 'Heiden' bei Paulus*, pp. 37−38), including *Heiden* in passages that characterize the ἔθνη as godless and immoral (ibid., pp. 27−28, referring to Rom 2:24; 1 Cor 5:1; 12:2; Gal 2:15; 1 Thess 4:5). In response to this perspective, HECKEL argues that Paul normally uses ἔθνη in the negative sense of *Heiden*, in contrast to the Jews, Israel, the Jewish people, or the circumcised ("Das Bild der Heiden und die Identität der Christen bei Paulus," pp. 270−271). In passages referring to Paul's mission, however, HECKEL acknowledges that Paul uses the term positively in the sense of *Völker* (ibid., p. 291−292). Neither DABELSTEIN nor HECKEL seems to recognize, however, that the distinction between *Völker* and *Heiden* as translations for ἔθνη is not

Israel (e.g., the citation of Gen 12:3 [+18:18] in Gal 3:8).[435] Although Paul never calls Israel a "nation" per se, he frequently refers to it as a λαός,[436] which, as we have seen, is often synonymous with ἔθνος in the OT.[437] Furthermore, as we shall see below on Rom 11:25, Paul has a concept of the traditional 70 or 72 nations of the world based on the Table-of-Nations tradition. Second, the plural is used of the non-Jewish "nations." In Rom 15:10−11, the citations of Deut 32:43 (ἔθνη is contrasted to the λαός of God) and Ps 117(116):1 (πάντα τὰ ἔθνη is parallel to πάντες οἱ λαοί) provide good examples of this usage. In Rom 1:5, Paul writes that through Jesus Christ "we (apostolic plural) have received grace and apostleship for the obedience of faith ἐν πᾶσιν τοῖς ἔθνεσιν...."[438] As the subsequent context makes clear, Paul means the ἔθνη composed of "Greeks" and "barbarians" (Rom 1:13−14).[439] Hence, Paul demonstrates familiarity with a usage of πάντα τὰ ἔθνη that we observed a number of times in the OT in the sense of "all the nations" of the earth apart from the "nation" of Israel.[440] In a number of passages, we can deduce the meaning of ἔθνη in this sense by the contrasting term.[441] Third, the plural is used of the "Gentiles," that is, individuals of any nation other than the nation of the Jews.[442] The third sense of ἔθνη retains the idea of nation and does not denote merely "pagan" although

just the difference between positive and negative terms but, rather, a difference in quantity between a collective noun and individualizing one.

[435] On Gal 3:8, see further below.

[436] Cf. Rom 10:21; 11:1−2; 15:10; 1 Cor 14:21.

[437] Cf., e.g., Ex 19:5−6.

[438] Cf. Rom 15:18, which also speaks of the "obedience of the ἔθνη."

[439] Cf. Dietrich-Alex Koch, *Die Schrift als Zeuge des Evangeliums. Untersuchungen zur Verwendung und zum Verständnis der Schrift bei Paulus* (BHT 69; Tübingen: Mohr-Siebeck, 1986), p. 124; Heckel, "Das Bild der Heiden und die Identität der Christen bei Paulus," p. 292.

[440] Cf. Ex 19:5−6; 23:22; Deut 4:6−8; Ezek 37:21−23; Esth 3:8; 1 Macc 13:6; also Zech 12:3.

[441] In 2 Cor 11:26, for example, ἔθνη is juxtaposed to γένος, which is often used of the nation Israel (cf. Josephus *BJ* 7.43; *Ant.* 10.183; Phil 3:5; for the opposition of γένος το ἔθνη, see Tob 1:10; 2 Macc 8:9; 3 Macc 6:9; Josephus *Ant.* 1.235; 5.98; *T. Levi* 5:6; *T. Sim.* 7:2; *T. Naph.* 8:3). Furthermore, when Ἰσραήλ (a nation!) is juxtaposed to ἔθνη (cf. Rom 9:30−31; 11:25−26), we must suppose that the latter denotes "nations." Cf. *T. Ash.* 7:3 (τὸν Ἰσραὴλ καὶ πάντα τὰ ἔθνη); *T. Jos.* 19:6 (πάντα τὰ ἔθνη καὶ τὸν Ἰσραήλ); *T. Sim.* 7:2; *T. Ben.* 3:8. On the other hand, Heckel argues that when the immediate context implies a direct opposition to the Jews, ἔθνη should be translated *Heiden* ("Das Bild der Heiden und die Identität der Christen bei Paulus," p. 292).

[442] The national overtones of this third use of ἔθνη can be illustrated in a passage like Eph 2:11−22: As τὰ ἔθνη ἐν σαρκί, i.e., individuals from a nation other than the nation of Israel, the addressees were formerly (πότε) alienated from the commonwealth of Israel (ἡ πολιτεία τοῦ Ἰσραήλ) and strangers to the covenants of the promise (ξένοι τῶν διαθηκῶν τῆς ἐπαγγελίας). But now (νυνὶ δέ), that has all changed: Gentiles and Jews have become joined together in Christ so that the addressees are no longer strangers and aliens (ξένοι καὶ πάροικοι) but, rather, fellow citizens with the saints (συμπολῖται τῶν ἁγίων). As Ephesians 3 goes on to say, "the Gentiles" are now "fellow heirs" (συγκληρονόμα) with the Jews and partakers of the Promise in Christ Jesus (v. 6).

negative connotations are often associated with the term in both the second and the third senses.[443] As we have seen in the OT and other "Hellenistic-Jewish" literature, it is often difficult to distinguish between the second and third uses of ἔθνη. The distinction is especially difficult to ascertain in Paul's writings, where several senses of the term can be mingled in the same passage.[444] We have clear evidence of this third usage, for example, when Paul applies the term to his addressees as a group of (former) "Gentiles" (cf. Rom 11:13; 1 Cor 12:2; also Eph 2:11). We may also suspect it in the antithesis between Ἰουδαῖοι and ἔθνη.[445]

Again, ἔθνος is not used in the singular for a single "Gentile." If Paul wants a term to contrast with the singular Ἰουδαῖος, he uses Ἕλλην (cf. Rom 2:9; 10:12; Gal 3:28; Col 3:11).[446] Here, however, it is difficult to know whether Ἕλλην is used simply as a substitute for ἔθνος. For although ἔθνη and Ἕλληνες appear at times to be used synonymously,[447] the use of Ἕλλην in Rom 1:16 may indicate the particular focus of Paul's mission.[448] Already in Rom 1:13–14, τὰ

---

[443] On several occasions, Paul uses an attributive participle to characterize the ἔθνη: They are those "who do not know God" (1 Thess 4:5; the nations who do not know God/the Lord [cf. 4 Kgdms 17:26; Jer 10:25 (ἔθνη τὰ μὴ εἰδότα σε); Ps 78:6 (ἔθνη τὰ μὴ γινώσκοντά σε), will one day know him [cf. Ezek 36:23; 37:28; 38:16; 39:7; 2 Macc 1:27]), "who do not have the Law" (Rom 2:14), and "who do not pursue righteousness" (Rom 9:30). Gal 2:15 reflects the traditional perspective of the ἔθνη as sinners. When Paul wants to describe the enormity of the immorality in the Corinthian church, he characterizes it as kind "which is found not even among the ἔθνη" (1 Cor 5:1; cf. Jer 18:13; Nah 3:4–5). As former "Gentiles," the Corinthians were led astray to dumb idols (1 Cor 12:2). See further Eph 4:17 (cf. Lev 20:23; 4 Kgdms 17:8, 15; Jer 3:17).

[444] We find the same kind of polysemy in other key Pauline terms, such as νόμος or even Ἰσραήλ. On the latter, see Otfried Hofius, "Das Evangelium und Israel. Erwägungen zu Römer 9–11," in *Paulusstudien* (WUNT 51; Tübingen: Mohr-Siebeck, 1989), pp. 175–202 (esp. p. 179 n. 15).

[445] Cf. Rom 3:29; 9:24; 1 Cor 1:23; Gal 2:15.

[446] For the opposition Ἰουδαῖοι – Ἕλληνες, see 1 Cor 1:22, 24. Compare also the contrast between ἡ περιτομή and ἡ ἀκροβυστία, which Paul often uses to divide humanity into two groups (cf. Rom 2:25, 26; 3:30; 4:9, 10; 1 Cor 7:18; Gal 2:7; 5:6; 6:15). Sometimes, Paul contrasts ἡ περιτομή and τὰ ἔθνη (cf. Gal 2:8–9).

[447] Cf., e.g., Rom 1:16; 1 Cor 1:22–23.

[448] Cf. Hans Windisch, *TWNT*, " Ἕλλην," 2 (1933) 510: "Mit Ἕλληνες bezeichnet somit [sc. with the formula "to the Jew first but also to the Greek"] Paulus den nichtjüdischen Teil der Menschheit. Die Formel ist bestimmt durch den Standort des Juden, speziell durch den des anatolischen Diasporajuden, des vom Judentum ausgehenden Missionars, der, sowie er die Grenzen des jüdischen Weltghettos überschreitet, in das Kulturbereich der Ἕλληνες gerät. Voraussetzung der Formel ist eben die wesentlich durch griechische Sprache und Zivilisation bestimmte einheitliche Kultur der Mittelmeerländer, daneben aber auch die Tatsache, daß Paulus als Heidenmissionar nicht den ganzen Umkreis der Heidenwelt umgreift, sondern sich auf die Ἕλληνες in Vorderasien, in Makedonien, Illyrien und Alt-Hellas beschränkt hat: Mit Αἰγύπτιοι oder Χαλδαῖοι hat er nie zu tun gehabt. Auf die Anwendung gesehen, gibt die Formel Ἰουδαῖοι καὶ Ἕλληνες zunächst die universalistische Bestimmung des Evangeliums überhaupt, die des paulinischen Evangeliums insbesondere, an. Ἕλληνες sind der durch Sprache, Abstammung und Kultur von den Juden unterschiedene Teil der Menschheit, also die wesentlich hellenistische Gesamtbewohnerschaft des Imperium Romanum, abgerechnet

ἔθνη are divided, in accordance with Hellenistic(-Jewish) usage,[449] into two groups – Ἕλληνες and βάρβαροι – to which Paul feels himself obligated.[450] If, as we shall discuss in the next chapters, Paul's mission is limited primarily to the land traditionally allotted to the Japhethites (Asia Minor and Europe), then Ἕλλην may well indicate the particular focus of Paul's mission. This is strengthened by the fact that in Jewish tradition, Greek is considered the language of Japheth since Javan (= Ἕλλην) is one of the sons of Japheth (cf. Gen 10:2, 4). Furthermore, Col 3:11 uses Ἕλλην in a series of contrasts that includes the "Scythian" (Σκύθης): ὅπου οὐκ ἔνι Ἕλλην καὶ Ἰουδαῖος, περιτομὴ καὶ ἀκροβυστία, βάρβαρος, Σκύθης, δοῦλος, ἐλεύθερος, ἀλλὰ τὰ πάντα καὶ ἐν πᾶσιν Χριστός. Josephus identifies the Scythians with biblical Magog, another son of Japheth (*Ant.* 1.123). To the one trained in Judaism, the very juxtaposition of "Jew" and "Greek" in Rom 1:16 may recall that Shem, the ancestor of the Semites (including the nation of the Jews), and Japheth, the ancestor of the Greeks, are brothers.

Method. In the following discussion, we shall examine Paul's use of ἔθνος under two broad headings. First, we shall survey the use of the term of Paul himself and of his mission to the ἔθνη. Second, we shall look at the use of the term as an appropriation of the OT and Jewish concept of ἔθνη. As we shall see, ἔθνος occurs in many of the same salvation-historical contexts that we have already observed in the OT and other literature of the Greco-Roman period.

Paul, the Apostle to the Ἔθνη

As a result of a revelation of the resurrected Christ as Son of God, which he received on his way to Damascus, Paul understands himself as the "apostle to the nations" (ἐθνῶν ἀπόστολος),[451] one who has been given grace by God to be a "minister of Christ Jesus to the nations" (λειτουργὸν Χριστοῦ Ἰησοῦ εἰς τὰ ἔθνη).[452] As such, Paul is called to preach the gospel "among the nations" (ἐν

---

die Juden." Cf. also HECKEL, "Das Bild der Heiden und die Identität der Christen bei Paulus," p. 273.

[449] Philo, in particular, has a very developed hierarchy in which the nations are divided into the same two groups. Cf., e.g, Philo *Spec. Leg.* 2.166: "Whereas the Greeks and barbarians wrongly failed to acknowledge God as Creator, this was corrected by the nation of the Jews, which passed over all created objects and chose service to the Uncreated and Eternal God." See further Wolfgang SPEYER and Ilona OPELT, "Barbar I," *RAC Suppl.*, 1.5/6 (1992) 811–895; Bernd FUNCK, "Studie zu der Bezeichnung βάρβαρος," in *Untersuchungen ausgewählter altgriechischer sozialer Typenbegriffe* (ed. Elizabeth C. Welskopf; Soziale Typenbegriffe in alten Griechenland und ihr Fortleben in den Sprachen der Welt 4; Berlin: Akademie-Verlag, 1981), pp. 26–51; UMEMOTO, "Juden, 'Heiden' und das Menschengeschlecht in der Sicht Philos von Alexandria," pp. 25–26.

[450] Thus Titus, who was a Ἕλλην, seems to be included among the ἔθνη to whom Paul has preached the gospel (Gal 2:2–3).

[451] Rom 11:13.

[452] Rom 15:15–16.

τοῖς ἔθνεσιν).[453] The language that Paul uses to describe this call is derived, in part, from the commission of Jeremiah, the great "prophet to the nations" (προφήτης εἰς ἔθνη).[454]

The churches founded by the Apostle belong to what he calls collectively πᾶσαι αἱ ἐκκλησίαι τῶν ἐθνῶν.[455] What does this expression mean – "all the churches of the *Gentiles*" or "all the churches of the *nations*"? Paul's other uses of αἱ ἐκκλησίαι with the genitive are suggestive (αἱ ἐκκλησίαι τῆς Γαλατίας,[456] αἱ ἐκκλησίαι τῆς ᾿Ασίας,[457] αἱ ἐκκλησίαι τῆς Μακεδονίας,[458] and αἱ ἐκκλησίαι τῆς ᾿Ιουδαίας[459]), for in each case, the genitive is a toponym indicating a Roman province or, from a Hellenistic-Jewish perspective, an ἔθνος:[460] Galatia,[461] Asia,[462] Macedonia,[463] and Judea.[464] Therefore, πᾶσαι αἱ ἐκκλησίαι τῶν ἐθνῶν in Rom 16:4 might well mean "all the churches of the *nations*." This is strengthened by the fact that the next verse goes on to mention Asia (v. 5).

Paul held that the gospel applied equally to Israel and the other nations of the world (cf. Rom 3:30; 1 Cor 1:24) even if it was to the Jew first (Rom 1:16). In the course of his mission activity, however, Paul experienced persecution both from the ἔθνη and from his own people (2 Cor 11:26), who tried to hinder him from speaking to the ἔθνη (1 Thess 2:14–16), for to the ᾿Ιουδαῖοι, Paul's message of the crucified Christ was a stumbling-block; to the ἔθνη, it was foolishness (1 Cor 1:23). The Apostle also encountered significant opposition to his gospel from Jewish believers whom he calls "false brethren" (Gal 2:4; 2 Cor 11:26).

Some 14 years after his first visit to Jerusalem (or after his conversion), Paul

---

453 Gal 1:15–16; cf. 2:2 (τὸ εὐαγγέλιον ὃ κηρύσσω ἐν τοῖς ἔθνεσιν); Rom 1:5; Eph 3:8; 1 Tim 2:7; 3:16; 2 Tim 4:17.

454 Gal 1:15–16; cf. Jer 1:5; also Isa 49:5–6. See further Karl Olav SANDNES, *Paul – One of the Prophets? A Contribution to the Apostle's Self-Understanding* (WUNT 2.43; Tübingen: Mohr-Siebeck, 1991), pp. 61, 63–64.

455 Rom 16:4.

456 Gal 1:2; 1 Cor 16:1.

457 1 Cor 16:19.

458 2 Cor 8:1.

459 Gal 1:22.

460 Cf. W.M. RAMSAY, *A Historical Commentary on St. Paul's Epistle to the Galatians* (London: Hodder and Stoughton, 1899), p. 134: "In other Provinces of the Roman State the fiction was usually maintained that there was only one 'tribe' or 'nation.' Even in provinces which were composed of many distinct nations, such as Asia, the official form admitted only one 'nation,' *viz.*, the Roman idea, the Province: in other words, the 'nation' officially was the Province. 'The nation Asia' (ἡ ᾿Ασία τὸ ἔθνος) was the technical Greek form translating the Latin *Asia Provincia* [Dio Cass. 54.30]." But see also SHERWIN-WHITE, "The Roman World as *Omnes Gentes* or Τὰ ῎Εθνη," pp. 437–444.

461 On Galatia as an ἔθνος, see Josephus *Ant.* 1.123; *BJ* 2.358–360; *Sib. Or.* 5.598–599.

462 On Asia as an ἔθνος, see *Sib. Or.* 3.598–599; also Josephus *BJ* 2.366. The continent of Asia is composed of many "nations" (cf. Philo *Mos.* 1.263; 2.19; *Legat.* 11, 144).

463 On Macedonia as an ἔθνος, see *Sib. Or.* 3.172; Josephus *BJ* 2.360.

464 On Judea as an ἔθνος, see Philo *Legat.* 214–215; Josephus *Ant.* 10.184; 12.141; 14.184.

went up to Jerusalem with Barnabas and Titus to lay before the Jerusalem apostles "the gospel which I preach among the ἔθνη" (Gal 2:1–2). Since circumcision seems to have been the issue that prompted this "Apostolic Council" (cf. Acts 15:1–29), it is significant that Titus was not forced to become circumcised even though he was a Ἕλλην (Gal 2:3).[465] Furthermore, without adding anything to Paul's message (v. 6), the "pillar" apostles – James, Cephas, and John – formally acknowledged both Paul's God-given "(apostleship) to the ἔθνη" and his "gospel to the uncircumcision" as equal to Peter's God-given "apostleship to the circumcision" and his "gospel to the circumcision" (Gal 2:7–8).[466] They then gave Paul and Barnabas the right hand of fellowship, "in order that we might go to the ἔθνη, and they to the circumcision" (v. 9). We shall return to this division of labor and the reasons behind it in our discussion of Pauline territoriality.[467]

As the divinely appointed Apostle to the ἔθνη, Paul viewed himself as a defender and preserver of the "truth of the gospel" for the sake of his Gentile churches (cf. Gal 2:5). Thus, when Peter withdrew from table fellowship with the ἔθνη in Antioch for fear of the men from James (characterized also as οἱ ἐκ περιτομῆς), and the other Ἰουδαῖοι (including Paul's own missionary partner!) followed Peter's example, Paul publicly denounced Peter to his face, recognizing that the "truth of the gospel" was at stake (Gal 2:11–14). Paul charges Peter with compelling the ἔθνη to live like Jews (ἰουδαΐζειν)[468] in order to be accepted in the community of believers (v. 14).[469] We may compare Esth 8:17: "And many of the nations were circumcised and lived like Jews for fear of the Jews."[470]

---

[465] Circumcision was considered a sign of membership in the nation of the Jews (cf. James D. G. DUNN, "What was the Issue between Paul and 'Those of the Circumcision'?," in *Paulus und das antike Judentum. Tübingen-Durham-Symposium im Gedenken an den 50. Todestag Adolf Schlatters* [ed. Martin Hengel and Ulrich Heckel; WUNT 58; Tübingen: Mohr-Siebeck, 1991], pp. 295–317 [here pp. 303–305]). According to Josephus (*Ant.* 12.241; cf. 13.4; 1 Macc 1:14), the attempt of many Jews during the reign of Antiochus Ephiphanes to conceal their circumcision in order to be Greeks (Ἕλληνες) even when unclothed was tantamount to giving up the "national customs" and imitating "the works of the other nations" (τὰ τῶν ἄλλων ἐθνῶν ἔργα).

[466] Cf. Rom 3:29–30, where we find the contrast between Ἰουδαῖοι and ἔθνη, on the one hand, and between περιτομή and ἀκροβυστία, on the other.

[467] See Chap. 3 below.

[468] Cf. O. BETZ, "ἰουδαΐζω κτλ.," *EWNT*, 2 (1992) 470–472.

[469] Did the believing Jews want thereby to make proselytes of the Gentiles in Antioch and thereby include them in their own nation? In Philo, proselytes are described as those who have abandoned their own kin, country, and customs in order to be loved as "kinfolk" (συγγενεῖς) by the "nation" (ἔθνος) of the Jews (*Virt.* 102–103).

[470] καὶ πολλοὶ τῶν ἐθνῶν περιετέμοντο καὶ ἰουδάιζον διὰ τὸν φόβον τῶν Ιουδαίων. That ἔθνη here denotes "nations" is supported not only by the use of the term in the previous context of Esther, which is heavily influenced by the Table-of-Nations tradition (cf., e.g., Esth 3:12; 4:17m), but also by Josephus' paraphrase of this passage in *Ant.* 11.285, which refers to "other nations." In Esther, Israel is understood as a "nation" among "all the nations" of Artaxerxes' empire (cf. Esth 3:8).

Paul's Appropriation of the OT/Jewish Concept of Ἔθνη

The Table of Nations. Paul's geographical horizon is determined by the OT and thus extends to "all the earth" (πᾶσα ἡ γῆ) and "the ends of the inhabited world" (τὰ πέρατα τῆς οἰκουμένης).[471] Given this worldwide perspective, it is significant that Rom 11:25 refers to "the full number of the nations" (τὸ πλήρωμα τῶν ἐθνῶν), which must come in before all Israel (i.e., all twelve tribes[472]) will be saved at the Parousia (v. 26).[473] This expectation is probably based on the traditional 70 or 72 nations of the world from Deut 32:8 and the Table-of-Nations tradition.[474] Deuteronomy 32 (and indeed Deuteronomic tradition in general) is crucial to Paul's argument in Romans 9–11.[475]

If Rom 11:25 appropriates the Jesus tradition of Mk 13:10, that before the Parousia of the Son of Man, "the gospel must first be preached to all the ἔθνη,"[476] we may ask further whether or not Paul's use of the Table-of-Nations tradition in the same verse represents another appropriation of Jesus tradition. For already in Rom 10:14–17 (cf. also 1 Cor 9:14), Paul argues on the basis of the Synoptic tradition of the Sending of the Seventy (Lk 10:1–12 par.),[477] in which the number 70 (*v.l.* 72) probably represents the 70 (or 72) nations of the

---

[471] Rom 10:18, citing Ps 18:5.

[472] As an "Israelite" (᾿Ισραηλίτης), Paul claims in Rom 11:1 that he is a member of the "tribe of Benjamin" (φυλὴ Βενιαμίν), which presupposes the twelve tribes of Israel. Hence, in Rom 11:26, "all Israel" (πᾶς ᾿Ισραήλ) should be seen in light of its Septuagintal usage as an expression denoting either the ten northern tribes (e.g., 2 Kgdms 5:5; 3 Kgdms 12:1, 12, 16) or all twelve tribes of Israel (e.g., 1 Kgdms 3:20; 2 Kgdms 17:11 [cf. 24:2]). Paul is arguing in context that whereas a "remnant" of Israel has already come to faith (including Paul himself as a representative of the tribe of Benjamin), "all Israel" will be saved in the future. He thereby looks forward to the regathering of "all the tribes of Jacob" (Sir 36:10; cf. *Pss. Sol.* 17:44). For further considerations on the expression "all Israel," see Hofius, "Das Evangelium und Israel," pp. 194–196.

[473] Note that the Deliverer is expected from Zion (Rom 11:26, citing Isa 59:20). On the importance of Jerusalem in Paul's thinking, see Chap. 3.

[474] Cf. Thomas Willi, *Chronik* (BKAT 24.1; Neukirchen-Vluyn: Neukirchener Verlag, 1991), p. 51; Bell, "Jealousy Motif," pp. 180–182, 195, 239–240. Hence, the numerical relationship between the "full number" of the nations and "all Israel" is already traditional. See Chap. 3 on Paul's Speech on the Areopagus, which alludes to Deut 32:8 (cf. Acts 17:26). Note that Isa 34:2 refers to πάντα τὰ ἔθνη and to their "number" (τὸν ἀριθμὸν αὐτῶν). We may wonder whether or not Rom 3:29 ("Is God the God of the Jews only, or also of the ἔθνη?") also recalls Deut 32:8 ("When the Most High divided the nations [ἔθνη], when he scattered the sons of Adam, he set the bounds of the nations [ὅρια ἐθνῶν] according to the number of the angels of God"), for Deut 32:9 goes on to state that Israel became "the portion of the Lord." On the reign of God over the ἔθνη, see further 1 Chr 16:31; Ps 46:2–3, 9; Mal 1:14; *Jos. As.* 19:5.

[475] Richard B. Hays goes so far as to call Deuteronomy 32 "Romans in nuce" (*Echoes of Scripture in the Letters of Paul* [New Haven and London: Yale University Press, 1989], p. 164). See further J. Scott, "Paul's Use of Deuteronomic Tradition," *JBL*, 112/4 (1993) 645–665.

[476] Cf. Peter Stuhlmacher, "Zum Thema: Das Evangelium und die Evangelien," in *Das Evangelium und die Evangelien* (ed. P. Stuhlmacher; WUNT 28; Tübingen: Mohr-Siebeck, 1983), pp. 1–26 (here p. 23).

[477] Cf. P. Stuhlmacher, "Jesustradition im Römerbrief? Eine Skizze," *TBei* 14/1 (1983)

earth in the Table of Nations.[478] Therefore, Jesus tradition could have influenced Paul's concept of "the full number of the nations."

As we shall discuss in the next chapter, evidence of the Table-of-Nations tradition can also be seen in the description of Paul's mission to Spain in Romans 15.

The Abrahamic Promise.

I. The Promise of Nationhood for Abraham and his Seed. To support the idea that Abraham is "the father of us all" (Rom 4:16), Paul introduces a citation of Gen 17:5: "just as it is written, I have made you a father of many nations" (πατέρα πολλῶν ἐθνῶν τέθεικά σε).[479] Since "us all" apparently includes Paul and other Jews as well as Gentiles, πολλὰ ἔθνη should be translated here "many nations." This is, of course, how the term would normally be understood, not only on the basis of the original context of the citation (cf. Gen 17:6) but otherwise as well.[480]

II. The Promise of Land for Abraham and his Seed. Although Paul does not use ἔθνος in reference to this aspect of the Abrahamic Promise, it is worth noting that Rom 4:13 includes the traditional expectation that Abraham and his seed will be "heir of the world" (κληρονόμος κόσμου).[481] Hence, those who are in Christ, the Abrahamic heir (Gal 3:16) and κύριος πάντων (Rom 10:12), enjoy universal sovereignty as joint heirs with Christ (Rom 8:17, 32; Gal 4:1; cf. Dan 7:14, 18, 22, 28).

III. The Promise of Blessing for all Nations in Abraham and his Seed. In Gal

---

240–250 (here pp. 248–249); idem, "Zum Thema," pp. 21–24; idem, "Das paulinische Evangelium," in *Das Evangelium und die Evangelien*, pp. 157–182 (here pp. 172–174).

[478] As we noted in Chap. 1, both numbers – seventy and seventy-two – are represented in the Jewish tradition of the Table of Nations, which makes the textual problem in Lk 10:1 difficult to solve (cf. Bruce METZGER, "Seventy or Seventy-two Disciples?" *NTS* 51958–59] 299–306). In either case, interpreters are divided as to whether the number refers to the traditional 70 (72) nations based on the Table of Nations. In favor of seeing a connection, I. Howard MARSHALL points out that Lk 10:3 ("I send you out as lambs in the midst of wolves") implies the 70 nations of the world, which, in Jewish literature, are described as seventy "wolves" (*The Gospel of Luke: A Commentary on the Greek Text* [NIGTC; Exeter: Paternoster Press, 1978], pp. 414–415). For the opposing perspective, see Joseph A. FITZMYER, *The Gospel according to Luke (X–XXIV)* (AB 28A; New York: Doubleday, 1985), pp. 845–846; Stephen G. WILSON, *The Gentiles and the Gentile Mission in Luke-Acts* (SNTSMS 23; Cambridge: Cambridge University Press, 1973) pp. 45–47.

[479] Rom 4:17. The text goes on to explain in v. 18 that Abraham believed that he would become the father of many nations on the basis of the promise in Gen 15:5, "So shall your descendants be."

[480] Cf., e.g., Ps 134:10 (ἔθνη πολλά introduces a list of nations); Ezek 38:12 (Israel is an ἔθνος gathered ἀπὸ ἐθνῶν πολλῶν); Zech 8:22 (λαοὶ πολλοὶ καὶ ἔθνη πολλά); *Jos. As.* 15:6 (ἔθνη πολλά stands in parallel with λαοὶ πολλοί); *Sib. Or.* 3.598 (ἄλλων ἔθνεα πολλά introduces a list of nations).

[481] See pp. 93–94 above. Philo *Somn.* 1.175 takes Gen 28:14 as a promise rendering its possessor the "heir of the world" (τοῦ κόσμου κληρονόμος).

3:8, Paul cites Gen 12:3 to show that scripture expected that God would justify τὰ ἔθνη by faith: προϊδοῦσα δὲ ἡ γραφὴ ὅτι ἐκ πίστεως δικαιοῖ τὰ ἔθνη ὁ θεὸς προευηγγελίσατο τῷ Ἀβραὰμ ὅτι Ἐνευλογηθήσονται ἐν σοὶ πάντα τὰ ἔθνη. As the following synoptic table shows, the citation is modified by the closely related passage in Gen 18:18:[482]

Gen 12:3 (24:14)	Gal 3:8	Gen 18:18
ἐνευλογηθήσονται ἐν σοὶ πᾶσαι αἱ φυλαὶ τῆς γῆς.	ἐνευλογηθήσονται ἐν σοὶ πάντα τὰ ἔθνη.	ἐνευλογηθήσονται ἐν αὐτῷ πάντα τὰ ἔθνη τῆς γῆς.

D.-A. KOCH argues that Paul understands πάντα τὰ ἔθνη in the citation in the sense of the preceding τὰ ἔθνη, that is, "nicht als Beschreibung der Vielzahl der einzelnen Völkerschaften der Erde (unter Einschluß der Juden), sondern als Bezeichnung für die Gesamtheit der Nichtjuden ('Heiden')."[483] In particular, KOCH takes the omission of τῆς γῆς from the citation as an indication that Paul had changed the meaning of the original text and applied it to "the Gentiles."[484]

Four points need to be considered in response to KOCH's argument. First of all, πάντα τὰ ἔθνη is normally used in the sense of "all the nations," whether of all the nations of the world[485] or of a more limited area.[486] Therefore, it would be unusual for Paul to use the expression in another way, especially since πάντα τὰ ἔθνη in Paul's modified citation of Gen 12:3 (+18:18) refers back in its original context to the Table of Nations in Genesis 10.[487] Furthermore, the parallelism between πάντα τὰ ἔθνη and πάντες οἱ λαοί in the citation of Ps 117:1 in Rom 15:11 shows that Paul is aware of the normal meaning of the expression. Second, Paul's understanding of Gen 12:3 (+18:18) is filtered through Ps 71:17 LXX, where πάντα τὰ ἔθνη clearly means "all nations" (cf.

---

[482] Cf. KOCH, *Schrift als Zeuge*, pp. 162–163.

[483] Ibid., p. 124.

[484] Ibid., p. 124.

[485] Cf., e.g., Deut 2:25; Ps 48:2; 85:9; 116:1; Isa 14:26; 66:18, 20; Hab 2:5; Zech 12:3; Jer 32:15 (with a *pars pro toto* list of nations in vv. 18–26); Jdt 3:8. In Amos 9:11, the expression is used of "all the nations of the world" apart from Israel.

[486] Cf. 1 Chr 18:11; 2 Chr 33:9; Esth 3:8.

[487] Cf. Demetrius in Eusebius *Pr. Ev.* 9.21.16, 18 ("Abraham was chosen from among the nations [ἐκ τῶν ἐθνῶν]"). We may surmise that Paul substitutes πάντα τὰ ἔθνη from Gen 18:18b for πᾶσαι αἱ φυλαὶ τῆς γῆς in order (1) to bring out even more strongly the relationship between Gen 12:3 and the Table of Nations (although αἱ φυλαί of Noah's sons are mentioned in the concluding verse of the Table [Gen 10:32]) and thus (2) to make the citation conform to his point in Gal 3:8, i.e., that the Scripture foresaw that God would justify τὰ ἔθνη by faith.

also v. 11).[488] Ps 71:17 looks forward to the fulfillment of Gen 12:3 in the (messianic) King, who is thereby identified as the seed of Abraham: "And all the tribes of the earth (αἱ φυλαὶ τῆς γῆς) will be blessed in him; all nations (πάντα τὰ ἔθνη) shall call him blessed." With this understanding of Gen 12:3 in light of Ps 71:17 (cf. Sir 44:21), Paul goes on to identify Christ/Messiah as the seed of Abraham (Gen 3:16).[489] Therefore, all nations – including Israel, from whom the Messiah stems (Rom 9:5) – need to be in Christ in order to participate in the Abrahamic Promise (Gal 3:28–29).[490] In Christ, the ἔθνη share in the Abrahamic Promise with Israel (cf. Rom 11:17–24; 15:27; Eph 2:11–22; 3:6). Third, Paul's citation of Gen 12:3 is introduced as a preliminary announcement of the gospel to Abraham (προευηγγελίσατο τῷ Ἀβραάμ). Since the gospel is to the Jew first (Rom 1:16), it would seem most plausible that Paul included the Jews in πάντα τὰ ἔθνη. Fourth, even if τὰ ἔθνη in Gal 3:8a is used in the sense of "the Gentiles," this would not necessarily affect the translation of πάντα τὰ ἔθνη in the citation since Paul often mingles the various uses of the term in any one context.[491]

The Covenant with Israel.

I. The Sin of Israel. Following Peter's lead, the Jews in Antioch withdrew from table fellowship with the Gentiles;[492] therefore, Paul rebukes Peter before

---

[488] Note also that Isa 19:23–24 combines the Abrahamic blessing of Gen 12:3 with the motif of Israel in the middle of the nations (cf. Ezek 5:5).

[489] Cf. SCOTT, *Adoption*, pp. 180–181.

[490] Cf. HECKEL, "Das Bild der Heiden und die Identität der Christen bei Paulus," p. 282: "Da durch die Abrahamsverheißung auch die Heiden in den Segen Gottes einbezogen, die Juden dabei aber natürlich nicht ausgeschlossen sind, sollte man πάντα τὰ ἔθνη in Gal 3,8 (cf. V 14) nicht wie die Lutherübersetzung mit dem ausgrenzenden Terminus 'die Heiden', sondern (analog zu den früheren Revisionen in Röm 4,16f.18) mit dem neutraleren Begriff 'alle Völker' wiedergeben." For the same reason, πάντα τὰ ἔθνη in Gal 3:8 also cannot be restricted to the non-Jewish nations (*pace* K. L. SCHMIDT, "ἔθνος," 2:367).

[491] We stand before the same dilemma in Gal 3:13–14, where Paul explains that Christ redeemed "us," "in order that in Christ the blessing of Abraham might be to τὰ ἔθνη, in order that *we* might receive the promise of the Spirit through faith."

[492] Eating "of the food of the nations" (ἐκ τῶν ἄρτων τῶν ἐθνῶν) was considered a defilement to which Jewish exiles succumbed (Tob 1:10), in accordance with prophecy of Ezekiel, that "the sons of Israel will eat unclean things among the nations" (Ezek 4:13). In order to avoid uncleanness, Jews sought hospitality among other Jews: "And he [sc. Elijah] went and found the widow and her son, for he could not stay with uncircumcised people . . ." (*VP* 10:4). According to *Ep. Arist.* 139 (cf. § 142), "In his wisdom the legislator [i.e. Moses], in a comprehensive survey of each particular part, and being endowed by God for the knowledge of universal truths, surrounded us with unbroken palisades and iron walls to prevent our mingling with any other nations in any manner (ὅπως μηθενὶ τῶν ἄλλων ἐθνῶν ἐπιμισγώμεθα κατὰ μηδέν), being thus kept pure in body and soul, preserved from false beliefs, and worshipping the only God omnipotent over all creation." As the *Epistle of Aristeas* goes on to state, this separation from the nations extends to every area of life, including food (*Ep. Arist.* 139). For Paul, however, the barriers between Israel and the other nations are broken down in Christ (cf. Gal 3:28). Cf. Eph 2:14–15: "For he [sc. Christ] is our peace, who has made us both

the assembly for compelling the Gentiles to live like Jews (Gal 2:11–14). In v. 15, Paul continues by stating, "We are Jews by birth and not sinners of the nations/Gentiles (ἡμεῖς φύσει Ἰουδαῖοι καὶ οὐκ ἐξ ἐθνῶν ἁμαρτωλοί)." This ironic *concessio*[493] not only flies in the face of what the Jewish believers actually know to be true (v. 16) but also contradicts OT and Jewish tradition. As we have seen, Israel is consistently portrayed not only as having followed after the sinful practices of the nations but also as having gone beyond the other nations in doing evil (4 Kgdms 21:9; Jer 18:13).[494] According to Ezek 5:5–6, Jerusalem, which had been given pride of place "in the midst of the nations" (cf. Ezek 38:12), became "the lawless one of the nations" (ἡ ἄνομος ἐκ τῶν ἐθνῶν). The exiles continue to be a "nation of sinners" that stands in need of repentance before it can be returned from the (sinful) nations among which it has been scattered (cf. Tob 13:8[6]). Furthermore, Paul assumes that "as many as are of works of the Law are under a curse" (Gal 3:10a), that is, the Deuteronomic curse for covenant violation that came upon Israel in 722/586 B.C. and persisted thereafter in the protracted Exile (v. 10b).[495] The fundamental problem is that "all the nations (πάντα τὰ ἔθνη) are uncircumcised in the flesh, and the whole house of Israel are uncircumcised in their hearts" (Jer 9:25; cf. Rom 2:25–29).

II. The Exile of Israel. In Rom 2:24, the citation of Isa 52:5 ("For, as it is written, 'The name of God is blasphemed among the nations because of you'") assumes that the contemporary Israel that Paul is castigating is in Exile, scattered among the nations.[496] This is in accordance with much Jewish tradi-

---

[sc. τὰ ἔθνη and Israel (cf. vv. 11–12)] and has broken down the dividing wall, that is, the hostility between us. He has abolished the law with its commandments and ordinances, that he might make the two in himself one new man, thus making peace." On the impurity of the nations and of eating with Gentiles, see further M. HENGEL, *The Pre-Christian Paul* (London: SCM Press; Philadelphia: Trinity Press International, 1991), pp. 31–33; *Jub.* 22:16; Philo *Mos.* 1.278; 1 Macc 1:47–48, 62–63; 2 Macc 6:18–21; 7:1; *Jos. As.* 7:1.

493 By thus contrasting the Jews to the sinful ἔθνη (cf., e.g., *Jub.* 23:22–23; 1 Macc 2:48; *Pss. Sol.* 17:22, 24), Paul at first gives credence to a basic Jewish prejudice only to undermine it in the subsequent context (Gal 2:16–21).

494 See above on the Sin of Israel. Jeremiah predicts Yahweh's judgment on the "circumcised who are uncircumcised" and groups Judah with Egypt, Edom, Ammon, Moab, and those who live in the desert: "For all nations are uncircumcised, and all the house of Israel is uncircumcised of their heart" (Jer 9:24–25; cf. Rom 2:29). See further 2 Kgs 17:7–8, 11, 15; *T. Jud.* 23:2; *Jub.* 1:8–9; 4QFlor 1.8–9. Cf. HECKEL, "Das Bild der Heiden und die Identität der Christen bei Paulus," pp. 285–286; DABELSTEIN, *Die Beurteilung der 'Heiden' bei Paulus*, p. 27.

495 Note the citation of Deut 27:26 (+ 29:19) in Gal 3:10b which substantiates v. 10a. See further SCOTT, "'For as many as are of works of the Law are under a curse' (Galatians 3.10)," pp. 187–220. See now Frank THIELMAN, *Paul and the Law: A Contextual Approach* (Downers Grove, IL: InterVarsity, 1994), pp. 125–127 et passim.

496 Cf. HAYS, *Echoes of Scripture in Paul*, 46 (emphasis mine): "The quotation of Isa. 52:5 works metaphorically in Paul's argument only if the reader castigated by the text imaginatively takes the role of *Israel in exile*." On the dishonoring of God among the nations through Israel, see *T. Naph.* 8:6.

tion that, as we have seen, views Israel as still in Exile. Since the gospel has gone out to the ends of the inhabited world (Ps 18:5), where Israel is dispersed,[497] and thus Israel has definitely heard the message (Rom 10:18), Paul interprets the predominantly negative response of the Jews to the gospel as stemming from Jewish jealousy of the Gentile mission (v. 19). Paul cites in this regard Deut 32:21, referring to the exilic situation of Israel: "I will make you jealous of those who are not a nation (οὐκ ἔθνει); with a foolish nation (ἐπ᾽ ἔθνει ἀσυνέτῳ) I will make you angry." A hardening has come upon part of Israel until the full number of the nations comes in (Rom 11:25; cf. 10:21).

III. The Restoration of Israel. If we read Rom 13:1–7 in the context of Paul's imminent expectation of the Parousia (13:11–12) and the Final Judgment (12:19), then the exhortation to the Roman addressees to be subject to the divinely ordained government presupposes that Rome is the Fourth Empire of Daniel,[498] the final empire before the Kingdom of God is established and the saints of the Most High rule the world.[499] As we have seen, Jewish writings of the Greco-Roman period presuppose that, in the succession of empires, God has now given Rome sovereignty over the nations of the world; therefore, resistance to its authority is futile.[500] In the interim, Paul the Apostle is able to use both his Roman citizenship[501] and the Pax Romana – the result of Rome's universal sovereignty – to the advantage of his mission to the nations.

Indirectly, the goal of Paul's mission to the nations is the salvation of Israel, whether by making his fellow Jews jealous and thus saving some of them (Rom 11:11, 13–14)[502] or by contributing to the coming in of the full number of the nations, whereby all Israel will be saved when the Deliverer comes from Zion (11:25–26).[503] Paul's concept of the coming in of the nations derives

---

[497] Cf. Koch, *Schrift als Zeuge*, p. 281 n. 18.

[498] Otto Betz makes a similar suggestion on the "restrainer" of 2 Thess 2:6–7 and draws the comparison to Rom 13:1–7 ("Der Katechon," in *Jesus, Herr der Kirche. Aufsätze zur biblischen Theologie II* [WUNT 52; Tübingen: Mohr-Siebeck, 1990], pp. 293–311). On the influence of Daniel on Paul, see further Betz, *Jesus und das Danielbuch, Band II. Die Menschensohnworte Jesu und die Zukunftserwartung des Paulus (Daniel 7,13–14)* (ANTJ 6.2; Frankfurt a.M.: Lang, 1985).

[499] On Paul's expectation of the reign of believers with Christ over the world, see above on the Abrahamic Promise of universal sovereignty (Rom 4:13; 8:17, 32; Gal 4:1; 1 Cor 6:2). See further Scott, *Adoption*, pp. 130–135, 147, 248–252.

[500] See above on Philo *Quod Deus* 176; Josephus *BJ* 5.367. We may also compare the oath that the initiate must swear upon admission to the Essene community: ". . . he will forever keep faith with all men, especially with the powers that be, since no ruler attains his office except by the will of God. . ." (*BJ* 2.137–142 [here § 140]).

[501] Cf. Hengel, *The Pre-Christian Paul*, pp. 6–15.

[502] Note that, unlike in Rom 10:19, the jealousy of the ἔθνη by the Jews is seen here in a positive light.

[503] According to Romans 11, all Israel will be saved, for the gifts and calling of God are irrevocable (vv. 26, 29). Hence, Paul's thinking remains thoroughly Jewish: The distinction between Israel and "nations" is maintained despite the existence of the church, and the promises to Israel are not eliminated because of the church.

from the OT expectation of the eschatological pilgrimage of the nations to Zion (cf. Isa 2:2−4 = Mic 4:1−3).[504]

In Rom 9:24, Paul argues that God has called "us" not only ἐξ Ἰουδαίων but also ἐξ ἐθνῶν. In support of this statement, the Apostle cites Hos 2:25 and 2:1,[505] both of which contain the word καλεῖν: "Those who were not my people (τὸν οὐ λαόν μου) I will call 'my people' (λαὸν μου). . . . And in the very place where it was said to them, 'You are not my people' (οὐ λαός μου ὑμεῖς), they will be called 'sons of the living God'" (Rom 9:25−26). Whereas these OT passages originally looked forward to the Restoration of Israel after the Exile, Paul applies them to believing Jews and Gentiles who are made the people and sons of God.[506] This is in accordance with the expectation of Zech 2:14−15,[507] which applies the Covenant Formula to the ἔθνη in the time of the Restoration of Israel: "And many nations (ἔθνη πολλά) will flee for refuge to the Lord in that day, and they shall be to him as a people (καὶ ἔσονται αὐτῷ εἰς λαόν), and they shall dwell in the midst of you [sc. daughter of Zion]. . . ."[508]

As we have seen in our discussion of the OT, the ultimate goal of the Restoration is that Israel and the nations might worship the Lord together in Zion.[509] Therefore, it is no surprise that Paul quotes Deut 32:43, a passage that looks forward to this joint worship at the time of Israel's Restoration: "Rejoice, O nations (ἔθνη), with his people" (Rom 15:10). This citation comes within a catena of OT quotations (Rom 15:9b-12), which are drawn from the Psalms, the Torah, and the Prophets, tied together by the word ἔθνη, and adduced in support of Paul's contention that τὰ ἔθνη should glorify God for his mercy (v. 9a).[510] In the same catena, Paul cites Isa 11:10: "The root of Jesse shall come, he who rises to rule the nations (ἐθνῶν); in him shall the nations (ἔθνη) hope" (Rom 15:12).[511]

---

[504] If the image of the pilgrimage of the nations in Isa 2:2−5 has been used here, the order has been reversed, for in Paul's scenario, the nations do not come to Israel because they see Israel's glory; rather, Israel comes to the nations because she sees the salvation and glory that they have in Christ. As Hofius suggests, however, Paul may have in mind certain OT texts that put the eschatological pilgrimage of the Gentiles before the Restoration of Israel ("Das Evangelium und Israel," p. 324).

[505] Cf. Koch, *Schrift als Zeuge*, pp. 104−105, 166−167, 173−174, 279−280.

[506] Cf. 2 Cor 6:16, 18, which applies the Covenant Formula and the Adoption Formula to the Gentile-Christian addressees in Corinth. See further Scott, *Adoption*, pp. 195−213.

[507] Cf. also *Jos. As.* 15:7.

[508] Elsewhere, the Covenant Formula applies to Israel of the Restoration (cf. Scott, *Adoption*, pp. 198−199).

[509] Cf., e.g., Ps 85:9: "All nations (πάντα τὰ ἔθνη), as many has you have made, will come and worship you, O Lord, and shall glorify your name."

[510] Cf. Koch, *Schrift als Zeuge*, pp. 281−284. The expression τὰ ἔθνη δοχάσαι is evidently to be interpreted as an imperatival infinitive construction, of which several other examples can be found in Paul (cf. BDR § 389).

[511] Cf. *Pss. Sol.* 17:34: "He [sc. the future Davidic King] will be merciful to all the nations before him in fear."

Conclusion

In our study of Paul's use of ἔθνος, we have been particularly interested in showing how the Apostle to the nations appropriates the OT and Jewish concept of the interplay between Israel and the other nations of the world. Paul clearly thinks in terms of "nations," not just of individual "Gentiles." His perspective is fundamentally Jewish. Even after becoming an apostle, Paul never ceased to be an "Israelite" and a "Hebrew of Hebrews" (2 Cor 11:22; Phil 3:5; Rom 11:1).[512] He begins with the presupposition that the Table of Nations provides an inventory of the "full number" of the nations of the world, which traditionally comprises 70 (or 72) nations. The Abrahamic Promise, which Paul regards as a prior annunciation of the gospel itself, anticipates that the nations of the world, as listed in the Table of Nations, will be blessed in Abraham and his seed. For Paul, the seed of Abraham is Christ. Therefore, the promise-fulfillment trajectory of the Abrahamic Promise culminates in Christ, the hope of the nations. Although most of Israel remains temporarily hardened to the gospel, her salvation and restoration will be complete when the full number of the nations "comes in" through the ongoing eschatological pilgrimage to Zion, a time that also coincides with the Parousia. Therefore, Paul works indefatigably toward the expeditious completion of the Gentile mission. For Paul, the goal of history is that all nations worship God with Israel in Zion.

These considerations provide the essential background for Paul's missionary strategy as presented in Romans 15.

---

[512] Cf. Karl-Wilhelm Niebuhr, *Heidenapostel aus Israel. Die jüdische Identität des Paulus nach ihrer Darstellung in seinen Briefen* (WUNT 62; Tübingen: Mohr-Siebeck, 1992).

Chapter 3

The Table of Nations in Paul

Japheth bezog die Hütten Sems, und Sem
mußte weichen.[1]

Introduction

As we saw in Chap. 1, the Table of Nations exerted a strong influence on the OT and early Judaism. It provided the fundamental point of orientation for describing Israel's place among the nations of the world and the basis for envisioning world geography and ethnography for both the present and the eschatological future. Furthermore, our study of ἔθνος in Chap. 2 began to show that Paul appropriates the OT and Jewish tradition of the Table of Nations. As the "Apostle to the nations" (Rom 11:13), Paul devotes himself to a mission to the nations for the sake of Israel. In Gal 3:8, he traces his gospel back to the Abrahamic Promise in Gen 12:3 (+ 18:18): "In you shall all the nations (πάντα τὰ ἔθνη) be blessed." In the OT context of Paul's modified citation, "all the nations[2] (of the earth)" refers back to the Table of Nations in Genesis 10. Paul's missionary strategy is to bring in "the full number of the nations" (τὸ πλήρωμα τῶν ἐθνῶν), at which time "all Israel" (i.e., all twelve tribes) will be saved (Rom 11:25−26). As we have suggested, this "full number of the nations" probably refers to the 70 or 72 of nations in the world in accordance with Deut 32:8 and the Table-of-Nations tradition.[3] As we shall see, Romans 15 provides further evidence that Paul's conception of his mission is influenced by regional geography and ethnography in the Table-of-Nations tradition.

---

[1] Adolf von HARNACK, *Die Mission und Ausbreitung des Christentums in den ersten drei Jahrhunderten, Bd. 1: Die Mission in Wort und Tat* (4th ed.; Leipzig: Hinrichs, 1927), p. 77. The allusion is to Gen 9:27.

[2] As we have seen, Paul substitutes πάντα τὰ ἔθνη from Gen 18:18b for πᾶσαι αἱ φυλαί of Gen 12:3.

[3] According to Deut 32:8 MT, the number of the nations (i.e., 70 or 72) was established according to the number of the sons of Israel. Hence, the numerical relationship in Rom 11:25−26 between the "full number" of the nations and "all Israel" is already traditional.

The Table of Nations and Romans 15

Context

Romans 15 provides an important glimpse into the geographical orientation of Paul's mission to the nations, for it includes actual landmarks that delineate the progress of Paul's mission within a section on Paul's apostolic ministry to the "nations" (vv. 14–21). Having just finished the paraenetic section of the letter, Paul explains why he has written to the Romans so boldly on some points (v. 15a), reminding them of his apostolic authority for doing so (v. 15b), for in words reminiscent of the superscription of the letter, where Paul first establishes the relationship between his readers and himself, introducing himself as having "received grace and apostleship to call people from among all ἔθνη to the obedience of faith" (Rom 1:5) and placing the Romans within the sphere of his apostolic commission (v. 6),[4] Paul now contends that he has the authority to write to them boldly, "because of the grace given to me by God to be a minister of Christ Jesus to the ἔθνη in the priestly service of the gospel of God, in order that the ἔθνη might become an offering acceptable to God, sanctified by the Holy Spirit" (15:15b-16). As a God-appointed minister, therefore, Paul has reason to be proud of his work for God (v. 17), for it is based on what Christ has done through him and in the power of the Holy Spirit for the obedience of the ἔθνη (vv. 18–19a). The result of this Spirit-empowered ministry to the nations through Christ is given in v. 19b: As the Apostle to the nations for the sake of Israel, Paul has "fulfilled" (πεπληρωκέναι) the gospel of Christ "from Jerusalem – and in a circle – to Illyricum" (ἀπὸ Ἰερουσαλὴμ καὶ κύκλῳ μέχρι τοῦ Ἰλλυρικοῦ). This marks Paul's progress in the process of stimulating "the full number of the nations" to come in and of thus bringing about the ultimate salvation of his people Israel at the Parousia (Rom 11:25–26).[5] Let us examine the *crux interpretum* of Rom 15:19b in more detail.

"From Jerusalem and in a Circle"

Jerusalem as the Starting Point of Paul's Mission. From the context, it is clear that the geographical movement "from Jerusalem ... to Illyricum" applies to Paul's own apostolic ministry.[6] Therefore, ἀπὸ Ἰερουσαλήμ cannot be sepa-

---

[4] The fact that Rom 15:14ff. picks up thoughts from the introductory section of the letter is shown (1) by the allusion in 15:14 to the positive evaluation of the Romans in the thanksgiving (1:8) and (2) by the reiteration in 15:23–24, 32 of Paul's longstanding desire to visit the Romans (1:10–13).

[5] Cf. Peter Stuhlmacher, *Der Brief an die Römer* (NTD 6; Göttingen: Vandenhoeck & Ruprecht, 1989), pp. 210, 212.

[6] Whereas A.S. Geyser argues that this expression is not to be taken geographically but rather as Paul's way of authenticating his apostolate ("Un essaie d'explication de Rm. XV 19," *NTS* 6 [1959–60] 156–159), Paul's use of concrete toponyms (e.g., Jerusalem, Rome, and

rated out as a reference to the starting point of the whole Christian mission[7] even though we know that the gospel went out originally from Jerusalem (cf. Acts 1:8). In that case, however, it may seem strange at first that Paul should choose to mention Jerusalem as the starting point (ἀπὸ Ἰερουσαλήμ)[8] of his own mission to the nations,[9] for Paul emphasizes in Galatians 1–2 that his apostolic authority and his gospel are independent of the Jerusalem authorities. Indeed, in the earliest period after his call, Paul had only the barest association with Jerusalem Christianity: His contact with its leaders was limited to Peter and James, and he was personally unknown to the churches in Judea (Gal 1:15–24). Does that mean, however, that he distanced himself from the Holy City itself, or that his mission did not, in some sense, begin there?

Acts reports that Paul preached in Jerusalem on several occasions, including the period just after his Damascus Road experience (cf. Acts 9:29; 26:20). According to Acts, furthermore, Paul received a vision in the Temple in which God himself commissioned Paul to preach among the nations (Acts 22:17–21).[10] It is in Jerusalem that the Apostolic Council gives Paul official recognition for his gospel and apostleship to the nations (Gal 2:7–9; see further below). Hence, there are many reasons why Paul could say that his mission to the nations proceeds "from Jerusalem." On the other hand, we must reckon with the very likely possibility that "from Jerusalem" indicates the special significance of the place itself for Paul's mission and not just an event that took place in Jerusalem associated with his mission.[11] We shall come back to the question of Paul's relationship to Jerusalem below. For the moment, however,

---

Spain) in the context of a discussion of his apostleship shows that these two ideas should not be played off against one another.

[7] So, correctly, Martin HENGEL, *The Pre-Christian Paul* (London: SCM; Philadelphia: Trinity Press International, 1991), p. 24; idem, "Der vorchristliche Paulus," in *Paulus und das antike Judentum* (ed. M. Hengel and Ulrich Heckel; Tübingen: Mohr-Siebeck, 1991), pp. 177–293 (here pp. 291–292); Rainer RIESNER, *Die Frühzeit des Apostels Paulus. Studien zur Chronologie, Missionsstrategie und Theologie* (WUNT 71; Tübingen: Mohr-Siebeck, 1994), pp. 213ff.

[8] The debate on whether the preposition ἀπό here includes or excludes Jerusalem seems inconsequential. The point of the passage is not that Paul preached in Jerusalem (cf. Acts 9:28–29) but rather that his mission to the ἔθνη originated from there.

[9] In fact, as part of his argument that Romans 15 as a whole is non-Pauline, Ferdinand Christian BAUR goes so far as to argue on 15:19b that Paul himself would never have indicated Jerusalem as the starting point: "Ist diess nicht gar zu deutlich eine den Judenchristen gemachte Concession, nach deren Ansicht freilich jeder Verkündiger des Evangeliums nur von Jerusalem ausgehen konnte?" (*Paulus, der Apostel Jesu Christi. Sein Leben und Wirken, seine Briefe und seine Lehre* [2 vols.; 2nd ed.; ed. Eduard Zeller; Leipzig: Fues's Verlag, 1866], 1:397).

[10] Cf. Otto BETZ, "Die Vision des Paulus im Tempel von Jerusalem. Apg 22, 17–21 als Beitrag zur Deutung des Damaskuserlebnisses," in *Jesus, der Herr der Kirche. Aufsätze zur biblischen Theologie II* (WUNT 52; Tübingen: Mohr-Siebeck, 1990), 91–102.

[11] Cf. RIESNER, *Frühzeit*, p. 214.

we shall concentrate on Rom 15:19b, in which the much-debated words καὶ κύκλῳ seem to hold the interpretive key. [12]

And in a Circle (of Jerusalem). The phrase καὶ κύκλῳ is usually interpreted in one of two ways: (1) as indicating the semi-circular path of Paul's missionary activity between Jerusalem and Illyricum ("from Jerusalem and around to Illyricum")[13] or (2) as describing the surroundings of Jerusalem ("from Jerusalem and round about to Illyricum").[14] The first alternative may have more grammatical support,[15] but it falters on the normal meaning of κύκλῳ (literally "in a circle").[16] Furthermore, if Paul had wanted to describe the path from Jerusalem to Illyricum and all that lay in between, then ἀπό ... μέχρι would have sufficed, for the infinitive πεπληρωκέναι itself indicates that the intervening territory was covered. It is likely, therefore, that Paul added καὶ κύκλῳ in order to emphasize the centrality of Jerusalem to his mission rather than to describe the path that he took to Illyricum.

In the OT, κύκλῳ is used frequently in connection with Jerusalem,[17] especially to describe the "nations" (ἔθνη) or "peoples" (λαοί) round about it.[18] This coincides with the Table-of-Nations tradition, which views Jerusalem as the "navel of the world" (Ezek 38:12). For the interpretation of Rom 15:19, the most interesting OT parallel is Ezek 5:5, which describes the supremacy of Jerusalem in terms of her geographical centrality in the world: "Thus says the Lord, 'This is Jerusalem: I have set her in the midst of the nations (ἐν μέσῳ τῶν ἐθνῶν) and the countries in a circle around her (καὶ τὰς κύκλῳ αὐτῆς χώρας).'" Here, we find two parallel lines that express the same fact about Jerusalem.[19]

---

[12] As evidence of the difficulty of Rom 15:19b in the history of its transmission, the textual tradition varies in its placement of καὶ κύκλῳ, whether after Ἰερουσαλήμ or after Ἰλλυρικοῦ (so D, F, G, m). See further William Paul Bowers, "Studies in Paul's Understanding of his Mission," (Ph.D. diss., Cambridge University, 1976), p. 23 n. 5.

[13] Cf., e.g., Ernst Käsemann, *An die Römer* (4th ed.; HNT 8a; Tübingen: Mohr-Siebeck, 1980), p. 380; Riesner, *Frühzeit*, p. 214; Bowers, "Paul's Understanding," pp. 23–25; James D. G. Dunn, *Romans* (2 vols.; WBC 38; Dallas: Word Books, 1988), 2:864, 872; C. E. B. Cranfield, *The Epistle to the Romans* (2 vols.; ICC; Edinburgh: T. & T. Clark, 1980–1981), 2:761.

[14] Cf., e.g., Ulrich Wilckens, *Der Brief an die Römer* (3 vols.; EKK 6; Zürich: Benziger Verlag; Neukirchen-Vluyn: Neukirchener Verlag, 1978–1982), 3:120; J. Knox, "Romans 15:14–33 and Paul's Conception of His Apostolic Mission," *JBL* 83 (1964) 1–11 (here p. 11).

[15] The καί is most naturally taken as a coordinating conjunction linking ἀπό and κύκλῳ. Proponents of this view point out that if καὶ κύκλῳ modified Ἰερουσαλήμ, then we would expect the article and an expression such as καὶ τῆς κύκλῳ χώρας, καὶ τοῦ κύκλῳ, or καὶ τῶν κύκλῳ. Cf. Cranfield, *Romans*, 2:761; Riesner, *Frühzeit*, p. 214.

[16] Cf. Knox, "Romans 15:14–33," p. 10–11; although, Bowers adduces three examples in which κύκλος is used of "a curving route alone, with no thought of a complete circuit": Xenophon *Anab.* 7.1.14; Appian *Mithrid.* 101; Philo *Legat.* 250 ("Paul's Understanding," pp. 24–25).

[17] Cf. Ps 78:3; 124:2; Jer 39:44; 40:13; Ezek 34:26.

[18] Cf. Ezek 5:5, 6; Zech 12:2; also Jer 4:17; 6:3.

[19] Cf. Walther Zimmerli, *Ezechiel* (2 vols.; 2nd ed.; BKAT 13; Neukirchen-Vluyn: Neukirchener Verlag, 1979), 1:132: "Die Verbindung גוים (bzw. עמים) – ארצות, die man sachgemäß

The first line states that Jerusalem was set "in the midst of the nations," which is another way of saying that Jerusalem is the "navel of the world." The second line portrays the countries as arrayed "in a circle" (κύκλῳ) around Jerusalem. Therefore, in light of Ezek 5:5 and the whole Table-of-Nations tradition, it seems likely that Rom 15:19 portrays Paul's mission to the nations from the perspective of Jerusalem as the center of a circle (κύκλος) embracing the whole inhabited world. Interestingly enough, John KNOX comes close to the same conclusion: "May I suggest the possibility . . . that it occurred to Paul to describe the territory already evangelized in Palestine, Syria, Asia Minor, and Greece in circular terms – to speak of it as lying within a circle – because he is thinking of the whole evangelistic enterprise to which he is committed as lying within *the circle of nations* around the Mediterranean Sea?"[20] Nevertheless, by failing to consider the OT and Jewish background, KNOX misses the relationship between the circle of nations and their center in Jerusalem.

The fact that Paul views Jerusalem as the center of the world can be shown already in Gal 4:21–31, where he provides geographical information intended to support his typological argument.[21] Thus when the Apostle refers to "the Jerusalem above" (v. 26), this can be seen in terms of Jewish world geography, in which the correspondence between the heavenly Jerusalem and the earthly Jerusalem implies that the earthly Jerusalem is "the navel of the world."[22] Furthermore, Paul's statement that Mount Sinai in Arabia (Hagar)[23] "corresponds to the present Jerusalem" (v. 25) also has a marked

---

wiedergeben könnte mit 'Heidenvölker – Heidenländer', ist für Ez besonders charakteristisch (5,5f.; 6,8; 11,16; 12,15; 20,23.32; 22,4.15; 29.12; 30,23.26; 36,19.24; vgl. 20,34.41; 25,7; 34,13). Sie wird hier im gehobenen Stil einer Aussage im parallelismus membrorum verwendet, um die Besonderheit Jerusalems als des Ortes der 'Mitte' der ganzen Völkerwelt herauszuheben."

[20] KNOX, "Romans 15:14–33," p. 11 (emphasis mine).

[21] Cf. Hartmut GESE, "Τὸ δὲ ῾Αγὰρ Σινᾶ ὄρος ἐστὶν ἐν τῇ ᾽Αραβίᾳ," in *Vom Sinai zum Zion. Alttestamentliche Beiträge zur biblischen Theologie* (BEvT 64; Munich: Kaiser, 1974), pp. 49–62. Gese's identification of Sinai with Hegra, which has been criticized (cf. G.I. DAVIES, "Hagar, El-Hegra and the Location of Mount Sinai," *VT* 22 [1972] 152–163), now finds targumic support (cf. M.G. STEINHAUSER, "Gal 4,25a: Evidence of Targumic Tradition in Gal 4,21–31?" *Bib* 70 [1989] 234–240). See further Paul MAIBERGER, *Topographische und historische Untersuchungen zum Sinaiproblem* (OBO 54; Freiburg: Universitätsverlag; Göttingen: Vandenhoeck & Ruprecht, 1984), pp. 73–82.

[22] Cf. Beate EGO, *Im Himmel wie auf Erden. Studien zum Verhältnis von himmlischer und irdischer Welt im rabbinischen Judentum* (WUNT 2.34; Tübingen: Mohr-Siebeck, 1989), pp. 86–91 et passim; Samuel TERRIEN, "The Omphalos Myth and Hebrew Religion," *VT* 20 (1970) 315–338 (here p. 317). EGO reports that Gal 4:26 is the earliest reference to the heavenly Jerusalem (ibid., p. 15). See also Peter HAYMAN, "Some Observations on Sefer Yesira: (2) The Temple at the Centre of the Universe," *JSS* 35 (1984) 176–182.

[23] According to Jewish tradition, Hagar was the mother of Ishmael, the founder of the "nation" (ἔθνος) of the Arabs who lived in Arabia (cf. Josephus *Ant.* 1.214; 2.213; see further Fergus MILLAR, "Hagar, Ishmael, Josephus and the Origins of Islam," *JJS* 44 [1993] 23–45). If, despite the doubt of Hans Dieter BETZ (*Galatians: A Commentary on Paul's Letter to the Galatians* [Hermeneia; Philadelphia: Fortress, 1979], p. 245), Paul had this fact in mind when he wrote Gal 4:22ff., this would be further evidence that Paul's geographical orientation is fundamentally biblical. In a personal communication, Professor Martin HENGEL expressed to

geographical dimension, for the point of this illustration does not seem to be that Mount Sinai and Jerusalem are identical but rather that they "correspond to one another" geographically.[24] In that case, the Table-of-Nations tradition in *Jubilees* 8–9 may provide the key for understanding what this means, for in the context of describing Zion as "the middle of the navel of the world" in accordance with Ezek 5:5 and 38:12, *Jub.* 8:19 conceives of the three holy places – Eden, Sinai, and Zion – as "facing [or corresponding to] one another," all within the territory of Shem. As P. S. ALEXANDER plausibly argues, "This probably means that they are at right angles to each other, i.e., a median runs east-west through the centre of Paradise and Zion, and another north-south through Zion and Sinai. It is not hard to guess that the east-west median went out through the Straits of Gibraltar. ...."[25] Even the idea of the Jerusalem above as "our Mother" in Gal 4:26 may be based on this Jerusalem-centric perspective, for as we saw in our discussion of Philo *Legat.* 281 in Chap. 2, Jerusalem is a μητρόπολις in the sense of the "capital city" of the world, for Isa 1:26 foresees that at the time of the Restoration, Jerusalem would be called "the faithful Metropolis Zion," in a context that portrays Zion as "the highest of the mountains," to which "all nations" (πάντα τὰ ἔθνη) will come (Isa 2:2). In this way, Paul is able to turn a cartographic correspondence into a typological correspondence that has the ring of plausibility for his readers.[26]

---

me the opinion that after Paul's call to preach the gospel among the nations, the Apostle went immediately to "Arabia" (Gal 1:17) precisely because the Arabs were the descendants of Ishmael, the son of Abraham, whose territory was part of the messianic kingdom. Günter STEMBERGER, "Die Bedeutung des 'Landes Israel' in der rabbinischen Tradition," *Kairos* 25 (1983) 176–199 (here pp. 192–193). HENGEL intends to elaborate on this point in his forthcoming book entitled *Paulus zwischen Damaskus und Antiochien. Die siebzehn unbekannten Jahre.*

[24] Cf. Gerhard DELLING, "συστοιχέω," *TWNT*, 7 (1964) 669: "Since in v. 24 Paul has already given an interpretation of Hagar, he does not equate her directly with the earthly Jerusalem but simply says that 'she belongs in the same series' (sie gehört in eine gemeinsame Reihe mit ihm)."

[25] Philip S. ALEXANDER, "Notes on the 'Imago Mundi' of the Book of Jubilees," *JJS* 33 (1982) 197–213 (here p. 204). Similarly, Gustav HÖLSCHER, *Drei Erdkarten. Ein Beitrag zur Erdkenntnis des hebräischen Altertums* (Sitzungsberichte der Heidelberger Akademie der Wissenschaften, Philosophisch-historische Klasse, Jahrgang 1944/48, 3. Abhandlung; Heidelberg: Winter, 1948), p. 69: "In diese Grenzen Shêms fügt sich die Aufzählung der ihm zugesprochenen Gebiete ein (8, 17–21). Shêm gehören die drei Heiligtümer Gottes auf Erden, der Garten 'Eden, der Berg Sinai in der Wüste und der Zion, die 'Mittes des Nabels der Erde' (8,19). Sie liegen 'einer dem andern gegenüber', Zion im Mittelpunkt der Erde, der Sinai auf demselben Längengrad südlich davon, 'Eden auf demselben Breitengrade östlich davon." Also, Francis SCHMIDT, "Jewish Representations of the Inhabited Earth during the Hellenistic and Roman Periods," in *Greece and Rome in Eretz Israel: Collected Essays* (ed. A. Kasher, et al.; Jerusalem: Yad Izhak Ben-Zvi/The Israel Exploration Society, 1990), pp. 119–134 (here p. 128).

[26] On the significance of Jerusalem for Paul, see further Peter STUHLMACHER, "Die Stellung Jesu und des Paulus zu Jerusalem," *ZTK* 86 (1989) 140–156 (esp. pp. 148–156); HENGEL, *The Pre-Christian Paul*, pp. 24–25 et passim.

"To Illyricum" and Beyond

Paul's Mission and the Tripartite Division of the World. If καὶ κύκλῳ in Rom 15:19 thus refers to the centrality of Jerusalem in accordance with Ezek 5:5 and the Table-of-Nations tradition, this has ramifications for the interpretation of the rest of Romans 15, for, as we saw in Chap. 1, the Table-of-Nations tradition presupposes that Jerusalem stands at the center of a world divided among the three sons of Noah. According to this conception, furthermore, Jerusalem is the point at which the three spheres of Shem, Ham, and Japheth intersect.

Thus, when Paul claims to have fulfilled the gospel of Christ from Jerusalem "to Illyricum," readers who share the Apostle's presupposed world map based on the Table of Nations[27] realize that Paul conceives of his missionary activity as focused on the sphere of the Japhethites,[28] for the swath of territory thereby described includes all of Asia Minor (with Galatia!) and Europe as far as the Adriatic Sea, which amounts to approximately half of the territory traditionally ascribed to Japheth and his sons.[29] This could be part of the κανών, or extent, of Paul's mission field, which, according to 2 Cor 10:13–16, Paul saw as particularly apportioned to him by God.[30] Furthermore, as the subsequent context of Romans 15 reveals, Paul evidently plans to complete the evangelization of the territory of Japheth, for, in announcing his intention to use Rome as a way station,[31] Paul makes it clear that his ultimate goal – after taking the collection to Jerusalem (vv. 25–28) – is to reach Spain with the gospel (vv. 22–24, 28–29).[32] Rome, of course, had already been evangelized,[33] and, since Paul insisted on doing pioneering missionary work rather than building on another's foundation (cf. vv. 20–21), he looked from the vantage point of Illyricum beyond the imperial capital to Spain, the next territory further west-

---

[27] Georg EICHHOLZ quite rightly emphasizes that to comprehend what Paul is saying in Romans 15, one must consult "the map of that day" (*Die Theologie des Paulus* [6th ed.; Neukirchen-Vluyn: Neukirchener Verlag, 1988], p. 23). Of course, the question really is this: Which map was Paul consulting?

[28] What possible role does Paul's place of birth in Tarsus play in the fact that the Apostle feels himself particularly called to evangelize the Japhethites? On Tarsus as Paul's birthplace, see now HENGEL, *The Pre-Christian Paul*, pp. 1–17.

[29] On the other hand, von HARNACK conceives of Illyricum as marking here the end of the Hellenic world and the beginning of the Latin world (*Die Mission und Ausbreitung des Christentums*, pp. 80, 82).

[30] See further below on Pauline territoriality.

[31] According to Acts 19:21, Paul plans to see Rome after going to Jerusalem although nothing is said of using Rome as a rest stop on the way to Spain.

[32] Hence, Jerusalem, the center of the world, stands in the middle between the two halves of Paul's mission to the Japhethites!

[33] By whom? Missionaries from Syrian Antioch? Returnees from Pentecost? See, e.g., Peter LAMPE, *Die stadtrömischen Christen in den ersten beiden Jahrhunderten. Untersuchungen zur Sozialgeschichte* (2nd ed.; WUNT 2.18; Tübingen: Mohr-Siebeck, 1989), pp. 1–4; EICHHOLZ, *Die Theologie des Paulus*, pp. 26–27.

ward.[34] In fact, Spain traditionally represents the westernmost portion of the territory of Japheth[35] (or of the inhabited world for that matter[36]). Both *Jubilees* (8:23, 26; 9:12) and Josephus (*Ant.* 1.122) mention Gadir/Gadeira near the Straights of Gibraltar in southern Spain in their respective expositions of the Table of Nations.[37]

Josephus writes that the sons of Japheth, "beginning by inhabiting the mountains of Taurus and Amanus, advanced in Asia up to the river Tanais and in Europe as far as Gadeira, occupying the territory upon which they lit . . ." (*Ant.* 1.122). Interestingly enough, this migration of the sons of Japheth corresponds to the intended scope and actual direction of Paul's mission to the nations as described in Romans 15. The northwesterly path of Paul's mission from Jerusalem also corresponds to the way in which the nations are listed in the Table of Nations of 1 Chronicles 1, for as as we observed in Chap. 1, 1 Chronicles 1 lists the nations of the world "in a circle" which proceeds counter-clockwise – from the North, to the West, to the South, and to the East – from the perspective of Jerusalem as the geographic center.[38]

Toponymy. If Paul has the Table of Nations in view when he describes his ministry to the nations, it may seem surprising that he does not use the names of

---

[34] Cf. Dieter ZELLER, "Theologie der Mission bei Paulus," in *Mission im Neuen Testament* (QD 93; ed. Karl Kertelge; Freiburg: Herder, 1982), pp. 164–187 (here p. 182).

[35] In the Table-of-Nations tradition, Spain is identified either with Meshech (cf. *Jub.* 9:12), with Tubal (cf. Josephus *Ant.* 1.124, depending on whether Ἴβηρες refers here to the Iberians in Spain [cf. *Ap.* 2.40] or to those in the territory of modern Georgia between the Black and Caspian Seas [cf. *Ant.* 13.421; 18.97]), or with Tarshish (cf. Édouard LIPINSKI, "Les Japhétites selon Gen 10,2–4 et 1 Chr 1,5–7," *ZAH* 3 [1990] 40–53 [here pp. 51–52]; Werner HUSS, *Geschichte der Karthager* [Handbuch der Altertumswissenschaft 3.8; Munich: C.H. Beck-'sche Verlagsbuchhandlung, 1985], pp. 29–30).

[36] That Spain lay at the "ends of the earth" is often stressed (cf. BOWERS, "Paul's Under-standing," pp. 77–78; Roger D. AUS, "Paul's Travel Plans to Spain and the 'Full Number of the Gentiles' of Rom. xi. 25," *NovT* 21 (1979) 232–262 [here pp. 242–246]). According to Henry A. REDPATH, Spain is the westernmost limit of the names occurring in the Septuagint ("The Geography of the Septuagint," *AJT* 7 [1903] 289–307 [here p. 307]; cf. p. 304, referring to 1 Macc 8:3; cf. HÖLSCHER, *Drei Erdkarten,* p. 23). Evidently presupposing that Paul was able to accomplish his journey to Spain, 1 Clem. 5:6–7 calls him a herald in the East as in the West, who taught the whole world (ὅλον τὸν κόσμον) righteousness and went to the termina-tion of the West (τὸ τέρμα τῆς δύσεως). See further E. Earle ELLIS, "'Das Ende der Erde' (Apg 1,8)," in *Der Treue Gottes trauen. Beiträge zum Werk des Lukas für Gerhard Schneider* (ed. Claus Bussmann and Walter Radl; Freiburg: Herder, 1991), pp. 277–286 (here pp. 284–285); idem, "'The End of the Earth' (Acts 1:8)," *Bulletin for Biblical Research* 1 (1991) 123–132.

[37] According to ALEXANDER's reconstruction of the Jubilees world map, a median runs east-west through the center of Eden, Zion, and Gadir ("Imago Mundi," p. 204). See Map 1.

[38] In contrast, Strabo's description of Homer's comprehensive knowledge of τὰ ἔσχατα καὶ τὰ κύκλῳ τῆς οἰκουμένης names the countries in a counterclockwise circle but mentions no center: Beginning with the Pillars of Heracles and moving eastward across North Africa, Strabo then takes us northward up the coast of Phoenicia, and then westward across Asia Minor and Europe to end at the point of origin in Iberia (*Geogr.* 1.1.10). Almost the same counterclockwise circumnavigation of the Mediterranean is found in Arrian's description of the lands under Roman control (*Prooem.* 1–3).

the Japhethites to refer to the territories he has covered or intends to cover.[39] Instead, Paul speaks here, as often elsewhere, in terms of Roman provinces.[40] However, this can be explained on the basis of both Paul's missionary situation and the Table-of-Nations tradition itself. On the one hand, since Paul is a Hellenistic Jew writing to a Hellenistic audience, it makes sense that he would write in a manner familiar to his readers. On the other hand, the Table-of-Nations tradition itself is a witness to the repeated attempt by Jews to "update" the original list of Genesis 10, often in terms of Roman provinces (see Table 3).[41] In fact, the Targumim often use the loanword איפרכייה (= ἐπαρχεία, "province") to introduce the contemporary identifications of the sons of Noah.[42] Furthermore, as we have seen in his exposition of the Table of Nations, Josephus blames "the Greeks" for changing the original nomenclature (*Ant.* 1.121) and then proceeds to give the contemporary equivalent for the territories founded by the sons and grandsons of Noah, often using the names of Roman provinces (e.g., Galatia [§ 123] and Cilicia [§ 127]). Likewise, Paul filters the Table of Nations through contemporary geographical categories. Again, John KNOX comes very close to this point, without mentioning the Jewish background: "In view of the way Paul speaks so consistently in provincial terms, one

---

[39] In Col 3:11, Paul does not speak of the Japhethites Ashkenaz or Magog but rather of the Scythians. While Ashkenaz is the biblical name for the Scythians, Josephus identifies them with Magog (*Ant.* 1.123).

[40] Note the references, in context, to the Roman provinces of Illyricum (Rom 15:19), Macedonia (v. 26), Achaia (v. 26), and Spain (vv. 24, 28). Elsewhere, too, Paul thinks in terms of Roman provinces (cf. HENGEL, *The Pre-Christian Paul*, pp. 10–11; RIESNER, *Frühzeit*, p. 227; W.M. RAMSAY, *A Historical Commentary on St. Paul's Epistle to the Galatians* [London: Hodder and Stoughton, 1899], p. 314). When he speaks, for example, of initial converts, they become "the firstfruits of Achaia" (1 Cor 16:15) or "the firstfruits of Asia" (Rom 15:5). His Aegean work hardly underway, Paul already thinks of the Thessalonians as examples of believers "in Macedonia and in Achaia" (1 Thess 1:7), and it is to the brethren "in all Macedonia" that they are found to have demonstrated love (1 Thess 4:10). Writing from Ephesus, Paul conveys greetings from "the churches of Asia" (1 Cor 16:19). His troubles there become afflictions "in Asia" (2 Cor 1:8). Those who supplied him with aid while in Corinth are "from Macedonia" (2 Cor 11:9). And it is "in the regions of Achaia" that he will let none stop his boast of never having been a financial burden (2 Cor 11:10). Perhaps most significant of all, when Paul is making arrangements for the collection that will mark the conclusion of his eastern mission, the participants become "the churches of Galatia" (1 Cor 16:1), "the churches of Macedonia" (2 Cor 8:1), "those of Macedonia" (2 Cor 9:2, 4), "Achaia" (2 Cor 9:2), and "Macedonia and Achaia" (Rom 15:26).

[41] We must add to our considerations one other point: Unlike the sons and descendants of Shem and Ham, who are mentioned in numerous places throughout the Hebrew Bible, the sons and descendants of Japheth are conspicuous by their absence from most of the OT. Outside the genealogical tables in Genesis and Chronicles, four of Japheth's sons – Gomer, Javan, Tubal, and Meshech – are mentioned chiefly in two books: Isa 66:19 (Javan, Tubal, and Meshech) and Ezek 27:13; 32:26; 38:2, 3, 6; 39:1, 6 (Gomer and Tubal). Of Japheth's descendants, the best known are two of Javan's sons: Tarshish (mentioned about 29 times in the Hebrew Bible) and Kittim (mentioned 5 times). In view of the relative obscurity of the names of the Japhethites, Paul may have preferred their Greco-Roman equivalents.

[42] See Chap. 1 above.

may wonder if by 'nations' he would not have meant simply the Roman provinces."[43] The traditional Japhethite territory corresponded approximately to the contemporary Roman Empire,[44] the realm of the Kittim (descendants of a grandson of Japheth).[45] According to Gen 10:4, Kittim is the son of Javan (Greece), and we have suggested that Paul's mission "to the Greek" (Rom 1:16) may be connected with the fact that, according to Jewish tradition, Greek was considered the language of Japheth.[46] We have also suggested that Paul considers Rome the Fourth Empire of Daniel, in which case it is significant that Daniel also mentions the Kittim (11:30 = Rome).[47] Therefore, even if Paul's mission was focussed on the Japhethites, it would not be unusual for him to use Greco-Roman nomenclature.

In light of these considerations, it makes little difference whether Paul actually evangelized in the Roman province of Illyricum or not,[48] for in the Table-of-Nations tradition, Illyricum could be included in the same traditional territory as Macedonia (i.e., Javan or Madai),[49] which Paul had already covered to his own satisfaction. It seems that for Paul, preaching the gospel to a representative number of any particular Japhethite nation counts as having fully evangelized the whole territory.[50] This might explain, on the one hand,

---

[43] KNOX, "Romans 15:14–33," p. 3. Similarly, BOWERS, "Paul's Understanding," p. 71: "Perhaps it [sc. Paul's differentiation between geographical regions] is based on taking τὰ ἔθνη not only as a category but also as a collection, not only as 'the Gentiles' but also as 'the nations'. These may have been discriminated in Paul's thought in terms of the units of the Empire, so that the provinces or regions stood each for a 'nation' and collectively for 'the Gentiles' to which he was called." As we discussed in the study of Paul's use of ἔθνος, the expression αἱ ἐκκλησίαι τῶν ἐθνῶν in Rom 16:4 is best understood in terms of churches of the Roman provinces, each of which can also be considered an ἔθνος: αἱ ἐκκλησίαι τῆς Γαλατίας (Gal 1:2; 1 Cor 16:1); αἱ ἐκκλησίαι τῆς Ἀσίας (1 Cor 16:19); αἱ ἐκκλησίαι τῆς Μακεδονίας (2 Cor 8:1); αἱ ἐκκλησίαι τῆς Ἰουδαίας (Gal 1:22). Cf. RAMSAY, *Galatians*, p. 134: "In other Provinces of the Roman State the fiction was usually maintained that there was only one 'tribe' or 'nation.' Even in provinces which were composed of many distinct nations, such as Asia, the official form admitted only one 'nation,' *viz.*, the Roman idea, the Province: in other words, the 'nation' officially was the Province. 'The nation Asia' (ἡ Ἀσία τὸ ἔθνος) was the technical Greek form translating the Latin *Asia Provincia* [Dio Cassius 54.30]." See further A. N. SHERWIN-WHITE, "The Roman World as *Omnes Gentes* or Τὰ Ἔθνη," in *The Roman Citizenship* (2nd ed.; Oxford: Clarendon Press, 1973), pp. 437–444.

[44] For example, Gadeira was considered the most westerly extent not only of Japhethite territory (Josephus *Ant.* 1.122) but of the Roman Empire as well (*BJ* 2.363).

[45] On the identification of the Romans with the Kittim (Gen 10:4), see Chap. 1. The *War Scroll* even refers to "the Kittim of Asshur" (1QM 1.2) and "the Kittim in Egypt" (1QM 1.4), which shows that as rulers of a world empire, the Japhethite nation of the Kittim had encroached on and stationed legions in the territories of Shem and Ham, respectively.

[46] See Chap. 2 above.

[47] See Chap. 1 above.

[48] As with the question of ἀπὸ Ἱερουσαλήμ, commentators are usually preoccupied with whether Paul means Illyricum inclusively or exclusively (cf., e.g., WILCKENS, *Römer*, 3:583).

[49] Cf. the Targumim and *b. Yoma* 10a, respectively.

[50] Perhaps this is because, as DUNN argues (*Romans*, 2:864, 881; cf. also CRANFIELD, *Romans*, 2:762, 766), Paul was responsible only for laying the foundation (cf. Rom 15:20). Paul assumes that from major centers like Thessalonica, the gospel radiates out to the

how Paul can claim that he had "fulfilled" the gospel of Christ in the eastern half of the Mediterranean (Rom 15:19) and that he had no further "place" (τόπος) to work in these "regions" (κλίματα)[51] (v. 23), for he had already preached the gospel to a representative number of each of the sons of Japheth and had established churches in their territories.[52] On the other hand, this insight might also explain why, skipping over the land that lay between Rome and Spain (e.g., Gallia), Paul thinks that his next and final evangelistic goal is to reach Spain,[53] for that may have been the last of the seven sons of Japheth who needed to hear the gospel before, in accordance with the OT and Jewish expectation of the eschatological pilgrimage of the nations to Jerusalem,[54] "the full number of the nations" would have come in (cf. Rom 11:25).[55] Thereupon, the salvation of all Israel in connection with the Parousia (v. 26) completes the winning of all nations on earth.

We have already seen above how the Table-of-Nations tradition is taken up in the expectation of the eschatological pilgrimage of the nations to Jerusalem, particularly in Isa 66:18−20. Hence, Rainer RIESNER's suggestion that Rom

---

surrounding country and beyond (cf. 1 Thess 1:8). For additional considerations, see AUS, "Paul's Travel Plans," pp. 257−260. In a letter responding to the present chapter, Professor Hengel suggested to me the interesting idea that Paul's commission is to win the "firstfruits" (cf. Rom 16:5; 1 Cor 16:15) of each of the nations in the territory of Japheth; the sum total of these "firstfruits" would then be the "fullness" of the nations.

[51] Paul elsewhere uses κλίματα as a geographical term referring to Roman provinces: τὰ κλίματα τῆς Ἀχαῖας (2 Cor 11:10); τὰ κλίματα τῆς Συρίας καὶ τῆς Κιλικίας (Gal 1:21).

[52] Cf. KÄSEMANN, *Römer*, p. 380; Günther BORNKAMM, *Paulus* (4th ed.; Urban-Taschenbücher 119; Stuttgart: Kohlhammer, 1979), p. 73: "Er denkt über die einzelne Gemeinde hinaus immer sofort in Ländern und Landschaften. Jede Gemeinde, kaum zum Leben erwacht, steht für ihn jeweils für eine ganze Landschaft: Philippi für Macedonien (Phil 4, 15), Thessalonisch für Macedonien und Achaia (1Thess 1, 7f.), Korinth für Achaia (1Kor 16, 15; 2Kor 1, 1) und Ephesus für Asia (Röm 16, 5; 1Kor 16, 19; 2Kor 1,8). Die Formulierung von Röm 15, 19 ist also keineswegs nur eine zufällige, übertreibende Wendung." Similarly, EICHHOLZ, *Die Theologie des Paulus*, pp. 25−26; Johannes MUNCK, *Paulus und die Heilsgeschichte* (Acta Jutlandica 26.1; Aarhus: Universitetsforlaget, 1954), p. 45. Contra CRANFIELD, *Romans*, 2:766−768, who, ignoring the OT/Jewish background of the Table of Nations, rejects the idea that Paul thinks in terms of "lists of countries" because such an idea could be based only on "the extremely improbable assumption that Paul both had a very inadequate conception of the number of nations embraced within the Roman Empire of his time and also regarded the multitude of nations outside its bounds as being beyond God's concern."

[53] Cf. Friedrich SCHMIDTKE, *Die Japhetiten der biblischen Völkertafel* (Breslauer Studien zur historischen Theologie 7; Breslau: Müller & Seiffert, 1926), p. 95: "Die drei großen Halbinseln Südeuropas: Pyrenänen-, Apenninen-, Balkan-halbinseln sind durch je ein Volk repräsentiert: Tarshish, Tiras, und Jawan; denn Jawan umfaßt nicht nur die Griechen an der kleinasiatischen Küste, sondern auch das eigentliche Griechenland. Tarshish aber ist die Pyrenäen-, Tiras die Apenninen-Halbinsel."

[54] Cf. Otfried HOFIUS, "Das Evangelium und Israel," in *Paulusstudien* (WUNT 51; Tübingen: Mohr-Siebeck, 1989), pp. 175−202 (here p. 202).

[55] If Paul's primary reason in wanting to evangelize Spain is to complete the mission to Japheth, then the question of whether or not Paul's intention to visit Spain presupposes the presence of Jews there (e.g., Salo W. BARON, *A Social and Religious History of the Jews* [18 vols.; New York: Columbia University Press, 1952−1983], 1:170) is beside the point.

15:19 should be seen in light of Isa 66:19[56] deserves careful consideration. According to RIESNER, the movement in Isa 66:19 from Jerusalem, whence God presumably comes to gather all nations to Zion (cf. vv. 18, 20), in a northwestern semicircle to the extreme west (the "distant islands") corresponds to the concept on which Rom 15:19 is based.[57] In response to this suggestion, several observations need to be made. First of all, this interpretation seems plausible insofar as it affirms that Paul is appropriating the tradition in which Isa 66:19 stands,[58] for Isa 66:19 belongs to the same Table-of-Nations tradition of which Romans 15 also partakes. Furthermore, the list of nations in Isa 66:19 mentions mostly sons of Japheth (Tarshish, Tubal, and Javan), the very nations that seem to be the particular focus of Paul's mission in Romans 15. If, as we have seen above, Isa 66:19 is to be understood as a promise that God will gather "all nations and tongues" to Jerusalem (cf. vv. 18, 20),[59] the list of nations in v. 19 provides concrete examples of nations drawn from the Table of Nations, including representatives from all three sons of Noah. Given the crucial importance of Isaiah in the Pauline letters, and particularly in the letter to the Romans,[60] Paul would surely have viewed himself as *part* of the eschatological missionary enterprise to the ἔθνη portrayed in Isa 66:19,[61] for, as Richard B. HAYS aptly observes, "Isaiah offers the clearest expression in the Old Testament of a universalistic, eschatological vision in which the restoration of Israel in Zion is accompanied by an ingathering of Gentiles to worship the Lord [cf. Rom 15:9−11!]; that is why the book is both statistically and substantively the

---

[56] RIESNER, *Frühzeit*, pp. 216−225. RIESNER arrives at this interpretation independently of the work of AUS, "Paul's Travel Plans," 232−262, which comes to the same basic conclusion with minor variations in detail (cf. RIESNER, *Frühzeit*, p. 217 n. 55). On AUS' suggestion that "the offering of the Gentiles/nations" (ἡ προσφορὰ τῶν ἐθνῶν) in Rom 15:16 should be seen in light of Isa 66:20 and the "offering" (δῶρον) of the Jewish remnant brought to the Lord from all nations, see ZELLER, "Theologie der Mission bei Paulus," p. 184 n. 69.

[57] RIESNER, *Frühzeit*, p. 224.

[58] RIESNER considers Isa 66:19 one contributing factor in Paul's choice of the course of his mission: "Es soll hier weder behauptet werden, daß sich die paulinischen Missionspläne von Anfang an Jes. 66,19 orientierten, noch daß in dieser Prophetie der einzige oder wichtigste Grund für die vom Apostel beschrittenen Routen liegt. Im folgenden ist aber die Möglichkeit zu prüfen, ob Paulus an entscheidenden Stationen seines Weges *auch* von dieser alttestamentlichen Missionsweissagung beeinflußt wurde" (ibid., pp. 224−225 [author's emphasis]).

[59] Cf. *Pss. Sol.* 17:31, which expects "nations (ἔθνη) to come from the ends of the earth to see his [sc. Messiah's] glory, to bring as gifts (δῶρα) her [Jerusalem's] sons who had been driven out...." For the tradition based on Isa 66:18−20, see also 4QDibHam 4.4−12.

[60] According to Dietrich-Alex KOCH (*Die Schrift als Zeuge des Evangeliums. Untersuchungen zur Verwendung und zum Verständnis der Schrift bei Paulus* [BHT 69; Tübingen: Mohr-Siebeck, 1986], p. 33), Paul cites Isaiah 28 times, Psalms 20 times, and Genesis and Deuteronomy each 15 times. No other book is quoted more than 5 times. See further RIESNER, *Frühzeit*, p. 217 n. 57.

[61] Since Isa 66:19 includes mostly Japhethites in its partial list of the nations, corresponding perhaps to the fact that the Japhethites are listed first in Genesis 10, Paul may have considered his mission to this group the most significant part of the world-wide mission to the ἔθνη.

most important scriptural source for Paul."[62] Indeed, even though it is not explicitly cited in the NT, this text may have been perhaps a basis for recognizing a division of labor among the apostles (see further on Gal 2:7–9 below). Second, however, RIESNER's interpretation would be more convincing if it were not so constrained to fit every detail of Isa 66:19 into the concept of Paul's mission in Romans 15. Here are a few points to consider on the geographical aspects of this interpretation: (1) Isa 66:19 does not explicitly refer to the two geographical limits of Paul's mission mentioned in Romans 15, i.e., Jerusalem and Spain. On the one hand, the Isaiah text does not explicitly state that the survivors proceed from Jerusalem nor even that God proceeds from Jerusalem. This is an inference from the text. Hence, it is not clear that ἀπὸ Ἰερουσαλήμ in Rom 15:19 is necessarily explained by the Isaiah text. On the other hand, even if the "distant islands" do refer to the ends of the earth,[63] that does not seem to help us directly with Romans 15, which explicitly mentions Spain as Paul's ultimate destination. According to RIESNER's reading, Tarshish in Isa 66:19 does not refer to Spain.[64] Indeed, it could not, if the direction of Paul's mission is reflected in the Isaiah passage, for Tarshish appears as the first nation in the list. (2) The scope of Isa 66:19 is broader than the more limited scope of Paul's mission in Romans 15. For example, Paul does not go to all the nations listed in Isa 66:19. In particular, it is curious that Paul is actually prohibited from preaching in Asia (Acts 16:6), which RIESNER rightly equates with Lud/Lydia. Furthermore, Isa 66:19 wants to be understood as a promise that God will gather "all nations and tongues," not just a select few.[65] The list of nations in v. 19 provides concrete examples of nations drawn from the Table of Nations, including representatives from all three sons of Noah. Hence RIESNER's attempt to locate all the lands in v. 19 exclusively in Asia Minor or Europe – i.e. Tarsus, Cilicia, Lydia, Mysia, Bithynia, Macedonia, and the far west – is problematic even if it is assumed that Isa 66:19 is being read in part from a special, first-century Jewish perspective.[66] Put, for example, as a son of Ham, is more naturally equated with Libya than with Cilicia.[67]

---

[62] Richard B. HAYS, *Echoes of Scripture in the Letters of Paul* (New Haven: Yale University Press, 1989), p. 162.

[63] RIESNER, *Frühzeit*, p. 224.

[64] RIESNER opts instead for the identification of Tarshish with Tarsus in Cilicia made by Josephus and the Rabbis (*Frühzeit*, p. 222).

[65] Cf. Claus WESTERMANN, *Das Buch Jesaja Kapitel 40–66* (3rd ed.; ATD; Göttingen: Vandenhoeck & Ruprecht, 1976), p. 336, who suggests that vv. 18, 19, and 21 are "controlled by a movement to the nations in the whole world, a movement of missionary witness which is to reach all people. . . ."

[66] RIESNER, *Frühzeit*, p. 224. Modifying my thesis in the present study, RIESNER argues that the movement in Isa 66:19 corresponds remarkably to the distribution of the sons of Japheth according to Genesis 10 (ibid., p. 224 n. 96). In effect, therefore, both of us agree that Paul's mission as described in Romans 15 is directed particularly towards the Japhethites.

[67] Cf. ibid., pp. 223; Johann MAIER, "Zu ethnographisch-geographischen Überlieferungen über Japhetiten (Gen 10,2–4) im frühen Judentum," *Henoch* 13 (1991) 157–194 (here p. 185).

Romans 15:19 and Later Church Tradition

If our analysis of Rom 15:19 is correct, Paul views his mission as part of a worldwide evangelistic enterprise that is shared by other apostles. In this regard, it is interesting to note how later church tradition interpreted Rom 15:19. According to widespread Christian tradition, the apostles divided the world into twelve parts, thus giving each one his own missionary territory.[68] However, in a fragment of Book 3 of Origen's Commentary on Genesis (c. A.D. 229) preserved in Eusebius' *Ecclesiastical History* (3.10.1–3), the world is divided among only five apostles, and Paul's territoriality is described in terms of Rom 15:19:

> But when the holy apostles and disciples of our Lord were dispersed over the whole inhabited world (οἰκουμένη), *Parthia* was allotted (εἴληχεν) to Thomas, according to tradition, while *Scythia* was allotted to Andrew, and *Asia* to John, with whom also he lived, dying at *Ephesus*. But Peter, it seems, preached in *Pontus* and *Galatia* and *Bithynia*, in *Cappadocia* and *Asia*, to those Jews who were of the Diaspora [1 Pet 1:1]. He also at the last came to *Rome*, and was crucified head down; for he requested that he might suffer thus. Why is it necessary to speak of Paul, who from *Jerusalem* even unto *Illyricum* has fully preached the gospel of Christ [Rom 15:19], and afterward was martyred at *Rome* under Nero?
>
> These are the express terms which Origen uses in the third book of his Commentaries on Genesis (ταῦτα Ὠριγένει κατὰ λέξιν ἐν τρίτῳ τόμῳ τῶν εἰς τὴν Γένεσιν ἐξηγητικῶν εἴρηται).[69]

Adolf von HARNACK argues that the first part of this summary about the division of the earth among the apostles stems not from Origen but from Eusebius (1) because the alleged quote is composed of two parts that stand in tension to one another, (2) because Origen does not mention this division of the earth elsewhere in his extant works, and (3) because "holy" (ἱερός) is characteristic of Eusebius' religious language, especially in reference to the apostles

---

[68] Cf. Wolfgang A. BIENERT, "Das Apostelbild in der altchristlichen Überlieferung," in *Neutestamentliche Apokryphen in deutscher Übersetzung, Bd. 2: Apostolisches, Apokalypsen und Verwandtes* (5th ed.; ed. Edgar Hennecke and Wilhelm Schneemelcher; Tübingen: Mohr-Siebeck, 1989), pp. 6–28 (here p. 19). See also the Apostle Map of Beatus of Liébana (cf. Anna-Dorothee von den BRINKEN, *Fines Terrae. Die Enden der Erde und der vierte Kontinent auf mittelalterlichen Weltkarten* [Monumenta Germaniae Historica-Schriften 36; Hannover: Hahnsche Buchhandlung, 1992], pp. 56–58, Pl. 17).

[69] Cf. Eduard SCHWARTZ, *Eusebius Werke, Bd. 2: Die Kirchengeschichte* (GCS 2.1; Leipzig: Hinrichs, 1903), pp. 188–189. See, however, the opinion of Wanda WOLSKA-CONUS ("Geographie," *RAC* 10 [1978] 155–222 [here col. 211]): "Die Texte über die christl[iche] Missionen bieten außerordentlich wenig an geographischem Gehalt. Sie geben lediglich eine Aufzählung der Völker, die das Christentum in der Oikumene 'von einem Ende zum anderen' angenommen haben, 'von Süden nach Norden' u[nd] 'vom Osten bis zum Westen', so z.B. Tertullian (adv. Iud. 7), Sozomenos (h.e. 2, 6), Arnobius (nat. 2, 12) u[nd] Irenaeus (haer. 1, 10, 2 . . .), der nur die Kirchen von Germanien, Iberien, Gallien, Libyen, Ägypten u[nd] des Orients nennt, außerdem die in jenen Teilen der Erde gegründeten, die er als αἱ κατὰ μέσα τοῦ κόσμου bezeichnet. . . ."

and the gospel.[70] Nevertheless, if we read this summary as part of a commentary on Genesis, then the idea that the whole world was divided by lot among less than twelve apostles may go back to the *Jubilees* tradition of the Table of Nations, according to which the world was divided by lot among the three sons of Noah.[71] As we have seen in Chap. 1, the *Jubilees* tradition had an important influence on Christian writings and possibly even on Christian cartography.[72] Furthermore, Origen's writings contain several allusions to Genesis 10 and the distribution of the earth among the sons of Noah.[73] Thus, although the case cannot be solved definitively, there is possibly more plausibility to Eusebius' attribution of the fragment than is sometimes assumed.

This use of Rom 15:19 in the context of the division of the world among the other apostles leads to the question of apostolic territoriality. How did Paul view the issue of territoriality elsewhere in his letters?

The Table of Nations and Pauline Territoriality

Although Paul evidently understood himself as the "Apostle to the nations" from the time of his apostolic call (cf. Gal 1:15–16), his strategy of focusing on a systematic mission to the Japhethites seems to have unfolded somewhat later, perhaps during the Apostolic Council (Gal 2:1–10; cf. Acts 15)[74] or even

---

[70] Adolf von HARNACK, *Der kirchengeschichtliche Ertrag exegetischen Arbeiten des Origenes, 1. Teil: Hexateuch und Richterbuch* (TU 42.3; Leipzig: Hinrichs, 1918), pp. 14–16; idem, *Die Mission und Ausbreitung des Christentums*, pp. 109–110. See further Eric JUNOD, "Origène, Eusèbe et la tradition sur la répartition des champs de mission des apôtres (Eusèbe, *Histoire ecclésiastique*, III, 1, 1–3)," in *Les actes apocryphes des apôtres. Christianisme et monde païen* (Publications de la Faculté de Théologie de l'Université de Genève 4; Paris: Labor et Fides, 1981), pp. 233–248.

[71] Cf. *Jub.* 8:11; *Sib. Or.* 3.110–114 (τρισσαὶ δὴ μερίδες γαίης κατὰ κλῆρον ἑκάστου). For other possible backgrounds for the idea of lot here, see JUNOD, "Origène, Eusèbe et la tradition sur la répartition des champs de mission des apôtres," pp. 242–245.

[72] For example, the Madaba Mosaic Map may have been influenced by the *Jubilees* tradition (see Chap. 1). On the possibility that the Madaba map was originally worldwide in scope and designed to show the missionary journeys of Paul, see Michael AVI-YONAH, *The Madaba Mosaic Map with Introduction and Commentary* (Jerusalem: Israel Exploration Society, 1954), p. 15.

[73] Cf., e.g., Origen's commentary to Jn 8:37: ἔξεστιν τοίνυν μὴ ὄντα σπέρμα τοῦ Ἀβραάμ, τῷ πάντως διὰ τὴν κατὰ τὸν κατακλυσμὸν ἱστορίαν ἀπὸ Νῶε τοὺς ἑξῆς γεγονέναι, εἶναι σπέρμα Νῶε· εἰ δὲ τοῦτο, καὶ σπέρμα Ἐνώχ, πάντως δὲ καὶ σπέρμα Ἐνὼς καὶ Σήθ· ἄδηλον δ᾽ ἡμῖν ἐπὶ τῶν πολλῶν κατωτέρω τοῦ Νῶε, τίς σπέρμα τοῦ Σὴμ καὶ τίς τοῦ Χὰμ καὶ τίς τοῦ Ἰάφεθ καὶ τῶν ἔτι κατωτέρω· πλὴν οὐκ ἔστιν τις μηδαμῶς μετέχων σπέρματος δικαίων (ed. Erwin PREUSCHEN, *Origenes Werke, Bd. 4: Der Johanneskommentar* [GCS 10; Leipzig: Hinrichs, 1903], p. 330).

[74] Cf. WILCKENS, *Römer*, 3:120: "Hinter Röm. 15,19 steht eine heilsgeschichtliche Missionskonzeption; und man mag fragen, ob diese als solche nicht in den Verhandlungen des Apostelkonzils (vgl. Gal. 2,9) die Stunde ihrer Geburt – oder doch jedenfalls ihrer ersten offiziellen Markierung – und von daher gesamtkirchlich-ökumenische Geltung gewonnen hat." See further DUNN, *Romans*, 2:863.

thereafter,[75] for it is after this point (and the incident at Antioch) that Paul began his own independent missionary enterprise. As C. Dietzfelbinger stresses, however, "What is historically tangible only later was there *in nuce* from the time of the Damascus event on. ..."[76] Rom 1:10−15 shows that Paul had the *Drang nach Westen* from a very earlier period because for some time, he had cast his gaze on the Roman capital. Yet in the time between his call and his second visit to Jerusalem, Paul's activities reveal no grand, worldwide strategy, for the Apostle records only that he went away into "Arabia" and returned again to Damascus (Gal 1:17) and that, after a short visit to Jerusalem (vv. 18−19), he went into the regions of Syria and Cilicia (v. 21).[77] Perhaps this contact with his native land of Cilicia, the threshold of the traditional Japhethite territory sprawling to the west, provided an impulse to Paul's further, independent missionary work. Nevertheless, Paul's description of the Apostolic Council provides the earliest account of his own view of "territoriality." For the purpose of the following discussion, we shall use "territoriality" in the sense formulated by R. D. Sack: a strategy by an individual or group to affect, influence, or control people, phenomena, and relationships by delimiting and asserting control over a geographic area.[78] When Paul's mission is viewed in light of a territorial strategy based on the Table of Nations, many aspects of his relationship to the Jerusalem apostles and his opponents begin to fall into place.

---

[75] Cf. M. Hengel, "The Origins of the Christian Mission," in *Between Jesus and Paul* (trans. John Bowden; London: SCM Press, 1983), pp. 48−64 (here p. 50): "Did Paul have this world-wide view of mission from the beginning, or did he develop it only at a later stage? Presumably the latter is the case. For about fourteen years his activity was limited to the Roman province of Syria and Cilicia, to which according to Acts 13 and 14 we must add nearby Cyprus and the immediately adjacent areas of Asia Minor. We can also assume Acts to be correct in showing that during this period Paul was working not primarily as a missionary on his own authority but – for at least part of the time – together with Barnabas and under the aegis of the church in Antioch. He also went to Jerusalem with Barnabas as a representative of the church. From this we may conclude that a *development* took place in Paul's understanding and strategy of mission which was influenced above all by the positive outcome of the Apostolic Council (AD 48), his parting from Barnabas and his separation from Antioch. Paul the missionary was not the same man after the Apostolic Council and the incident in Antioch (Gal. 2.11 ff.): only after this point on does his missionary activity take on its world-wide aspect and its forward impetus." See further Hengel, "Origins," pp. 52, 54; similarly, Bornkamm, *Paulus*, pp. 68−69; von Harnack, *Die Mission und Ausbreitung des Christentums*, p. 80.

[76] Christian Dietzfelbinger, *Die Berufung des Paulus als Ursprung seiner Theologie* (2nd ed.; WMANT 58; Neukirchen-Vluyn: Neukirchener Verlag, 1989), p. 144. Gal 1:16 does not necessarily imply that Paul began his work as apostle to the nations immediately after his call to apostleship. We are not told exactly when Paul went to Arabia (v. 17), what he did there, and how long he stayed. Perhaps the purpose of the revelation of the Son of God (ἵνα εὐαγγελίζω-μαι αὐτὸν ἐν τοῖς ἔθνεσιν) became apparent to him gradually in terms of its scope and direction.

[77] See Hengel's forthcoming book, *Paulus zwischen Damaskus und Antiochien. Die siebzehn unbekannten Jahre* (described in n. 23 above).

[78] Cf. Robert David Sack, *Human Territoriality: Its Theory and History* (Cambridge Studies in Historical Geography 7; Cambridge: Cambridge University Press, 1986), pp. 5, 19 et passim.

Territoriality and the Apostolic Council (Gal 2:1–10)

According to Gal 1:15–16, Paul was called to apostleship by a divine revelation to preach the gospel of the Son of God "among the nations."[79] Since in the autobiographical section of the letter, Paul wants to establish his independence from the Jerusalem apostles, he emphasizes that after his call to apostleship, he waited three years before going to Jerusalem for a brief visit with Cephas and James (1:16b-20) and fourteen years before returning to Jerusalem according to a revelation in order to lay before the apostles "the gospel which I preach among the nations" (Gal 2:1–2). Paul's concern about whether he was running in vain or had run in vain (v. 2) points to a successful preaching of the gospel in the past, including, presumably, the First Missionary Journey (Acts 13–14). The so-called Apostolic Council was to be a test case for the recognition of the legitimacy of Paul's gospel (cf. Acts 15) and a crucial point for the future of Paul's mission.[80]

The outcome of the Council is given in Gal 2:7–9.[81] First, the "pillar" apostles – James, Cephas, and John[82] – recognize that Paul's God-given apostleship to the nations and gospel of the uncircumcision are equal to Peter's God-given apostleship and gospel of the circumcision (vv. 7–8).[83] This clarifies the issue of circumcision, which presumably led to the Council in the first place (cf. Acts 15:1; Gal 2:3–5).[84] Second, the apostles agree to a division of labor and jurisdiction: that Paul (and his associates) should go "to the nations" (εἰς τὰ ἔθνη) and that Peter (and his associates) should go "to the circumcision" (εἰς τὴν περιτομήν) (v. 9).

How are we to understand this agreement of jurisdiction: (1) as a mutually

---

[79] For this translation of ἐν τοῖς ἔθνεσιν, see the word study in Chap. 2.

[80] The present study assumes, with most NT scholars, that Gal 2:1–10 presents Paul's version of the Apostolic Council (Acts 15) and that Gal 2:11–14 (the incident at Antioch) follows that event chronologically. For a recent challenge to these presuppositions, see Gerd LUEDEMANN, *Paul, Apostle to the Gentiles: Studies in Chronology* (trans. F. Stanley Jones; Philadelphia: Fortress, 1984), and the rebuttal by Alfred SUHL, "Der Beginn der selbständigen Mission des Paulus. Ein Beitrag zur Geschichte des Urchristentums," *NTS* 38 (1992) 430–447. On the date of the Apostolic Council, see, e.g., Andreas SCHMIDT, "Das historische Datum des Apostelkonzils," *ZNW* 81 (1990) 122–131.

[81] The first-person singular perspective of these verses shows that they do not constitute the official protocol of the Council. See further Bradley H. McLEAN, "Galatians 2.7–9 and the Recognition of Paul's Apostolic Status at the Jerusalem Conference: A Critique of G. Luedemann's Solution," *NTS* 37 (1991) 67–76 (esp. pp. 70–74); A. SCHMIDT, "Das Missionsdekret in Galater 2.7–8 als Vereinbarung vom ersten Besuch Pauli in Jerusalem," *NTS* 38 (1992) 149–152.

[82] On the primacy of James in this list, see M. HENGEL, "Jakobus der Herrenbruder – der erste 'Papst'?" in *Glaube und Eschatologie. Festschrift für Werner Georg Kümmel zum 80.Geburtstag* (ed. Erich Gräßer and Otto Merk; Tübingen: Mohr-Siebeck, 1985), pp. 71–104.

[83] The parallelism between vv. 7 and 8 allows the second occurrence of εὐαγγέλιον and ἀποστολή to be elided in each case. Cf. McLEAN, "Galatians 2.7–9," pp. 68–70.

[84] Paul is totally silent on his reason for going to Jerusalem in the first place, stating only that he went up "according to revelation" (Gal 2:2).

exclusive division of geographical territory (e.g., Judea assigned to Peter and the other nations to Paul)[85] or (2) as a geographically overlapping division according to ethnicity (world Jewry assigned to Peter and all non-Jews to Paul)?[86] For the following reasons, the second possibility seems improbable, at least as the Pauline understanding of the agreement.[87] First, Paul stands for a mission to both Israel and the nations and a church of mixed composition. Even after the Council, Paul himself never gave up trying to evangelize the Jews directly (cf. 1 Cor 9:20).[88] Paul's gospel was "to the Jew first" (Rom 1:16), and his missionary mandate extended to "all nations" (Rom 1:5). Some Pauline

---

[85] Cf. Albrecht OEPKE, *Der Brief des Paulus an die Galater* (3rd. ed.; THKNT 9; Berlin: Evangelische Verlagsanstalt, 1979), pp. 81–82, 85; Theodor ZAHN, *Der Brief des Paulus an die Galater* (3rd ed.; Kommentar zum Neuen Testament 10; Leipzig: Scholl, 1922; reprint ed., Wuppertal: Brockhaus, 1990), p. 107; Ernst de Witt BURTON, *A Critical and Exegetical Commentary on the Epistle to the Galatians* (ICC; Edinburgh: T. & T. Clark, 1921), pp. 97–98; Heinrich SCHLIER, *Der Brief an die Galater* (12th ed.; Kritisch-exegetischer Kommentar über das Neue Testament 7; Göttingen: Vandenhoeck & Ruprecht, 1962), pp. 79–80; John BLIGH, *Galatians: A Discussion of St. Paul's Epistle* (Householder Commentaries 1; London: St. Paul Publications, 1969), p. 168. Franz MUßNER seems to support this position (*Der Galaterbrief* [4th ed.; HTKNT 9; Freiburg: Herder, 1981], pp. 122–123), stressing, however, that a purely geographical interpretation of the agreement in the sense of a division of missionary territories would be erroneous (ibid., p. 123 n. 120).

[86] Cf. BETZ, *Galatians*, p. 100; Dieter GEORGI, *Remembering the Poor: The History of Paul's Collection for Jerusalem* (Nashville: Abingdon, 1992), p. 32; See, however, Walter SCHMITHALS, "Paulus als Heidenmissionar und das Problem seiner theologischen Entwicklung," in *Jesus Rede von Gott und ihre Nachgeschichte im frühen Christentum. Beiträge zur Verkündigung Jesu und zum Kerygma der Kirche. Festschrift für Willi Marxsen zum 70. Geburtstag* (ed. Dietrich-Alex Koch, et al.; Gütersloh: Mohn, 1989), pp. 235–251 (here pp. 248–249). MUNCK's tertium quid (*Paulus und die Heilsgeschichte*, p. 112) seems implausible: The division to which the apostles agreed was simultaneously "religious" (Peter to the Jews, Paul to the Gentiles) *and* geographical (Peter: Palestine, Syria, and oriental regions; Paul: the Roman Empire from Syria westwards). Ragnar BRING vacillates between the alternatives (*Der Brief des Paulus an die Galater* [Berlin: Lutherisches Verlagshaus, 1968], p. 74). See further Nicholas TAYLOR, *Paul, Antioch and Jerusalem: A Study in Relationships and Authority in Earliest Christianity* (JSNTSup 66; Sheffield: JSOT Press, 1992), pp. 113–115.

[87] Of course, the agreement is open to interpretation and may have been ambiguously formulated from the beginning. Cf. BLIGH, *Galatians*, p. 167: "It [sc. the agreement] appears to have been a rather vague, unwritten, gentlemen's agreement, of the sort that often leads to disputes. [...] Paul may have understood this agreement to mean that Peter would refrain from exercising his authority outside of Palestine, but Peter may not have intended this. And Peter may have understood Paul to mean that he would go and preach directly to the Gentiles; in fact, whenever Paul entered a Gentile city he preached first to the Jews and then to the Greeks. If the agreement was as ill-defined as Gal 2:9 suggests, it was bound to lead to disputes."

[88] Acts portrays Paul as regularly beginning his missionary effort in a new area by attending the local synagogue, where his message would reach both Jews and God-fearers (cf. Acts 9:20; 13:5, 14; 14:1; 16:13; 17:2, 10, 17; 18:4, 19; 19:8), a perspective that 2 Cor 11:24 tends to support. In his farewell address to the Ephesian elders, Paul emphasizes that he testified "both to Jews and to Greeks" (Acts 20:21; cf. 9:15; 17:30; 26:17, 20). On Gentile "God-fearers," see further n. 92 below.

churches were obviously composed of both Jews and Gentiles.[89] In fact, as the Antioch incident shows, Paul considers it a grave violation of the truth of the gospel for Jewish believers to separate themselves from their Gentile brethren, destroying the unity and fellowship of the church (Gal 2:11−14). For Paul, the wall of separation between the two groups had been broken down in Christ (cf. Eph 2:11−18, which reflects a genuinely Pauline position on the new situation),[90] and there was no longer any distinction between them (cf. Gal 3:28; Col 3:11; 1 Cor 7:19; 12:13). On the other hand, a division of apostolic jurisdictions along such lines would have led inevitably to separation between Jews and Gentiles in the church.[91] Second, a division of apostolic jurisdictions along ethnic lines would have been practically impossible to implement since one of the prime targets of Paul's missionary activity were the "God-fearers," that is, Gentile adherents of the Jewish synagogue who had stopped short of full conversion to Judaism.[92] As long as this fringe group existed, Paul could never ignore the synagogue in his mission. In that case, both the Gentile mission and the Jewish mission would be bound to tangle themselves in each others' affairs, without the possibility of true cooperation. Third, the idea that the Apostolic Council resulted in a division of apostolic jurisdictions along ethnic lines seems

---

[89] The church in Corinth, for example, was composed mostly of former Gentiles (cf. 1 Cor 12:2), with a Jewish-Christian minority (Prisca and Aquila, Crispus, Sosthenes).

[90] Cf. Peter STUHLMACHER, "'Er ist unser Friede' (Eph 2,14)," in *Versöhnung, Gesetz und Gerechtigkeit. Aufsätze zur biblischen Theologie* (Göttingen: Vandenhoeck & Ruprecht, 1981), pp. 224−245 (here pp. 234 ff.).

[91] Cf. M. HENGEL, *Zur urchristlichen Geschichtsschreibung* (Stuttgart: Calwer, 1979), p. 101.

[92] Although the existence of "God-fearers" as a separate class is sometimes disputed (cf., e.g., A. Thomas KRAABEL, "The Disappearance of the 'God-fearers,'" *Numen* 28 [1981] 113−126; reprinted in J. Andrew OVERMAN and Robert S. MACLENNAN, eds., *Diaspora Jews and Judaism: Essays in Honor of, and in Dialogue with, A. Thomas Kraabel* [South Florida Studies in the History of Judaism 41; Atlanta, GA: Scholars Press, 1992], pp. 119−130, with additional discussion on pp. 131−152), nevertheless, an inscription from Aphrodisias found in 1976 provides solid, third-century evidence of this intermediate group (θεοσεβής) and, to some extent, corroborates the witness of Acts as to the existence of σεβόμενοι τὸν θεόν and φοβούμενοι τὸν θεόν in the first century (cf. Acts 10:2, 22, 35; 13:16, 26, [43], 50; 16:14; 17:4, 17; 18:7). The secondary literature on this subject is enormous. See merely Martin HENGEL, "Der alte und der neue 'Schürer'," *JSS* 35 (1990) 19−72 (here p. 43); J. REYNOLDS and R. TANNENBAUM, *Jews and Godfearers at Aphrodisias* (CPSSup 12; Cambridge: Cambridge Philological Society, 1987); Louis H. FELDMAN, *Jew and Gentile in the Ancient World: Attitudes and Interactions from Alexander to Justinian* [Princeton: Princeton University Press, 1993], pp. 342−382; Paul R. TREBILCO, *Jewish Communities in Asia Minor* [MSSNTS 69; Cambridge: Cambridge University Press, 1991], pp. 145−166; SCHÜRER, *Hist.*, 3.1:162−173; Pieter W. van der HORST, "Das Neue Testament und die jüdischen Grabinschriften aus hellenistisch-römischer Zeit," *BZ* 36 (1992) 161−178 (here pp. 169−171); Gary GILBERT, "The Making of a Jew: 'God-fearer' or Convert in the Story of Izates," *USQR* 44 (1991) 299−313; Terence L. DONALDSON, "Proselytes or 'Righteous Gentiles'? The Status of Gentiles in Eschatological Pilgrimage Patterns of Thought," *JSP* 7 (1990) 3−27; Conrad H. GEMPF, "The God-fearers," in Colin J. HEMER, *The Book of Acts in the Setting of Hellenistic History* (WUNT 49; Tübingen: Mohr-Siebeck, 1989), pp. 444−447.

improbable because Paul came to the Council with the awareness that he had been called to preach the gospel "among the nations" (Gal 1:16; 2:2).[93] As the Apostle to the "nations" (ἔθνη), Paul understood his mission as geographically determined from the beginning even if the scope and direction of his mission developed in the course of time. Therefore, from Paul's perspective, the Jerusalem accord almost certainly acknowledged a division of territorial jurisdictions among the apostles. This is substantiated by the accumulation of toponyms ('Ιεροσόλυμα, 'Αραβία, Δαμασκός, τὰ κλίματα τῆς Συρίας καὶ τῆς Κιλικίας, 'Ιουδαία, 'Αντιόχεια) and other related terms (τὰ ἔθνη, ῞Ελλην) in the autobiographical section of the letter (1:13−2:21).

This division of territorial jurisdiction among the apostles may be based on the Table of Nations of Genesis 10.[94] This can be shown, first, by the so-called Apostolic Decree that, according to Acts 15:23−29 (cf. v. 20), issued from the Apostolic Council as a directive "to the brethren who are of the nations (ἔθνη) in Antioch and Syria and Cilicia," for the letter exhorts the Gentile believers to "abstain from what has been sacrificed to idols and from blood and from what is strangled and from fornication" (v. 29). As generally acknowledged, this goes back to the "Noachic commandments" of Gen 9:1−7 (cf. also Leviticus 17−18),[95] called in Rabbinic tradition "the seven laws of the sons of Noah,"[96] which have been incumbent on all humanity since the Flood. Hence, even if it is

---

[93] This is especially true insofar as Paul casts his call to apostleship in the mold of Jeremiah's call to be a "prophet to the nations" (Gal 1:15; cf. Jer 1:5), for Jeremiah prophesied not only to Judah but to "all nations" as well (Jer 32:15, 18−26).

[94] Early Christian tradition frequently mentions Noah's family. Heb 11:7 recalls that Noah constructed an ark "for the saving of his household" (εἰς σωτηρίαν τοῦ οἴκου αὐτοῦ). According to 1 Pet 3:20−21, the water of the Flood through which eight persons (i.e., Noah and his wife, and Noah's three sons and their wives) were saved is an antitype of the baptism that now saves believers. Moreover, 2 Pet 2:5 states that God preserved Noah with seven other persons when he brought a flood upon the world of the ungodly.

[95] Cf. David Flusser and Shmuel Safrai, "Das Aposteldekret und die Noachitischen Gebote," in *"Wer Tora vermehrt, mehrt Leben." Festgabe für Heinz Kremers zum 60. Geburtstag* (ed. Edna Brocke and Hans-Joachim Barkenings; Neukirchen-Vluyn: Neukirchener Verlag, 1986), pp. 173−192; Claus Westermann, *Genesis* (3 vols.; 3rd ed.; BKAT 1; Neukirchen-Vluyn: Neukirchener Verlag, 1983), 1:628; F.F. Bruce, *The Acts of the Apostles: The Greek Text with Introduction and Commentary* (2nd ed.; London: Tyndale Press, 1970), p. 299; idem, "Noah," *NIDNTT*, 2 (1976) 681−683 (here p. 682); Otto Böcher, "Das sogenannte Aposteldekret," in *Vom Urchristentum zu Jesus. Für Joachim Gnilka* (ed. Hubert Frankemölle and Karl Kertelge; Freiburg: Herder, 1989), pp. 325−336 (here pp. 327−328); Oepke, *Galater*, pp. 83−84; W. A. Strange, *The Problem of the Text of Acts* (SNTSMS 71; Cambridge: Cambridge University Press, 1992), pp. 87−105 (esp. pp. 96, 98, 101). I have not seen C.K. Barrett, "The Apostolic Decree of Acts 15:29," *AusBR* 35 (1987) 50−59. For a different view, see Matthias Klinghardt, *Gesetz und Volk Gottes. Das lukanische Verständnis des Gesetzes nach Herkunft, Funktion und seinem Ort in der Geschichte des Urchristentums* (WUNT 2.32; Tübingen: Mohr-Siebeck, 1988), pp. 176−180.

[96] Cf. Schürer, *Hist.*, 3.1:171−172; Str-B, 2:721, 729−740; 3:37−38. These "Noachic commandments" include prohibitions against idolatry, incest and adultery, murder, and eating flesh with the blood.

to be viewed as historically secondary,[97] the Apostolic Decree shows that Noachic tradition was associated with the Apostolic Council from an early period. In that case, the agreement to divide the world among the apostles may have been based on the division of the world among the sons of Noah. Given Paul's appropriation of the OT expectation of the eschatological pilgrimage of the nations (cf. Rom 11:25), we may wonder what role, if any, Isa 66:18−21 may have had in the Jerusalem agreement on apostolic jurisdictions, for Isaiah 66 expects that God will gather "all nations" (πάντα τὰ ἔθνη) to Jerusalem, by "sending" (ἐξαποστελῶ) a Jewish remnant "to the nations" (εἰς τὰ ἔθνη), a representative selection of which are named from each of the three sons of Noah in the Table of Nations (v. 19).

That the territorial jurisdiction agreed to at the Apostolic Council may be based on the Table of Nations can be shown, second, by the nature of the question that presumably required the Council to convene in the first place, that is, whether the Gentiles must be circumcised in order to be included in the Abrahamic Covenant.[98] Paul's answer at the Council may have been similar to that in Galatians: The promise in Gen 12:3 (+ 18:18), that all nations of the earth (i.e., all the nations in the Table of Nations in Genesis 10) will be blessed in Abraham and his seed, is fulfilled in Christ, the seed of Abraham (cf. Gal 3:8, 14, 16). We have seen that Qumran interpreted Gen 9:27 in light of Gen 12:3 as a promise for all three sons of Noah in the Table of Nations.[99] If, therefore, the answer to the basic issue at the Council was formulated in terms of the Table-of-Nations tradition, the division of jurisdictions among the apostles may well have been based on the same tradition.

That the territorial jurisdiction agreed to at the Apostolic Council may be based on the Table of Nations can be shown, third, by comparison to the actual scope and direction of Paul's mission after the Council. As we have seen in Romans 15, Paul focuses his mission to the "nations" (ἔθνη) on Asia Minor and Europe while keeping Jerusalem in the center. By the time of the writing of Romans, he had covered "from Jerusalem and in a circle to Illyricum" (v. 19). Since there was no longer any room in these regions for further evangelistic

---

[97] Paul himself makes no mention of the Decree and gives no indication of having accepted its restrictions (cf. Gal 2:6). Even in 1 Corinthians 8−10 and Romans 14, where the issue of food arises, Paul makes no reference to the Apostolic Decree. HENGEL argues that James was the author of the Apostolic Decree after the Antioch incident as a compromise formula to facilitate the reestablishment of the disturbed table fellowship ("Jakobus der Herrenbruder," pp. 94−95). HENGEL also suggests that Paul possibly recommended adhering to the decree in 1 Corinthians 8 and Romans 14 without mentioning it by name and for a totally different reason (ibid., p. 94). Furthermore, Alan F. SEGAL provides evidence of the Noachic commandments in Paul's letters (*Paul the Convert: The Apostolate and Apostasy of Saul the Pharisee* (New Haven: Yale University Press, 1990), pp. 194−201.

[98] Cf. Peter STUHLMACHER, *Biblische Theologie des Neuen Testaments, Bd. 1: Grundlegung. Von Jesus zu Paulus* (Göttingen: Vandenhoeck & Ruprecht, 1992), p. 215.

[99] See Chap. 1 on 4Q252 2.6−7.

work, Paul planed, after delivering the collection to Jerusalem,[100] to continue his westward mission, travelling by way of Rome to Spain (vv. 22–29). Seen from the perspective of the Table-of-Nations tradition, the territory that Paul thus stakes out for himself corresponds to that allotted to Japheth and his sons; the westerly direction that Paul travels corresponds to the direction that the Japhethites originally took to migrate from Tarsus in Cilicia to Gadeira in Spain; and Jerusalem is the center of the nations of the world. If, therefore, Paul's missionary strategy in Romans 15 is based on the Table of Nations, and if, as many scholars suggest, Paul's missionary strategy in Romans 15 goes back to the Apostolic Council,[101] then the Jerusalem agreement to divide the world into missionary territories may have been based on the Table of Nations.[102] In that case, Peter's jurisdiction may have included the whole territory of Shem, rather than just Jerusalem and Judea. Indeed, 1 Pet 5:13 presupposes that Peter's letter to the διασπορά in Asia Minor (i.e., Pontus, Galatia, Cappadocia, Asia, and Bithynia) was written from "Babylon." Although this reference to "Babylon" is usually interpreted as a cryptogram for Rome,[103] A. SCHLATTER, among others, takes it as a reference to the literal Babylon in Mesopotamia.[104] As to who may have been responsible for the territory of Ham,[105] we can only speculate, since little is known about the first-century

---

[100] Note that Rom 15:26 mentions neither Galatia nor Asia as participating in the collection despite the fact that they are known elsewhere to have been involved (cf. 1 Cor 16:1 [Galatia]; Acts 20:4 [Asia]).

[101] See n. 74 above. The connection between Paul's missionary strategy in Romans 15 and the Apostolic Council in Gal 2:1–10 is further strengthened by the fact that both passages are concerned with the collection for the "poor" (πτωχοί) of the saints in Jerusalem (cf. Gal 2:10; Rom 15:26).

[102] In that case, Paul's description of himself as having received an apostleship for the obedience of faith ἐν πᾶσιν τοῖς ἔθνεσιν (Rom 1:5) does not necessarily imply that he would reach "all nations" singlehandedly (cf. KNOX, "Romans 15:14–33," pp. 1–11, who argues that the Apostle hoped to make "one great journey beginning and ending at Jerusalem, but encompassing the whole Mediterranean world in its scope" [here p. 11]; EICHHOLZ, *Die Theologie des Paulus*, pp. 20–21, 24, 27). Paul neither initially nor at a later time went northeastward on a Mesopotamian mission nor southwestward on an Egyptian mission. The territories of Shem and Ham were presumably the responsibility of other apostles. Cf. DUNN, *Romans*, 2:864 (also p. 872), on Rom 15:19: "We should not exclude the possibility that Paul saw his work not only as an arc but as the top half of a circle which presupposed that others were engaged in the bottom sweep (through Egypt, Alexandria, and North Africa). . . ." Furthermore, Paul seems to expect the full number of the nations to come in soon, probably upon the completion of his mission to Spain.

[103] Cf., e.g., Carsten P. THIEDE, "Babylon, der andere Ort. Anmerkungen zu 1. Petr. 5,13 und Apg 12,17," in *Das Petrusbild in der neueren Forschung* (ed. C. P. Thiede; Theologische Verlagsgemeinschaft Monographien 316; Wuppertal: Brockhaus, 1987), pp. 221–229; M. HENGEL, *Studies in the Gospel of Mark* (London: SCM Press, 1985), p. 151 n. 58.

[104] Cf. A. SCHLATTER, *Petrus and Paulus nach dem ersten Petrusbrief* (Stuttgart: Calwer, 1937), pp. 176–179; also J. MUNCK, *Paulus und die Heilsgeschichte*, p. 270. Is this the "other place" to which Peter went during the persecution of Jerusalem believers under Herod Agrippa I (Acts 12:17)?

[105] The Gnostic *Apocalypse of Adam* refers to "the illuminator [lit. 'light'] of knowledge"

mission to Africa.[106] In Gal 2:1−10, Paul's portrayal of the Apostolic Council is not concerned with this aspect.[107]

---

whose mission is to "the seed of Noah and the sons of Ham and Japheth" (76.8−15), apparently to the exclusion of Shem (cf. Douglas M. PARROTT, "The 13 Kingdoms of the Apocalypse of Adam: Origin, Meaning and Significance," *NovT* 31 [1989] 67−87 [here p. 69]). In *T. Ben.* 11:2, the beloved of the Lord who will arise from Benjamin's seed (i.e., the Apostle Paul) is seen as "the light of knowledge" who "enlightens all nations with new knowledge" (γνῶσιν καινὴν φωτίζων πάντα τὰ ἔθνη). In Acts 13:47, Isa 49:6 (φῶς ἐθνῶν) is applied to Paul and Barnabas. Perhaps, therefore, the illuminator in the *Apocalypse of Adam* is to be identified as Paul, in which case, we have evidence for a (Christian) tradition that conceives the scope of Paul's mission to the nations in terms of the Table of Nations, particularly the territories of Ham and Japheth.

[106] Cf. HENGEL, *Zur urchristlichen Geschichtsschreibung*, pp. 90−91. See further below on Acts 8:26−40; also Mk 15:21; Acts 2:10; 6:9; 11:20−21; 13:1. Is it coincidence, however, that the parties in 1 Cor 1:12 are named in terms of three men who stem from the territories allotted to Noah's three sons, beginning in the north and proceeding counterclockwise (in accordance with the Table-of-Nations tradition?): Paul of Tarsus (Japheth), Apollos of Alexandria (Ham), and Cephas of Bethsaida/Capernaum (Shem)? Of course, Apollos was not present at the Apostolic Council since he was apparently an "outsider" until somewhat later (cf. Acts 18:24−26). Eusebius' *Ecclesiastical History* (2.16) preserves a tradition that Mark was the first evangelist in Egypt: "Now it is said that this Mark journeyed to Egypt and was the first to preach the gospel there, which also he had written, and that he was the first to form churches at Alexandria itself." See further John J. GUNTHER, "The Association of Mark and Barnabas with Egyptian Christianity (Part I)," *EvQ* 54 (1982) 219−232; idem, "The Association of Mark and Barnabas with Egyptian Christianity (Continued)," *EvQ* 55 (1983) 21−29; Birger A. PEARSON, "Earliest Christianity in Egypt: Some Observations," in *The Roots of Egyptian Christianity* (ed. B. A. Pearson and James E. Goehring; Studies in Antiquity and Christianity; Philadelphia: Fortress, 1986), pp. 132−159; C. Wilfred GRIGGS, *Early Egyptian Christianity from its Origins to 451 C. E.* (Coptic Studies 2; Leiden: Brill, 1990), pp. 13−43. Cf. also RIESNER, *Frühzeit*, p. 235: "Paulus hätte über Alexandria in den Süden nach Lybien (Lud) oder Karthago (Tharschisch?) gehen können. Wenn er schon damals seinem Grundsatz folgte, möglichst in nichtmissioniertem Gebiet zu arbeiten, dann sprach das wahrscheinlich gegen dieses Ziel. Wir sind zwar, vor allem auch wegen der fast völligen Ausrottung des ägyptischen Judentums (115−117 und 132−135 n. Chr.), weitgehend auf Mutmaßungen angewiesen, aber es ist doch recht wahrscheinlich, daß schon in frühester Zeit, vermutlich direkt von Jerusalem aus (vgl. Apg. 18,25D), unter der starken Judenschaft Ägyptens judenchristliche Gemeinden entstanden. Auch die zahlreichen Juden der Kyrenaika (Jos, Ant XIV 114), deren vielfache Beziehungen zur heiligen Stadt sich beiläufig im Neuen Testament spiegeln (Mk. 15,21 Parr.; Apg. 2,10; 6,9; 11,19f vgl. 13,1), dürfen schon sehr früh vor der Mission der palästinischen Judenchristen erfaßt worden sein. Man kann fragen, ob nicht einige der aus Jerusalem kyrenischen Hellenisten (Apg. 11,20) in ihre Heimat zurückkehrten."

[107] Adolf DEISSMANN (*Paulus. Eine kultur- und religionsgeschichtliche Skizze* [2nd ed.; Tübingen: Mohr-Siebeck, 1925], pp. 176−177 [emphasis mine]) considers the question of why Paul did not go to Egypt, not even to the world center of the Jewish Diaspora in Alexandria: "Hat er Alexandrien . . . wegen seiner so großen Judenschaft nicht für Heidenland, sondern für 'Beschneidung' [Gal 2,9], also für Missionsfeld des *Petrus* gehalten? Er ist ja eifersüchtig darauf bedacht, daß jeder Missionar seinen Bezirk hat und nicht überschreitet [2 Kor 10,13ff.; Röm 15,20], und insbesondere das Abkommen mit den Säulenaposteln [Gal 2,9] hat er gewiß treu gehalten. Oder waren in Aegypten etwa schon frühe andere christliche Missionare gewesen? Die Anfänge des ägyptischen Christentums liegen leider ganz im Dunkeln." According to GUNTHER ("The Association of Mark and Barnabas with Egyptian Christianity

Territoriality and the Conflict in Antioch (Gal 2:11−14)

After the description of the Apostolic Council in Gal 2:1−10 and the agree-
ment of the apostles to respect the God-given territories of each, Paul goes on
to report an incident in 2:11−14 that stands in stark contrast to this agreement:
Leaders of the Jerusalem church and their delegates came to Antioch! Thus,
Paul writes: "But when Cephas came to Antioch, I opposed him to his face. . ."
(v. 11). Even before detailing the central theological issue at stake in Antioch,
Paul emphasizes that he opposed Peter when the latter came to Antioch.[108]
Furthermore, even when Paul starts to unveil the underlying issue, he does so at
first in terms of another unexpected arrival in Antioch: "certain men came from
James" (v. 12). Paul evidently considers Peter and the men from James as
intruders, infringing on his missionary territory by attempting to exercise
control over an area that was outside their sphere of direct influence/jurisdic-
tion.[109] Although the Taurus-Amanus mountain range just north of Antioch
was usually considered the northern border both of the Land of Israel and of
Shem's territory,[110] there is some evidence to suggest that the territorial status
of Antioch and its environs may have been ambiguous in Jewish circles.[111]

[Part I]," p. 229), "the most satisfactory explanation for the exclusion of north Africa from
Paul's possible missionary territoriality is that he did not wish to trespass in the domain of
Barnabas, the other apostle to the Gentiles. Why else did Paul not plan to stop in Alexandria
and Cyrene on the way from Jerusalem to Rome after delivering his gift to 'the saints'?
Barnabas stayed out of Paul's territory, even in Asia Minor where he had been on their 'first
journey'. They subsequently acted as if they had made an agreement on the division of
missionary territory when they personally parted ways."

[108] Viewing the Apostolic Council as establishing completely separate Jewish and Gentile
missions, SCHMITHALS ("Paulus als Heidenmissionar," pp. 248−249) suggests another reason
why Peter's arrival in Antioch was so problematic for Paul: Peter had evidently violated the
Jerusalem accord by having table fellowship with Gentile Christians on a previous missionary
journey in Asia Minor (Galatia).

[109] According to Acts 11:22, Barnabas had been sent to oversee affairs of the nascent
church in Antioch before Paul became involved in the work. As a result of the Apostolic
Council, however, the territorial jurisdiction of Paul was sharply divided from that of Peter, so
that, from Paul's perspective, Peter should not have tried to exert his influence there.

[110] See Chap. 1 on *Jub.* 8:19; 1QapGen 21.16−17; Josephus *Ant.* 1.122.

[111] In Paul's day, Antioch was part of the Roman province composed of Syria and Cilicia; it
is possible, therefore, that there was some ambiguity about the status of Antioch from the
perspective of the Table-of-Nations tradition. Paul may have reckoned it with Cilicia as
Japhethite territory, whereas the Jerusalemites may have regarded it as Shemite territory. As
we have seen in Chap. 1, there was a dispute in the Table-of-Nations tradition as to whether
Asia Minor should be reckoned to the territory of Shem (so *Jubilees*) or to Japheth (so
Josephus and the majority position). Furthermore, the Nazareans, a Jewish-Christian group
cited by Jerome in his commentary on Isaiah, do not refer to "Galilee of the nations" (Isa 8:23
cited in Matt 4:15) but rather to "the borders of the nations," following the translation of
Symmachus who renders גליל הגוים by ὅριον τῶν ἐθνῶν. Thus, they make a twofold application of the text: Jesus removed the heavy yoke of Jewish tradition from the land of Zebulun
and Naphtali, and afterwards, Paul brought the gospel of Christ to the borders of the nations.
Cf. A.F.J. KLIJN, "Jerome's Quotations from a Nazarean Interpretation of Isaiah," *RSR* 60
(1972) 241−255. According to Jdt 2:25, Holofernes, a general of Nebuchadnezzar, seized the

Of course, the issue that develops in Antioch after these men arrive runs much deeper than a merely territorial dispute; Paul claims that Peter stands condemned of violating the gospel itself (v. 11; cf. v. 14).[112] Nevertheless, from Paul's perspective, that the situation develops at all is precisely because these Jews came into his territory and attempted a strategy to extend their influence over "the Gentiles," i.e., individuals from a nation other than the nation of the Jews. This was evidently in contravention of their agreement, according to which Paul – and not the pillar apostles – was recognized as the one divinely called to the nations.

Territoriality and Paul's Opponents (2 Cor 10:13–16)

In 2 Corinthians 10, Paul begins a defence of his apostolic authority in the face of opponents who are criticizing him, commending themselves, and encroaching on his missionary territory with a different gospel during his absence (cf. 11:4). In vv. 13–16, therefore, Paul makes a definite distinction between what is properly his missionary territoriality and what is the territoriality of others, making it clear that his territoriality has been violated by his opponents. Unlike his opponents, Paul claims in v. 13 that he does not boast "beyond (proper) limits" (εἰς τὰ ἄμετρα) but keeps to "the limit of the jurisdiction God has apportioned to us, to reach out even as far as you" (κατὰ τὸ μέτρον τοῦ κανόνος οὗ ἐμέρισεν ἡμῖν ὁ θεὸς μέτρου, ἐφικέσθαι ἄχρι καὶ ὑμῶν). In other words, the Corinthian church falls within the swath of territory divinely allotted to Paul. Unlike his opponents, who are trying to exert their influence on Corinth and thus to usurp Paul's territory, overstepping the limits of their commission, Paul has not gone beyond the jurisdiction that God apportioned to him.

This territorial interpretation of Paul's apostolic "jurisdiction" (κανών)[113] is confirmed by the subsequent context. So far, the swath of Paul's divinely

---

territory of Cilicia and then came "to the borders of Japheth which are to the south facing Arabia" (ἕως ὁρίων Ιαφεθ τὰ πρὸς νότον κατὰ πρόσωπον τῆς Ἀραβίας). Does this assume that the borders of Japheth extend below the Taurus-Amanus range? Verse 26 goes on to state that Holofernes surrounded all the sons of Midian, whose land is traditionally located in northwest Arabia (e.g., Josephus *Ant.* 2.257).

[112] The issue essentially is that Peter and the other Jewish Christians in the mixed congregation of Antioch suddenly changed their tolerant attitude towards their fellow Gentile believers after the arrival of the men from James by withdrawing from table fellowship. This action upset the unity and fellowship of the church, called the Gentiles' position in Christ into question, and compelled the Gentiles to conform to Jewish practice in order for fellowship to be restored.

[113] For this translation of κανών, see Victor Paul Furnish, *II Corinthians* (AB 32A; New York: Doubleday, 1984), p. 471; also Ralph P. Martin, *2 Corinthians* (WBC 40; Waco, TX: Word, 1986), pp. 320–321; E. A. Judge, "The Regional *Kanon* for Requisitioned Transport," in *New Documents Illustrating Early Christianity: A Review of the Greek Inscriptions and Papyri Published in 1976* (ed. G. H. R. Horsley; North Ryde, Australia: The Ancient History Documentary Research Centre, Macquarie University, 1981), pp. 36–45 (esp. pp. 44–45).

allotted territoriality extends to Corinth,[114] but it is expected to go well beyond that. According to v. 14, Paul has reached all the way to the Corinthians with the gospel of Christ (ἄχρι γὰρ καὶ ὑμῶν ἐφθάσαμεν ἐν τῷ εὐαγγελίῳ τοῦ Χριστοῦ). Paul did the pioneering missionary work there. In keeping with his principle of not building on another's foundation (cf. Rom 15:20), Paul does not boast "beyond limit" (εἰς τὰ ἄμετρα), that is, in other men's labors (2 Cor 10:15a). This insinuates that the opponents have done just that. Furthermore, according to v. 16, Paul's desire is "to preach the gospel in lands beyond you (εἰς τὰ ὑπερέκεινα ὑμῶν εὐαγγελίσασθαι), without boasting of work already done in another's jurisdiction (κανών)." Given the fact that in vv. 13 and 14, Paul has come "as far as" (ἄχρι) the Corinthians, who are identified with Achaia (cf. 1:1; 9:2; 11:9−10), the idea of "beyond" in v. 16a is most naturally taken geographically as indicating lands to west of Achaia, perhaps including Spain (cf. Rom 15:24, 28).[115]

From this description, it is clear that Paul has a conception of the scope and direction of his mission that is comparable to that in Romans 15.[116] In the westward course that he is pursuing, Paul seems confident that there are lands beyond the Corinthians where he can preach without encroaching on another's (Peter's?) jurisdiction[117] and that, at the same time, are legitimately part of the jurisdiction allotted to him. In all likelihood, this confidence goes back to the Apostolic Council, where the respective jurisdictions of the apostles (esp. those of Peter and of Paul) were formally acknowledged and agreed upon (Gal 2:7−9).[118] As Apostle to the nations, Paul was laying claim to his territorial jurisdiction over the Corinthian church, in which the opponents are "properly to be seen as interlopers and usurpers of apostolic prerogative."[119]

If Paul's argument in 2 Cor 10:13−16 is based on the agreement of the Apostolic Council, it is interesting to speculate about who Paul's opponents

---

[114] Cf. MARTIN, *2 Corinthians*, p. 322.

[115] Cf. Charles Kingsley BARRETT, *The Second Epistle to the Corinthians* (HNTC; New York: Harper & Row, 1973), p. 268: "What Paul has in mind is an evangelistic journey leading from his present Aegean field to Rome, and further to Spain." Rom 1:10−15 shows that Paul had a strong desire to go westward from a very earlier period, for he had long set his sights on reaching the Roman capital.

[116] Compare especially Rom 15:19 with 2 Cor 10:14b, both of which refer to "the gospel of Christ."

[117] Note in v. 16 that Paul does admit that there is a jurisdiction other than his.

[118] Cf. BARRETT, *Second Epistle to the Corinthians*, pp. 264−65; MARTIN, *2 Corinthians*, p. 322: "... and so he [sc. Paul] claims to have staked out Corinth as his territory (κανών), since this strategy was his by design (Rom 15:17−20) and indeed by the concurrence of the 'pillar' apostles in Jerusalem (Gal 2:6, 7)." But see FURNISH, *II Corinthians*, pp. 471−472, 481. Friedrich LANG traces the origin of the *kanon* back to Paul's call to be an apostle to the Gentiles (*Die Briefe an die Korinther* [NTD 7; Göttingen: Vandenhoeck & Ruprecht, 1986], p. 333). Although 2 Cor 10:13−16 does not explicitly refer to the Jerusalem accord, it is only natural in a situation in which Paul's opponents are calling his apostleship into question and are infringing on his jurisdiction that his stance would go back to the Council, which had officially recognized his apostleship and his territoriality.

[119] MARTIN, *2 Corinthians*, p. 322.

may have been. Some scholars think that there may have been a connection between the opponents and Peter himself.[120] Certainly it is curious that Peter's name keeps reappearing in the Corinthian correspondence, especially in the context of factions in Corinth (cf. 1 Cor 1:12; 3:22).[121] Even if one cannot go as far as F.C. BAUR in postulating an ongoing conflict in the early Church between Petrine and Pauline positions that is resolved in so-called "early Catholicism," one must admit that Peter or his emissaries frequently intrude into what Paul considers his territory. As we have seen in Gal 2:11–14, Peter comes to Antioch even after the agreement of the Apostolic Council and tries to exert his influence there over the Gentiles. According to Christian tradition based on 1 Pet 1:1,[122] Peter's mission overlapped significantly with that of Paul's, extending to Pontus, Galatia, Cappadocia, Asia, and Bithynia.[123] Yet if the prevailing Table-of-Nations tradition stands behind the Jerusalem accord and Peter was primarily responsible for the territory of Shem, then the only one of these lands that would have come under his jurisdiction was the province of Asia, the heart of which was composed of the Shemite territory of Lud.[124] If, on the other hand, Peter assumes the Table-of-Nations tradition in *Jubilees* 8–9,[125] then all of Asia

---

[120] Cf., e.g., HENGEL, "Origins," p. 170 n. 26: "Possibly Peter-Cephas himself later became more and more of a missionary to the Gentiles, despite Gal. 2:7–9, under the impact of the failure of the mission to the Jews described by Paul in Rom. 10.3,16; 11.6f., etc., a failure which is also hardly open to dispute in the non-Pauline Roman community. 1 Cor. 1.12; 3:10ff., 22 could also indicate this. Might Paul's opponents in II Cor. even be emissaries of Peter's mission? In that case II Cor. 11.5, which is akin to Gal. 2.6, could refer to the authorities in the background and 11.13 to the emissaries themselves. This would also be a particularly good explanation of the dispute over missionary territory in II Cor. 10.15–16, cf. Rom. 15.20, as of the fact that Paul makes his opponents anonymous. Of course it is impossible to do more than guess here. The mission legend in Acts 10.1–11.18 also shows a connection between Peter and the mission to the Gentiles; there he is made its real author...." See further idem, *Zur urchristlichen Geschichtsschreibung*, pp. 83–84, 104; idem, "Petrus und die Heidenmission," in *Das Petrusbild in der neueren Forschung* (ed. Carsten Peter Thiede; Theologische Verlagsgemeinschaft Monographien 316; Wuppertal: Brockhaus, 1987), pp. 163–170 (here pp. 168–169); MARTIN, *2 Corinthians*, p. 323.

[121] Cephas' name also appears in 1 Cor 9:5; 15:5.

[122] Cf. 1 Pet 1:1: "Peter, an apostle of Jesus Christ, to the exiles of the Diaspora in Pontus, Galatia, Cappadocia, Asia, and Bithynia." Does this passage presuppose a Petrine mission *before* the Apostolic Council, as Carsten P. THIEDE suggests (*Simon Peter: From Galilee to Rome* [Exeter: Paternoster, 1986], p. 155)? See further Terence V. SMITH, *Petrine Controversies in Early Christianity: Attitudes towards Peter in Christian Writings of the First Two Centuries* (WUNT 2.15; Tübingen: Mohr-Siebeck, 1985).

[123] See above on Book 3 of Origen's Commentary on Genesis in Eusebius *Hist. eccl.* 3.10.1–3; cf. also 3.4.2.

[124] By the same token, Paul did not encroach on the territory of Lud. See further below on Acts 16:6b.

[125] As we saw in Chap. 1, *Jubilees* breaks with the normal Table-of-Nations tradition by dividing the land among the sons of Noah according to three continents separated by two rivers (i.e., the Gihon [= the Nile] and the Tanais): Shem received Asia, Ham received Africa, and Japheth received Europe.

Minor would belong to his jurisdiction. Was this is a point of contention or misunderstanding among the apostles?

Territoriality and the Roman Addressees (Rom 1:5−6)

The superscription of Paul's letter to the Romans (Rom 1:1−6) establishes a relationship between the Apostle and the believers in Rome. Particularly in vv. 5−6, Paul almost directly states that the Romans fall within the jurisdiction of his apostolic commission, for the grace of apostleship given to him through Jesus Christ makes him responsible for the obedience of faith among all nations, "among whom also you are called of Jesus Christ." This shows that even if Paul did not want to build on another's foundation (Rom 15:20), there were churches like those in Rome that had been established by other missionaries but that nevertheless were located within the nations of Paul's divinely allotted missionary territory from Cilicia to Spain and thus fell under his apostolic authority (cf. 15:15ff.).

The Table of Nations and Acts 17:26

If Paul's own letters show evidence of the Table-of-Nations tradition in conjunction with Paul's gospel and missionary strategy, it is interesting to note that, as we shall see on Acts 17:26, Luke's portrayal of Paul confirms this impression. Furthermore, Luke-Acts itself shows influence from the same tradition. [126]

The Table of Nations in Acts

The Nations in Luke-Acts. In a special way, Luke's two-volume work focuses on the "nations" (ἔθνη) [127] and the whole "inhabited world" (οἰκουμένη). [128] In the Gospel, for example, Jesus sends out the Twelve (Lk 9:1−6), representing

---

[126] See further my recent essay, "Luke's Geographical Horizon," in *The Book of Acts in Its First Century Setting, Vol. 2: The Book of Acts in Its Graeco-Roman Setting* (ed. David W. J. Gill and Conrad Gempf; Grand Rapids: Eerdmans; Carlisle: Paternoster, 1994), pp. 483−544.

[127] Cf. Stephen G. WILSON, *The Gentiles and the Gentile Mission in Luke-Acts* (SNTSMS 23; Cambridge: Cambridge University Press, 1973).

[128] Cf. Lk 2:1 (the decree of Caesar Augustus went out that "all the world should be registered"); 4:5 (the devil showed Jesus "all the kingdoms of the world"); 21:25−26 (before the coming of the Son of Man, signs upon the earth will cause "distress among nations" and foreboding of what is coming "upon the world"); Acts 11:28 (there would be a great famine "over the whole inhabited world"); 17:6 (Paul and his companions "have been turning the inhabited world upside down"), 31 (God "will judge the world"); 19:27 ("all Asia and the inhabited world" worship Artemis); 24:5 (Paul was found to be "an agitator among all the Jews throughout the world"). This list could be greatly expanded by the many references in Luke-Acts to γῆ in the sense of the "earth" (cf. Lk 2:14; 5:24; 10:21; 11:31; 12:49, 51, 56; 16:17; 18:8;

the number of the tribes of Israel (cf. 22:30), and then the Seventy(-two) (10:1−12), the traditional number of nations in the world based on the Table of Nations. [129] Then, just before his ascension, Jesus explains to his disciples what scripture says about him: "This is what is written: The Christ will suffer and rise from the dead on the third day, and repentance and forgiveness of sins will be preached in his name *to all nations* (εἰς πάντα τὰ ἔθνη), beginning at Jerusalem" (Lk 24:46−47). [130] Evidently, this mission "to all nations" is viewed as the continuation of the mission of the Seventy(-two), [131] for the same sequence of numbers is at least implied at the beginning of Acts: *twelve* apostles (1:26; 2:14) and *seventy* (cf. 2:5: "every nation under heaven"). [132]

The Table of Nations and Acts 1:8. Acts takes up where Luke's Gospel leaves off, with Jesus' final words to his disciples before his ascension (Acts 1:1−11). The idea that the disciples would preach "to all nations (εἰς πάντα τὰ ἔθνη) beginning at Jerusalem" (Lk 24:46−47) is reiterated in Acts 1:8, where Jesus promises, "and you will be my witnesses in Jerusalem, and in all Judea and Samaria, and to the ends of the earth." [133] Acts 1:8 is often understood as broadly programmatic for the structure of Acts: The witness begins in Jerusalem (Acts 1−7), spreads to Judea and Samaria as a result of persecution (8:1, 4−8), and eventually reaches "the ends of the earth" [134] through the

---

21:23, 25, 33, 35; 23:44; Acts 1:8; 2:19; 3:25; 4:24, 26; 7:49; 8:33; 10:11, 12; 11:6; 13:47; 14:15; 17:24, 26; 22:22).

[129] As we noted in Chap. 1, both numbers – 70 and 72 – are represented in the Jewish tradition of the Table of Nations, which makes the textual problem in Lk 10:1 difficult to solve (cf. Bruce METZGER, "Seventy or Seventy-two Disciples?" *NTS* 5 [1958−59] 299−306). In either case, interpreters are divided as to whether the number refers to the traditional 70(72) nations based on the Table of Nations (or, for example, to the number of elders whom Moses chose to assist him [Num 11:24]). For example, *pro*: I. Howard MARSHALL, *The Gospel of Luke: A Commentary on the Greek Text* (NIGTC; Exeter: Paternoster Press, 1978), pp. 414−415, pointing out that Lk 10:3 ("I send you out as lambs in the midst of wolves") implies the 70 nations of the world, which in Jewish literature are pictured as 70 "wolves"; *con*: Joseph A. FITZMYER, *The Gospel according to Luke (X−XXIV)* (AB 28A; New York: Doubleday, 1985), pp. 845−846; WILSON, *The Gentiles*, pp. 45−47. Note that Luke's Gospel mentions Noah several times. In conformity with the universalistic emphasis of Luke's Gospel, Lk 3:23−38 traces the lineage of Jesus from Joseph (v. 23), through Noah (v. 36), to Adam (v. 38), in a way that mirrors the Table of Nations in 1 Chr 1:1−2:2 beginning with Adam (1:1). And, Lk 17:26−27 compares the days of the Son of Man to the days of Noah.

[130] Yet, Luke's account of the Cleansing of the Temple (Lk 19:45−46) omits the part of the citation of Isa 56:7 that states that "My house shall be (called) a house of prayer *for all nations* (πᾶσιν τοῖς ἔθνεσιν)," whereas Mk 11:17 includes it.

[131] On the connection between the mission of the Seventy(-two) and Acts, see Robert C. TANNEHILL, *The Narrative Unity of Luke-Acts: A Literary Interpretation, Vol. 1: The Gospel according to Luke* (Foundations and Facets; Philadelphia: Fortress, 1986), pp. 232−237.

[132] On the connection between Rom 10:14−17 and the Synoptic Sending tradition in Paul's concept of the apostolic mission, see Chap. 2.

[133] Daniel R. SCHWARTZ tries to argue that γῆ here refers to the end of the "land" of Israel and refers only to the mission to Jews in Palestine ("The End of the GH [Acts 1:8]: Beginning or End of the Christian Vision?" *JBL* 105 [1986] 669−676).

[134] On the Septuagintal usage of this expression (cf. *Pss. Sol.* 8:16 [Rome?]; Deut 33:17; Isa

ministry of Paul (Acts 28:14–31). Yet as an explication of what it means that the disciples would preach "to all nations," the concentric circles radiating out from Jerusalem[135] in a northwesterly direction to the ends of the earth suggests influence from the Table-of-Nations tradition, for as we have seen, 1 Chronicles 1 lists the nations of the world "in a circle" that proceeds counterclockwise – from the North, to the West, to the South, and to the East – with Jerusalem in the center. Likewise in Ezek 5:5, Jerusalem is in the center of a "circle" of nations.[136] This would correlate with the normal meaning of the "the ends of the earth" as the furthest points on the edge of the inhabited world, including Scythia in the North, India in the East, Ethiopia in the South, and Spain in the West.[137] Furthermore, the expression "to the ends of the earth" (ἕως ἄκρων τῆς γῆς) in 1 Macc 1:3 is influenced by the

---

48:20; 49:6; 62:11; Ps 46:10[9]; 48:11[10]; 72:8; Prov 17:24; Job 28:24; Mic 5:3[4]; Zech 9:10; 1 Macc 3:9), see esp. W. C. van UNNIK, "Der Ausdruck ἕως ἐσχάτου τῆς γῆς (Apostelgeschichte I 8) und sein alttestamentlicher Hintergrund," in *Sparsa Collecta, Part 1: Evangelia, Paulina, Acta* (NovTSup 29; Leiden: Brill, 1973), pp. 386–401 (esp. pp. 395–399). On the concept, see further HENGEL, "Luke the Historian and the Geography of Palestine in the Acts of the Apostles," in *Between Jesus and Paul*, pp. 97–128 (here p. 101); Othmar KEEL, *Die Welt der altorientalischen Bildsymbolik und das Alte Testament am Beispiel der Psalmen* (Zürich: Benziger Verlag; Neukirchen: Neukirchener Verlag, 1972), pp. 17–20 (on Ps 72:8); James S. ROMM, *The Edges of the Earth in Ancient Thought: Geography, Exploration, and Fiction* (Princeton, NJ: Princeton University Press, 1992); Klaus KARTUNNEN, "Expedition to the End of the World: An Ethnographic τόπος in Herodotus," *StudOr* 64 (1988) 177–181.

[135] The Book of Acts as a whole is strongly centered on Jerusalem (cf. Rudolf PESCH, *Die Apostelgeschichte* [2 vols.; EKK 5; Zürich: Benziger Verlag; Neukirchen-Vluyn: Neukirchener Verlag, 1986], 1:38, who uses this fact against seeing Acts 1:8 as an organizing principle of the book; also Dennis D. SYLVA, "Death and Life at the Center of the World," in *Reimaging the Death of the Lukan Jesus* [ed. D.D. Sylva; BBB 73; Frankfurt a.M.: Hain, 1990], pp. 153–217). Peder BORGEN argues that from a geographical perspective, Ephesus is to Luke what Alexandria is to Philo ("Philo, Luke and Geography," in *Paul Preaches Circumcision and Pleases Men and Other Essays on Christian Origins* [Relieff 8; Dragvoll-Trondheim: TAPIR, 1983], pp. 59–71).

[136] See further in Chap. 1 on the concentric circles of diminishing holiness radiating out from Jerusalem to the nations (cf. *m. Kelim* 1:6–9). Furthermore, *1 Enoch* 26:1 describes Jerusalem as "the center of the earth," from which Enoch makes a journey to the four corners of the earth – East (chaps. 28–33), North (34), West (35), and South (36) – in a counterclockwise direction that corresponds approximately to the orientation and movement of the Table of Nations in 1 Chronicles 1. We may also note that in Acts 6:9 the peoples and nations represented in the Jerusalem synagogues are listed counterclockwise: "the synagogue of the Freedmen . . ., and of the Cyrenians, and of the Alexandrians, and of those from Cilicia and Asia. . . ." On Acts 6:9, see further HENGEL, *The Pre-Christian Paul*, p. 56.

[137] Cf. ELLIS, "'Das Ende der Erde' (Apg 1,8)," pp. 279–281. On the basis of this usage, ELLIS argues that in Acts 1:8, ἐσχάτος (singular!) refers specifically not to Rome but to Spain and that despite the allusion to Isa 49:6 and the commission to all the apostles, Acts 1:8 cannot refer to the whole universal witness to the ends of the earth. But, see Hans CONZELMANN, *Die Apostelgeschichte* (2nd ed.; HNT 7; Tübingen: Mohr-Siebeck, 1972), p. 27: "Der Ausdruck [sc. (ἕως) ἐσχάτου τῆς γῆς] meine immer die Enden der Erde. Das würde im Fall des Paulus auf Spanien weisen. Dagegen spricht PsSal 8,15 und der lukanische Geschichtszusammenhang."

Table of Nations tradition, as shown by the use of "Kittim" (v. 1) and the repeated occurrence of "nations" (vv. 3, 4) in the context.

The Table of Nations and Acts 2:5—11. Further evidence for the influence of the Table-of-Nations tradition on the book can be seen in Acts 2:5—11. On the day of Pentecost, Jews "from every nation (ἀπὸ παντὸς ἔθνους) under heaven" were staying in Jerusalem (v. 5). Having stated that these Diaspora Jews are amazed about hearing the disciples speak in their own "tongues" (γλῶσσαι) (vv. 6—8; cf. v. 11), the text goes on to supply a *partial* list of the nations represented by these Jews: "Parthians and Medes and Elamites; and residents of Mesopotamia, Judea and Cappadocia, Pontus and Asia, Phrygia and Pamphylia, Egypt and the parts of Libya belonging to Cyrene; and visitors from Rome,[138] both Jews and proselytes; Cretans and Arabs" (vv. 9—11). This list has generated much discussion about its apparent lack of structure and uniformity[139] and its possible background in Greco-Roman astrology.[140] Curiously, however, this table of nations has not been examined against the background of the Table-of-Nations tradition.

Acts 2:9—11 shares several features in common with the Table-of-Nations tradition. First of all, it contains a *pars pro toto* list of nations similar to those in the Table-of-Nations tradition. Already in Isaiah 66, Yahweh's promise to gather "all nations and tongues" (v. 18; cf. Gen 10:5, 20, 31)[141] is explicated by a partial list of "the nations" drawn from the Table of Nations (v. 19). Similarly in *Sib. Or.* 3.512—519, the prophecy that Yahweh will send afflictions on "all nations" of the earth is elaborated by a partial list of the nations, including Magog. The closest parallel to Acts 2:9—11 is found in Philo *Legat.* 281—283, which gives a *pars pro toto* list of the nations to which Jews have been sent out from the "Metropolis" Jerusalem in order to form colonies throughout the whole inhabited world.[142]

---

[138] Rome is the only European city mentioned in this list.

[139] Cf., e.g., Werner STENGER, "Beobachtungen zur sogenannten Völkerliste des Pfingstwunders (Apg 2,7—11)," *Kairos* 21 (1979) 206—214, who perceives in the list a convoluted pattern of correspondences based on the opposition of the four points of the compass.

[140] On the usual view that the astrological text of Paulus Alexandrinus is the closest parallel to Acts 2:9—11 (e.g., Eberhard GÜTING, "Der geographische Horizont der sogenannten Völkerliste des Lukas [Acta 2,9—11]," *ZNW* 66 [1975] 149—169 [here p. 151]), see Bruce METZGER, "Ancient Astrological Geography and Acts 2:9—11," in *New Testament Studies: Philological, Versional and Patristic* (NTTS 10; Leiden: Brill, 1980), pp. 46—56; Gerhard SCHNEIDER, *Die Apostelgeschichte* (2 vols.; HTKNT 5; Freiburg: Herder, 1980), 1:254—255. For further parallels to Acts 2:9—11, see Pieter W. van der HORST, "Hellenistic Parallels to the Acts of the Apostles (2.1—47)," *JSNT* 25 (1985) 49—60 (here pp. 53—54); Manfred GÖRG, "Apg 2,9—11 in außerbiblischer Sicht," *Biblische Notizen* 1 (1976) 15—18. CONZELMANN denies an astrological background for the table, explaining it instead as a list describing the kingdoms of the Diodochoi (*Apostelgeschichte*, p. 31).

[141] Cf. Acts 2:5 ("every nation"), 7, 8 ("language").

[142] As we suggested in Chap. 1, a list of nations or even a map based on the Table of Nations was probably kept by priestly circles in Jerusalem in order to keep track of the Temple tax delivered by the Jewish Diaspora as well as other offerings associated with the pilgrimage festivals.

Second, Acts 2:9–11 shares the apparent lack of structure and uniformity often found in the Table-of-Nations tradition. Not every list of nations in this tradition has the same counterclockwise structure observed in 1 Chronicles 1.[143] Some lists, such as the ones just mentioned, have a more random structure.[144] Furthermore, such texts often vacillate between names of peoples and names of lands in much the same way as Acts 2:9–11 does.[145] We can see this seemingly haphazard alternation already in Genesis 10 and 1 Chronicles 1.[146]

Third, Acts 2:9–11 shares many of the names of nations and lands commonly found in the Table-of-Nations tradition. In fact, approximately 50 percent of these names can be matched by the toponyms in Josephus' "updated" version of the Table of Nations in *Ant.* 1.122–147. This includes Ἰουδαία, which has often been thought to be out of place in Acts 2:9.[147] Moreover, the connection between Cretes and Arabs at the end of the list (v. 11), which has long perplexed scholars,[148] receives a possible explanation on the basis of the Table of Nations: Both peoples are descendants of Mizraim (Egypt) whose progeny settled in the contiguous territories of Palestine and Nabatea, respectively.[149]

---

[143] Nevertheless, without referring to the Table-of-Nations tradition, METZGER ("Ancient Astrological Geography," pp. 54–55) suggests that Acts 2:9–11 lists the nations in a counterclockwise, circular direction (beginning from countries or peoples in the upper part of the Fertile Crescent and then moving generally westward, eventually turning south and finally southeast). Note, however, that there are several clockwise deviations from this general pattern (e.g., Asia then Phrygia, Egypt then Libya, Libya then Rome).

[144] Philo's list (*Legat.* 281–283) has a highly structured, three-part framework, but the list of nations within each part is more random.

[145] Names of *peoples*: Parthians, Medes, Elamites, Romans, Cretans, and Arabs; names of *lands*: Mesopotamia, Judea, Cappadocia, Pontus, Asia, Phrygia, Pamphylia, Egypt, and Arabia.

[146] Names of *peoples*: Kittim, Rodanim, Mizraim, and Ludim; names of *lands*: Canaan, Sidon, Aram, and Asshur.

[147] Cf. METZGER, "Ancient Astrological Geography," p. 56; GÜTING, "Der geographische Horizont der sogenannten Völkerliste des Lukas (Acta 2,9–11)," pp. 149–151, 153, 162–164. Because of the order of the toponyms (Judea comes between Mesopotamia and Cappodocia in v. 9), Martin DIBELIUS conjectures Γαλατίαν or Γαλλίαν instead of Ἰουδαίαν ("Der Text der Apostelgeschichte," in *Aufsätze zur Apostelgeschichte* [5th ed.; ed. Heinrich Greeven; FRLANT 60; Göttingen: Vandenhoeck & Ruprecht, 1968], pp. 76–83 [here p. 82]), although the middle term is still "out of order" in that case.

[148] Cf., e.g., Jürgen ROLOFF, *Die Apostelgeschichte* (NTD 5; Göttingen: Vandenhoeck & Ruprecht, 1981), p. 46. G. D. KILPATRICK suggests that the collocation goes back to the Lucianic manuscripts of the Septuagint at Ezek 30:5 ("Persians and *Cretans* and Lydians and Libyans and all *Arabia*"), which likewise comes within an eschatological context ("A Jewish Background to Acts 2:9–11?" *JJS* 26 [1975] 48–49). A. M. SCHWEMER compares the Arabs to the Cretans in terms of their reputations as merchants in the ancient world: "Die Händler par excellence der Antike waren zu Land die Araber; ihnen entsprechen die Kreter, die Handelsmacht auf dem Meer" ("Elija als Araber. Die haggadischen Motive in der Legende vom Messias Menahem ben Hiskija (yBer 2,4 5a; EkhaR 1,16 § 51) im Vergleich mit den Elija- und Elischa-Legenden der Vitae-Prophetarum," in *Die Heiden. Juden, Christen und das Problem des Fremden* [ed. Reinhard Feldmeier and Ulrich Heckel; WUNT 70; Tübingen: Mohr-Siebeck, 1994], pp. 108–157 [here p. 124 n. 65]).

[149] As generally acknowledged, the Caphtorim, who descended from Mizraim and gave rise

Fourth, Acts 2:9–11 shares a similar context to that of the Table-of-Nations. P. S. ALEXANDER argues that "if the outpouring of the Spirit at Pentecost is seen in Acts as a reversal of God's confusion of tongues after the Flood (Gen 11:7), then the catalogue of nations is most obviously related to Genesis 10. The brief list in Acts is only an allusion to the longer Table in Genesis."[150] As Acts brings out in a subsequent chapter, Peter had reported the reversal of Babel in yet another respect: "God himself has intervened in order to take from the nations (ἐξ ἐθνῶν) a people (λαός) for his name" (15:14).[151] Remaining "one people" and "one lip" had been the ill-fated goal of those who built the tower (cf. Gen 11:4–5 LXX) and the political hope of many empires.[152]

In light of these considerations, the table of nations in Acts 2:9–11 seems to reflect the Table-of-Nations tradition. In that case, the list has the same geographic orientation as the programmatic verse of Acts.

The Table of Nations and the Structure of Acts. If the programmatic verse of Acts is influenced by the Table-of-Nations tradition (1:8; cf. 2:9–11), we may ask whether the whole Book of Acts, with its strong geographical orientation, its emphasis on the nations of the world, and its dependence on the OT, is influenced to a certain extent by this tradition. Seen in this light, the Spirit-impelled witness that goes out from Jerusalem – the center – to the ends of the earth can be broadly divided into three missions according to the three sons of Noah, whose progeny constitute the Table of Nations: *Shem* (Acts 2:1–8:25), *Ham* (8:26–40), and *Japheth* (9:1–28:31).[153] Perhaps this outline can shed new light on the difficult question of the structure of Acts.[154]

---

to the Philistines (Gen 10:13–14), are to be identified with the Cretans (cf., e.g., WESTER-MANN, *Genesis*, 1:693). According to Josephus, the Arabs descended from Ishmael, the son of Abraham by Hagar the Egyptian, who likewise took an Egyptian wife (*Ant.* 1.214, 220–221; cf. MILLAR, "Hagar, Ishmael, Josephus and the Origins of Islam," pp. 23–45). The Arabs occupied Nabatea (*Ant.* 1.221), the land adjacent to Palestine. The latter was named after the Philistines (§ 136).

[150] ALEXANDER, "Geography and the Bible (Early Jewish)," *ABD*, 2 (1992) 977–988 (here p. 983); Christoph UEHLINGER, *Weltreich und "eine Rede". Eine neue Deutung der sogenannten Turmbauerzählung (Gen 11,1–9)* (OBO 101; Freiburg: Universitätsverlag Freiburg; Göttingen: Vandenhoeck & Ruprecht, 1990), pp. 264–266. But, see CONZELMANN, *Apostelgeschichte*, p. 31: "An die apokalyptische Erwartung, daß es in der Endzeit nur *eine* Sprache geben werde (Jes 66,18; Test Jud 25,3 . . .), ist nicht gedacht."

[151] See further J. DUPONT, "Un peuple d'entre des nations (Actes 15.14)," *NTS* 31 (1985) 321–335.

[152] According to 1 Macc 1:41, for example, Antiochus Epiphanes wrote to his whole kingdom (i.e., Syria, Palestine, Mesopotamia, Persia, and parts of Asia Minor) that all should be "one people" (λαὸν ἕνα), that is, unified in language, religion, and culture.

[153] Although it may be objected that this outline focuses disproportionately on the missions to Shem and Japheth, this corresponds to the generally acknowledged emphasis in Acts on Peter and Paul, respectively. Therefore, the novelty of this outline lies in the suggestion that the pericope on the Ethiopian Eunuch (8:26–40) constitutes a second major division of Acts nestled between the primary foci. Possible reasons for the disproportionateness will be considered below.

[154] Acts has frequently been divided on the basis of Luke's interest either in Peter (chaps.

I. The Mission to Shem (Acts 2:1–8:25). Beginning on the day of Pentecost, the Spirit-impelled witness promised in Acts 1:8 goes out with great success to the Jews who were assembled in Jerusalem from every nation under heaven, resulting in 3,000 believers being added that day (2:1–41). The nascent Jerusalem church immediately begins to thrive (2:42–47; 4:32–5:11; 6:1–7), and a strong apostolic witness continues to impress the residents of the city despite growing official opposition and persecution (3:1–4:31; 5:12–42; 6:8–8:3). Even while concentrating on Jerusalem, however, Acts does not lose sight of the mission to the nations, for Peter's speech in Solomon's Colonnade includes a modified citation of Gen 22:18; 26:4 (καὶ ἐν τῷ σπέρματί σου [ἐν]ευλογηθήσονται πᾶσαι αἱ πατριαὶ τῆς γῆς),[155] which, through the original promise in Gen 12:3, alludes to the Table of Nations.[156] Thus when severe persecution breaks out after the stoning of Stephen,[157] (Hellenistic) Jewish Christians are forced to leave Jerusalem and, in fulfillment of Acts 1:8, begin to evangelize Judea and Samaria (8:1, 4–25; cf. 9:40). With this mission to the Samaritans – a collective name for deportees into the region of Samaria from various Mesopotamian "nations" (cf. 2 Kgs 17:24–41)[158] – Acts shows that the mission to Shem is well under way.[159]

1–12) and Paul (13–28) or in the geographical expansion of the apostolic witness from Jerusalem (1–7) to Samaria and Judea (8–10) and to the ends of the earth (11–28). The summaries about the growth of the word of God or of the church in 6:7; 9:31; 12:24; 16:5; 19:20 have been used to divide the book into six sections. On the various outlines of Acts, see, e.g., Schneider, *Apostelgeschichte*, 1:65–68; Roloff, *Apostelgeschichte*, pp. 12–14; Pesch, *Apostelgeschichte*, 1:36–42.

[155] Acts 3:25.

[156] Cf. already Acts 2:39, in which "all those are afar off" refers to the Gentiles in an allusion to Isa 57:19.

[157] Stephen's final provocative statement, which led directly to his being stoned, was that he saw "the Son of man standing at the right hand of God" (Acts 7:56). This alludes to Daniel 7, where the one like a Son of man, who was brought near to the Ancient of Days (v. 13), "was given dominion and glory and kingship, that all peoples, nations, and tongues should serve him" (v. 14). Therefore, Stephen's allusion may imply the Table of Nations, since, as we saw in Chap. 1, the Book of Daniel has been influenced by this tradition.

[158] For example 4 Kgdms 17:26 refers to the ἔθνη that the king of Assyria removed from Mesopotamia and resettled in the cities of Samaria (cf. vv. 29, 32, 33, 41). Cf. James D. Purvis, "The Samaritans," *The Cambridge History of Judaism, Vol. 2: The Hellenistic Age* (ed. W. D. Davies, et al.; Cambridge: Cambridge University Press, 1989), pp. 591–613 (here pp. 591–592): Whereas the Samaritans themselves claimed to be the surviving remnant of the old Israelite tribes of Ephraim, Manasseh, and Levi, the Jewish community regarded them as "descendants of the colonists who had been settled in northern Palestine by the Assyrians in the late eighth century BC. The Jewish account of that settlement, found in 2 Kings 17:24–41, contains a severe indictment of those colonists for their syncretistic religious practices, half-pagan, half-Yahwistic. The Samaritans were consequently called the *Kûtîm* by the Pharisees (so too Josephus, *Antiquities* IX.288, and *passim*) after *Kûtâh*, one of the five Mesopotamian cities from which the colonists were said to have been brought. The insinuation in the use of this untoward sobriquet was clear: Samaritanism was no more Israelite religion than were the Samaritans the descendants of Israelites." According to Josephus *Ant.* 9.279 (cf. also § 288), "After removing other nations (ἔθνη) from a region called Chuthos . . . , he [sc. Salmanasses]

II. The Mission to Ham (Acts 8:26–40). If the Book of Acts unfolds along the lines of the Table of Nations, then Philip's transitory mission to the Ethiopian eunuch occupies a more important place in the structure of Acts than is usually appreciated. The account is often lumped together with the preceding account of the mission to Judea and Samaria, which may be legitimate insofar as Acts 6–8 is derived (in whole or in part) from a Hellenistic source that records the rise and expansion of Hellenistic Christianity in Jerusalem and Judea and in adjoining regions.[160] Nevertheless, Luke's own particular use of this material must also be taken into consideration. As it stands, Acts 8:26–40 is isolated in the narrative of Acts and not immediately connected with anything that precedes or follows it.[161] Having finished the story of Peter and James among the Samaritans (8:14–25), Luke abruptly begins the account of the Ethiopian eunuch with the angel of the Lord instructing Philip to go from Jerusalem to Gaza (v. 26), and he also ends it abruptly with Philip being caught up by the Spirit and taken to other regions (vv. 39–40).[162] Therefore, the text gives the impression of being a separate section in the narrative structure of Acts.

---

settled them in Samaria and in the country of the Israelites." In *Ant.* 10.184, Josephus refers to these resettled "nations" as τὸ τῶν Χουθαίων ἔθνος. One of Herod's nine wives was also "one of the nation of the Samaritans" (*Ant.* 17.20: τοῦ Σαμαρέων ἔθνους μία). "The nation of the Samaritans (τὸ Σαμαρέων ἔθνος) too was not exempt from disturbance" (*Ant.* 18.85). Note that Josephus also mentions a resettlement of "the nations of the Assyrians" in Damascus (*Ant.* 9.253), which is not found in the OT. Sir 50:25–26 refers to "those who live on the mountain of Samaria" as a "nation" (ἔθνος). On Josephus' concept of the Samaritans as foreign colonists, cf. also *Ant.* 9.288–291; 10.184; 11.303; 12.257. In *Ant.* 11.340, however, Josephus describes the Samaritans as "apostates from the nation of the Jews." See further Rita EGGER, *Josephus Flavius und die Samaritaner. Eine terminologische Untersuchung zur Identitätsklärung der Samaritaner* (NTOA 4; Freiburg: Universitätsverlag; Göttingen: Vandenhoeck & Ruprecht, 1986), pp. 313–316 and *passim*; R.J. COGGINS, "The Samaritans in Josephus," in *Josephus, Judaism and Christianity* (ed. Louis H. Feldman and Gohei Hata; Leiden: Brill, 1987), pp. 257–273; also Alan David CROWN, *A Bibliography of the Samaritans* (ATLA Bibliography Series 10; Metuchen, NJ/London: ATLA/Scarecrow Press, 1984). That Luke-Acts views the Samaritans as "foreigners" (non-Jews) is shown not only by Lk 17:18, where Jesus refers to a Samaritan (cf. v. 16) as ὁ ἀλλογενὴς οὗτος (on the use of ἀλλογενής for foreigners [from a Jewish perspective], see Friedrich BÜCHSEL, *TWNT*, 1 [1933] 266–267; EGGER, *Josephus*, pp. 200–201), but also by Acts 8:9, which explicitly states that Samaria is a separate "nation" (τὸ ἔθνος τῆς Σαμαρείας).

159 Beyond Samaria is "Galilee of the nations" (גליל הגוים), the former the land of Zebulun and Naphtali (cf. Isa 8:23; Matt. 4:12–15), which is composed of several nations (cf. Josephus *Ant.* 12.331: "Ptolemais, Tyre and Sidon and the other nations of Galilee" [καὶ τῶν ἄλλων ἐθνῶν τῆς Γαλιλαίας]; but see the parallel passage in 1 Macc 5:15 [Γαλιλαίαν ἀλλοφύλων]).

160 Cf. F.F. BRUCE, "Philip and the Ethiopian," *JSS* 34 (1989) 337–386 (here p. 377). According to ROLOFF, Luke took this account from "einem in den Kreisen der Hellenisten tradierten Kranz von Philippus-Legenden" (*Apostelgeschichte*, p. 138; cf. p. 139).

161 Cf. BRUCE, "Philip and the Ethiopian," p. 378. According to PESCH, "Die nach 8,4–13 zweite Philippus-Erzählung, 'eine in sich geschlossene Missionserzählung', ist wohl kaum, wie insbesondere die Stilunterschiede vermuten lassen, zusammen mit der ersten und im Anschluß an sie in der Lukas zugekommenen Tradition weitergegeben worden" (*Apostelgeschichte*, 1:287).

162 On the concentric formal structure of Acts 8:25–40, see R.F. O'TOOLE, "Philip and the Ethiopian Eunuch (Acts VII 25–40)," *JSNT* 17 (1983) 25–34. According to this suggestion,

In light of the evidence for the Table-of-Nations tradition that we have seen so far in Acts, the point of this section, with its pronounced geographical orientation, is not difficult to surmise, for the text emphasizes that the eunuch is an "Ethiopian" in the court of the queen of the "Ethiopians" (v. 27). Ethiopia is the Greek name for the territory of Cush,[163] the first son of Ham (cf. Gen 10:6, 7). In the Septuagint, the inhabitants of Cush are usually rendered by Αἰθίοπες, and Αἰθιοπία stands in general for the Hebrew כוש; only in the Table of Nations itself does the transliteration Χοῦς occur (Gen 10:6, 7, 8; 1 Chr 1:8, 9, 10).[164] For example, Jer 38(45):7–13 knows of an Ethiopian eunuch (סריס [MT only]) in the palace of Zedekiah in Jerusalem who rescued Jeremiah from the cistern and who was therefore spared by God during the destruction of Jerusalem (cf. Jer 39[46]:15–18). The Hebrew text calls him a "Cushite" (כושי), and the Septuagint translates it "Ethiopian" (Αἰθίοψ). Acts 8:26ff. may even be alluding to this account when it portrays the Ethiopian eunuch as active in Jerusalem (v. 27), as serving in a royal court (v. 27), and as being saved by God for trusting in him (vv. 36–37; cf. Jer 39[46]:18). Yet, the interpretation of the text does not depend on a obscure allusion to the OT, for "Cushite" was widely used, even in NT times, to refer to the Ethiopians.[165] In his exposition of the Table of Nations, Josephus explains that "of the four sons of Ham, the name of one, Chusaeus [Cush], has escaped the ravages of time: the Ethiopians, his subjects, are *to this day* called by themselves and by all in Asia Chusaeans [Cushites]" (*Ant.* 1.131). Thus, for the reader trained in Judaism, the mention of an Ethiopian eunuch would recall not only that the man was a Cushite but

---

the passage would be linked to the previous context at least by the formal correspondence between vv. 25 and 40.

[163] So also Erich DINKLER, "Philippus und der ΑΝΗΡ ΑΙΘΙΟΨ (Apg 8,26–40). Historische und geographische Bemerkungen zum Missionsablauf nach Lukas," in *Jesus und Paulus. Festschrift für Werner Georg Kümmel zum 70. Geburtstag* (ed. E. Earle Ellis and Erich Gräßer; Göttingen: Vandenhoeck & Ruprecht, 1975), pp. 85–95 (here p. 90).

[164] See further REDPATH, "The Geography of the Septuagint," pp. 292–293. Thus, the association of Gog and Magog with Ethiopia in *Sib. Or.* 3:319 is probably due to the mention of Cush (LXX: Αἰθίοπες) in Ezek 38:5, whose whole immediate context (Ezekiel 38–39) stands in the Table-of-Nations tradition (see Chap. 1). Whereas Num 12:1 refers to the "Cushite woman" whom Moses had married, Josephus speaks of Moses' having married "Tharbis, the daughter of the king of the Ethiopians" (*Ant.* 2.252–253; cf. Tessa RAJAK, "Moses in Ethiopia: Legend and Literature," *JJS* 29 [1978] 111–122).

[165] Cf. Torgny SÄVE-SÖDERBERGH, "Kusch," in *Lexikon der Ägyptologie,* 3 (1980) 888–893; Jean LECLANT, "Kuschitenherrschaft," ibid., cols. 893–901. Inge HOFMANN (*Studien zum meroitischen Königtum* [Monographies Reine Élisabeth 2; Brussels: Fondation Égyptologique Reine Élisabeth, 1971], p. 10) notes, however, that the modern usage of "Cush" is more limited than the ancient: "Seit dem Mittleren Reich bezeichneten die Ägypter das Gebiet südlich des 2. Kataraktes als 'Kusch', welcher Name später für das gesamte, südlich an Ägypten grenzende Territorium verwendet wurde. Von einem 'kuschitischen' Königreich zu sprechen, führt aber unweigerlich zu Missverständnissen, da seit Lepsius der Begriff 'kuschitisch' für die hamito-semitischen Sprachen zwischen Nil und Rotem Meer reserviert ist und ethnologisch für die verhältnismässig einheitliche Kultur Abessiniens Anwendung findet."

also that Cush was the first son of Ham.[166] If the mission to the Ethiopian stands for the mission to Ham,[167] it does not "compete" with the story of the Roman Cornelius in Acts 10:1–11:18, which describes the basis for the mission to Japheth.[168]

The representative nature of Philip's mission to the Ethiopian is reinforced by the fact that the eunuch was an official in the court of Candace, the queen of the Ethiopians (Acts 8:27),[169] whose Christian influence could have been expected to spread in the territory of Ham in accordance with his high position. The text makes it clear that the eunuch continued on his way back from Jerusalem to Ethiopia after his encounter with Philip (cf. Acts 8:27–28, 39), presumably to become the first missionary to that area of the world.[170] This illustrates for the first time in Acts that, again in fulfillment of Acts 1:8, the Spirit-impelled witness radiating out from Jerusalem went "to the ends of the earth" since Ethiopia was considered one of the ends of the earth.[171] Further-

---

[166] Not only is Cush the first son of Ham, but the eponymous nation that he represents (Ethiopia) is considered one of the most populous nations on the African continent (cf. Josephus *BJ* 2.382).

[167] That one of the descendants of Ham (here Cush/Ethiopia) could stand for the whole territory of Ham is made even more plausible by Psalm 105, where "the land of Ham" stands in parallel to Egypt (vv. 23, 27). See also Ps 78:51, where "the tents of Ham" stands in parallel to Egypt.

[168] Often, the story of the Ethiopian is thought to "compete" with the story of Cornelius in Acts 10:1–11:18 for the claim of who was the first Gentile to become a believer in Jesus. Actually, however, they are complementary accounts (cf. DINKLER, "Philippus und der ANHP ΑΙΘΙΟΨ," pp. 86–87; but see pp. 94–95; see further below) that describe the mission to Ham, on the one hand, and the mission to Japheth, on the other. Seen in this light, the difficult and highly controversial question of whether the eunuch was a full proselyte or merely a God-fearer becomes irrelevant, for the text wants to emphasize that the man was an Ethiopian, that is, a Cushite, a descendant of Ham. Insofar as Acts is concerned with the question of the Restoration of Israel (cf. 1:6), the prohibition against the admission of eunuchs into the people of God (cf. Deut 23:2) has come to an end, for according to Isa 56:3–5, at the time of the Restoration, "the eunuch" (הסריס, ὁ εὐνοῦχος) actually has a preferred status among the people of God. Cf. WESTERMANN, *Das Buch Jesaja Kapitel 40–66*, p. 250: "Die alte Bestimmung Dt. 23,2 wird außer Kraft gesetzt; von jetzt ab wird dem Verschnittenen ausdrücklich und feierlich ein Platz in der Gemeinde Jahwes gewährt."

[169] Cf. HOFMANN, *Studien zum meroitischen Königtum*, pp. 36–40.

[170] Cf. PESCH, *Apostelgeschichte*, 1:294; DINKLER, "Philippus und der ANHP ΑΙΘΙΟΨ," pp. 92, 94, 95; SCHNEIDER, *Apostelgeschichte*, 1:499. On Acts 8:39 ("he went on his way rejoicing"), Irenaeus adds that the man became a preacher in Ethiopia of the coming of Christ (*Adv. haer.* 4.23.2; cf. 3.12.10).

[171] Cf., e.g., HENGEL, *Zur urchristlichen Geschichtsschreibung*, p. 70; PESCH, *Apostelgeschichte*, 1:295; DINKLER, "Philippus und der ANHP ΑΙΘΙΟΨ," pp. 85, 86, 92, 94; SCHNEIDER, *Apostelgeschichte*, 1:499, 500–501. According to Strabo, the idea that the Ethiopians live at "the ends (ἔσχατοι) of the earth, on the banks of the Oceanus ...," goes back to Homer (*Geogr.* 1.1.6). In subsequent Greek cartographic tradition, Ethiopia was often considered one of the ends of the earth (cf. ELLIS, "'Das Ende der Erde' [Apg 1,8]," pp. 279–281). In Luke-Acts, however, the idea goes back more directly to the OT/Jewish tradition of the Queen of Sheba/Ethiopia. It is no coincidence that the only two occurrences of βασίλισσα in Luke-Acts are used of "the Queen of the South (νότου)," i.e., the Queen of Sheba, who came "from

more, Acts 8:26 emphasizes the direction Philip was to go: "toward the south" (κατὰ μεσημβρίαν)[172] to the road that "goes down" (καταβαίνουσα) from Jerusalem to Gaza. This is desert." As REDPATH suggests about the Septuagint's paraphrastic translation of "south" (נגב) as ἡ ἔρημος,[173] "This may perhaps illustrate the use of ἔρημος in Acts 8:26, where 'the way that goeth down from Jerusalem unto Gaza' is followed by the expression αὕτη ἐστὶν ἔρημος – for Gaza stands on the border of the Negeb."[174] Diodorus Siculus (18.6.4) refers to this region as "the desert" (ἡ ἔρημος) through which the Nile makes its way, dividing Syria and Egypt and the very hot countries "to the south" (κατὰ μεσημβρίαν) from those "to the north" (πρὸς ἄρκτους). Clearly, this presupposes the concept of the three continents in which the Nile is regarded as the boundary between Asia and Libya-Africa (cf. Strabo *Geogr.* 1.4.7).[175] Seen in this light, ἔρημος in Acts 8:26 underscores again the representative nature of Philip's mission to the Ethiopian eunuch as a mission to the South,[176] that is, to

---

the ends of the earth" (Lk 11:31 par.), and of Candice, "the Queen of the Ethiopians" (Acts 8:27). According to Josephus, the Queen of Sheba was the "queen of Egypt and Ethiopia" (*Ant.* 8.159, 165, 175), and Saba (Sheba) was the capital of the Ethiopian realm (*Ant.* 2.249). Although Lou H. SILBERMAN considers Josephus idiosyncratic at this point ("The Queen of Sheba in Judaic Tradition," in *Solomon & Sheba* [ed. James B. Pritchard; London: Phaidon Press, 1974], pp. 65–84), Josephus' connection between the Queen of Sheba and Ethiopia is confirmed by *Vitae Prophetarum* 1:8 (see the word study on ἔθνος in Chap. 2 above). In the Table of Nations, furthermore, Sheba is the son of Raamah, the son of Cush (Gen 10:7). Therefore, the title βασίλισσα in Lk 11:31 and Acts 8:27 refers to the queen of the Ethiopians (*pace* Edward ULLENDORFF, "Candace [Acts VII.27] and the Queen of Sheba," *NTS* 2 [1955–56] 53–56 [here p. 54]), and both texts emphasize the South. In that case, both queens are seen as dwelling at the ends of the earth.

172 The phrase κατὰ μεσημβρίαν can mean "at midday" (cf. Diodorus Siculus 4.22.3; Diogenes Laertius *Vita Phil.* 1.109; Philostratus *Vita Phil.* 5.30; 8.26; Lucianus *Navigium* 35.15; Philo *Somn.* 1.202; Philostratus Major *Imagines* 2.11.1; Strabo *Geogr.* 2.5.37; 8.3.28; 15.1.63; 15.3.10; 17.1.48), but here, it more likely means "toward the South." Κατὰ μεσημβρίαν frequently occurs in enumerations of the four points of the compass – North, East, South, and West (cf. Dionysius of Halicarnassus *Ant. Rom.* 14.1.1; Philo *Somn.* 1.175; *Legat.* 89) – and in oppositions of northern to southern (cf. Josephus *BJ* 7.347 [of city walls]; Diodorus Siculus 18.6.4). Most importantly for our considerations, the phrase is used in reference to Ethiopia: "In the Ethiopian and in the Arab and in all those toward the South (κατὰ μεσημβρίαν), the nature of the skin . . . is hard, dry and black" (Galen *De temperamentis libri iii* 1.628).

173 Cf. Gen 12:9; 13:1, 3; Num 13:19(17), 23(22); 21:1; Deut 34:3; Josh 15:21; Isa 21:1; 30:6.

174 REDPATH, "The Geography of the Septuagint," p. 305. The referent of the feminine singular demonstrative pronoun may be either ὁδόν or Γάζαν. Since αὕτη follows directly on Γάζαν, the latter is more likely. On the interpretation of αὕτη ἐστὶν ἔρημος as an allusion to the destruction of Gaza in A. D. 66, see HEMER, *The Book of Acts in the Setting of Hellenistic History*, p. 371 (also p. 368 n. 10).

175 See further Chap. 1.

176 As we saw in our discussion of Ps 71:9 LXX in Chap. 1, the Ethiopians are representative of southern part of the messianic empire, which extends "to the ends of the earth" (v. 8; cf. also Isa 11:11–12). DINKLER ("Philippus und der ΑΝΗΡ ΑΙΘΙΟΨ," pp. 86–87; cf. pp. 94–95) makes a similar point in comparing the account of the Ethiopian and that of Cornelius: ". . . einerseits (1,8) ἕως ἐσχάτου τῆς γῆς in Richtung κατὰ μεσημβρίαν (8,26): nach Süden, ja zu

the sons of Ham,[177] for, according to Jewish tradition based on the Table of Nations, the sons of Ham occupy the hot, southern portion of the world, i.e., the continent of Africa.[178]

III. The Mission to Japheth (Acts 9:1–28:31). According to our proposed outline, the third section of Acts – the bulk of the book – is concerned with Paul's mission to Japheth.[179] Although this section is not completely unified, it begins and ends with Paul and concentrates on him for the most part (cf. Acts 9:1–30; 11:19–30; 13:1–28:31). Even the voluminous material on Peter in the early part of this section serves, to a large degree, either as a presupposition for Paul's mission to the Japhethites (cf. Acts 10:1–11:18, which describes the prototypical conversion of a Roman centurion of the "*Italian* Cohort")[180] or as a digression inserted into the account of Paul's famine-relief visit to Jerusalem (12:1–23).[181]

---

den Quellen des Nils, andererseits in Richtung Westen: nach Rom. Und sobald man dies beachtet, wird man wohl doch eine bewußte Koordinierung der beiden durch sehr unterstrichenes Handeln und Eingreifen Gottes gekennzeichneten Geschichten nicht übersehen können." Nevertheless, DINKLER emphasizes "the ends of earth" to such an extent that he denies Luke had any particular interest in the evangelization of Ethiopia (ibid., p. 94). More likely, however, Luke was interested in the mission to each of the sons of Ham.

[177] One may wonder why Acts gives far less scope to the mission to Ham than to the other two missions. Several possibilities suggest themselves: (1) The mission to Ham was little known; (2) it was beyond the horizons of the author and his audience; (3) it was held to be less significant. This last possibility deserves special consideration because according to Strabo, Africa (coextensive with the territory of Ham) is considered the smallest and least significant continent (*Geogr.* 17.3.1).

[178] Cf. *Jub.* 8:22–24. Hence, DINKLER is quite right to point out that Gaza is the border between Asia and Africa (cf. Gen 10:19) and that Luke's account of the expansion of the gospel is oriented on the three continents: Asia, Africa, and Europe ("Philippus und der ANHP AIΘIOΨ," pp. 89, 95; cf. SCHNEIDER, *Apostelgeschichte*, 1:499).

[179] If a reason is sought for this disproportionate emphasis on the mission to Japheth, several possibilities suggest themselves: (1) Japheth is featured more prominently than the other two sons of Noah in the Table-of-Nations tradition (e.g., Japheth is to dwell in the tents of Shem [Gen 9:27]; Japheth is given pride of place in Genesis 10 and is better represented in the list of nations in Isa 66:19); (2) the mission to Japheth interests Luke the most since Luke is probably a travelling companion of Paul to that territory (cf. Claus-Jürgen THORNTON, *Der Zeuge des Zeugen. Lukas als Historiker der Paulusreisen* [WUNT 56; Tübingen: Mohr-Siebeck, 1991]); (3) Luke is writing to Theophilus, who is possibly a Japhethite; (4) Japheth represents the last frontier before the restoration of the kingdom to Israel (cf. 1:6; 28:31). See further GUNTHER, "The Association of Mark and Barnabas with Egyptian Christianity (Part I)," pp. 220–221, who suggests that Luke concentrates on the progress of Paul from Jerusalem to Rome and ignores the origins of Egyptian Christianity because its catechesis was deemed imperfect (cf. the verdict on Apollos' instruction before coming to Ephesus [Acts 18:24–25]).

[180] On Cornelius as the name of a Roman soldier, see HEMER, *The Book of Acts in the Setting of Hellenistic History*, pp. 177, 226–227. A *cohors II Italic(a) c(iuium) R(omanorum)* is attested in Syria in A.D. 69 (*ILS* 9168). Note also that the revelation to Peter that God has declared all things clean, which goes back to the Noachic commandment (Gen 9:3–4), prepares the way for the Apostolic Council and its Decree (Acts 15:20, 29; 21:25), which goes back to the same Noachic commandment (see further above).

[181] The church in Antioch entrusted Barnabas and Saul to take the famine relief to

The section begins with Paul's call to apostleship on the way to Damascus (9:1-9). Paul is presented as the one who is called to carry the name of Jesus before the "nations" (ἔθνη) and their kings (9:15),[182] as the one who, again in fulfillment of Acts 1:8 (ἕως ἐσχάτου τῆς γῆς), has been commissioned to be "the light for the nations ... to the ends of the earth" (ἕως ἐσχάτου τῆς γῆς).[183] He was sent "far away to the ἔθνη" (Acts 22:21).[184] He was sent to the λαός (Israel) and to the ἔθνη (Acts 26:17, 23). What this means concretely begins to take shape already in 9:30, when Paul returns to his home in Tarsus; however, it becomes obvious only after the Apostolic Council, when he separates from Barnabas (with whom he had previously worked in Antioch, Cyprus, and Asia Minor) and ventures out for the first time on his own independent missionary enterprise, the so-called Second Missionary Journey (Acts 15:36-18:22).

From this point onwards, the Apostle focuses almost exclusively on Asia Minor and Europe, which together compose the traditional territory of Japheth. This agrees completely with Paul's own description of the scope and direction of his mission in Romans 15 and 1 Cor 10:13-16 (see above). Thus, starting from Syria and Cilicia (Acts 15:41) and proceeding ever westward, Paul took the overland route to Derbe and Lystra (16:1), passed through "the region of Phrygia and Galatia" (v. 6a),[185] and, having been forbidden by the Holy Spirit to speak the word in Asia (v. 6b), went on to Troas (v. 8). When he received the "Macedonian Call" in Troas (v. 9), Paul then crossed from Asia Minor into Macedonia (vv. 11-12), his first station in Europe (16:13-17:15). Encountering opposition in Macedonia, however, Paul continued his missionary activity in Achaia (17:16-18:17) before returning by way of Ephesus to Antioch (18:18-22). Therefore, Paul's first independent missionary journey begins where, according to Josephus (cf. *Ant.* 1.123), the Japhethites began their settlement (Cilicia), and it proceeds in the same westward direction through Asia Minor and Europe that the Japhethites had originally migrated along. Paul even bypasses the one territory in Asia Minor that does not belong the Japhethites, for the Roman province of Asia, which the Holy Spirit mysteriously forbade Paul to enter (Acts 16:6b),[186] includes at

---

Jerusalem (Acts 11:30). Then after completing their mission, Barnabas and Saul returned from (to?) Jerusalem (12:25).

[182] On Paul as a "witness," see Acts 22:15 (πρὸς πάντας ἀνθρώπους), 18; 23:11; 26:16, 22.

[183] Acts 13:47, citing Isa 49:6. On Paul's commission to the nations, see Gal 1:15-16 and Acts 26:23. See also on *Apoc. Adam* 76.8-15 above.

[184] The allusion is to Isa 57:19; cf. Acts 2:39; Eph 2:13-17.

[185] On this translation of τὴν Φρυγίαν καὶ Γαλατικὴν χώραν, see Chap. 4.

[186] Except for his involvement in Ephesus (see below), Paul's ministry in Asia remained mostly indirect. The influence of Paul's gospel went out from Ephesus to the whole province of Asia (Acts 19:10), and Paul wrote letters to individuals in this area. The letter to Philemon is written to a man who is evidently a resident of Colossae (Philemon's slave Onesimus hails from Colossae [Col 4:9]). Although Paul does not seem to have met Philemon personally (cf.

its heart the traditional territory of Lud, a son of Shem (Gen 10:22),[187] whom Josephus identifies with the Lydians of Asia Minor (*Ant.* 1.144).[188] In fact, F. F. Bruce suggests that a narrower sense of "Asia" corresponding to the dimensions of Lydia may actually be intended in Acts 16:6 if the subsequent context (vv. 7−8) implies a distinction between Asia and Mysia (which is included in the Roman province of Asia).[189] In any case, Ephesus would not be affected by this prohibition, because it falls within the territory of Javan, a Japhethite whom Josephus identifies with Ionia (§ 124).[190] It appears, therefore, that Paul is retracing the steps of the Japhethites.

If this analysis is correct, Luke probably does not consider Paul's very impressive mission as having reached its completion by Acts 28, for despite the fact that, from the perspective of Jerusalem, Rome may be viewed as "the ends of the earth" (cf. *Pss. Sol.* 8:16),[191] the imperial capital does not mark the westernmost extent of the territory of Japheth. Furthermore, Acts realizes that there are already believers in Rome (cf. 28:15). Therefore, Acts may presuppose that Paul's mission would continue beyond Rome to Spain, just as the Apostle himself expected in Rom 15:24, 28, based on the Table-of-Nations

---

Phlm 5), he apparently hopes to visit him in the near future (v. 22). Paul wrote another letter to the saints at Colossae although Epaphras had founded the church (cf. Col 1:7; 4:12), and Paul had never visited it (cf. 2:1). Nevertheless, Paul may have considered Colossae part of his missionary territory if he means to describe Epaphras as "a faithful minister of Christ *on our behalf*" (Col 1:7). Much depends on whether the text should read ὑπὲρ ὑμῶν ("for you"; cf. 4:13) or ὑπὲρ ἡμῶν ("on our behalf"). Cf. Bruce M. Metzger, *A Textual Commentary on the Greek New Testament: A Companion Volume to the United Bible Societies' Greek New Testament (third edition)* (rev. ed.; London/New York: United Bible Societies, 1975), pp. 619−620: "Although on the basis of superior Greek evidence (P[46] and early Alexandrian and Western authorities) ἡμῶν might seem to be preferable, a majority of the Committee, impressed by the widespread currency of ὑμῶν in versional and patristic witnesses, considered it probable that copyists introduced the first person pronoun under the influence of the preceding ἡμῶν and the following ἡμῖν."

[187] But what would explain the report that the Spirit also prohibited Paul from entering Bithynia (Acts 16:7)? Cf. Riesner, *Frühzeit*, pp. 259−260.

[188] According to most interpreters, Gen 10:22 itself presupposes the identification of Lud with the Lydians (cf. Westermann, *Genesis*, 1:684−685). Lydia bordered in the north on Mysia, in the east on Phrygia, in the south on Caria, and in the west on Ionia (cf. Hans Treidler and Günter Neumann, "Lydia," *Der Kleine Pauly*, 3 [1975] 797−800 [here col. 797]). In 133 BC, Lydia was incorporated into the Roman province of Asia (ibid., col. 799). See further C. Habicht, "New Evidence on the Province of Asia," *JRS* 65 (1975) 64−91.

[189] Cf. F.F. Bruce, *The Acts of the Apostles: The Greek Text with Introduction and Commentary* (3rd ed.; Grand Rapids: Eerdmans, 1990), pp. 354−355.

[190] Having reached Achaia on the Second Missionary Journey, Paul went back to Antioch by way of Ephesus, where he ministered in the synagogue for a while (Acts 18:18−21). On his Third Missionary Journey, Paul came back to Ephesus and ministered there for two years (Acts 19:1−41). This mission in Ephesus is sometimes explained as Paul's attempt to close the gap between Macedonia and Achaia, on the one hand, and Galatia, on the other (cf. Riesner, *Frühzeit*, pp. 264−265; Pesch, *Apostelgeschichte*, 2:157−158). It could also be explained as an attempt to consolidate his mission to Javan since Javan includes the Greeks not only in Greece but also in Ionia.

[191] But see Ellis, "'Das Ende der Erde' (Apg 1,8)," p. 279.

tradition.[192] If so, Paul's preaching in Rome about "the kingdom of God" may indicate an expectation that the mission would soon be completed.[193]

Summary. We have suggested that Acts presents the mission of the early church as proceeding according to the programmatic statement in Acts 1:8, which is based on the Table-of-Nations tradition. As such, the Spirit-impelled witness that proceeds from Jerusalem – the center – to the ends of the earth is divided into three missions according to the three sons of Noah who constitute the Table of Nations: Shem in the middle of the world, Ham to the South, and Japheth to the North. Ethiopia, the representative mission to Ham, is traditionally considered one of the ends of the earth, and Paul's mission is expressly concerned with bringing salvation "to the ends of the earth" (Acts 13:47). None of these three missions is considered already completed, but rather somewhere between just beginning (Ham), well under way (Shem), or nearing completion (Japheth?). The crucial link between all three missions is clearly the Stephen Circle.[194] Most importantly for our considerations here, Acts presents Paul as the main apostle to Asia Minor and Europe, the traditional territory of Japheth. Paul seems to be retracing the steps of the Japhethites. As we shall see next, Paul's missionary preaching on the Areopagus includes the Table-of-Nations tradition (Acts 17:26).

The Table of Nations in Paul's Speech on the Areopagus

Paul's Allusion to Genesis 10. In his speech on the Areopagus (Acts 17:22–31), Paul is reported first to have established common ground with his Athenian audience, which included Epicurean and Stoic philosophers (v. 18), by proclaiming to them the "unknown god" invoked on one of their local altar inscriptions (vv. 22–23). Then, foreshortening the story line of Genesis 1–10, Paul goes on to describe this God as (1) the one "who made the world and everything in it" (Acts 17:24–25; cf. Gen 1:1–25) and as (2) the one "who made from one man [sc. Adam] every nation (ἔθνος) of men to dwell on all the face of the earth (ἐπὶ παντὸς προσώπου τῆς γῆς), having determined allotted periods and the boundaries of their habitation" (Acts 17:26a; cf. Gen 1:26–28;

---

[192] Cf. ELLIS, "'Das Ende der Erde' (Apg 1,8)," pp. 277–286, who argues that "the end of the earth" refers to specifically to Spain and demonstrates Luke's knowledge of Paul's (planned) mission to Spain.

[193] At the beginning of Acts, Jesus' preaching about "the kingdom of God" is associated with an imminent expectation (1:3, 6).

[194] Stephen begins the witness in Jerusalem itself (Acts 6:8–7:53). When persecution breaks out after the death of Stephen, Philip, one of the seven Hellenistic Jews in the Stephen Circle (cf. Acts 6:5), extends the gospel beyond Jerusalem to Judea and Samaria (cf. Acts 8:4–25, 40), and, through the eunuch, to Ethiopia (8:26–40). Furthermore, members of the Stephen Circle who were scattered as a result of the persecution began the mission to "the Greeks" in Antioch (11:19–20). Through Paul and Barnabas, who were also associated with the church in Antioch, the witness is extended to Asia Minor and Europe.

9:1, 7, 19; 10:1–32).[195] This foreshortening of the narrative is consistent with the Genesis account itself, for the mandate to "Be fruitful and multiply, and fill the earth (γῆ)" in Gen 1:28 is reiterated verbatim to Noah and his sons in Gen 9:1 (cf. v. 7).[196] Indeed, according to Gen 9:19, it was from these sons of Noah that people spread out "over the whole earth" (ἐπὶ πᾶσαν τὴν γῆν). Therefore, the idea of "every nation" (πᾶν ἔθνος) in Paul's speech clearly alludes to the Table of Nations itself, which concludes with the statement: "These are the tribes of the sons of Noah, according to their generations, according to their nations (ἔθνη); from them were the islands of the nations (ἔθνη) scattered over the earth (γῆ) after the flood" (Gen 10:32). A similar compression of Genesis 1–10 occurs in the Table of Nations in 1 Chr 1:1–2:2, which explicitly begins with Adam (1:1) and then proceeds to list the descendants of Noah (vv. 4ff.). There, the name of Peleg, one of Shem's descendants, receives the etymological explanation: "for in his days the earth was divided (נפלגה)" (1 Chr 1:19; Gen 10:25).

In Jewish tradition based on the Table of Nations, the distribution of the nations on the earth was considered an act of God. In Josephus' exposition of the Table of Nations, for example, we read that after the confusion of tongues at the building of the Tower of Babel, humanity was scattered over the face of the earth, God leading them and determining their dwelling-places (*Ant.* 1.120). In his detailed examination of the Areopagus speech, B. GÄRTNER makes a direct comparison between this Jewish tradition and Acts 17:26.[197]

Paul's Allusion to Deut 32:8. This interpretation of Acts 17:26 in light of the Table-of-Nations tradition is further substantiated by the allusion to Deut 32:8:[198] "When the Most High divided the nations (ἔθνη), when he separated the sons of Adam, he set the bounds of the nations (ὅρια ἐθνῶν) according to the number of the angels of God (MT: sons of Israel)." This provides the allusion to Adam in Acts 17:26.[199] Furthermore, just as Deut 32:8 refers to God's having set the "bounds" (ὅρια) of the nations, so also Acts 17:26b refers to God's having set the "boundaries" (ὁροθεσία) of the nations' habitation. If,

---

[195] Sir 17:1–17 contains a somewhat similar foreshortening of Genesis 1–10, beginning with the Creation (vv. 1–6) and concluding with an allusion to the Table of Nations: "For each nation he set a ruler..." (v. 17). See also 4Q266 8–10: "He [sc. the priest] is to stand and say, 'Blessed are you; you are all; everything is in your hand and (you are) the maker of everything, who established [the peo]ples according to their families and their national languages'" (Robert EISENMAN and Michael WISE, *The Dead Sea Scrolls Uncovered: The First Complete Translation and Interpretation of 50 Key Documents Withheld for over 35 Years* [Rockport, MA: Element, 1992], pp. 218–219).

[196] On the other hand, both Philo (*Abr.* 40) and 4 Ezra (3:7–10) presuppose the existence of antediluvian nations that were destroyed by the Flood. The latter speaks explicitly of nations that sprang from Adam.

[197] Bertil GÄRTNER, *The Areopagus Speech and Natural Revelation* (ASNU 21; Lund: Gleerup, 1955), p. 151.

[198] Less likely is the suggestion that the text alludes here to Ps 74:17 (PESCH, *Apostelgeschichte*, 2:137–138).

[199] Cf. 1 Clem. 29:2, which cites Deut 32:8.

as several investigators have recently emphasized, Deuteronomy 32 plays an important role in Paul's argument in Romans 9−11 and if the "full number of the nations" in Rom 11:25 alludes to Deut 32:8,[200] then the allusion to Deut 32:8 in Acts 17:26 has a claim to being genuinely Pauline[201] despite the general reluctance of NT scholarship to acknowledge the authenticity of the theology in the speech.[202] Moreover, if Deut 32:8 stands in the Table-of-Nations tradition (see Chap. 1), then the influence of the Table of Nations in Acts 17:26a does not merely reflect Luke's program in Acts[203] but Paul's own point of view as well.[204]

---

[200] See further above.

[201] Paul's concept of the unity of humanity as stemming from one man, based as it is on the OT and Jewish tradition, differs radically from the pantheistic concept of the unity of humanity espoused by the Stoic philosophers in Paul's audience although his citation of the Stoic poet Aratus (Acts 17:28: τοῦ γὰρ καὶ γένος ἐσμέν) may at first seem to obscure the differences (cf. M. HENGEL, *Der Sohn Gottes. Die Entstehung der Christologie und die jüdisch-hellenistische Religionsgeschichte* [2nd ed.; Tübingen: Mohr-Siebeck, 1977], pp. 39−40). Paul is probably appropriating a Hellenistic-Jewish topos that views Abraham as the prototypical proselyte to Judaism when, as an idolatrous polytheist, he suddenly recognized God as the Creator-Father of all mankind and was then adopted by God in a more particular and personal sense (cf. J. SCOTT, *Adoption as Sons of God: An Exegetical Investigation into the Background of ΥΙΟΘΕΣΙΑ in the Pauline Corpus* [WUNT 2.48; Tübingen: Mohr-Siebeck, 1992], pp. 88−96). In this way, Judaism sought to give credence to the unity of humanity as a point of contact with the pagan world and still hold to the election of Israel (cf., e.g., Josephus *Ant.* 2.94, which views "all men" as equal "by virtue of their kinship" [κατὰ συγγένειαν]). Even in his own letters, Paul considers God "the Father, from whom are all things" (1 Cor 8:6). Cf. Hans CONZELMANN, "The Address of Paul on the Areopagus," in *Studies in Luke-Acts: Essays Presented in Honor of Paul Schubert* (ed. Leander E. Keck and J. Louis Martyn; Nashville/ New York: Abingdon, 1966), pp. 217−230 (here p. 221): "After the *biblical* coloring of vss. 24−25, Stoic color dominates vss. 26−28. But the same motifs without exception can be found within Hellenistic Judaism (including the quotation of Aratus in v. 28! [Aristobulus frg. 4 in Eusebius *Praep. Evang.* XIII, 12, 3 ff.])."

[202] Cf. B. GÄRTNER, *Areopagus Speech*, p. 40 (also pp. 248−252): "As a rule the speech is attributed to Luke, and is thought to breathe his theology rather than Paul's."

[203] For example, Helga BOTERMANN ("Der Heidenapostel und sein Historiker. Zur historischen Kritik der Apostelgeschichte," *TBei* 24 [1993] 62−84) argues that Paul conducted his mission through the synagogue, where he had contact with Jews and God-fearers, who would have had the background to understand his message. She goes so far as to stress, however, that Luke himself is responsible for portraying the early Christian mission as worldwide and for presenting Paul's mission as to the "Gentiles." "Aus den Gottesfürchtigen sind die 'Heiden' schlechthin geworden" (ibid., p. 84). For BOTERMANN, the climax of this universalistic Lukan portrayal comes in the un-Pauline Areopagus speech (ibid., p. 84).

[204] According to Acts 13:19, Paul's speech at Pisidian Antioch also contains a reference to "nations" that goes back ultimately to the Table-of-Nations tradition: the "seven nations" (ἔθνη ἑπτά) that God destroyed in the land of Canaan (Deut 7:1; cf. Gen 10:15−18). On the other hand, in light of the citation of Aratus' *Phaenomena* in Acts 17:28, we may ask whether the mention of "allotted periods" and "boundaries of their habitation" in v. 26 presupposes the widely influential celestial globe of Eudoxus, for Aratus' frequently copied *Phaenomena* is a verse rendering of Eudoxus' work by the same name, which was written to accompany his globe and to facilitate its interpretation (cf. J. B. HARLEY and David WOODWARD, *The History of Cartography, Vol. 1: Cartography in Prehistoric, Ancient, and Medieval Europe and the Mediterranean* [Chicago: University of Chicago, 1987], pp. 141−143, 164−165).

What is particularly interesting about Paul's speech on the Areopagus is that his allusion to the Table of Nations and Deut 32:8 comes in the context of his preaching to the Gentiles during the Second Missionary Journey, that is, in the time after the Apostolic Council. Although Luke's portrayal of the Council in Acts 15 does not mention a division of territorial jurisdictions among the apostles, the corresponding passage in Galatians (2:7−9) does.

Conclusion

We have seen evidence in Paul's letters and in Acts that the Apostle to the nations had a missionary strategy based on the Table of Nations. The earliest evidence of this tradition is found in Galatians. In Gal 3:8, Paul traces the gospel back to the promise in Gen 12:3 (+ 18:18), that all the nations of the earth – i.e., all the nations in the Table of Nations of Genesis 10 – will be blessed in Abraham and his seed. Hence, it is not surprising that the Table-of-Nations tradition becomes part of Paul's missionary message (cf. Acts 17:26). The missionary strategy that results from this understanding of the gospel can be seen in the outcome of the so-called Apostolic Council in Gal 2:7−9, where the apostles agree to observe territorial jurisdictions in their respective missions, probably drawn along the lines of the sons of Noah in the Table of Nations. The book of Acts also seems to be structured along these lines.

After the Apostolic Council, territoriality becomes an increasingly important factor for the Pauline mission. On the one hand, it focuses the scope and direction of Paul's mission on reaching Asia Minor and Europe even as it maintains his orientation on the center, Jerusalem. This is seen most clearly in Romans 15, where Paul describes his mission to the "nations" as proceeding from Jerusalem and – "in a circle" (καὶ κύκλῳ) – extending to date as far as Illyricum (15:19b; cf. also 2 Cor 10:13−14). The expression "in a circle" can be explained in terms of Ezek 5:5, which states that God has set Jerusalem "in the middle of the nations (ἐν μέσῳ τῶν ἐθνῶν) and the countries in a circle (κύκλῳ) around her." Furthermore, when Paul announces his plans to continue his mission as far as Spain (Rom 15:24, 28; cf. 2 Cor 10:16), he thereby unveils the full scope and direction of his mission. The Apostle has evidently focused his mission on the territory of the Japhethites, that is, of the descendants of the third son of Noah who settled in the region of Asia Minor and Europe from Cilicia to Spain.[205] Acts presents the scope and direction of Paul's mission in much the same light – a mission radiating out from Jerusalem "to the ends of the

---

[205] The Japhethite territory with which Paul is concerned corresponds approximately to the contemporary Roman Empire, the realm of the Kittim. Hence, W.M. Ramsay's concept of Paul as a strategist intent on taking the gospel to the Roman Empire seems more plausible than W.D. Davies' opposing notion of an "a-territorial," universal Pauline mission (*The Gospel and the Land: Early Christianity and Jewish Territorial Doctrine* [Berkeley: University of California Press, 1974], pp. 180−182, 375).

earth" (cf. Acts 1:8; 13:47), concentrating on Asia Minor and Europe, and complementing the missions to Shem (2:1–8:25) and Ham (8:26–40). Thus, the geographical orientation of the Table-of-Nations tradition provides a fundamental point of departure for comparing the Paul of the letters and the Paul of Acts.[206]

On the other hand, after the Apostolic Council, territoriality becomes an increasingly important factor for the Pauline mission insofar as Paul now has a strong sense of his own territorial jurisdiction vis-à-vis that of others (2 Cor 10:13–16). Paul wants to do pioneering missionary work and not to build on another's foundation (2 Cor 10:15; Rom 15:20) although all churches in his jurisdiction, whether founded by him or not, stand under his authority (cf. Rom 1:5–6). Paul does not infringe on the territory of the Jerusalem apostles, and he expects that they (and/or their emissaries) will not infringe on his. When it happens, however, that despite the Jerusalem accord, the pillar apostles (and/ or their emissaries) violate Paul's jurisdiction by coming into his territory and tampering with the gospel or calling his apostleship into question, Paul does not hesitate to respond either offensively (Gal 2:11–14) or defensively (2 Cor 10:13–16). For Paul, such actions are an attempt to usurp his territory and to undermine his mission.

---

[206] See also the use of Isa 49:5–6 both in Paul's own letters (Gal 1:15–16) and in Acts (13:47).

Chapter 4

The Table of Nations and the Destination of Galatians

Introduction

So far, we have gained an overview of Paul's mission to the nations from the perspective of the Table-of-Nations tradition, that is, the OT and Jewish conception of world geography and ethnography. From Rom 15:19, we have been able to see that the scope of Paul's mission is limited primarily to the territory of the Japhethites. Even the direction of Paul's mission to the ἔθνη seems to retrace the steps of the original migration of the Japhethites from Cilicia to Spain. Furthermore, the official Roman provincial nomenclature that Paul often uses in this regard is probably based on the Table-of-Nations tradition, which updates the names of peoples and countries in Genesis 10 in terms of their equivalent Roman provinces.

The purpose of this chapter is to explore the implications of Paul's use of the Table-of-Nations tradition for the North and South Galatian Hypotheses. The crucial question in this debate has been: Who may be addressed as "Galatians" in Paul's day? Our considerations will add a whole new dimension to this debate, as we examine the question not only from a Greco-Roman perspective but also from an OT and Jewish point of view. In order to set the stage, we begin our discussion with a survey of the history of Galatia and its people.

The History of Galatia and the Galatians

When considering the identity of the Galatian addressees, particularly from a Hellenistic-Jewish perspective, it is helpful to recall the basic contours of the history of Galatia and the Galatians. Our survey encompasses the period from the Phrygian Empire to the Roman Empire, for, as we shall see, Jewish tradition based on the Table of Nations compresses this history, based on the assumption that at most only the names of nations have changed in the course of time. From this perspective, the ethnography of the eternally viable Table of Nations remains relatively constant.

The Phrygians

The Phrygians, regarded by Herodotus (2.2) in the fifth century B.C. as the most ancient of all nations, migrated from Macedonia and Thrace in the twelfth century B.C., flowed over most of the western Anatolian plateau, and displaced the Hittites as the dominant power in central Asia Minor.[1] The earliest settlement of the Phrygians may be by the Mygdones, the tribe of the eponymous Phrygian hero Mygdon, who traditionally lived around Lake Ascania, by Nicea. The southern limit of the Phrygians' conquest is obscure, but it is worth noting that another Lake Ascania is found in Pisidia near Sagalassus, north of which was located the tomb of Mygdon, on the road running south towards Lycia.

The ultimate Phrygian Empire was probably a federation of several tribes with both western and eastern elements. The Phrygians seem to have represented the western element, with their capital at Gordium (approx. 50 miles southwest of Ancyra). At Gordium, the Phrygian kings bore the alternate dynastic names Midas and Gordios. The situation of Gordium, commanding the trade routes between the Hellespont and the Cilician Gates, was symbolized in the famous "Gordian knot": Whoever untied it would control all Asia Minor. The eastern element of the federation was formed both by Mushki (biblical Meshech),[2] with its capital at Mazaca,[3] and by Tabal (biblical Tubal).[4]

The Cimmerians

The power of Phrygia was broken by the Cimmerians (biblical Gomer; Akkadian *Gimmirai*),[5] who invaded from the Russian steppes in 714 B.C.[6] Herodotus (4.11−13) relates that the Cimmerians were driven south over the

---

[1] Cf. R.D. BARNETT, "Phrygia and the Peoples of Anatolia in the Iron Age," in *The Cambridge Ancient History, Vol. II.2: History of the Middle East and the Aegean Region c. 1390−1000 B.C.* (3rd ed.; ed. I.E.S. Edwards, et al.; Cambridge: Cambridge University Press, 1975), pp. 417−442 (here pp. 417−426); Peter CARRINGTON, "The Heroic Age of Phrygia in Ancient Literature and Art," *Anatolian Studies* 27 (1977) 117−126. For a revision of this history, see now Gertrud LAMINGER-PASCHER, "Lykaonien und die Ostgrenze Phrygiens," *Epigraphica Anatolica* 1 (1990) 1−13. For a comprehensive treatment of the matters discussed in the present chapter, see now Stephen MITCHELL, *Anatolia: Land, Men, and Gods in Asia Minor* (2 vols.; Oxford: Clarendon, 1993).

[2] Meshech: Gen 10:2; 1 Chr 1:5; Ezek 27:13; 32:26; 38:2, 3; 39:1.

[3] Cf. Josephus *Ant.* 1.125.

[4] Tubal: Gen 10:2; 1 Chr 1:5; Isa 66:19; Ezek 27:13; 32:26; 38:2−3; 39:1.

[5] Gomer: Gen 10:2−3; 1 Chr 1:5−6; Ezek 38:6.

[6] Cf. Ashold I. IVANTCHIK, *Les Cimmeriens au Proche-Orient* (OBO 127; Fribourg: Éditions Universitaires Fribourg Suisse; Göttingen: Vandenhoeck & Ruprecht, 1993); A. KAMMENHUBER, "Kimmerier," *Reallexikon der Assyriologie und vorderasiatischen Archäologie*, 5 (1980): 594−596. Although the Assyrians distinguished between the Cimmerians and the Scythians, later texts of the Neo-Babylonians and Persians (6th-5th centuries B.C.) use the term *Gimmirai* also for the Scythians. Biblical Ashkenaz (Gen 10:3; 1 Chr 1:6; Jer 51:27) is known in nonbiblical sources as the Scythians (Akkadian *Ishkuza*; Greek Σκύθης).

Caucasus by the Scythians (biblical Ashkenaz)[7] as the Scythians themselves were being pushed westward by other tribes.

The Cimmerians swept into eastern and central Anatolia. According to classical sources, they seized the Greek colony of Sinope on the north shore of Anatolia. In ca. 676 B.C., they destroyed Gordium, the Phrygian capital of the legendary Midas. According to Strabo, Midas so despaired at the defeat that he committed suicide by drinking bull's blood (*Geogr.* 1.61). The chief effect of the Cimmerian invasion, which terrorized Asia Minor for eighty years, was to destroy the Phrygian Empire, the heart of which they appear to have occupied.

Gen 10:3 presents Gomer, the oldest son of Japheth and grandson of Noah, as the father of Ashkenaz, Riphath, and Togarmah. Ezek 38:2–6 pictures Gomer's descendants, including Togarmah, as being allied in support of Gomer's brothers, Magog, Meshech, and Tubal. They are to be defeated as part of God's judgment on Gog, the king of Magog.

The Persians

When the Cimmerian invasion receded, Lydia (biblical Lud), with its capital at Sardis, emerged as the leading Anatolian power, extending its dominion over Phrygia as far east as the Halys River. From then on, Phrygia was subject to one imperial power after another – to the Persians after Cyrus' overthrow of the Lydian Croesus in 546 B.C. and to the Macedonians after Alexander's conquest of Asia Minor in 333 B.C.

Under the Persian Empire, Phrygia was divided into two satrapies, Greater Phrygia and Lesser – or Hellespontine – Phrygia.[8] The dimensions of this realm are provided by the itinerary of Cyrus II, who in 401 B.C. led his army of Greeks east from Sardis in his bid to seize the Persian throne from his brother Artaxerxes II (Xenophon *An.* 1.20.6–19). Here is a summary of their route through Phrygia:

> They crossed the Maeander from Lydia into Phrygia; then one day's march of 24 miles took them through Phrygia to Colossae, "a large and prosperous city." From there, a three days' march of 60 miles took them to Celaenae, where Cyrus was joined by reinforcements from other parts of the Greek world. Then they advanced to Peltae (a two days' march of 30 miles to the northwest), to Potters' Market (a two days' march of 36 miles), and to Cayster Plain (a three days' march of 60 miles). A two day's march from there (30 miles) took them to Thymbrion, where there was a fountain named after Midas. Another two days' march of 30 miles took them to Tyriaion, from which a three days' march of 60 miles took them to "Iconium, the last city of Phrygia." Upon leaving Iconium, they crossed from Phrygia into Lycaonia.

---

[7] Ashkenaz: Gen 10:3; 1 Chr 1:6; Jer 51:27.

[8] On the subdivisions of Phrygia, see further below.

Alexander and the Diodochoi

Alexander the Great also passed through Phrygia, on his way from the Granicus in northwest Mysia to Issus in southwest Cilicia (334−333 B.C.). Having reached Pamphylia, Alexander and his army set out northward through what would later be called the province of Galatia (Arrian *Anab.* 1.26.1−2.4.1).[9] Beginning at Perga (1.27.5), Alexander marched past Telmissus (= Termessus? [1.27.5]) and Sagalassus (1.28.2) in Pisidia, past Lake Ascania (1.29.1), past Celaenae (1.29.1), which later became Apamea, to Gordium (1.29.3; 2.3.1) and Ancyra (2.4.1).[10] It was at Gordium in 333 B.C. that Alexander is said to have ensured his mastery over Asia Minor by "cutting the Gordian knot."

After Alexander's death (323 B.C.), Antigonus, his governor of Phrygia, was proclaimed king by his army; but Ptolemy and Seleucus, with Lysimachus of Thrace and Cassander of Macedonia, allied themselves against him and killed him at the battle of Ipsus in central Phrygia (301 B.C.). Lysimachus then gained control of Asia Minor but soon lost most of it, including Phrygia, to Seleucus.

The Gauls and the Galatians

In 278/277 B.C., three tribes of migrant Gauls (Γαλάται) from Europe crossed the Hellespont[11] into Asia Minor at the request of the king of Bithynia, who hoped to use them as mercenaries against his enemies.[12] For more than a generation, these Gauls, who are sometimes called οἱ ἐν 'Ασίᾳ Γαλάται[13] or οἱ Γαλλογραικοί[14] to distinguish them from their relatives in the West but most often simply Γαλάται,[15] menaced their neighbors in Asia Minor[16] until a series

---

[9] Cf. Barbara LEVICK, *Roman Colonies in Southern Asia Minor* (Oxford: Clarendon Press, 1967), pp. 12, 15.

[10] For details on Alexander's expeditions, see William W. TARN, *Alexander the Great* (2 vols.; Cambridge: Cambridge University Press; New York: Macmillan, 1948).

[11] *Sib. Or.* 3.508−511 describes an earlier phase of this same migration, the Gaulic invasion of Thrace in 280 B.C.: "Woe to you, Thrace, how you will come to a yoke of slavery! When the Gauls (Γαλάται) mingled with Dardanidae ravage Greece with a swoop, then will evil come upon you."

[12] Cf. Felix STÄHELIN, *Geschichte der kleinasiatischen Galater* (2nd ed.; Stuttgart: Teubner, 1907; reprint ed., Osnabrück: Zeller, 1973), pp. 6−7; H.D. RANKIN, "The Galatians," in *Celts and the Classical World* (London: Croom Helm, 1987), pp. 188−207; Franz FISCHER, "Die Ethnogenese der Kelten aus der Sicht der Vor- und Frühgeschichte," in *Ethnogenese europäischer Völker aus der Sicht der Anthropologie und Vor- und Frühgeschichte* (ed. Wolfram Bernhard and Anneliese Kandler-Pálsson; Stuttgart/New York: Fischer, 1986), pp. 209−224.

[13] Polybius *Hist.* 21.38.1; Plutarch *Mor.* 258 E − F. See further n. 136 below.

[14] Cf. Appian *Mithrid.* 560 (114): "He made Deiotarus and others tetrarchs of the Gallogrecians (Γαλλογραικοί), who are now the Galatians (Γαλάται) bordering on Cappadocia."

[15] This leads, of course, to the problem of equivocation in some texts. See below on 1 Macc 2:8.

[16] On the extent of the Galatian plundering, see now Andreas MÜLLER-KARPE, "Neue

of defeats at the hands of Attalus I, king of Pergamum, confined them to the territory that had formerly been northeastern Phrygia but that was afterwards known as Γαλατία (232 B. C.). Their territory was organized on the Celtic tribal basis. The three tribes – the Tolistobogii, Tectosages, and the Trocmi – occupied separate areas around their respective capitals (i.e., Pessinus, Ancyra, and Tavium), each tribe being divided into four parts under tetrarchs.

The occasion for the ascendancy of Attalus I over the Galatians was the so-called "War of the Brothers," between Seleucus II, the legitimate king of the Seleucid Empire, and his brother Antiochus Hierax, who was supported mainly by Galatian mercenaries (240/39 – *c.* 237 B. C.).[17] In antiquity, the Galatians were known as mighty warriors[18] and were therefore often used as mercenaries.[19] In 240 or 239 B. C., Seleucus suffered a crushing defeat at the hands of his brother near Ancyra, which gave Antiochus Hierax the sovereignty over Asia Minor. Thereupon, Antiochus allied with the Galatians and attacked Attalus. In the course of several battles, Antiochus was defeated, and the Galatians succumbed to the Pergamene troops. As a consequence, Attalus took the title of king and received the cognomen Soter (Savior). The Attalids celebrated the containment of the Gauls to central Anatolia as a victory of Hellenic civilization over barbarism. This is seen particularly in the famous representations of the victories over the Gauls in Pergamene art.[20] In the sacred enclosure of the Pergamene city goddess, Athene, Attalus had works of sculpture (e.g., the statue of the Dying Gaul) erected that were intended to portray Pergamum as a center of Hellenistic culture and Attalus himself as its champion against the barbarians. (According to Jewish tradition based on Ezek 38:2–6, it was actually Alexander the Great who had shut the fearsome descendants of Japheth behind iron gates until the end of time.)[21]

---

galatische Funde aus Anatolien," *Istanbuler Mitteilungen des deutschen Archäologischen Instituts* 38 (1988) 189–199. On the ethnography and settlement of the Anatolian Celts, see now MITCHELL, *Anatolia*, 1:42–58.

[17] Cf. H. HEINEN, "The Syrian-Egyptian Wars and the new kingdoms of Asia Minor," in *The Cambridge Ancient History* (8 vols; 2nd ed.; ed. F. W. Walbank, et al.; Cambridge: Cambridge University Press, 1984), 7.1:412–445 (here pp. 428–432); François CHAMOUX, "Pergame et les Galates," *Revue des Études Grecques* 101 (1988) 492–500.

[18] Cf. Appian *Syr.* 22.4 [6]; Lucian *Dial.* 13.1; Polybius *Hist.* 22.21.4.

[19] M. LAUNEY, *Recherches sur les armées hellénistiques* (2 vols.; Paris: de Boccard, 1949–50), 1:490–534.

[20] Cf. HEINEN, "The Syrian-Egyptian Wars and the new kingdoms of Asia Minor," pp. 423–424, 431.

[21] Cf. Josephus *BJ* 7.245; Helmut van THIEL, *Leben und Taten Alexanders von Makedonien. Der griechischen Alexanderroman nach der Handschrift L* (Texte zur Forschung 13; Darmstadt: Wissenschaftliche Buchgesellschaft, 1983), pp. 248–251; Bernhard HELLER, "Gog und Magog im jüdischen Schrifttum," in *Jewish Studies in Memory of George A. Kohut 1874–1933* (ed. Salo W. Baron and Alexander Marx; New York: The Alexander Kohut Memorial Foundation, 1935), pp. 350–368 (here 351–353); Friedrich PFISTER, "Studien zur Sagengeographie," *SO* 35 (1959) 5–39 (esp. 22–28); idem, *Alexander der Grosse in den Offenbarungen der Griechen, Juden, Mohammedaner und Christen* (Deutsche Akademie der Wissenschaften zu Berlin: Schriften der Sektion für Altertumswissenschaft 3; Berlin:

The Galatians retained their independence and enjoyed a resurgence in the first century B.C., when their leaders proved to be stalwart allies of Rome in the wars against Mithridates VI of Pontus (95—63 B.C.).[22] They were rewarded with important territorial grants by Pompey and Mark Antony between 63 and 36 B.C. At the beginning of the principate of the emperor Augustus, a single Galatian ruler, Amyntas, controlled the whole of central Anatolia, and his kingdom even reached to the Mediterranean. During this period, the Galatians retained much of their traditional Celtic culture: They spoke a Celtic dialect that survived in rural areas at least until the fourth century A.D.[23]; Celtic personal and place names are widely present[24]; and they had a distinctive Celtic form of religious and political organization.[25]

The Roman Province of Galatia

When Amyntas fell in battle in 25 B.C., his expanded kingdom became the Roman province of Galatia, governed directly by a Roman legate.[26] At this date, the province included the following: the original area of Galatian settle-

---

Akademie-Verlag, 1956), pp. 30—31. See further *Sib. Or.* 3:319—322, 508—513; *1 Enoch* 56:5; Str-B, 3:831—840.

[22] In the third war between Rome and Mithradates, Galatian auxiliaries distinguished themselves by almost capturing Mithradates himself and then by assisting Lucullus against Tigranes. For these and other accomplishments, the Romans granted Deiotarus kingship over Galatia, thus transforming Galatia from a tribal society to a kingdom.

[23] Cf. Johann SOFER, "Das Hieronymuszeugnis über die Sprachen der Galater und Treverer," *Wiener Studien* 55 (1937) 148—158; Rüdiger SCHMITT, "Die Sprachverhältnisse in den östlichen Provinzen des römischen Reiches," in *ANRW* II.29.2 (ed. Wolfgang Haase; Berlin: de Gruyter, 1983), pp. 554—586 (here pp. 567—568).

[24] Cf., e.g., Stephen MITCHELL, *Regional Epigraphic Catalogues of Asia Minor, Vol. 2: The Ankara District. The Inscriptions of North Galatia* (BAR International Series 135.4; Ankara: Oxford British Institute of Archaeology at Ankara, 1982), nos. 191, 296, 346, 362, 498; idem, "Population and the Land in Roman Galatia," in *ANRW* II.7.2 (ed. Hildegard Temporini; Berlin: de Gruyter, 1980), pp. 1053—1081 (here pp. 1058—1060).

[25] Cf., e.g., Richard D. SULLIVAN, "Priesthoods of the Eastern Dynastic Aristocracy," in *Studien zur Religion und Kultur Kleinasiens. Festschrift für Friedrich Karl Dörner zum 65. Geburtstag am 28. Februar 1976* (2 vols.; ed. Sencer Sahin, et al.; EPRO 66; Leiden: E.J. Brill, 1978), pp. 914—939 (930—934).

[26] Cf. Robert K. SHERK, "Roman Galatia: The Governors from 25 B.C. to A.D. 114," in *ANRW* II.7.2 (ed. Hildegard Temporini; Berlin: de Gruyter, 1980), 954—1052 (here pp. 955—963). See further Bernard RÉMY, *Les fastes sénatoriaux des provinces Romains d'Anatolie au Haut-Empire (31 av. J.-C. — 284 ap. J.C.) (Pont-Bithynie, Galatie, Cappadoce, Lycie-Pamphylie et Cilicie)* (Institut Français d'Études Anatoliennes; Paris: Éditions Recherche sur les Civilisations, 1988), pp. 95—118; idem, *Les carrières sénatoriales dans les provinces Romaines d'Anatolie au Haut-Empire (31 av. J.-C. - 284 ap. J. C.) (Pont-Bithynie, Galatie, Cappadoce, Lycie-Pamphylie et Cilicie)* (Varia Anatolica 2; Istanbul/Paris: Institut Français d'Études Anatoliennes et Éditions Divit, 1989), pp. 127—151; Gerd R. STUMPF, *Numismatische Studien zur Chronologie der römischen Statthalter in Kleinasien (122 v. Chr. — 163 n. Chr.)* (Saarbrücker Studien zur Archäologie und Alten Geschichte 4; Saarbrücken: Saarbrücker Druckerei und Verlag, 1991), pp. 125—131, 166—170, 217—225. See now esp. MITCHELL, *Anatolia*, 1:59ff.

ment around Ancyra; ancient Ancyra itself, which was henceforth the chief provincial city; the central Anatolian plateau of East Phrygia and Lycaonia; the mixed Pisido-Phrygian area around Pisidian Antioch and Apollonia; the mountainous tribal region of Isauria and Pisidia; and the Pamphylian plain. This vast and diverse area was further enlarged between 6 B.C. and A.D. 64 by the addition of Paphlagonia to the north (6/5 B.C.) and the Pontic regions to the northeast (Pontus Galaticus in 3–2 B.C. and Pontus Polemoniacus in A.D. 64).[27]

Previous Research on the Destination of Galatians

The foregoing survey sets the historical context for answering the question of the destination of Galatians. The two main answers have been the so-called "North Galatian Hypothesis" and the "South Galatian hypothesis." Again, the fundamental question is one of usage: Who may be called a Galatian in Paul's day? From the answer to this question comes two very different historical reconstructions.

The North Galatian Hypothesis

The Question of Usage. Proponents of the North Galatian Hypothesis argue that, in Paul's day, "Galatians" properly applied only to the ethnic Galatians of North Galatia, that is, the original three tribes who settled in Phrygian territory.[28] The support for this position is often sought by the negation of the central tenets of South Galatian Hypothesis. Thus, Hans HÜBNER writes: "Für die Landschaftshypothese sprechen vor allem folgende Gründe: Der südliche Teil der Provinz wird im 'zeitgenössischen Sprachgebrauch' ... nicht Galatien genannt, ebensowenig deren Bewohner Galater. Undenkbar ist, daß Paulus 3,1 etwa Pisidier oder Lykaonier als 'dumme Galater' angeredet hätte."[29] The question of usage, then, becomes the crucial factor in this debate. Proponents of the North Galatian Hypothesis emphasize that the Roman province was not called "Galatia" but rather that "Galatia" constitutes only one part of the whole. Appeal is made to inscriptions that list "Galatia" as a component territory within the province, albeit, as the seat of government, the most important territory.[30]

---

[27] Cf. B. RÉMY, *L'évolution administrative de l'Anatolie aux trois premiers siècles de notre ère* (Collection du Centre d'Études Romaines et Gallo-Romaines N.S. 5; Lyon: Boccard, 1986), pp. 21–47, with a series of maps on the territorial accretion (pp. 22, 26, 31, 36, 38, 42, 44).

[28] Cf., e.g., Heinrich SCHLIER, *Der Brief an die Galater* (12th ed.; Kritisch-exegetischer Kommentar über das Neue Testament 7; Göttingen: Vandenhoeck & Ruprecht, 1962), pp. 15–16; Albrecht OEPKE, *Der Brief des Paulus an die Galater* (THKNT 9; Berlin: Evangelische Verlagsanstalt, 1979), p. 24; Franz MUßNER, *Der Galaterbrief* (4th ed.; HTKNT 9; Freiburg: Herder, 1981), p. 8.

[29] H. HÜBNER, "Galaterbrief," *TRE* 12 (1984) 6.

[30] For example, *CIL* 3.291 (= *Suppl.* 3.6818): *leg(atus) Aug(usti) pro pr(aetore) provinc(iae*

The Historical Reconstruction. If Paul's use of "Galatians" refers only to the North Galatians, then a certain historical reconstruction based primarily on the Book of Acts logically follows, for if the letter itself makes it clear that Paul founded the churches to which he is writing (cf. Gal 4:13–19), the question then becomes this: When did Paul found churches in North Galatia? Paul gives us little to go on in the letter itself.[31] On the basis of the Book of Acts, there is really only one recorded occasion on which Paul might have founded the churches of Galatia, that is, on the so-called Second Missionary Journey, in the period referred to in Acts 16:6, after Paul and his companions had been forbidden by the Spirit to preach the gospel in Asia. Yet even if that text means that Paul and the others went through "Phrygia and the Galatic region" in the sense of North Galatia,[32] there is still no explicit mention of his having founded any churches in that region.[33] This must be inferred from Acts 18:23, which presupposes that, by the beginning of Paul's Third Missionary Journey, the Apostle had made "disciples" in

---

or -*iarum*) *Gal(atiae) Pisi[d](iae) Phryg(iae) Luc(aoniae) Isaur(iae) Paphlag(oniae) Ponti [G]ala[t](ici) Ponti Polemonian(i) A[r]m(eniae)*; 3.6819. Also the Galatian milestones in *CIL* 3.312 and 318, both from the time of Domitian: *vias provinciarum Galatiae Cappadociae Ponti Pisidae Paphlagoniae Lycaoniae Armeniae Minoris.* See further Colin J. HEMER, *The Book of Acts in the Setting of Hellenistic History* (WUNT 49; Tübingen: Mohr-Siebeck, 1989), pp. 296–297.

[31] Very little weight can be put on the interpretation of τὸ πρότερον in Gal 4:13, whether "formerly" on his prior visit or on the first of two visits (Acts 16:6; 18:23). The use of τὸ πρότερον with εὐηγγελισάμην would seem to suggest the latter possibility since the verb εὐαγγελίζειν is normally used of the initial proclamation of the gospel (cf. Paul N. TARAZI, "The Addressees and the Purpose of Galatians," *Vladimir's Theological Quarterly* 33 [1989] 159–179).

[32] On the geographical difficulties with this view, see the discussion below. Travel between Ancyra and Antioch was extremely difficult: There was always the Sultan Dagh, the mountain range that divided Antioch from Iconium, to be circumvented or crossed (cf. LEVICK, *Roman Colonies in Southern Asia Minor*, pp. 121–123). Nevertheless, the route that the North Galatian Hypothesis postulates for Paul can be documented to some degree in ancient sources. The Roman consul Gnaeus Manlius may have taken a similar route: He and a company of ten legates "left Apamea [approx. 60 miles southwest of Antioch!] and proceeded toward the Hellespont, intending *on their way* (κατὰ τὴν πάροδον) to put matters in Galatia on a safe footing" (Polybius *Hist.* 21.45.12). This makes it sound as if Manlius made an even bigger detour to the northeast than that suggested by the North Galatian Hypothesis (see, however, the parallel passage in Livy 38.40.1: "Having published these treaties and decrees, Manlius with the ten legates and all the army set out for the Hellespont, *summoning thither the chiefs of the Gauls* [evocatis eo regulis Gallorum], and stated the terms on which they should observe peace with Eumenes…"). See also Arrian *Anab.* 1.26.1–2.4.1 (discussed above).

[33] On the attempt to infer the evangelization of North Galatia from the verb διῆλθον in Acts 16:6 (e.g., James MOFFATT, *An Introduction to the Literature of the New Testament* [3rd ed.; International Theological Library; Edinburgh: T. & T. Clark, 1918], p. 95; Rudolf PESCH, *Die Apostelgeschichte* [2 vols.; EKK 5; Zürich: Benziger Verlag; Neukirchen-Vluyn: Neukirchener Verlag, 1986], 2:100), see Rainer RIESNER, *Die Frühzeit des Apostels Paulus. Studien zur Chronologie, Missionsstrategie und Theologie* (WUNT 71; Tübingen: Mohr-Siebeck, 1994), pp. 250–251.

"the Galatian region and Phrygia," who now needed to be strengthened by another apostolic visit. Is there any other evidence for this hypothesis?

Possible Additional Evidence. While arguments based on supposed characteristics of ethnic Galatians may be safely ignored,[34] there are some other references in the letter that deserve brief notice as possible indications of a North Galatian destination of the letter. For example, the Sarah-Hagar Allegory in Gal 4:21–31, which is based in part on the story of Ishmael's birth in Genesis 16, has an interesting parallel in the North Galatian story of Stratonice in Plutarch's *Mulierum Virtutes* (*Mor.* 242E – 263C):

> Stratonice, well knowing that her husband desired children from her to succeed to the kingdom, but having no child herself, prevailed upon him to have a child by another woman, and to connive at its being passed off as her own. Deiotarus thought highly of the idea, and did everything in dependence on her judgment, and she procured a comely maiden from the prisoners, Electra by name, and sealed her to Deiotarus. The children that were born she brought up with loving care and in royal state as if they had been her own.[35]

Nevertheless, the parallel to Gen 16:1–6 seems superficial, especially since, unlike Sarah, Stratonice is said to have accepted the child and to have raised it as her own.

Another possible indication of a North Galatian destination for the letter is the reference to castration in Gal 5:12: "I wish that those who disturb you would emasculate themselves!" The Phrygian cult of Magna Mater (Cybele) and Attis, whose center was in Pessinus of North Galatia, featured the so-called Galli (Γαvλλοι), the priests of Cybele who castrated themselves in frenzied

---

[34] Whereas J. B. LIGHTFOOT argued that Paul's characterization of his addressees points to a North Galatian destination of the letter (*Saint Paul's Epistle to the Galatians* [10th ed.; London: Macmillan, 1892], pp. 13–16), Stephen MITCHELL has recently argued that Paul's characterization of his addressees as "foolish" points to a South Galatian destination of the letter ("Galatia," *ABD*, 2 [1992] 870–872 [here p. 871]; cf., similarly, Heinz-Werner NEUDORFER, "Mehr Licht über Galatien?" *Jahrbuch für evangelikale Theologie* 5 [1991] 47–62 [here p. 61]). On this kind of argument, see F. F. BRUCE, "Galatian Problems, 2: North or South Galatians," *BJRL* 52 (1969–70) 243–266 (here pp. 249–250); RANKIN, *Celts and the Classical World*, p. 205. In any case, the evidence of the reputation of the Galatians seems to be mixed. On the one hand, the adjective Γαλατικός is used with ἄγριος and βάρβαρος in a negative sense (cf. Plutarch *Mor.* 1049B), and Galatians are often considered "lawless" barbarians (cf. Polybius *Hist.* 3.3.5; 21.40.1; *Anth. Gr.* 7.492; *Sib. Or.* 3:599–600). On the other hand, however, there is some evidence from antiquity that, as barbarians, the Galatians were well respected: "Yes, mourning is very feminine, and weak, and ignoble, since women are more given to it than men, and barbarians more than Greeks, and inferior men more than better; and of the barbarians themselves, not the most noble, Celts and Galatians (Κελτοὶ καὶ Γαλάται), and all who are filled with a more manly spirit, but rather, if such there are, the Egyptians and Syrians and Lydians and all those who are like them" (Plutarch *Mor.* 113A). HEMER provides evidence that "Γαλάτης was a widely used and honourable self-designation, that it was applicable to persons of Phrygian rather than Celtic origin, and that it corresponded rather generally to 'Galatia' in the shifting senses of that term" (*Acts*, pp. 304–305).

[35] Plutarch *Mor.* 258D.

worship of Cybele.[36] The prohibition of pork in Pessinus is linked with the same cult.[37] Is it possible, however, that Paul's sarcastic remark could be linked with Isa 56:4–5, where the eunuchs who keep the Law are promised privileges better than those of sons and daughters?

The South Galatian Hypothesis

The Question of Usage. Proponents of the South Galatian Hypothesis argue that, in Paul's day, Γαλάται applies not only to the North Galatians but to the whole heterogeneous population of the more extensive Roman province of Galatia.[38] Thus, anyone who resided within the confines of the province could legitimately be called a "Galatian." By the time Paul wrote his letter to the Galatians in the 50's, the Roman province of Galatia had been in existence for some 75 years, presumably enough time for the name "Galatians" to become well established in contemporary usage for the provincials. What evidence can be adduced in support of this contention?

First, there is adequate evidence that, by the first century at least, the province as a whole was called "Galatia." For example, an official honorary inscription of A.D. 54 from the Roman colony of Iconium,[39] on the border of Phrygia and Lycaonia in South Galatia, refers to L. Pupius Praesens as the "Procurator ... of the Galatian Province" (ἐπίτροπος ... Γαλατικῆς ἐπαρχείας).[40] We note here that the province is given a single name, without listing

---

[36] See further Garth THOMAS, "Magna Mater and Attis," in *ANRW* II.17.3 (ed. Wolfgang Haase; Berlin: de Gruyter, 1984), pp. 1500–1535 (here pp. 1504, 1510, 1512, 1525–1526, 1527); Giula Sfameni GASPARRO, *Soteriology and Mystic Aspects in the Cult of Cybele and Attis* (EPRO 103; Leiden: E.J. Brill, 1985), pp. 26–29, 56, 105–106.

[37] Cf. Pausanias 7.17.10, which explicitly mentions Attis.

[38] Cf., e.g., HEMER, *Acts*, pp. 277–307; Martin HENGEL, in the "Foreword" to Theodor ZAHN, *Der Brief des Paulus an die Galater* (3rd ed.; Kommentar zum Neuen Testament 9; Leipzig/Erlangen: Deitertsche Verlagsbuchhandlung, 1922; reprint ed., Wuppertal/Zürich: Brockhaus, 1990), pp. vi-vii; idem, *The Pre-Christian Paul* (London: SCM Press; Philadelphia: Trinity Press International, 1991), p. 11; Peter STUHLMACHER, *Biblische Theologie des Neuen Testaments, Bd. 1: Grundlegung. Von Jesus zu Paulus* (Göttingen: Vandenhoeck & Ruprecht, 1992), p. 226; F.F. BRUCE, *The Epistle to the Galatians: A Commentary on the Greek Text* (NIGTC; Grand Rapids: Eerdmans, 1982), pp. 3–18; idem, "Galatian Problems 2. North or South Galatians?" *BJRL* 52 (1969–70) 243–266; G. Walter HANSEN, "Galatia," in *The Book of Acts in Its First Century Setting, Vol. 2: The Book of Acts in Its Graeco-Roman Setting* (ed. David W.J. Gill and Conrad Gempf; Grand Rapids: Eerdmans; Carlisle: Paternoster, 1994), pp. 377–395 (here pp. 389–390).

[39] On Iconium as a Roman colony, see Stephen MITCHELL, "Iconium and Ninica," *Historia. Zeitschrift für alte Geschichte* 28 (1979) 409–438.

[40] *CIG* 3991: "The people of Claud[iconium] honored Lucius Pupius Praesens, son of Lucius, of the Sabatina Tribe, military tribune, prefect of the Picentine Calvary Squadron, Procurator of Caesar on the Tiber Banks, Procurator of Tiberius Claudius Caesar Augustus Germanicus and Nero Claudius Caesar Augustus Germanicus of the province of Galatia, their benefactor and founder."

the component territories.[41] Likewise, an undated Latin inscription from Ephesus refers to C. Rutilius Gallicus, the governor of Galatia from A.D. 56–64(?), as *legatus provinciae Galaticae* (ILS 9499).[42] There are many other indications that the province as a whole was called "Galatia,"[43] including the very likely possibility that the κοινὸν τῶν Γαλατῶν[44] or the κοινὸν Γαλατίας[45] – the assembly in charge of managing the imperial cult at the provincial level – was active in both North and South Galatia.[46] The geographer Claudius Ptolemaeus (ca. A.D. 90–168), who collected information from his predecessors, especially from Marinus of Tyre (fl. A.D. 100),[47] very precisely describes the borders of the various lands of the world.[48] In Book 5, which covers Asia Minor, Armenia, Cyprus, Syria, Palestine, Arabia Petraea, Mesopotamia, Arabia Deserta, and Babylonia, Ptolemy describes the borders of Galatia, with coordinates, as extending from Pontus in the north to Pamphylia in the south and from Bithynia and Asia on the west to Cappodocia on the east (*Geogr.* 5.4).[49] Within these borders, Ptolemy also gives an extensive list of the regions

---

[41] Despite C. G. BRANDIS, "Galatia," *PW*, 7 (1912) 519–559 (here cols. 555–556).

[42] Republished in Helmut ENGELMANN, eds., et al., *Die Inschriften von Ephesos, Teil III* (Inschriften Griechischer Städte aus Kleinasien 13; Bonn: Habelt, 1980), pp. 114–115 (no. 715). Cf. also *CIL* 3.254, from Ancyra: *Leg(atus) Augustorum pr(o) pr(aetore) provinc(iae) Galat(iae)*.

[43] Cf. HEMER, *Acts*, pp. 290–305.

[44] Cf., e.g., *IGRR* 3.157, of A.D. 14, the dedication of the Temple of Rome and Augustus at Ancyra.

[45] Cf., e.g., Warwick WROTH, *Catalogue of the Greek Coins of the British Museum: Catalogue of the Greek Coins of Galatia, Cappadocia, and Syria* (Bologna: Arnaldo Forni, 1964), pp. xviii, 5–7.

[46] Cf. Jürgen DEININGER, *Die Provinziallandtage der römischen Kaiserzeit von Augustus bis zum Ende des dritten Jahrhunderts n. Chr.* (München/Berlin: C.H. Beck'sche Verlagsbuchhandlung, 1965), pp. 68–69, 175; Stephen MITCHELL, "Galatia under Tiberius," *Chiron* (1986) 17–33 (here p. 31); Marc WAELKENS, "The Imperial Sanctuary at Pessinus: Archaeological, Epigraphical and Numismatic Evidence for its Date and Identification," *Epigraphica Anatolica* 7 (1986) 37–72 (here pp. 71–72). Note that three years after Paphlagonia was added to the Roman province of Galatia (6/5 B.C.), the inhabitants of Paphlagonia swore an oath of allegiance to Augustus and his house (cf. SHERK, "Roman Galatia: The Governors from 25 B.C. to A.D. 114," pp. 960–961; idem, *Rome and the Greek East to the Death of Augustus* [Cambridge: Cambridge University Press, 1984], pp. 135–136). Perhaps this provides additonal evidence of the activity of the Koinon of the Galatians, working to consolidate and Romanize the province by means of propagating the imperial cult (cf. Peter HERRMANN, *Der römische Kaisereid. Untersuchungen zu seiner Herkunft und Entwicklung* [Hypomnemata 20; Göttingen: Vandenhoeck & Ruprecht, 1968], pp. 96–99). A similar oath of allegiance in the Augustan period, which like the oath of the Pamphlagonians applied to a whole territory, was the oath that Herod made the Jews swear in ca. 6 B.C. (Josephus *Ant.* 17.42; cf. 15.368).

[47] Cf. Ptolemy *Geogr.* 1.6–7.

[48] See further Wilhelm KUBITSCHEK, *Studien zur Geographie des Ptolemäus, I: Die Ländergrenzen* (οἱ περιορισμοί) (Akademie der Wissenschaften in Wien, Philosophisch-historische Klasse, Sitzungsberichte 215.5; Wien/Leipzig: Hölder-Pichler-Tempsky, 1934), pp. 94–95.

[49] One of the ancient maps based on Ptolemy's *Geographica*, attributed to Agathodaemon of Alexandria (biographical dates unknown), clearly shows these borders of Galatia and includes Pisidian Antioch, among other South Galatian cities, within them (see the reproduc-

and cities of Galatia, including many from the southern part of the province.[50] Hence, both in official and popular usage, the name of the province was generally known as "Galatia."[51]

Far less certain is, second, that the name "Galatian" was applied not just to the inhabitants of North Galatia but to those of South Galatia as well. On the one hand, it could be argued that all residents of the Roman province of "Galatia" should be called "Galatians" and that, pragmatically speaking, this is the only comprehensive term that was available to Paul to address such a heterogeneous group of people as were found in the churches of Galatia.[52] On the other hand, however, evidence of this usage of Γαλάται in reference to the South Galatians is surprisingly sparse and controvertible. Only four possible examples have so far been adduced. In an inscription of A. D. 222, a man from Apollonia thanks Zeus for bringing him back safely "to my home in the land of the Galatians" (καὶ Γαλατῶν γαίης ἤγαγες ἐς πατρίδα).[53] Upon closer examination, however, this example fails to demonstrate a broader usage of Γαλάτης, for the inscription itself reveals a special relationship between the Apollonians and the Trocmi of North Galatia.[54] There is also evidence that Apollonia was reckoned to North Galatia rather than to South Galatia.[55] Another possible example of a broader use of "Galatians" comes from Tacitus: *simul Pontica et Galatarum Cappadocumque auxilia* (*Ann.* 15.6). If the three modifiers of *auxilia* indicate that the auxiliary troops were drawn from the three provinces of

---

tion in *Tübinger Atlas des Vorderen Orients* 10 [1985] BS1: Weltkarten der Antike 1.1: "Karten des Klaudios Ptolemaios"). Vetius Valens, an astrologer of the second century A.D., provides another approach to the integration of Galatia into the broader scheme of things. In his section on the "Twelve Signs of the Zodiac" in Book 1 of his *Anthologies*, the astrologer describes the κλίματα subjugated to Leo as follows: "At the head, Gaul (Κελτική) and the places under its control; the frontals, Bithynia; to the right, Macedonia and the places under its control; to the left, Propontis; at its feet, Galatia (Γαλατία); the abdomen, [Gaul]; at the shoulders, Thrace; to the sides, Phoenicia, the Adriatic Sea, Libya; in the middle, Phrygia (Φρυγία) and Syria; at the tail, Pessinus (Πισινοῦς)." For text, commentary, and translation, see Joëlle-Frédérique BARA, *Vettius Valens d'Antioche, Anthologies, Livre 1: Etablissement, traduction et commentaire* (EPRO 111; Leiden: Brill, 1989), p. 61.

[50] See further HEMER, *Acts*, pp. 294–295.

[51] Cf. Stephen MITCHELL, "Galatia," *ABD*, 2 (1992) 870–872 (here p. 871): "In the mid 1st century A.D. it was normal to refer to the whole province and not just the Celtic region as Galatia (Eutropius 7.10; *ILS* 9499; *IG Rom.* 3.263)."

[52] Cf. BRUCE, "Galatian Problems," pp. 263, 264; HENGEL, "Forward," p. VII; W.M. RAMSAY and C.J. HEMER, "Galatia," *ISBE*, 2 (1982) 377–379 (here p. 379).

[53] *MAMA* 4.140. The text is from the copies made in 1833 and 1850, when the stone was more complete. See further *Supplementum Epigraphicum Graecum* 30 (1980) 417.

[54] The local people are referred to as "the godly Trocmi." Cf. HEMER, *Acts*, p. 293, who suggests on the basis of this that Apollonia may have been incorporated into a structure based on that of the old Celtic tribes of the north. See further William M. CALDER, "Colonia Caesareia Antiocheia," *JRS* 2 (1912) 79–109 (here pp. 85–86).

[55] Cf. J. FRIEDRICH, "Phrygia," *PW* 20.1 (1941) 781–891 (here col. 803), who argues against W.M. Ramsay that Apollonia belongs to "Phrygia towards Pisidia" (South Galatia), maintaining instead that it belongs to "Greater Phrygia" (North Galatia).

Pontus, Galatia, and Cappadocia,[56] then genitive plural *Galatarum* ("of Galatians") could include South Galatians as well although that is not explicitly stated in the text. We must note, however, that "Galatians" were spoken of as being included among the Roman auxiliaries well before Galatia became a Roman province in 25 B.C.[57] An inscription of Pednelissus, on the border between Pisidia and Pamphylia, ascribed to the first century, appears to designate that city as ἡ πόλις Γαλατῶν.[58] Finally, in the temple in Ancyra built by the Koinon of the Galatians in the early Augustan period (ca. 25−20 B.C.),[59] an inscription was discovered − besides the *Res Gestae* − that contains a list of "those who are priests of the Galatians to the Divine Augustus and the Goddess Roma" ([Γα]λατῶν ο[ἱ] [ἱε]ρασάμενοι θεῶι Σεβαστῶι καὶ θεᾳ ῾Ρώμηι).[60] On the one hand, we might assume that "Galatians" refers here to all of the inhabitants of the province since, as we have seen, the Koinon operated throughout the Roman province of Galatia.[61] On the other hand, however, the inscription refers explicitly to "the three nations" (τὰ τρία ἔθνη),[62] that is, to the original three tribes of the ethnic Galatians.[63]

As C. HEMER himself admits at the conclusion of his extensive study of the terms "Galatia" and "Galatians," "The crucial difficulty in all this subject is in fact the matter of *usage*, and its difficulty puts a weapon into the hand of the objector."[64] However, we shall see further evidence below that will bolster the South Galatian Hypothesis at this very point.

---

[56] So MUßNER, *Galaterbrief*, p. 8, citing the authority of H. Bengston from personal correspondence. Note that these three provinces appear in the same order in the adscription of 1 Peter (1:1), presumably also referring to provinces in each case (cf. BRUCE, *Galatians*, p. 14, with n. 58).

[57] Cf. Cicero's letter to Atticus, dated 26 June 50 B.C.: "My army is weak − the auxiliaries are pretty good but are made up of Galatians, Pisidians, and Lycians (*Galatarum, Pisidarum, Lyciorum*); such is the backbone of my force" (*Att.* 6.5.3).

[58] HEMER, *Acts*, p. 301.

[59] Cf. Ronald MELLOR, "The Goddess Roma," in *ANRW* II.17.2 (ed. Wolfgang Haase; Berlin: de Gruyter, 1981), pp. 950−1030 (here pp. 979).

[60] Cf. Daniel KRENCKER and Martin SCHEDE, *Der Tempel in Ankara* (Archäologisches Institut des deutschen Reiches: Denkmäler antiker Architektur 3; Berlin/Leipzig: de Gruyter, 1936), p. 52 (col. II).

[61] Cf. Helmut HALFMANN, "Zur Datierung und Deutung der Priesterliste am Augustus-Roma-Tempel in Ankara," *Chiron* 16 (1986) 35−42 (here p. 41).

[62] Cf. KRENCKER and SCHEDE, *Der Tempel in Ankara*, p. 53 (col. IX).

[63] Cf. Strabo *Geogr.* 12.5.1, which refers to the three Galatian tribes − the Trocmi, the Tolistobogii and the Tectosages − as ἔθνη τρία.

[64] *Acts*, p. 306 [emphasis mine]. Even an ardent defender of the South Galatian Hypothesis and an expert on Anatolia like Stephen MITCHELL ("Galatia," *ABD*, 2 [1992] 870−872 [here p. 871]) must admit: "Certainly this word [sc. 'Galatians' in Gal 3:1] would not be a natural mode of address to the inhabitants of cities which had few if any Celtic inhabitants, but that is precisely the point. It is part of Paul's reproach to his correspondents that he equates them with the barbarous and unsophisticated people who had given their name to the province and who, throughout antiquity, had a quite independent reputation for simplemindedness." But see now MITCHELL, *Anatolia,* 2:4: ". . . in the mid-first century it was normal to refer to the whole province, quite simply, as Galatia [cf. Eutropius 7.10; *ILS* 9499; *IGR* 3.263]. Thus, in AD 50 it

Historical Reconstruction. If Γαλάται can be used of all inhabitants of the Roman province of Galatia, then the churches to which Paul addressed his letter could, theoretically, be located anywhere from Pontus on the Black Sea to Pamphylia on the Mediterranean. The usage of the term in itself would not be sufficient to narrow the field. The question then becomes this: Where did Paul found churches in provincial Galatia? The Book of Acts records that, on his so-called First Missionary Journey, Paul founded churches in several cities of South Galatia (Derbe, Lystra, Iconium, and Antioch).[65] If, as seen above, nothing concrete is known about his having founded churches in North Galatia, then these southern churches would be likely candidates as the Galatian addressees of Paul's letter.

How does the South Galatian Hypothesis deal with Acts 16:6? After the Apostolic Council (Acts 15:1−29), Paul and Barnabas wanted to return and visit the brethren "in every city" (κατὰ πόλιν πᾶσαν) where they had preached on the First Missionary Journey to see how they were doing (v. 36) and to deliver the Apostolic Decree (cf. 15:22; 16:4). Hence, after Paul and Barnabas broke up over the issue of Mark[66] and went their separate ways (vv. 37−39), Paul, together with Silas, departed for Asia Minor on the so-called Second Missionary Journey (Acts 15:40).[67] Proceeding from Syrian Antioch, they went through Syria and Cilicia (v. 41), and from there, through the Cilician Gates to the north of Tarsus, they came by means of the *Via Sebaste*[68] to the cities of Derbe and Lystra in the province of Galatia, where Paul had already been with Barnabas on his previous missionary journey (16:1a; cf. 14:20−21). In Lystra, the missionaries added Timothy to their entourage (vv. 1b-3).

The following verses (vv. 4−6) apparently provide a *summary* of the method and effects of Paul's ministry with Silas and Timothy in this area.[69] There are several indications that this section is a summary. First of all, up to this point in the narrative, nothing has been said about the ministry of Paul and his companions in the cities already named (i.e., Derbe, Lystra, and Iconium [vv. 1−2]) but only that Timothy was added to their company in Lystra. Therefore, τὰς πόλεις in v. 4 may well stand for all "the cities" with previously established

---

was as natural to refer to the churches of Antioch, Iconium, Lystra, and Derbe as churches of Galatia, as it was to call that of Corinth a church of Achaea."

[65] Cf. Acts 13:14; 14:1, 6, 21. On the route that Paul traveled, see David FRENCH, "Acts and the Roman Roads of Asia Minor," *The Book of Acts in Its Graeco-Roman Setting*, pp. 49−58 (here pp. 50−53, 55−56); HANSEN, "Galatia," pp. 384−385.

[66] As the incident at Antioch shows (Gal 2:11−14), the issue between Paul and Barnabas probably ran much deeper.

[67] On the route that Paul traveled, see FRENCH, "Acts and the Roman Roads of Asia Minor," pp. 53−54, 56, 57.

[68] On the *Via Sebaste*, see D. H. FRENCH, "The Roman Road-System of Asia Minor," in *ANRW* II.7.2 (ed. Hildegard Temporini; Berlin/New York: de Gruyter, 1980), pp. 698−729 (here pp. 707−708); idem, "Acts and the Roman Roads of Asia Minor," pp. 52−53; F. J. Foakes JACKSON and Kirsopp LAKE, *The Acts of the Apostles* (5 vols.; The Beginnings of Christianity 1; Grand Rapids: Baker, 1979), 5:225−226.

[69] V. 5 is often spoken of as a summary (cf., e.g., PESCH, *Apostelgeschichte*, 2:96).

churches that Paul and his companions visited in this area, including both those that have already been named and Pisidian Antioch, which was evangelized on the First Missionary Journey (cf. Acts 13:14–50) but is not explicitly mentioned in our text. Alternatively, the text may be referring just to the cities that Paul visited after leaving Lystra. Much depends on which cities are considered part of "the region of Phyrgia and Galatia" (see further below). Second, the series of imperfect verbs (διεπορεύοντο, ἐστερεοῦντο, ἐπερίσσευον) summarizes the travellers' normal procedure at this time and in this area – their going through the cities, with the result that the churches were being strengthened in the faith and were increasing in number daily.[70] The emphasis is on an overall process that took place in the past rather than on a certain itinerary. The immediately preceding context provides a closely parallel example of this use of the imperfect in a summary of Paul's mission: διήρχετο δὲ τὴν Συρίαν καὶ [τὴν] Κιλικίαν ἐπιστηρίζων τὰς ἐκκλησίας (Acts 15:41). Third, the account remains very general and sketchy, just like a summary. The cities that they went through are not named but are merely implied. The direction of travel is not mentioned although it would most likely be northwesterly. What happened in each place is ignored, except for the one triumphant outcome – the edification of the church.[71] As a summary, vv. 4ff. are not interested in the particulars about each place but in a general schema. Fourth, the section concludes in v. 6 by giving the general extent of their travels in this area: "And they went through the Phrygian and Galatic region, having been forbidden by the Holy Spirit to speak the word in Asia." Whereas the North Galatian Hypothesis takes v. 6 as signalling a departure into new territory to the north (i.e., the land of the three tribes of Galatia),[72] and the South Galatian Hypothesis usually explains the same verse as a continuation of Paul's travels from v. 1 (Derbe and Lystra) to the other cities (Iconium and Antioch),[73] we would like to suggest seeing v. 6 as part of the summary in vv. 4ff.[74] Thus, whereas v. 4 summarizes that they were "going *through*" (διεπορεύοντο) the cities, v. 6 recapitulates the general extent of the

---

[70] The use of the imperfect in such summaries is characteristic of Luke's style. Cf. Acts 2:47 (ὁ δὲ κύριος προσετίθει τοὺς σῳζομένους καθ' ἡμέραν ἐπὶ τὸ αὐτό); 6:7 (καὶ ὁ λόγος τοῦ θεοῦ ηὔξανεν, καὶ ἐπληθύνετο ὁ ἀριθμὸς τῶν μαθητῶν ἐν Ἰερουσαλὴμ σφόδρα, πολύς τε ὄχλος τῶν ἱερέων ὑπήκουον τῇ πίστει); 9:31 (ἡ μὲν οὖν ἐκκλησία ... εἶχεν εἰρήνην, ... καὶ ... ἐπληθύνετο); 12:24 (ὁ δὲ λόγος τοῦ θεοῦ ηὔξανεν καὶ ἐπληθύνετο); 13:49 (διεφέρετο δὲ ὁ λόγος τοῦ κυρίου δι' ὅλης τῆς χώρας); 14:28 (διέτριβον δὲ χρόνον οὐκ ὀλίγον σὺν τοῖς μαθηταῖς); 19:20 (οὕτως κατὰ κράτος τοῦ κυρίου ὁ λόγος ηὔξανεν καὶ ἴσχυεν).

[71] We are reminded of similar summaries in Acts (cf., e.g., 2:41–42, 43–47; 3:32–35). See the previous note.

[72] Cf., e.g., MOFFATT, *Introduction*, pp. 92–93.

[73] Cf. HEMER, *Acts*, pp. 282–283; RIESNER, *Frühzeit*, p. 253; BRUCE, "Galatian Problems," p. 258. But see Claus-Jürgen THORNTON, *Der Zeuge des Zeugen. Lukas als Historiker der Paulusreisen* (WUNT 56; Tübingen: Mohr-Siebeck, 1991), p. 88 n. 7: "If Iconium and Antioch were in view for the first time in 16:6, one would have to ask which cities were meant in 16:4."

[74] Cf. W. M. RAMSAY, *The Church in the Roman Empire before A. D. 170* (7th ed.; London: Hodder & Stoughton, 1903), p. 77; HEMER, *Acts*, p. 281.

territory that they actually "went *through*" (διῆλθον).[75] In other words, the process described in v. 4 is described as completed action in v. 6, and "the cities" of v. 4 are circumscribed, whether in whole or in part,[76] within a region in South Galatia. To which region does the text specifically refer?

The South Galatian Hypothesis argues that τὴν Φρυγίαν καὶ Γαλατικὴν χώραν in v. 6 signifies "the Phrygian and Galatian region" or, on the analogy of the well-attested Pontus Galatica, simply "Phrygia-Galatica." The single article before χώραν suggests that both Φρυγίαν and Γαλατικήν are to be taken as adjectival modifiers of the noun, forming together a unified concept.[77] HEMER provides examples of Φρυγία being used adjectivally.[78] What, then, is the evidence for a region of South Galatia called "Phrygia-Galatica"?

Excursus: The Subdivisions of Phrygia

Phrygia was originally a unified empire extending through much of Asia Minor, but at the end of the fifth century B. C. it was divided into two major regions: Lesser Phrygia (Φρυγία μικρά, also called Phrygia Epictetus and Phrygia Hellespontica)[79] in the northwest and Greater Phrygia to the south and east.[80] According to Strabo, Greater Phrygia (Φρυγία μεγάλη) itself was divided into three parts: the main part, called "Phrygia Paroreios" (ἡ Παρώρειος), consisting of the low ground along the north and the south of the Sultan Dagh mountain range running between Philomelion and "Anti-

---

[75] A similar case is found in Acts 14:24, where "having gone through Pisidia" concludes a passage concerning a visit to Pisidian Antioch.

[76] THORNTON objects that the South Galatian Hypothesis does not account for the fact that in Acts 13:14 and 14:24 Luke erroneously ascribes Antioch and Iconium to Pisidia ('Αντιόχεια ἡ Πισιδία) rather than to Phrygia, to which they really belong (*Der Zeuge des Zeugen*, p. 85 n. 4). This ignores, however, the complex issue of the changing political and ethnic subdivisions of Phrygia. The Roman colony of Antioch stood on the border between Phrygia and Pisidia. Strabo knew that it was only 'Αντιοχεία ἡ πρὸς τῇ Πισιδίᾳ (*Geogr.* 12.6.4). As LEVICK points out, however, Pisidia was a geographical concept that Augustus illegitimately extended after the formation of the province of Galatia to include certain southern colonies that were to be used in restraining the mountain tribes of Taurus, loosely called Pisidians (*The Roman Colonies in Southern Asia Minor*, pp. 33–38). On the ambiguous position of Iconium, see n. 85 below. On the position of Antioch, see HEMER, Acts, pp. 109, 201, 228; FRIEDRICH, "Phrygia," col. 793; RIESNER, *Frühzeit*, p. 243 n. 45.

[77] Cf. BURTON, *A Critical and Exegetical Commentary on the Epistle to the Galatians* (ICC; Edinburgh: T. & T. Clark, 1980), p. xxxi; LIGHTFOOT, *Galatians*, p. 22; BRUCE, "Galatian Problems," p. 255; HEMER, *Acts*, pp. 283–284; OEPKE, *Galater*, p. 25.

[78] Cf. HEMER, *Acts*, p. 283, with n. 21; G. H. R. HORSLEY, *New Documents Illustrating Early Christianity: A Review of the Greek Inscriptions and Papyri Published in 1979* (North Ryde, Australia: The Ancient History Documentary Research Centre, Macquarie University, 1987), p. 174.

[79] For example, the mention of Phrygia in Anthony's route as given in Appian *BCiv.* 5.7 ("Phrygia, Mysia, Galatia, Cappadocia, Cilicia, Syria Coele, Palestine …") would seem strangely out of place if we did not consider that "Phrygia" probably means "Phrygia Minor" in northwest Asia Minor.

[80] Cf. FRIEDRICH, "Phrygia," cols. 801–803.

ocheia towards Pisidia"; a second part, called "Phrygia towards Pisidia" (ἡ πρὸς Πισι-
δίαν), occupying the southwestern slope of the Sultan Dagh and including the territory
from Antioch to the Pisidian border; and a third part around Amorium, Eumeneia and
Synnada (τὰ περὶ ᾿Αμόριον καὶ Εὐμένειαν καὶ Σύνναδα).[81] The Galatians originally
settled on Phrygian territory.[82] At one point, Strabo even seems to identify Greater
Phrygia with Galatia[83] although the former is actually divided between the provinces of
Galatia and Asia. Here, we begin to see the distinction, which must often be made in
discussing Phrygia, between political boundaries and ethnic borders.[84] In the course of
time, the political boundaries of Phrygia often shifted, and the same place belonged in
different times to different political regions.[85] It is necessary to recognize this fact in
order to avoid misunderstanding.

W. M. CALDER argues that a Neo-Phrygian inscription of ca. A. D. 250 honoring a
"regional centurion" (ἑκατόνταρχον ῥεγεωνάριον)[86] in the name of Pisidian Antioch
and the district of "Mygdonia" (a poetic synonym for "Phrygia")[87] is to be understood as
referring to the *regio* of Phrygia in the sense of "the Phrygic and Galatic territory" in Acts

---

[81] Cf. Strabo *Geogr.* 12.8.13.

[82] Cf. Strabo *Geogr.* 12.1.1 ("the Galatians who settled in Phrygia and extended as far as the
Lycaonians"); 12.2.8 ("the country of the Galatians who held Phrygia"); 12.3.9 ("the Galatians who settled among them [sc. the Phrygians]").

[83] Cf. Strabo *Geogr.* 2.5.31, which divides Phrygia into two parts: Phrygia Epictetus and
"Galatia of the Gallo-Grecians." Elsewhere, however, Strabo seems to exclude Galatia from
Greater Phrygia (cf. 12.4.10: "to the south of the Paphlagonians are the Galatians; and still to
the south of these is Greater Phrygia").

[84] Cf. FRIEDRICH, "Phrygia," col. 790.

[85] For example, Iconium, on the southeastern border of Phrygia, was sometimes considered
part of Lycaonia. Cf. MITCHELL, "Population and the Land in Roman Galatia,"
pp. 1061–1062; FRIEDRICH, "Phrygia," col. 790.

[86] *IGRR* 3.301 reads instead λεγεωνάριον at this point, but the "Addenda et Corrigenda"
(ibid., p. 511 [no. 1490]) correct the reading to ῥεγεωνάριον on the authority of Theodor
MOMMSEN, *Römisches Strafrecht* (Systematisches Handbuch der deutschen Rechtswissenschaft 1.4; Leipzig: Duncker & Humblot, 1899), p. 312 n. 1. On the correctness of the textual
reading ῥεγεωνάριον and on ῥεγιών or ῥεγεών as a Greek transliteration of the Latin *regio* in
the epigraphy of Asia Minor, see further HEMER, *Acts*, p. 295 n. 52. For the opposing
argument, see JACKSON and LAKE, *Acts*, 5:235.

[87] Cf. CALDER, "Colonia Caesareia Antiocheia," pp. 81–82, citing RAMSAY: "The country
Mygdonia at Antioch can of course be nothing but Phrygia expressed by a poetic synonym.
Mygdon was an ancient Phrygian king, and Mygdonia was either a district of Phrygia or
Phrygia as a whole. Pliny [*Nat. Hist.* 5.145] indeed distinguishes Mygdonia from Phrygia,
placing it on the southern frontier of Asian Phrygia (i.e. Phrygia in so far as it belonged to
province Asia) adjoining Pisidia and Lycaonia. This is an excellent description of Galatic
Phrygia and agrees exactly with the evidence of the inscription before us. Hence I cannot see
any loophole for escaping the conclusion that a certain region of the province Galatia, having
Antioch as its metropolis and centre, was called Phrygia or Mygdonia." On the χώρα as the
territory of a city, see Mireille CORBIER, "City, Territory and Taxation," in *City and Country in
the Ancient World* (ed. John Rich and Andrew Wallace-Hadrill; Leicester-Nottingham
Studies in Ancient Society 2; London/New York: Routledge, 1991), pp. 211–239 (here esp.
pp. 211, 217–220, 229); E. M. de Ste. CROIX, "Polis and Chora," in *The Class Struggle in the
Ancient Greek World* (London: Duckworth, 1981), pp. 9–19. Note that according to Acts
13:50, Paul and Barnabas were driven out from the city limits of Antioch (ἀπὸ τῶν ὁρίων
αὐτῶν) and went to Iconium (v. 51).

16:6 or "Phrygia Galatica"[88] – that is, that part of Phrygia within the Roman province of Galatia that excludes Galatia proper.[89] In this sense, Phrygia lies below Galatia,[90] even though the Phrygian population of Galatia was evidently more extensive than this.[91] On the basis of this evidence, CALDER concludes: "Future discussion of the Φρυγία καὶ Γαλατικὴ χώρα in Acts, xvi, 6 must reckon with the position that there was a district stretching westwards and northwards from the boundary of the territory of Lystra which was felt by its inhabitants to be Phrygian as well as Galatian, known as a *regio* or χώρα, and called Mygdonia or Phrygia."[92] This would correlate with the fact that "the Phrygian and Galatic region" that Paul and his companions traversed was evidently bounded by Asia, for the Holy Spirit had previously forbidden them from evangelizing in Asia (Acts 16:6).[93]

---

[88] Compare the well-attested part of *Provincia Galatia* called "Pontus Galaticus" (cf., e.g., Ptolemy *Geogr.* 5.2, 4; *CIL Suppl.* 3.6818 (cited above); also HEMER, *Acts*, pp. 205 n. 86, 284–285, 290 n. 37, 294). By the same token, if the western part of Phrygia was known as Asian Phrygia (cf. Galen *De aliment. facultat.* 1.13.10), then its eastern part may well have been known as Galatic Phrygia. See also HEMER, *Acts*, pp. 281–282; RIESNER, *Frühzeit*, p. 253.

[89] Cf. W. M. CALDER, "The Boundary of Galatic Phrygia," in *MAMA* 7:ix-xvi (esp. pp. xi-xiii); idem, "Colonia Caesareia Antiocheia," pp. 81–84. On "Phrygia Galatica," see further HEMER, *Acts*, pp. 294–295. Cf. also A. H. M. JONES, *The Cities of the Eastern Roman Provinces* (2nd ed.; Oxford: Clarendon, 1971), pp. 139–140: "Antioch was the most important of Augustus' Pisidian colonies; it alone was granted the *ius Italicum*. It must have possessed a large territory, but its limits are unknown. On the north and east its frontier coincided with that of the province of Galatia. On the south it was bounded by the Cillianian plain."

[90] Cf. Pausanias 10.36.1 ("the Galatians who are above Phrygia"); Pliny *Nat. Hist.* 5.146 ("Galatia, which lies above Phrygia and holds lands that for the most part were taken from that country, as was Gordium, its former capital"); Strabo *Geogr.* 12.5.2; 12.5.4; 12.13.1. Cf. MITCHELL, "Population and the Land in Roman Galatia," p. 1060: "The area to the south of Galatia, the Προσειλημμένη of Ptolemy [*Geogr.* 5.4.8], is called Phrygia by both Strabo and Pliny, and their evidence is fully supported by the epigraphic remains."

[91] On the Phrygian population of Galatia and its extent, see MITCHELL, "Population and the Land in Roman Galatia," pp. 1058, 1060–1062; HEMER, *Acts*, p. 304 (the population of Roman Galatia was largely Phrygian in both the north and the south). See, however, Gertrud LAMINGER-PASCHER, "Lykaonien und die Ostgrenze Phrygiens," *Epigraphica Anatolica* 16 (1990) 1–14, who criticizes attempts to identify "Phrygian" areas of Central Anatolia during the Roman Empire.

[92] CALDER, "Colonia Caesareia Antiocheia," p. 84; cf. RAMSAY, *Galatians*, p. 209. Stephen MITCHELL ("Galatia," *ABD*, 2 [1992] 870–872 [here p. 871]) writes in a similar vein: "Paul did not visit N. Galatia. The book of Acts relates that he passed through a region called Phrygia and the Galatic country after leaving Derbe and Lystra, as a stage in a journey that led through Mysia to Troas (Acts 16:6). This cannot have been Galatia, which lay some 200 km NE of any natural route between Lystra and Mysia in NW Asia Minor. The phrase is naturally understood as denoting the country of Phrygia Paroreius which lay on either side of Sultan Dagh, the mountain range that divided Pisidian Antioch from Iconium, an area that was ethnically Phrygian but which was divided between the Roman provinces of Asia and Galatia." MITCH-ELL (ibid., p. 871) goes on to explain "the Galatic country and Phrygia" (Acts 18:23) as another reference to Phrygia Paroreius, adding the that the Pontic bishop, Asterius of Amasea, in the late fourth century understood the passage to refer to Lycaonia and Phrygia (*Homilia VIII in SS. Petrum et Paulum* [*PG* 40:293D]) not to Galatia in the ethnic sense.

[93] The aorist participle κωλυθέντες should not be interpreted as describing an action subsequent to that of διῆλθον (so HEMER, *Acts*, pp. 281–282; G. M. LEE, "Two Linguistic

The subsequent route of Paul is often thought to militate against this interpretation of Acts 16:6. For if Paul went through "the Phrygian and Galatian region" in the sense of South Galatia, then "it is impossible that Paul's route through this district brought him out anywhere near Mysia."[94] Acts 16:6−8 reads as follows: "And they went through the Phrygian and Galatian region, having been forbidden by the Holy Spirit to speak the word in Asia. And when they had come opposite Mysia (κατὰ τὴν Μυσίαν), they attempted to go into Bithynia, but the Spirit of Jesus did not allow them; so, passing by Mysia, they went down to Troas." According to the North Galatian interpretation of this passage, Paul travelled northward from Lystra and Iconium to the territory of the ethnic Galatians.[95] Since this also does not bring Paul out anywhere near Mysia, proponents of the North Galatian Hypothesis are sometimes forced to suppose that Γαλατικὴ χώρα includes the cities of Nacoleia and Dorylaeum, which lay to the west of Galatia proper.[96] However, the South Galatian Hypothesis can explain Paul's subsequent route without resort to such expedients: Paul travelled westward on the *Via Sebaste* from Lystra, through Iconium, to Pisidian Antioch, where the road branches towards Apamea, the Lycus Valley, and Ephesus.[97] Having previously been prohibited by the Holy Spirit from evangelizing in Asia (Shemite territory),[98] Paul proceeded in a northwesterly direction. However, when he came "opposite Mysia," possibly at the Dorylaeum or Cotiaeum, his attempt to enter Bithynia was also blocked by the Spirit, and so, passing by Mysia, he continued on to Troas.[99]

Possible Additional Evidence. It is possible that, on the so-called First Missionary Journey, Paul and Barnabas went directly from Cyprus to South Galatia as a result of their encounter with Sergius Paulus, the proconsul of Cyprus who became a believer through their missionary activity (Acts 13:7, 12).[100] Sergius

---

Parallels from Babrius," *NovT* 9 [1967] 41−42; idem, "The Aorist Participle of Subsequent Action [Acts 16:6]," *Bib* 51 [1970] 235−237; idem, "The Past Participle of Subsequent Action," *NovT* 17 [1975] 199), for the participle does not necessarily imply that the travellers were already on the borders of Asia before the prohibition came; it may have come, for example, already at Lystra (cf. BRUCE, "Galatian Problems," p. 257).

[94] JACKSON and LAKE, *Acts*, 5:235−236.

[95] Cf., e.g., PESCH, *Apostelgeschichte*, 2:101.

[96] Cf. Gerhard SCHNEIDER, *Die Apostelgeschichte* (2 vols.; HTKNT 5; Freiburg: Herder, 1980), 2:205 n. 12; JACKSON and LAKE, *Acts*, 5:236. See the evaluation of RIESNER, *Frühzeit*, pp. 251−252, and MITCHELL, *Anatolia*, 2:3−4.

[97] Cf. RIESNER, *Frühzeit*, p. 253. This accords best with Acts 18:23, where Paul is again said to have gone "through the region of Galatia and Phrygia" on his way to Ephesus. If the North Galatian Hypothesis were correct, Paul would have deviated sharply northward from his westerly course, adding 300 miles to his journey.

[98] On the interpretation of κωλυθέντες, see n. 93 above.

[99] Cf. RIESNER, *Frühzeit*, pp. 259−260.

[100] Cf. MITCHELL, "Population and the Land in Roman Galatia," p. 1074 n. 134; idem, *Anatolia*, 2:7; RIESNER, *Frühzeit*, pp. 245−246; Alanna NOBBS, "Cyprus," in *The Book of Acts in Its Graeco-Roman Setting*, pp. 279−289 (here p. 287). Cilliers BREYTENBACH of the Kirchliche Hochschule in Berlin is preparing a monograph on Sergius Paullus and the Galatians.

Paulus and his family were landed aristocrats in Galatia.[101] A new funerary inscription from Iconium (on the border between Lycaonia and Phrygia), dated to the first or second century A. D. based on paleography, mentions a certain Παῦλος[102] as the (eldest) son of a δοῦλος πραγματευτής, that is, a "slave" and a "manager."[103] Since the name Παῦλος is extremely rare among non-Romans, especially in the Greek-speaking East,[104] we may ask how the slave's son may have received this name. The editor of the inscription suggests the slave himself may have already had the name Παῦλος,[105] noting however that the family of the Sergii Paulli were established in this area.[106] If the slaveholder, whose name evidently ends in the genitive -ου in the inscription (Παῦλος?), was a member of the family of the Sergii Paulli, is it possible that the patron conferred his name upon the eldest son of his administrator, perhaps in the process of manumission?[107] If so, this would illustrate the precise means, if not the exact family,[108]

---

[101] Cf. MITCHELL, "Population and the Land in Roman Galatia," pp. 1073–1074; RIESNER, *Frühzeit*, pp. 122–126.

[102] Note that a *tria nomina*, characteristic of Roman citizens (cf. Plutarch *Mar.* 1; Juvenal 5.127), is absent. For an example of the *tria nomina* in Roman Galatia, see the first- or second-century inscription referring to a certain Titus Flavius Valention, a Roman citizen evidently enfranchised by one of the Flavian emperors (cf. MITCHELL, *Regional Epigraphic Catalogues of Asia Minor, Vol. 2: The Ankara District. The Inscriptions of North Galatia* , no. 398).

[103] Cf. Norbert ERHARDT, "Eine neue Grabinschrift aus Iconium," *Zeitschrift für Papyrologie und Epigraphik* 81 (1990) 185–188. The text reads as follows:

> [– – – – ca. 15–17 – – – –]
> [ ]ου δοῦλος πραγμα-
> [τ]ευτὴς ἔτι ζῶν ἑαυτῷ
> [τ]ὴν λάρνακα καὶ τὸν
> [β]ωμὸν σὺν τοῖς περι-
> [κ]ειμένοις θωρακείο[ις]
> κατεσκεύασεν καὶ το[ῖς]
> τέκνοις αὐτοῦ Παύλῳ
> καὶ Στράτωνι κ{η}αὶ Φιλο[υμέ-]
> νη καὶ τοῖς τέκνοις τοῦ Σ[τρά-]
> τωνος Στράτωνι καὶ Στ[ρα-]
> τωνίδι.

[104] Cf. HENGEL, *The Pre-Christian Paul*, pp. 8–9.

[105] Cf. EHRHARDT, "Eine neue Grabinschrift aus Iconium," p. 187.

[106] Ibid., p. 187 n. 16. The son of L. Sergius Paulus – L. Sergius L. f. Paullus filius – is known from an inscription from Pisidian Antioch (cf. Helmut HALFMANN, *Die Senatoren aus dem östlichen Teil des Imperium Romanum bis zum Ende des 2. Jahrhunderts n. Chr.* [Hypomnemata 58; Göttingen: Vandenhoeck & Ruprecht, 1979], p. 105; LEVICK, *Roman Colonies in Southern Roman Asia Minor*, p. 112; MITCHELL, "Population and the Land in Roman Galatia," p. 1074).

[107] Freedmen normally took over the *nomen* and *praenomen* of their patron (cf. HENGEL, *The Pre-Christian Paul*, p. 9, with n. 73). This is definitely not a case of adoption by the slave-owner since the inscription still regards Paulus as the son of the slave. On manumission and adoption, see Jane F. GARDNER, "The Adoption of Roman Freedmen," *Phoenix* 43 (1989) 236–257; J. SCOTT, *Adoption as Sons of God: An Exegetical Investigation into the Background of ΥΙΟΘΕΣΙΑ in the Pauline Corpus* (WUNT 2.48; Tübingen: Mohr-Siebeck, 1992), pp. 85–88.

[108] It would be imprudent to speculate about a possible relationship of the Apostle Paul's

by which, as HENGEL suggests, the Apostle's father originally received the name Paul.[109] On the other hand, the very fact that Paulus is regarded as the son of a slave seems to presuppose his own slave status. In that case, the name might have been given to the son as a token of honor or gratitude for the (namesake) slaveholder. For the moment, however, our question is different: Does Paul have a special interest in the evangelization and edification of the southern part of the Roman province of Galatia because of the presence of the Sergii Paulli there? If so, is this an additional argument that Paul's mission to Galatia was confined to the southern part of the province?

Galatia and the Table-of-Nations Tradition

Having surveyed the two contending hypotheses on the question of the Galatian addressees, we are now in a position to examine the problem from a distinctively OT and Jewish perspective. We have seen that Paul's understanding of his mission to the nations is very likely influenced by the Table-of-Nations tradition. How then might this tradition affect his perception of the Galatian addressees? Josephus' exposition of the Genesis 10 provides a convenient point of departure to answer this question.

Josephus' Identification of Gomer with the Galatians

As we observed in Chap. 1, Josephus' exposition of the Table of Nations in *Ant.* 1.122−147 "updates" Genesis 10 by providing the modern equivalents for the descendants of Noah's sons. For Josephus, as for Judaism in general, the Table of Nations was not an obsolete relic of the past but rather a perennially-relevant description of the nations of the world both in the present and in the eschatological future. From this perspective, the Table could be glossed, but it could never be superseded. In this section, we are interested primarily with Josephus' identification of the sons of Japheth, especially Gomer, to whom Paul's mission was particularly directed (see Chap. 3).

After explaining that the sons of Japheth originally gave their own names to the nations that they founded, Josephus proceeds to illustrate how the Greeks (who are themselves Japhethites!) changed the nomenclature, beginning with Gomer, the first son of Japheth:

---

family to the Sergii Paulli although the self-conscious switch in Acts from "Saul" to "Paul" after the encounter with Sergius Paulus is striking (cf. Acts 13:9). Cf. MITCHELL, *Anatolia*, 2:7.

[109] Cf. HENGEL, *The Pre-Christian Paul*, p. 9. Compare HENGEL's argument that Paul's forebears received Roman citizenship when they were freed by a Roman citizen (ibid., p. 14). On the granting of Roman citizenship by manumission, see A.N. SHERWIN-WHITE, *The Roman Citizenship* (2nd ed.; Oxford: Clarendon Press, 1973), pp. 322−334; GARDNER, "The Adoption of Roman Freedmen," pp. 236−257. Other scholars have suggested that Paul was connected with Sergius Paulus as a freedman of the same gens (cf. NOBBS, "Cyprus," p. 289).

Thus those whom the Greeks now (νῦν) call Galatians were named Gomarites, having been founded by Gomar. [. . .] Gomar had three sons, of whom Aschanaxes founded the Aschanaxians, whom the Greeks now call Rheginians, Riphathes the Riphataeans – the modern Paphlagonians – and Thugrames the Thugramaeans, whom the Greeks thought good to call Phrygians.[110]

According to this text, Gomer corresponds to those who are now called Galatians by the Greeks.[111] Two issues need to be discussed at this point: (1) Josephus' procedure in updating the text and (2) the reason for the identification of Gomer with Galatia.

Josephus' Procedure. As already commonly in the Ancient Near East, the Greeks and the Romans consider the population of the whole world and each of its parts as completely divided into "nations."[112] Therefore, Josephus' task is simply to establish the proper correspondences between the biblical Table of Nations and the contemporary Roman "nations." The tendency to "update" Genesis 10 by identifying the original names with peoples and places in his own day (νῦν) is a practice that Josephus has in common with much Jewish exegesis (see Table 3). In fact, the *Chronicles of Jerahmeel* 31:4 also identifies Gomer with the Galatians.[113] As we have seen, Josephus' method is similar to that in the Targumim, where the loanword איפרכייא (= ἐπαρχεία, "province") is often used to introduce the contemporary identifications of the sons of Noah.

Exactly when the name change took place, Josephus does not mention, for he is not so much interested in history at this point as in the abiding relevance of the Table of Nations. The province of Galatia that Josephus knew was not formed until 25 B.C., when Augustus subjected the territory of Amyntas to direct rule by a Roman governor.[114] However, the territory was called "Galatia" long before that[115] although it underwent some additions and subtractions when it became a Roman province.[116] For Josephus, the Roman Empire was the ruling world power; therefore, he naturally identified the biblical Table of Nations in terms of Roman nomenclature that were familiar to him even though he claimed that the "Greeks" were responsible for the name changes.[117]

---

[110] *Ant.* 1.123, 126.

[111] See Chap. 1 above.

[112] Cf. Fritz GSCHNITZER, "Volk, Nation, Nationalismus, Masse (II. Altertum)," in *Geschichtliche Grundbegriffe. Historisches Lexikon zur politisch-sozialen Sprache in Deutschland*, 7 (1992) 151–171 (here p. 165).

[113] However, this may be evidence of the *Chronicles'* dependence on Josephus at this point.

[114] Cf. Dio Cassius *Hist. Rom.* 53.26.3.

[115] Cf. Polybius [3rd-2nd cent. B.C.] *Hist.* 24.14.2, 6; 24.15.7; 25.2.4; 30.30.2. Writing just after the time that Galatia became a Roman province (cf. *Geogr.* 12.5.1), Strabo also refers to the pre-provincial territory as "Galatia" (cf. 2.5.31; 12.5.1).

[116] Cf. SHERK, "Roman Galatia: The Governors from 25 B.C. to A.D. 114," pp. 958–959; RAMSAY, *Galatians*, pp. 113–127; LEVICK, *Roman Colonies in Southern Asia Minor*, pp. 29ff. On provincial boundaries in Asia Minor from 25 B.C. to A.D. 235, see MITCHELL, *Anatolia*, 2:151–157.

[117] See further in Chap. 2 on Josephus' use of ἔθνος. Josephus views the Greeks as the Third Kingdom of Daniel and the Romans as the Fourth Kingdom.

When Josephus identifies Gomer with Galatia, he evidently thinks that the boundaries of Provincia Galatia coincide exactly with the territory originally allotted to Gomer[118] since, for him, only the names of the territories have changed not the territories themselves. This is confirmed by the way that Josephus divides the territory of Gomer among the three sons of Gomer using the principle of "blocking-in,"[119] for, as we will discuss further below, Paphlagonia (Riphathes) formed the northernmost part of the Roman province of Galatia, Phrygia (Thugrames) also formed a distinct part of Galatia, and therefore, in all probability, Rhegines (Ashkenaz), whose identification remains obscure, also formed a part of Galatia.

Let us examine each part of this tripartite division of Galatia in more detail. (a) When Josephus identifies Riphathes (biblical Riphath), the second son of Gomer/Galatia, with the Paphlagonians, he betrays a conception of the extent of Galatia that postdates 6/5 B. C., when Paphlagonia was incorporated into the Roman province.[120] Hence, in conformity with contemporary usage, Josephus does not restrict the designation of "Galatia" to the landlocked territory of the original three tribes of ethnic Galatia in central Asia Minor but extends it to more recently incorporated territories as well.[121] That means that Josephus also includes in Galatia the whole middle section of Asia Minor: all of the territory from Pontus on the north (bordering on the Black Sea) to Pamphylia on the south (bordering on the Mediterranean), including the so-called South Galatian territory, which was part of the Roman province of Galatia from its formation in 25 B. C. Moreover, Josephus does not just incorporate these three "sons of Gomer" into the territory of Galatia but actually allows them to be brought under the heading of those peoples who are called "Galatians," for according to *Ant.* 1.123, Gomer founded the Gomarites, whom the Greeks call "Galatians" (Γαλάται). We may loosely compare the official Roman inscription referring to a "procurator ... of Galatia and [its] *related* nations" (ἐπίτροπος ... ἐπαρχείας Γαλατίας καὶ τῶν σύνεγγυς ἐθνῶν).[122] Here, at last, is

---

[118] On the composition of the Roman province of Galatia from 25 B. C. to A. D. 64, see SHERK, "Roman Galatia: The Governors from 25 B. C. to A. D. 114," pp. 958–963: "By now, that province had assumed a vast and complicated design that stretched all the way from the southeastern border of the province of Asia to the foothills of the Caucasus" (p. 962). The unity of the whole Roman province around the imperial cult was apparently the concern of the Koinon of Galatia (cf. Jürgen DEININGER, *Die Provinziallandtage der römischen Kaiserzeit von Augustus bis zum Ende des dritten Jahrhunderts n. Chr.* [Munich/Berlin: Beck'sche Verlagsbuchhandlung, 1965], pp. 68–69; Stephen MITCHELL, "Galatia under Tiberius," pp. 31, 33; WAELKENS, "The Imperial Sanctuary at Pessinus," pp. 71–72).

[119] On this principle, see Chap. 1.

[120] Cf. SHERK, "Roman Galatia: The Governors from 25 B. C. to A. D. 114," pp. 960–961; RAMSAY, *Galatians*, p. 121.

[121] However, Josephus does not explicitly mention two other, more recent additions to the northeastern part of the Roman province of Galatia: Pontus Galaticus (3–2 B. C.) and Pontus Polemoniacus (A. D. 64). Cf. SHERK, "Roman Galatia: The Governors from 25 B. C. to A. D. 114," pp. 961–962.

[122] *IGRR* 3.70. Although these "related nations" could refer to the "three nations" (ἔθνη

evidence that, at least from a Jewish perspective, all those who belonged to the Roman province of Galatia could be called "Galatians," including the South Galatians.

(b) When Josephus identifies Thugrames (biblical Togarmah), the third son of Gomer/Galatia, with the Phrygians, he could have one of several things in mind, depending on what he means by "Phrygia." We have seen that in the course of time, Phrygia was divided into various regions and districts (see the excursus above). Hence, there are a number of senses in which Josephus could be using the term "Phrygia" here. Precisely which one he intends when referring to Togarmah can be ascertained only after considering one final point.

(c) When Josephus identifies Aschanaxes (biblical Ashkenaz), Gomer's first son, with the Rheginians ('Ρήγινες), his meaning is at first puzzling, for "Rheginians" as the name of a people is attested only of the inhabitants of Rhegium ('Ρηγῖνοι),[123] a city on the narrows between Italy and Sicily,[124] whereas in context, we would expect the Rheginians to be located somewhere within Roman Galatia, like the other two sons of Gomer. We consider it likely, therefore, that Josephus associates Aschanaxes (LXX: Ασχαναζ) with Ascania ('Ασκανίη), which is probably an ancient name for Phrygia or a territory in Phrygia.[125] The words 'Ασκαία (referring to the Antioch valley) and 'Ασ-

---

τρία) that constitute the ethnic Galatians (cf. Strabo *Geogr.* 12.5.1), that is, the Trocmi, the Tolistobogii and the Tectosages, they more likely refer to the component territories of provincial Galatia that are often listed in official inscriptions and sometimes explicitly include Phrygia (cf. *CIL* 3.291, cited above). On the other hand, CALDER ("Colonia Caesareia Antiocheia," p. 83 n. 7) interprets "the related nations" as meaning other provinces and compares *CIL* 3.6994 (*proc. per Asiam et adhaerentes provincias*).

[123] Cf., e.g., Diodorus Siculus 11.52.3, 5; 14.40.1, 6; Dionysius of Halicarnassus *Ant. Rom.* 20.4.1, 2. Since the form 'Ρήγινες is unique to Josephus, we may perhaps suspect a corruption in the text (note the many textual variants listed in B. NIESE's edition: ῥίγηνες, ῥηγίνες, ῥιγῖνες, ῥηγῆνες, *regini*, Reginos).

[124] Thomas W. FRANXMAN actually suggests this as a possible interpretation of our term (*Genesis and the "Jewish Antiquities" of Flavius Josephus* [BibOr 35; Rome: Biblical Institute Press, 1979], pp. 105–106). He also considers it possible that 'Ρήγινες is a corruption of Bithynoi and thus refers to Bithynia, for Aschanaxes sounds like Ascania, the lake upon which the principle city of Bithynia was situated, and the two brothers of Aschanaxes occupy adjacent territories to Bithynia (i.e., Riphath occupied Paphlagonia and Togarmah Phrygia). See also now Johann MAIER, "Zu ethnographisch-geographischen Überlieferungen über Japhetiten (Gen 10,2–4) im frühen Judentum," *Henoch* 13 (1991) 157–194 (here p. 189).

[125] Cf., e.g., Strabo *Geogr.* 12.4.5 (also 14.5.29): "And in fact one should thus interpret the words of the poet [sc. Homer] when he says, 'And Phorcys and godlike Ascanius led the Phrygians from afar, from Ascania' [*Il.* 2.862], that is, the Phrygian Ascania. ..." See further B. MADER, "'Ασκανίη," *Lexikon des frühgriechischen Epos*, 1 (1979) 1403–1404; RAMSAY, *Galatians*, pp. 27–29; Fritz HOMMEL, *Ethnologie und Geographie des alten Orients* (Handbuch des Altertumswissenschaft 3.1.1; Munich: Beck, 1926), p. 212, with n. 4; Th. ARLDT, "Die Völkertafeln der Genesis und ihre Bedeutung für die Ethnographie Vorderasiens," *Wiener Zeitschrift für die Kunde des Morgenlandes* 30 (1917) 264–317 (here pp. 271–272). Note that Jer 28(51):27 LXX associates the "kingdoms of Ararat" with "the Ashkenazis" in the context of the fall of Babylon. This may be significant insofar as Ararat was sometimes located in Phrygia (see above, Chap. 1).

καηνός or Ἀσκαῖος (used of the moon-god Men centered near Antioch)[126] are common in Phrygia.[127] A recent study argues for the equation of Men's epithet Ἀσκαηνός with biblical Ashkenaz in order to see Scythian influence in the cult.[128] According to W. M. RAMSAY, "It is generally said that Ashkenaz ... in Genesis X 3, is the name of the Phrygian people...."[129] If all this is correct, then Josephus makes two references to Phrygia (or parts of Phrygia) in his identification of the sons of Gomer/Galatia. How does Josephus intend for us to distinguish between them?

In accordance with the aforementioned subdivisions of Phrygia, we may infer that Josephus makes a distinction here between two parts of Phrygia that lay within the contemporary province of Galatia: (1) Greater Phrygia (Togarmah), which, as we have seen, is particularly associated with Galatia proper, and (2) "Phrygia Galatica" or "Phrygia towards Pisidia" (Ashkenaz). This second reference to Phrygia might explain Josephus' identification of Aschanaxes with the *Rheginians*, for, as mentioned above, CALDER suggests, on the basis of inscriptional evidence, that there is a *regio* of Phrygia in the sense of "the Phrygic and Galatic territory" of Acts 16:6.[130] Thus, Josephus refers not only to

126 On Pisidian Antioch as a major center of the Men-cult, see Eugene N. LANE, "Men: A Neglected Cult of Roman Asia Minor," in *ANRW* II.18.3 (ed. Wolfgang Haase; Berlin/New York: de Gruyter, 1990), pp. 2161–2174 (here pp. 2163–2166).

127 Cf. CALDER, "Colonia Caesareia Antiocheia," pp. 94–95; E. N. LANE, "The Italian Connection: An Aspect of the Cult of Men," *Numen* 22 (1975) 235–239 (here p. 235–236). As mentioned above, there are two lakes called Ascania in Phrygia.

128 Cf. Agnès van HAEPEREN-POURBAIX, "Recherche sur les origines, la nature, et les attributs du dieu Mên," in *Archéologie et religions de l'Anatolie ancienne. Mélanges en l'honneur du professeur Paul Naster* (ed. R. Donceel and R. Lebrun; Homo Religiosus 10; Louvain: Centre d'Histoire des Religions, 1983), pp. 221–257 (here pp. 239–242). LANE argues that since Ἀσκαηνός automatically recalls Aeneas' son Ascanius, the Romans deliberately fostered the cult of Men, particularly in Pisidian Antioch, for the purposes of propaganda, thereby encouraging the idea of the supposed racial affinity between Italians and Anatolians ("The Italian Connection: An Aspect of the Cult of Men," pp. 235–239; idem, *Corpus Monumentorum Religionis Dei Menis [CMRDM], Vol. 3: Interpretations and Testamonia* [EPRO 19; Leiden: Brill, 1976], p. 72).

129 RAMSAY, *Galatians*, p. 28; cf. CALDER, "Colonia Caesareia Antiocheia," p. 95. For the equation of Ashkenaz with Askania (Phrygia), see, e.g., Gustav HÖLSCHER, *Drei Erdkarten. Ein Beitrag zur Erdkenntnis des hebräischen Altertums* (Sitzungsberichte der Heidelberger Akademie der Wissenschaften, Philosophisch-historische Klasse, Jahrgang 1944/48, 3. Abhandlung; Heidelberg: Winter, 1948), p. 22 n. 9. Note that in later Jewish tradition, Ashkenaz is identified with Asia (cf. the Targumim; *y. Meg.* 71b; *Gen. Rab.* 37:1). P.S. ALEXANDER suggests that the Rabbinic identification of Ashkenaz with Asia is based on the knowledge, mediated through the Diaspora, of the frequent occurence of the names Ascanius and Ascania for geographical features in the region of Roman Asia ("The Toponymy of the Targumim, with Special Reference to the Table of Nations and the Boundaries of the Land of Israel" [D. Phil. thesis, Oxford University, 1974], p. 110). Today, Ashkenaz is usually identified with the Scythians.

130 A. SCHALIT also explains Josephus' uses of Rhegines in terms of the Latin *regio* albiet as the Greek expression for the inhabitants of the *regiones* into which Asia Proconsularis was divided at the time of Sulla (*Namenwörterbuch zu Flavius Josephus* [Leiden: Brill, 1968], p. 101).

that part of the land of the Phrygians that long before that had been invaded by the Kimmerioi (= Assyrian *Gimmirai* = biblical Gomer) and later became known as "Galatia," but also to that part of Phrygia to the south of Galatia proper.

When Josephus identifies Gomer with Galatia and Phrygia, he stands in the same tradition as the Targumim and *Gen. Rab.* 37:1, which identify Gomer with Phrygia (see Table 3).[131] Furthermore, Hippolytus appears to link the Galatians with both the Paphlagonians and the Phrygians (cf. *Chron.* 200 [43]). We are beginning to see that Josephus' method is informed by Jewish tradition. Let us probe in more detail the reason behind Josephus' identification of Gomer and the Galatians.

The Reason for the Identification. Surely, Josephus must know that historically the Galatians did not migrate from Armenia into Asia Minor, as he supposes the Gomerites did along with the rest of the sons of Japheth, but rather that the Gauls, i.e. those whom he normally calls Γαλάται,[132] migrated from Europe into Asia Minor.[133] Even if he is aware of it, however, Josephus says nothing about the historical nexus between the Γαλάται of Asia Minor and those of Western and Central Europe.[134] Indeed, Josephus seems to know little

---

[131] Cf. ALEXANDER, "Toponymy," pp. 106–108. ALEXANDER argues convincingly that אפריקי refers to "Phrygia" in these instances (ibid., pp. 107–108; so also Martin McNAMARA, *Targum and Testament: Aramaic Paraphrases of the Hebrew Bible: A Light on the New Testament* [Shannon: Irish University Press, n.d.], p. 198) rather than to "Africa" (so Samuel KRAUSS, "Die biblische Völkertafel im Talmud, Midrasch und Targum," *MGWJ* N.F. 3 [1895] 1–11 pp. [here pp. 2–7]). We may note the same problem with the use of *'Afrêg* in the description of the portion of Japheth in *Jub.* 8:27: R.H. CHARLES takes it as as referring to Phrygia (*APOT*, 2:26 n.; followed by O.S. WINTERMUTE, *OTP*, 2:74 n. *x*), whereas HÖLSCHER takes it as referring to Africa (*Drei Erdkarten*, p. 71).

[132] Cf. Josephus *Ant.* 15.217 (Caesar presented Herod with a body guard of four hundred Gauls); 17.198 (Gauls as part of the honor guard at Herod's funeral), 344 (Archelaus is sent into exile in Vienna, a city in Gaul); *Ap.* 1.67 ("about Gauls and Iberians," there is a great deal of ignorance among historians); *BJ* 1.5 (the Romans were preoccupied with their neighbors the Gauls and with the Celts); 1.397 (Caesar presented Herod with a body guard of four hundred Gauls), 437 (Herod has his brother-in-law Aristobulus drowned by the Gauls), 673 (Gauls as part of the honor guard at Herod's funeral); 2.364 (the wealth of the Gauls), 371–372 (the Gauls have the best chances of revolting from Rome by virtue of their location, surrounded by magnificant natural ramparts [i.e., the Alps, the Rhine, the Pyrenees, the ocean], and their abundant population of three hundred and five nations); 4.440 (Gaul revolted from Nero), 494 (the war in Gaul), 547 (the battle at Bedriacum in Gaul), 634 (Cremona, a town in Gaul); 7.76 (the Gauls join with their neighbors, the Germans, in revolting against Rome), 88 (Domitian settled affairs in Cisalpine Gaul).

[133] Cf. RANKIN, *Celts and the Classical World*, pp. 188–190; HEINEN, "The Syrian-Egyptian Wars and the new kingdoms of Asia Minor," pp. 422–425. Still important is STÄHELIN, *Geschichte der kleinasiatischen Galater*. See now MITCHELL, *Anatolia*, 1:13–19.

[134] *Jubilees* 8–9 seems even less informed in this regard although 8:26 does mention the "Mountains of Qelt" in Japheth's portion, which are probably in some way connected with the Celts (cf. P.S. ALEXANDER, "Notes on the 'Imago Mundi' of the Book of Jubilees," *JJS* 33 [1982] 197–213 [here p. 208]).

about these people and their pre-Roman history,[135] declaring that sound information about the Γαλάται (and the Iberians) is not even achieved by the most eminent historians (cf. *Ap.* 1.67).[136] In making his identification between Gomer and the Galatians, he completely ignores the complex historical development of the region in the time between the Flood and the Roman Empire. For example, he fails to make the connection between the Cimmerians and the Scythians who later occupied their land,[137] opting instead to identify those whom the Greeks call the Scythians with Magog. He apparently begins with the assumption that the Gomerites settled in central Anatolia and then translates that territory into its contemporary equivalent. As we have seen, this amounts to superimposing the Roman province of Galatia onto the original territory of the Gomerites. There is reason to believe, however, that Josephus' basic assumption was neither arbitrary nor superficial[138] but rather informed by OT and Ancient Near Eastern tradition,[139] for the biblical Gomerites are now generally recognized to be the *Gimmirai*, that is, the Cimmerians who de-

---

[135] Apart from his exposition of the Table of Nations (*Ant.* 1.123) and possibly one other text (*Ant.* 12.414 [see further below]), Josephus does not discuss the Galatians of central Anatolia. Furthermore, his information about the Gauls of western and central Europe is confined to the recent Roman period (see n. 131 above).

[136] Cf., similarly, Strabo *Geogr.* 1.3.21. Diogenes Laertius (*Vitae* 5.83) reports, however, that a certain Demetrius of Byzantium wrote a thirteen-volume history of the migration of the Gauls from Europe into Asia.

[137] Cf. Herodotus 4.11: ". . . for the country which the Scythians now inhabit is said to have belonged of old to the Kimmerians."

[138] ALEXANDER argues that Josephus' identification of a name in the Table of Nations basically depended on whether the modern equivalent resembled in some recognizable way the ancient name ("Geography and the Bible [Early Judaism]," *ABD*, 2 [1992] 983). He regards Josephus' identification of the Gomerites with the Galatians as "exceedingly tenuous" ("Toponymy," p. 60).

[139] In describing "the principles of Rabbinic toponymy," ALEXANDER adduces Josephus' equation of the Gomerites with the Galatians as a classic example of the belief in the primacy of the Biblical account in preserving the original names and places of settlement of peoples of the world. However, he does not consider the possibility that this equation could be based on a plausible OT tradition rather than on a mere word play. In ALEXANDER's words ("Toponymy," p. 53), "Greek archaeologists made a similar assumption as to their tradition, the body of myths and legends found in Homer and related texts. Take the following example: in 279/8 BC the Galatians crossed the Hellespont and poured into Asia Minor. They appeared on the Greek scene 'out of the blue', and the question of their origin was naturally raised. Two of the leading Greek scholars of the time, Callimachus and Timaeus, provided a typical answer: they were descendants of Galates, the son of Polyphemus and the nymph Galatea. These same Galatians are said by Josephus (*AJ* I 123) to be the sons of the Biblical Gomer, the son of Japhet and grandson of Noah. The method of the Greek and Jewish writers is the same: each presupposes the primacy of his respective traditions, and his archaeology consists of finding a niche in those traditions for the particular nation or nations which he is considering. The part played by the manipulation of names in the process should be observed." Cf. ibid., p. 55: "Given that the Biblical account of the origin of nations is primary, Josephus' task is then to marry it and the world as he actually knew it. The union was effected primarily through the manipulation of proper names." On the Greek myth, see further RANKIN, *Celts and the Classical World*, p. 81; Herbert Jennings ROSE, "Galatea," *OCD*, p. 453.

stroyed Gordium, the capital of the Phrygian Empire and later a city in North Galatia, and settled in Phrygia in the seventh century B. C.[140] Thus, Josephus' identification of Gomer with Phrygia and Galatia is not at all arbitrary. Perhaps a vestige of the ancient name of the Gomerites (Γομαρεῖς) is preserved in Γοργορωμεῖς, the name of a people in the southwestern part of Roman Galatia on the northeastern shore of Lake Trogitis.[141]

The identification of Gomer and the Galatians may have been facilitated by Ezek 38:2−6, where Gomer and Magog appear as wild tribes from the north on the fringes of the civilized world and dangerous opponents of Israel.[142] Interestingly enough, Hippolytus identifies Magog with the "Celts and the Galatians" (Μαγὼγ, ἀφ᾿ οὗ Κελτοὶ καὶ Γαλάται)[143] and thus stands in the same tradition as Josephus.[144] Furthermore, after Attalus I (241−197 B. C.) gained mastery over the Gauls, the wild barbarians from the north who had crossed over the Hellespont into Asia Minor in 278/7 B. C. and were oppressing all of Asia Minor, the Attalids celebrated the containment of the Gauls to central Anatolia as a victory of Hellenic civilization over barbarianism. This is seen particularly in the famous representations of the victories over the Gauls in Pergamene art (see further above). Hence, there is a direct comparison between the Gomerites and the Galatians as invading barbarians from the north although they come from two different directions in the north.

The Galatians in Other Jewish Tradition

Other than the examples that we have already examined, there are very few unequivocal references to Galatia and the Galatians in early Jewish literature. This corresponds perhaps to the marginal political and religious significance that Galatia seems to have had for Jews. Palestinian Jews had the opportunity to become acquainted with Galatia and its people by two basic means: (1) by firsthand information both from the emissaries who were sent out from Jerusalem and from the Jews of Asia Minor who came to Jerusalem to study, to worship, and/or to live[145] and (2) by literary traditions. As an example of the

---

[140] Cf. Claus Westermann, *Genesis* (3 vols.; 3rd ed.; BKAT 1; Neukirchen-Vluyn: Neukirchener Verlag, 1983), 1:674; Édouard Lipiński, "Les Japhétites selon Gen 10,2−4 et 1 Chr 1,5−7," *ZAH* 3 (1990) 40−52 (here pp. 40−41). See further Kammenhuber, "Kimmerier," pp. 594−596.

[141] Cf. A. S. Hall, "The Gorgoromeis," *Anatolian Studies* 21 (1971) 125−166.

[142] Cf. Alexander, "Toponymy," p. 68.

[143] *Chron.* 58. This shows that Hippolytus knows the historical connection between the Celts and the Galatians.

[144] Hippolytus identifies Gomer with the Cappadocians (*Chron.* 57), whereas Josephus identifies the latter with Meshech (*Ant.* 1.125).

[145] Cf. Alexander, "Toponymy," pp. 27−29. On the other hand, Louis H. Feldman argues that there was little traffic between Palestine and Asia Minor, particularly between Palestine and the interior of Asia Minor (*Jew and Gentile in the Ancient World: Attitudes and Interactions from Alexander to Justinian* [Princeton, NJ: Princeton University Press, 1993], pp. 72−73).

first means of information, we may refer to R. Aqiba, who is said to have visited Galatia (גליא) on one of his many travels (*b. Rosh. Hash.* 6a), and to "Nahum the Galatian," who evidently resettled in Palestine to become a respected Jewish authority (*b. Ketub.* 60a).[146] Alexander Jannaeus (107–78 B. C.) is said to have used mercenaries from Pisidia (Josephus *BJ* 1.88; *Ant.* 13.374).[147] In later years, there might even have been some contact between the Jews and the Legion XXII Deiotariana, the army of the Galatian king Deiotarus that passed over intact into the Roman army when the client kingdom of Galatia was incorporated into the Empire in 25 B. C. and that later contributed to Roman forces in both Jewish wars.[148]

As an example of the second means of information (literary tradition), we may cite 1 Macc 8:2, which Josephus appropriates in *Ant.* 12.414: "He [sc. Judas] had been told of their [sc. the Romans'] wars and of the brave deeds that they were doing among the Galatians/Gauls (Γαλάται), how they had defeated and forced them to pay tribute...." The very brief context in 1 Maccabees leaves open whether Γαλάται is used in the sense of "Galatians" or "Gauls,"[149] for elsewhere in classical literature, the term is capable of either meaning, even within the same context.[150] The historical arguments for the meaning of the

---

[146] Nahum was evidently an old authority, for he does not bear the title "Rabbi", and his ruling is repeated as a Tannaitic tradition. Naomi G. COHEN argues that R. Meir, a third-generation Tannaite and student of R. Aqiba (cf. Hermann L. STRACK and Günter STEM-BERGER, *Einleitung in Talmud und Midrasch* [7th ed.; Munich: Beck, 1982], p. 82), was of Anatolian origin and that his name was Phrygian ("R. Meir, A Descendant of Anatolian Proselytes: New Light on his Name and the historic Kernel of the Nero Legend in Gittin 56a," *JJS* 23 [1972] 51–59). It appears that R. Meir died in Asia (cf. *y. Kil.* 32a).

[147] See further Jonathan A. GOLDSTEIN, *II Maccabees: A New Translation with Introduction and Commentary* (Garden City, NY: Doubleday, 1976), p. 332. On the Galatians as mercenaries, see n. 19 above. The practice of hiring foreign mercenaries was established by John Hyrcanus (cf. Josephus *Ant.* 13.249) and may have been indirectly denounced in 11QTemple 57.1–7 (cf. Johann MAIER, *The Temple Scroll: An Introduction, Translation and Commentary* [JSOTSup 34; Sheffield: JSOT Press, 1985], pp. 125–126).

[148] Cf. L. J. F. KEPPIE, "The History and Disappearance of the Legion XXII Deiotariana," in *Greece and Rome in Eretz Israel: Collected Essays* (ed. A. Kasher, et al.; Jerusalem: Yad Izhak Ben-Zvi; the Israel Exploration Society, 1990), pp. 54–61. On the possiblity that in A. D. 132, XXII was the second legion of the permanent garrison in Judea, see ibid., pp. 59–61. On the history of XXII, see now MITCHELL, *Anatolia*, 1:136–137.

[149] Cf. Henry A. REDPATH, "The Geography of the Septuagint," *AJT* 7 (1903) 289–307 (here p. 304).

[150] To cite just one of many examples, Polybius begins by using Γαλάται almost exclusively of the Gauls of Europe (e.g., *Hist.* 1.6.2, 3, 6; 1.77.1, 5; 1.79.8; 1.80.1; 2.5.4, 5; 2.7.5; 2.15.8 [Γαλάται Τρανσαλπίνοι]; 2.21.4 [οἱ ἐκ τῶν Ἄλπεων Γαλάται]; except 3.3.5, referring to the "lawlessness [παρανομία] of the Galatians" in Asia [on the "lawlessness" of the Galatians, see also 21.40.1; *Anth. Gr.* 7.492; *Sib. Or.* 3:599–600]) until he comes to his discussion of "the war against the Gauls/Galatians in Asia" (τὸν περὶ τὴν Ἀσίαν πρὸς τοὺς Γαλάτας πόλεμον) conducted by Gnaeus Manlius (Polybius *Hist.* 21.33.1); thereafter, he uses the term almost exclusively of the "Galatians" in Asia Minor (e.g., 21.35.5; 21.37.1, 2, 3; 21.37.9; 21.38.1, 4; 21.39.1, 6, 9; 29.22.4 [οἱ κατὰ τὴν Ἀσίαν Γαλάται]). Likewise, the text of 2 Tim 4:10 vacillates between Γαλλίαν and Γαλατίαν.

term here seem about equally balanced. On the one hand, a case can be made that Γαλάται refers to the Cisalpine Gauls who were conquered by the Romans in 190 B. C., since Spain ('Ιβηρία) is mentioned in connection with these people in the very next verse, and the Asiatic Galatians were apparently not required to pay tribute. On the other hand, a case can also be made that Γαλάται refers to the Galatians of central Anatolia since Galatia was conquered by the Roman army under Manlius in 189 B. C., probably less than thirty years before the time of 1 Macc 8:2. What is interesting to note is that 1 Maccabees 8 goes on to list further nations conquered by the Romans (vv. 1−13), including the Kittim (v. 5). This shows that the Table-of-Nations tradition always lies just below the surface of the text.

Seleucus I is said to have granted citizenship to Jewish settlers in cities that he founded in "Asia and Lower Syria" (Josephus *Ant.* 12.119). Among these, Pidisian Antioch is probably to be included.

The victory of Attalus I over the Galatians provides the backdrop to 2 Macc 8:20, according to which, Judas Maccabeus rallied his men before the battle of Emmaus by recounting the success that Babylonian Jews had had in the service of the Seleucid army in an unspecified battle against the Galatians: "And he [sc. Judas] told them of the battle that they had in Babylon with the Galatians (Γαλάται), how they came but 8000 in all to the business, with 4000 Macedonians; yet when the Macedonians were hard pressed, the 8000, by the help that came to them from heaven, destroyed 120,000 Galatians and took a great amount of booty." This probably refers neither to the "elephant battle" that Antiochus I fought against the Gauls in Asia Minor (275 or 270 B. C.) nor to an undocumented campaign against the Galatians in the time of Antiochus III but to the "War of the Brothers," part of which was fought in Babylonia.[151] Hence, just as the Attalids could celebrate their ultimate victory over the barbarian Galatians, so also the Jews could take courage in their victorious battle against the fearful (and more numerous) Galatians in the same period.

Josephus quotes three documents ascribed to Antiochus III, the third of which is a letter to Zeuxis, the governor of Lydia in western Asia Minor (*Ant.* 12.147−153), written between 212 and 205/4 B. C.[152] Antiochus instructs Zeuxis concerning the relocation of 2000 Jewish families from Mesopotamia and Babylonia to form military colonies in Phrygia and Lydia and thus quell the revolts in these areas.[153] Numbering probably more than 10,000 persons in all,

---

[151] Cf. B. Bar-Kochva, "On the Sources and Chronology of Antiochus I's Battle against the Galatians," *Proceedings of the Cambridge Philological Society* N. S. 19 (1973) 1−8 (esp. pp. 5−7), who explains the fact that the Seleucid army is called "the Macedonians" as "pseudo-national," adding that the practice is quite common in Jewish literature (ibid., p. 7). On the interpretive possibilities, see also Christian Habicht, *2. Makkabäerbuch* (JSHRZ 1.3; Gütersloh: Gerd Mohn, 1979), p. 240 n. 20a.

[152] For an actual letter of Antiochus III to Zeuxis from the same period, see now Hasan Malay, "Letter of Antiochus III to Zeuxis with two Covering Letters (209 B. C.)," *Epigraphica Anatolica* 10 (1987) 7−15.

[153] Cf. A. Schalit, "The Letter of Antiochus III to Zeuxis regarding the establishment of

these families laid the foundation of the Jewish Diaspora in Asia Minor.[154] The
settlement in Phrygia almost certainly included Apamea, an important city in
Phrygia where a large and influential Jewish community flourished.[155] Jews of
Apamea may have migrated into the nearby region that would later be called
the Roman province of Galatia.[156]

There is some evidence for the presence of Jews in Roman Galatia.[157]
Besides the evidence of the New Testament itself,[158] we may cite the Roman
circular of 139 B.C. to the Hellenistic cities and states, which preserves impor-

---

Jewish military colonies in Phrygia and Lydia," *JQR* 50 (1960) 289–318; Harald HEGERMANN,
"The Diaspora in the Hellenistic Age," in *The Cambridge History of Judaism, Vol. 2: The
Hellenistic Age* (ed. W.D. Davies, et al.; Cambridge: Cambridge University Press, 1989),
pp. 145–146; D. MUSTI, "Syria and the East," in *The Cambridge Ancient History, Vol. 7.1:
The Hellenistic World* (2nd ed.; ed. F.W. Walbank, et al.; Cambridge: Cambridge University
Press, 1984), pp. 175–220 (here pp. 198–201). When Antiochus III succeeded to the Seleucid
throne in 221 B.C., he had to win back Lydia and Phrygia from his rebellious kinsman
Achaeus, who seized those regions and had himself crowned king at Laodicea (220 B.C.).
When Antiochus recovered these regions, he settled the Jewish families from Babylonia there
to ensure their continued allegiance.

[154] Cf. Paul R. TREBILCO, *Jewish Communities in Asia Minor* (SNTSMS 69; Cambridge:
Cambridge University Press, 1991), pp. 5–6.

[155] Cf. ibid., pp. 85–103.

[156] Cf. Lea ROTH, "Galatia," *EncJud*, 7 (1972) 262. LIGHTFOOT (*Galatians*, pp. 9–11) argues
that after the Roman conquest of Galatia in 189 B.C., there must have been a spillover into
Galatia from the Jewish military colony established in Phrygia by Antiochus the Great, for
Galatia would have had many features that would have attracted these Jews: commercial
opportunities in a fertile land situated on major trade routes. Although the influence of the
Jews in Galatia might be seen in the reported abstinence from eating pork in Pessinus (cf.
Pausanias 7.17.10), it is more likely reflective of a practice that is common to many eastern
peoples. See further Menahem STERN, *Greek and Latin Authors on Jews and Judaism, edited
with Introduction, Translations and Commentary* (3 vols.; Jerusalem: The Israel Academy of
Sciences and the Humanities, 1974–84), 1:559 (Cretans); 2:159, 257, 286 (Egyptians); 2.434
(Phoenicians); 2.676–678 (Syrians). We may also point out that Pausanius 7.170.10–12 deals
with the Phrygian cult of Magna Mater (Cybele) and Attis, whose center was in Pessinus in
North Galatia. This cult featured the so-called Galli, who castrated themselves in frenzied
worship of Cybele. This has nothing do do with Jewish circumcision. See further Garth
THOMAS, "Magna Mater and Attis," in *ANRW* II.17.3 (ed. Wolfgang Haase; Berlin: de
Gruyter, 1984), pp. 1500–1535; Giula Sfameni GASPARRO, *Soteriology and Mystic Aspects in
the Cult of Cybele and Attis* (EPRO 103; Leiden: E.J. Brill, 1985).

[157] Cf. TREBILCO, *Jewish Communities in Asia Minor*, pp. 137, 243 n. 49; SCHÜRER, *Hist.*,
3.1: 34–35; S. MITCHELL, *Regional Epigraphic Catalogues of Asia Minor, Vol. 2: The Ankara
District. The Inscriptions of North Galatia*, nos. 133, 141, 246, 400, 418, 509–512; LEVICK,
Roman Colonies in Southern Asia Minor, p. 128. Julia Severa of Acmonia is honored as a
Jewish πρῶτος ἄρχων (*MAMA* 6.263; *IGRR* 4.655–656). Though considered by some a
daughter of Julius Severus (i.e., a descendant of the Galatian tetrarch Deiotaurus and other
kings or tetrarchs of Galatia), she is more likely his ancestor, which would make her a Galatian
dynast (cf. SULLIVAN, "Priesthoods of the Eastern Dynastic Aristocracy," pp. 931–932;
LEVICK, *Roman Colonies in Southern Asia Minor*, pp. 106–107).

[158] Note, for example, the existence of Jewish synagogues in South Galatia: Pisidian
Antioch (cf. Acts 13:14); Iconium (14:1). The nations listed in Acts 2:9–11 include Phrygia
and Pamphylia (v. 10), parts of which belonged to Galatia (see further below).

tant evidence of the distribution of Jews in Asia Minor (1 Macc 15:22−23).[159] It
explicitly mentions Pamphylia and its chief city Side (v. 23). After the formation of the Roman province of Galatia in 25 B. C., some part of Pamphylia
belonged to Galatia, and, as R. K. SHERK suggests, it may have included Side, a
city and harbor on the coast of Pamphylia.[160] In A. D. 25, however, Side
became the capital of the newly formed province of Pamphylia.

Josephus tells of an edict of Augustus published in Ancyra, capital of Galatia,
granting Jews, among other privileges, the right to practice their ancestral
traditions and to transfer funds to Jerusalem (*Ant.* 16.162−165). That could
presuppose a sizeable Jewish population in this area. However, "Ancyra"
(Ἀγκύρῃ) is merely a conjecture proposed by J. J. Scaliger.[161]

The Galatian Addressees

In light of all these considerations, who are the "Galatians" whom Paul
addresses in Gal 3:1? Let us begin with the evidence that can be gleaned from
the letter itself.

Internal Evidence

The Approach of Literatursoziologie. Whereas most scholars claim that Paul
communicates little or nothing about the identity of the Galatian addressees,[162]
Verena JEGHER-BUCHER tries to dig deeper by applying the methods of
Literatursoziologie − "the investigation of the reciprocal contingency of literature and society"[163] − in order to ascertain the explicit and the implicit readers
of the letter.[164]

The question of the "explicit readers" is handled only briefly, the Galatians
being identified somewhat indefinitely as the inhabitants of the Roman pro-

---

[159] Cf. SCHÜRER, *Hist.*, 3.1:4 n. 2, 33.

[160] SHERK, "Roman Galatia: The Governors from 25 B. C. to A. D. 114," p. 958, with n. 17.

[161] Cf. SCHÜRER, *Hist.*, 3.1:34−35.

[162] Cf., e.g., Jürgen BECKER, *Paulus − der Apostel der Völker* (Tübingen: Mohr-Siebeck,
1989), p. 287: "Da auch Paulus in seinem Brief zum Hintergrund der Gemeinde nichts mitteilt,
außer daß ihre jetzigen Mitglieder einst Heiden waren (Gal 4,8f.), bleiben uns die Adressaten
des Briefes praktisch unbekannt."

[163] The definition comes from Michael BÜNKER, *Briefformular und rhetorische Disposition
im 1. Korintherbrief* (GTA 28; Göttingen: Vandenhoeck & Ruprecht, 1984), p. 16: "Literatursoziologie läßt sich ganz allgemein definieren als die Untersuchung der wechselseitigen
Bedingtheit von Literatur und Gesellschaft. Bei dieser Untersuchung hat sie vornehmlich die
Trias von Autor (die Produktion), Werk (das Medium und die Distribution) und Gesellschaft
(die Konsumation) im Blick."

[164] Verena JEGHER-BUCHER, *Der Galaterbrief auf dem Hintergrund antiker Epistolographie
und Rhetorik. Ein anderes Paulusbild* (ATANT 78; Zürich: Theologischer Verlag, 1991),
pp. 98−115.

vince of Galatia.[165] The only evidence offered for this identification is that it corresponds to the fact that the letter wants to be understood as an official, public document.[166]

More attention is given to the "implicit readers" of the letter. Proceeding on the assumption that every ancient author was obligated to adapt his written or oral communication according to the characteristics of his readership or audience (e.g., sex, age, education, vocation), JEGHER-BUCHER compares the various components of the Galatian letter (e.g., form, argumentation, rhetoric, language) to what was known and usual in that day in order to deduce who may have been particularly addressed in each case. For example, the "crass humor" of Gal 5:12 ("I wish those who unsettle you would emasculate themselves!") may have been intended for the soldiers of the Roman garrison.[167] On the basis of such a survey, JEGHER-BUCHER concludes: "In the Letter to the Galatians, Paul addresses predominantly everyone [i.e., members of all social levels] and in special sections 'Jews' [i.e., σεβόμενοι!]."[168] Thus, even on the basis of a method that strives for a more profiled glimpse of the Galatian addressees, little can be known with certainty.[169]

It seems doubtful, however, that this literary-sociological approach is even appropriate for a circular letter that is addressed not to individuals but "to the churches" of a particular region, for in that case, Paul is writing with the collective whole in mind and not so much the individual constituents. Furthermore, 2 Pet 3:16 shows that Paul's letters were sometimes hard to understand and could easily be misconstrued by some readers.[170] If Paul did not always succeed in adequately adapting his message to his addressees, then inferring the specific kinds of intended readers from statements in the letters themselves becomes problematic.

Paul's Description of the Galatians. More important for our considerations is Paul's own description of who the Galatians were before they came to faith. In Gal 4:8—9, the Apostle contrasts the Galatians' present status as emancipated and adopted sons of God and heirs of Abraham through God (cf. vv. 1—7) with

---

[165] JEGHER-BUCHER, *Der Galaterbrief*, p. 98. The subsequent attempt to define these Roman provincial Galatians becomes even more nebulous: "die Einwohner der in dieser Provinz gelegenen Städte und größeren Ortschaften entlang der alten Karawanenstraßen – heute würden wir sie 'Westanatolier' nennen" (ibid., pp. 98—99).

[166] Ibid., p. 98.

[167] Ibid., p. 115.

[168] Ibid., p. 114. The fact that in Galatians, Paul continually appropriates OT citations and Jewish traditions suggests that the addressees were God-fearers, i.e., Gentile adherents of the synagogue who had not undergone circumcision and were not therefore full proselytes. According to Acts, Paul often preached in the synagogues of the cities he visited and won many converts among the God-fearers (cf. Acts 13:16, 26, 43, 50; 16:14; 17:4, 17; 18:7). On the God-fearers, see Chap. 3.

[169] We are reminded of similarly uncertain attempts to reconstruct the so-called *Sitz im Leben* based upon an assumption of what lies behind a text. Cf. M. HENGEL, *Zur urchristlichen Geschichtsschreibung* (Stuttgart: Calwer, 1979), p. 23.

[170] See merely the Corinthians' misunderstanding of the previous letter (1 Cor 5:9—11).

their former status, into which they are currently in danger of relapsing by keeping the Law:

But formerly (ἀλλὰ τότε), when you did not know God (οὐκ εἰδότες θεόν), you were enslaved to beings that by nature are not gods. Now, however, that you have come to know God, or rather to be known by God, how can you turn back again to the weak and beggarly elements? How can you want to be enslaved to them again?"

This description puts the Galatians in the category of the nations who do not know God[171] and who worship the "gods of the nations."[172] This may be an important clue as to how Paul views the Galatians. He does not see them merely as individuals but collectively as part of several churches in a defined land (Galatia). As we have seen in the word study on ἔθνος, the expression "the churches of Galatia" can be compared with Paul's reference in Rom 16:4 to "all the churches of the nations" (πᾶσαι αἱ ἐκκλησίαι τῶν ἐθνῶν). For Paul, as for other Jewish writers of the period, Galatia is a "nation" (cf. Josephus *Ant.* 1.123; *BJ* 2.358–360; *Sib. Or.* 5.598–599).

The Galatian Addressees and the Table of Nations

If Paul views the Galatians as one of the nations, then it is significant that Josephus' exposition of the Table of Nations equates Gomer, the first son of Japheth, with the Galatians and that he identifies the sons of Gomer with parts of Roman Galatia, including the southern portions all the way to the Mediterranean, which were added to the original Roman province in 25 B.C. From this perspective, therefore, the usual distinction between "North Galatia" and "South Galatia" becomes artificial, for all peoples in the contemporary Roman province are genealogically related to one another as sons of Gomer. According to the Table-of-Nations tradition reflected in Josephus' *Antiquities*, the so-called "South Galatians" are no less Gomerites/Galatians than the so-called "ethnic Galatians" of North Galatia.

In that case, one of the main obstacles to the South Galatian Hypothesis is removed, that of the usage of Γαλάται.[173] As we have seen, the North Galatian Hypothesis has always been able to claim that contemporary usage of Γαλάται excludes the possibility that Paul could use the term of those living in the southern portion of the Roman province. Indeed, the previous evidence for a broader usage of the term has been meager and controvertible. Now, however, we have evidence of the broader usage of Γαλάται from the same Table-of-Nations tradition that seems to have influenced Paul's thinking elsewhere in his letters. As we have seen, Josephus' exposition of the Table of Nations is derived

---

[171] Cf. 1 Thess 4:5 (τὰ ἔθνη τὰ μὴ εἰδότα τὸν θεόν); Jer 10:25 (ἔθνη τὰ μὴ εἰδότα σε); Ps 78:6 (ἔθνη τὰ μὴ γινώσκοντά σε).

[172] See the word study on ἔθνος in Chap. 2. Gal 5:2–3; 6:12–13 shows conclusively that the addressees are uncircumcised and therefore non-Jews.

[173] So also RIESNER, *Frühzeit*, p. 256 n. 41.

at least in part from Jewish tradition that dates to the third or second century B.C. (*Jubilees* 8–9 and the Third Sibyl);[174] therefore, Paul too may have appropriated the same tradition.

If the usage of "Galatians" is no longer an obstacle to the South Galatian Hypothesis, then we are left essentially with our interpretation of the pertinent passages in Acts (16:6; 18:23) in order to decide the case. Could Paul be referring to the churches of South Galatia that he founded on his First Missionary Journey? These appear to be the only churches of Galatia that are explicitly mentioned in Acts.

Conclusion

Previous attempts to ascertain the destination of Paul's letter to the Galatians have been based on Greco-Roman conceptions of ethnography and geography. From this perspective, it is usually argued that the term Γαλάται can refer only to the ethnic Galatians in the northern part of the Roman province of Galatia and not to the mixed population in the southern part.

Yet, the question of the Galatian addressees has never been examined from the perspective of Jewish geography and ethnography based on the Table of Nations. As we discussed in Chap. 1, the Table-of-Nations tradition provides the fundamental and eternally valid orientation to the nations of the world and Israel's relationship to them, a static perspective in which, at most, the names may change with the passing of time, but the "map" itself remains the same. Thus, Josephus identifies Gomer, the first son of Japheth, as the contemporary Galatians (*Ant.* 1.123). As we can ascertain from his identifications of Gomer's three sons (§ 126), Josephus considers the ancient territory of Gomer to be coextensive with the Roman province of Galatia, which is divided into three parts among each of the three sons. Thus, from a Jewish perspective, each of these sons, including the Ashkenaz in the south, has as much right to be called in contemporary terms a Gomerite/Galatian as the twelve sons of Jacob and their descendants have a right to be called Israelites. From this perspective, there is no distinction between ethnic Galatians and non-ethnic Galatians. That imposes a false dichotomy onto this territory. From a Jewish point of view, all inhabitants of Roman Galatia are Gomerites/Galatians.

If this is correct, then Paul is most likely sending his letter to the churches of Ashkenaz, the firstborn son of Gomer, the first son of Japheth. Or, to update that in contemporary Greco-Roman terms, Paul was sending his letter to the churches of Phrygia-Galatica, which he founded on his First Missionary Journey and then visited again on his Second Missionary Journey.

---

[174] As we observed in Chap. 1, the provenance of the Third Sibyl is Apamea, a city on the Phrygian mainland bordering Galatia on the west. A rich Noachic tradition is associated with the whole Apamea area.

Conclusion

P. M. FRASER aptly observes that "full understanding of the outlook of any individual in antiquity – or indeed at any period before the modern era – depends to a considerable extent on our ability to assess his geographical horizon."[1] This is especially true of Paul, whose apostolic ministry consists essentially of a series of missionary journeys to found churches within the confines of the contemporary Roman Empire. Our study seeks therefore to assess Paul's geographical horizon. How does he view the geography and ethnography of the world? Which "map" is he using? What geographical tradition informs his missionary strategy? When he thinks, for example, of Galatia and the Galatians, how does he integrate them into his *imago mundi*? These rather neglected issues are far from trivial; they are actually fundamental to any proper understanding of Paul's missionary enterprise.

Paul is generally acknowledged to be the Apostle to the nations, and yet little attention has been given to what Paul himself means by "nation." The present study explores the possibility that in developing his missionary strategy, the former Pharisee and Hebrew of Hebrews appropriated the OT and Jewish tradition of the Table of Nations (Genesis 10; 1 Chr 1:1−2:2). In Chap. 1, we saw that the Table of Nations exerted a significant influence on OT and Jewish literature. Despite some differences of interpretation and emphasis, both Hellenistic- and conservative-Jewish schools of thought considered Genesis 10 the fundamental point of orientation for describing Israel's place among the nations of the world and the basis for envisioning world geography and ethnography in both the present and the eschatological future (cf., e.g., Josephus *Ant.* 1.122−147; *Jubilees* 8−9). From a Jewish perspective, the Table of Nations was never superseded after Noah's descendants spread out over the face of the earth and occupied their respective territories: Shem in Asia, Ham in Africa, and Japheth in Asia Minor and Europe. Genesis 10 provided an eternally valid "map" of the nations of the world, with Israel and especially Zion in the geographical center. The Kittim of old were now world rulers, and Magog and other sons of Japheth were expected to menace in the eschatological future. At most, the Table needed to be "updated" by giving the contemporary equivalents for the biblical nations, often in terms of Roman provincial names. Given the enduring relevance of the Table of Nations, we are not surprised to find that, appropriating OT and Jewish tradition, the NT expects "the nations which

---

[1] P. M. FRASER, *Ptolemaic Alexandria* (3 vols.; Oxford: Clarendon Press, 1972), 1:520.

are at the four corners of the earth" (τὰ ἔθνη τὰ ἐν ταῖς τέσσαρσιν γωνίαις τῆς γῆς), identified with Gog and Magog (cf. Gen 10:2), to gather for the final eschatological battle against the saints and Jerusalem (Rev 20:7–10; cf. Ezekiel 38–39).

In Chap. 2, we began to investigate Paul's own conception of the nations by a extensive study of his use of ἔθνη against the OT and Jewish background. We were able to ascertain that in using ἔθνη, the Apostle very often thinks in terms of "nations" and not only of individual "Gentiles." Paul apparently begins with the presupposition that the Table of Nations provides an inventory of the "full number" of the nations of the world, which traditionally comprise 70 (or 72) nations (cf. Rom 11:25). The Abrahamic Promise (Gen 12:3), which Paul regards as a prior annunciation of the gospel itself (Gal 3:8), expects that the nations of the world as listed in the Table of Nations (Genesis 10) will be blessed in Abraham and his seed. For Paul, the seed of Abraham is Christ (Gal 3:16). Therefore, the promise-fulfillment trajectory of the Abrahamic Promise culminates in Christ, the hope of the nations (cf. Rom 15:12). Although most of Israel remains temporarily hardened to the gospel, her salvation and restoration will be complete when the full number of the nations "comes in" through the ongoing eschatological pilgrimage to Zion, a time that coincides also with the Parousia. Therefore, Paul works indefatigably toward the expeditious completion of his mission to the nations. For Paul, the goal of history is that all nations would worship God with Israel in Zion (Rom 15:10).

In Chap. 3, we turned our attention to specific passages that reveal the geographical aspects of Paul's missionary strategy. If Paul traces the gospel back to the promise in Gen 12:3, that all the nations of the earth – i.e., all the nations in the Table of Nations of Genesis 10 – will be blessed in Abraham and his seed, then the missionary strategy that results from this understanding of the gospel can be seen in the outcome of the so-called Apostolic Council in Gal 2:7–9, where the apostles agree to observe territorial jurisdictions in their respective missions, probably drawn along the lines of the sons of Noah in the Table of Nations. After the Apostolic Council, territoriality becomes increasingly important to Paul as he seeks to do pioneering missionary work within his own territorial jurisdiction and expects that others will desist both from infringing upon his domain and from trying to exercise their influence over his Gentile converts (Gal 2:11–14; 2 Cor 10:13–16; Rom 15:20). The scope and direction of Paul's mission now focuses on Asia Minor and Europe while maintaining an orientation on the geographical center, Jerusalem. This is seen most clearly in Rom 15:19, where Paul describes his mission to the "nations" (ἔθνη) as proceeding from Jerusalem and – "in a circle" (καὶ κύκλῳ) – extending to date as far as Illyricum (cf. also 2 Cor 10:13–14). The expression "in a circle" can be explained in terms of Ezek 5:5, which states that God has set Jerusalem "in the middle of the nations (ἐν μέσῳ τῶν ἐθνῶν) and the countries in a circle (κύκλῳ) around her." Jerusalem as the center of the world is a fundamental tenet of the Table-of-Nations tradition (cf. Ezek 38:12; *Jub.* 8:19). Furthermore, when

Paul announces his plans to continue his mission as far as Spain (Rom 15:24, 28; cf. 2 Cor 10:16), he thereby unveils the full scope and direction of his mission. The Apostle evidently focuses his mission on the territory of the Japhethites, that is, of the descendants of the third son of Noah who settled in the region of Asia Minor and Europe from Cilicia to Spain (cf. Josephus *Ant.* 1.122). Acts presents the scope and direction of Paul's mission in much the same light – a mission radiating out from Jerusalem "to the ends of the earth" (cf. Acts 1:8; 13:47), concentrating on Asia Minor and Europe, and complementing the missions to Shem (2:1–8:25) and Ham (8:26–40). Thus, the geographical orientation of the Table-of-Nations tradition provides a fundamental point of departure for comparing the Paul of the letters and the Paul of Acts.

In Chap. 4, we adduced an example of how this conception of Paul's missionary strategy might help in solving a long-standing problem of NT introduction, specifically the problem of the destination of Galatians, for if Paul bases his strategy on the Table of Nations, this puts the old question of Paul's Galatian addressees in a wholly new light. Previous attempts to ascertain the destination of Galatians relied exclusively on Greco-Roman conceptions of ethnography and geography. From this perspective, it is usually argued by proponents of the North Galatian Hypothesis that the term Γαλάται can refer only to the ethnic Galatians in the northern part of the Roman province of Galatia and not, as the South Galatian Hypothesis assumes, to the mixed population in the southern part. Seen in light of the Table-of-Nations tradition, however, a broader use of Γαλάται can be observed, for in his exposition of the Table of Nations, Josephus identifies Gomer, the first son of Japheth, with the "Galatians" (Γαλάται), who are understood as occupying the whole Roman province of Galatia, including South Galatia (*Ant.* 1.123, 126). Josephus, in effect, superimposes the Roman province of Galatia on the ancient territory of Gomer and his three sons. Hence, from a Jewish perspective, all the inhabitants of Roman Galatia are ethnic Gomerites/Galatians. In that case, the main obstacle to the South Galatian Hypothesis – that of usage – is removed. Paul is most likely sending his letter to the churches of Ashkenaz, the firstborn son of Gomer, the first son of Japheth. Or, to update that in contemporary Greco-Roman terms, Paul was sending his letter to the churches of Phrygia-Galatica, which he founded on his First Missionary Journey and then visited again on his Second Missionary Journey.

Our study of Paul's missionary strategy in light of the Table-of-Nations tradition does not claim to be exhaustive. It provides merely one example of what can be done if we remain sensitive to the OT and Jewish background of Paul's letters. Further investigation is needed in order to assess the full extent to which this tradition influences both the Pauline letters and the rest of the NT.

Selected Bibliography

Primary Sources

Old Testament and Jewish Texts

ABERBACK, MOSES and BERNARD GROSSFELD, eds. *Targum Onkelos to Genesis: A Critical Analysis together with an English Translation of the Text.* New York: Ktav, 1982.

BEYER, KLAUS, *Die aramäischen Texte vom Toten Meer.* Göttingen: Vandenhoeck & Ruprecht, 1984.

BRAUDE, WILLIAM G., *Pesikta Rabbati: Discourses for Feasts, Fasts, and Special Sabbaths.* 2 vols. Yale Judaica Series, 18. New Haven/London: Yale University Press, 1968.

BURCHARD, CHRISTOPH, "Ein vorläufiger griechischer Text von Joseph und Aseneth." *Dielheimer Blätter zum Alten Testament* 14 (1979) 2–53.

CHARLESWORTH, JAMES H., ed. *The Old Testament Pseudepigrapha.* 2 vols. Garden City, NY: Doubleday, 1983–1985.

COHN, LEOPOLD, ed., et al. *Philo von Alexandria. Die Werke in deutscher Übersetzung.* 7 vols. Berlin: Walter de Gruyter, 1962–1964.

DELCOR, M., *Les Hymnes de Qumran (Hodayot).* Paris: Letouzey et Ané, 1962.

DENIS, ALBERT-MARIE, ed. *Fragmenta Pseudepigraphorum quae supersunt graeca.* PVTG 3. Leiden: Brill, 1970.

DRAZIN, ISRAEL, *Targum Onkelos to Deuteronomy: An English Translation of the Text with Analysis and Commentary (Based on A. Sperber's Edition).* New York: Ktav, 1982.

DUPONT-SOMMER, ANDRÉ, *The Essene Writings from Qumran.* Translated by Geza Vermes. Oxford: Blackwell, 1961; reprint ed., Glouchester/Magnolia, MA: Peter Smith, 1973.

EISENMAN, ROBERT and MICHAEL WISE, *The Dead Sea Scrolls Uncovered: The First Complete Translation and Interpretation of 50 Key Documents Withheld for over 35 Years.* Rockport, MA: Element, 1992.

ELLIGER, K. and RUDOLPH, W., eds., et al. *Biblia Hebraica Stuttgartensia.* Stuttgart: Deutsche Bibelstiftung, 1977.

FREEDMAN, H. and MAURICE SIMON, *Midrash Rabbah.* 10 vols. 2nd ed. London: Soncino, 1951.

FRIEDLANDER, GERALD, *Pirkê de Rabbi Eliezer.* London: Kegan Paul; New York: Block, 1916.

GASTER, M., ed. *The Chronicles of Jerahmeel.* London: Oriental Translation Fund, 1899; reprint ed., New York: Ktav, 1971.

GEFFCKEN, JOH., *Die Oracula Sibyllina.* Die griechischen christlichen Schriftsteller der ersten drei Jahrhunderte, 8. Leipzig: J. C. Hinrich, 1902.

GINSBURGER, M., ed. *Pseudo-Jonathan (Thargum Jonathan ben Usiël zum Pentateuch) nach der Londoner Handschrift (Brit. Mus. add. 27031)*. Berlin: S. Calvary, 1903.

HARRINGTON, DANIEL J., *The Hebrew Fragments of Pseudo-Philo's Liber Antiquitatum Biblicarum Preserved in the Chronicles of Jerahmeel*. SBLTT 3; SBLPS 3. Missoula, MT: Society of Biblical Literature, 1974.

–, *Pseudo-Philon, Les Antiquités Bibliques*. 2 vols. Translated by Jacques Cazeaux. SC 229–230. Paris: Cerf, 1976.

HOLLADAY, CARL R., *Fragments from Hellenistic Jewish Authors*. Vol. 1: *Historians*. SBLTT 20; SLBPS 10. Chico, CA: Scholars Press, 1983.

–, *Fragments from Hellenistic Jewish Authors, Vol. 2: Poets*. SBLTT 30; SBLPS 12. Atlanta, GA: Scholars Press, 1989.

JAMES, M. R., *The Biblical Antiquities of Philo now first translated from the Old Latin Version*. Translations of Early Documents: Series I, Palestinian Jewish Texts. London: Society for Promoting Christian Knowlege, 1917.

JONGE, M. DE, *The Testaments of the Twelve Patriarchs: A Critical Edition of the Greek Text*. PVTG 1.2. Leiden: Brill, 1978.

KISCH, GUIDO, *Pseudo-Philo's Liber Antiquitatum Biblicarum*. Publications in Mediaeval Studies, 10. Notre Dame: University of Notre Dame, 1949.

KITTEL, BONNIE PEDROTTI, *The Hymns of Qumran: Translation and Commentary*. Society of Biblical Literature Dissertation Series, 50. Chico, CA: Scholars Press, 1981.

KRAFT, ROBERT A. and ANN-ELIZABETH PURINTUN, *Paraleipomena Jeremiou*. SBLTT 1; SBLPS 1. Missoula, MT: Society of Biblical Literature, 1972.

KÜMMEL, WERNER G., *Jüdische Schriften aus hellenistisch-römischer Zeit*. 5 vols. (in fasc.). Gütersloh: Gerd Mohn, 1973–1984.

LAUTERBACH, JACOB Z., ed. *Mekilta de-Rabbi Ishmael: A Critical Edition on the Basis of the Manuscripts and early Editions with an English Translation, Introduction and Notes*. 3 vols. The Schiff Library of Jewish Classics. Philadelphia: Jewish Publication Society of America, 1933–1935.

LOHSE, EDUARD, E., *Die Texte aus Qumran. Hebräisch und Deutsch*. 2nd ed. Darmstadt: Wissenschaftliche Buchgesellschaft, 1971.

MAHER, MICHAEL, *Targum Pseudo-Jonathan: Genesis*. The Aramaic Bible 1B. Edinburgh: Clark, 1992.

MAIER, JOHANN, *The Temple Scroll: An Introduction, Translation and Commentary*. JSOTSup 34. Sheffield: JSOT Press, 1985.

NEUSNER, JACOB, *The Talmud of the Land of Israel, Vol. 19: Megillah*. Chicago Studies in the History of Judaism. Chicago: University of Chicago Press, 1987.

–, *The Tosefta Translated from the Hebrew: Second Division: Moed (The Order of Appointed Times)*. New York: Ktav, 1981.

PELLETIER, A., *Lettre d'Aristée à Philocrate*. SC 89. Paris: Cerf, 1962.

PHILONENKO, MARC, *Joseph et Aséneth: Introduction, texte critique, traduction et notes*. Studia post-Biblica, 13. Leiden: Brill, 1968.

PICARD, J. C., ed. *Apocalypsis Baruchi Graece*. PVTG 2. Leiden: Brill, 1967.

RAHLFS, ALFRED, ed. *Septuaginta*. 2 vols in 1. Stuttgart: Deutsche Bibelstiftung, 1935.

SCHERMANN, T., ed. *Prophetarum vitae fabulosae indices apostolorum discipulorumque Domini Dorotheo, Epiphanio, Hippolyto aliisque vindicate*. Leipzig: Teubner, 1907.

Septuaginta. Vetus Testamentum Graecum auctoritate Societatis Litterarum Gottingensis editum. 12 vols. in 18. Göttingen: Vandenhoeck & Ruprecht, 1931–1986.

SMALLWOOD, E. MARY, *Philonis Alexandrini Legatio ad Gaium: Edited with an Introduction, Translation and Commentary.* 2nd ed. Leiden: Brill, 1970.

SCHULLER, EILEEN M., *Non-Canonical Psalms from Qumran: A Pseudepigraphic Collection.* HSS 28. Atlanta: Scholars Press, 1986.

TISCHENDORF, KONSTANTIN, *Apocalypses Apocryphae.* Leipzig, 1866; reprint ed., Georg Olms, 1966.

TORREY, CHARLES C., *The Lives of the Prophets: Greek Text and Translation.* JBLMS 1. Philadelphia: Society of Biblical Literature and Exegesis, 1946.

VERMES, GEZA, *The Dead Sea Scrolls in English.* 3rd ed. Sheffield: JSOT, 1987.

YADIN, YIGAEL, *The Scroll of the War of the Sons of Light against the Sons of Darkness.* Translated by Batya and Chaim Rabin. Oxford: Oxford University Press, 1962.

–, *The Temple Scroll.* 3 vols. Jerusalem: The Israel Exploration Society/The Institute of Archaeology of the Hebrew University of Jerusalem/The Shrine of the Book, 1983.

Greco-Roman Texts

All references are adapted from the Loeb Classical Library unless otherwise indicated in the text. For these exceptions, see Luci Berkowitz and Karl A. Squitier, *Thesaurus Linguae Graecae: Canon of Greek Authors and Works* (New York/Oxford: Oxford University Press, 1986); John F. Oates, et al., eds., *Checklist of Editions of Greek Papyri and Ostraca,* 3rd ed., Bulletin of the American Society of Papyrologists Supplements, 4 (Chico, CA: Scholars Press, 1985); and François Bérard, et al., eds., *Guide de l'Épigraphiste. Bibliographie choisie des épigraphies antiques et médiévales,* Bibliographie de l'École Normale Supérieure: Guides et inventaires bibliographiques, 2 (Paris: Presses de l'École normale supérieure, 1986). That leaves only the following to be mentioned here:

BARA, JOËLLE-FRÉDÉRIQUE, *Vettius Valens d'Antioche, Anthologies, Livre 1: Etablissement, traduction et commentaire.* EPRO 111. Leiden: Brill, 1989.

BRUNT, P. A. and J. M. MOORE, eds. *Res Gestae Divi Augusti: The Achievements of the Divine Ausustus with An Introduction and Commentary.* Oxford: Oxford University Press, 1967.

ERHARDT, NORBERT, "Eine neue Grabinschrift aus Iconium." *Zeitschrift für Papyrologie und Epigraphik* 81 (1990) 185–188.

HEAD, BARCLAY V., *Catalogue of Greek Coins: Central Greece (Locris, Phocis, Boeotia and Euboea).* Bologna: Arnaldo Forni, 1963.

KRENCKER, DANIEL and MARTIN SCHEDE, *Der Tempel in Ankara.* Archäologisches Institut des deutschen Reiches: Denkmäler antiker Architektur 3. Berlin/Leipzig: de Gruyter, 1936.

MITCHEL, STEPHEN, *Regional Epigraphic Catalogues of Asia Minor, Vol. 2: The Ankara District. The Inscriptions of North Galatia.* BAR International Series 135.4. Ankara: Oxford British Institute of Archaeology at Ankara, 1982.

MÜLLER, KARL, *Geographi Graeci minores.* 2 vols. Paris: Didot, 1861.

SELTMAN, CHARLES, *Greek Coins: A History of Metallic Currency and Coinage down to the Fall of the Hellenistic Kingdoms.* 2nd ed. Methuen's Handbook of Archaeology. London: Methuen, 1955.

STERN, MENACHEM, *Greek and Latin Authors on Jews and Judaism.* 3 vols. Jerusalem: The Israel Academy of Sciences and Humanities, 1984.

New Testament and Other Christian Texts

ALAND, KURT, et al., eds. *The Greek New Testament*. 3rd ed. New York: United Bible Societies, 1975.

BAUER, ADOLF, ed. *Die Chronik des Hippolytus in Matritensis Graecus 121*. TU 19.1. Leipzig: Hinrichs, 1905.

– and RUDOLF HELM, eds. *Hippolytus Werke, Bd. 4: Die Chronik*. 2nd ed. GCS 46. Berlin: Akademie-Verlag, 1955.

FRANKENBERG, WILHELM, *Die syrischen Clementinen mit griechischen Paralleltext. Eine Vorarbeit zu dem literargeschichtlichen Problem der Sammlung*. TU 48.3. Leipzig: Heinrichs, 1937.

HENNECKE, EDGAR and WILHELM SCHNEEMELCHER, eds. *Neutestamentliche Apokryphen in deutscher Übersetzung*. 2 vols. 5th ed. Tübingen: Mohr-Siebeck, 1989.

MRAS, K., *Eusebius Werke 8.1, Praeparatio Evangelica*. GCS 43.1. Berlin: Akademie-Verlag, 1954–56.

NESTLE, EBERHARD, et al., eds. *Novum Testamentum Graece*. 26th ed. Stuttgart: Deutsche Bibelstiftung, 1979.

PREUSCHEN, ERWIN, *Origenes Werke, Bd. 4: Der Johanneskommentar*. GCS 10. Leipzig: Hinrichs, 1903.

REHM, BERNARD, *Die Pseudoklementinen II. Rekognitionen in Rufins Übersetzung*. GCS 51. Berlin: Akademie-Verlag, 1965.

SCHWARTZ, EDUARD, *Eusebius Werke, Bd. 2: Die Kirchengeschichte*. GCS 2.1. Leipzig: Hinrichs, 1903.

STONE, MICHAEL, *Signs of the Judgment, Onomastica Sacra, and the Generations from Adam*. University of Pennsylvania Armenian Texts and Studies 3. Chico, CA: Scholars Press, 1981.

Reference Works

BLASS, F., and DEBRUNNER, ALBERT, *A Greek Grammar of the New Testament and Other Early Christian Literature*. 9th/10th ed. Edited by Robert W. Funk. Chicago/London: University of Chicago Press, 1961.

BLASS, FRIEDRICH, and DEBRUNNER, ALBERT, *Grammatik des neutestamentlichen Griechisch*. 15th ed. Edited by Friedrich Rehkopf. Göttingen: Vandenhoeck & Ruprecht, 1979.

BOTTERWECK, G. JOHANNES, and RINGGREN, HELMER, eds. *Theologisches Wörterbuch zum Alten Testament*. 5 vols. Stuttgart/Berlin: Kohlhammer, 1973–1986.

BUTTRICK, G. A., ed. *Interpreter's Dictionary of the Bible*. 4 vols. Nashville: Abingdon Press, 1962.

EBELING, ERICH, ed., et al. *Reallexikon der Assyriologie*. 6 vols. Berlin: de Gruyter, 1932–1983.

HAMMOND, N. G. L., and SCULLARD, H. H., eds. *The Oxford Classical Dictionary*. 2nd ed. Oxford: Clarendon Press, 1970.

HELCK, WOLFGANG, and OTTO, EBERHARD, eds. *Lexikon der Ägyptologie*. 6 vols. with 6 Index vols. Wiesbaden: Harrassowitz, 1975–1986.

JENNI, ERNST, and WESTERMANN, CLAUS, eds. *Theologisches Handwörterbuch zum Alten*

Testament. 2 vols. 3rd. ed. Munich: Chr. Kaiser; Zürich: Theologischer Verlag, 1978–1979.

KLAUSER, THEODOR, ed., et al. *Reallexikon für Antike und Christentum. Sachwörterbuch zur Auseinandersetzung des Christentums mit der antiken Welt.* 13 vols. + 5 fasc. + 4 Suppl. Stuttgart: Hiersemann, 1950–1988.

KRAUSE, GERHARD, and MÜLLER, GERHARD, eds. *Theologische Realenzyklopädie.* 16 vols. Berlin/New York: de Gruyter, 1977–1987.

PAULY, AUGUST, ed., et al. *Der kleine Pauly. Lexikon der Antike. Auf der Grundlage von Pauly's Realencyclopädie der classischen Altertumswissenschaft.* 5 vols. Munich: Alfred Druckenmüller, 1964–1975.

–, et al. *Paulys Realencyclopädie der classischen Altertumswissenschaft.* 6 vols. in 8 (1st Series), 19 vols. (N. F.) with 15 Suppl. vols. and a Register. Munich: Alfred Druckenmüller, 1839–1980.

ROTH, CECIL and WIGODER, GEOFFREY, eds. *Encyclopaedia Judaica.* 16 vols. Jerusalem: Keter Publishing House, 1971–1972.

SOKOLOFF, MICHAEL, *A Dictionary of Jewish Palestinian Aramaic of the Byzantine Period.* Dictionaries of Talmud, Midrash and Targum 2. Ramat-Gan, Israel: Bar Ilan University Press, 1990.

Secondary Sources

AALEN, SVERRE, "'Reign' and 'House' in the Kingdom of God in the Gospels." *NTS* 8 (1961–1962) 215–240.

AHARONI, YOHANAN, *The Land of the Bible: A Historical Geography.* London: Burns & Oates, 1979.

– and MICHAEL AVI-YONAH, *The Macmillan Bible Atlas.* 2nd ed. Translated by A. F. Rainey. New York: Macmillan; London: Collier, 1968.

ALEXANDER, LOVEDAY, ed. *Images of Empire.* JSOTSup 122. Sheffield: JSOT Press, 1991.

ALEXANDER, PHILIP S. "Jewish Aramaic Translations of Hebrew Scriptures." In *Mikra: Text, Translation, Reading and Interpretation of the Hebrew Bible in Ancient Judaism and Early Christianity*, pp. 217–254. CRINT 2.1. Assen: Van Gorcum; Philadelphia: Fortress, 1988.

–, "Notes on the 'Imago Mundi' of the Book of Jubilees." *JJS* 33 (1982) 197–213.

–, "Retelling the Old Testament." In *It is Written: Scripture Citing Scripture. Essays in Honour of Barnabas Lindars*, pp. 99–121. Edited by D. A. Carson and H. G. M. Williamson. Cambridge: Cambridge University Press, 1988.

–, "The Toponymy of the Targumim, with Special Reference to the Table of Nations and the Boundaries of the Land of Israel." D. Phil. thesis, Oxford University, 1974.

AMARU, BETSY HALPERN, "Land Theology in Josephus' *Jewish Antiquities*." *JQR* 71 (1980–81) 201–229.

–, "Land Theology in Philo and Josephus," in *The Land Of Israel: Jewish Perspectives*, pp. 65–93. Edited by Lawrence A. Hoffman. University of Notre Dame Center for the Study of Judaism and Christianity in Antiquity 6. Notre Dame: University of Notre Dame, 1986.

ARENTZEN, JÖRG-GEERD, *Imago Mundi Cartographica. Studien zur Bildlichkeit mittelalterlicher West- und Ökumenekarten unter besonderer Berücksichtigung des Zusam-*

menwirkens von Text und Bild. Münstersche Mittelalter-Schriften 53. Munich: Wilhelm Fink, 1984.

ARLDT, TH., "Die Völkertafeln der Genesis und ihre Bedeutung für die Ethnographie Vorderasiens." *Wiener Zeitschrift für die Kunde des Morgenlandes* 30 (1917) 264–317.

AUS, ROGER D., "Paul's Travel Plans to Spain and the 'Full Number of the Gentiles' of Rom. xi. 25." *NovT* 21 (1979) 232–262.

AVIGAD, NAHMAN and YIGAEL YADIN, *A Genesis Apocryphon: A Scroll from the Wilderness of Judaea.* Jerusalem: The Magnes Press of the Hebrew University and Heikhal Ha-Sefer, 1956.

AVI-YONAH, MICHAEL, *The Madaba Mosaic Map with Introduction and Commentary.* Jerusalem: Israel Exploration Society, 1954.

BAR-KOCHVA, B., "On the Sources and Chronology of Antiochus I's Battle against the Galatians." *Proceedings of the Cambridge Philological Society* N. S. 19 (1973) 1–8.

BARRETT, C. K., *A Commentary on the Epistle to the Romans.* HNTC. New York/London: Harper & Row, 1957.

–, *A Commentary on the Second Epistle to the Corinthians.* HNTC. New York: Harper & Row, 1973.

–, *The First Epistle to the Corinthians.* Harper's New Testament Commentaries. New York/London: Harper & Row, 1968.

BASSER, HERBERT W., *Midrashic Interpretations of the Song of Moses.* American University Studies 7.2. New York/Frankfurt a.M./Berne: Peter Lang, 1984.

BASTOMSKY, S. J., "Noah, Italy, and the Sea-Peoples." *JQR* 67 (1977) 146–153.

BAUR, FERDINAND CHRISTIAN, *Paulus, der Apostel Jesu Christi. Sein Leben und Wirken, seine Briefe und seine Lehre.* 2 vols. 2nd ed. Edited by Eduard Zeller. Leipzig: Fues's Verlag, 1866.

BECKER, JÜRGEN, *Paulus. Apostel der Völker.* Tübingen: Mohr-Siebeck, 1989.

BELL, RICHARD H., "The Origin and Purpose of the Jealousy Motif in Romans 9–11: A Case Study in the Theology and Technique of Paul." Dr. theol. dissertation, University of Tübingen, 1990.

BERGER, P.-R., "Ellasar, Tarschisch und Jawan, Gn 14 und 10." *Die Welt des Orients* 13 (1982) 50–78.

BERNHARD, WOLFRAM and ANNELIESE KANDLER-PÁLSSON, *Ethnogenese europäischer Völker aus der Sicht der Anthropologie und Vor- und Frühgeschichte.* Stuttgart/New York: Fischer, 1986.

BETZ, HANS DIETER, *Galatians: A Commentary on Paul's Letter to the Churches in Galatia.* Hermeneia. Philadelphia: Fortress Press, 1979.

BETZ, OTTO, *Jesus, Herr der Kirche. Aufsätze zur biblischen Theologie II.* WUNT 52. Tübingen: Mohr-Siebeck, 1990.

–, *Jesus und das Danielbuch. Band II. Die Menschensohnworte Jesu und die Zukunftserwartung des Paulus (Daniel 7,13–14).* ANTJ 6.2. Frankfurt a.M.: Lang, 1985.

BICKERMAN, ELIAS J., "Origines Gentium." *CP* 47 (1952) 65–81.

BLIGH, JOHN, *Galatians: A Discussion of St Paul's Epistle.* Householder Commentaries, 1. London: St Paul Publications, 1969.

BÖCHER, OTTO, "Das sogenannte Aposteldekret." In *Vom Urchristentum zu Jesus. Für Joachim Gnilka,* pp. 325–336. Edited by Hubert Frankemölle and Karl Kertelge. Freiburg: Herder, 1989.

BORGEN, PEDER, "Philo, Luke and Geography." In *Paul Preaches Circumcision and*

Pleases Men and Other Essays on Christian Origins, pp. 59–71. Relieff 8. Dragvoll-Trondheim: TAPIR, 1983.

BORNKAMM, GÜNTHER, *Paulus*. 4th ed. Kohlhammer Urban-Taschenbücher. Stuttgart: Kohlhammer, 1979.

BORSE, UDO, *Der Brief an die Galater*. RNT. Regensburg: Friedrich Pustet, 1984.

BORST, ARNO, *Der Turmbau von Babel. Geschichte der Meinungen über Ursprung und Vielfalt der Sprachen und Völker*. 4 vols. in 6. Stuttgart: Hiersemann, 1957–1963.

BOTERMANN, HELGA, "Der Heidenapostel und sein Historiker. Zur historischen Kritik der Apostelgeschichte." *TBei* 24 (1993) 62–84.

BOWERS, WILLIAM PAUL, "Studies in Paul's Understanding of his Mission." Ph.D. dissertation, Cambridge University, 1976.

BRING, RAGNAR, *Der Brief des Paulus an die Galater*. Berlin: Lutherisches Verlagshaus, 1968.

BRINKEN, VON DEN, ANNA-DOROTHEE, *Fines Terrae. Die Enden der Erde und der vierte Kontinent auf mittelalterlichen Weltkarten*. Monumenta Germaniae Historica-Schriften 36. Hannover: Hahnsche Buchhandlung, 1992.

BRUCE, F. F., *1 and 2 Corinthians*. New Century Bible. London: Oliphants, 1971.

–, *The Acts of the Apostles: The Greek Text with Introduction and Commentary*. 3rd ed. Grand Rapids: Eerdmans, 1990.

–, *The Epistle to the Galatians*. NIGTC. Grand Rapids: Eerdmans, 1982.

–, "Galatian Problems 2. North or South Galatians?" *BJRL* 52 (1969–70) 243–266.

–, "Philip and the Ethiopian." *JSS* 34 (1989) 337–386.

BÜNKER, MICHAEL, *Briefformular und rhetorische Disposition im 1. Korintherbrief*. GTA 28. Göttingen: Vandenhoeck & Ruprecht, 1984.

BULTMANN, RUDOLF, *Der zweite Brief an die Korinther*. Kritisch-exegetischer Kommentar über das Neue Testament, Sonderband. Edited by Erich Dinkler. Göttingen: Vandenhoeck & Ruprecht, 1976.

BURTON, ERNEST DE WITT, *A Critical and Exegetical Commentary on the Epistle to the Galatians*. ICC. Edinburgh: Clark, 1921.

BYRNE, BRENDAN, *'Sons of God' – 'Seed of Abraham': A Study of the Idea of the Sonship of God of all Christians against the Jewish Background*, AnBib 83. Rome: Biblical Institute Press, 1979.

CALDER, WILLIAM M., "Colonia Caesareia Antiocheia." *JRS* 2 (1912) 79–109.

CARRINGTON, PETER, "The Heroic Age of Phrygia in Ancient Literature and Art." *Anatolian Studies* 27 (1977) 117–126.

CHAMOUX, FRANÇOIS, "Pergame et les Galates." *Revue des Études Grecques* 101 (1988) 492–500.

CHARLESWORTH, JAMES H., "Jewish Interest in Astrology during the Hellenistic and Roman Period." In *ANRW* II.20.2, pp. 926–952. Edited by Wolfgang Haase. Berlin/New York: de Gruyter, 1987.

COHEN, NAOMI G., "R. Meir, A Descendant of Anatolian Proselytes: New Light on his Name and the historic Kernel of the Nero Legend in Gittin 56a." *JJS* 23 (1972) 51–59.

COLLINS, JOHN J., *The Sibylline Oracles of Egyptian Judaism*. SBLDS 13. Missoula, MT: Scholars Press, 1974.

–, "Was the Dead Sea Sect an Apocalyptic Movement?" In *Archaeology and History in the Dead Sea Scrolls: The New York University Conference in Memory of Yigael Yadin*. Edited by Lawrence H. Schiffman. JSPSup 8; JSOT/ASOR Monographs 2. Sheffield: JSOT, 1990.

CONZELMANN, HANS, "The Address of Paul on the Areopagus." In *Studies in Luke-Acts: Essays Presented in Honor of Paul Schubert*, pp. 217–230. Edited by Leander E. Keck and J. Louis Martyn; Nashville/New York: Abingdon, 1966.

–, *Die Apostelgeschichte*. 2nd ed. HNT 7. Tübingen: Mohr-Siebeck, 1972.

–, *Der erste Brief an die Korinther*. 2nd ed. Kritisch-exegetischer Kommentar über das Neue Testament, 5. Göttingen: Vandenhoeck & Ruprecht, 1981.

CORBIER, MIREILLE, "City, Territory and Taxation." In *City and Country in the Ancient World*, pp. 211–239. Edited by John Rich and Andrew Wallace-Hadrill; Leicester-Nottingham Studies in Ancient Society 2. London/New York: Routledge, 1991.

CRANFIELD, C. E. B., *A Critical and Exegetical Commentary on the Epistle to the Romans*. 2 vols. ICC. Edinburgh: T. & T. Clark, 1980–81.

CROIX, E. M. de Ste. *The Class Struggle in the Ancient Greek World*. London: Duckworth, 1981.

CROSBY, STEVEN, "Kinship, Territory, and the Nation in the Historiography of Ancient Israel." *ZAW* 105 (1993) 3–18.

DABELSTEIN, ROLF, *Die Beurteilung der 'Heiden' bei Paulus*. BBET 14. Frankfurt a.M.: Peter Lang, 1981.

DAVIES, G. I., "Hagar, El-Hegra and the Location of Mount Sinai." *VT* 22 (1972) 152–163.

DAVIES, GRAHAM, "The Destiny of the Nations in the Book of Isaiah." In *The Book of Isaiah/Le Livre d'Isaïe. Les oracles et leurs reflectures unité complexité de l'ouvrage*, pp. 93–120. Edited by Jacques Vermeylen. BETL 81. Leuven: University Press, 1989.

DAVIES, PHILIP R., *1QM, the War Scroll from Qumran: Its Structure and History*. BibOr 32. Rome: Biblical Institute Press, 1977.

–, "Eschatology at Qumran." *JBL* 104 (1985) 39–55.

DAVIES, W. D., ed. *The Cambridge History of Judaism, Vol. 2: The Hellenistic Age*. Cambridge: Cambridge University Press, 1989.

–, *The Gospel and the Land: Early Christianity and Jewish Territorial Doctrine*. Berkeley: University of California Press, 1974.

DEININGER, JÜRGEN, *Die Provinziallandtage der römischen Kaiserzeit von Augustus bis zum Ende des dritten Jahrhunderts n. Chr.* Munich/Berlin: C. H. Beck'sche Verlagsbuchhandlung, 1965.

DEISSMANN, ADOLF, *Paulus. Eine kultur- und religionsgeschichtliche Skizze*. 2nd. ed. Tübingen: Mohr-Siebeck, 1925.

DHORME, ÉDOUARD, "Les peuples issus de Japhet." In *Études bibliques et orientales*, pp. 167–189. Paris: Imprimerie Nationale, 1951.

DIBELIUS, MARTIN, "Der Text der Apostelgeschichte." In *Aufsätze zur Apostelgeschichte*, pp. 76–83. 5th ed. Edited by Heinrich Greeven. FRLANT 60. Göttingen: Vandenhoeck & Ruprecht, 1968.

DIETZFELBINGER, CHRISTIAN, *Die Berufung des Paulus als Ursprung seiner Theologie*. 2nd ed. WMANT 58. Neukirchen-Vluyn: Neukirchener Verlag, 1989.

DILKE, O. A. W., *Greek and Roman Maps*. Aspects of Greek and Roman Life. London: Thames and Hudson, 1985.

–, "Cartography in the Byzantine Empire." In *The Hisktory of Cartography, Vol. 1: Cartography in Prehistoric, Ancient, and Medieval Europe and the Mediterranean*, pp. 258–275. Edited by J. B. Harley and David Woodward. Chicago: University of Chicago Press, 1987.

DINKLER, ERICH, "Philippus und der ANHP AIΘIOΨ (Apg 8,26−40). Historische und geographische Bemerkungen zum Missionsablauf nach Lukas." In *Jesus und Paulus. Festschrift für Werner Georg Kümmel zum 70. Geburtstag*, pp. 85−95. Edited by E. Earle Ellis and Erich Gräßer. Göttingen: Vandenhoeck & Ruprecht, 1975.

DONALD, LESLIE D., "Japhet in China." *JAOS* 104 (1984) 403−409.

DONALDSON, TERENCE L., "Proselytes or 'Righteous Gentiles'? The Status of Gentiles in Eschatological Pilgrimage Patterns of Thought." *JSP* 7 (1990) 3−27.

DONNER, HERBERT and HEINZ CÜPPERS, *The Mosaic Map of Madaba: An Introductory Guide*. Palaestina Antiqua 7. Kampen: Kok Pharos, 1992.

−, *Die Mosaikkarte von Madeba, Teil 1: Tafelband*. Abhandlungen des deutschen Palästinavereins. Wiesbaden: Otto Harrassowitz, 1977.

−, "Die Restauration und Konservierung der Mosaikkarte von Madeba." *ZDPV* 83 (1967) 1−33.

−, "Transjordan and Egypt on the Mosaic Map of Madaba." *Annual of the Department of Antiquities, Jordan* 18 (1984) 249−257.

DROGE, ARTHUR J., *Homer or Moses? Early Christian Interpretation of the History of Culture*. HUT 26. Tübingen: Mohr-Siebeck, 1989.

DUNN, JAMES D. G., *Romans*. 2 vols. WBC 38. Dallas: Word Books, 1988.

EGO, BEATE, *Im Himmel wie auf Erden. Studien zum Verhältnis von himmlischer und irdischer Welt im rabbinischen Judentum*. WUNT 2.34. Tübingen: Mohr-Siebeck, 1989.

EICHHOLZ, GEORG, *Die Theologie des Paulus im Umriß*. 6th ed. Neukirchen-Vluyn: Neukirchener Verlag, 1988.

ELLIS, E. EARLE, "'Das Ende der Erde' (Apg 1,8)." In *Der Treue Gottes trauen. Beiträge zum Werk des Lukas für Gerhard Schneider*, pp. 277−286. Edited by Claus Bussmann and Walter Radl. Freiburg: Herder, 1991.

−, "'The End of the Earth' (Acts 1:8)." *Bulletin for Biblical Research* 1 (1991) 123−132.

EVANS, CRAIG A., "The Genesis Apocryphon and the Rewritten Bible." *RevQ* 49−52 (1988) 153−165.

FELDMAN, LOUIS H., "Hellenizations in Josephus' Portrayal of Man's Decline." In *Religions in Antiquity: Essays in Memory of Erwin Ramsdell Goodenough*, pp. 336−353. Edited by Jacob Neusner. Studies in the History of Religions 14. Leiden: Brill, 1968.

−, *Jew and Gentile in the Ancient World: Attitudes and Interactions from Alexander to Justinian*. Princeton, NJ: Princeton University Press, 1993.

−, "Josephus' Commentary on Genesis." *JQR* 72 (1981/82) 121−131.

−, "Josephus' Portrait of Noah and Its Parallels in Philo, Pseudo-Philo's *Biblical Antiquities*, and Rabbinic Midrashim." *PAAJR* 55 (1988) 31−57.

FELDMEIER, REINHARD and ULRICH HECKEL, eds. *Die Heiden. Juden, Christen und das Problem des Fremden*. WUNT 70. Tübingen: Mohr-Siebeck, 1994.

FITZMYER, JOSEPH A., *The Dead Sea Scrolls: Major Publications and Tools for Study*. Rev. ed. SBLRBS 20. Atlanta, GA: Scholars Press, 1990.

−, *The Genesis Apocryphon of Qumran Cave 1: A Commentary*. 2nd ed. BibOr 18A. Rome: Biblical Institute Press, 1971.

−, *The Gospel according to Luke*. 2 vols. AB 28−28A. Garden City, NY: Doubleday, 1981−1985.

FLUSSER, DAVID and SHMUEL SAFRAI, "Das Aposteldekret und die Noachitischen Gebote." In *"Wer Tora vermehrt, mehrt Leben." Festgabe für Heinz Kremers zum*

60. Geburtstag, pp. 173—192. Edited by Edna Brocke and Hans-Joachim Barkenings. Neukirchen-Vluyn: Neukirchener Verlag, 1986.

Fox, Michael V., *Character and Ideology in the Book of Esther*. Studies on Personalities of the Old Testament. Columbia, SC: University of South Carolina, 1991.

Franxman, Thomas W., *Genesis and the "Jewish Antiquities" of Flavius Josephus*. BibOr 35. Rome: Biblical Institute Press, 1979.

Fraser, P. M., *Ptolemaic Alexandria*. 3 vols. Oxford: Clarendon Press, 1972.

French, David, *Roman Roads and Milestones of Asia Minor*. British Institute of Archaeology at Ankara Monograph 9; BAR International Series 391(i). Oxford: BAR, 1988.

–, "The Roman Road-System of Asia Minor." In *ANRW* II.7.2, pp. 698—729. Edited by Hildegard Temporini. Berlin/New York: de Gruyter, 1980.

Furnish, Victor Paul, *II Corinthians*. The Anchor Bible, 32A. Garden City, NY: Doubleday & Co., 1984.

Gärtner, Bertil, *The Areopagus Speech and Natural Revelation*. ASNU 21. Lund: Gleerup, 1955.

Gardner, Jane F., "The Adoption of Roman Freedmen." *Phoenix* 43 (1989) 236—257.

Gasparro, Giula Sfameni, *Soteriology and Mystic Aspects in the Cult of Cybele and Attis*. EPRO 103. Leiden: Brill, 1985.

Georgi, Dieter, *Remembering the Poor: The History of Paul's Collection for Jerusalem*. Nashville: Abingdon, 1992.

Gese, Hartmut, *Alttestamentliche Studien*. Tübingen: Mohr-Siebeck, 1991.

–, *Vom Sinai zum Zion. Alttestamentliche Beiträge zur biblischen Theologie*. BevT 64. Munich: Chr. Kaiser, 1974.

Gilbert, Gary, "The Making of a Jew: 'God-fearer' or Convert in the Story of Izates." *USQR* 44 (1991) 299—313.

Gill, David W. J. and Conrad Gempf, eds. *The Book of Acts in Its First Century Setting, Vol. 2: The Book of Acts in Its Graeco-Roman Setting*. Grand Rapids: Eerdmans; Carlisle: Paternoster, 1994.

Ginzberg, Louis, *The Legends of the Jews*. 7 vols. Philadelphia: Jewish Publication Society of America, 1909—1938.

Görg, Manfred, "Apg 2,9—11 in außerbiblischer Sicht." *Biblische Notizen* 1 (1976) 15—18.

–, "Ophir, Tarschisch und Atlantis. Einige Gedanken zur symbolischen Topographie." *Biblische Notizen* 15 (1981) 76—86.

Goldstein, Jonathan A., *II Maccabees: A New Translation with Introduction and Commentary*. Garden City, NY: Doubleday, 1976.

Gowan, Donald E., *Eschatology in the Old Testament*. Philadelphia: Fortress Press, 1986.

–, "The Exile in Jewish Apocalyptic." In *Scripture in History and Theology: Essays in Honor of J. Coert Rylaarsdam*, pp. 205—223. Edited by Arthur Merrill and Thomas W. Overholt. PTMS 17. Pittsburg: Pickwick Press, 1977.

Griggs, C. Wilfred, *Early Egyptian Christianity from its Origins to 451 C. E.* Coptic Studies 2. Leiden: Brill, 1990.

Güting, Eberhard, "Der geographische Horizont der sogenannten Völkerliste des Lukas (Acta 2,9—11)." *ZNW* 66 (1975) 149—169.

GUNDEL, HANS GEORG, *Zodiakos. Tierkreisbilder im Altertum: Kosmische Bezüge und Jenseitsvorstellungen im antiken Alltagsleben.* Kulturgeschichte der antiken Welt 54. Mainz am Rhein: Philipp von Zabern, 1992.

GUNTHER, JOHN J., "The Association of Mark and Barnabas with Egyptian Christianity (Part I)." *EvQ* 54 (1982) 219–232.

–, "The Association of Mark and Barnabas with Egyptian Christianity (Continued)." *EvQ* 55 (1983) 21–29.

GUTSCHMID, ALFRED VON, *Kleine Schriften, Vol. 5: Schriften zur römischen und mittelalterlichen Geschichte und Literatur.* Edited by Franz Rühl. Leipzig: Teubner, 1894.

HAEPEREN-POURBAIX, AGNÈS VAN, "Recherche sur les origines, la nature, et les attributs du dieu Mên." In *Archéologie et religions de l'Anatolie ancienne. Mélanges en l'honneur du professeur Paul Naster*, pp. 221–257. Edited by R. Donceel and R. Lebrun. Homo Religiosus 10. Louvain: Centre d'Histoire des Religions, 1983.

HALFMANN, HELMUT, *Die Senatoren aus dem östlichen Teil des Imperium Romanum bis zum Ende des 2. Jahrhunderts n. Chr.* Hypomnemata 58. Göttingen: Vandenhoeck & Ruprecht, 1979.

–, "Zur Datierung und Deutung der Priesterliste am Augustus-Roma-Tempel in Ankara." *Chiron* 16 (1986) 35–42.

HALL, A. S., "The Gorgoromeis." *Anatolian Studies* 21 (1971) 125–166.

HAMLIN, JOHN, "Three Metaphors for the Inhabited World." *Proceedings of the Eastern Great Lakes and Midwest Bible Societies* 9 (1989) 49–58.

HARDWICK, MICHAEL E., *Josephus as an Historical Source in Patristic Literature through Eusebius.* BJS 128. Atlanta, GA: Scholars Press, 1989.

HARE, DOUGLAS R. A. and DANIEL J. HARRINGTON, "'Make Disciples of all Gentiles' (Mt 28:19)." *CBQ* 37 (1975) 359–369.

HARL, MARGUERITE, *La Langue de Japhet. Quinze études sur la Septante et le grec des chrétiens.* Centre Lenain de Tillemont. Paris: Cerf, 1992.

HARLEY, J. B. and DAVID WOODWARD, eds. *The History of Cartography, Vol. 1: Cartography in Prehistoric, Ancient, and Medieval Europe and the Mediterranean.* Chicago: University of Chicago Press, 1987.

HARNACK, ADOLF VON, *Der kirchengeschichtliche Ertrag exegetischer Arbeiten des Origenes, 1. Teil: Hexateuch und Richterbuch.* TU 42.3. Leipzig: Hinrichs, 1918.

–, *Die Mission und Ausbreitung des Christentums in den ersten drei Jahrhunderten, Bd. 1: Die Mission in Wort und Tat.* 4th ed. Leipzig: Hinrichs, 1927.

HAYMAN, PETER, "Some Observations on Sefer Yesira: (2) The Temple at the Centre of the Universe." *JSS* 35 (1984) 176–182.

HAYS, RICHARD B., *Echos of Scripture in the Letters of Paul.* New Haven/London: Yale University Press, 1989.

HEGERMANN, HARALD, "The Diaspora in the Hellenistic Age." In *The Cambridge History of Judaism, Vol. 2: The Hellenistic Age*, pp. 145–146. Edited by W. D. Davies, et al. Cambridge: Cambridge University Press, 1989.

HELLER, BERNHARD, "Gog und Magog im jüdischen Schrifttum." In *Jewish Studies in Memory of George A. Kohut 1874–1933*, pp. 350–368. Edited by Salo W. Baron and Alexander Marx. New York: The Alexander Kohut Memorial Foundation, 1935.

HEMER, CONRAD H., *The Book of Acts in the Setting of Hellenistic History.* Edited by Conrad H. Gempf. WUNT 49. Tübingen: Mohr-Siebeck, 1989.

HENGEL, MARTIN, *Studies in the Gospel of Mark*. London: SCM, 1985.

–, *The 'Hellenization' of Judaea in the First Century after Christ*. London: SCM Press; Philadelphia: Trinity Press International, 1989.

–, "Jakobus der Herrenbruder – der erste 'Papst'?" In *Glaube und Eschatologie. Festschrift für Werner Georg Kümmel zum 80.Geburtstag*, pp. 71–104. Edited by Erich Gräßer and Otto Merk. Tübingen: Mohr-Siebeck, 1985.

–, *Judentum und Hellenismus. Studien zu ihrer Begegnung unter besonderer Berücksichtigung Palästinas bis zur Mitte des 2.Jh.s v.Chr*. 3rd ed. WUNT 10. Tübingen: Mohr-Siebeck, 1973.

–, "Luke the Historian and Geographer in the Acts of the Apostles." In *Between Jesus and Paul: Studies in the Earliest History of Christianity*, pp. 97–128. Translated by John Bowden. London: SCM Press, 1983.

–, "Messianische Hoffnung und politischer 'Radikalismus' in der 'jüdisch-hellenistischen Diaspora'. Zur Frage der Voraussetzungen des jüdischen Aufstandes unter Trajan 115–117 n. Chr." In *Apocalypticism in the Mediterranean World and the Near East: Proceedings of the International Colloquium on Apocalypticism, Uppsala, August 12–17, 1979*, pp. 655–686. 2nd ed. Edited by David Hellholm. Tübingen: Mohr-Siebeck, 1983.

–, "The Origins of the Christian Mission." In *Between Jesus and Paul*, pp. 48–64. Translated by John Bowden. London: SCM Press, 1983.

– and ULRICH HECKEL, *Paulus und das antike Judentum. Tübingen-Durham-Symposium im Gedenken an den 50.Todestag Adolf Schlatters*. WUNT 58. Tübingen: Mohr-Siebeck, 1991.

–, *The Pre-Christian Paul*. London: SCM Press; Philadelphia: Trinity Press International, 1991.

–, *Der Sohn Gottes. Die Entstehung der Christologie und die jüdisch-hellenistische Religionsgeschichte*. 2nd ed. Tübingen: Mohr-Siebeck, 1977.

–, *Studies in the Gospel of Mark*. Transl. by John Bowden. London: SCM Press, 1985.

–, *Die Zeloten. Untersuchungen zur jüdischen Freiheitsbewegung in der Zeit von Herodes I. bis 70 n. Chr*. AGJU 1. Leiden: Brill, 1976.

–, *Zur urchristlichen Geschichtsschreibung*. Stuttgart: Calwer, 1979.

HERRMANN, ALBERT, *Die Erdkarte der Urbibel*. Braunschweig: Westermann, 1931.

HERRMANN, PETER, *Der römische Kaisereid. Untersuchungen zu seiner Herkunft und Entwicklung*. Hypomnemata 20. Göttingen: Vandenhoeck & Ruprecht, 1968.

HÖLSCHER, GUSTAV, *Drei Erdkarten. Ein Beitrag zur Erdkenntnis des hebräischen Altertums*. Sitzungsberichte der Heidelberger Akademie der Wissenschaften, Philosophisch-historische Klasse, Jahrgang 1944/48, 3. Abhandlung. Heidelberg: Winter, 1948.

HOFIUS, OTFRIED, *Paulusstudien*. WUNT 51. Tübingen: Mohr-Siebeck, 1989.

HOLLANDER, H.W., and JONGE, M. DE, *The Testaments of the Twelve Patriarchs: A Commentary*. SVTP 8. Leiden: Brill, 1985.

HOMMEL, FRITZ, *Ethnologie und Geographie des alten Orients*. Handbuch des Altertumswissenschaft 3.1.1. Munich: Beck, 1926.

HOROWITZ, WAYNE, "Mesopotamian Cosmic Geography." Ph.D. dissertation, University of Birmingham, 1986.

–, "The Babylonian Map of the World." *Iraq* 50 (1988) 147–163.

–, "The Isles of the Nations: Genesis X and Babylonian Geography." In *Studies in the Pentateuch*, pp. 35–43. Edited by J. A. Emerton. VTSup 41. Leiden: Brill, 1990.

HORSLEY, G. H. R., ed. *New Documents Illustrating Early Christianity: A Review of the Greek Inscriptions and Papyri Published in 1976.* North Ryde, Australia: The Ancient History Documentary Research Centre, Macquarie University, 1981.

–, *New Documents Illustrating Early Christianity: A Review of the Greek Inscriptions and Papyri Published in 1979.* North Ryde, Australia: The Ancient History Documentary Research Centre, Macquarie University, 1987.

HORST, PIETER W. VAN DER, "Hellenistic Parallels to the Acts of the Apostles (2.1–47)." *JSNT* 25 (1985) 49–60.

–, "Das Neue Testament und die jüdischen Grabinschriften aus hellenistisch-römischer Zeit." *BZ* 36 (1992) 161–178.

IVANTCHIK, ASHOLD I., *Les Cimmeriens au Proche-Orient.* OBO 127 Fribourg: Éditions Universitaires Fribourg Suisse; Göttingen: Vandenhoeck & Ruprecht, 1993.

JACKSON, F. J. FOAKES and KIRSOPP LAKE, *The Acts of the Apostles.* 5 vols. The Beginnings of Christianity, 1. Grand Rapids: Baker, 1979.

JACOBY, ADOLF, *Das geographische Mosaik von Madaba. Die älteste Karte des heiligen Landes.* Studien über christliche Denkmäler 3. Leipzig: Dieterisch'sche Verlagsbuchhandlung, 1905.

JEGHER-BUCHER, VERENA, *Der Galaterbrief auf dem Hintergrund antiker Epistolographie und Rhetorik. Ein anderes Paulusbild.* ATANT 78. Zürich: Theologischer Verlag, 1991.

JONES, A. H. M., *The Cities of the Eastern Roman Provinces.* 2nd ed. Oxford: Clarendon, 1971.

JONGE, MARIANUS DE, "Josephus und die Zukunftserwartung seines Volkes." In *Josephus-Studien. Untersuchungen zu Josephus, dem antiken Judentum und dem Neuen Testament. Otto Michel zum 70. Geburtstag gewidmet,* pp. 205–219. Edited by Otto Betz, et al. Göttingen: Vandenhoeck & Ruprecht, 1974.

JUNOD, ERIC, "Origène, Eusèbe et la tradition sur la répartition des champs de mission des apôtres (Eusèbe, *Histoire ecclésiastique,* III, 1, 1–3)." In *Les actes apocryphes des apôtres. Christianisme et monde païen,* pp. 233–248. Publications de la Faculté de Théologie de l'Université de Genève 4. Paris: Labor et Fides, 1981.

KARTUNNEN, KLAUS, "Expedition to the End of the World: An Ethnographic τόπος in Herodotus." *StudOr* 64 (1988) 177–181.

KARTVEIT, MAGNAR, *Motive und Schichten der Landtheologie in I Chronik 1–9.* ConBOT 28. Stockholm: Almquist & Wiksell, 1989.

KÄSEMANN, ERNST, *An die Römer.* 4th ed. HNT 8a. Tübingen: Mohr-Siebeck, 1980.

KASHER, ARYEH, *The Jews in Hellenistic and Roman Egypt: The Struggle for Equal Rights.* Texte und Studien zum Antiken Judentum 7. Tübingen: Mohr-Siebeck, 1985.

KEEL, OTHMAR, et al. *Orte und Landschaften der Bibel.* 2 vols. Zürich: Benziger Verlag; Göttingen: Vandenhoeck & Ruprecht, 1982–84.

–, *Die Welt der altorientalischen Bildsymbolik und das Alte Testament am Beispiel der Psalmen.* Zürich: Benziger Verlag; Neukirchen: Neukirchener Verlag, 1972.

KEGLER, JÜRGEN, *Synopse zum Chronistischen Geschichtswerk.* Beiträge zur Erforschung des Alten Testaments und des antiken Judentums 1. Frankfurt a.M.: Lang, 1984.

KEPPIE, L J. F., "The History and Disappearance of the Legion XXII Deiotariana." In *Greece and Rome in Eretz Israel: Collected Essays,* pp. 54–61. Edited by A. Kasher, et al. Jerusalem: Yad Izhak Ben-Zvi; The Israel Exploration Society, 1990.

KILPATRICK, G. D., "A Jewish Background to Acts 2:9–11?" *JJS* 26 (1975) 48–49.

KLIJN, A. F. J., "Jerome's Quotations from a Nazarean Interpretation of Isaiah." *RSR* 60 (1972) 241–255.

KLINGHARDT, MATTHIAS, *Gesetz und Volk Gottes. Das lukanische Verständnis des Gesetzes nach Herkunft, Funktion und seinem Ort in der Geschichte des Urchristentums.* WUNT 2.32. Tübingen: Mohr-Siebeck, 1988.

KNIBB, MICHAEL A., "Exile in the Damascus Document." *JSOT* 25 (1983) 99–117.

–, "The Exile in the Literature of the Intertestamental Period." *HeyJ* 17 (1976) 253–272.

KNOX, JOHN, "Romans 15:14–33 and Paul's Conception of His Apostolic Mission." *JBL* 83 (1964) 1–11.

KOCH, DIETRICH-ALEX, *Die Schrift als Zeuge des Evangeliums. Untersuchungen zur Verwendung und zum Verständnis der Schrift bei Paulus.* BHT 69. Tübingen: Mohr-Siebeck, 1986.

KOCH, KLAUS, *Das Buch Daniel.* Erträge der Forschung, 144. Darmstadt: Wissenschaftliche Buchgesellschaft, 1980.

KRAABEL, A. THOMAS, "The Disappearance of the 'God-fearers.'" *Numen* 28 (1981) 113–126.

KRAUSS, SAMUEL, "Die biblische Völkertafel im Talmud, Midrasch und Targum." *MGWJ* N. F. 3 (1895) 1–11, 49–63.

–, "Die Zahl der biblischen Völkerschaften." *ZAW* 19 (1899) 1–14.

–, ed. *Monumenta Talmudica, Bd. 5.1: Geschichte – Griechen und Römer.* Monumenta Hebraica 1; Vienna/Leipzig: Orion-Verlag, 1914.

–, "Zur Zahl der biblischen Völkerschaften." *ZAW* 20 (1900) 38–43.

KRONHOLM, TRYGGVE, *Motifs from Genesis 1–11 in the Genuine Hymns of Ephrem the Syrian with Particular Reference to the Influence of Jewish Exegetical Tradition.* ConBOT 11. Lund: Gleerup, 1978.

KUBITSCHEK, WILHELM, *Studien zur Geographie des Ptolemäus, I: Die Ländergrenzen* (οἱ περιορισμοί). Akademie der Wissenschaften in Wien, Philosophisch-historische Klasse, Sitzungsberichte 215.5. Wien/Leipzig: Hölder-Pichler-Tempsky, 1934.

KÜMMEL, WERNER, *Einleitung in das Neue Testament.* 21th Ed. Heidelberg: Quelle & Meyer, 1983.

LACROIX, LEON, "L'omphalos, attribut d'Asclépios, selon le témoinage des monnaies." *Revue belge de Numismatique* 97 (1951) 6–18.

LAMINGER-PASCHER, GERTRUD, "Lykaonien und die Ostgrenze Phrygiens," *Epigraphica Anatolica* 1 (1990) 1–13.

LAMPE, PETER, *Die stadtrömischen Christen in den ersten beiden Jahrhunderten. Untersuchungen zur Sozialgeschichte.* 2nd ed. WUNT 2.18. Tübingen: Mohr-Siebeck, 1989.

LANE, EUGENE N., "The Italian Connection: An Aspect of the Cult of Men," *Numen* 22 (1975) 235–239.

–, "Men: A Neglected Cult of Roman Asia Minor." In *ANRW* II.18.3, pp. 2161–2174. Edited by Wolfgang Haase. Berlin/New York: de Gruyter, 1990.

LANG, FRIEDRICH, *Die Briefe an die Korinther.* NTD 7. Göttingen: Vandenhoeck & Ruprecht, 1986.

LAUNEY, M., *Recherches sur les armées hellénistiques.* 2 vols. Paris: de Boccard, 1949–50.

LEVICK, BARBARA, *The Government of the Roman Empire: A Sourcebook.* London/Sydney: Croom Helm, 1985.

–, *Roman Colonies in Southern Asia Minor.* Oxford: Clarendon Press, 1967.

LEVY, B. BARRY, *Targum Neophyti 1: A Textual Study, Vol. 1: Introduction, Genesis,*

Exodus. Studies in Judaism. Lanham, NY/London: University Press of America, 1986.

LEWIS, JACK P., *A Study of the Interpretation of Noah and the Flood in Jewish and Christian Literature.* Leiden: Brill, 1968.

LICHTENBERGER, HERMANN, *Studien zum Menschenbild in Texten der Qumrangemeinde.* SUNT 15. Göttingen: Vandenhoeck & Ruprecht, 1980.

LIETZMANN, HANS, *An die Galater.* 4th ed. HNT 10. Tübingen: Mohr-Siebeck, 1971.

–, *An die Korinther I.II.* HNT 9. Tübingen: Mohr-Siebeck, 1969.

LIGHTFOOT, J. B., *Saint Paul's Epistle to the Galatians.* 10th ed. The Epistles of St Paul 2.3. London: Macmillan, 1892.

LIM, TIMOTHY H., "Notes on *4Q252* fr.1, cols. i-ii." *JJS* 44 (1993) 121–126.

LINDNER, HELGO, *Die Geschichtsauffassung des Flavius Josephus im Bellum Judaicum. Gleichzeitig ein Beitrag zur Quellenfrage.* AGJU 12. Leiden: Brill, 1972.

LIPINSKI, ÉDOUARD, "Les Japhétites selon Gen 10,2–4 et 1 Chr 1,5–7." *ZAH* 3 (1990) 40–52.

LUEDEMANN, GERD, *Paul, Apostle to the Gentiles: Studies in Chronology.* Translated by F. Stanley Jones. Philadelphia: Fortress, 1984.

MACH, MICHAEL, *Entwicklungsstadien des jüdischen Engelglaubens in vorrabbinischer Zeit.* Texte und Studien zum Antiken Judentum 34. Tübingen: Mohr-Siebeck, 1992.

McLEAN, BRADLEY H., "Galatians 2.7–9 and the Recognition of Paul's Apostolic Status at the Jerusalem Conference: A Critique of G. Luedemann's Solution." *NTS* 37 (1991) 67–76.

McNAMARA, MARTIN, *Targum and Testament: Aramaic Paraphrases of the Hebrew Bible: A Light on the New Testament.* Shannon: Irish University Press, n.d.

MAIER, JOHANN, "Zu ethnographisch-geographischen Überlieferungen über Japhetiten (Gen 10,2–4) im frühen Judentum." *Henoch* 13 (1991) 157–194.

MALAY, HASAN, "Letter of Antiochus III to Zeuxis with two Covering Letters (209 B. C.)." *Epigraphica Anatolica* 10 (1987) 7–15.

MARSHALL, I. HOWARD, *The Gospel of Luke: A Commentary on the Greek Text.* NIGTC. Exeter: Paternoster Press, 1978.

MARTIN, RALPH P., *2 Corinthians.* WBC 40. Waco, TX: Word Books, 1986.

MARTINEZ, FORENTINO G., "4QMess AR and the Book of Noah." In *Qumran and Apocalyptic: Studies on the Aramaic Texts from Qumran,* pp. 1–44. STDJ 9. Leiden: Brill, 1992.

MASON, HUGH J., *Greek Terms for Roman Institutions: A Lexicon and Analysis.* American Studies in Papyrology 13. Toronto: Hakkert, 1974.

MEIER, I. P., "Nations or Gentiles in Matthew 28:19?" *CBQ* 39 (1977) 94–102.

MELLOR, RONALD, "The Goddess Roma." In *ANRW* II.17.2, pp. 950–1030. Edited by Wolfgang Haase. Berlin: de Gruyter, 1981.

MENDELS, DORON, *The Land of Israel as a Political Concept in Hasmonean Literature: Recourse to History in Second Century B. C. Claims to the Holy Land.* Texte und Studien zum Antiken Judentum 15. Tübingen: Mohr-Siebeck, 1987.

METZGER, BRUCE M., "Ancient Astrological Geography and Acts 2:9–11." In *New Testament Studies: Philological, Versional and Patristic,* pp. 46–56. NTTS 10. Leiden: Brill, 1980.

–, "Seventy or Seventy-two Disciples?" *NTS* 5 (1958–59) 299–306.

–, *A Textual Commentary on the Greek New Testament:* A COMPANION VOLUME TO THE UNITED BIBLE SOCIETIES' GREEK NEW TESTAMENT (THIRD EDITION). Rev ed. London/ New York: United Bible Societies, 1975.

MEYER, R., "Die Bedeutung des Deuteronomium 32,8f.43 (4Q) für die Auslegung des Moseliedes," in *Verbannung und Heimkehr. Beiträge zur Geschichte und Theologie Israels im 6. und 5. Jahrhundert v. Chr. Wilhelm Rudolf zum 70. Geburtstag*, pp. 197–210. Edited by Arnulf Kuschke. Tübingen: Mohr-Siebeck, 1961.

MILLAR, FERGUS, "Hagar, Ishmael, Josephus and the Origins of Islam." *JJS* 44 (1993) 23–45.

MITCHELL, STEPHEN, *Anatolia: Land, Men, and Gods in Asia Minor.* 2 Vols. Oxford: Clarendon, 1993.

–, "Galatia under Tiberius." *Chiron* (1986) 17–33.

–, "Iconium and Ninica." *Historia. Zeitschrift für alte Geschichte* 28 (1979) 409–438.

–, "Population and the Land in Roman Galatia." In *ANRW* II.7.2, pp. 1053–1081. Edited by Hildegard Temporini. Berlin: de Gruyter, 1980.

MOFFATT, JAMES, *An Introduction to the Literature of the New Testament.* 3rd ed. International Theological Library. Edinburgh: Clark, 1918.

MOMMSEN, THEODOR, "Der Religionsfrevel nach römischen Recht." *Historische Zeitschrift* 64 (1890) 389–429.

–, *Römisches Strafrecht.* Systematisches Handbuch der deutschen Rechtswissenschaft 1.4. Leipzig: Duncker & Humblot, 1899.

MÜLLER, KLAUS E., *Geschichte der antiken Ethnographie und ethnologischen Theoriebildung von den Anfängen bis auf die byzantinischen Historiographen.* 2 vols. Studien zur Kulturkunde 29 and 52. Wiesbaden: Franz Steiner Verlag, 1972–80.

MÜLLER-KARPE, ANDREAS, "Neue galatische Funde aus Anatolien." *Istanbuler Mitteilungen des deutschen Archäologischen Instituts* 38 (1988) 189–199.

MUNCK, JOHANNES, *Paulus und die Heilsgeschichte.* Acta Jutlandica 26.1. Aarhus: Universitetsforlaget, 1954.

MUßNER, FRANZ, *Der Galaterbrief.* 4th ed. HTKNT 9. Freiburg: Herder, 1981.

NA'AMAN, NADAV, *Borders and Districts in Biblical Historiography: Seven Studies in Biblical Geographical Lists.* Jerusalem Biblical Studies 4; Jerusalem: Simor, 1986.

NEIMAN, DAVID, "The Two Genealogies of Japhet." In *Orient and Occident: Essays Presented to Cyrus H. Gordon on the Occasion of his Sixty-fifth Birthday*, pp. 119–126. Edited by Harry A. Hoffner, Jr. AOAT 22. Kevelaer: Verlag Butzon & Becker; Neukirchen-Vluyn: Neukirchener Verlag, 1973.

NEUBAUER, ADOLPHE, *La géographie du Talmud.* Amsterdam: Meridian, 1965.

NEUDORFER, HEINZ-WERNER, "Mehr Licht über Galatien?" *Jahrbuch für evangelikale Theologie* 5 (1991) 47–62.

NICKELSBURG, GEORGE W. E., *Jewish Literature between the Bible and the Mishnah: A Historical and Literary Introduction.* Philadelphia: Fortress Press, 1981.

NICOLET, CLAUDE, *Space, Geography, and Politics in the Early Roman Empire.* Jerome Lectures 19. Ann Arbor: University of Michigan Press, 1991.

NIEBUHR, KARL-WILHELM, *Heidenapostel aus Israel. Die jüdische Identität des Paulus nach ihrer Darstellung in seinen Briefen.* WUNT 62. Tübingen: Mohr-Siebeck, 1992.

NORTH, ROBERT, *A History of Biblical Map Making.* Beihefte zum Tübinger Atlas des vorderen Orients B32. Wiesbaden: Ludwig Reichert Verlag, 1979.

ODED, B., "The Table of Nations (Genesis 10) – A Socio-cultural Approach." *ZAW* 98 (1986) 14–31.

OEPKE, ALBRECHT, *Der Brief des Paulus an die Galater.* 3rd ed. THKNT 9. Berlin: Evangelische Verlagsanstalt, 1979.

OEMING, MANFRED, *Das wahre Israel. Die "genealogische Vorhalle" 1 Chronik 1−9.* BWANT 7.8. Stuttgart: Kohlhammer, 1990.

O'TOOLE, R. F., "Philip and the Ethiopian Eunuch (Acts VII 25−40)." *JSNT* 17 (1983) 25−34.

OVERMAN, J. ANDREW and ROBERT S. MACLENNAN, eds. *Diaspora Jews and Judaism: Essays in Honor of, and in Dialogue with, A. Thomas Kraabel.* South Florida Studies in the History of Judaism 41. Atlanta, GA: Scholars Press, 1992.

PEARSON, BIRGER A, "Earliest Christianity in Egypt: Some Observations." In *The Roots of Egyptian Christianity*, pp. 132−159. Edited by B. A. Pearson and James E. Goehring. Studies in Antiquity and Christianity. Philadelphia: Fortress, 1986.

PESCH, RUDOLF, *Die Apostelgeschichte.* 2 vols. EKKNT 5. Zürich: Benziger Verlag; Neukirchen-Vluyn: Neukirchener Verlag, 1986.

PFISTER, FRIEDRICH, *Alexander der Grosse in den Offenbarungen der Griechen, Juden, Mohammedaner und Christen.* Deutsche Akademie der Wissenschaften zu Berlin: Schriften der Sektion für Altertumswissenschaft 3. Berlin: Akademie-Verlag, 1956.

−, "Studien zur Sagengeographie." *SO* 35 (1959) 5−39.

POZNANSKI, SAMUEL, "Zur Zahl der biblischen Völker." *ZAW* 24 (1904) 301−308.

PRINGENT, PIERRE, *Le Judaïsme et l'image.* Texte und Studien zum Antiken Judentum 24. Tübingen: Mohr-Siebeck, 1990.

RAD, GERHARD VON, "Gerichtsdoxologie." In *Gesammelte Studien zum Alten Testament*, 2:245−254. 2 vols. Edited by Rudolf Smend. Munich: Chr. Kaiser Verlag, 1973.

RAJAK, TESSA, "Josephus and the 'Archaeology' of the Jews." *JJS* 33 (1982) 465−477.

−, "Moses in Ethiopia: Legend and Literature." *JJS* 29 (1978) 111−122.

RAMSAY, WILLIAM M., *The Church in the Roman Empire before A. D. 170.* 7th ed. London: Hodder & Stoughton, 1903.

−, *A Historical Commentary on St. Paul's Epistle to the Galatians.* London: Hodder and Stoughton, 1899.

RANKIN, H. D., *Celts and the Classical World.* London: Croom Helm, 1987.

REDPATH, HENRY A., "The Geography of the Septuagint." *AJT* 7 (1903) 289−307.

REININK, G. J., "Das Land 'Seiris' [Shir] und das Volk der Serer in jüdischen und christlichen Traditionen." *JSJ* 6 (1975) 72−85.

RÉMY, BERNARD, *L'évolution administrative de l'Anatolie aux trois premiers siècles de notre ère.* Collection du Centre d'Études Romaines et Gallo-Romaines N. S. 5. Lyon: Boccard, 1986.

−, *Les carrières sénatoriales dans les provinces Romaines d'Anatolie au Haut-Empire (31 av. J.-C. − 284 ap. J. C.) (Pont-Bithynie, Galatie, Cappadoce, Lycie-Pamphylie et Cilicie).* Varia Anatolica 2. Istanbul/Paris: Institut Français d'Études Anatoliennes et Éditions Divit, 1989.

−, *Les fastes sénatoriaux des provinces Romains d'Anatolie au Haut-Empire (31 av. J.-C. − 284 ap. J. C.) (Pont-Bithynie, Galatie, Cappadoce, Lycie-Pamphylie et Cilicie).* Institut Français d'Études Anatoliennes. Paris: Éditions Recherche sur les Civilisations, 1988.

REYNOLDS, J. and R. TANNENBAUM, *Jews and Godfearers at Aphrodisias.* CPSSup 12. Cambridge: Cambridge Philological Society, 1987.

RIESNER, RAINER, *Die Frühzeit des Apostels Paulus. Studien zur Chronologie, Missionsstrategie und Theologie.* WUNT 71. Tübingen: Mohr-Siebeck, 1994.

RIESSLER, PAUL, "Zur Geographie der Jubiläen und der Genesis." *TQ* 96 (1914) 341−367.

ROLOFF, JÜRGEN, *Die Apostelgeschichte*. NTD 5. Göttingen: Vandenhoeck & Ruprecht, 1981.

ROMM, JAMES S., *The Edges of the Earth in Ancient Thought: Geography, Exploration, and Fiction*. Princeton, NJ: Princeton University Press, 1992.

ROSENBERG, SHALOM, "The Link to the Land of Israel in Jewish Thought: A Clash of Perspectives." In *The Land of Israel: Jewish Perspectives*, pp. 139–169. Edited by Lawrence A. Hoffman. University of Notre Dame Center for the Study of Judaism and Christianity in Antiquity 6. Notre Dame: University of Notre Dame, 1986.

ROSS, ALAN P., "The Table of Nations in Genesis 10 – Its Structure." *BSac* 137 (1980) 340–353.

–, "The Table of Nations in Genesis 10 – Its Content." *BSac* 138 (1981) 22–34.

ROST, LEONHARD, "Die Bezeichnungen für Land und Volk im Alten Testament." In *Das kleine Credo und andere Studien zum Alten Testament*, pp. 76–101. Heidelberg: Quelle & Meyer, 1965.

SACK, ROBERT DAVID, *Human Territoriality: Its Theory and History*. Cambridge Studies in Historical Geography 7. Cambridge: Cambridge University Press, 1986.

SAFRAI, SHMUEL, *Die Wallfahrt im Zeitalter des Zweiten Tempels*. Forschungen zum jüdisch-christlichen Dialog 3. Neukirchen-Vluyn: Neukirchener Verlag, 1981.

SANDERS, E. P., *Judaism: Practice and Belief 63 BCE – 66 CE*. London: SCM; Philadelphia: Trinity Press International, 1992.

SANDNES, KARL OLAV, *Paul – One of the Prophets? A Contribution to the Apostle's Self-Understanding*. WUNT 2.43. Tübingen: Mohr-Siebeck, 1991.

SCHALIT, A., "The Letter of Antiochus III to Zeuxis regarding the establishment of Jewish military colonies in Phrygia and Lydia." *JQR* 50 (1960) 289–318.

–, *Namenwörterbuch zu Flavius Josephus*. Leiden: Brill, 1968.

SCHALLER, BERNDT, "Philon von Alexandreia und das 'Heilige Land.'" In *Das Land Israel in biblischer Zeit. Jerusalem-Symposium 1981 der Hebräischen Universität und der Georg-August-Universität*, pp. 172–187. Edited by Georg Strecker. GTA 25. Göttingen: Vandenhoeck & Ruprecht, 1983.

SCHLATTER, A., *Petrus and Paulus nach dem ersten Petrusbrief*. Stuttgart: Calwer, 1937.

SCHLIER, HEINRICH, *Der Brief an die Galater*. 12th ed. Kritisch-exegetischer Kommentar über das Neue Testament 7. Göttingen: Vandenhoeck & Ruprecht, 1962.

–, *Der Römerbrief*. 2nd ed. HTKNT 6. Freiburg: Herder, 1979.

SCHMIDT, ANDREAS, "Das historische Datum des Apostelkonzils." *ZNW* 81 (1990) 122–131.

–, "Das Missionsdekret in Galater 2.7–8 als Vereinbarung vom ersten Besuch Pauli in Jerusalem." *NTS* 38 (1992) 149–152.

SCHMIDT, FRANCIS, "Géographie politique et espaces imaginaires dans le Judaïsme à l'époque hellénistique et romaine." *Annuarie de l'École pratique des Hautes Études, Vᵉ Section (Sciences Religieuses)* 89 (1980–81) 443-449.

–, "Imago mundi et pèlerinage." In *Moïse Géographe. Recherches sur les représentations juives et chrétiennes de l'espace*, pp. 13–30. Edited by Alain Desreumaux and F. Schmidt. Études de Psychologie et de Philosophie 24. Paris: Librairie philosophique J. Vrin, 1988.

–, "Jewish Representations of the Inhabited Earth during the Hellenistic and Roman Periods." In *Greece and Rome in Eretz Israel: Collected Essays*, pp. 119–134. Edited by A. Kasher, et al. Jerusalem: Yad Izhak Ben-Zvi/The Israel Exploration Society, 1990.

–, "Naissance d'une géographie juive," in *Moïse géographie. Recherches sur les représentations juives et chrétiennes de l'espace*, pp. 13–30. Edited by Alain Desreumaux and Francis Schmidt. Études de Psychologie et de Philosophie 24. Paris: Librairie philosophique J. Vrin, 1988.

SCHMIDTKE, FRIEDRICH, *Die Japhetiten der biblischen Völkertafel*. Breslauer Studien zur historischen Theologie 7. Breslau: Velag Müller & Seiffert, 1926.

SCHMITHALS, WALTER, "Paulus als Heidenmissionar und das Problem seiner theologischen Entwicklung." In *Jesus Rede von Gott und ihre Nachgeschichte im frühen Christentum. Beiträge zur Verkündigung Jesu und zum Kerygma der Kirche. Festschrift für Willi Marxsen zum 70. Geburtstag*, pp. 235–251. Edited by Dietrich-Alex Koch, et al. Gütersloh: Mohn, 1989.

SCHNEIDER, GERHARD, *Die Apostelgeschichte*. 2 vols. HTKNT 5. Freiburg: Herder, 1980.

SCHNELLE, UDO, *Gerechtigkeit und Christusgegenwart. Vorpaulinische und paulinische Tauftheologie*. GTA 24. Göttingen: Vandenhoeck & Ruprecht, 1983.

SCHÜRER, EMIL, *The History of the Jewish People in the Age of Jesus Christ (175 B. C. – A. D. 135)*. 3 vols. in 4. Rev. ed. Edited by Geza Vermes, et al. Edinburgh: Clark, 1973–1987.

SCHWARTZ, DANIEL R., *Agrippa I: The Last King of Judaea*. Texte und Studien zum Antiken Judentum 23. Tübingen: Mohr-Siebeck, 1990.

–, "The End of the GH (Acts 1:8): Beginning or End of the Christian Vision?" *JBL* 105 (1986) 669–676.

SCHWEMER, ANNA MARIA, "Studien zu den frühjüdischen Prophetenlegenden. Vitae Prophetarum, Band 1: Die Viten der großen Propheten: Jesaja, Jeremia, Ezechiel und Daniel, eingeleitet, übersetzt und kommentiert." Dr. Theol. diss., Eberhard-Karls-Universität Tübingen, 1993.

SCOBIE, CHARLES H.H., "Israel and the Nations: An Essay in Biblical Theology," *TynBul* 43/2 (1992) 283–305.

SCOTT, JAMES M., *Adoption as Sons of God: An Exegetical Investigation into the Background of ΥΙΟΘΕΣΙΑ in the Pauline Corpus*. WUNT 2.48. Tübingen: Mohr-Siebeck, 1992.

–, "'For as many as are of works of the Law are under a curse' (Galatians 3.10)," in *Paul and the Scriptures of Israel*, pp. 187–220. Edited by James A. Sanders and C.A. Evans. JSNTSup 83; SSEJC 1. Sheffield: JSOT Press, 1993.

–, "Luke's Geographical Horizon." In *The Book of Acts in Its First Century Setting, Vol. 2: The Book of Acts in Its Graeco-Roman Setting*, pp. 483–544. Edited by David W.J. Gill and Conrad Gempf. Grand Rapids: Eerdmans; Carlisle: Paternoster, 1994.

"The Restoration of Israel." In *The Dictionary of Paul and his Letters*, pp. 796–805. Edited by R.P. Martin, et al. Downers Grove: InterVarsity Press, 1993.

SCOTT, JAMIE and PAUL SIMPSON-HOUSLEY, eds. *Sacred Places and Profane Spaces: Essays in the Geographics of Judaism, Christianity, and Islam*. New York: Greenwood, 1991.

SEGAL, ALAN F., *Paul the Convert: The Apostolate and Apostasy of Saul the Pharisee*. New Haven: Yale University Press, 1990.

SEGAL, PERETZ, "The Penalty of the Warning Inscription from the Temple of Jerusalem." *IEJ* 39 (1989) 79–84.

SETERS, JOHN VAN, *Prologue to History: The Yahwist as Historian in Genesis*. Zürich: Theologischer Verlag, 1992.

SHERK, ROBERT K., "Roman Galatia: The Governors from 25 B.C. to A.D. 114." In

ANRW II.7.2, pp. 954–1052. Edited by Hildegard Temporini. Berlin: de Gruyter, 1980.

–, *Rome and the Greek East to the Death of Augustus.* Cambridge: Cambridge University Press, 1984.

SHERWIN-WHITE, A. N., *The Roman Citizenship.* 2nd ed. Oxford: Clarendon Press, 1973.

SILBERMAN, LOU H., "The Queen of Sheba in Judaic Tradition." In *Solomon & Sheba*, pp. 65–84. Edited by James B. Pritchard. London: Phaidon Press, 1974.

SIMONS, J., *The Geographical and Topographical Texts of the Old Testament.* Leiden: Brill, 1959.

–, "The 'Table of Nations' (Gen. X): Its General Structure and Meaning." *OTS* 10 (1954) 155–184.

SKINNER, JOHN, *A Critical and Exegetical Commentary on Genesis.* 2nd ed. ICC. Edinburgh: Clark, 1930.

SMITH, TERENCE V., *Petrine Controversies in Early Christianity: Attitudes towards Peter in Christian Writings of the First Two Centuries.* WUNT 2.15. Tübingen: Mohr, 1985.

SOFER, JOHANN, "Das Hieronymuszeugnis über die Sprachen der Galater und Treverer." *Wiener Studien* 55 (1937) 148–158.

SPEISER, E. A., *Genesis.* AB 1. Garden City, NY: Doubleday, 1964.

STADELMANN, LUIS I. J., *The Hebrew Conception of the World: A Philological and Literary Study.* AnBib 39. Rome: Pontifical Biblical Institute, 1970.

STÄHELIN, FELIX, *Geschichte der kleinasiatischen Galater.* 2nd ed. Stuttgart: Teubner, 1907; reprint ed., Osnabrück: Zeller, 1973.

STECK, ODIL HANNES, *Israel und das gewaltsame Geschick der Propheten. Untersuchungen zur Überlieferung des deuteronomistischen Geschichtsbildes im Alten Testament, Spätjudentum und Urchristentum.* WMANT 23. Neukirchen-Vluyn: Neukirchener Verlag, 1967.

–, "Das Problem theologischer Strömungen in nachexilischer Zeit." *EvT* 28 (1968) 445–458.

STEGNER, WERNER, "Beobachtungen zur sogenannten Völkerliste des Pfingstwunders (Apg 2,7–11)." *Kairos* 21 (1979) 206–214.

STEINHAUSER, M. G., "Gal 4,25a: Evidence of Targumic Tradition in Gal 4,21–31?" *Bib* 70 (1989) 234–240.

STEMBERGER, GÜNTER, "Die Bedeutung des 'Landes Israel' in der rabbinischen Tradition." *Kairos* 25 (1983) 176–199.

STERN, MENAHEM, "Josephus and the Roman Empire as Reflected in The Jewish War." In *Josephus, Judaism, and Christianity*, pp. 71–80. Edited by Louis H. Feldman and Gehei Hata. Leiden: Brill, 1987.

(STRACK, HERMANN L.), and BILLERBECK, PAUL, *Kommentar zum Neuen Testament aus Talmud und Midrasch.* 6 vols. 6th ed. Munich: Beck, 1975.

–, and STEMBERGER, GÜNTER, *Einleitung in Talmud and Midrasch.* 7th ed. Beck'sche Elementarbücher. Munich: Beck, 1982.

STRANGE, W. A., *The Problem of the Text of Acts.* SNTSMS 71. Cambridge: Cambridge University Press, 1992.

STUHLMACHER, PETER, ed. *Biblische Theologie des Neuen Testaments, Bd. 1: Grundlegung. Von Jesus zu Paulus.* Göttingen: Vandenhoeck & Ruprecht, 1992.

–, *Der Brief an die Römer.* NTD 6. Göttingen: Vandenhoeck & Ruprecht, 1989.

–, *Das Evangelium und die Evangelien*. WUNT 28. Tübingen: Mohr-Siebeck, 1983.

–, "Jesustradition im Römerbrief? Eine Skizze." *TBei* 14/1 (1983) 240–250.

–, *Das paulinische Evangelium, Teil 1: Vorgeschichte*. FRLANT 95. Göttingen: Vandenhoeck & Ruprecht, 1968.

–, "Die Stellung Jesu und des Paulus zu Jerusalem." *ZTK* 86 (1989) 140–156.

–, *Versöhnung, Gesetz und Gerechtigkeit. Aufsätze zur biblischen Theologie*. Göttingen: Vandenhoeck & Ruprecht, 1981.

STUHLMANN, RAINER, *Das eschatologische Maß im Neuen Testament*. FRLANT 132. Göttingen: Vandenhoeck & Ruprecht, 1983.

STUMPF, GERD R., *Numismatische Studien zur Chronologie der römischen Statthalter in Kleinasien (122 v. Chr. – 163 n. Chr.)*. Saarbrücker Studien zur Archäologie und Alten Geschichte 4. Saarbrücken: Saarbrücker Druckerei und Verlag, 1991.

SUHL, ALFRED, "Der Beginn der selbständigen Mission des Paulus. Ein Beitrag zur Geschichte des Urchristentums." *NTS* 38 (1992) 430–447.

SULLIVAN, RICHARD D., "Priesthoods of the Eastern Dynastic Aristocracy." In *Studien zur Religion und Kultur Kleinasiens. Festschrift für Friedrich Karl Dörner zum 65. Geburtstag am 28. Februar 1976*, pp. 914–939. 2 vols. Edited by Sencer Sahin, et al. EPRO 66. Leiden: Brill, 1978.

SYLVA, DENNIS D., "Death and Life at the Center of the World." In *Reimaging the Death of the Lukan Jesus*, pp. 153–217. Edited by D. D. Sylva. BBB 73. Frankfurt a.M.: Hain, 1990.

TALMON, S., "*Tabûr ha'arez* and the Comparative Method." *Tarbiz* 45 (1975–76) 163–177.

TANNEHILL, ROBERT C., *The Narrative Unity of Luke-Acts: A Literary Interpretation, Vol. 1: The Gospel according to Luke*. Foundations and Facets. Philadelphia: Fortress, 1986.

TARN, WILLIAM W., *Alexander the Great*. 2 vols. Cambridge: Cambridge University Press; New York: Macmillan, 1948.

TARAZI, PAUL N., "The Addressees and the Purpose of Galatians." *Vladimir's Theological Quarterly* 33 (1989) 159–179.

TAYLOR, NICHOLAS, *Paul, Antioch and Jerusalem: A Study in Relationships and Authority in Earliest Christianity*. JSNTSup 66. Sheffield: JSOT Press, 1992.

TERRIEN, SAMUEL, "The Omphalos Myth and Hebrew Religion." *VT* 20 (1970) 315–338.

THIEDE, CARSTEN P., ed. *Das Petrusbild in der neueren Forschung*. Theologische Verlagsgemeinschaft Monographien 316. Wuppertal: Brockhaus, 1987.

–, *Simon Peter: From Galilee to Rome*. Exeter: Paternoster, 1986.

THIEL, HELMUT VAN, *Leben und Taten Alexanders von Makedonien. Der griechischen Alexanderroman nach der Handschrift L*. Texte zur Forschung 13. Darmstadt: Wissenschaftliche Buchgesellschaft, 1983.

THOMA, CLEMENS, "Die Weltvölker im Urteil rabbinischer Gleichniserzähler," in *Judentum – Ausblicke und Einsichten. Festgabe für Kurt Schubert zum siebzigsten Geburtstag*, pp. 115–133. Edited by Clemens Thoma, et al. Judentum und Umwelt 43. Frankfurt a.M.: Lang, 1993.

THOMAS, GARTH, "Magna Mater and Attis." In *ANRW* II.17.3, pp. 1500–1535. Edited by Wolfgang Haase. Berlin: de Gruyter, 1984.

THORNTON, CLAUS-JÜRGEN, *Der Zeuge des Zeugen. Lukas als Historiker der Paulusreisen*. WUNT 56. Tübingen: Mohr-Siebeck, 1991.

TREBILCO, PAUL R., *Jewish Communities in Asia Minor*. SNTSMS 69. Cambridge: Cambridge University Press, 1991.

UEHLINGER, CHRISTOPH, *Weltreich und "eine Rede". Eine neue Deutung der sogenannten Turmbauerzählung (Gen 11,1−9)*. OBO 101. Freiburg: Universitätsverlag Freiburg; Göttingen: Vandenhoeck & Ruprecht, 1990.

ULLENDORFF, EDWARD, "Candace (Acts VII.27) and the Queen of Sheba." *NTS* 2 (1955−56) 53−56.

UNNIK, W. C. VAN, "Der Ausdruck ἕως ἐσχάτου τῆς γῆς (Apostelgeschichte I 8) und sein alttestamentlicher Hintergrund." In *Sparsa Collecta, Part 1: Evangelia, Paulina, Acta*, pp. 386−401. NovTSup 29. Leiden: Brill, 1973.

−, *Das Selbstverständnis der jüdischen Diaspora in der hellenistisch-römischen Zeit*. Edited by Pieter Willem van der Horst. AGJU 17. Leiden: Brill, 1993.

VANDERKAM, J. C., "1 Enoch 77,3 and a Babylonian Map of the World." *RevQ* 11 (1983) 271−278.

−, *Textual and Historical Studies in the Book of Jubilees*. HSM 14. Missoula, MT: Scholars Press, 1977.

VERMES, GEZA, "Josephus' Treatment of the Book of Daniel." *JJS* 42 (1991) 149−166.

−, *Scripture and Tradition in Judaism: Haggadic Studies*. SPB 4. Leiden: Brill, 1961.

WAELKENS, MARC, "The Imperial Sanctuary at Pessinus: Archaeological, Epigraphical and Numismatic Evidence for its Date and Identification." *Epigraphica Anatolica* 7 (1986) 37−72.

WESTERMANN, CLAUS, *Das Buch Jesaja Kapitel 40−66*. 3rd ed. ATD. Göttingen: Vandenhoeck & Ruprecht, 1976.

−, *Genesis*. 3 vols. 3rd. ed. BKAT 1. Neukirchen-Vluyn: Neukirchener Verlag, 1983.

WILCKENS, ULRICH, *Der Brief an die Römer*. 3 vols. EKKNT 6. Zürich: Benziger Verlag; Neukirchen-Vluyn: Neukirchener Verlag, 1978−1982.

WILLI, THOMAS, *Chronik*. BKAT 24.1. Neukirchen-Vluyn: Neukirchener Verlag, 1991.

WILSON, ANDREW, *The Nations in Deutero-Isaiah: A Study on Composition and Structure*. Ancient Near Eastern Texts and Studies 1. Lewiston, NY: Edwin Mellen Press, 1986.

WILSON, STEPHEN G., *The Gentiles and the Gentile Mission in Luke-Acts*. SNTSMS 23. Cambridge: Cambridge University Press, 1973.

WINKLE, D. W. VAN, "The Relationship of the Nations to Yahweh and to Israel in Isaiah xl − lv." *VT* 35 (1985) 446−458.

WISEMAN, D. J., ed. *Peoples of Old Testament Times*. Oxford: Clarendon Press, 1973.

ZAHN, THEODOR, *Der Brief des Paulus an die Galater*. 3rd ed. Kommentar zum Neuen Testamemt 10. Leipzig: Scholl, 1922; reprint ed., Wuppertal: Brockhaus, 1990.

ZEITLIN, SOLOMON, "Did Agrippa write a letter to Gaius Caligula?" *JQR* N. S. 56 (1965) 22−31.

−, "The Jews: Race, Nation or Religion − Which? A Study Based on the Literature of the Second Jewish Commonwealth." *JQR* N. S. 26 (1935−36) 313−347.

ZELLER, DIETER, "Theologie der Mission bei Paulus." In *Mission im Neuen Testament*, pp. 164−187. Edited by Karl Kertelge. QD 93. Freiburg: Herder, 1982.

ZIMMERLI, WALTHER, *Ezechiel*. 2 vols. 2nd ed. BKAT 13. Neukirchen-Vluyn: Neukirchener Verlag, 1979.

Index of Ancient Writings

I. Old Testament

II. New Testament

III. Pseudepigrapha

Testaments of the Twelve Patriarchs

IV. Dead Sea Scrolls

V. Philo

VI. Josephus

VII. Rabbinic Writings

VIII. Greco-Roman Literature

VIII. Early Christian Writings

Index of Modern Authors

Wissenschaftliche Untersuchungen zum Neuen Testament

Alphabetical Index
of the first and second series

Frenschkowski, Marco: Offenbarung und Epiphanie. Volume I 1995. *Volume II/79.* – Volume II 1996. *Volume II/80.*

Frey, Jörg: Eugen Drewermann und die biblische Exegese. 1995. *Volume II/71.*

Fridrichsen, Anton: Exegetical Writings. Ed. by C. C. Caragounis and T. Fornberg. 1994. *Volume 76.*

Garlington, Don B.: The Obedience of Faith. 1991. *Volume II/38.*

– Faith, Obedience and Perseverance. 1994. *Volume 79.*

Garnet, Paul: Salvation and Atonement in the Qumran Scrolls. 1977. *Volume II/3.*

Grässer, Erich: Der Alte Bund im Neuen. 1985. *Volume 35.*

Green, Joel B.: The Death of Jesus. 1988. *Volume II/33.*

Gundry Volf, Judith M.: Paul and Perseverance. 1990. *Volume II/37.*

Hafemann, Scott J.: Suffering and the Spirit. 1986. *Volume II/19.*

– Paul, Moses, and the History of Israel. 1995. *Volume 81.*

Heckel, Theo K.: Der Innere Mensch. 1993. *Volume II/53.*

Heckel, Ulrich: Kraft in Schwachheit. 1993. *Volume II/56.*

– see *Feldmeier.*

– see *Hengel.*

Heiligenthal, Roman: Werke als Zeichen. 1983. *Volume II/9.*

Hemer, Colin J.: The Book of Acts in the Setting of Hellenistic History. 1989. *Volume 49.*

Hengel, Martin: Judentum und Hellenismus. 1969, [3]1988. *Volume 10.*

– Die johanneische Frage. 1993. *Volume 67.*

Hengel, Martin and *Ulrich Heckel* (Ed.): Paulus und das antike Judentum. 1991. *Volume 58.*

Hengel, Martin and *Hermut Löhr* (Ed.): Schriftauslegung. 1994. *Volume 73.*

Hengel, Martin and *Anna Maria Schwemer* (Ed.): Königsherrschaft Gottes und himmlischer Kult. 1991. *Volume 55.*

– Die Septuaginta. 1994. *Volume 72.*

Herrenbrück, Fritz: Jesus und die Zöllner. 1990. *Volume II/41.*

Hofius, Otfried: Katapausis. 1970. *Volume 11.*

– Der Vorhang vor dem Thron Gottes. 1972. *Volume 14.*

– Der Christushymnus Philipper 2,6 – 11. 1976, [2]1991. *Volume 17.*

– Paulusstudien. 1989, [2]1994. *Volume 51.*

Holtz, Traugott: Geschichte und Theologie des Urchristentums. Ed. by Eckart Reinmuth and Christian Wolff. 1991. *Volume 57.*

Hommel, Hildebrecht: Sebasmata. Volume 1. 1983. *Volume 31.* – Volume 2. 1984. *Volume 32.*

Hvalvik, Reidar: The Struggle of Scripture and Covenant. 1996. *Volume II/82.*

Kähler, Christoph: Jesu Gleichnisse als Poesie und Therapie. 1995. *Volume 78.*

Kamlah, Ehrhard: Die Form der katalogischen Paränese im Neuen Testament. 1964. *Volume 7.*

Kim, Seyoon: The Origin of Paul's Gospel. 1981, [2]1984. *Volume II/4.*

– »The ›Son of Man‹« as the Son of God. 1983. *Volume 30.*

Kleinknecht, Karl Th.: Der leidende Gerechtfertigte. 1984, [2]1988. *Volume II/13.*

Klinghardt, Matthias: Gesetz und Volk Gottes. 1988. *Volume II/32.*

Köhler, Wolf-Dietrich: Rezeption des Matthäusevangeliums in der Zeit vor Irenäus. 1987. *Volume II/24.*

Korn, Manfred: Die Geschichte Jesu in veränderter Zeit. 1993. *Volume II/51.*

Koskenniemi, Erkki: Apollonios von Tyana in der neutestamentlichen Exegese. 1994. *Volume II/61.*

Kuhn, Karl G.: Achtzehngebet und Vaterunser und der Reim. 1950. *Volume 1.*

Lampe, Peter: Die stadtrömischen Christen in den ersten beiden Jahrhunderten. 1987, [2]1989. *Volume II/18.*

Lieu, Samuel N. C.: Manichaeism in the Later Roman Empire and Medieval China. 1992. *Volume 63.*

Löhr, Hermut: see *Hengel.*

Löhr, Winrich A.: Basilides und seine Schule. 1995. *Volume 83.*

Maier, Gerhard: Mensch und freier Wille. 1971. *Volume 12.*

– Die Johannesoffenbarung und die Kirche. 1981. *Volume 25.*

Markschies, Christoph: Valentinus Gnosticus? 1992. *Volume 65.*

Marshall, Peter: Enmity in Corinth: Social Conventions in Paul's Relations with the Corinthians. 1987. *Volume II/23.*

Meade, David G.: Pseudonymity and Canon. 1986. *Volume 39.*

Meadors, Edward P.: Jesus the Messianic Herald of Salvation. 1995. *Volume II/72.*

Mell, Ulrich: Die »anderen« Winzer. 1994. *Volume 77.*

Mengel, Berthold: Studien zum Philipperbrief. 1982. *Volume II/8.*

Merkel, Helmut: Die Widersprüche zwischen den Evangelien. 1971. *Volume 13.*

Merklein, Helmut: Studien zu Jesus und Paulus. 1987. *Volume 43.*

Metzler, Karin: Der griechische Begriff des Verzeihens. 1991. *Volume II/44.*

Niebuhr, Karl-Wilhelm: Gesetz und Paränese. 1987. *Volume II/28.*

– Heidenapostel aus Israel. 1992. *Volume 63.*

Nissen, Andreas: Gott und der Nächste im antiken Judentum. 1974. *Volume 15.*

Noormann, Rolf: Irenäus als Paulusinterpret. 1994. *Volume II/66.*

Okure, Teresa: The Johannine Approach to Mission. 1988. *Volume II/31.*

Park, Eung Chun: The Mission Discourse in Matthew's Interpretation. 1995. *Volume II/81.*

Philonenko, Marc (Ed.): Le Trône de Dieu. 1993. *Volume 69.*

Pilhofer, Peter: Presbyteron Kreitton. 1990. *Volume II/39.*

Pöhlmann, Wolfgang: Der Verlorene Sohn und das Haus. 1993. *Volume 68.*

Probst, Hermann: Paulus und der Brief. 1991. *Volume II/45.*

Räisänen, Heikki: Paul and the Law. 1983, [2]1987. *Volume 29.*

Rehkopf, Friedrich: Die lukanische Sonderquelle. 1959. *Volume 5.*

Rein, Matthias: Die Heilung des Blindgeborenen. 1995. *Volume II/73.*

Reinmuth, Eckart: Pseudo-Philo und Lukas. 1994. *Volume 74.*

– see *Holtz.*

Reiser, Marius: Syntax und Stil des Markusevangeliums. 1984. *Volume II/11.*

Richards, E. Randolph: The Secretary in the Letters of Paul. 1991. *Volume II/42.*

Riesner, Rainer: Jesus als Lehrer. 1981, [3]1988. *Volume II/7.*

– Die Frühzeit des Apostels Paulus. 1994. *Volume 71.*

Rissi, Mathias: Die Theologie des Hebräerbriefs. 1987. *Volume 41.*

Röhser, Günter: Metaphorik und Personifikation der Sünde. 1987. *Volume II/25.*

Rose, Christian: Die Wolke der Zeugen. 1994. *Volume II/60.*

Rüger, Hans Peter: Die Weisheitsschrift aus der Kairoer Geniza. 1991. *Volume 53.*

Salzmann, Jorg Christian: Lehren und Ermahnen. 1994. *Volume II/59.*

Sänger, Dieter: Antikes Judentum und die Mysterien. 1980. *Volume II/5.*

– Die Verkündigung des Gekreuzigten und Israel. 1994. *Volume 75.*

Sandnes, Karl Olav: Paul – One of the Prophets? 1991. *Volume II/43.*

Sato, Migaku: Q und Prophetie. 1988. *Volume II/29.*

Schaper, Joachim: Eschatology in the Greek Psalter. 1995. *Volume II/76.*

Schimanowski, Gottfried: Weisheit und Messias. 1985. *Volume II/17.*

Schlichting, Günter: Ein jüdisches Leben Jesu. 1982. *Volume 24.*

Schnabel, Eckhard J.: Law and Wisdom from Ben Sira to Paul. 1985. *Volume II/16.*

Schutter, William L.: Hermeneutic and Composition in I Peter. 1989. *Volume II/30.*

Schwartz, Daniel R.: Studies in the Jewish Background of Christianity. 1992. *Volume 60.*

Schwemer, A. M.: see *Hengel.*

Scott, James M.: Adoption as Sons of God. 1992. *Volume II/48.*

– Paul and the Nations. *Volume 84.*

Siegert, Folker: Drei hellenistisch-jüdische Predigten. Part 1. 1980. *Volume 20.* – Part 2. 1992. *Volume 61.*

– Nag-Hammadi-Register. 1982. *Volume 26.*

– Argumentation bei Paulus. 1985. *Volume 34.*

– Philon von Alexandrien. 1988. *Volume 46.*

Simon, Marcel: Le christianisme antique et son contexte religieux I/II. 1981. *Volume 23.*

Snodgrass, Klyne: The Parable of the Wicked Tenants. 1983. *Volume 27.*

Söding, Thomas: see *Thüsing.*

Sommer, Urs: Die Passionsgeschichte des Markusevangeliums. 1993. *Volume II/58.*

Spangenberg, Volker: Herrlichkeit des Neuen Bundes. 1993. *Volume II/55.*

Speyer, Wolfgang: Frühes Christentum im antiken Strahlungsfeld. 1989. *Volume 50.*

Stadelmann, Helge: Ben Sira als Schriftgelehrter. 1980. *Volume II/6.*

Strobel, August: Die Stunde der Wahrheit. 1980. *Volume 21.*

Stuckenbruck, Loren: Angel Veneration and Christology. 1995. *Volume II/70.*

Stuhlmacher, Peter (Ed.): Das Evangelium und die Evangelien. 1983. *Volume 28.*

Sung, Chong-Hyon: Vergebung der Sünden. 1993. *Volume II/57.*

Tajra, Harry W.: The Trial of St. Paul. 1989. *Volume II/35.*

– The Martyrdom of St. Paul. 1994. *Volume II/67.*

Theissen, Gerd: Studien zur Soziologie des Urchristentums. 1979, [3]1989. *Volume 19.*

Thornton, Claus-Jürgen: Der Zeuge des Zeugen. 1991. *Volume 56.*

Thüsing, Wilhelm: Studien zur neutestamentlichen Theologie. Ed. by Thomas Söding.
     1995. *Volume 82.*

Twelftree, Graham: Jesus the Exorcist. 1993. *Volume II/54.*

Visotzky, Burton L.: Fathers of the World. 1995. *Volume 80.*

Wagener, Ulrike: Die Ordnung des ›Hauses Gottes‹. 1994. *Volume II/65.*

Wedderburn, A. J. M.: Baptism and Resurrection. 1987. *Volume 44.*

Wegner, Uwe: Der Hauptmann von Kafarnaum. 1985. *Volume II/14.*

Welck, Christian: Erzählte ›Zeichen‹. 1994. *Volume II/69.*

Wilson, Walter T.: Love without Pretense. 1991. *Volume II/46.*

Wolff, Christian: see *Holtz.*

Zimmermann, Alfred E.: Die urchristlichen Lehrer. 1984, [2]1988. *Volume II/12.*

For a complete catalogue please write to the publisher
J. C. B. Mohr (Paul Siebeck), P. O. Box 2040, D-72010 Tübingen.